M. TVLLI CICERONIS
TVSCVLANARVM DISPVTATIONVM
LIBRI QVINQVE

M. TVLLI CICERONIS
TVSCVLANARVM DISPVTATIONVM
LIBRI QVINQVE

A REVISED TEXT
WITH INTRODUCTION AND COMMENTARY AND
A COLLATION OF NUMEROUS MSS.

BY

THE LATE

THOMAS WILSON DOUGAN
PROFESSOR OF LATIN IN QUEEN'S COLLEGE, BELFAST

AND

ROBERT MITCHELL HENRY, M.A.
PROFESSOR OF LATIN IN QUEEN'S UNIVERSITY, BELFAST

VOLUME II

CONTAINING BOOKS III–V

CAMBRIDGE
AT THE UNIVERSITY PRESS
1934

CAMBRIDGE
UNIVERSITY PRESS

University Printing House, Cambridge CB2 8BS, United Kingdom

Cambridge University Press is part of the University of Cambridge.

It furthers the University's mission by disseminating knowledge in the pursuit of education, learning and research at the highest international levels of excellence.

www.cambridge.org
Information on this title: www.cambridge.org/9781107497627

© Cambridge University Press 1934

First published 1934
First paperback edition 2015

A catalogue record for this publication is available from the British Library

ISBN 978-1-107-49762-7 Paperback

Cambridge University Press has no responsibility for the persistence or accuracy of URLs for external or third-party internet websites referred to in this publication, and does not guarantee that any content on such websites is, or will remain, accurate or appropriate.

PREFACE

WHEN on the death of the late Professor Dougan his papers were examined it was found that the second volume of his edition of Cicero's *Tusculan Disputations*, upon which he had been engaged up to the last, was in a very incomplete condition. He had left a fair copy of the explanatory notes upon Book III and the first 34 paragraphs of Book IV, and there were several notebooks containing his collations of various MSS. His widow (now Mrs Bor), to whom he entrusted the task of seeing that the book should be completed, and his executor, Mr William Dougan, handed these over to the present editor with the request that he should finish the work. The editor has accordingly printed as it stood that portion of the commentary which had been finished before Professor Dougan's death, adding only a few notes of his own enclosed in square brackets, and has himself written the commentary upon the remainder of Book IV and the whole of Book V, together with the *Introduction* containing a detailed analysis of the three books and a discussion of the question of Cicero's sources. Deciding to keep the critical notes uniform with those of the first volume, he used Professor Dougan's collations as far as they went, but collated himself for this volume the following MSS, E 1 E 2 R 1 R 6 R 7 R 10 R 16 R 17 V and P.

To the list (vol. I, p. ix) of editions consulted should be added for this volume that of L. W. Hasper (Gotha, 1883–5) (Ha.).

The editor desires to record his sincere thanks to the Syndics of the Press for their kindness in undertaking the publication of this volume and for their great patience in the long delay that has occurred in the completion of the work. He must also thank the readers of the press for the care and skill which detected errors that but for them might have passed unnoticed; and his friend Professor R. K. McElderry for his kindness in reading the proofs of the text and commentary.

R. M. H.

QUEEN'S UNIVERSITY
BELFAST

CONTENTS

INTRODUCTION

THE ARGUMENT

BOOK III

On relieving annoyance

THOUGH we possess a mind as well as a body, it is a strange thing that while the science of medicine exists for the benefit of the latter and is in high esteem, the corresponding science, philosophy, is either neglected or disliked—because, perhaps, while the mind appreciates a bodily disorder, the body has no sense of mental disorder and a diseased mind is unaware of its own condition. Nature who might have ordered otherwise has so designed our constitutions that the sparks or seeds of virtue which, if cultivated, ensure health of mind are easily destroyed. The process of destruction begins almost at birth under the influence of nurses, parents, teachers, literature and public opinion which teach us to mistake the false for the true, and to aim at material rather than moral success: we aim in consequence at the false rather than at the true glory, the counterpart of virtue, seduced by popular opinion rather than in reliance upon the judgment of the wise. Blinded by these false notions men are involuntarily the instruments of disaster to others as well as to themselves. Must we not try to find some remedy for this unhealthy state of mind, which is far more serious than any bodily disorder? Anxiety and lust are, for instance, worse than disease; and surely the human mind which has invented a cure for diseases can discover, and has discovered, a cure for the mind more reliable even than the science of medicine; this cure is to be found in philosophy, and it is surely important enough to be taken seriously. The general question has already been discussed in the *Hortensius*; here Cicero will only reproduce the aspect of the matter discussed upon this particular occasion, as following up the discussion of the two preceding days he and his friends discussed upon the third day the truth of a general proposition laid down by one of their number, §§ 1–7.

The proposition was: *The wise man is subject to annoyance.* Cicero contends in reply that as *aegritudo* is only one of several disorders of the mind, the mind which is subject to one may be subject to all and

H. *b*

become so thoroughly unhealthy as to be practically *insane*, a word which taken literally means "in an unhealthy state," which (according to philosophers) a mind under such conditions undoubtedly is—Latin brings this point out better than Greek. A mind under the sway of passion is out of its own control, though here two states of mind must be distinguished: one, temporary, called *furor* or μελαγχολία, to which even wise men are subject, and the other (*insania* or μανία), a state inconsistent with true wisdom, §§ 7–11.

The position to be combatted is one that appeals to human nature on its tender side; and there is much to be said for Crantor's view that total absence of feeling can only be secured at the cost of brutality of mind and torpor of body. And yet Cicero fears that this view merely humours our weakness. We must remove this emotion; yet so deep-rooted is it that an ineradicable minimum will probably be left. And we must deal with the other emotions, too, but with this one first, §§ 12, 13.

A. Cicero now proceeds to put forward compressed Stoic arguments in syllogistic form to prove that the wise man is not affected by annoyance, §§ 14–21.

(*a*) Fear and annoyance are concerned with the same objects: the man who is liable to the one is also liable to the other: the wise man is not liable to fear, therefore he is not liable to annoyance, § 14.

(*b*) The wise man is too high-spirited to regard human concerns and being so must be superior to annoyance, § 15.

(*c*) The mind which is annoyed, like the eye which is inflamed, cannot do its work. The mind of the wise man is always equal to its work: therefore it is always free from annoyance.

(*d*) The wise man is self-controlled (σώφρων), and therefore calm, and therefore free from annoyance, c. 8, §§ 16–18.

(*e*) If the wise man were liable to annoyance he would also be liable to anger, §§ 18, 19.

(*f*) The wise man cannot fall into a state of envy or compassion; but the former is annoyance at the good fortune, and the latter annoyance at the evil fortune, of another; therefore the wise man cannot fall into annoyance, §§ 20, 21.

B. These fine-drawn arguments must be considerably expanded, but still principally according to Stoic views, for the Peripatetic theory of the mean as applied to emotions does not recommend itself to Cicero, § 22.

The original question: "Is the wise man affected by annoyance?" (except for the passage in the end of § 25 '*id enim sit propositum, quando-*

quidem eam tu uideri tibi in sapientem cadere dixisti, quod ego nullo modo existimo') is now tacitly dropped (cf. § 80 *'sed nescio quo pacto ab eo quod erat a te propositum aberrauit oratio, tu enim de sapiente quaesieras...'*), and Cicero divides his main subject into two parts, the setting forth of the cause of annoyance and the discovery of its cure, § 23.

I. The cause of annoyance, §§ 24–75.

1. The relation of *aegritudo* to the other emotions, and its definition:—

The whole cause of the irrational emotions is a false opinion. Every *perturbatio* is *'animi motus uel rationis expers uel rationem aspernans uel rationi non oboediens.'* Irrational emotions are related thus, §§ 24, 25:—

Perturbationes *ex opinione*	*boni*	*praesentis,* *absentis,*	*laetitia,* *cupiditas,*	ἡδονή ἐπιθυμία
	mali	*praesentis,* *absentis,*	*aegritudo* *metus,*	λύπη φόβος.

We must remove all these, and *aegritudo* now. *Aegritudo* is defined as *'opinio magni mali praesentis, et quidem recens opinio talis mali, ut in eo rectum uideatur esse angi, id autem est ut is qui doleat oportere opinetur se dolere.'*

2. Analysis of the nature of *aegritudo*:—

It is—

(*a*) *opinio magni mali praesentis*, §§ 28–61.

The Epicureans held that this opinion was inevitably produced by every present great evil, the Cyrenaics only where such evil was unexpected. Cicero admits that the unexpected character of an evil tends to intensify the resulting annoyance, § 28.

Hence ills that have been anticipated by reflexion fall upon a man less heavily. Illustrations from the Telamon (?) of Ennius, from the Theseus of Euripides, from Anaxagoras, from the Phormio of Terence, §§ 28–30.

Cicero accepts from the Cyrenaics this principle of *praemeditatio* as a weapon against annoyance but sees in its effect a proof that annoyance is due to opinion, not, as they held, to inevitable necessity, § 31.

Of the Cyrenaics in more detail anon : the view of the Epicureans must first be dealt with. They held that where a man thinks himself to be in evil he must necessarily be in annoyance, even though the evil has been foreseen or is long-established. They even condemned the practice of anticipatory reflexion upon evils, which may or may not occur, as a gratuitous undertaking of additional annoyance, § 32.

There were, according to them, two means for the abatement of annoyance: (*a*) to call off the attention from the source of trouble; (*b*) to divert it to some pleasant thought such as might be supplied by memory or anticipation, § 33.

But they are wrong to reject *praemeditatio rerum futurarum* and their remedy, which consists in diverting the attention from the cause of annoyance, is useless, § 34.

Praemeditatio secures a double advantage: (*a*) by meditating upon the circumstances amid which we live a man performs the true duty of a philosopher; (*b*) when misfortunes confront a man he has a threefold consolation: (*a*) he has long anticipated the possibility of the occurrence; (*β*) he knows that the incidents of the human lot must be borne with resignation; (*γ*) he knows that there is no evil where there is no moral blame.

And who are the Epicureans to bid us ignore the annoyance at the very moment when it pierces us and yet deny us all healing influence from time? And, by the way, what are these good things to which they would call off our attention? § 35.

Here Cicero loses the thread of his subject in a tirade against the views of Epicurus, §§ 36–51.

Pythagoras or Socrates or Plato might well rouse a man who was thus succumbing to annoyance; they might bid him consider the four cardinal virtues in turn, but Epicurus bids us think of pleasures, and those pleasures the pleasures of sense. Epicureans need not deny it: the assertion is proved out of the mouth of their cleverest man, Zeno of Sidon, §§ 36–8, and from the work of Epicurus himself on the chief good, §§ 41–42.

A fine life they prescribe and fine reflexions they would provide for the solace of a Thyestes or an Aeetes or a Telamon or a captive Andromache in distress, §§ 39, 40, 43–46.

Some may seek to defend Epicurus. It is true that he has uttered many noble sentiments, but his statement of the chief good is only too plain, c. 20, § 46.

It need not be urged that he places the essential cause of happiness in repose of mind. He contradicts himself, and he fails to distinguish between pleasure and absence of pain, and he separates pleasure from the chief good, § 47.

But it may be urged that he often praises virtue. What of that? C. Gracchus praised economy with regard to the public money. But look to his acts, which the story of Piso Frugi serves to illustrate. So Epicurus may assert that virtuous living is essential to happy living; he may deny that fortune has any power over the wise man; he may award the preference to frugal fare; he may assert that the wise man is at all times happy—all these utterances are inconsistent with his doctrine with regard to pleasure, §§ 48, 49.

Epicureans complain that this is to attack Epicurus in the spirit of a partisan. A very likely story! This is no exciting question and yet even exciting questions such as questions of war can be argued without acrimony, as the case of Cato and Lentulus shows, §§ 50, 51.

To return to the view of the Cyrenaics: they hold that where annoyance arises the occurrence which causes it is unexpected. This is an important point: and Chrysippus also holds that the blow is heavier where it is unexpected. But this is due to two causes: (*a*) the suddenness of the occurrence prevents us from rightly measuring its true dimensions: (*b*) the annoyance is increased by a feeling of self-accusation due to the idea that the occurrence might have been foreseen, § 52.

That this explanation is correct is shown by the case of enslaved captives: though their evils continue unchanged their annoyance is not only abated but in many instances removed by lapse of time. Examples are furnished by Carthaginians, Macedonians, Corinthians, § 53.

When Carthage was destroyed Clitomachus thought it necessary to console his fellow-countrymen with a book which we have read. Had he delayed the sending of it for a number of years there would have been no wounds to heal, § 54.

Accordingly it is not because they are unexpected that misfortunes loom large upon us but because they have newly occurred; *quia recentia sunt maiora uidentur, non quia repentina*, § 55.

There are two ways in which we may ascertain the real dimensions of a seeming evil (or a seeming good)—We may examine its real nature, take e.g. the case of poverty; or we may illustrate it from the behaviour of individual men, e.g. Socrates, Diogenes, Caecilius' philosopher in a mean cloak, Fabricius: such instances, when placed before us, gradually bring us to a perception of the true dimensions of the supposed evil (or good). And previous reflexion upon possible future evils brings about the same result as is produced by lapse of time: the true dimensions of the supposed evil are better seen, §§ 56–59.

Antiochus writes that Carneades used to blame Chrysippus for quoting from Euripides in illustration of the inevitability of pain and woe, asserting that such sentiments could only bring consolation to spiteful persons. But Cicero thinks otherwise, holding that the inevitability of the human lot forbids us to fight with the deity and that the citation of examples is calculated not to delight the spiteful but to bring people to resolve to endure what they find that many have endured, §§ 59–60.

Annoyance is a terrible thing, compare Chrysippus' derivation of the word λύπη, but it will be rooted out now that its cause is set forth. This cause is nothing else than *opinio et iudicium magni praesentis et urgentis mali*, § 61.

(*b*) *aegritudo* is intensified where to the idea of a great present evil is added the idea that it is our duty to be annoyed at what has occurred, §§ 62–74.

To this idea are due disgusting modes of displaying grief, tearing the cheeks, plucking out the hair; to the same idea is due the blame bestowed by others upon those who fail to display the expected measure of grief, e.g. the blame which Aeschines cast upon Demosthenes.

Owing to the same idea some, when in grief, rush to the desert; some become dumb, others rabid, hence the legends of Niobe and Hecuba; others, like the nurse in Ennius, tell their sorrows to the desert air, §§ 62, 63. And all act in these various ways because they think it is their duty to grieve. That this is so is shown by the fact that, if those in mourning forget their grief for a moment, they blame themselves for doing so and purposely recall their grief, and if children, in time of mourning, do not display the proper air of gloom their elders take measures to produce it artificially. Notice, too, the word '*decrevi*' in the play of Terence, a plain indication that grief is an evil voluntarily, and not inevitably, incurred. This fact explains why people can abstain from grief where the circumstances forbid it, e.g. where men are daily falling in numbers on the battle-field. It also explains why those who witnessed the murder of Pompey were able to make good their flight to Tyre before their grief burst forth, §§ 64–66. And just because grief is a voluntary matter nothing is more effective in bringing about its abandonment than the persuasion that it does no good. And, because grief is a voluntary matter and they have found that it does no good, men, who have suffered much, endure their woes with more patience, § 67.

The voluntary character of annoyance is further shown by the fact that though the greatest philosophers recognise that they are in a most evil state, since they are *insipientes*, inasmuch as they have not yet attained to perfect wisdom, they nevertheless do not lament because in their case there is no idea that it is a matter of duty to lament. The greatest philosophers, e.g. Aristotle and Theophrastus, have admitted that there was much that they did not know, §§ 68, 69.

Again where a man thinks it unmanly to mourn he proves able to abstain from mourning, §§ 70 *fin.*, 71 *init.*

Even those who deny that any man would voluntarily give way to grief, and maintain that it is unavoidable, admit that men go further than is necessary in giving way to it, in other words they admit that a portion of it is voluntarily incurred, § 71 *fin.*

But there are motives which actually cause men voluntarily to incur grief:—

(*a*) the conception of an evil as of such magnitude that we *must* grieve;

(*β*) the idea that our mourning is acceptable to the dead;

(*γ*) the idea that the gods are pleased at our self-abasement beneath their stroke.

The inconsistency of these popular views is apparent from the fact that men are praised for meeting their own death calmly though they are blamed for taking that of another in the same way, for it is nonsense to suppose that anyone could love another more than himself, §§ 72, 73 *init.*

Objections are untenable: if some are not influenced by consolatory addresses this, so far from proving that their grief is not a matter of will, serves only to show that they have made up their minds to grieve. If some are too illogical to apply to their own case the good advice they give to others in distress (e.g. Oileus, § 71) they are not more inconsistent than misers who blame the avaricious or than ambitious men who condemn ambition. It is will that operates in all cases. Thus where grief seems healed by time it is really by reflexion, for which time has given opportunity, and not by time, that the cure is wrought. The Peripatetic theory of the mean cannot apply. For if grief is a matter of inevitable necessity why do they employ consolation? If, on the other hand, it is incurred by an act of will, why not root it out entirely? Cicero sums up the result of the enquiry as far as this point in the words '*satis dictum esse arbitror aegritudinem esse opinionem mali praesentis, in qua opinione illud insit ut aegritudinem suscipere oporteat,*' §§ 73, 74.

(*c*) Lastly Cicero says that Zeno rightly adds to the definition of *aegritudo* the qualification that it be *recens*, this word not being limited to a strictly temporal meaning but applying so long as the belief in the evil retains fresh vigour and force. The grief of Artemisia, for instance, remained *recens* in this sense until she died through its effect, § 75.

II. The remedial treatment of annoyance, §§ 75–79 end.

Different remedies are put forward by different philosophers. Some combine all these remedies, since some are affected by one, some by another; this is the method adopted in Cicero's own *Consolatio* where he tried every possible remedy; still, as Prometheus says in Aeschylus, one must wait for a suitable opportunity for administering the proper treatment.

In administering consolation one will show that the evil is non-existent or very small; that it is incident to the human lot; that grieving

over it is of no avail. Cleanthes' remedy which consisted in pointing out
that there was no evil where there was no disgrace is not a practical one.
His statement is not even always true; it was not true, for instance,
when Alcibiades grieved because he did not possess virtue, §§ 77, 78.

To point out to a sufferer that his misfortune is a common one does
not bring conviction in every case. The truest remedy, but one not easy
to apply while the annoyance is at its height, is that of Chrysippus, which
consists in convincing the sufferer that his grief is due to his own volition,
and to an idea that it is demanded by duty. We must vary our mode of
treatment according to the person treated, § 79.

EPILOGUE. The discussion has digressed from the original question
which was "Is the wise man affected by annoyance?" Instead of dealing
with that question we have discovered that the evil which is involved in
annoyance results not from inevitable and necessary causes but from an
act of will and erroneous opinion, § 80. Moreover we have dealt chiefly
with one form of annoyance, grief for the dead (*luctus*), this being the
severest of all its subdivisions, but the same treatment applies to all the
rest, §§ 81–4.

BOOK IV

On the remaining irrational emotions

Abstract of contents:—

Introduction, §§ 1–7.

The theme for discussion, §§ 8–10.

Main Division A. Stoic division and definitions of the emotions,
§§ 11–33.

B. Refutation of the Peripatetic defence of the emotions, §§ 34–57.

C. The treatment of the emotions, §§ 58–81.

Epilogue, §§ 82–4.

Introduction, §§ 1–7.

Our ancestors made early progress in constitutional development and
in the military art, § 1; and Cicero sees reason for thinking that they
had also acquired some knowledge of philosophy. His reasons are the
following:—

(*a*) It is not likely that the early Romans were deaf to the
doctrines of Pythagoras taught in Magna Graecia and widely celebrated, § 2.

(*b*) The fiction that Numa was a Pythagorean seems to indicate
an early Roman admiration for the Pythagoreans.

(*c*) The Pythagoreans and the early Romans alike are said to have sung to instrumental accompaniment and the poem of Appius Caecus seems to show Pythagorean influence, §§ 2–4.

Though the Romans have been philosophic from of old, no Roman philosopher can be named before the age of Laelius and Scipio. When these were young men the embassy of Diogenes, Carneades (and Critolaus) was sent to Rome in 155 B.C., § 5.

The philosophy of the schools founded by Plato and Aristotle is hardly as yet represented in Latin literature, but the Epicurean writings of Amafinius have had much influence, § 6.

The theme for discussion, §§ 8–10.

The question for the day's discussion is "Is the wise man free from all irrational emotions?" Annoyance was disposed of the previous day; fear is so closely connected with annoyance that the same decision applies to each. Exultant joy and desire remain to be considered, § 8.

The Stoics give much attention to the classification and definition of the several emotions. The Peripatetics disregard this department and attend rather to the remedial treatment of the emotions. Cicero will deal with classification and division first, §§ 9, 10.

A. Stoic division and definitions of the emotions, §§ 11–33.

(*a*) *Perturbatio* and its genera and their subdivisions defined, §§ 11–22.

Zeno defines *perturbatio* as ' *auersa a recta ratione contra naturam animi commotio*.' There are four main divisions (cf. iii 11, 24 and table on p. xxxi), viz. desire and joy, annoyance and fear, § 11.

All *perturbationes* are due to a mental decision and to the forming of a mere opinion, § 14. The forming of such an opinion is a weak act of assent, § 15. *Constantia* is opposed to *perturbatio*, being a movement of the soul in accordance with reason (εὐπάθεια). The *constantia* opposed to desire is reasonable wish (*uoluntas*, βούλησις): to unrestrained mirth (*laetitia gestiens*) is opposed joy (*gaudium*, χαρά, εὔλογος ἔπαρσις), a tranquil movement; to fear (*metus*) is opposed prudence (*cautio*, εὐλάβεια); annoyance (*aegritudo*) has no *constantia* opposed to it, §§ 12–15.

Each separate *perturbatio* has its subdivisions, § 16.

Definitions of the several subdivisions of each *perturbatio*, §§ 17–21. The source of all irrational emotions is want of self-control (*intemperantia*, ἀκράτεια), § 22.

(*b*) Stoic comparison between diseases of the mind and diseases of the body, §§ 23–32.

Disordered states of the mind arise from the disturbing effect of emotions just as similar states of the body arise from corruption of blood, or redundancy of phlegm or bile.

From *perturbationes* spring diseased cravings (*morbi*) and vicious habits (*aegrotationes*, ἀρρωστήματα), and, as errors of an opposite kind, diseased aversions (*offensiones*). The Stoics, and especially Chrysippus, push this parallel between diseases of the body and those of the mind too far, § 23.

These *morbi*, *aegrotationes* and *offensiones* are illustrated in detail, §§ 24-7.

Further parallelism between the health of the body and that of the mind, §§ 27-8.

And, as in the body we find diseases, chronic ailing states and deformity, we find corresponding evils in the mind. Definition of *uitiositas*, §§ 28, 29.

And there is the same parallelism between good conditions of the mind and those of the body as there is in the case of evil conditions, §§ 30, 31.

They differ in this that the mind while sound cannot be assailed by disease but the body can, c. 14, § 31.

How the clever differ from the dull as regards the irrational emotions. *Morbi* and *aegrotationes* are more difficult to uproot than *uitia animorum*, § 32.

(*c*) Transition to the second division of the subject, § 33.

B. Refutation of the Peripatetic defence of the emotions, §§ 34-57.

Virtue being a settled and laudable state of the mind, giving rise to good desires and actions, and its opposite *uitiositas*, which the Greeks call κακία, giving rise to irrational and disturbing desires, the only method of getting rid of these evil results is to be found in virtue, § 34.

Nothing can be more wretched and revolting than the sight of a man who is the slave of an emotion, for instance, of fear (like Tantalus): and foolish men are always such ; emotions like desire and exultation are just as foolish; the only person who is free from them all is the wise man, §§ 35, 36.

The wise man free from these disturbing emotions is certainly happy. How can he be mistaken in his judgment of the importance of any event who has studied the constitution of things and is on guard against surprise? His keen vision sees that the only home of peace is a quiet mind, free from disturbing emotion, while a mind ill at ease loses its health, §§ 37, 38.

How then can the Peripatetics adopt the effeminate view that a certain limited amount of emotion is necessary to man? The emotions are all contrary to reason, and nothing that is so can be tolerated.

Besides no limit is possible. One may under a single misfortune give way to emotion, and if misfortune be repeated the emotion will increase till it passes all bounds, §§ 39, 40. To try to set a limit to what is in itself a *uitium* is to try to stop oneself in mid air after leaping from a cliff; a mind once upon the downward track will go on; the disease will increase; without reason the mind has no strength; it is no protection against vice to be moderately vicious, §§ 41, 42.

Besides the Peripatetics declare the emotions to possess a certain utility; (*a*) anger, for instance, whets the courage of warriors and inspires orators; a man who cannot be angry is no man; (*b*) Themistocles was roused to energy by jealousy of Miltiades; (*c*) even philosophers have a *greed* for knowledge; (*d*) annoyance has its moral uses when men are annoyed at their own faults—and so they argue about (*e*) pity, envy, fear and all the rest, of which they approve in moderation, §§ 41–46.

Cicero is not going to join in the bout of sparring between the Peripatetics and the Stoics, the only question being for an impartial enquirer " What is the true definition of *perturbatio*?" Can a better than that of Zeno be found, "an unnatural movement of the mind away from right reason"? Cicero now takes the Peripatetics up point by point: (*a*) *Anger*: to say that a man cannot be brave unless he is angry is to degrade a brave man to the level of the gladiator in Lucilius. Was not Ajax joyful instead of angry when he challenged Hector, as is apparent from their colloquy before their duel? The bravery of Torquatus, Marcellus, Africanus, Hercules borrowed nothing from anger. Bravery is the deliberate judgment of the mind that death and pain are to be despised and endured: anger is a kind of madness, as much akin to valour as is drunkenness. The definitions of bravery given by Sphaerus and Chrysippus support this view (the Stoics are right when they say that all but the wise are mad). Again, anger can hardly be said to be of use in domestic life. It is true that an orator or a poet may simulate anger, but that is a different thing; (*b*) *Greed*: to say that philosophers are *greedy* for knowledge is an abuse of language; (*c*) *Annoyance*: the moral uses of annoyance have nothing to do with a wise man; (*d*) *Pity*, *jealousy* and the rest are similarly useless; a wise man should help, not pity, and there is little utility in envy and jealousy, §§ 47–56.

If a man has any of these vices even to a slight degree he is so far to be blamed, and cannot be called a wise man; the only safe remedy is not to prune but to eradicate, § 57.

C. The treatment of the emotions, §§ 58–81.

Cicero is not sure that the friend who laid down the general proposition of § 8 may not, under the guise of an abstract discussion, be anxious for some personal guidance; and happily nature has provided a remedy for moral as well as bodily disorders, § 58.

There are many methods of dealing with mental disturbance: one may either argue the general question whether one ought ever to allow his mind to be disturbed, or the particular question whether the patient has in a given instance any adequate reason for disturbing his mind: the former is the better course, as it can be applied to all cases. One may then show (*a*) that the object of fear or annoyance is not an evil or the object of desire and delight not a good; or (*b*) that a state of mental disturbance is in itself vicious, unnatural and unnecessary. Even those who will not yield to argument (*a*) may still be persuaded to moderate their emotions, and it must be admitted with regard to (*b*) that it is not always successful or of general utility. Different arguments must of course be used with those whose annoyance proceeds from consciousness of a lack of virtue and desire to obtain it: but the view that emotion (whatever be our view as to the value of the exciting cause) is inconsistent with the grave and serious character of a philosopher ought to be admitted universally, §§ 59–61.

In dealing with *libido* or desire, even for virtue, one ought to deal not with the value of the object desired, but dwell upon the effects which this emotion produces in the mind; *aegritudo* or annoyance can be cured by a consideration of the universal lot, though this point has been dealt with in the previous book and in the *Consolatio*. Fear (an uneasy emotion with regard to the future as annoyance is with regard to the present) may be dispelled by the consideration (*a*) of its debasing effect upon the character; (*b*) of the harmless nature of the chief objects of fear, pain and death, which have been dealt with in Books I and II, §§ 62–64.

Cicero now passes to the emotions caused by supposed goods, i.e. *delight* and *desire*. Here again the preferable method is to show, not that the supposed goods are not real goods but that these emotions, even if the objects of them be granted to be good, must not be carried to excess (immoderate laughter ex. gr. is offensive) and are as vicious in their own way as their opposites, §§ 65–67.

A special case of the emotion of delight is the passion of *love*, the most unworthy of all emotions. The poets praise it and attribute it to the gods, and even philosophers have been found to patronize it: the former even have praised unnatural vice. Stoic philosophers speak of a kind of love which is a mere overture for friendship inspired by the sight of beauty; if there be such an emotion it is harmless and calls for no cure; but the passion as ordinarily conceived is more akin to madness and is so represented by the poets, §§ 68–74.

Here the proper course is either to show (*a*) the trivial character of the pleasure aimed at, or (*b*) to inspire the lover with other interests, or (*c*) to get rid of one passion by means of another, or (*d*) to show that the passion is really insane and disgusting, and in any case a voluntary and not a necessary affection, §§ 75, 76.

Anger is still more clearly a form of insanity; here the patient is to be treated by the withdrawal of the object of his anger, or by being induced to defer its satisfaction, as Archytas voluntarily did, §§ 77, 78. How absurd then is the view that anger is either natural or useful! If the former, all men would be equally angry, and no one need ever repent of its results as did Alexander: like other emotions it is purely voluntary and proceeds from a false estimate of the value of objects; like other emotions it may be cured, and it is true of it as of the others that some men are naturally prone to it, and if it be not checked in time it becomes incurable, §§ 79–81.

EPILOGUE. The four days' discussion has shown that next to the knowledge of final good and ill there is nothing more useful than the discussion of such subjects. It has been shown (*a*) that death, and (*b*) that pain are to be despised and endured, (*c*) that annoyance, and (*d*) that all emotions are evil and can be cured. Annoyance is perhaps worse than the others and so has been treated in a separate book; but they are all effects of wrong judgment and can be cured, nor while they remain uncured can we be really happy or of sound mind, §§ 82–4.

BOOK V

Virtue is sufficient for a happy life.

Abstract of Contents :—

Introduction, §§ 1–11.

The consideration of the fifth day's subject, the self-sufficiency of virtue to ensure happiness, must end the discussions; this thesis, though difficult to prove, is the most important message of philosophy; the desire to secure happiness gave rise to philosophical speculation, and if happiness is to be secured by philosophy, who would not be a philosopher? If virtue cannot secure happiness amid the accidents of fortune we must despair, as Cicero confesses he sometimes does himself, of ever attaining it. Our bodies are so subject to disease and pain that one sometimes fears the mind must necessarily be subject to a similar fortune; this fear proceeds from a distrust of the power of virtue, which can raise us above all accidents of life and fate, by giving us true views of the world, §§ 1–4.

Philosophy alone can correct our mistaken views and ensure our happiness. Cicero breaks into an impassioned apostrophe of the philosophy which has created society, literature and civilization; whose precepts make a moment of time more precious than immortality; which has destroyed the fear of death. But in spite of such services to man, it is not merely neglected but despised and its history forgotten.

Though the word philosophy is new, the subjects it deals with are old: the Seven Wise Men, Lycurgus and others were philosophers in fact though not in name, the name being coined by Pythagoras who considered the contemplation of nature the most liberal pursuit, and the knowledge of it the most precious possession: he advanced the study of science and applied it in the public and private life of Magna Graecia. Until Socrates philosophers studied merely geometry, arithmetic, physics, astronomy; Socrates was the first to study moral science; his dialectical skill and intellectual power can be seen in the dialogues of Plato; he was the real founder of the Academic method, of which Carneades was the most celebrated exponent, to which Cicero will adhere in this discussion—the method of suspension of judgment and refusal to dogmatize, §§ 7–11.

The theme for discussion, §§ 12–14.

The proposition is laid down by one of the company that virtue is not sufficient to ensure a life of happiness. From this Cicero strongly dissents; he asserts that virtue is sufficient to ensure a life of goodness, rectitude, and honour and that such a life is a happy life. His opponent retorts that a man may live such a life and yet be unhappy, if for example he is subjected to torture. Cicero refuses to believe that happiness will not unite itself to the company of the virtues even though they be in the hands of the torturer. The reply of his opponent is a refusal to be put off with Stoic figures of speech; he demands that leaving abstractions aside Cicero should deal with the facts of life and with the dictates of common sense which declares that pain and happiness are incompatible. This Cicero promises to do though denying the right of his opponent to prescribe the method of proof to be adopted, §§ 12–14.

Proof of the Proposition that Virtue is Sufficient for a Happy Life, §§ 15–82.

A. The proof in syllogistic form, §§ 15–20.

If the results arrived at in the discussions of the precedings days are valid (as they admittedly are) then the matter is easily disposed of; for, (1) men who are under the influence of such emotions as fear, annoyance, lust, etc. are unhappy; (2) men who are subject to none of these are tranquil and therefore happy; (3) this tranquillity is produced by virtue; therefore virtue is in itself sufficient to produce happiness, §§ 15–17; Cicero's opponent admits the premiss that freedom from emotion and passion produces happiness, while he also grants that the further premiss that the wise man is free from emotion and passion has been proved on the preceding days, and it seems as if there were no more to be said, § 17.

But Cicero admits that a proof by axioms, after the style of geometers and Stoics, is unsatisfactory in a philosophical discussion which requires and is conceded, even by the Stoics, a broader treatment. Besides, the conclusion is too important to be dismissed so briefly; happiness, which even Xerxes with all his power and wealth could not secure, must be put beyond the reach of doubt, §§ 18–20.

B. Detailed consideration of various arguments, §§ 21–82.

Cicero's opponent here declares himself ready to admit the logical validity of the two positions (a) The only good is what is *honestum*, therefore virtue produces happiness, and (b) A happy life consists in virtue, therefore virtue is the only good; but he objects that other philosophers, such as Aristus and Antiochus, hold the existence of other goods than virtue. Cicero's reply is that the question of the agreement with their own premisses displayed in the conclusions of others must be discussed elsewhere; he has discussed the matter with the philosophers named; his own position was, and is, that if bodily infirmities and misfortune be evil, then since the wise man can be subject to such things, and no man can be happy surrounded by evils, it is possible for the wise man not to be happy. Antiochus holds that while such things are evils yet happiness (like most words of the kind) is a relative term, and that a man may be happy, even though he is subject to some evils. Since Cicero will not go into the question at this stage he contents himself with saying that he cannot conceive degrees of happiness, nor can he see how, if of the three kinds of evils (bodily, external and moral) a man is subject to the first two, he can be described even as relatively happy, §§ 21–23. Theophrastus, he proceeds (still labouring the digression), felt the difficulty; admitting the existence of external and bodily evils, he could not take a very lofty tone ; he is blamed for this, but he has at least the merit of consistency ; he is universally blamed also for his view that fortune, not philosophy, is the mistress of human life ; but here again he is quite consistent. Why should we imitate the inconsistencies of Epicurus who holds both that pleasure is the only good, and that abstemiousness is praiseworthy; that pleasure is happiness and yet that no one can be happy who does not live virtuously ; that pain is the greatest, nay the only evil, and yet that fortune has little to do with the wise man? Metrodorus too defies fortune in language which might become Zeno or Aristo but is inconsistent in the mouth of a follower of Epicurus, §§ 24–27. Uneducated persons are taken in by the language of these men but a trained mind detects their inconsistency. Cicero's own position (the good are always happy) is, however, free from this reproach; by the good (or the wise) he means those equipped with all virtue; by happiness he means the full possession of all good and the exclusion of all evil; it is necessary then to deny the existence of any good except goodness, or virtue; pain, poverty, slavery may befall the wise man, but as they are not evils they cannot interfere with his happiness. Philosophers like Aristotle and others who hold misfortunes to be evils are then inconsistent when they say that the wise man is always happy. If they wish to deserve the honourable name of philosophers they should despise misfortune and seek happiness within; but they must not adopt at once the language of the crowd and of philosophy; this is to be as inconsistent as Epicurus who speaks as if he did not understand his own theories, §§ 28–31.

Cicero's opponent here interjects that, though all this is plausible, it is entirely inconsistent with the statement in the Fourth Book of the *De Finibus* that Zeno differs from the Peripatetics only in terminology; if this be so why should they not be allowed to use the same language in regard to virtue in its relation to happiness? Cicero protests strongly against an Academic being tied down to previous statements, and points out that in any case he is at present only concerned with the mere question of logical validity. If Brutus (for instance) wishes as a Peripatetic to hold that the wise man is always happy that is his own affair ; and Cicero only differs from him in holding that the wise man is always *absolutely* happy, §§ 32–34 init.

Besides, if Zeno be a parvenu in philosophy, one can go back to Plato for the truth of the Stoic position : Plato makes Socrates in the *Gorgias* identify happiness with virtue and in the *Epitaphios* he lays stress upon the self-dependence of the wise man and his superiority to external fortune or misfortune. It is entirely upon the authority of Plato that Cicero will rely, §§ 34–36.

Where then must we search for our premisses? Clearly in nature, which aims in everything at self-development and perfection. This is true not only of the vegetable, but specially of the animal, world; every species remains true to its own natural development; and much more of man, whose principle of development is the divine principle of reason, whose cultivation brings enlightenment and whose perfection is virtue: and since to be perfect is to be happy, then all virtuous men are happy. So far the Peripatetics go: but Cicero goes farther and holds this happiness to be absolute, since happiness which cannot be depended upon to continue is not happiness at all, and if there be such goods as bodily and external goods (upon which no one can depend) real happiness is unattainable; the happiness which such goods confer is like the merchant's fortune tied to his rigging—nothing that may be lost can confer happiness. True happiness is at once indefectible and complete, just like courage (ex. gr.) which fears, not little, but nothing. Such happiness is impossible if there be any good but virtue, the only possession which confers confidence and independence; the virtuous man is like the Lacedemonian state which no threat could terrify nor death dismay—such fortitude combined with self-control is of the essence of virtue, §§ 37–42.

If it be true, as it is, that fancied goods and fancied evils produce mental disturbance at variance with reason, must not the man who is free from these be happy? The wise man who is always free from them is therefore always happy. Further every good gives pleasure; what gives pleasure is to be well spoken of, and what is to be well spoken of is glorious and so praiseworthy, that is to say virtuous or *honestum*, and therefore 'the good' is identical with virtue: but no one would call an external good *honestum*, such a 'good' therefore is not 'the good.' Must not a man in possession of all possible external goods be wretched if he is unjust, intemperate or cowardly; how then can such things which cannot confer happiness be called good? A happy life must be homogeneous, it cannot admit of anything but what is good. The good is an object of desire, and therefore of approbation, and of worth and deserving of praise; nothing but virtue is such, §§ 43–45.

We must abandon this view if other things are to be called good: if riches, birth, popularity, beauty are goods, philosophers are no better than the crowd. The Stoics call such things 'objects of preference' (*producta, praecipua*) but not 'goods' and not capable of producing happiness: even the Peripatetics admit they do not confer absolute happiness, the only happiness we are concerned with. A man is what he feels; what a man says, he is; his life is as his doctrines; a good man's feelings are praiseworthy, so is his life and therefore his life, being praiseworthy, is virtuous. A good man's life then is happy. What else has all that has been said been intended to prove? How can a man be good whose feelings and acts do not proceed from what is praiseworthy? What can be praiseworthy but virtue? Virtue therefore ensures happiness, §§ 46–48.

We may reach the same conclusion by another line of reasoning. In a wretched life (or in one that is neither happy nor wretched) there is nothing praiseworthy, nothing to be well spoken of. There must be some kind of life in which there is something of this kind; a happy life is such, for there is nothing to be well spoken of but happiness; but unless a virtuous life be a happy one there is something better than happiness (virtue of course being better)—an absurd conclusion: and if vice produces misery why should its opposite not produce the opposite? Is not this the real teaching of Critolaus' illustration of the balance? Why, if he admits virtue to be so superior to everything else, does he not admit its power to confer absolute happiness? Annoyance produces fear and servility of mind—the opposite of the freedom conferred by virtue; if virtue produces a good, i.e. a brave and lofty, life it must produce a happy life, free from regret, abundant, unhampered and (unlike the life of the foolish man) contented, §§ 49–54.

Was not Laelius, who was virtuous and wise, happier than Cinna, though the latter was consul four times and Laelius only once? There are of course men who would prefer to be Cinna; but can a man like Cinna, stained with the murder of Octavius, Crassus, Caesar and others, be called happy? He was wretched, not merely because he was a murderer, but because he had the heart of a murderer. Was Marius not happier when he shared his glory with Catulus than when, without a rival, he gave orders to murder him? Of the two Catulus was happier even in death than the man who stained his glory and his last days with crime, §§ 54–56.

Dionysius of Syracuse, though temperate and energetic, was malicious and unjust and, so, miserable; in spite of his birth, high position and crowds of favourites he practically lived in a prison owing to his suspicion of everyone, even of his two wives; a boy who made a harmless jest was executed on suspicion of having meant more than he said. The episode of Damocles showed what value Dionysius set upon his own happiness: yet so deeply was he involved in evil that he could not extricate himself even if he wished. True friendship was denied him; his artistic and musical, even his literary, talent could find no satisfaction; he had to pass his life in the company of barbarians and ruffians, §§ 57–63.

To compare the life of a Plato or an Archytas with his would be absurd. Archimedes, the mathematician of Syracuse, is a better parallel.

Even the site of Archimedes' grave had been forgotten until Cicero discovered it when he was a quaestor at Syracuse; yet what cultivated man would not prefer his life to that of Dionysius?—the one exercised his mind and reason in scientific investigation, the other in murder. What wealth or power can compare with the life of a philosopher, who enjoys the exercise of the best part of his nature, and is happy because he is virtuous? §§ 64–67. But more cogent arguments can be advanced : let us call up in imagination the character of the man distinguished for virtue, intellect and mental energy, full of zeal for knowledge of nature, of the laws of conduct and of thought : can we imagine any greater pleasure than such a person derives from the study and contemplation of nature as seen in the heavens, in the facts of biology or physics? He is led on from these to the realization of the truth of the Delphic maxim, "Know thyself," and to imitation of the gods who are the upholders of the order of the universe. What peace and joy, what independence of mind and feeling, are the result! He understands what virtue is and how to live virtuously and happily; his trained mind is incapable of yielding to false appearances. If he should engage in public life, his knowledge and justice benefit the community; he enjoys the blessings of friendship. What life can be happier? Is not such virtue identical with happiness? §§ 68–72.

If Epicurus, who places all pleasure in sensation, can claim that the wise man under the most cruel torments will smile at them with contempt, what is to be said of the really wise man who is armed against bodily pain by the virtues of firmness and fortitude, and has not to depend in his pain merely upon the memory of past pleasures? If Epicurus can take up this position why may not the Peripatetics? For even granting their doctrine of the existence of other goods than virtue, provided these others are allowed to be inferior to virtue, the virtuous man should be supremely happy. Is pain to affright a philosopher, who, as we have seen, is superior to the fear of death and other disturbing feelings? Even youths in Sparta treat it with contempt ; Indian sages are superior to heat and cold ; widows in India are not afraid to be burned along with a dead husband; the superstitious Egyptian would endure any torture rather than injure one of his sacred animals ; even brutes despise cold and hunger and will die for their young ; ambition and love lead men to endure anything, §§ 73–79.

The fact is that happiness and virtue are inseparable, and even pain and torture cannot effect their divorce : the virtuous man has nothing to regret, his every action is noble and right, he is proof against the surprises of fortune, he is stable and independent. Nothing can confer greater happiness than this. The Stoics define the final good as a life in harmony with nature; such a life is the duty of the wise man and is possible for him, and therefore happiness is within his reach. Nothing more can be said about happiness than this, §§ 80–82 *init.*

Cicero's opponent grants the validity of the argument so far; but he would like Cicero to develope a statement made during his argument (in § 75) that even the Peripatetics should admit that the wise man was supremely happy; he is not sure that this would be consistent with their main position, § 82.

The proposition true from the standpoint of all philosophers, §§ 83–118.

Cicero promises, availing himself of the liberty accorded him as a member of the New Academy, leaving the Stoic view aside (which, as has been sufficiently demonstrated, supports his conclusion), to prove the consistency of his thesis with the doctrine of the good held by rival schools, §§ 83, 84 *init.*

The philosophic schools may be divided into two classes, according as they regard the chief good as (*a*) simple, or (*b*) composite: (*a*) to the first class belong the Stoics (whose chief good is virtue), the Epicureans (pleasure), the school of Hieronymus (absence of pain), the school of Carneades (enjoyment of *naturae prima bona*); (*b*) to the second class belong the Peripatetics and Old Academy (who divide the good into *bona animi, bona corporis* and *bona externa*); the followers of Dinomachus and Callipho (pleasure and virtue); the followers of Diodorus (virtue and absence of pain). The schools of Aristo, Pyrrho and Erillus are out of date, §§ 84, 85.

These are now taken one by one: (α) The Peripatetics, who assert that the *animi bona* are immeasurably superior to the other two, can assent to the view expounded by Cicero, by regarding the absence of the *bona corporis* and *bona externa* as negligible or by understanding "happy" to mean "happy *multo maiore ex parte.*" (β) The followers of Callipho and Diodorus can speak of virtue as producing happiness because they admit virtue to be immeasurably preferable to pleasure and absence of pain. (γ) The Epicureans and the followers of Hieronymus and Carneades will be harder put to it, yet even they will admit that the mind being judge for itself of what is good and bad can rise superior to mere appearances, §§ 85–88.

If the truth of our position can be proved even from the premises of Epicurus it must be admitted to be consistent with the premises of all the others. Now Epicurus proclaims his indifference to death (for as it means annihilation it need not concern us) and to pain (which can be relieved either by recollections of past pleasure or by the thought that severe pain cannot last, while pain which lasts cannot be severe). No philosopher takes up a nobler position in regard to these two sources of unhappiness. What about poverty? Epicurus is an adherent of the simple life; and indeed a man who keeps far from him the passions which money is required to gratify has no need of money. Anacharsis the Scythian might be an example to Greek and Roman philosophers in this respect; and all might imitate with advantage the contempt for wealth that was displayed by Socrates, Xenocrates and Diogenes, §§88–92.

Epicurus' division of the desires into (*a*) those natural and necessary, (*b*) those natural and unnecessary, (*c*) those neither natural nor necessary, while not very scientific, is useful: for (*a*) the first class are satisfied with next to nothing, (*b*) the second class are more or less a matter of indifference, and (*c*) the third class should not be satisfied at all. On these points the Epicureans point out that ex. gr. the passion of love, which falls under the second class, can be gratified easily and easily done without; and Epicurus' doctrine of the wisdom of enduring pain in the hope of securing greater future pleasure, and of the function of the mind in deciding what pleasure is, makes it possible for the wise man to be perpetually happy, at any rate with the help of recollection and anticipation, §§ 93–96.

This has its bearing upon the gratification of appetite; hunger and thirst make anything sweet; exercise produces a healthy appetite, the gratification of which gives pleasure even though the food be coarse, as we see in the case of the Spartans and Persians; simple fare and abstinence ensure health, and consequently pleasure; on the other hand rich food and gluttony produce discomfort and disease, as the anecdotes told of Timotheus and Plato show. A Sardanapallus was little better than a brute, §§ 97–101. Nor is wealth required for the satisfaction of the artistic tastes, which are gratified not by possession of works of art but by contemplation of them, § 102.

Again obscurity or unpopularity need not cause unhappiness. Men like Demosthenes or Democritus should be above the judgment of the vulgar, as even a flute blower is in the practice of his profession. A community often hates or neglects its most eminent citizen, as the people of Ephesus and of Athens did in the cases of Hermodorus and Aristides: a life of ease and contemplation is better than a public career after all, §§ 103–105.

Many men fear exile, unreasonably; but its usual cause, unpopularity, and its frequent concomitant, poverty, have been already shown to be of no consequence, and merely to be absent from one's country is not a misfortune; many go abroad for gain, many philosophers to acquire knowledge—if one is exiled for crime that is a different matter. A philosopher is equally at home in every place where he is well off. Of this history furnishes many examples, §§ 106–109.

The best antidote to annoyance is a mind pleasantly occupied, as Epicurus teaches. Such a mind is unaffected even by the awful calamity of blindness, which might seem to deprive us of the noblest sense. A philosopher can meditate in the dark, witness the examples of Diodotus and Democritus: Homer was blind and yet how lifelike are his descriptions; if Polyphemus bewails his blindness to the ram, it is because the one was no more a philosopher than the other, §§ 113–115.

Deafness, again, which is reckoned a misfortune, is what we all suffer from (in a sense) without pain; for everyone is deaf in respect of a language he does not understand; and if a deaf man misses music, he misses along with it many unpleasant sounds, and he can always converse with himself, § 116.

If, finally, a man is overwhelmed with all these at once, the remedy is in his own hands—he need not continue to live; like a guest at a banquet unable to partake of the good cheer he had better depart at once. Epicurus and Hieronymus both sanction this remedy, §§ 117, 118.

EPILOGUE. If Epicurus, to whom virtue is an empty name, can say what he does of the happiness of the philosopher, why should not the followers of Socrates and Plato who lay so much stress upon virtue in comparison with everything else say at least as much? After all, the difference between the Stoics and the Peripatetics is a mere matter of terminology.

The five days' discussion being now over, Cicero promises to write an account of them in five books which he will dedicate to Brutus in the hope that they may confer upon others the same comfort that the discussion has brought to himself, §§ 119–121.

THE SOURCES OF BOOKS III—V.

BOOK III.

The most divergent views have been propounded as to Cicero's sources for this book. Posidonius, Chrysippus, Crantor, Antiochus, Philo have each been named as Cicero's principal authorities, though the possibility of his having used such subsidiary sources as Panaetius, Plato and Dicaearchus is admitted even by those who hold to the doctrine of one main and principal authority.

It is hardly necessary to criticize each of these views in detail: it will be sufficient to give the main grounds upon which the claims of each authority have been urged, and develope any necessary criticism of them in the analysis which follows.

TABLE OF THE *PERTURBATIONES* AND THEIR EFFECTS, TO ILLUSTRATE IV 5, 11 ff.

PERTVRBATIONES (πάθη) oriuntur

A ex bono opinato praesente — laetitia [ἡδονή] (uoluptas) [opp. to *gaudium* [χαρά]]

- maleuolentia [ἐπιχαιρεκακία]
- delectatio [κήλησις]
- iactatio
- (et similia)

quae inueterata fiunt → morbi (νοσήματα) / aegrotationes (ἀρρωστήματα):
- auaritia [φιλοχρηματία]
- gloriae cupiditas [φιλοτιμία] (ambitio)
- mulierositas (φιλογυνία) [λαγνεία]
- peruicacia [προσπάθεια]
- ligurritio [γαστριμαργία]
- uinulentia [οἰνοφλυγία]
- cuppedia [φιλοψία]
- (et similia)

B ex bono opinato futuro — libido [ἐπιθυμία] [opp. to *uoluntas* [βούλησις]]

- ira [ὀργή]
- excandescentia [θύμωσις]
- odium [μῆνις]
- inimicitia [μῖσος, κότος]
- discordia
- indigentia [σπάνις]
- desiderium [πόθος, ἵμερος]
- (et similia)

C ex malo opinato praesente — aegritudo [λύπη]

- inuidentia [φθόνος]
- aemulatio [ζῆλος]
- obtrectatio [ζηλοτυπία]
- misericordia [ἔλεος]
- angor [ἄχθος]
- luctus [πένθος]
- maeror [ἄχος]
- aerumna [ὀδύνη]
- dolor
- lamentatio [γόος, κλαυσις]
- sollicitudo [φροντίς]
- molestia [ἀνία]
- adflictatio [ἐνόχλησις, ἄση]
- desperatio [ἀθυμία]
- (et similia)

D ex malo opinato futuro — metus [φόβος] [opp. to *cautio* [εὐλάβεια]]

- pigritia [ὄκνος]
- pudor [αἰσχύνη]
- terror [ἔκπληξις]
- timor [δέος]
- pauor [δέος]
- exanimatio [ἀγωνία]
- conturbatio [θόρυβος]
- formido [ὀρρωδία]

quae inueterata fiunt → offensiones [προσκοπαί]:
- odium mulierum [μισογυνία]
- odium generis humani [μισανθρωπία]
- inhospitalitas

Greek words within round brackets are given in the text: the rest are supplied from the sources mentioned in the commentary.

R. Hirzel (*Untersuchungen zu Ciceros philosophischen Schriften*, iii, pp. 414 ff.), rejecting the views of Poppelreuter (*Quae ratio intercedat inter Posidonii περὶ παθῶν πραγματείας et Tusc. Disp. Ciceronis*, Bonn, 1883), who claims Posidonius as the source, and of Heine (Einleitung p. xxi) and Zietzschmann (*De Tusc. Disp. fontibus*, Halle, 1868), who hold that Chrysippus was the source, argues in favour of the view that Cicero derived his material and method of treatment from Philo. He puts aside possible claims in favour of Panaetius and of Antiochus, of the former on the ground that he admits "naturgemässe Lust" in opposition to the view championed by Cicero, and of the latter on the ground that though noted for his Stoic leanings and quoted incidentally on a particular point by Cicero (25, 59) he would not have subscribed to Cicero's polemic against the Peripatetics. The claims of Posidonius are easily disposed of, as the view of the origin of the emotions apparently taken by Cicero is opposed to all that Galen tells us of his doctrines in the fourth and fifth books of his "De placitis Hippocratis et Platonis" (pp. 330 ff. ed. Müller). Hirzel also claims that the known views of Chrysippus on the proper method of curing the πάθη and of the value of time as a remedial agent are inconsistent with the possibility of any work of his being the authority upon which Cicero relied. He takes the general tone of the treatment to be evidence that a writer of sceptical tendencies was the source. This consideration combined with the marked Stoic leanings shown in the book points to Philo as the writer upon whom Cicero relied.

Buresch (*Consolationum a Graecis Romanisque scriptarum Historia Critica* in *Leipziger Studien* ix pp. 1–170) considers that Cicero relied upon Crantor and the other writers whom he had consulted in writing his *Consolatio*, with occasional reference to Dicaearchus, Chrysippus and others. He regards the following passages as either due directly to Crantor or repeated from the *Consolatio* (1, 2; 6, 12; 13, 28, 29; 14, 30; 16, 34; 22, 54; 24, 58; 26, 63; 28, 66; 28, 70, 71; 30, 73; 31, 76).

Pohlenz, in his article in *Hermes* (xli pp. 321–355, *Das Dritte und Vierte Buch der Tusculanen*), finds much in the book to point to Chrysippus as the source or to be at least not inconsistent with his views, while there are some points in which his doctrines are in contradiction to those expounded by Cicero. This latter he holds to be perhaps most distinctly the case in regard to the question of the effect of time upon the cure of *aegritudo* (cf. 22, 54; 24, 58; 30, 74 with the sketch of Chrysippus' opinions given in Galen *op. cit.* pp. 394 ff.). It is however possible, according to Pohlenz, that Cicero while holding in the main to Chrysippus slurred over (as indeed Chrysippus himself may have done) the critical point upon which Posidonius (as quoted by

Galen *l.c.*) afterwards laid so much stress. It is possible that Cicero may have been indebted to Antiochus, who defended Chrysippus against Posidonius, for some hints on the treatment of the subject.

J. von Arnim (*Stoicorum ueterum fragmenta* i, pp. xx ff.) draws attention to the confused and inconsistent treatment of the natural causes of *perturbationes* and of their cure, as also of the criticism of the Cyrenaics and Epicureans. He regards the crucial question to be whether §§ 28 ff. are to be referred to Chrysippus or to Posidonius and decides in favour of the latter, partly on the ground that the importance given by Cicero to *praemeditatio* seems more consistent with the general position taken up by Posidonius. On the other hand §§ 24, 25, which are inconsistent with Posidonius' views, are to be referred to some authority who tried to mediate between the rival views of Zeno and Chrysippus, traces of the same authority being also seen in §§ 28, 52, 58, 59 and 62. This authority is most probably Antiochus.

Kühner (Prolegomena, p. 7, to his edition of the Tusculan Disputations, Hanover, 1874) regards Chrysippus' treatise περὶ παθῶν as the source not only of Cicero's description of the passions but of his quotations from Euripides and Anaxagoras. He allows the translation of Epicurus περὶ τέλους in 18, 41 f. to be Cicero's own and thinks he may also owe something to Cleanthes, Crantor, Clitomachus and Antiochus.

Philipp Finger (*Die beiden Quellen des III Buches der Tusculanen Ciceros* in Philologus LXXXIV pp. 51 ff. and pp. 320 ff.) finds two sources for this book, one a Stoic, and the other the eclectic Antiochus. He divides the book between them as follows: §§ 28–31 Stoic criticism of the Cyrenaics; §§ 32–37 Stoic criticism of the Epicureans; §§ 38–51 criticism of the Epicureans after Antiochus, §§ 52–61 criticism of the Cyrenaics according to Antiochus, §§ 62–71 after Antiochus, §§ 72–84 from the Stoic standpoint. He finds clear evidence of Antiochus being followed in the paragraphs assigned to him above; in ex. gr. §47 '*uirtus* maxime *expetatur*' and §50 '*mihi* summum *in animo bonum uidetur*,' where an orthodox Stoic would have said '*uirtus sola*' and '*solum bonum*'; again in §58 '*intellecto eo, quod rem continet, illud malum quod opinatum sit esse maximum nequaquam esse tantum ut uitam beatam possit euertere*' contains, he says, the kernel of the teaching of Antiochus in opposition to that of the Stoics whose view was '*nullum malum nisi culpa.*' The Stoic source he believes to have been Posidonius, the Stoic sections of this book being a faithful reflexion of the teaching of Posidonius as reported by Seneca, Epp. 87, 31 ff. The dualistic psychology of Posidonius which appears in the introduction to the book (ex. gr. §11, cf. iv, §34) has neither in Cicero nor in Seneca any influence upon his teaching with regard to the moral character of the πάθη. Finger however admits the difficulty of coming to a definite conclusion in regard to many phrases, as Cicero evidently made an attempt to cover up the fact that his sources were at variance on important points.

The two principal philosophical questions discussed in the book are (a) the nature of the *perturbatio* (πάθος) known as *aegritudo* (λύπη) and (b) the proper method of its treatment. Cicero defines *aegritudo* in 11, 25 as '*opinio magni mali praesentis, et quidem recens opinio talis mali ut in eo rectum uideatur esse angi.*' This definition must be interpreted however in the light of the general definition of *perturbatio* given in the preceding paragraph, '*animi motus uel rationis expers uel rationem aspernans uel rationi non oboediens, isque motus aut boni aut mali opinione citetur.*' According to this general definition a *perturbatio* is a *motus animi* which takes its rise in an *opinio*: while according to the special definition of *aegritudo* this particular *perturbatio* is an *opinio*. This apparent looseness or inconsistency of expression is characteristic of the whole book: it is one thing to say of *perturbationes* that '*causa omnis in opinione est,*' it is another to say that every *perturbatio* is an *opinio*; and yet the expressions are used interchangeably by Cicero: examples of the former are to be found in 12, 26 (where '*in opinione mali*' must be interpreted by '*tumor animi*' preceding, though in 28, 71 *in opinione* is used in a context which belongs to the other definition); 29, 72 '*sed plures sunt* causae *suscipiendi doloris. primum illa opinio mali, quo uiso atque persuaso aegritudo* insequitur *necessario*': examples of the latter are 25, 61 '*est enim nulla alia* (sc. *aegritudo*) *nisi opinio et iudicium magni praesentis . . . mali*'; 26, 62; 28, 68; 31, 74 '*satis dictum esse arbitror aegritudinem esse opinionem mali praesentis*': in the case of other passages such as 13, 28 '*tum aegritudinem existere, cum quid ita uisum sit, ut magnum quoddam malum adesse . . . uideatur*' and 34, 82 '*aegritudinem omnem procul abesse a sapiente, quod . . . non natura exoriatur, sed iudicio, sed opinione*' it is somewhat difficult to say under which head they should be classed. This looseness of expression is all the more remarkable when we remember that it relates to a point which was the subject of a historic difference of opinion between Zeno and Chrysippus, who are both referred to by Cicero as being responsible for the views he expounds without any indication of their opinions having differed: in fact Zeno is quoted with commendation in 31, 75 as the author of an addition to a definition which, according to Galen, was framed not by him but by his critic Chrysippus. With regard to the general difference of opinion Galen says (de placitis Hippocratis et Platonis p. 405 M. [p. 429 K.]) Χρύσιππος μὲν οὖν ἐν τῷ πρώτῳ περὶ παθῶν ἀποδεικνύναι πειρᾶται κρίσεις τινὰς εἶναι τοῦ λογιστικοῦ τὰ πάθη, Ζήνων δὲ οὐ τὰς κρίσεις αὐτὰς ἀλλὰ τὰς ἐπιγινομένας αὐταῖς συστολὰς καὶ διαχύσεις ἐπάρσεις τε καὶ πτώσεις ἐνόμιζεν εἶναι τὰ πάθη (cf. *op. cit.* p. 337 M. [367 K.]). This passage brings out clearly, as do many others in Galen, the distinction between the rival views, Zeno holding that *aegritudo* was an abnormal state of mind resulting from a *recens opinio praesentis mali* while Chrysippus held that the *aegritudo* was the *opinio* itself. But as not every *opinio* resulted in a *perturbatio* it was necessary for Chrysippus to define more closely than had been done by Zeno the particular kind of *opinio* which in his opinion constituted an *aegritudo*: he had in fact to include as part of the definition of the *opinio* what according to Zeno was a distinct condition to which the *opinio* gave rise. This Chrysippus did by the addition of the words which appear in Cicero's translation (11, 25; cf. 31, 74) as *ut in eo rectum uideatur esse angi*. That this addition is due to Chrysippus is plain both from its logical consistency with Chrysippus' general position (Zeno's doctrine accounting for the same facts in another way) and from the testimony of Galen *op. cit.* p. 370 M. [p. 398 K.] where Posidonius' criticism of Chrysippus' view is quoted: εἰ γὰρ τὸ μέγεθος τῶν φαινομένων ἀγαθῶν ἢ κακῶν κινεῖ τὸ νομίζειν καθῆκον καὶ κατὰ ἀξίαν εἶναι παρόντων αὐτῶν ἢ παραγινομένων μηδένα λόγον προσίεσθαι περὶ τοῦ ἄλλως δεῖν ὑπὸ αὐτῶν κινεῖσθαι, τοὺς ἀνυπέρβλητα νομίζοντες εἶναι τὰ περὶ αὐτοὺς τοῦτο ἔδει πάσχειν; *ibid.* p. 371 M. [p. 399 K.] τὸ δὲ ὑπολαμβάνειν κατὰ ἀξίαν εἶναι τῶν συμβεβηκότων οὕτως κεκινῆσθαι ὥστε ἀποτρέφεσθαι τὸν λόγον, μέγα δὲ πάθος ἐμφαίνειν, οὐ καλῶς ὑπολαμβάνειν ἐστί: cf. also 31, 76 '*Chrysippus autem caput esse censet in consolando detrahere illam opinionem maerenti, si se officio fungi putet iusto atque debito*' (see Hirzel, *Untersuchungen* iii, 416 f.; von Arnim, *Stoic. Vett. Fragm.* i, xxiii; Heine, *de fontibus T. D.* 15). Yet Cicero in 31, 74 can speak of Zeno having made an addition to the definition of *aegritudo* which contains the words '*in qua opinione illud insit ut aegritudinem suscipere oporteat.*'

This halting between two opinions, or failure to perceive the radical inconsistency between the two views, might be confidently set down to Cicero's own carelessness, indifference or lack of acumen, were it not that Chrysippus himself is chargeable with precisely the same fault: Galen *op. cit.* p. 337 M. [p. 367 K.] ἐν μὲν δὴ τούτοις τοῖς ὅροις ὁρμὰς καὶ δόξας καὶ κρίσεις ὑπάρχειν οἴεται τὰ πάθη, κατὰ δέ τινας τῶν ἐφεξῆς Ἐπικούρῳ καὶ Ζήνωνι μᾶλλον ἢ τοῖς ἑαυτοῦ δόγμασιν ἀκόλουθα γράφει· τήν τε γὰρ λύπην ὁριζόμενος μείωσιν εἶναί φησι ἐπὶ φευκτῷ δοκοῦντι ὑπάρχειν ... καὶ γὰρ αἱ μειώσεις καὶ αἱ ἐπάρσεις καὶ αἱ συστολαὶ καὶ αἱ διαχύσεις, καὶ γὰρ τούτων ἐνίοτε μέμνηται ... ὃ καὶ θαυμάζειν ἐπέρχεταί μοι τἀνδρὸς ἐν ἐπαγγελίᾳ λογικῆς τε ἅμα καὶ ἀκριβοῦς διδασκαλίας οὐκ ἀκριβοῦντος. This being so it seems somewhat dangerous to assume either that the inconsistencies of statements in Cicero are due to a reliance upon different sources in different passages or to the use of an authority who attempted to combine both views.

The views of both Zeno and Chrysippus were subjected to a penetrating examination by Posidonius, who, as the result, probably, of Academic criticism, abandoned the traditional Stoic psychology and adopted the Platonic threefold division of the soul into τὸ λογικόν, τὸ θυμοειδές and τὸ ἐπιθυμητικόν. His view of the emotions (expounded by Galen in books iv and v of the De placitis Hippocratis et Platonis) is thus radically distinct from that adopted by Cicero in T.D. iii. Regarding the emotions as due to the irrational elements of the soul, he could not of course subscribe to any definition which regarded them as originating in, or being identical with, an *opinio* or δόξα which was a function of the rational intelligence: nor could he regard the corruption of human nature as due primarily to the evil influence of training and environment, a view which is the natural consequence (though not always the consistent lesson) of the doctrine of Zeno and Chrysippus. Of this view there is no trace in Cicero's discussion here, and if we except one passage there is nothing in Cicero's treatment of the question which can fairly be interpreted as due to an acquaintance with the teaching of Posidonius. That apparent exception is the passage in which Cicero deals with an objection to the Chrysippean view of the possibility of *aegritudo* in the case of a philosopher, which, as it concerns the treatment proper to be adopted in such a case, will be discussed later.

From the discussion of the nature of *aegritudo* Cicero passes to the question of its appropriate treatment and cure. Setting aside the view of Epicurus that the mind of the patient should be induced to dwell upon pleasurable experiences or anticipations (15, 33; 31, 76), he enumerates the various methods recommended by experience or philosophy; these are (*a*) the effect of time (16, 35; 22, 53 f.; 30, 74; 31, 76); (*b*) *praemeditatio* (14, 29; 16, 34; 22, 52; 23, 55; 25, 60); (*c*) consideration of the real nature of the object which has given rise to the feeling of *aegritudo* (23, 56; 31, 76; 32, 77); (*d*) consideration of the nature of the feeling itself (25, 61); (*e*) reflexion upon the irrational and useless character of the feeling (27, 64; 28, 66; 31, 76 f.; 33, 79; 34, 82); (*f*) the appeal to the experiences of others (23, 56; 33, 79). To each of these Cicero allows some weight, as in the case of his own bereavement he had experienced their value when for his *Consolatio* he had collected and tried them all (31, 76), though he admits that their values vary.

(*a*) The value of time as an agent of healing resides in the *cogitatio diurna* for which it affords opportunity. This is a point upon which the views of Chrysippus had been criticized by Posidonius. The view of the former is given by Galen op. cit. p. 394 M. [p. 419 K.] ὅτι δὲ ἐν

χρόνῳ μαλάττεται τὰ πάθη κἂν αἱ δόξαι μένωσι τοῦ κακόν τι αὐτοῖς γεγονέναι
καὶ ὁ Χρύσιππος ἐν τῷ δευτέρῳ περὶ παθῶν μαρτυρεῖ γράφων ὧδε· 'ζητῆσαι δὲ
ἄν τις καὶ περὶ τῆς ἀνέσεως τῆς λύπης πῶς γίνεται πότερον δόξης τινος μετα-
κινουμένης ἢ πασῶν διαμενουσῶν καὶ διὰ τί τοῦτο ἔσται.' εἶτα ἐπιφέρων φησί
'δοκεῖ δέ μοι ἡ μὲν τοιαύτη δόξα διαμένειν ὅτι κακὸν αὐτό, ὃ δὴ πάρεστιν, ἐγ-
χρονιζομένης δὲ ἀνίεσθαι ἡ συστολὴ καί, ὡς οἶμαι, ἡ ἐπὶ τὴν συστολὴν ὁρμή·
τυχὸν δὲ καὶ ταύτης διαμενούσης οὐχ ὑπακούσεται τὰ ἑξῆς διὰ ποιὰν ἄλλην
ἐπιγενομένην διάθεσιν ἀσυλλόγιστον τούτων γινομένων κτλ.' It is clear from
this passage that Chrysippus acknowledged the psychological fact that
emotion becomes less vehement by the mere lapse of time, though he
seems to have found this fact somewhat difficult to reconcile with his
view that emotion was a δόξα upon which time in itself could not have
any effect. Posidonius seized upon his difficulty and in a forcible
passage (*op. cit.* p. 399 M. [p. 424 K.]) developed the view that the
gradual cessation of the emotions was to be attributed to the satisfaction
or exhaustion of the irrational elements of the soul. Of this difficulty
and controversy there is not the slightest hint in Cicero, another proof
that he cannot have drawn in this book upon a work of Posidonius.

But Chrysippus, while admitting a certain element of uncertainty in
the psychological details, was sure that in some cases the value of time
in these matters lay in the opportunity for reflexion which it afforded.
He is quoted by Galen (*op. cit.* p. 398 M. [p. 422 K.]) for the remark
καθ' ὃν λόγον οὐκ ἂν ἀπελπίσαι τις οὕτως τῶν πραγμάτων ἐγχρονιζομένων καὶ
τῆς παθητικῆς φλεγμονῆς ἀνιεμένης τὸν λόγον παρεισδυόμενον καὶ οἱονεὶ χώραν
λαμβάνοντα παριστάναι τὴν τοῦ πάθους ἀλογίαν—a passage which Cicero
seems almost to quote in 27, 64, '*ipsa remissio luctus cum est consecuta
intellectumque est nihil profici maerendo*' and again in 12, 26 '*et
quidem inueterato malo, cum tumor animi resedisset.*' Cicero's treatment
of the effect of time then is entirely opposed to that of Posidonius and
partially identical with that of Chrysippus, though he slurs over the
difficulty which the Greek philosopher frankly admitted.

(*b*) The value of *praemeditatio* was fully acknowledged by Chrysippus,
Galen *op. cit.* p. 392 M. [p. 417 K.]) καί φησι διότι πᾶν τὸ ἀμέτρητον καὶ
ξένον ἀθρόως προσπῖπτον ἐκπλήττει τε καὶ τῶν παλαιῶν ἐξίστησι κρίσεων
ἀσκηθὲν δὲ καὶ συνεθισθὲν καὶ χρονίσαν ἢ οὐδὲ ὅλως ἐξίστησιν ὡς κατὰ πάθος
κινεῖν, ἢ ἐπὶ μικρὸν κομιδῇ· διὸ καὶ προενδημεῖν δεῖν φησι τοῖς πράγμασι μήπω
τε παροῦσιν οἷον παροῦσι χρῆσθαι—where προενδημεῖν expresses what Cicero
means by *praemeditari*.

(*c*) The consideration of the real nature and quality of the object
which has caused the emotion is recommended by Cleanthes (31, 76),
who held that the proper remedy for *aegritudo* was to show that the
object was not *malum*, and by the Peripatetics (*ib.*) who recommended

the consideration that it was not *magnum malum*. To this Cicero raises two objections: (1) that it is a method only suitable in the case of a *sapiens*, '*qui consolatione non eget*,' and (2) that it cannot be employed in the case of a person whose grief is due to the fact that he is not virtuous or wise. The first objection is at bottom identical with the view of Chrysippus. Galen (*op. cit.* p. 371 M. [p. 398 K.]) quotes from Posidonius the clause εἴτε πρὸς τῷ μεγέθει τῶν φαινομένων καὶ τὴν ἀσθένειαν τῆς ψυχῆς αἰτιάσονται καὶ διὰ τοῦτο τοὺς μὲν σοφοὺς τὸ παράπαν ἐροῦσιν ἀπηλλάχθαι τῶν παθῶν κτλ., in which, as the context shows, the arguments of Chrysippus and his followers are under discussion. The second objection will be more conveniently discussed when we come to consider the arguments that are to be mentioned under (*e*).

(*d*) The method of dealing with *aegritudo* which consists in the explanation that it is merely an *opinio et iudicium magni praesentis atque urgentis mali* (25, 61), though separately discussed and briefly dismissed by Cicero, is really identical with (*c*).

(*e*) The view, variously expressed by Cicero, that a satisfactory cure or *consolatio* can be secured by the reflexion that, whatever be the object which has caused the *aegritudo*, grief is useless and unnecessary and not a matter of duty, is expressly attributed to Chrysippus in 31, 76 and adopted by Cicero (33, 79; 34, 82) as on the whole the most satisfactory, though the practical application of it may cause difficulty when the emotion is still fresh and strong. It affords the only satisfactory reply to the objection urged by Posidonius, that if an emotion be a δόξα that the object which arouses it is very good or very bad then οἱ προκόπτοντες must be in a perpetual state of mental disturbance: the sight of the virtue which they hope to attain and of the evil which they desire to avoid, giving rise to an opinion of their nature which cannot be refuted, must fill them either with unseemly desire or unseemly grief. So far as the actual fragments of Chrysippus go there is no direct evidence that he raised or considered the point, while we know from Galen that Posidonius made much of it (*op. cit.* p. 370 M. [p. 397 K.]). But the general trend of the views of Chrysippus as well as particular expressions in his extant fragments leave little doubt both that he raised the question and answered it by the argument which Cicero lays such stress upon (see Hirzel *op. cit.* iii pp. 436 sqq.: Pohlenz *Fleck. Jahrb.* XXIV pp. 569, 613). If this be so it must be assumed that the discussion of this point in 28, 68 is derived not from Posidonius (who solved the difficulty by the argument that in the persons concerned the rational faculty was so powerful as to keep the emotions in check) but, either mediately or immediately, from Chrysippus.

(*f*) The attempt to cure *aegritudo* by adducing examples of persons who have suffered already may be regarded from one point of view as a subdivision of *praemeditatio*. If, however, the method be employed without regard to the circumstances of the particular case it may do more harm than good (33, 79). There is nothing here which is inconsistent with the general standpoint adopted in the book.

It remains to discuss in detail the method adopted by Cicero and to endeavour to discover whether any particular treatise or author can be shown to be the source probably followed in the dialogue. The introduction (§§ 1–7) is admitted on all hands to be Cicero's own; but it is important to keep in mind that the view adopted in § 2 of the origin of human depravity can hardly be reconciled with any psychological doctrine other than that professed by the strict Stoic. The corruption of human nature is there referred entirely to the environment and upbringing of human beings: it is *mali mores opinionesque* (imbibed from nurses, parents, schools, literature and life) which quench the original sparks of virtue: there is not a word about the irrational faculties, τὸ θυμοειδές and τὸ ἐπιθυμητικόν, the traitors within the soul, upon which Posidonius laid so much stress. In fact no two views of the matter could well be more inconsistent than that expounded by Cicero here and that attributed to Posidonius in Galen *op. cit.* p. 465 M. [p. 483 K.]. The general parallelism between diseases of the body and those of the soul, though in some points of detail differently expressed by Posidonius and Chrysippus, is too vaguely sketched in Cicero to afford a satisfactory clue to his sympathies in this minor discussion.

The subject of the dialogue is stated and expounded in 4, 7–6, 13. Here the material which can be directly referred to any Greek source is no more than the text upon which Cicero dilates: the digressions upon points of translation and etymology are Cicero's addition and they are so worked in with the rest that the result owes more to Cicero than to any probable source. The definition of πάθη as '*motus animi rationi non obtemperantes*' is one to which, it is true, Posidonius might have subscribed if he had been allowed to interpret *ratio* as τὸ λογιστικόν and *animus* as the whole which comprised both it and the irrational elements of τὸ θυμοειδές and τὸ ἐπιθυμητικόν. But Chrysippus also used such phrases as ἄλογος and ἀπειθὲς λόγῳ and ἀπεστραμμένον τοῦ λόγου, for which (and especially in the case of ἄλογος) he was charged with an unscientific ambiguity (Galen *op. cit.* pp. 348 ff. M. [pp. 377 ff. K.]). The quotation from Crantor in 6, 12 is probably derived from the materials amassed for the *Consolatio*, in which Cicero had collected the views of all philosophers who had written upon the subject. The passage is in any case only quoted to be refuted and Crantor's general position was one which both here and elsewhere is combatted by Cicero. While it is true that Cicero often quoted from him in this book either directly or indirectly, he is at best only a subsidiary source.

The remark in 6, 13 that, while *aegritudo* may be cured, yet the root of it will remain, must not be pressed into an expression of even partial or guarded sympathy with a view which regarded a certain amount of *perturbatio* as natural and necessary, a view expressly disclaimed in 10, 22 and other passages. Cicero seems to mean here no more than what Zeno himself admitted (cf. 22, 54 n. on '*cicatricibus*'), though using a different metaphor.

Cicero concludes this section with the statement that he will adopt first the Stoic style of treatment and then following his own bent allow himself a free rein.

The "Stoic treatment" is to be found in 7, 14 to 10, 21. So far as the question of form is concerned it is "Stoic" in the style of Zeno and Chrysippus, not in that of Posidonius. The references in 7, 14 to *infractio animi* and *demissio animi* are consistent either with Zeno's or Chrysippus' expressions of their views and the phrases in 8, 17 '*motus animi adpetentis regere*' and '*aduersantem libidini…seruare constantiam,*' while perfectly consistent with the doctrine of Posidonius, are not out of keeping with the occasional loose phraseology of Chrysippus.

The digression on *frugalitas* is clearly derived either from Plato (see the nn. *ad. loc.*) or more probably from Panaetius whom Cicero followed in that section of the *de Officiis* (i 27, 93 ff.) in which the virtue of *decorum* (τὸ πρέπον) is dealt with. The view there expounded of the relation of σωφροσύνη to the other virtues is that of Panaetius (see Schmekel *Die Phil. d. Mittl. Stoa* pp. 36 ff.) and is in marked contrast to the doctrine of Zeno (whom Chrysippus seems to have followed in the main) that the virtue which comprised all the others was φρόνησις (cf. Plut. *de uirt. mor.* 2 ἔοικε δὲ καὶ Ζήνων εἰς τοῦτό πως ὑποφέρεσθαι ὁ Κιτιεύς, ὁριζόμενος τὴν φρόνησιν ἐν μὲν ἀπονεμητέοις δικαιοσύνην, ἐν δὲ διαιρετέοις σωφροσύνην, ἐν δὲ ὑπομενετέοις ἀνδρείαν· ἀπολογούμενοι δ' ἀξιοῦσιν ἐν τούτοις τὴν ἐπιστήμην φρόνησιν ὑπὸ τοῦ Ζήνωνος ὠνομάσθαι and Dyroff (*Die Ethik d. alt. Stoa* pp. 79 ff.)).

With regard to the quotations of Dionysius (9, 18) and Theophrastus (10, 21) there is no reason why we should not assume that they may have been derived from the materials collected for the *Consolatio*.

The whole section is interspersed with Cicero's usual Latin digressions, discussions and quotations.

The following section (10, 22-3) furnishes a transition from the "Stoic" to the "freer," rhetorical treatment which Cicero prefers. He quotes the Peripatetic view of the *mediocritates* as one to which he cannot subscribe, thereby ranging himself on the side of the Stoics. He has the usual digression upon the superiority of Latin to Greek as an instrument of philosophical expression, though his idea of the strict meaning of πάθος is a mistaken one. There is nothing in this section to indicate direct reliance upon any Greek (or other) authority.

With 11, 24 Cicero enters upon the main subject of the book, the nature of *aegritudo* and the method of its cure. It has already been shown that the views taken of both these points are certainly not those of Posidonius, and that on the other hand they in many respects coincide with the known views of Chrysippus and are not in any case contradictory of what we know of his teaching. But the treatment is complicated by digressions upon the views of the Cyrenaics and the Epicureans. The Cyrenaics are criticized for their view of the origin of *aegritudo*, which referred it to an "unlooked for and unexpected evil," and they are praised for having seen that *praemeditatio* was a sound method of treatment. But there is only a very superficial attempt made to discuss their position; the superiority of Chrysippus' definition to theirs is asserted, not proved, and if Cicero had a Greek authority here he has either cut it down so as to exclude everything characteristic or its treatment must have been so superficial as to make it not worth consulting.

The same may be said of the criticism of Epicurus. With the views of the Epicureans Cicero had been acquainted for years. He had studied under Zeno the Epicurean, whose lectures indeed he quotes in 17, 38. There is nothing in his remarks upon Epicurus here, except the Ciceronian rhetoric, which was not common form; and it may safely be said that if Cicero was not capable of composing these sections without reference to a Greek handbook he was not capable, and never would have dreamed, of writing philosophical treatises at all. It will hardly be contended that the quotations from Epicurus in 18, 41 f. must have been derived from quotations in a Greek original. Cicero must have been familiar with the "liber qui continet omnem disciplinam Epicuri" and we need not assume that his quotations from it were not the result of his own reading and memory. The same remark must be made about the poetical quotations scattered through the book. The quotations from Latin poets (like the illustrations from Roman history) are admitted by all critics to be the result of Cicero's own reading. With the quotations from the Greek poets he must have been equally familiar, if not from the study of the poets themselves, then at least from his study of Greek philosophers in whose writings they seem to have occurred *ad nauseam*. The same passages were to be met in Chrysippus, Crantor and Posidonius, pressed by each into the service of his own particular theory or introduced for the embellishment of his pages. Many of them must have been long familiar to Cicero and if he had for his *Consolatio* read, as he says he did (Att. xii 14, 3), everything that had been written on the subject, it is idle to assume that a passage in which (e.g.) a fragment of Euripides occurs must have been borrowed from (say) Crantor merely because we know that Crantor quoted that particular fragment, and have no direct evidence that any other writer on the same subject either did or did not.

Cicero quotes (or professes to quote) the following Greek authors in this book: Crantor (6, 12), Dionysius (9, 18), Theophrastus (10, 21), Zeno the Epicurean (17, 38), Epicurus (18, 41 f.; 20, 46), Chrysippus (22, 52; 25, 61 (?); 31, 76), Clitomachus (22, 54), Antiochus (25, 59), Aristotle (28, 69), Cleanthes (31, 76 (?)), Lycon (32, 78). It is not necessary to assume that all these quotations are at first hand: but it seems like trifling with evidence to assert that this was *not* so in the cases of Crantor, Epicurus, Chrysippus, Clitomachus and Antiochus: while Zeno is quoted from Cicero's recollections of lectures which he attended at Athens.

On the whole it seems most probable that Cicero followed in the main in this book the doctrines of Chrysippus on the origin of *aegritudo* and the method of its cure; that he relied for his knowledge upon his own acquaintance with the works of Chrysippus and (perhaps) other writers of the Chrysippean school; that he made extensive use of the works of other authors whom he had read for the purposes of his *Consolatio* (e.g. Crantor and Clitomachus); that he introduced, when necessary, recollections of his reading of other authors both Greek (e.g. Panaetius) and Latin; and that in arranging his materials he was guided by his own judgment and fancy.

BOOK IV.

The subject which was begun in Book iii is continued in Book iv, which deals with the remaining *perturbationes* and their cure. Hirzel *op. cit.* iii pp. 456 ff. thinks that it is therefore to be referred to the same source: we have, he argues, the same sceptical tone which is against the assumption of a dogmatic source, and the polemic against the Peripatetics which excludes Antiochus; Posidonius is excluded since Cicero adopts the views of Chrysippus which Posidonius combatted as to the parallelism between mental and bodily diseases. He concludes that Philo is the source. Pohlenz *l.c.* pp. 339 ff. argues that the subdivision of the πάθη, the polemic against the Peripatetics, the method advocated for curing the πάθη, all point to an orthodox Stoic source. This is most probably some work of Chrysippus, and perhaps the Θεραπευτικός.

Von Arnim *l. c.* pp. xxvi ff. considers that the book is of composite origin; §§ 11–33 come from a source which while it is not a work of Chrysippus inclines on the whole to his doctrines. The rest of the book is from some other source, as no one holding the views of Chrysippus would use the arguments urged here against the Peripatetics.

Heine (*de fontibus Tusc. Disp.* Weimar 1863 pp. 13 ff.) holds that in cc. 4–15 a handbook based upon Chrysippus' περὶ παθῶν was the source: in cc. 15–27 the same book, supplemented by Crantor περὶ πένθους, was the ultimate source; while the remainder of the book is based not upon a philosophical but upon a rhetorical treatise.

Ph. Finger *op. cit.* p. 348 considers that the sources of this book, as of the preceding, are Antiochus and Posidonius, whose influence he divides as follows: §§ 37–46 after Posidonius; §§ 47–56 after Antiochus; §§ 57–65 after Posidonius; §§ 66–78 after Antiochus; §§ 79 ff. after Posidonius.

Upon the question of the origin and nature of the πάθη Cicero adopts in this book practically the same ground as in the preceding book. In 5, 9, 11 he names "Chrysippus et Stoici" as the philosophers who devoted most attention to the classification and definition of the emotions and declares his intention of following them in this part of his work; and where he quotes his authority for a definition it is always a Stoic, e.g. 6, 11 (Zeno), 14, 33 (Stoici), 21, 47 (Zeno), 24, 53 (Sphaerus and Chrysippus). But with regard to the question in dispute between Zeno and Chrysippus as to whether the δόξα, *opinio*, constituted the emotion or caused it we have the same uncertainty and vacillation as in the previous book. In 6, 11 a *perturbatio* is an *animi commotio*, which is Zeno's definition: in 6, 14 *aegritudo* is an *animi contractio*; while five lines lower down it is defined as an *opinio...in quo demitti contrahique animo rectum esse uideatur.* In 7, 15 he regards the *perturbationes* as the source of the *recessus animi* and the other mental states which Zeno considered to constitute the *perturbationes.* Again in 15, 34 the definition of *perturbationes* as *turbidi motus* is Zenonian and in 21, 47 Zeno's own definition is quoted with approval. In 27, 59 two other and shorter definitions *adpetitus uehementior* (ὁρμὴ πλεονάζουσα) and *aspernatio rationis* (ἄλογος κίνησις) are adopted, which though Zeno's (Diog. L. vii 110) do not raise the immediate point of controversy and may be reconciled with either view.

It is therefore surprising to find Cicero in 5, 10 announcing that while he intends to employ Stoic definitions (i.e. the definitions of Zeno and Chrysippus) he is an adherent of the rival view, derived from Pythagoras and Plato, which regards the soul as partly rational and partly irrational: the latter being the seat of the emotions of anger and desire (τὸ θυμοειδές and τὸ ἐπιθυμητικόν), the former the placid and quiet seat of the controlling reason. Not only is the contradiction between this general position and the subsequent definitions formal and complete, but it is hard to see why the statement should have been introduced at all, and if introduced why it should not have been made earlier. If the general distinction between the irrational soul, the source of the *perturbationes*, and the rational soul, the seat of the controlling influence, was relevant in any way to Cicero's discussion, the place to draw it was when he began the treatment of the most obstinate of the *perturbationes* in the third book. It is not even hinted at there: why then is it introduced here?

This casual and careless method of dealing with fundamental questions renders it very difficult to avoid the conclusion that if Cicero really held to the Platonic psychology (as he says he did) he either did not understand, or considered irrelevant for his purpose, the distinction between the Stoic and the Platonic view of the emotions. If he had read Posidonius' criticisms of Chrysippus (upon which there is no direct evidence either positive or negative) he cannot have failed to understand the difference or have regarded it as psychologically unimportant. But his immediate object being not scientific but practical, he seems to have put the question to one side, content to assume that the practical results could be reached independently of theoretical presuppositions. That the Stoic definitions could not be accepted as they stood by any adherent of the Platonic psychology ought to have been self-evident; that the Peripatetic doctrine of the *mediocritates*, so vigorously repudiated by Cicero, is not easily to be set aside if the Platonic psychology be admitted, does not seem to have been considered by him with sufficient care: and he may have been the more readily induced to gloss over distinctions by the ease with which words may be chosen to conceal them. It is not hard to see how (e.g.) the definition '*auersa a recta ratione contra naturam animi commotio*' might be interpreted and applied by a Platonist: how "adpetitiones animi" might be held to be either the ὁρμαί of Chrysippus or τὸ ἐπιθυμητικόν of Posidonius. Expressions seem to slip in which it is difficult to interpret from a purely Stoic standpoint. How are we to reconcile with pure Stoicism the phrase in 25, 55 '*utile est enim uti motu animi qui uti ratione non potest*'?

For this and similar inconsistencies of expression Cicero might have pleaded the example of Chrysippus himself, who, as Galen (De plac. Hipp. et Plat. p. 331 M. (362 K.) ff.) points out, was in the habit at least of accommodating his language to the conceptions of a Platonist if not, as Galen believes, of actually contradicting himself. One might even go the length of conjecturing that Cicero's apparent indifference to important doctrinal distinctions may have been encouraged by Chrysippus' indifference to the importance of verbal consistency.

And with the importance of the practical end tending to overshadow in his mind the importance of scientific accuracy, Cicero might have appealed in defence of his comparative carelessness of philosophical pedantry to the dictum of Chrysippus that whatever be the view held as to the ultimate values of things the πάθη ought to be eradicated. Origen (c. Celsum viii 51) quotes from Chrysippus' περὶ παθῶν θεραπευτικός the sentence κἂν γὰρ τρία ᾖ γένη τῶν ἀγαθῶν καὶ οὕτω θεραπευτέον τὰ πάθη· οὐ περιεργαζόμενον ἐν τῷ καιρῷ τῆς φλεγμονῆς τῶν παθῶν τὸ προκαταλαβὸν δόγμα τὸν ὑπὸ τοῦ πάθους ἐνοχλούμενον, a statement which evidently underlies Cicero's discussion in 28, 60. This will not, of course, excuse indifference to distinctions of doctrine in a philosophical treatise, but it is an assertion of the occasional importance of the practical in contrast to the theoretical which is capable of a wider application than Chrysippus intended.

The conclusion seems to be that Cicero, while an adherent in principle of the Platonic psychology (espoused by Posidonius), did not consider the points of controversy between the Chrysippean and Platonic forms of Stoicism sufficiently relevant to his object to prevent his adopting the phraseology of the Chrysippean school in dealing with the *perturbationes* : but that he judged it necessary to state briefly his own personal preferences in the matter (perhaps merely to satisfy himself or to guard against criticism); and that it being a matter of indifference where this statement was made its appearing here rather than elsewhere is largely accidental.

The introduction (cc. 1–5) is of course Cicero's own both in expression and content. His sketch of the history of "philosophy" in Italy and his insistence upon the influence of Pythagoras and the necessity for a "cultured" philosophy perhaps led him by an association of ideas to a declaration of his own personal preference for the Pythagorean-Platonist school. But he makes it plain (5, 9) that while he will adhere to Chrysippus and the Stoics in matters of definition and proof, he will adopt the more humane methods of their rivals when it comes to the application of the lesson.

The following chapters (cc. 6–14) are derived from Zenonian and Chrysippean sources. This is shown not merely by the direct testimony of Cicero (6, 11 (Zeno), 10, 23 (Chrysippus)) but by the character of the whole passage. The minute subdivision of the various πάθη into meticulously defined particulars is eminently characteristic of Chrysippus, to whose σμῆνος ἀρετῶν an equally elaborated σμῆνος κακιῶν was no doubt contrasted.

The passages (10, 23 f., 12, 27 f.) in which the comparison between physical and moral disorders is referred to seems to exclude the possibility of any use of Posidonius, who criticized Chrysippus in detail upon this very point. Galen, *op. cit.* p. 408 M. [p. 433 K.], οὐκουν ὀρθῶς εἰκάζεσθαί φησιν ὑπὸ τοῦ Χρυσίππου τὴν μὲν ὑγίειαν τῆς ψυχῆς τῇ τοῦ σώματος ὑγιείᾳ τὴν δὲ νόσον τῇ ῥᾳδίως εἰς νόσημα ἐμπιπτούσῃ καταστάσει τοῦ σώματος.... ἀλλὰ δικαιότερον εἶναι προσεικάζειν τὰς τῶν φαύλων ψυχὰς ἤτοι τῇ σωματικῇ ὑγιείᾳ ἐχούσῃ τὸ εὐέμπτωτον εἰς νόσον, οὕτω γὰρ ὠνόμασεν ὁ Ποσειδώνιος, ἢ αὐτῇ τῇ νόσῳ, εἶναι γὰρ ἤτοι νοσώδη τινὰ ἕξιν ἢ ἤδη νοσοῦσαν. Cicero adopts the Chrysippean parallelism of *morbus corporis* to *morbus animi* in such a way as to ignore the criticism by making no attempt to avoid it. Further the definition of *sanitas animi* given in 13, 30 f. is in exact accord with the views of Chrysippus as criticized by Galen following Posidonius (*op. cit.* pp. 416 ff. M. [pp. 440 ff. K.]). Chrysippus had said διὸ καὶ καλὴ ἢ αἰσχρὰ ψυχὴ ἀνάλογον ῥηθήσεται κατὰ συμμετρίαν τε τινα καὶ ἀσυμμετρίαν τοιῶνδε τινῶν μερῶν, in which Posidonius scented a contradiction lurking in the word μέρη; which however it seems from a later passage (p. 422) was used by Chrysippus in conformity with his view that the λόγος was ἐννοιῶν τε τινῶν καὶ προλήψεων ἄθροισμα : this corresponds precisely to Cicero's *iudicia opinionesque concordant.*

There is therefore no ground for assuming any except a Chrysippean source for these chapters.

With c. 15 Cicero begins the more rhetorical treatment of his subject in which, though still adhering to the Stoic position in principle, he allows himself to "spread his sails." His definition of virtue in 15, 34 is Stoic as is the definition of *perturbationes* in the same paragraph. The substance of 16, 36 repeats iii 8, 16 f. and the *praemeditatio* recommended in 17, 37 f. is τὸ προενδημεῖν of Chrysippus. There follows (17, 38) a criticism of the Peripatetic view of the mean, which extends with digressions to the end of c. 26. In it the Stoic standpoint is defended against the criticisms alike of the Peripatetics and the New Academy (21, 47; 24, 53). The comparison in 18, 41 f. of a man under the influence of a πάθος to a man falling from a precipice or standing upon a slope is also derived from Chrysippus, who is quoted by Galen (*op. cit.* p. 360 M. [p. 388 K.]) for the sentence: οἱ δὲ κατὰ τὸν λόγον κινούμενοι ὡς ἂν ἡγεμόνα καὶ τούτῳ οἰακίζοντες τὰς κατὰ μέρος δηλονότι κινήσεις τῆς ψυχῆς κρατοῦσι τῶν κατὰ αὐτὰς ὁρμῶν ἀνάλογον τοῖς περιπατοῦσι ἀλλ' οὐχ ὑπὸ αὐτῶν ἐκφέρονται βιαίως ὥσπερ οἱ κατὰ πρανοῦς θέοντες. Here again Cicero ignores the criticisms of Posidonius, who, as reported by Galen, pointed out that the inability to stop when running down a slope was due to causes outside the person concerned, and that in the case of the mind such a comparison, if relevant, implied that other than purely rational causes must be postulated. According to him, then, the comparison was in Chrysippus' mouth inept and inconsistent with his psychological assumptions. This is ignored by Cicero in a way which seems unlikely if he were here in any way dependent upon Posidonius. On the other hand the particular use made of the comparison here suggests rather a reminiscence than a reference, unless we assume a recurrence of the illustration in some other work of Chrysippus than the περὶ παθῶν.

The historical examples and poetical quotations in this section are about equally Latin and Greek and Cicero turns so naturally from one to the other as to make it appear that Greek as well as Latin examples and quotations are not copied from some original but drawn from his own wide reading.

The remainder of the book from c. 27 to the end is devoted to a discussion of the remedies for *perturbatio*. On this head, as Cicero confesses (5, 9), the Stoics had little to say, whereas the Peripatetics devoted much attention to it. Cicero could therefore, if he relied upon a Stoic source, do little more than expand brief hints. But, as in Book III, when it comes to a question of *consolatio*, the practical outweighs the theoretical, and he takes into account methods of cure for mental disorders which cannot be reconciled with strictly Stoic principles. In doing so he had the authority (and perhaps the example) of Chrysippus who both deprecated the insistence upon philosophical subtleties in the case of acute πάθη (29, 63) and laid stress upon the desirability and possibility of curing the *perturbationes* no matter what philosophical principles were espoused either by the patient or the practitioner. In this respect the standpoint of 28, 60 f. and 31, 66 is the same as that of Chrysippus as quoted by Origen (see p. xlv above). Where this eclectic standpoint is not assumed Cicero is entirely in the matter of the *curatio* on the side of the Stoics who assumed *perturbatio* to be purely a matter of opinion (δόξα), e.g. in 31, 65; 34, 76; 35, 74; 37, 79; 37, 81; 38, 82 f. And the psychological view implied in 35, 78 (see explanatory notes there) is emphatically that of the older Stoics.

There is nothing then in this book to induce us to assume that Cicero had any other authority or source than either Chrysippus or some Stoic who adopted the Chrysippean standpoint. As in the preceding book the evidence does not seem to point to any more than a general dependence upon this source except in the case of the list of definitions in 7, 14 ff. where it is not unreasonable to assume that Cicero is copying directly either from some handbook or, perhaps, from a list compiled for his use.

BOOK V.

Zietzschmann *op. cit.* pp. 32–70 gives a long and careful analysis of the possible sources of the book. He discovers evident traces of Posidonius in the introduction; the view that philosophy is the source of civilisation (2, 5) is expressly attributed by Seneca (Epp. 90, 5) to Posidonius. The treatment in cc. 5–26 is obviously Stoic: the arguments in 15, 43 ff. are drawn from Chrysippus (Plut. *de Stoic. repugn.* 13, p. 1039 Stob. *Ecl.* ii. 126, 202): so is the treatment of fear in 18, 52 (cf. Stob. *Ecl.* ii 172 Diog. Laert. vii 112); and the long digression about Dionysius is like Chrysippus '*qui totos libros adscribere solebat.*' But it is not necessary to assume an immediate dependence on Chrysippus: it is more likely that Cicero's source is some controversial Stoic hand-book composed to defend Stoicism against the Peripatetics and Academics. Since the tenets of Antiochus seem to be often in view it is probable that the source was contemporary with him. And of the generation of Antiochus what Stoic was so prominent as Posidonius? It accords with this that the ascription of the premier place in philosophy to physics, not logic (24, 68), is characteristic of Posidonius in contrast to Chrysippus (Diog. Laert. vii. 40), and the position accorded to Plato (e.g. 12, 34) points in the same direction. If Posidonius be the source of this part of the book his ἠθικὸς λόγος (Diog. Laert. vii 91) was probably drawn upon chiefly. A short passage (27, 76–28, 82) is probably Cicero's own and serves to introduce his next source Antiochus whose *De fine bonorum* is responsible for the matter of 29, 82–31, 88: the argument of 31, 86 is indeed expressly attributed to Antiochus in 8, 22. The remainder of the book is from an Epicurean source, as may be seen, if detailed proof be required, from a comparison of 33, 93 with Diog. Laert. x 130; of 33, 95 with Diog. Laert. x 129 and of 34, 97–99 with Diog. Laert. x 130–131. It is not however any work of Epicurus, but that of some later Epicurean writer, upon which Cicero draws; and this may be either Zeno or Phaedrus or possibly Apollodorus: in any case, it was the same as the source of Plutarch *de exilio.* Hirzel *op. cit.* iii pp. 468 ff. holds that the case for regarding Posidonius as one of Cicero's sources is weak. He thinks that the references to Plato are not sufficient in themselves to prove it and that it is impossible to suppose that a Stoic like Posidonius could have used the language of 12, 34 with regard to Zeno. Nor is the case for Antiochus any stronger. The view defended by Cicero that, no matter what view may be taken of the *summum bonum*, the practice of virtue is sufficient to ensure happiness is the view not of Antiochus but of Carneades: indeed it is plain from De Finn. v. that Antiochus would have denied this if *uoluptas* or *uacuitas doloris* were assumed to be the *summum bonum*.

Again while the Peripatetic standpoint is most prominent in De Finn. v (which is known to be derived from Antiochus) it is thrown into the shade in T. D. v in which the Stoic standpoint is predominant. Cicero's whole treatment of the questions discussed in the book is not dogmatic but sceptical: he assumes the Stoic position, not because he is convinced that it is the truth, but because it furnishes the most logical and consistent proof of the thesis which he was really interested to maintain, that virtue was sufficient for happiness. This must have been the treatment adopted in his source, which cannot have been a treatise of Carneades, who fought bitterly against the Stoics, but of some other adherent of the school of the Sceptics. This source was probably Philo. This assumption is not contradicted by 24, 68, which seems to be due to some dogmatic source, since the threefold division of philosophy there referred to may be an addition of Cicero's or due to the retention, for the sake of convenience, by Philo of a division which is as old as Plato.

The introduction to the book (1, 1–4, 11) is admittedly Cicero's addition to whatever source may be assumed for the book as a whole. The praise of philosophy in 2, 5 is (though closely resembling sentiments quoted from Posidonius by Seneca) more or less of a common-place and the matter of 3, 7 ff. is Stoic in content where it is not directly borrowed from Heraclides of Pontus. Cicero concludes his introduction by a statement that he intends to employ, not the dogmatic, but the sceptical method in the discussion, a method derived from Socrates by Carneades. It may also be assumed without discussion that the section 5, 12 to 7, 20 need not be directly referred to any literary source.

With 8, 22 begins the formal discussion of the question which is the principal thesis of the book, that virtue ensures absolute happiness. This, Cicero contends, can only be maintained by assuming that virtue is the only good, the philosophers who, admitting other *bona* besides virtue, yet insisted that virtue was productive of happiness, being logically inconsistent. The discussion of this point occupies the section 8, 22 to 26, 75.

Cicero begins with the assertion that he discussed the question often with Antiochus and recently with Aristus during a visit to Athens. Antiochus asserted the position (defended in his books) that virtue produced happiness: this happiness was not absolute, there being certain *bona* which virtue alone could not confer; but the happiness conferred by virtue was sufficiently great to justify both the disregard of the partial unhappiness that might be caused by the absence or loss of the other *bona* and the general statement that the virtuous man was, on the whole, happy. Cicero argues from the Stoic standpoint that there are no degrees in happiness and that to admit other *bona* besides virtue is, not to dilute happiness, but to destroy it altogether.

Cicero's statement as to the fact of his discussing the question himself with Antiochus must be accepted: the only question remaining is whether the treatment of the matter here is such as to make it necessary to assume that he was copying or adapting the published work of some other person who had opposed Antiochus' conclusions from the same standpoint as himself.

In 9, 24 he quotes and criticizes Theophrastus: the statement '*non usquam id quidem dicit omnino, sed, quae dicit, idem ualent*' seems undoubtedly to show that Cicero was relying upon his own knowledge of the writings of Theophrastus, as well as his acquaintance with the "libri et scholae omnium philosophorum" (9, 25) who criticized his views. The references to, or quotations from, Epicurus in 9, 26 and 10, 31 are so general as to make it absurd to assume that Cicero must have borrowed or copied them from some previous writer. Nor is it any more than an assumption that the quotations from Plato in 12, 35 f. must have been borrowed either from a platonizing Stoic like Posidonius or from some other opponent of Antiochus. The references to Critolaus (17, 51) and to Xenocrates (18, 51) are in both cases sufficiently superficial and general to obviate the necessity of searching for a particular authority. The passages (14, 41; 15, 43–45; 16, 48; 18, 53) in which Cicero makes conspicuous use of the *laquei Stoicorum* point undoubtedly to an acquaintance with the method of argument employed by Chrysippus and the earlier Stoics, and the "chain-arguments" reproduced in these paragraphs are no doubt translations or close imitations of the arguments of some Greek Stoic. The long digression (20, 57 ff.) in which the evil case of Dionysius is expounded is, no doubt, reminiscent of the habit of Chrysippus: but it falls very far short of being evidence of direct dependence by Cicero upon Chrysippus or upon any one else. The somewhat contemptuous reference to Zeno in 12, 34 which Pohlenz thinks to be an argument against regarding Posidonius as the source of this section is not an argument either for or against anyone: it is, if anything, an argument for Cicero's independence of any direct source, being a dramatic adaptation of the expression to the situation. Cicero is protesting against the assumption that he is bound to have adopted as his own conviction the philosophical view which he may happen to be advocating at the moment. His interlocutor is on the Peripatetic side, and he is pressing the Stoic point of view not (he says) because he is committed to its truth, but because it '*nostros animos probabilitate percussit*,' "but," he says, "if Zeno of Citium, that mere outsider and low verbal mechanic, be considered to have wormed his way into philosophy" then let us take Plato and leave him aside. To attempt to use such a phrase as evidence either for or against a particular literary "source" is childish.

It is extremely unsafe to infer from 24, 68 fin. in which philosophy is divided into physics, ethics and logic that the section in which the divisions are arranged in this order must be derived from Posidonius. It is true that he adopted this particular order: but so did Panaetius, as is expressly stated by Diogenes Laertius (vii 40, Παναίτιος δὲ καὶ Ποσειδώνιος ἀπὸ τῶν φυσικῶν ἄρχονται), who makes it plain that there was considerable divergence among the Stoics on the point. In any case an order which goes back to Panaetius is not valid evidence that a passage in which it occurs ought probably to be referred to a work of Posidonius.

There is nothing in the section which compels us to assume direct dependence upon any particular author or treatise. Cicero was no doubt aware of what was to be said, and had been said, from the Stoic standpoint against the views of Antiochus. He took his arguments where he found them, and he may have found some of them in Posidonius, though most of them are sufficiently obvious to have occurred to any one interested in the discussion. But if he discussed the matter often with Antiochus (by which he certainly does not mean that he repeated to him extracts out of Posidonius) there is no reason why he should not have composed this section without taking a treatise of either Posidonius or Philo as the groundwork of his treatment.

Having shown that the Stoic ethics alone furnished an absolutely satisfactory basis for his main thesis, Cicero proceeds to examine what may be said for it upon the basis of other ethical systems (27, 76 ff.). Assuming the threefold division of *bona*, he enquires whether, supposing the *bona corporis* and the *bona externa* to be practically equivalent to the Stoic προηγμένα, the same result will not follow. Of course, if these two classes of *bona* are sufficiently depressed the result is the same as on the Stoic hypothesis, and Cicero refers to the discussion in the previous books, as well as to fresh examples (27, 77 ff.), to sustain the inference, repeating some of the more extravagant statements of the Stoics and declaring that their statement is the most courageous that can be made (28, 80 ff.). No one seems inclined to look for any source here beyond Cicero himself.

He proceeds in 29, 82 ff. to examine the question how far it is logically consistent with the views of the Peripatetics and Academics to assert '*sapientis esse semper beatissimos*.' Carneades had asserted that no matter what view was held *de finibus* virtue possessed '*satis ad uitam beatam praesidii*' (29, 83), and this being already proved in regard to the

Stoics, the other sects are passed in review in the light of Carneades'
dictum. After enumerating the *fines* adopted by the various schools (30,
84) he proceeds to examine them in order. The case of the Peripatetics,
which he takes first (30, 85), is the easiest. With the exception of
Theophrastus, they rank the *bona corporis* and the *bona externa* so low
in comparison with the *bona animi*, that the happiness derived from the
latter overshadows any unhappiness due to the loss of the former: besides,
the argument which Cicero had learned from Antiochus (8, 22) applies—
life can be called happy if it is predominantly so. He proceeds to argue
that the Peripatetics can all consistently speak with the extravagance of
the Stoics. So may Callipho and Diodorus. The case of others is more
difficult; but that of Epicurus being, to outward seeming, most difficult
of all, he offers to show that even he may consistently speak of virtue as
sufficient to ensure happiness. The only argument in this section is one
which Cicero confessedly borrowed from Antiochus, whose teaching,
whether written or oral, may legitimately be regarded as the "source"
of this section.

From 31, 88 to the end of the book Cicero is engaged upon a
demonstration of the compatibility of a belief in his thesis with adherence
to the teaching of Epicurus. Epicurus, he asserts, despises death and
pain and poverty: he is abstemious, and free from avarice like Anacharsis,
Socrates, Xenocrates and Diogenes. The Epicurean division of *cupiditates* is insisted upon to prove on the one hand that the Epicureans did
not attach an excessive value to the satisfaction of particular desires, and
on the other that to the Epicurean the mind was the standard of pleasure,
the body being merely the percipient. This being so, the life of the
Epicurean philosopher, aided by recollection and anticipation, would be
a long and unbroken series of pleasures. The moderation in eating and
drinking exemplified by Epicurus is dwelt upon and enforced (34, 97–
35, 102) by other examples: examples are given of philosophical indifference to *ignobilitas* (36, 103–105), and to exile (37, 106–38, 110), to
blindness (38, 111–39, 115), to loss of hearing (40, 116–117), to pain
(40, 117–41, 119). In all these cases he asserts that on the principles of
Epicurus the *sapiens* is able to derive enough pleasure from life to
overbalance his calamities and may therefore be called happy or may
in the last resort escape from pain by suicide.

Thus he concludes (41, 120) the judgment of Carneades as to the
essential agreement of all schools of philosophy upon the sufficiency of
virtue for a happy life is proved to be sound.

In this section Cicero, as he says both at the beginning (29, 83) and
at the end (41, 120), is defending a view of Carneades. It is a natural
presumption that he became acquainted with this view from the works

of the disciples of Carneades who recorded his doctrines (Diog. Laert. iv 65): but it would seem to follow from Cicero's references to Carneades that, while he laid down the general position '*quaecumque dissentientium philosophorum sententia sit de finibus, tamen uirtus satis habeat ad uitam beatam praesidii*' (29, 83), his "proof" of it was mainly a discussion of the apparent discrepancies between the Peripatetics and the Stoics (cf. 41, 120: '*nam cum, quaecumque bona Peripateticis, eadem Stoicis commoda uiderentur, neque tamen Peripatetici plus tribuerent diuitiis, bonae ualetudini, ceteris rebus generis eiusdem quam Stoici, cum ea re non uerbis ponderarentur, causam esse dissidendi negabat*'; 29, 83: '*Carneadem disputare solitum accepimus; sed is, ut contra Stoicos, quos studiosissime semper refellebat*'). In the detailed discussion of the application of Carneades' dictum to the Epicurean ethics there is no mention of Carneades, and it may be inferred that the substance of 31, 88–41, 119 is not directly due to any recorded discussion of his.

In these sections Cicero quotes Epicurus (or professes acquaintance with his works) more than once: 31, 88, '*eum diem quo moritur beatum appellat*'; 32, 89, '*nemo de tenui uictu plura dixit*'; 33, 93 '*uides, credo, ut Epicurus cupiditatum genera diuiserit*'; 33, 95, '*totumque hoc de uoluptate sic ille praecipit ut...*'; 38, 110, '*non sine causa igitur Epicurus ausus est dicere.*' He refers also to the writings of the Epicureans, 33, 94, '*hoc loco multa ab Epicureis disputantur*'; 34, 97, '*atque his similia ad uictum etiam transferuntur*'; 38, 111, '*quidam etiam disputent.*' He notes the verbal agreement between Epicurus and Hieronymus, 41, 118, '*haec eadem quae Epicurus, totidem uerbis dicit Hieronymus.*' To assume, in view of the enormous number of treatises left by Epicurus (Diog. Laert. x 26, γέγονε δὲ πολυγραφώτατος ὁ Ἐπίκουρος, πάντας ὑπερβαλλόμενος πλήθει βιβλίων), of his epistles containing a compendium of his doctrines, of his κύριαι δόξαι, of his philosophical importance, of the popularity of his doctrines in Rome, of Cicero's lifelong devotion to Greek philosophy and his constant study of it, that he did not take these references directly from Epicurus, but borrowed them from some later Epicurean or some Sceptic like Philo, is an impossible position. On the other hand, it is plain that he owed a good deal to Epicurean apologists, eager to show that Epicurus was not so bad as his opponents painted him. Of such apologies it is plain that there was a very considerable number. They did not prove that *uirtus* was sufficient to ensure complete happiness: but they did endeavour to show (what Cicero, with no very exacting philosophical conscience, held to be practically the same thing) that it was possible for a man who held *uoluptas* to be the chief good to be consistently happy, through recollection, anticipation and the selection of simple pleasures. For Cicero's treatment of the matter we need not, with the evidence before us, assume any other "source" than a moderate acquaintance with the works of Epicurus and of Epicurean apologists. It may be that he relied principally upon some particular writer; but to assert that he did, still more to name the writer or to select one of such a writer's works, is to go far beyond what the evidence will warrant.

NOTES ON THE *APPARATUS CRITICUS*.

THE MS designated V (V 1) in the critical notes is (as stated in the Introduction to Vol. I, p. xxxi) damaged at the end of Book v: the second column of the *recto* of f. 96 is imperfect and stained though still legible and the same applies to the first column of f. 96 *verso;* the second column, ending *in surditate uero* (v 40, 116), is practically undamaged: f. 97 is imperfect and much stained, the *verso* being almost illegible. A second scribe has recopied these two leaves, i.e. from *aegritudinesque obliuione leniuntur* (v 38, 110) to the end of the book. Where V is still legible its readings are quoted, the readings from the folios written by the later hand are denoted by v. A slight inaccuracy in the statement made in Vol. I, p. xxxi may here be rectified: the note added by the original copyist is *M. Tullii Ciceronis Tusculanarum līb V explicit feliciter.*

The Bodleian fragment published by Professor A. C. Clark in *Mélanges pour H. Chatelain* (Paris 1910) pp. 169 ff. is called F in the critical notes; Professor Clark proposed to call it O, but that designation was already in use for the group of Oxford MSS.

It may be added that, where a letter (*ex. gr.* R) used to denote a group of MSS is employed without a number following, it denotes the MS numbered (1) in that particular group; and that where MSS are quoted for any reading and nothing is said about other MSS the others have not been collated for that reading.

M. TVLLI CICERONIS

TVSCVLANARVM DISPVTATIONVM

LIBER TERTIVS

I. 1. Quidnam esse, Brute, causae putem, cur, cum constemus ex animo et corpore, corporis curandi tuendique causa quaesita sit ars atque eius utilitas deorum inmortalium inuentioni consecrata, animi autem medicina nec tam desiderata 5 sit, ante quam inuenta, nec tam culta, posteaquam cognita est, nec tam multis grata et probata, pluribus etiam suspecta et inuisa? an quod corporis grauitatem et dolorem animo iudicamus, animi morbum corpore non sentimus? ita fit ut animus de se ipse tum iudicet, cum id ipsum quo iudicatur aegrotet.

I. § 1, 3. ars eius atque R 1 6 7 17 V P 1–3 G B 1 3 K 2 S E 1–3 L 1–6
                 +ei
W 1 2 M 1 2 D C Π J O 1–3 7 ed. H. ar^feius atque K 1 (i.e. arei *in* ars et
mut. nigriore atr. et ei *eod. atr. superscr.*) ars eius sit atque O 8. ars atque eius
corr. Manutius. ‖ inmortalium R V P G S K. immortalium L. 4. inuentione L. ‖
desidera[∢] R (*sic*). desidera^{ta} V (*manu ant. superscr.*) desidera G desiderata
B 1 K 1 2 L 1 W 1 2 D C Π O 1–3. 9. quo iudicatur R 1 7 17 V P 1–3
B 1 3 K 1 2 S L 1 W 2 M 1 2 D C Gr. ‖ quod R 6 E 2 W 1 Π O 1 7.
q̃uĩdẽ J (i.e. quidem *in* quod idem *mut.*) ‖ iudicatus G (*sed* t *expunx. et* m *superscr.*
alt. man.) iudicat ed. H.

I. § 1. **quaesita**: the word implies that the want was *felt*, cf. *desiderata* below. Contrast *inuenta* below for which see i 47, 114 n.

atque eius utilitas, 'and deemed so useful that it has had the honour of being ascribed to immortal gods as its discoverers.' So Anon. in Olivet 'Ars medendi propter suam utilitatem diis assignata fuit tanquam inuentoribus.' For this opinion Dav. compares Pliny, H.N. xxix 1 (medicina) 'diis primum inuentores suos adsignauit et caelo dicauit.'

deorum...inuentioni = *dis inuentoribus,* cf. Naegelsbach, *op. cit.* § 74, who quotes Or. ii 58, 237 'parcendum maxime est caritati hominum' = *hominibus caris.*

deorum: especially Apollo and Aesculapius.

consecrata = *cum huius artis consecratione tributa,* Naegelsbach, *Stil.* § 102. Cf. p. Sest. 68, 143 'hanc opinionem si in illo sanctissimo Hercule consecratam uidemus'; N.D. iii 24, 61

'quarum rerum utilitatem uideo, uideo etiam consecrata simulacra.'

animi...medicina : sc. *philosophia.*

tam...tam...tam...: sc. *quam corporis medicina.*

pluribus: sc. *quam grata est.*

an: cf. ii 18, 42 n.

corporis grauitatem: an oppressed feeling is denoted. The expression is not found elsewhere in classical Latin. Dav. quotes it from Celsus i pref. *ad fin.* ; i 10; ii 7, p. 65; and the similar use of βαρύτης, Porphyrius, de Abstin. i ch. 51; Plutarch, de Sanit. Tuenda ii p. 127 D; p. 128 B βαρύτητα καὶ πλησμονὴν σώματος [cf. also grauedo, καρηβαρία ad Att. x, 16, 6, Catullus xliv, 13]. Editors are wrong in referring to Fin. iv 12, 31. There Madv. rightly adopts Bentley's emendation *prauitate membrorum.* Lucr. iii 478 has 'grauitas membrorum.' *grauis* is a common epithet of *morbus,* cf. 'grauitatem morbi' N.D. iii 31, 76.

ita fit ut, 'whence it follows that...,' ii 6, 16 n. Dav. compares Plut. Animine

10 **2.** quodsi talis nos natura genuisset, ut eam ipsam intueri et perspicere eademque optima duce cursum uitae conficere possemus, haud erat sane quod quisquam rationem ac doctrinam requireret. nunc paruulos nobis dedit igniculos, quos celeriter malis moribus opinionibusque deprauati sic restinguimus, ut nusquam naturae
15 lumen appareat. sunt enim ingeniis nostris semina innata uirtutum, quae si adolescere liceret, ipsa nos ad beatam uitam natura perduceret. nunc autem, simul atque editi in lucem et suscepti sumus, in omni continuo prauitate et in summa opinionum peruersitate uersamur, ut paene cum lacte nutricis errorem suxisse

§ **2**, 10. talis R V P G B K E L W 2 D.   tales S J *alii.*   tales W 1 (e *ex* i *mut. ut uid.*)   11. optima R V G B K.   12. haud W 1   ᵸaut V (h *manu ant. superscr.*) ⊦aub (*sic*) K 1 (i.e. aut *in* haub *man. rec. mut.*)   aut R G L.   ‖ rationem R 6 O 1 2   rōnē J.   rationē V (*fort. ead. man.*)   rationē S (*linea super* e *leuiter impressa et a recent. glossatore ut uid. addita*).   ratione R 1 17   P 1–3   G B K 1 E 1 L 1 M 2 C Π O 3.   ratiōe O 7.   ratōe O 8.   rōne R 7   B 3   E 2 W 2 D Gr.   rōe K 2   W 1   M 1.   rāōeȝ E 3 (*at* m *alio atr. add.*) ‖ ac R 1 6 7 17   V P 1 3   B 1 3   K S E 2   L 1   W 2   M Π J   O 1 7 ed. H. hac G (h. *expunx. et conf. man. ant.*)   ad O 2.   et P 2   E 1   W 1   D O 3 Gr.   aut O 8.   ‖ doctrinam R 6   O 1 2.   doctrinā E 3   J.   doctrina R 1 7 17   V P 1–3   G   B 1 3   K S E   L 1   W   M D C Π   O 3 7 8 Gr.   doctrinam ac rationem O 1.   ‖ requiret G (*at* re *superscr.*)   13. paruulos R V G K L. 14. deprauati B 1.   deprauatiṣ V.   deprauatiᶠ E 1 (*eod. atr. superscr.*)   deprauatis R 1 6 7 10   P B 3   K 1   S E 2   L 1 2 5 6   W 2   M 1   Π O 2 3 7 8.   depratis G (*at* ua *superscr.*)   deprautis K 2.   deprauatos R 17   P 2 3   W 1   M 2 D C J O.   deprauatos E 3 (*al. atr.*)   depṇat̊ R 16.   ‖ restringimus Π. ‖ unusquam G (*at* t *alt. man. superscr.*)   15. appareat R V P G K S E L. ‖ semita G. 16. adholescere G (h *conf. alt. man.*).   19. poene G. ‖ nutriscis G (s *punctis not.* alt. man.).   ‖ suxisse R 1 *alio atr.*

an corp. affect. s. p. p. 500 F τῶν μὲν γὰρ περὶ τὸ σῶμα νοσημάτων ἐρρωμένος ὁ λογισμὸς αἰσθάνεται, τοῖς δὲ τῆς ψυχῆς συννοσῶν αὐτὸς οὐκ ἔχει κρίσιν ἐν οἷς πάσχει, πάσχει γὰρ ᾧ κρίνει.

When the body is ill the mind, which studies it, is well, but when the mind is ailing, it, though ailing, has to study itself.

§ **2. ut eam ipsam:** i.e. *ut naturam ipsam.* For *eam* see Küh. *Gr.* ii § 117 anm. 1 p. 437; Gild. and Lodge § 309 n. 1 ; Madv. 490 (c) obs. 3. The argument is from the point of view of the Stoics who made the chief good consist in living in harmony with nature, cf. v 28, 82 'Stoicorum...qui...finem bonorum esse senserint congruere naturae cumque ea conuenienter uiuere.'

erat: Madv. 348 e.

rationem ac doctrinam, 'systematic instruction,' cf. i 1, 1 n.

nunc, 'but as it is.' This contrasted use of *nunc* is very common. So *nunc autem* (as below), *nunc uero* and in Gk. νῦν, νῦν δέ.

paruulos...igniculos, 'only tiny rays of light,' cf. ii 18, 42 n. on *contortulis conclusiunculis.*

deprauati: the nominative, proposed by Lamb., is supported by V² B1 and by *in...peruersitate uersamur* below, which = *deprauamur* as Mo. notes, and it is intrinsically preferable to *deprauatis.*

lumen, 'a glimpse,' ii 24, 58 n.

semina innata uirtutum: cf. Fin. iv 7, 18 'his initiis et, ut ante dixi, seminibus a natura datis...omnis honestas perfecte absoluta est'; v 7, 18 'quorum similia sunt prima in animis, quasi uirtutum igniculi et semina'; 15, 43 'in pueris uirtutum quasi scintillas uidemus.'

editi: sc. *a matre.*

suscepti: cf. Att. xi 9, 3 'utinam susceptus non essem.' For the custom implied in this word see Ramsay, *Rom. Ant.* p. 475.

[*Nutricis*: Old Roman custom seemed to have expected that the mother should nurse her own child : Cato's wife did so (Plut. Cato 20): but the custom seems to

20 uideamur. cum uero parentibus redditi, dein magistris traditi sumus, tum ita uariis inbuimur erroribus, ut uanitati ueritas et opinioni confirmatae natura ipsa cedat.

II. **3.** Accedunt etiam poëtae, qui cum magnam speciem doc trinae sapientiaeque prae se tulerunt, audiuntur, leguntur, ediscuntur et inhaerescunt penitus in mentibus; cum uero eodem quasi maximus quidam magister populus accessit atque omnis undique

20. redditi dein V. deinde R 6 B 3 O 8. dein M 1. demum B 1 S E 1 2. demū D C II. reddit idem G. redditidem R (*eod. atr. superscr.*) idem P *al. atr.* redditi idē W 2. redditi id est P 3 K 2 M 2 O 2. redditi id ē L 1 J. redditi iisdem O 3. redditi & W 1. redditi uel O 1. 21. imbuimur V G B S. inbuimur R P K E. imbuamur L. 22. opinio G *at* ni *superscr.*

alt. man. ‖ confirmatae M 2. confirmata V *al. atr. suppl.* confirmata R 1 6 7 G B 1 K S E 1 L 1 5 M 1 D C II O 2 8. confirmate W 1. confirmate R 17 B 3 O 1 E 3 (*at* e *in ras. alio atr.*) confirmare O 3. conformata O 7 *om.* W 2.

II. § **3, 2.** tulerunt R V P 3 G B 1 3 K S E L M D C II O 1-3 7. tulerē P 1. tulunt W 2. tullerūt J. tulerint R 6 W 1 O 8 (i *ex u ras. mut.*) 3. inherescunt punitus G (pun. *in* pen. *alt. man. corr.*) ‖ accidit eodem M 1 2. accedit eodem E 2 O 7 E 3 (*habet al. atr. suppl.*) eodem accedit D C.

4. maximus R V G. maximus P (u *in* i *ras. mut.*) maximus K (*atr. nigr.* superscr.) ‖ accessit V *al. man. superscr.* accedit R 6 7 S II. accidit P 3 B 3 O 2 3 *om.* R 1 17 P 1 G B 1 K E L W M J O 1 7.

have died out at least among the rich and the well-to-do. Plutarch (de lib. educ. 5) has some good remarks on the question; his own daughter had a τίτθη (Consol. ad ux. 2 p. 608 D), but not his eldest son (*ib.* p. 609 E). See Marquardt, *das Privatleben d. Röm.* p. 56. Inscrr. show the esteem and affection which often prevailed between nurses and their charges, v. Orelli-Henzen 6260, 6291, 6484.]

cum uero parentibus redditi: the parents are apt to set a bad example, Juv. xiv *passim*; Sen. de ira ii 21 9—10 'nutricum et paedagogorum...patrem...': Leg. i 17, 47 'nam sensus nostros non parens, non nutrix, non magister, non poeta, non scaena deprauat, non multitudinis consensus abducit a uero. animis omnes tenduntur insidiae, uel ab eis, quos modo enumeraui, qui teneros et rudes cum acceperunt inficiunt et flectunt, ut uolunt; uel ab ea, quae penitus in omni sensu implicata insidet, imitatrix boni, uoluptas.'

magistris: e.g. *paedagogis.* These men were often ignorant and vicious. Cf. Tac. dial. 29; Pseudo-Plut. de educ. 7, Mayor on Juv. vii 218.

uanitati, 'falsehood.' Cf. N.D. ii 21, 56 and Mayor's n.; Nonius, p. 416.

opinioni confirmatae, 'rooted prejudice.' Cf. ii 26, 63 n. on *opinio.*

II. § **3.** For this view of the influence of the poets cf. ii. 11, 27 and notes there.

et inhaerescunt, 'and as a result take root....' *inhaerescunt* is not a fourth member to the asyndetic series but gives the result of the series. Cf. v 5, 12.

cum uero eodem......multitudo: Galen says (de Hipp. et Plat. Plac. v p. 459) that Posidonius censured Chrysippus for holding that men are born with a tendency to the good alone, ᾠκειῶσθαι πρὸς μόνον τὸ καλόν, that Chrysippus had a difficulty in explaining why children go wrong and that he referred their doing so (p. 462) to two causes, ἑτέραν μὲν ἐκ κατηχήσεως τῶν πολλῶν ἀνθρώπων ἐγγινομένην, ἑτέραν δὲ ἐξ αὐτῆς τῶν πραγμάτων τῆς φύσεως. The former of the two causes we have here in almost so many words 'quasi maximus quidam *magister* populus atque *omnis* undique ad uitia consentiens *multitudo.*'

quidam: i 12, 27 n.

accessit: the verb, though absent from all the best MSS except V², cannot be omitted. The tense must be perfect and the mood indicative, cf. ii 11, 27 'ad malam domesticam disciplinam...cum accesserunt etiam poetae' and ii 2, 5 n. on *occurrit.* For the sentiment cf. Seneca, Ep. 115, 11—12 'admirationem nobis *parentes* auri...fecerunt...deinde totus

5 ad uitia consentiens multitudo, tum plane inficimur opinionum
prauitate a naturaque desciscimus, ut nobis optime naturae uim
uidisse uideantur, qui nihil melius homini, nihil magis expetendum, nihil praestantius honoribus, imperiis, populari gloria
iudicauerunt. ad quam fertur optimus quisque ueramque illam
10 honestatem expetens, quam una natura maxime anquirit, in

6. optime R V P G K L.   optimam W 1. ‖ naturam R 1 6 17   V P G   B 1
K 1   E 2   L 1 4–6   M D C Π   O 1 3 8 Gr.   naturā B 3   S J.   natām K 2.
nãm E 3   W   O 2 7.   nã R 7   E 1 *om. charta pertusa.*   7. inuidisse R 1 6 7 17
V P G   B 1 3   K S   E 2 3   L 1 5 6   W M D C Π J   O 2 3.   ĭ uidisse L 2
                                     ĭdidisse
O 7.   inuiuisse O 1.   in iudice O 8 (*al. atr. suppl.*)   E 1 *om. charta pertusa.*
naturae uim uidisse *corr. Maduigius.*   9. optumus R V K.   obtumus G.
optimus L.   10. una R 1 6 7 17   V P G B K S E   L 1 3–6   W 1   M Π J   O 1 2 7 8 Gr.
unam C.   unā D.   nām W 2 *om.* L 2.   ‖ maxime R V G L.   ‖ inquirit
R 1 6 7 17   V P G B K S E   L 1–6   W M D C Π   O 1–3 7 8.   inqurat J.
anquirit *corr. Moser.*

populus…in hoc conuenit…accedunt deinde *carmina poetarum.*'

opinionum prauitate: stronger than *opinionibus prauis.* The corruption extends to *all* our opinions.

optime naturae uim uidisse, 'to have best perceived the true meaning of nature.' This emendation of Madv. in his n. on 'uis naturae perspici potest' Fin. iii 19, 62 has driven out Bentley's *optimam magistram inuidisse* which was accepted by Dav. Mo. and others. The conjecture of Keil *optime naturam ii uidisse* is clever but *uidisse naturam* is not quite the expression required.

honoribus, imperiis, 'civil and military preeminence.' So long as office and command were bestowed by vote of the people *popularis gloria* conduced to and resulted from the attainment of both. *populari gloria* therefore sums up the effect of *honoribus imperiis* and *ad quam* refers only to it, not, as Küh. holds, to the other two words as well.

ad quam fertur: trans. 'at this the best men among us aim and, though they desire the truly honourable, the search for which preeminently belongs to nature, they are occupied with the veriest un-realities and pursue no well-defined form of virtue but merely a shadowy semblance of glory.'

optimus quisque: from the social, not from the moral, point of view.

ueramque…expetens: by reason of the *paruulos igniculos*, the *ingeniis nostris semina innata uirtutum* of § 2. Cf. Seneca, Ep. 121, 14; Fin. iii 7, 23 and Madvig's n. They miss their aim, being *deprauati* by the *populus.*

It is well-known that the Stoics taught that every living thing tends to preserve its own nature; that nothing can be in harmony with the nature of any individual unless it be in harmony with the course of the universe (cf. Diog. L. vii 88 ἀκολούθως τῇ φύσει ζῆν); that a rational life in agreement with the general course of the world, is the highest good, or virtue; that virtue alone is good. See Zeller, *Stoics, etc.* c. x pp. 214—6.

quam una natura maxime anquirit: Küh. thinks *natura* here=*ii homines qui, naturam secuti, recta uel absoluta ratione instructi sunt.* But that meaning would be very obscurely expressed and *natura* here is certainly the same as *natura* in §§ 2 and 3. *natura* is animate, since 'the terms Soul of the world, Reason of the world, Nature, Universal Law, Providence, Destiny—all mean the same thing' Zeller, *Stoics, etc.,* c. vi p. 145. 'Nature seeks out the honourable' I take to mean (in more prosaic form) that the honourable is essential to harmony with nature or conformity to universal law.

una intensifies *maxime,* cf. Fin. ii 13, 42 'uoluptas quam unam uirtus minimi facit.' Trans. 'which nature preeminently seeks out.'

unam is read by Man. Lamb. and most modern editors except Mo. Kl. and Küh. The meaning with *unam* would be 'which is preeminently the thing that nature seeks out.' The objection of Küh. that this is the *only* thing that *natura* seeks out seems insuperable though he does not take *natura* in the same sense as I do. Virtue or the *honestum* is the only good; *natura* demands this alone, not this pre-

summa inanitate uersatur consectaturque nullam eminentem
effigiem uirtutis, sed adumbratam imaginem gloriae. est enim
gloria solida quaedam res et expressa, non adumbrata ; ea est
consentiens laus bonorum, incorrupta uox bene iudicantium de
15 excellenti uirtute, ea uirtuti resonat tamquam imago. quae quia
recte factorum plerumque comes est, non est bonis uiris repudianda. 4. illa autem, quae se eius imitatricem esse uolt, temeraria
atque inconsiderata et plerumque peccatorum uitiorumque lau-
datrix, fama popularis, simulatione honestatis formam eius
20 pulchritudinemque corrumpit. qua caecitate homines, cum quaedam etiam praeclara cuperent eaque nescirent nec ubi nec

12. uirtutis *om.* O 1. 14. bonorum & incorrupta V *al. atr. superscr.* 15. excellenti D C O 1 excellenti V (i.e. e *in* i *mut.*) excellente R P G B K S E L W M Π J
O 2 3 7 8. excelente B 3. ‖ gloriae *post* imago *habent* R 1 6 7 17 V G B K S
E W M D C Π J O 1 7 8. *non habent* P B 3 M 2 O 2 3. 16. rectae G. ‖
repudianda R G B S L W D *alii.* repudianda K *at* a *ex* e *eod. atr. mut.* repudienda V *eod. atr. superscr.* E *alio atr. superscr.* repudienda K 2.

§ 4, 17. uolt V G K. uolt R *eod. atr.* uult R 10 16 L. 19. forme G *at* e
puncto not. et ā *alt. man. superscr.*

eminently. *una* of the MSS seems to give
a good sense as taken above. *natura* or
universal law is not alone in demanding
this; men who are in harmony with
nature also seek it out.
 anquirit: *inquirit* of the MSS, 'inquires
into,' gives an unsuitable meaning. For
anquiro see ii 10, 25 n.; iv 21, 47; v 4,
10. In all three places inferior MSS have
the more familiar *inquirere* as a variant.
 eminentem effigiem: in these words
and in *solida* and *expressa* below we have
metaphors from sculpture; in *adumbratam*
a metaphor primarily from painting.
eminentem, 'filled out,' 'substantial,'
nearly = *expressam*, 'clearly defined,' for
which see Reid on p. Arch. 12, 30;
Wilkins on Hor. A.P. 32. The latter
word is used of clear bringing out of
details. *adumbratam* (= ἐσκιαγραφημένην)
is used of a mere sketch in outline, cf.
N.D. i 27, 75 'species quaedam deorum,
quae nihil concreti habeat, nihil solidi,
nihil expressi, nihil eminentis...cedo mihi
istorum adumbratorum deorum liniamenta
atque formas'; p. Caelio 5, 12; Fin. v
22, 61-2; Off. iii 17, 69; p. Planc. 12,
29 and Holden's n.
 effigiem uirtutis: some have omitted
uirtutis but the word is required to
correspond to *ueram honestatem* above,
to which *gloriae* could not correspond
since *gloria*, even when it is *solida*, is not
uera honestas but only the concomitant
of the latter.

est: emphatic by its position, cf. 3, 6
'est profecto animi medicina.'
 solida: the opposite of *inanis*.
 bene = *recte*.
 excellenti: it seems better, with most
editors, to follow V² against the majority
of the MSS and give the usual ablatival
form of the participle used as an adjective. Dav. Küh. Mo. Schiche read
excellente.
 tamquam imago: sc. *uocis*. 'This
responds to virtue as its echo.' Cf. Virg.
Geo. iv 50; Hor. Odes i 12, 4; i 20, 8.
Varro, R.R. iii 16 12 (of bees) 'primum
secundum uillam, potissimum ubi non
resonent imagines.' Val. Flacc. Argon.
iii 597; Statius Silu. i 3, 18. Gronovius
proposed to read and punctuate thus—
imago; gloriaque, quia recte factorum...
but Dav. rightly rejects this as a patch
devoid of Ciceronian colour. *gloriae*, of
most MSS, came in by dittography from
gloriae above or else as a marginal gloss.
 comes: cf. i 45, 109 'gloria...uirtutem
tamquam umbra sequitur.'
 § **4. corrumpit**, 'caricatures.' Hei.
 qua caecitate, 'by the blinding influence of which' = *cuius rei caecitate*.
Hei. after Schlenger quite unnecessarily
reads *qua caecati*.
 cum: concessive.
 etiam: with *praeclara*.
 eaque: for *que* see i 29, 71 n. Translate
'though they aimed at objects which were
even noble, yet, understanding neither

qualia essent, funditus alii euerterunt suas ciuitates, alii ipsi
occiderunt. atque hi quidem optima petentes non tam uoluntate quam cursus errore falluntur. quid? qui pecuniae cupiditate,
25 qui uoluptatum libidine feruntur, quorumque ita perturbantur
animi, ut non multum absint ab insania, [quod insipientibus
contingit omnibus], his nullane est adhibenda curatio? utrum
quod minus noceant animi aegrotationes quam corporis, an quod
corpora curari possint, animorum medicina nulla sit?

III. 5. At et morbi perniciosiores pluresque sunt animi
quam corporis; hoc enim ipso odiosi sunt, quod ad animum

22. euerterunt B E W M D C Π J   O 3 7 8.   euerterent R V P K.   euerterent
G L.   euertunt O 1.   23. adque G *at* d *in* t *mut. alt. man.* ‖ hi R V P G   B 3
K W M J   O 1 2 7   hii K 2   D C Π   O 8   ii S *at littera ante* ii *erasa.*
ii M 2   O 3.   i E *in* ſi *al. atr. mut.*   hẹc L 1.   alii ed. H.   ‖ optuma
R B K.   24. quid qui R 10 16   P E.   quidque R *al. atr. superscr.*   quidq; V.
quidq; G L.   27. contingit R V B K S E L W M D C Π   O 2 3 7 8.   contigit
P J   O 1   G *at* n *alt. man. superscr.*   ⁹tigit W 2.   ‖ his R V G B K E L W J
O 7.   hiis C D   O 8.   iis S.   ‖ nulla G *at* ne *superscr. ait. man.*   28. an...corporis
om. G *in marg. infer. add. alt. man.*
III. §5, 2. hi enim ipsi R 1 6 7   V G B K 1 S E 1   L 6   W M J   O 1 2 7   hii K 2
E 3   L 3-5   D C Π   O 8   L 2 (*om.* ipsi).   ii M 2   E 2   O 3 (*om.* ipsi).   ei P 3.
hi enim odiosi P 1 L 1.   hoc enim ipso *corr. Bakius.*

where these were to be found nor what
they really were....'

alii...alii: Cicero is thinking of Caesar
and Pompey, as Hei. notes.

atque...quidem, 'moreover,' 'and
indeed.' Cicero passes from the case of
ambition to the still stronger cases of
avarice, etc. The formula *atque...qui-
dem*...is suited to such transitions. See
Küh. here and Hand *Tursell*. 1 p. 492
foll. A personal or, as here, a demonstrative pronoun often follows to mark
the correspondence of clauses. *hi* is alone
right; the logical pronoun *ei* would not
suit for this purpose. 'And while such
men with the best of aims go wrong,...
though not wilfully it is true but through
a mistake with regard to the course,
what of those who are carried away by
avarice...?'

cursus: gen. of indirect object. See
Naegelsbach, *Stil*. § 120.

uoluptatum libidine: cf. Sen. 12, 39
uoluptatis auidae libidines'; 40 'libido
uoluptatis.'

quod insipientibus contingit omnibus:
this Stoic commonplace comes in most
ineptly here and is rightly bracketed by
Bake, whom Bai. and Hei. follow. Ml.
and others retain the words. T.S. would
make the inaccuracy Cicero's own and
Küh. thinks that in these hastily written

books we must not be too critical. But
though Cicero is often betrayed by haste
into inaccuracies of construction it is
hardly likely that so great an orator
would thus destroy his climax. The
clause seems evidently a mere gloss upon
the word *insania.*

III. § 5. at et: the clause *at et morbi
perniciosiores pluresque sunt animi quam
corporis* answers the question *utrum quod
minus noceant animi aegrotationes quam
corporis.* We ought therefore to have a
second *et*-clause to answer the second
part of the preceding double question
an...animorum medicina nulla est, such
clause running somewhat as follows—*et
animi medicina certe est,* but the intervention of the explanation why the diseases
of the mind are more harmful than those
of the body *hoc enim ipso...grauiores* has
caused the construction to be broken off
and the *an*-clause is answered in a new
sentence *qui uero probari potest...*leaving
et pendens.

hoc enim ipso: the correction of Bake
for *hi enim ipsi* of the MSS is accepted by
most editors except Sff. The argument
is 'diseases of the mind are more harmful
(and more numerous) than those of the
body. They are troublesome from the
very fact that it is the mind which they
affect and disturb; and the ailing mind

pertinent eumque sollicitant, 'animusque aeger,' ut ait Ennius,
'semper errat neque pati neque perpeti potest, cupere
5 numquam desinit.' quibus duobus morbis, ut omittam alios,
aegritudine et cupiditate, qui tandem possunt in corpore esse
grauiores? qui uero probari potest ut sibi mederi animus non
possit, cum ipsam medicinam corporis animus inuenerit, cumque
ad corporum sanationem multum ipsa corpora et natura ualeat
10 nec omnes, qui curari se passi sint, continuo etiam conualescant,
animi autem, qui se sanari uoluerint praeceptisque sapientium
paruerint, sine ulla dubitatione sanentur? 6. est profecto animi
medicina, philosophia; cuius auxilium non ut in corporis morbis
petendum est foris, omnibusque opibus uiribus ut nosmet ipsi

---

3. sollicitant B K L W 2.   solicitant R V G (*alt. man.*)   solicitāt W.
sol icitent S *unius litt. spatio post* l *rel.*   4 erra t V *litt. eras.* ‖ pati R 1 6 7 17
V P 1-4 G B K S E L W M D C J O 1-3 7 8.   parci E 2 II. ‖ neque
perpeti *om.* O 7.   5. obmittam G *at* b *conf. alt. man.*   9. ualeat R 1 6 7
V G B K S E L W 2 M J O 1-3 7 8.   u̇eleat P *al. atr.*   ualeant W D C II.
ualeāt E 2.   10. omnes V i *in e* ut uid. mut.   omnis R G.   om̅is E L W 2.
om̅s S W. ‖ passi sunt R 1 6 7 10 17 V P 3 G B K S E L W M D C II J
O 1-3 7 8.   s̅t P R 16.   î K 2.   passi sint *corr. Tregder.* ‖ conualescunt
G u *exp. et a superscr. alt. man.*   11. qui se R 1 6 V P G B K S E L W M II J
O 1-3 7 8.   se *om.* D C.

§ 6, 14. opibus uiribus R P G B L W 2 C O 3.   opibus & uiribus V *al. man.*
opibus et uiribus W J O 8.   opibus iuribusque R 6 7 B 3 M D O 2.   opibus
iuribusq; E *al. atr. suppl.*   operibus et uiribus O 1.   uiribus *om.* E 2 II O 7 Gr.

---

is ever wrong, a prey to annoyance and
desire, two evils than which, not to
mention any others, no ills of body can
be more grievous.' Cicero does not offer
any proof here that *morbi animi* are
plures for *plures* was only rhetorically
tacked on to *perniciosiores*, the latter being
the only word necessary to take up the
words *quod minus noceant*. Cicero's reason
for considering them to be *plures* is seen
from v 1, 3.

Sff. reading *hi enim ipsi* thinks that
these words refer to *morbi corporis* and
that the argument is 'even these affect
the mind and are on that account *odiosi*.
Hence *we infer* that the diseases of the
mind are *plures*, while the *animus aeger*
shows that they are also *perniciosiores*.'

Ennius: *Fragm. Scen.* 392 (ed. Vahlen):
the play from which the words are quoted
is unknown. [Ribbeck, *Scaen. Rom. Poes.
Frag.* i² 68, regards the lines as troch.
tetrameters: for *pati* he reads *poti* (from
potior) and *potis est* for *potest*, supposing
some word or words to have been lost
between *potis est* and *cupere*.]

pati: in *pati...perpeti* we have a gradation 'endure...hold out.' The allitera-

tive repetition is characteristic of old
Latin. [See Vahlen's n. *Enn. Poesis
Rell.* p. 194.] Sff. and Küh. follow Ribbeck in altering to *poti=potiri*, comparing 18, 41 *ut natura eis potiens dolore
careat*.

qui...probari potest: *probari*, when
negatived (*qui probari potest?=non probari potest*), lends itself to the construction
of result since the proposition is only a
mental conception: 'how can a view be
established which would make it out that
the mind...' Küh. In *Fin.* ii 33, 108 we
may have the same construction but Madv.
and Ml. there read *qui id probari potest*.
Küh. compares *non uerisimile est* with *ut*
and subj. and *uerisimile est* with acc. and
inf. See Madv. on *Fin.* ii 3, 6 'hoc uero
optimum, ut is...'and *Gram.* § 374 obs. 2.

corpora et natura: the two words are
looked upon as forming a single whole,
natura being the more important, 'the
constitution of the body'; the predicate
ualeat can therefore be in the singular.
Küh. *Gram.* II p. 32.

§**6. omnibusque:** for *que* see i 29, 71 n.
opibus uiribus, 'resources and forces,'
'might and main.' This reads like a

15 nobis mederi possimus elaborandum est. quamquam de uniuersa philosophia, quanto opere et expetenda esset et colenda, satis, ut arbitror, dictum est in Hortensio. de maximis autem rebus nihil fere intermisimus postea nec disputare nec scribere. his autem libris exposita sunt ea, quae a nobis cum familiaribus 20 nostris in Tusculano erant disputata. sed quoniam duobus superioribus de morte et de dolore dictum est, tertius dies disputationis hoc tertium uolumen efficiet. **7.** ut enim in Academiam nostram descendimus inclinato iam in posmeridianum tempus die, poposci eorum aliquem, qui aderant, causam dis-25 serendi. tum res acta sic est:

IV. *A.* Videtur mihi cadere in sapientem aegritudo.

M. Num reliquae quoque perturbationes animi, formidines,

16. quanto opere R V P G B K S E L D   O 3 Gr.   17. maxumis R V G B.

maxu̯mis P.   maximis K *atr. nigr.*   maximis L.   19. eaq̱ G.

§ 7, 22. incademiam G *alt. man. superscr.*   23. postmeridianum R 1 6 7 17 V
P 1–4 G B K S E L W M D C ΠJ O 1–3 7 8.   24. aliquid G *in* aliquē *alt. man. corr.* ‖ quid adherant G *sed* d *et* h *conf. alt. man.*
IV. *Litteras A et M ignorant* R 1 2 10 16   V B 1   K 1   O 7.   *habent* R 6 7
G B 3 W 1 O 3.   *B et M habet* R 17.   *D et T habet* Π.   *D et M habet* D.
Di et M habet O 1.   *B et T habet* O 8.   *Atti et Mar. habet* O 2.

proverbial expression, cf. *equis uiris*; *uentis remis*. The asyndeton might also be justified by the close connexion between the two ideas, cf. i 14, 31 n. It is retained by Küh. Hei. T.S. Ml. Writers are not limited to the proverbial form; thus in iii 11, 25 we have 'omnibus uiribus atque opibus repugnandum est.' For this Klotz compares Ter. Heaut. 904 'dictum factum' with Ter. And. 381 'dictum ac factum.' Dav. reads *et* before *uiribus*; Bent. Wes. Bai. (in Tauchnitz text) *atque*; Schiche *ac*; Tregder and Baiter-Orelli bracket *uiribus*.

de uniuersa philosophia: ii 1, 4 n. on 'uniuersam.'

esset: for the preference of the secondary sequence after a perfect see i 1, 1 n.

in Hortensio: see ii 2, 4 n.

scribere: after the Hortensius Cic. wrote the Academica and the de Finibus. See Introd. to Vol. 1 p. xv.

§ 7. **in Academiam:** ii 3, 9 n.

posmeridianum is read by T.S. This and not *pomeridianum*, which Orelli reads in his Oxford edition, is the form which Cic. in Or. 47, 157 professes to prefer. Most editors retain the reading of the MSS.

causam disserendi: 'a subject for discussion.' For *causa* in this sense cf. Or. ii 36, 153 'istorum omnium sum-matim causas et genera...gustaui.' The subject of discussion here is a general question ($\theta\acute{\epsilon}\sigma\iota\varsigma$, *quaestio infinita*); the term *causa* is more usually applied to a particular question ($\acute{\upsilon}\pi\acute{o}\theta\epsilon\sigma\iota\varsigma$, *quaestio finita*); cf. Topica 21, 79; de Inu. i 6, 8.

IV. **reliquae:** The Stoics divided irrational emotions (*perturbationes*, $\pi\acute{a}\theta\eta$) into four classes viz. $\lambda\acute{\upsilon}\pi\eta$, $\phi\acute{o}\beta o\varsigma$, $\acute{\epsilon}\pi\iota\theta\upsilon$-$\mu\acute{\iota}a$, $\acute{\eta}\delta o\nu\acute{\eta}$ or *aegritudo*, *metus*, *libido*, *laetitia gestiens*, cf. iv 4, 8; Fin. iii 10, 35; Zeller, *Stoics, etc.* p. 233. Each of these main divisions has several subordinate varieties and *iracundia* (*ira*) is a subdivision of *libido*, see iv 7, 16. Thus instead of enumerating the remaining three Cicero only mentions two and a subordinate species of one of the two. Hence emendations have been attempted, e.g. Fr. Fabricius proposed *iucunditates*. But an accurate enumeration is not necessary to Cicero's purpose in this book, where he deals only with *aegritudo*, as it is in book iv, where he deals with the remaining three emotions. Cf. *haec* and *fere* below and the plurals *formidines*, etc. 'fits of terror,' etc. Cicero is more rhetorical and less precise here. Similarly in iii 5, 11 he first co-ordinates *libido* and *iracundia* and then admits that *iracundia libidinis pars est*. Dav. cites other in-

libidines, iracundiae? haec enim fere sunt eius modi quae
Graeci πάθη appellant; ego poteram morbos, et id uerbum
5 esset e uerbo, sed in consuetudinem nostram non caderet. nam
misereri, inuidere, gestire, laetari, haec omnia morbos Graeci
appellant, motus animi rationi non obtemperantis, nos autem
hos eosdem motus concitati animi recte, ut opinor, perturbationes dixerimus, morbos autem non satis usitate, nisi quid
10 aliud tibi uidetur.

    8. A. Mihi uero isto modo.

    M. Haecine igitur cadere in sapientem putas?

    A. Prorsus existimo.

    M. Ne ista gloriosa sapientia non magno aestimanda est,
15 siquidem non multum differt ab insania.

    A. Quid? tibi omnisne animi commotio uidetur insania?

    M. Non mihi quidem soli, sed, id quod admirari saepe soleo,
maioribus quoque nostris hoc ita uisum intellego multis saeculis

---

    3. libidines R V G K S E L. ‖ ḷ'hu / ịiusmodi V *al. man. superscr.*   4. πάθη W.
pathe G *alii.*   7. obtemperantis V P G K L W 2 M 2 J O.   optemperantis B 1.
obtemperantis R *eod. atr. suppl.*   obtemperantes P 2 B 3 S E 2 W M D C Π
O 2 3 7 8.   optemperantes E.

    § **8, 12.** haecine G K.   heͅcine V.   haecine R *alio atr. suppl.*   heͅc E *alio
atr. suppl.*   h'cine O 7.   haeccine M 2   heͅccine W (t *an* c *incert.*)   heccine
B 3 S E 2 L W 2 M D C Π J O 1-3.   hecineͅ B.   hecne O 8.
14. ne R V P G B K S E L W 2 M D C Π J O 1-3 8.   nae W.   nec O 7. ‖
magno R V P G B K S E L W D C Π O 2 3 7 8.   magna O.   **17.** admirari K L W.
amirari R *eod. atr.*   amirari V O 7.   ammirari G.   **18.** intellego R V G K.
intelligo R 10 16 S E L.

---

stances—Off. i 20, 69 'uacandum autem
omni est animi perturbatione, cum cupiditate et metu, tum etiam aegritudine et
uoluptate nimia et iracundia'; i 29, 102
'licet ora ipsa cernere iratorum aut eorum
qui aut libidine aliqua aut metu commoti
sunt aut uoluptate nimia gestiunt.'

    haec: for the comprehensive use of the
neuter cf. ii 26, 62 n.

    ego poteram morbos: cf. Fin. iii 10, 35
'perturbationes animorum...quas Graeci
πάθη appellant, poteram ego uerbum
ipsum interpretans morbos appellare, sed
non conueniret ad omnia.'

    poteram: Madv. 348 (e) obs. 1.

    morbos: here as elsewhere Cic. is
incorrect in his moralising upon the
shortcomings of the Greek language.
morbus translates νόσος not πάθος. Cf.
his identification of πόνος with *labor* in
ii 15, 35.

    uerbum...e uerbo: sc. *exprimere* or

expressum. For similar phrases see Reid
on Ac. ii 6, 17.

    in consuetudinem nostram=*in cons.
nostri sermonis.*

    obtemperantis: accusative.

    dixerimus: perf. subj. Küh. *Gram.* II
p. 133, cf. iv 6, 12 n. on 'appellemus.'

    § **8. ne**: i 30, 74 n.

    magno: this abl. is found with *aesti-
mare* in Cic. as well as *magni.* For
magno cf. Verr. iv 7, 13; Fin. iii 3, 11;
v 30, 90; and perhaps Parad. vi 3, 51;
also *nihilo* Fin. iv 23, 62. For *magni* cf.
T.D. v 7, 20; Fin. iii 13, 43; p. Cluent.
58, 159 'maximi aestimare conscientiam
mentis suae' but MSS *maxime*; p. Mur.
37, 79 'magni interest...esse Kal. Ian. in
r. p. duo consules.'

    a quo...manauit: cf. Reid on Ac. i 4,
15—16 and reff. cited there; Zeller,
Socrates p. 39 E.T.[2] 'The pre-Socratic
philosophy was simply and solely a

ante Socraten, a quo haec omnis, quae est de uita et de moribus,
20 philosopnia manauit.

A. Quonam tandem modo ?

M. Quia nomen insaniae significat mentis aegrotationem
et morbum [, id est insanitatem et aegrotum animum, quam
appellarunt insaniam. **9.** omnis autem perturbationes animi

19. socraten R P K S.   socratem V   P 2 3   B 1   K 2   E 2   L M C   O 1–3.

socratē B 3   W D Π   O 7 8.   socrateṇ E 1.   socrantem G *sed* n *expunx. et conf.
alt. man.* ‖ et de moribus R V P G B K S E L M Π J   O 2 7 8.   de *om.* W D C
O 1 3.   moribus *om.* W 2.   23. et aegrotum animum R V P G B K S E L   W 2
D C Π   O 1–3 7 8 Gr.   et egrotum animum M.   et aegritudinem aī W.
24. appellarunt G K.   appellauerunt W.

§ 9. omnis V.   omnis R *eod. atr.*   omīs K E L   W 2.   omnes G.
omīs S.

philosophy of nature; the transitional philosophy of the Sophists was the first to leave nature for ethical and dialectical questions. After Socrates the dialectical tendency is supreme. His own attention was exclusively occupied with determining conceptions, and enquiries respecting virtue.'

For the triple division of philosophy cf. Ac. i 5, 19 'fuit ergo...philosophandi ratio triplex: una de uita et moribus, altera de natura et rebus occultis, tertia de disserendo et quid uerum sit, quid falsum, quid rectum in oratione prauomue, quid consentiens, quid repugnans iudicando,' and Reid's n.

de uita et de moribus = περὶ τῶν ἠθικῶν. For the double translation of a Greek term see ii 21, 47 n. on *eneruatum quodam modo et languidum.* The repetition of the preposition is strange, and unusual in such translations. It is probably intrusive.

mentis: the ruling portion of the *animus,* cf. § 11 'mentis cui regnum totius animi a natura tributum est' and N.D. ii 11, 29 quoted on i 10, 20 n.

id est insanitatem...insaniunt: this passage is open to much suspicion. The *id est* clause introduces an unnecessary explanation and an absurd repetition. The rest of the passage gives us the views of philosophers in a hackneyed Stoic syllogism to show that all non-philosophers are mad, though the point to be proved is not this but that the early Romans held mental disturbance to be identical with madness, and a view is thus attributed to philosophers which is limited to Stoic philosophers. Then with a change from present to past time and a meaningless *enim* we have the sentence *sanitatem...non posset* tacked on, with *philosophi*

instead of the required *maiores nostri* as its only possible subject, a construction which would leave us quite without explanation of the views of the early Romans.

Sff. emends and reads *id est insanitatem ex aegroto animo...nostri sanitatem animorum*...comparing for *ex*)(*et* the variants (inter alia) on i 39, 93 and accounting for the loss of *nostri* by the abbreviation n̄r̄ī and for the intrusion of *enim* by assuming dittography from the preceding *-em.* But the *id est* clause would still be unsatisfactory and the comparison which he finds between the view of the Stoics and that of the early Romans to shew that both arrived at the same conclusion would not be clearly expressed.

Bentley, followed by Dav. and others, declared the clause *id est...insaniam* to be spurious. Bake bracketed the whole passage *id est...insaniunt,* and the theory of a double gloss has found many adherents, among them Wes. Bai. Hei. T.S. Ml. Schiche.

Nissen Or. and Mo. retained the whole passage. Or. notes 'haec etymologica sunt, addita in eum finem ut, cur iam Romani antiqui diu ante Socratem rectum nomen illi animi commotioni indidissent, manifestius appareret.'

It seems best to suppose that the unconvincing nature of Cicero's argument has led to the fabrication of glosses to eke out his meaning, these glosses being compiled from §§ 9 and 10.

Hei. notes that the Stoic tendency to support argument by appeal to the popular consciousness often leads to strained interpretations. Of course Cic. did not find in his Greek sources a ref. to the views of the early Romans but he may have adapted an argument drawn from the views of the early Greeks.

25 morbos philosophi appellant negantqve stultum quemquam his
morbis uacare. qui autem in morbo sunt sani non sunt, et
omnium insipientium animi in morbo sunt; omnes insipientes
igitur insaniunt]. sanitatem enim animorum positam in tranquillitate quadam constantiaque censebant; his rebus mentem
30 uacuam appellarunt insaniam, propterea quod in perturbato
animo sicut in corpore sanitas esse non posset.

V. 10. Nec minus illud acute, quod animi adfectionem
lumine mentis carentem nominauerunt amentiam eandemque
dementiam. ex quo intellegendum est eos qui haec rebus
nomina posuerunt sensisse hoc idem, quod a Socrate acceptum
5 diligenter Stoici retinuerunt, omnis insipientes esse non sanos.
qui est enim animus in aliquo morbo (morbos autem hos per-
turbatos motus, ut modo dixi, philosophi appellant), non magis
est sanus quam id corpus quod in morbo est. ita fit ut sapientia
sanitas sit animi, insipientia autem quasi insanitas quaedam, quae

25. his morbis R V G B K E L W M   O 1 2 7.   hiis morbis D C Π   O 8.
iis morbis M 2 S (*at una litt. ut uid. ante* i *eras.*)   morbis his O 3.   31. non possit
R V P G K S E L W M (*non ut Küh.*) D C Π   O 2 3 7 8.   non poterit L 3 5·
non potit W 2.   non potest O 1 *om.* B.   posset *corr. Ernestius.*

V. § 10, 1. ille G *alt. man. corr.* ‖ occulte L *al. atr.* ‖ adfectionem V P G K E.
adfectionem R.   affectionem S L.   3. intellegendum R V P G K.   intellegendum L.
4. posuerunt R V P G B 3 K S E L M D C Π O 2 3 7 8.   posuere L 5 W 2 J O.
imposuerunt W.   imposuerunt B.   imposuere R 7. ‖ senisse G.   5. omnis
V B K O 2.   omnis R.   omīs W 2.   omnes G.   omīs L. ‖ insipientes
R V G B K S E L W 2 O 2.   6. qui S M.   quis P.   quis R V B K E M 2
D C J O 7 8.   Qis W 2.   qus G *alt. man. superscr.*   quid L O 1 2.
cuius R 7   W. ‖ est enim animus R V P G B K S E L W 2 (*at* sanus *in marg.*)
M J O 1–3.   enim *om.* C D.   est enim sanus M 2 B 3 (*at* animus *in marg.*)
enim est animus O 7.   enim animus est W.   animus enim qui est E 2 Π.

§ 9. mentem uacuam = *mentis uacuae
adfectionem.*

posset: i 4, 7 n. on *dedimus...aude-
remus. possit* of the best MSS could not
be defended by *possim* which may be
right in i 4, 7.

V. §10. amentiam...dementiam, 'lack
of mind'...'loss of mind.'

rebus nomina posuerunt: *inponere
nomen* is much more usual, but Dav.
compares N.D. i 17, 44 'sunt enim rebus
nouis noua ponenda nomina.'

a Socrate acceptum: the Stoic paradox
ὅτι πᾶς ἄφρων μαίνεται was never uttered
by Socrates. But the germ of the doctrine
may be found in his teaching, cf. Xen.
Mem. iii 9, 6 where he is said to have
pronounced the failing to know oneself
and the imagining that one knows what
one does not know to be ἐγγυτάτω μανίας.

Editors should not refer to the 'Second
Alcibiades' in this connexion, for Socrates
says there that while all madmen are
unwise all unwise men are not mad, Ps.-
Plato Alc. ii cc. 4—5 pp. 139—140. Cic.
makes similar assertions in Ac. ii 44, 136
and in Parad. 4.

qui est enim animus: the argument is
'They rightly named that state of mind
which lacks the control of reason *amentia*
and *dementia*. For the diseased mind
(and an excited mind is a diseased mind)
is not sound. Hence wisdom is a sound
state of mind and lack of wisdom may
be termed "unsoundness" of mind or,
in other words, madness or loss of
reason.'

ut modo dixi: c. 4 § 7.

quasi insanitas quaedam: the word
insanitas occurs in Cic. only here and in

10 est insania eademque dementia; multoque melius haec notata
sunt uerbis Latinis quam Graecis, quod aliis quoque multis locis
reperietur. sed id alias, nunc quod instat. **11.** totum igitur id,
quod quaerimus, quid et quale sit, uerbi uis ipsa declarat. eos
enim sanos quoniam intellegi necesse est, quorum mens motu
15 quasi morbo perturbata nullo sit, qui contra adfecti sint, hos
insanos appellari necesse est. itaque nihil melius quam quod est
in consuetudine sermonis Latini, cum exisse ex potestate dicimus eos qui ecfrenati feruntur aut libidine aut iracundia; quamquam ipsa iracundia libidinis est pars; sic enim definitur: iracundia
20 ulciscendi libido. qui igitur exisse ex potestate dicuntur, idcirco
dicuntur, quia non sint in potestate mentis, cui regnum totius

12. reperietur R V P B K E W M D C   O 2 3 8.   reperitur S   W 2   Π J O.
reperitur G (*ead. man.*)   reppperietur L.   reppitur E 2.
__§ 11, 14. quoniam R 1 7 V P G S E L 4   C Π   O 3 Gr.   quidem R 17   O 8.
qm K 2   E 2   L D.   qm̄ B.   quŏ K.   quomodo O 1 *om*. R 6   B 3   L 3 5 6
W M   O 2 7. ‖ intellegi R V P G B K.   intelligi S E L W C.   15. nullo B 3
E 2   W M D C Π   O 1–3 8.   nullo V (*ex* nulla *mut*.)   nullạ B.   nulla
R G K E L   O 7. ‖ adfecti V K E.   adfecti R d *in* f *al. atr. mut*.   affecti
G B L. ‖ sint R V P G B K S E L   W 2   M Π J   O 1 2 8.   sunt W D C
O 3 7.   16. insani G *alt. man. superscr*. ‖ appellari R V G B K E L.   apellari S.
18. ecfrenati B K.   ecfrenati R *al. atr. suppl*.   hecfrenati G *sed* h *conf. alt. man*.
hęcfrenati V.   effrenati R 6   P 2   S L W M 2   D C J   O 1 3 8.   & frenati E.
affrenati O 7. ‖ libidine R V P K L. ‖ iracondia G (*bis*).   19. libidinis R V P K L.
20. qui igitur R P G K.   quis igitur V.   quis igitur R 16   O 7. ‖ idcirco
R V P G K L.   iccirco B.   21. sint R V G B K S E 2   L   W 2   M Π J   O 3 7.
sin P *al. atr. suppl*.   sunt E D C   O 1 2 8.   st' W.

the suspected passage above, and here its
use is apologised for as involving an unfamiliar metaphor. Cf. i 12, 27 n.

multoque melius: cf. ii 15, 35 n. on
'amantis doloris.'

id alias: sc. *agemus*, cf. de Inu. ii 11, 37
'qua re ante factis omissis illud, quod
instet, agi oportere.'

§ 11. quid et quale sit, 'its nature
and quality.'

quoniam: for the position of the con-
junction after one or more emphasised
words see Madv. § 465 b.

exisse ex potestate, 'to have lost their
self-control.' Gk. ἐξίστασθαι ἑαυτῶν. Cf.
iv 36, 77 'exisse de potestate, id est de
consilio, de ratione, de mente; horum
enim potestas in totum animum esse
debet.' It is not necessary to adopt the
suggestion of Turnebus, *Aduers*. ii 11,
approved by Dav. that this expression
arose from the fact that *furiosi* were from
an early period subject to the *potestas* of

their *adgnati* and *gentiles*. Dav. quotes
Senec. de Ira i 12 'uenitque in alienam
potestatem, dum in sua non est.'

iracundia libidinis est pars: iv 7, 16
and iii 4, 7 n.

iracundia ulciscendi libido, 'for so
the definition runs: anger, a desire for
revenge,' much as we should say 'for so
the dictionary has it.' This punctuation,
adopted by Mo. and Küh., is better than
that of most editors 'sic enim definitur
iracundia: ulciscendi libido,' for Cicero
is evidently quoting as from a glossary.
Cf. Festus, passim. H. Stephanus in
Mo. takes Cic. to be translating this
definition from the Greek: ὀργή· τιμωρίας
ἐπιθυμία.

The well-known fact that *sic* is often
redundantly used, pointed out here by
Ml. 'for the benefit of Küh.,' does not
determine the point.

igitur: resuming, i 13, 30 n.; i 7, 14 n.

mentis, cui regnum: § 8 n.

animi a natura tributum est. Graeci autem μανίαν unde appellent, non facile dixerim; eam tamen ipsam distinguimus
nos melius quam illi. hanc enim insaniam, quae iuncta stultitia
25 patet latius, a furore disiungimus, Graeci uolunt illi quidem, sed
parum ualent uerbo; quem nos furorem, μελαγχολίαν illi uocant;
quasi uero atra bili solum mens ac non saepe uel iracundia grauiore
uel timore uel dolore moueatur; quo genere Athamantem,
Alcmaeonem, Aiacem, Orestem furere dicimus. qui ita sit ad-

22. Graecia G *sed a exp. et conf. alt. man.* ‖ appellent R 7 L 2 W.	appellant
R V P G B K S E L W 2 M D C Π J O 1–3 7 8.	*om.* R 6.	23. ipsa G.
24. stultitia P G L 5 W 2 O 1.	stultitiae R a *in æ al. atr. mut.*	stulticia R 1 7
L J.	stultitiae V P 3 K M 2 O 2 Gr.	stultitię B.	stulticiae R 6.
stulticię W.	stultitie P 2 4 S E 2 3 M C O 3 7.	stulticie B 3 K 2 E D Π
O 8.	25. disiungimus V G B K S E L W M 2 C Π O 8.	distinguimus R
eod. atr. distinguimus W 2 M D E 3 O 7.	26. melancholian G B.	27. hac non
G *sed* h *confossum.* ‖ saepae G.	28. dolorem G.

Graeci...μανίαν unde appellent: the
root man- from which μανία is derived is
found also in μαινάς and μάντις in Gk.
and in the Latin words *mens* and *moneo*:
Giles, *Manual of Comp. Phil.* pp. 32 ff.
distinguimus, 'subdivide.' Cic. takes
μανία to be the Gk. general term and
seems to find no particular term to correspond to *insania* and only an inadequate
term to correspond to *furor*. But he
does not indicate a Latin general term to
include *insania* and *furor* and his assertions with regard to μανία and μελαγχολία are incorrect, μανία not μελαγχολία
being the usual word for *furor* in Hippocrates and other pre-Ciceronian Gk.writers.
Cf. Sylburg in Mo., where it is also
pointed out that Cic. elsewhere fails to
observe his own distinction e.g. in Off.
iii 25, 95 'si gladium quis apud te sana
mente deposuerit, repetat insaniens,'
where *furiosus* would be the proper word
according to the distinction here drawn.
iuncta stultitia: examples of the abl.
without prep., to express that which is
united with something else, are rare and
are confined to the participle and gerundive, unless v 33, 96, where most editors
now follow Madv. in inserting *cum* after
tum, be an instance from the finite verb.
Instances are found in Att. ix 10, 4
'infinitum bellum iunctum miserrima
fuga'; Or. iii 14, 55 'magis probitate
iungenda summaque prudentia,' where
see Wilkins' n. Brut. 44, 162 quoted by
Küh. on v 33, 96 seems to require emendation; see Piderit's and Kellogg's n.
In Leg. iii 20, 47 'id est enim iunctum
magistratibus' the case may be dat. not
abl., or *cum* may have fallen out after
tum. coniungi is more common than

iungi and *coniunctus cum aliquo* or *cum
aliqua re* is usual. The simple abl. is
found in Phil. iii 14, 35 'ea summa
miseria est summo dedecore coniuncta';
v 7, 20 'huius mendicitas auiditate coniuncta.' The dat. is found with *iungor*
Ac. ii 14, 44 'posteriori superius non
iungitur,' but not in the same sense as in
our passage.
patet latius: being united with folly it
has a wide application since all *stulti* are
insani.
illi quidem: i 3, 6 n.
uerbo: abl. of means. 'They are un-
fortunate in their word.'
quasi uero: for the pres. subj. cf.
i 22, 50 n.
ac non=*ac non potius*, cf. i 7, 13 n.
on 'et non eos.'
Athamantem: Athamas, father of
Phrixus and Helle by Nephele, and of
Learchus and Melicerta by Ino, was
driven mad by Juno and slew Learchus
and pursued Ino, who jumped into the
sea with Melicerta, whereupon she was
changed into Leucothea and M. into
Palaemon. Cf. i 12, 28 n.; Ovid, Met.
iv 416—562.
Alcmaeonem: Amphiaraus joined the
expedition of the Seven against Thebes,
induced thereto by his wife Eriphyle,
who had been bribed with the gift of the
golden necklace. At Thebes the earth
opened and swallowed him together with
his chariot. Before quitting Argos, knowing the fate that was in store for him,
he charged his sons to avenge him upon
their mother when they should be grown
up. Alcmaeon accordingly slew his mother
and was in consequence driven mad and
persecuted by the Furies. Cf. ii 25, 60.

30 fectus, eum dominum esse rerum suarum uetant duodecim
tabulae; itaque non est scriptum 'SI INSANVS' sed 'SI FVRIOSVS
ESCIT.' stultitiam enim censuerunt constantia, id est sanitate,
uacantem posse tamen tueri mediocritatem officiorum et uitae

29. orestem R V P G K S L D.   orestē E.   horestem B W. ‖ adfectus V G K E.
                                                             i
aafectus R *al. atr. mut.*   affectus B S L.   30. duodecim G K.   duodecem R *eod.*
ut uid. atr. duodecem V. XII D.   31. furiosus esse incipit R V P G B K S E L M
D C II O 1–3 7 8.   ēē incepit W.   incipit J (esse *om.*)   ícip̄ W 2 (esse *om.*)
furiosus escit *corr. Bouhier.*   32. stultitiam R 1 6   P 3   B   L 2–6   W 2   M   O 1–3 7.
stultitiā R 7   K W J   O 8 Gr.   stultitiā R *et* P *linea alio atr. supra duct.*
  ti
stultiā V.   stulticiam K 2   E 2.   stulticiā B 3   E D II.   stultitia G.
stulticię R 10. ‖ ịnconstantiaṃ V.   inconstantia G.   inconstantiā B 3   K L 5
W M D̄   O 8.   īọstātiā W 2.   inconstantiam R 1 6   P B   K 2   S E L   M 2
O 1–3 7 Gr.   idest W 2   id ē L   O 8.   inconstanciam R 7 17   II. ‖ id est G K
O 1 3 7 Gr.   idest W 2   id ē L   O 8.   idē E 2.   id̄ B.   ·i· W.

Aiacem: i 41, 98 n.

Orestem: persecuted by the Furies for
slaying his mother Clytaemnestra who,
along with Aegisthus, had murdered his
father Agamemnon.

furere: present, because they appeared
upon the stage in plays then extant. Cf.
18, 42 n. on 'uolt.'

duodecim tabulae: see the extract and
reff. under ii 21, 48 n. on 'amicorum
propinquorumque custodiis.'

escit: an inchoative form = *esse incipit*
of the MSS, which is evidently due to an
explanatory gloss. That *escit* was rightly
restored by Bouhier is indicated by the
fact that Nonius, p. 443, quotes this
passage with *essit* and MSS of de Inu.
ii 50, 148 quote this law with *erit* and
those of ad Herenn. i 13, 23 with *existet*
or *existat. escit* occurs in Lucr. i 619 and
in Gellius xx 1, 25; *escunt* in Leg. iii 3, 9
'discordiae ciuium escunt' and it is also
no doubt the true reading lower down in
the same section 'ast quando consules...
nec escunt' and in ii 24, 60 'cui auro
dentes iuncti escunt.' Festus has *super-
escit* = *supererit* and Paulus from Festus
escit = *erit* and *obescit* = *oberit.*

stultitiam = *insaniam*, as maintained
in the preceding sections, and this = *insanos*, abstract for concrete. Nonius p. 443
quotes the passage thus 'insaniam enim
censuerunt...' but *insaniam...sanitate uacantem* would be intolerable and the
authority of Nonius is slight, cf. Muller's
Nonius 11² p. 257. Ern. proposed *stultitiam enim censuerunt, id est inconstantiam sanitate uacantem, posse...*

id est = *ergo etiam*. These words are
often used not to express identity but to
add something necessary to the argument,
cf. i 31, 75 n.

mediocritatem officiorum = *media officia*, but the idea in *media* receives more

prominence from the substantive, cf.
Naegelsbach, *Lat. Stil.* § 74. This use
is very common in Latin, cf. p. Ligario
11, 33 'hunc splendorem omnium' = *hos
omnes uiros splendidos*; Tac. Hist. iv 24
'unius senis ualetudine' = *ab uno sene
inualido.*

While the strict Stoic doctrine was
that only those actions that were done in
accordance with virtue as the outcome of
perfect intention (possible only to the
ideal wise man) were good—these being
καρορθώματα, *recte facta*—and that only
the direct opposites of these were evil—
ἁμαρτήματα, *peccata*—and that all things
except virtue and vice were matters of
indifference, ἀδιάφορα, *res indifferentes*,
virtue being an unchangeable condition
of the mind in accordance with right
reason, the Stoics were compelled as a
concession to the practical facts of life to
admit that whatever contributes to bodily
well-being must have a certain positive
value (ἀξία) and must be desirable (προηγμένα, *producta*) in all cases in which no
higher good suffers in consequence, and
that whatever is opposed to bodily well-
being, when higher duties are not involved,
must have a negative value (ἀπαξία) and
consequently deserve to be avoided (ἀπο-
προηγμένα, *reiecta*); and that an action
might be done in accordance with reason
even though the perfect intention necessary
to make it a right action were lacking.
All actions which occupied this intermediate position they called καθήκοντα
(appropriate actions), *officia* (duties); and
as καρορθώματα, right actions, were sometimes termed καθήκοντα τέλεια these
intermediate actions were sometimes
termed καθήκοντα μέσα, *media officia*.
The *stultus* (i.e. the non-philosopher)
cannot have the perfect intention necessary
to the performance of right actions but

communem cultum atque usitatum; furorem autem esse rati
35 sunt mentis ad omnia caecitatem. quod cum maius esse uideatur
quam insania, tamen eius modi est ut furor in sapientem cadere
possit, non possit insania. sed haec alia quaestio est; nos ad
propositum reuertamur.

VI. 12. Cadere opinor, in sapientem aegritudinem tibi
dixisti uideri.

A. Et uero ita existimo.

M. Humanum id quidem, quod ita existimas. non enim
5 silice nati sumus, sed est naturale in animis tenerum quiddam

34. cultum G c *in ras.*　　uisitatum G *in* usit. *corr.*　　38. praepositum G
prae *in* pro *alt. man. corr.*
VI. 12, 3. et uero R V P G B K S E L D C Π O 1 3 7 8 Gr.　　et uere B 3
M O 2. et $\overline{ue}$ W 2 J. ego uero W. ‖ existimo R V B K S E L. existumo G.
4. existimas S L. existumas R V G B K E. ‖ enim silice R K L W. enim silice V.
5. scilice E. ‖ naturale R 6 P 2　　E 2 L 5 W 1 Π J.　　naturabile V P 3.
naturabile R 1 7 1 7 P 1 4 G B 1 3 K E L M 1 2 D C O 2 3 7 8.　　nbile K 2.
file W 2. ‖ animis tenerum R 1 6 7 1 7 V P 1-4 G B 1 3 K 1 2 S E 1 2
L 1-6 W 2 M 1 2 D C Π J O 1-3 8.　　aio tenerum W 1.　　ais et'num O 7. ‖
quiddam B 1 3 K E 2 L W 1 2 M 2 C O 1 3.　　quidam R (*fort. eod. atr.*
suppl.) V.　　quiddam G *at* ddam *in ras.*　　quidam M O 2.

he may perform *officia.* Zeller, *Stoics etc.*,
c. xi pp. 261—274; Diog. L. vii 108;
Stob. Ecl. II 158 foll.; Off. i 3, 8; iii 3, 14;
Ac. i 10, 37; Fin. iii 17, 58.
ad: 'in respect of,' a common use.
Küh. compares (inter alia) 33, 79
'Chrysippi consolatio ad ueritatem firmissima est, ad tempus aegritudinis difficilis'; Livy xxi 54, 3 'hostem caecum ad
has belli artes habebitis.'
quod: sc. *ad omnia caecum esse.*
furor...insania: the *sapiens* cannot
have that form of madness which implies
weakness of intellect. Virtue is right-
ordered reason, iv 15, 34; and once
possessed it can never be lost, ii 14, 32 n.;
but *furor* may be produced by an over-
powering physical cause, cf. Diog. L.
vii 118 ἔτι δὲ οὐδὲ μανήσεσθαι· προσ-
πεσεῖσθαι μέντοι ποτὲ αὐτῷ φαντασίας
ἀλλοκότους διὰ μελαγχολίαν ἢ λήρησιν,
οὐ κατὰ τὸν τῶν αἱρετῶν λόγον, ἀλλὰ παρὰ
φύσιν, quoted by Dav. See also *ibid.* § 127,
quoted in v. Arnim's *Stoica* III 237.
possit, non possit: cf. ii 17, 39 n. on
'posset...non posset.'
VI. § 12. **et uero**: de R.P. i 32, 49;
vi 1, 1. See also ii 11, 26 n. on 'uero.'
non enim silice...: a ref. to those early
myths which represented men as sprung
from stocks and stones, cf. Hom. Od.
xix 163 οὐ γὰρ ἀπὸ δρυός ἐσσι παλαιφάτου,
οὐδ' ἀπὸ πέτρης; Il. xvi 33-5; Virg.

Aen. viii 315 'gensque uirum truncis et
duro robore nata,' and Conington's n.;
iv 366. See also Reid on Ac. ii 31, 101.
naturale: Lamb. read *natura*, followed
by Bai. and T.S. Some early editors read
naturabile with MSS, relying upon a variant
in Laelius 21, 80 'maxime naturali carent
amicitia,' but to this Bent. objected that
Cic., who wrote *naturalis* hundreds of
times, was not likely to write *naturabilis*
once or twice. Bent. himself proposed
natura fere which Dav. Lall. and Mo.
adopted. The emendation of Sff. *natura
tractabile in animis et tenerum* is very
plausible and has been adopted by Küh.
natura (*nra*) would pass into the MS
reading by quasihaplography and *et* might
readily fall out before *tenerum*. Moreover, the passage in Lael. 13, 48 cited by
Sff. in support of his reading is very
parallel and must have been taken from
the same source as our passage. There
we have a use of *humanitatem* similar to
that of *humanum* here, and then 'quid
enim interest...inter hominem et truncum
aut saxum...? neque enim sunt isti audi-
endi, qui uirtutem duram et quasi ferream
esse quandam uolunt: quae quidem est...
tenera atque tractabilis.'
naturale, however, read by Hei. Ml.
and Schiche, has MS support and gives
a good sense = *natura insitum*, as in
Diu. ii 12, 29, 'tauri opimi iecur...quid

atque molle, quod aegritudine quasi tempestate quatiatur, nec
absurde Crantor ille, qui in nostra Academia uel in primis fuit
nobilis, 'Minime,' inquit, 'adsentior iis, qui istam nescio
quam indolentiam magno opere laudant, quae nec potest
10 ulla esse nec debet. ne aegrotus sim ; si, inquit, fuero, sen-

6. qua G *in* quod *alt. man. corr.*   7. qui in nostra R 6 7   C D   O 8.   qui, n̄ra V.

q in n̄ra W 1.   qui n̄ra E (*al. atr. superscr.*)   qui nostra R 1 17   P G S   L 1 5
W 2   M 2   J   O 2 3.   qui n̄ra B 1 3   K 1   E 2 3   M Π.   qui n̄ram K 2.

8. adsentior R V.   assentior S L.   absentior B K.   absentior E *al. man. corr.* ‖
his R 1 10 16 V P G.   9. magnoopere V P.   magno-opere R (*al. atr. corr.*)   magno
opere L.   magno ope B 2.   magnopere R 10 16   B 1 3   S E. ‖   quęnec V (i *in*
ę *corr.*)   quęnec B (ę *ex* i *ut uid. mut.*)   qui nec B 2   G.   quinec R P E.

10. ullę G *alt. man. corr.* ‖   ne aegrotus sim G.   nec aegrotassem P B.   nec
ęgrotassē R.   nec egrotassem R 7 17   P 4   B 2   K 1 2   E 1 2   L 1 4   D C Π
O 7 8.   neç egrotassem V.   nec ęgrotasse S *at duarum uel trium litt. spatio post
hoc uerb. cum ras. rel.*   nec egrotasse L 5   J.   nec aegrotis est L 3.   nec
ęgrotis est P 2.   nec egrotis est B 3.   nec egrotus est P 3   M 1 2.   nec egroto
etiam R 6.   nec ęgroto etiam W.   nec egrotis est O 3.   nec aegrotis ē O 2.
nec egrotare L 6. ‖   si inquit R 1 17   B 1 2   K 1 2   S   E 2   L   W 2   D C Π J.
sị inquit V.   si inquid P *al. atr. superscr.*   si inquid O 7   G *at* d *in* t *alt. man.
corr.*   sinquid E.   si is qui R 7   B 3   L 2 4–6   M 1 2   O 1 8.   si hijs qui P 4. ‖

fuerat R 1 7   P 1 4   G   B 1–3   K S E   L 1 3 4 6   M 1 2   D Π J   O 1 8.   fuerat V.
fūat E 2   L 5.   fua't C (*sic*).   fuęāt O 7.   fuerāt L 2.   affua't K 2 (*sic*).
fui't R 1 7.   fuīt W 2.

habet naturale, quod declarare possit quid
futurum sit?' quoted by Ml. Cf. also
iv 26, 57 'nam quod aiunt nimia resecari
oportere, *naturalia* relinqui.' There seems
to have been some tendency in copyists
to confuse the terminations -*abilis* and
-*alis*.

[For the sentiment cf. ii 21, 47 est in
animis omnium fere natura molle quiddam, demissum, humile, eneruatum quodam modo et languidum.]

Crantor : i 48, 115 n. The passage
referred to is preserved in Plut. Cons. ad
Apollon. p. 102 C οὐ γὰρ ἔγωγε συμφέρομαι τοῖς τὴν ἄγριον ὑμνοῦσι καὶ σκληρὰν
ἀπάθειαν, ἔξω καὶ τοῦ δυνατοῦ καὶ τοῦ
συμφέροντος οὖσαν...'μὴ γὰρ νοσοῖμεν' φησὶν
ὁ ἀκαδημαϊκὸς Κράντωρ, 'νοσήσασι δὲ
παρείη τις αἴσθησις, εἴτ᾽ οὖν τέμνοιτό τι
τῶν ἡμετέρων εἴτ᾽ ἀποσπῷτο. τὸ γὰρ ἀνώ-
δυνον τοῦτ᾽ οὐκ ἄνευ μεγάλων ἐγγίγνεται
μισθῶν τῷ ἀνθρώπῳ· τεθηριῶσθαι γὰρ
εἰκὸς ἐκεῖ μὲν σῶμα τοιοῦτον ἐνταῦθα δὲ
ψυχήν.

indolentiam : a word invented by Cic.,
cf. Madv. on Fin. ii 4, 11. Crantor was
a contemporary of Zeno of Citium, the
founder of the Stoics, whose doctrine, in
its strictest form, demanded the suppres-
sion of all emotion (ἀπάθεια), Zeller,

Stoics, *etc.*, p. 238. For the εὐπάθεια,
a modification of the strict doctrine, see
ibid. p. 274. The question of the sup-
pression of the emotions must have been
much discussed at least from Plato's time
onwards, the germ of the doctrine being
found in Plato. See Grote's remarks upon
the Philebus, *Plato* II c. 30, pp. 608 foll.
Cf. also Democritus' εὐθυμία or ἀθαμβία,
Fin. v 29, 87; Diog. L. ix 45.

ne aegrotus sim...: Gronovius conjectured *ne aegrotassim, inquit, sin fuerit*
(sc. ut aegrotare debeam) *sensus adsit*;
P. Victorius, whom Dav. follows, *ne
aegrotassim; sin quid fuerit sensus adsit*;
Fr. Fabricius, followed by Küh., *ne
aegrotus sim, inquit; sed, si fuerim,
sensus adsit*; F.A.W. and Mo. *ne aegrotus sim; sin: is qui fuerat sensus adsit*;
Halm, followed by Bai., *ne aegrotus sim:
si sim, qui fuerat sensus adsit*; Sff.,
followed by T.S., Hei., Hasper and Ml.,
*ne aegrotus sim: si, inquit, fuero, sensus
adsit*; Schiche agrees with Sff. except
that he inserts *et* before *sensus*. The
reading of Victorius is open to the objection that the euphemism *si quid fuerit*
is only used of death; that of F.A.W.
presents an ellipse with *sim* for which it
would be hard to find parallels; to that

sus adsit, siue secetur quid siue auellatur a corpore.
nam istuc nihil dolere non sine magna mercede contingit inmanitatis in animo, stuporis in corpore.' **13.** Sed
uideamus ne haec oratio sit hominum adsentantium nostrae
15 inbecillitati et indulgentium mollitudini; nos autem audeamus
non solum ramos amputare miseriarum, sed omnis radicum fibras
euellere. tamen aliquid relinquetur fortasse; ita sunt altae stirpes
stultitiae; sed relinquetur id solum quod erit necessarium. illud
quidem sic habeto, nisi sanatus animus sit, quod sine philo-
20 sophia fieri non potest, finem miseriarum nullum fore. quam ob
rem, quoniam coepimus, tradamus nos ei curandos; sanabimur,
si uolemus. et progrediar quidem longius; non enim de aegritudine solum, quamquam id quidem primum, sed de omni animi,
ut ego posui, perturbatione, morbo, ut Graeci uolunt, explicabo.

12. istuc R V P 1 3   G   B 2 3   K L   M 1 2   O 1–3 7 8.   istud R 6   B S   E 1 2
W 1 2   D C II   J.   13. inmanitatis V P   B 2   K E L.   inmanitas R.   immanitatis
B S G *at* m *in* n *alt. man. mut.*

§ 13, 14. adsentantium R V G B K L.   assentantium B 2   S.   15. inbecillitati
R V G   B 2   K L.   imbecillitati B.   16. omnis R V G B K E L.   oīs W 2.   om̄s B 2.

17. altae R B.   altą V.   altę L W.   alte W 2   D   O 1 3 7 8.   alta G   B 2   K. ‖
scurpes G *ut uid.*; *in* stirpes *alt. man. corr.*   20. quam G, *in marg.* quam *alt.
man. adscr.*

of Halm, Sff. objects that the words *qui
fuerat* are unnecessary. The reading of
Sff. agrees closely with the MSS and with
the Gk original. The repetition of *inquit*
within the space of two lines has been
objected to, but Küh. refers to ii 19, 44;
N.D. i 7, 17; Or. ii 3, 13; 74, 298. See
especially Or. ii 3, 13. Schiche's *et* may
be right, but *fuerat* may have arisen out
of *fuero* owing to the following *s, s* and *t*
being often confused.

secetur: this and **auellatur** are subj.
because the *siue* clauses depend upon a
pure mental conception. Draeger, *H.S.*
I § 151, 5 h, puts these subjunctives under
the head of attraction. See also i 25, 60 n.
'siue ignis sit.'

mercede: cf. μισθῶν in the Gk, quoted
above. More usually of pay, here of cost,
as in p. Domo 11, 29 'data merces est
erroris mei magna'; Fam. i 9, 3 'te...
gaudeo eam fidem cognosse hominum non
ita magna mercede, quam ego maximo
dolore cognoram.' For the genitive cf.
i 15, 34 n. on 'mercedem gloriae.'

§ **13. uideamus ne**: a polite mode of
expressing warning and doubt, Küh. on
i 34, 83.

quod erit necessarium, 'which must
inevitably be retained,' i.e. without which

the man would cease to be a *homo*. See
ii 17, 39 n. on 'si quidem homo esset.'
Hieronymus, Ep. 133 (ad Ctesiphontem),
mentions the Stoic doctrine that the last
trace of the *perturbationes* must be rooted
out and says that this doctrine was disputed by the *Peripatetici...et Academici
noui, quos Tullius sequitur* and adds *hoc
est enim hominem ex homine tollere...et
optare potius quam docere.* Cicero in Off.
iii 5, 26 has *quid cum eo disseras qui
omnino hominem ex homine tollat?* but
he is not referring there to the *perturbationes.* Where Cicero uses *optare hoc
quidem est, non docere* (in ii, 13, 30) he
is referring to the despising of pain, and
Jerome may have found *hoc est enim
hominem ex homine tollere* with the same
reference in Cicero's Consolatio, a work
with which he was familiar.

sic habeto, 'of this be assured.'

ut ego posui, 'to use the expression
that I have adopted' in 4, 7. Cf. 20, 46
'non...uerbo solum posuit uoluptatem';
Fam. i 9, 21 'ut paulo ante posui.' Küh

primo: sc. as far as c. 10 § 22.

Stoicorum more: cf. iv 4, 9 foll. The
Stoic style is described in the introduction
to the Paradoxa § 2 'Cato autem, perfectus
mea sententia Stoicus, ... in ea est haeresi,

H.   2

25 et primo, si placet, Stoicorum more agamus, qui breuiter astringere solent argumenta; deinde nostro instituto uagabimur.

VII. **14.** Qui fortis est, idem est fidens, quoniam confidens
mala consuetudine loquendi in uitio ponitur, ductum uerbum
a confidendo, quod laudis est. qui autem est fidens, is profecto
non extimescit; discrepat enim a timendo confidere. atqui, in
5 quem cadit aegritudo, in eundem timor; quarum enim rerum
praesentia sumus in aegritudine, easdem inpendentes et uenientes
timemus. ita fit ut fortitudini aegritudo repugnet. ueri simile

25. astringere R V G   B 2   K S L.   adstringere B E.
VII. § **14**, 2.   uerbum a confidendo R 1 10 16   G   B 1 3   K L D   O 1 7 8.
               a
uerbum confidendo V.   uerbum confidendo E.   uerbum a confitendo B 2.
uerbum a fidendo W.   3. quod laudis R 1 10 16   G   B 2   E 2   W 1 2   M 1 2   D
               in
O 1 3 8.   quod laudis V.   quod laudi E.   quod laus O 7.   ‖   fidens G L.
9fidens V *al. man. superscr.*   4. atqui R 6   S   M 2   Π   E 2 (*at* qui *in ras. alio atr.*).
  i
atque R *al. atr. suppl.*   atq; P *al. atr. suppl.*   atque G.   atq; R 1 7   V
B 1 2   K 1 2   E L   W 1 2   J   O 1 3 7 8.   atq R 7   B 3   M 1   O 2.   at C D.
                              i
6. inpendentes R G K E L.   inpendentes V.   impendentes P   B 1 2.   uenientes
    i
G B.   uenientes V.   7. uere G e *in* i *alt. man. corr.*

quae nullum sequitur florem orationis
neque dilatat argumentum; minutis inter-
rogatiunculis quasi punctis quod proposuit
efficit.' See also ii 18, 42 n. and reff.
there.

astringere, 'compress,' cf. Brut. 90,
309 'eram cum Stoico Diodoto...a quo...
in dialectica exercebar, quae quasi contracta et adstricta eloquentia putanda est';
also Brut. 31, 120 quoted on § 22, below.

nostro instituto = *more oratorio.*

uagabimur: cf. 'neque dilatat argumentum' in Paradoxa § 2 above.

VII. § **14. quoniam**: elliptic = *hoc dico
quoniam* or *non dixi illum confidentem
quoniam hoc uerbum...*; cf. 9, 20 *non dixi
inuidiam*, compared by T.S.

confidens: the participle was more
usual at all times in a bad sense than in
a good one, cf. the exx. in Nonius 262;
it is used in a good sense in Ter. And.
v 2, 14 'ellum, confidens, catus.' The
good sense is more common with the
adverb *confidenter*. *Confidentia* has both
senses.

atqui was much used to introduce a
minor premiss in syllogistic argument, cf.
i 43, 104 n. on 'in corpore autem.' It is
therefore read here by editors generally,
though *atque* has much better MS support.
Fluctuations in MSS between *atque* and
atqui are very frequent, cf. v 15, 43 init.,
18, 53 init.; N.D. ii 15, 41 init. It may
be observed that *et* was sometimes thus
used (cf. § 18), and therefore *atque* 'and

further' does not seem in itself unsuitable
but the meaning yielded by *atqui* seems
better here [cf. the similar use of καὶ μήν
in Greek].

ita fit ut...repugnet: Hei., *Posen
Progr.* p. 19, maintains that these words
are a gloss summing up, out of place, the
argument which is again summed up lower
down in *non cadunt autem....*But the argument would not run on if these words
were cut out, and the conclusion to be
reached is not that the brave man is not
liable to annoyance but that the wise man
is not so.

We have in this chapter three chain
arguments to prove that the wise man
cannot suffer annoyance, the first occupying the whole of § 14; the second from
praeterea down to *non cadet igitur in
sap. aegritudo*; the third from *et quem ad
modum* to the end of § 15. The stages in
the first argument are the following: he
who is brave is also confident: he who is
confident does not fear: but he who is
liable to annoyance is also liable to fear:
hence liability to annoyance is out of
keeping with bravery. At this point
Cicero takes a new start and brings the
argument down to the same point by
another set of inferences, viz.—he who is
liable to annoyance would seem liable to
fear, loss of spirit, despondency: he who
is liable to these is liable to become a
slave, to admit defeat: he who is liable
to this is liable to timidity and cowardice:

est igitur, in quem cadat aegritudo, cadere in eundem timorem
et infractionem quidem animi et demissionem. quae in quem
10 cadunt, in eundem cadit ut seruiat, ut uictum, si quando, se esse
fateatur. quae qui recipit, recipiat idem necesse est timiditatem
et ignauiam. non cadunt autem haec in uirum fortem; igitur ne
aegritudo quidem. at nemo sapiens nisi fortis; non cadet ergo
in sapientem aegritudo. **15.** praeterea necesse est, qui fortis sit,
15 eundem esse magni animi; qui magni animi sit, inuictum; qui
inuictus sit, eum res humanas despicere atque infra se positas

8. igitur *om.* L. ‖ cadat R V P 4 B 1 2 K L W C O 1 2 7. cadat S *eod. atr.*
cadit R 6 7 P 1–3 G B 3 E 2 W 2 M 1 2 D J Π O 3 8. 9. quidem R 7 V P G
B 1–3 K E L 1 5 W 2 M 2 J O 1 3 8.   quandam R 6 P 4 S E 2 W M Π
O 2.   quamdam K 2 D C.   quādā O 7.   q̄ndā R *at in marg.* quidem
al. atr. adscr.　E 3 *om. at in marg.* quādam *habet.* ‖ et demissionem B 2 S L
W 1 2 D O 1.　et demissionē R 10 16.　et demisionem V.　et demisionē R
atr. nigr. suprascr.　et demisionem G K.　et demisione E. ‖ quae in quē
cad̄t G ē *et* dt *in ras. alt. man. scr.*　10. si quando se esse R 1 7 P 4 G B K 1 2
E W 2 J.　si quando esse P *al. atr. superscr.*　si quando se L esse *om.*
si quando esse se E 2.　se si quando esse D C O 7.　si quando ēē B 2 se *om.*
aliquando se esse V E 3.　aliquando esse se S *at ali in ras.*　se quandoque
esse P 2 3 B 3 M 1 2 O 3.　se quandoque O 1 esse *om.*　se quandocunque
esse R 6.　ſe quandoq̄ esse se Π *at* q̄3 *al. atr. suppl.* et ſe *mut. esse suspicor.*
se qn̄q; esse O 7.　si q̄n̄ ē e O 8 *al. atr. superscr.*　ut quandoque se uictum ēē W.
13. cadet R 1 6 P 4 G B 1 2 E 1 L 1 O 8.　cad& V *man. ant. suppl.*　cadat
P K 1 O 3.　cadit B 3 S E 2 W 1 2 M 1 2 D C J O 1 2 7.
§ **15**, 15. qui magni animi sit inuictum R 6 7 B 1 3 E 1 2 M 1 2 D J Π
O 1 2 7 8. qui animi magni sit inuictum C. qui magni animi inuictum W 1. qui magni
animi *om.* R 1 G B 2 E 3 L 1 O 3.　sit inuictum R *eod. atr.*　sit̥ inuictum
P *al. atr. corr.*　magni animi sit̠inuictū V.　qui magni animi *habet* K 1 *eod.*
atr. superscr.　qui magni sit inuictum K 2.　sic inuictum E 3.

the brave man is not liable to these:
therefore the brave man cannot be liable
to annoyance. Having now reached the
point which he had reached in the first
set of inferences Cicero adds two more
propositions which apply to both sets
alike, viz.—but no one is wise unless
brave: therefore the wise man cannot be
liable to annoyance.

cadat: for the subj. cf. § 15 'qui fortis sit';
9, 19 'qui...id concupierit.' The sentences
are conditional relative. The dependency
of the clauses makes the statements hypothetical. But the clauses above, e.g. *in
quem cadit*, are unconditional statements.

et infractionem quidem, 'and in fact a
weakening of spirit.' The idea in *timor*
is expanded to lead up to the next inference (*ut seruiat, ut...fateatur*). It seems,
therefore, unnecessary, with Küh. Mo.
and F.A.W. to alter *quidem* of the best
MSS to *quandam*, making that word

modify *infractionem* as a new word metaphorically used, for which use of *quidam*
cf. i 12, 27 n. The participles, especially
demissus, are common in this metaphorical
sense, cf. post Red. ad Quir. 8, 19 'non
modo non infracto animo...sed confir-
mato'; in L. Pison. 26, 62 'ita nescio
quid istuc fractum, humile, demissum';
T.D. iv 30, 64 'humile, summissum,
molle, effeminatum, fractum.'

si quando: Küh. compares for this
elegant elliptical use (sc. *est, accidit*) the
frequent use of *si forte.*

recipit, recipiat: i 22, 52 n. on 'esset,
non esset.'

igitur: for the position of this word
cf. i 2, 4 n.

cadet: for the future cf. *uacabit* § 15
and i 22, 53 n. on 'nesciet...sciet.'

§ 15. res humanas, 'the vicissitudes
of life,' cf. ii 14, 33 n. on 'humana contem-
nentem'; ii 27, 65 n. on 'humane.'

arbitrari; despicere autem nemo potest eas res propter quas
aegritudine adfici potest; ex quo efficitur fortem uirum aegritudine numquam adfici; omnes autem sapientes fortes; non
20 cadit igitur in sapientem aegritudo. et quem ad modum oculus
conturbatus non est probe adfectus ad suum munus fungendum,
et reliquae partes totumue corpus statu cum est motum deest
officio suo et muneri, sic conturbatus animus non est aptus
ad exsequendum munus suum. munus autem animi est ratione
25 bene uti, et sapientis animus ita semper adfectus est ut ratione
optime utatur; numquam igitur est perturbatus. at aegritudo
perturbatio est animi; semper igitur ea sapiens uacabit.

VIII. 16. Veri etiam simile illud est, qui sit temperans—
quem Graeci σώφρονα appellant eamque uirtutem σωφροσύνην
uocant, quam soleo equidem tum temperantiam, tum modera-
tionem appellare, non numquam etiam modestiam; sed haud
5 scio an recte ea uirtus frugalitas appellari possit, quod angustius
apud Graecos ualet, qui frugi homines χρησίμους appellant, id est
tantum modo utilis; at illud est latius; omnis enim abstinentia,

---

18. adfici (*hic et infra*) V E K.   adfici (*hic et inf.*) R *al. atr. mut.*   affici (*hic et
inf.*) B S L.   affici *hic habet* G *at* af *in ras. alt. man. scr. et ad ante* af *eraso: infra*
adfici.   21. adfectus V G K.   adfectus R.   affectus B S L.   24. exsequendum B L.
exequendum R V P G K O 2.   26. optime R V G B K E L.

  VIII. § 16, 1. illi G *man. alt. superscr.*   2. CΩΦPONA naappellant G.
NA *in ras. et* na *man. alt. confod.*   appellantur R 1 6 *spat. post rel.*   appellant
σώφρονα R 10.   3. tum temperantiam R V P G   B 1–3   K   E 1 2 W 1 2 M 1 2
D C II J O 2 3 8 7.   tum temperationem O 1. ‖ moderantiam O 1.   7. utilis
R V P G B 1 2 K E L J.   utiles S.

---

conturbatus: *conturbatio oculorum* is
used by Scribonius Largus, Comp. Med.
19, as a technical term for inflammation of
the eyes.

fungendum: the gerundive with personal constr. from *utor, fruor, fungor,
potior, uescor* and their compounds is in
classical use; the acc. with these verbs
is ante- and post-classical, except in the
case of *potior*, for which see i 37, 90 n.
on 'urbem nostram.' Cf. 17, 36 'quod
utendum acceperis'; Fin. i 1, 3 'non
paranda nobis solum ea, sed fruenda
etiam est.'

statu: the metaphor is the same as in
'de sententia esse deiectum' ii 5, 14 n.

deest: for the number of the predicate
when two or more subjects are connected
by a disjunctive particle see Madv. § 213 b,
obs. 1.

[at: cf. v 15, 43 n.]
VIII. § 16. qui sit temperans...: an

anacoluthon. Having set down *temperans* as an equivalent for the Gk σώφρων
Cicero pauses to consider the fitness of
the translation and develops a preference
for *frugi*, with *frugalitas* as an equivalent
for σωφροσύνη, and so loses the thread of
his construction, which he resumes in a
new sentence in § 18 in the words *qui sit
frugi igitur uel, si mauis, moderatus et
temperans, eum necesse est esse constantem....* F.A.W. compares the anacolou-
thon in Hor. Epp. i 15, 1—22.

quem...eamque: Cicero might have
written *cuiusque uirtutem...*; for the
transition from the relative to the demonstrative cf. v 3, 8 n. on 'eumque.'

haud scio an: cf. i 17, 41 n.

frugalitas, 'goodness.'

quod angustius apud Graecos ualet,
'an idea which the Greeks express by a
word of narrower meaning.' Orelli in his
notes on F. A. Wolf's lectures observes

omnis innocentia (quae apud Graecos usitatum nomen nullum
habet, sed habere potest ἀβλάβειαν ; nam est innocentia adfectio
10 talis animi quae noceat nemini)—reliquas etiam uirtutes frugalitas
continet. quae nisi tanta esset, et si iis angustiis, quibus plerique
putant, teneretur, numquam esset L. Pisonis cognomen tanto
opere laudatum. **17.** sed quia, nec qui propter metum praesidium
reliquit, quod est ignauiae, nec qui propter auaritiam clam de-
15 positum non reddidit, quod est iniustitiae, nec qui propter
temeritatem male rem gessit, quod est stultitiae, frugi appellari
solet, eo tris uirtutes, fortitudinem, iustitiam, prudentiam, fru-

9. adfectio V G.　　affectio R B K L.　　11. si his G B L.　　12. tanto opere V G
B 2 E.　　tanto-opere R *al. atr. corr.*　　tant opere S o *post* nt *eras.*　　tantoopere K.
tantopere B 1 L.
§ 17, 14. reliquit R 10 16 B 2 W 2.　　reli*n*quit V.　　relinquit R B K E W.
relinquid G *at* d *in* t *alt. man. mut.*　　17. tris R V G K E.　　tris P *al. atr. suppl.*
tres B 2 S L W J.　　tri B 1 *litt. eras.*

that the clause *quod angustius apud
Graecos ualet, qui frugi homines χρησίμους
appellant,* would be thus expressed in the
modern style, *quod Graece aliter reddi
nequit quam χρήσιμος, hoc autem est
angustius; nam apud nos χρήσιμος tantum est utilis; frugi autem latius patet.*
Dav. notes 'Glossae ueteres: Frugalis
χρήσιμος,' and he quotes Donatus on Ter.
Eun. iii 5, 60 and iv 7, 46 for *frugi = utilis,
necessarius,* and for the wider sense of the
word T.D. iv 16, 36 'quod nisi eo nomine
(frugalitatis) uirtutes continerentur, numquam ita peruolgatum illud esset, ut iam
prouerbii locum obtineret, hominem frugi
omnia recte facere,' and for both uses he
compares Quintil. i 6, 29 'M. Caelius se
esse hominem frugi uolt probare, non
quia abstinens sit, (nam id ne mentiri
quidem poterat,) sed quia utilis multis,
id est fructuosus, unde sit ducta frugalitas.'
**omnis enim abstinentia, omnis in-
nocentia:** another anacoluthon, the
consideration of the Gk equivalent leading
to the substitution of the active constr.
for the passive, *reliquae etiam uirtutes
frugalitate continentur.* Dav. compares
Ter. Hec. iii 1, 6 'nam nos omnes quibus
est alicunde aliquis obiectus labos, omne
quod est interea tempus prius quam id
rescitumst lucrost'; Hirtius, Bell. Afr.
c. 18 and c. 23.
ἀβλάβειαν: the noun does not seem to
occur before Plutarch, and there it has
the passive sense of *incolumitas,* 'freedom
from harm.' The adj. ἀβλαβής and the
adv. ἀβλαβῶς often have an active sense
in classical Greek (see Liddell and Scott)

and Dav. quotes 'Glossarium Graeco-
Latinum : Ἀβλάβεια, *innoxia, innocentia.*'
reliquas etiam uirtutes: sc. *prudentiam, fortitudinem, iustitiam.*
iis angustiis, quibus plerique putant:
angustiis = *angusta significatione.* The
word *frugi* was much applied to slaves,
cf. Plautus and Terence, passim. Cic. in
p. r. Deiot. 9, 26 quotes the sentiment
'frugi hominem dici non multum habet
laudis in rege' but expresses his own
dissent 'ego tamen frugalitatem, id est
modestiam et temperantiam, uirtutem
maximam iudico.' In Att. vii 4, 1 Cic.
says of Dionysius, a freedman of Atticus,
'quem quidem cognoui...frugi hominem
ac, ne ut libertinum laudare uidear, plane
uirum bonum,' with which Bouhier compares Mart. xii 30 'siccus, sobrius est
Aper. quid ad me ? | serum sic ego
laudo, non amicum.' For the cause of
this limitation of the application of the
word *frugi* Bouhier quotes Augustin. de
Beata Vita 31 'propter uolgarem dicendi
consuetudinem, qua frugalitas quasi parsimonia dici solet.'
L. Pisonis: L. Calpurnius Piso Frugi,
consul 133 B.C. and subsequently, as it
seems, censor, wrote annals, and as trib.
pl. in 149 carried the *lex Calpurnia de
repetundis,* by which the first of the
quaestiones perpetuae was established.
He adhered to the optimate party, cf. 20,
48.
cognomen: cf. pro Fonteio 17, 39.
§ 17. **eo tris uirtutes:** Hei. compares
Stob. Ecl. Eth. ii p. 112 τῆς δὲ σωφρο-
σύνης ἴδιον κεφάλαιόν ἐστι, τὸ παρέχεσθαι

galitas complexa est (etsi hoc quidem commune est uirtutum ;
omnes enim inter se nexae et iugatae sunt); reliqua igitur est,
20 quarta uirtus ut sit, ipsa frugalitas. eius enim uidetur esse
proprium motus animi adpetentis regere et sedare semperque
aduersantem libidini moderatam in omni re seruare constantiam;
cui contrarium uitium nequitia dicitur. **18**. frugalitas, ut
opinor, a fruge, qua nihil melius e terra, nequitia ab eo (etsi erit

19. omnis G.   omīs K. ‖ est quarta C.   ē quarta R 7.   et quarta
R 1 2 6 10 16 17 V P 1-4 G B 1 2 K 1 E 1 3 W 1 2 Π J O 1-3 7.   20. ut sit
R 1 2 6 7 10 16 17 P 1-4 G B 2 3 K 1 2 E 2 3 L 2 3 5 6 M 1 2 Π O 1-3 7.

ut sit V.   ut sit B 1.   sit ut sit E D C.   ut sit S *nihil in marg. add.*
ut W 2.   ut sunt L.   necesse est ut sit W 1 L 4. ‖ frugalitas eius enim R 1 2 7
V P 1-4 G B K S E 1 2 W 2 M 1 2 D C J O 2 3 8.   frugalitas eis enim B 2.
frugalitas necesse est eius enim R 6.   f. est necesse e. e. O 1.   frugalitas eius
enim Π *at in marg.* necesse est *add.*   21. adpetentis R V G E.   adpetentis
K 1 (*sic*) *eod. atr.*   appetentis P 2 B 1-3 S L 1-6 W 1 2 M 2 D J O 1 3 7 8.
appetentis P *at* p *post* a *in ras.*   apetētis E 3.   22. auersantem R 1.   aufantē
R 10.   auersantem G. ‖ libidini R V P G K L.   libini E.
§ 18, 24. melius e R V P 1 2 4   G B K S E 2 W M 2 Π O 2.   melius
ex B 2.   melius a K 2 L 1 W 2 J O 3 7.   melius in D C O 1.   melius ē a
O 8.   melius est a M 1.   *om.* E 1.

τὰς ὁρμὰς εὐσταθεῖς καὶ θεωρεῖν αὐτὰς
προηγουμένως, κατὰ δὲ τὸν δεύτερον λόγον
τὰ ὑπὸ τὰς ἄλλας ἀρετάς, ἕνεκα τοῦ ἀδια-
πτώτως ἐν ταῖς ὁρμαῖς ἀναστρέφεσθαι· καὶ
ὁμοίως τὴν ἀνδρείαν προηγουμένως μὲν πᾶν
ὃ δεῖ ὑπομένειν, κατὰ δὲ τὸν δεύτερον λόγον
τὰ ὑπὸ τὰς ἄλλας· καὶ τὴν δικαιοσύνην
προηγουμένως μὲν τὸ κατ' ἀξίαν ἑκάστῳ
σκοπεῖν, κατὰ δὲ τὸν δεύτερον λόγον καὶ τὰ
λοιπά. πάσας γὰρ τὰς ἀρετὰς τὰ πασῶν
βλέπειν, καὶ τὰ ὑποτεταγμένα ἀλλήλαις;
Plato Gorg. p. 507; Cic. Off. i 28, 100.
As *frugalitas* includes the other three
cardinal virtues Cicero concludes that
that word suitably translates σωφροσύνη.
etsi: for this corrective use see i 42,
99 n.
omnes...iugatae sunt: for this view
see ii 14, 32 n. and reff.; the words
hoc quidem...iugatae sunt are quoted by
Nonius p. 47.
**reliqua igitur est, quarta uirtus ut
sit, ipsa frugalitas**: this is the conjecture of Madv., adopted by T.S. Hei.
Sff. Ml. Schiche and Bai., though the
punctuation of Bai., *ut sit ipsa, frugalitas*, is not to be followed. The reading
involves practically no departure from
the MSS, *est* and *et* being specially liable
to be confused. Dav., followed by Mo.,
read *reliquum igitur est, quarta uirtus ut
sit ipsa frugalitas*. He also suggested
*relinquitur ut quarta uirtus sit ipsa
frugalitas*, and this reading, as improved

by Bake, who kept *ut* where the MSS
have it, before *sit*, is very Ciceronian.
Dav. supports this conjecture by ref. to
Fin. iii 9, 31 'circumscriptis igitur eis
sententiis, quas posui, et eis, si quae
similes earum sunt, relinquitur ut summum bonum sit uiuere scientiam adhi-
bentem...'
Lucr. v 795 'linquitur ut merito mater-
num nomen adepta | terra sit'; Varro
R.R. i 5 'relinquitur quot partes ea
disciplina habeat ut sit uidendum.' To
these examples may be added Diu. ii 5,
14 'ita relinquitur ut ea fortuita diuinari
possint...'; Ac. ii 38, 119; Att. x 8, 2
'relinquitur ut si uincimur in Hispania
quiescamus.'
adpetentis: accusative. *motus animi
adpetentis* = 'the desires,' τὰς ὁρμάς, cf.
the definition of σωφροσύνη quoted above
from Stobaeus.
aduersantem refers to the subject acc.
frugalitatem, not to *constantiam*.
§ 18. nihil melius: more effective
without *est* which Baiter (following Wesenberg) inserted, cf. 5, 11 'itaque nihil
melius quam quod...'
ab eo...ab eo: the repetition for the
sake of clearness is not uncommon after
a parenthesis or in a sentence of some
length, cf. 28, 71 'ergo id, quod alii...id hi
turpe putantes aegritudinem reppulerunt.'
nequicquam: the same erroneous etymology is given by Varro L.L. x 5 'ut

25 hoc fortasse durius, sed temptemus; lusisse putemur, si nihil sit)
ab eo, quod nequicquam est in tali homine, ex quo idem nihili
dicitur. qui sit frugi igitur uel, si mauis, moderatus et temperans,
eum necesse est esse constantem; qui autem constans, quietum ;
qui quietus, perturbatione omni uacuum, ergo etiam aegritudine.
30 et sunt illa sapientis; aberit igitur a sapiente aegritudo.

   IX. Itaque non inscite Heracleotes Dionysius ad ea disputat
quae apud Homerum Achilles queritur hoc, ut opinor, modo :
   Corque meum penitus turgescit tristibus iris,
   Cum decore atque omni me orbatum laude recordor.

   25. temptemus R V G B K L   O 13.   temnemus E.   temerius W 12   D C
O 7 Gr.   teme&ius S.   ‖ lusisse R 6   P 3   B 3   K 2   W 1 2   M 1 2   J   O 3.
                                                                    l
lu fiffe V (*ras. post* lu).   iusisse R 1.   luxisse R 7.   lussisse E 3 *eod. atr. corr.*
iussisse P 1 4   G   B 1   K 1   S   E 1 2   L 1   D C   O 1 7 Gr.   iuxisse P 2.
iusisse R 17.   iusse B 2.   et lusisse O 2.   etlis︿isse Π.   dixisse O 8.   ‖
                                                       ⏄
si ~~nihil~~ sit R 1 *al. atr. corr. et in marg.* mn⁹ *add.*   si nil G.   26. idem nihili V
i *fort. post. add.*   nihili idem R 6.   idem nihil R P 1 3   B 1 3   K S E   L 1–3 6
M 1 2   O 1–3.   idem nihil G *at litt. post* 1 *eras.*   idem nichil R 7   P 2 4   B 2
L 4 5   W 2   D C J Π   O 8.   idem nich' E 2.   idem nil K 2   O 7.   nihil
idem W 1 (*non ut Küh. et Mo.*).   idem nihili ed. H.   27. qui scit G *at* c *eras.*
                 n
28. costans G *alt. man. superscr.*
   IX. 1. insite G.   ‖   heracleotes R V G K.   eracleotes R 10 16   B.
yracleotes P.   dionisius V R 10 16.   dyonisius R.   dẏonisius P B K.
2. queritur P   B 1 2   K L.   queritur V *at* e *ex* ℮ *ras. corr. ut uid.*   quaeritur R G.

ex *non* et *uolo nolo*, sic ex *ne* et *quicquam*
item media extrita syllaba coactum est
nequam. itaque ut eum, quem putamus
esse *non hili* dicimus *nihili*, sic in quo putamus esse *nequicquam* dicimus *nequam.*'
   The similarity between the above extract and Cicero here, taken along with
the greater fulness and clearness of the
extract from Varro, gives some reason
for thinking that Cicero had Varro's
passage before him when writing, unless
both writers derived this etymology from
a common source. As early as 47 B.C.
Varro promised to dedicate to Cicero an
important work and he ultimately dedicated to him books v to xxv of the de
Lingua Latina, but he had probably not
done so when Atticus delivered to him
the copy of the second edition of the
Academica dedicated to him by Cicero,
and he certainly had not done so by the
28th of June 45 B.C. Cf. Att. xiii 12, 3
and xiii 18. The date of the letter which
records the delivery of the Academica to
Varro (Att. xiii 44, cf. § 2) is fixed by
O. E. Schmidt as 20 or 21 July 45 B.C.
The Tusculans were pretty certainly
finished by the end of September of that
year. Varro's work may possibly have
been delivered to Cicero in September,
a month not represented by any letters
in Cicero's correspondence.
   For the derivation of *nequam* see
Lindsay, Lat. Lang. p. 571.
   nihili: for the form Mo. compares
Varro, quoted above, and also L.L. viii
p. 111 (ix § 54 in Müller) 'dicimus hic
homo nihili est et huius hominis nihili et
hunc hominem nihili.' Wesenberg, Em.
II p. 4, refers to passages in Plautus and
to Q. Fr. i 2, 14 'noli spectare, quanti
homo sit ; parui enim pretii est, qui iam
nihil sit,' where the emendation *nihili* is
required by the play on words. The form
nihili has some MS support here and is
well supported in iv 35, 74.
   constantem, 'firm.'
   et: occasionally used to introduce the
minor premiss in a syllogism, cf. 7, 14 n.
on 'atqui.'
   IX. **Heracleotes Dionysius**: ii 25, 60 n.
   ad ea: i 4, 7 n.
   hoc, ut opinor, modo: introduces, with
some diffidence, Cicero's somewhat free
translation of Iliad ix 646—8
ἀλλά μοι οἰδάνεται κραδίη χόλῳ, ὁππότε
    κείνων
μνήσομαι, ὥς μ' ἀσύφηλον ἐν Ἀργείοισιν
    ἔρεξεν
Ἀτρεΐδης, ὡς εἴ τιν' ἀτίμητον μετανάστην.
   tristibus, 'gloomy,' cf. ii 8, 20 'tristis
Eurystheus.'

5 19. num manus adfecta recte est cum in tumore est, aut num
aliud quodpiam membrum tumidum ac turgidum non uitiose se
habet? sic igitur inflatus et tumens animus in uitio est. sapientis
autem animus semper uacat uitio, numquam turgescit, numquam
tumet; at iratus animus eius modi est; numquam igitur sapiens
10 irascitur; nam si irascitur, etiam concupiscit; proprium est enim
irati cupere, a quo laesus uideatur, ei quam maximum dolorem
inurere; qui autem id concupierit, eum necesse est, si id consecutus sit, magno opere laetari, ex quo fit ut alieno malo
gaudeat; quod quoniam non cadit in sapientem, ne ut irascatur
15 quidem cadit. sin autem caderet in sapientem aegritudo, caderet
etiam iracundia; qua quoniam uacat, aegritudine etiam uacabit.
20. etenim si sapiens in aegritudinem incidere posset, posset etiam
in misericordiam, posset in inuidentiam. non dixi inuidiam,

§ 19, 5. adfecta R V P G K.   affecta B.   afflicta L.   6. aliud qppiä W ɪ
(*non ut Küh.*).   aliud quippiam L 3.   aliud quidpiam O 3.   aliđ quippiam O 2.
aliquod quippiam R 1 7 17   V P 1–3   B 2 3   E 1–3   L 2–6   M 1 2   D C   O 1 7.

aliquod quippiam S *in marg.* aliud *man. ant.*   aliquid quippiam K ɪ *eod. atr.*
aliqđ quippiam R 10   G B L.   aliquid quippiam J.   aliqd' quidpiam K 2.

aliqd quippiam Π O 8.   aliq̣ qppiä W 2.   āqd quippiam R 16.   aliquot
quippiam P 4.   aut num quippiam R 6.   aliud quodpiam *corr. Turnebus*   7. uatio
G a *in* i *corr.*   9. at iratus R 1 6 7   P 1 3 4   G B 1–3   K 1 2   S   E 1 2   L
W 1 2   M D C Π J   O 1 3 8 7.   aut iratus O 2.   ac iratus M 2.   aut irati V
at i *in ras., duabus litt. eras.*   11. maxumum R V B.   maximum K *eod. atr.*
maximum G L.   12. sit G *alt. man. corr.*   13. magno opere G B 2.
magnoopere V.   magno opere R *punct. alio atr. supp.*   magnopere B ɪ K L.
magnope S E. ‖ aliaeno G.   16. iracondia G *alt. man. corr.* ‖ aegritudone G
o *in* i *corr.*
§ 20, 17. in aegritudine G.   18. dixi inuidiam R V P G B 1 3   K 1 2   E L
W 1 2   M 1 2   D C J   O 1–3 7 8.   dixi in inuidiam S Π ed. H.   dixi in
inuidam E 2.   dixi in uiam B 2.

§ 19. **aliud quodpiam**: for the form
aliquodpiam, proposed here by Gronovius
on Livy xli 6 and by some subsequent
scholars, see Neue, *Formenlehre* II³ 482,
where the subject is fully treated.

[**tumidum ac turgidum**: *tumidum*
medici dicunt praeter naturam inflatum:
turgidum cum ex tumore quippiam erumpere paratum est. Forc.]

in uitio est=*uitiosus est*, cf. i 39, 94 n.

iratus animus: but *sapientis animus*
in the contrasted clause. Hence some
have approved and Ern. adopted *irati* of
V². Cf. *proprium est enim irati*, below.

ex quo fit: not a conclusion but merely
an explanation, 'thus exulting in the ills
of another.' The wise man does not give
way to the irrational emotions of desire
or joy.

sin: the preceding *si*-clause begins at
nam si irascitur, of which all that follows
is a development, cf. i 49, 119 n.

§ 20. **etenim**, 'and in truth,' does not
refer to the clause immediately preceding
but continues the argument that the wise
man is free from *aegritudo*, by introducing
a new proof [cf. Madvig's note Fin. i
1, 3].

in misericordiam: pity was, according
to the Stoics, an irrational emotion inconsistent with the unruffled calm which
characterised the wise man, cf. Seneca
de Clementia ii 4, 4—6, 4.

inuidentiam, 'enviousness,' a word
coined by Cicero, who wanted a word
of active force only, since *incidere in
inuidiam* might be either active, 'to fall
into a state of envy,' or (more usually)

quae tum est cum inuidetur; ab inuidendo autem inuidentia
20 recte dici potest, ut effugiamus ambiguum nomen inuidiae, quod
uerbum ductum est a nimis intuendo fortunam alterius, ut est in
Melanippo:

> Quísnam florem líberum inuidít meum?

male Latine uidetur, sed praeclare Accius; ut enim 'uidere,' sic
25 'inuidere florem' rectius quam 'flori.' nos consuetudine pro-
hibemur; poëta ius suum tenuit et dixit audacius.

X. 21. Cadit igitur in eundem et misereri et inuidere. nam
qui dolet rebus alicuius aduersis, idem alicuius etiam secundis

19. quae tum est R 2 6 10 16 17　B 1 3　K　E 1 2　L　W 1　Π O 2 3 8 7.
quae tum est R 1 *an* t *mut. sit incert.*　　quae tūc est R 7.　　quae cum est G　B 2.
quae c̄um est V P c *in* t *mut.*　　quae tā ē W 2.　　20. rectae G a *conf. alt. man.* ‖
ut effugiamus R 1 10 16 V G　K 1　L 1　W 1 2　D　O 1–3 7 8.　ueffugiamus P.
ut effugiā K 2.　ut effugiam ed. H.　ut et fugiamus Non. cod. L (ap. Mueller,
p. 443).　21. dictum G *alt. man. superscr.*　22. melanippo R V P G B K.
melanipo J.　　menalippo S E L　W 1　D C.　23. quasnam G *in* quisnam
alt. man. mut.　24. accius R V P G B E L.　actius K S J.　25. florem B 1
K 2　E 2　D C　O 1–3.　　florē B 3　K 1　E 1　W 1 2　Π O 7 8.　florē R
at linea al. atr. supra duct.　flore V G　B 2　L.

X. § 21, 2. dolet B 1–3　S　E 1 2　W 2　M 1 2　D C Π J　O 2 3 8.　olet V
ras. ante o.　solet R *man. ant. superscr.*　solet P *al. atr. superscr.*　ṣolet K 1
eod. atr.　solet G　K 2　L 1. ‖ dolet alicuius etiam secundis W 1.　alicuius
dolet secundis O 1.

---

passive, 'to become an object of envy.'
This is more clearly shown in iv 7, 16
'quoniam inuidia non in eo qui inuidet
solum dicitur, sed etiam in eo cui inuidetur.' Hence *inuidia* is referred to
lower down as *ambiguum nomen.* Hence
too Dav. proposed to insert *et* (Bentley's
conj.) or *item*, and Bouh. *etiam*, before
tum, and Schiche reads *in qua etiam est.*
But Cicero wishes to limit *inuidia* to
the passive use, giving the active use to
inuidentia. The meaning therefore is
'I do not use the word *inuidia*, since
this word applies where one is the object of envy.' The extract *posset etiam
...nomen inuidiae* is quoted by Nonius
p. 443 M.
a nimis intuendo: lit. = 'over-regard-
ing.' For the separation of the prep.
from its case cf. i 43, 102 n. on 'de nihil
sentiendo.' Bentley's conj. *limis* for *nimis*
is unnecessary. Bouhier explains that the
eyes by prolonged regard were supposed
to shoot forth irresistible darts of love or
hatred, this action being termed *fascinare*
in the case of hatred. Bouh. compares
Pliny N.H. vii 2 'esse in Triballis et

Illyriis...qui uisu quoque effascinent in-
terimantque quos diutius intueantur.'
Melanippo: for the plot of Accius'
Melanippus (from which play the following
line is taken) see Ribbeck, *Röm. Trag.*
pp. 521–4; *Frag.* I² p. 190.
Quisnam: the line is quoted differently
by Nonius p. 500 'sic et *inuidit illam
rem* pro *illi rei* Accius Melanippo, unde
haec: *quis mortalis florem liberum inuidit meum.*' Ribbeck *Frag.* p. 190 reads
unde quis non mortalis... and *Röm. Trag.*
p. 523 *num quis non mortalis.* The
speaker is uncertain.
florem ... inuidit: lit. 'blighted the
bloom of my children' i.e. 'blighted my
fair children'; for *inuidere* of injuring by
spiteful glance cf. Catullus 5, 12 'aut
nequis malus inuidere possit.' *florem
liberum = florentes liberos*, cf. 5, 11 n.
'mediocritatem officiorum.' For the genitive form in *liberum* and *meum* cf. 24,
58 n.
male Latine sc. *dixisse.*
dixit audacius: F.A.W. notes that
this is no bold expression but the usual
constr. of Accius' day.

dolet, ut Theophrastus interitum deplorans Callistheni, sodalis
sui, rebus Alexandri prosperis angitur, itaque dicit Callisthenem
5 incidisse in hominem summa potentia summaque fortuna, sed
ignarum quem ad modum rebus secundis uti conueniret. atqui,
quem ad modum misericordia aegritudo est ex alterius rebus
aduersis, sic inuidentia aegritudo est ex alterius rebus secundis.
in quem igitur cadit misereri, in eundem etiam inuidere; non
10 cadit autem inuidere in sapientem; ergo ne misereri quidem.
quodsi aegre ferre sapiens soleret, misereri etiam soleret. abest
ergo a sapiente aegritudo.

    22. Haec sic dicuntur a Stoicis concludunturque contortius.
sed latius aliquanto dicenda sunt et diffusius, sententiis tamen

3. theophrastus K.   theophratus G *alt. man. superscr. et* theoph *in ras.* ‖

callisthenis R V G   B 1   K 1   M 2.   callisthe E *eod. atr.*   calisthenis S   W 1
D C.   callidis thenis B 2.   calisthem L 1.   4. callisthenem R V G   B 1 2.
calisthonē L 1.   11. egre ferre R 7   P 4.   hoc aegre ferre R 6   M 2   O 2.
hoc egre ferre P 3   B 3   E 3.   fi egre ferre M 1.   hẹc egre ferre O 3.   hec egre
ferre P 2   egre hec ferre E 2 Π.   egro h' referre O 7.   egre hec rẹferre S.
hẹc referre V *atr. uiridiore.*   haec referre R G   K 1.   hẹc referre B 1   L 1.

hoc referre J.   h' referre R 17   W 2   C.   h referre D.   fi reff're K 2.
qd' hec referre B 2.   hẹc sapiens referre W 1.   12. a sapiente R 1 10 16   G   B 1 2
K L.   sapiente V *eod. atr. suppl.*

§ 22, 13. sic dicuntur R 10   K 2   W 1 2   D   O 3 8.   sidicuntur R *eod. atr.*
B *eod. atr.* V *alia man. suppl.*   si dicuntur R 16   P   G   B 2   K L.

14. aliqñto D C.   aliqto L 4.   aliquando R 1 6 7   G   B 1 2   K 1 2   E 1 2
L 1 3 5   M 2   Π   O 1–3 8 ed. H.   aliqñ R 17   B 3   E 3   L 2 6   W 1 2   M J
O 7.   ali'qndo S *at* d *atr. nigriore script.*

    X. § 21. **ut Theophrastus**: sc. in his
Καλλισθένης ἢ περὶ πένθους, mentioned
by Diog. L. v 44 in a list of Theophrastus' works. Cf. v 9, 25. See also Buresch,
Leipz. Stud. IX p. 34.

    Callistheni: of Olynthus, a relative
and pupil of Aristotle, on whose recommendation he was taken by Alexander
the Great in 334 to the east, to record
the history of his Asiatic campaigns. By
his freedom of speech he gave offence
and was ultimately put to death by order
of the King. The circumstances are
variously related. He was arrested at
the same time as Hermolaus and his
fellow-conspirators. Q. Curtius viii 29
says that he was innocent and Diog. L.
v 5 only asserts that he was thought to
have conspired. Arrian, Anab. iv 14, says
that Aristobulus and Ptolemy Lagi (writers
contemporary with these events) stated
that the conspirators asserted that Callisthenes had instigated them to conspire;

that this was denied by most authorities;
but that as Alexander already disliked
Callisthenes, and the latter was very
intimate with Hermolaus, the King readily
believed the worst with regard to him.
[On the termination of the genitive cf.
v 16, 46 n.]

    hominem, i.e. Alexandrum.

    ne...quidem, 'not...either,' as often.

    aegre ferre = *aegritudine adfici*, cf. 26,
62.

    abest ergo: a false conclusion; to prove
that he is free from two forms of annoyance does not prove that he is free from
all annoyance.

    § 22. **concludunturque contortius**: see
ii 18, 42 n. on 'contortulis...conclusiun-
culis.'

    latius...diffusius, 'must be consider-
ably expanded and treated in detail.' Cf.
Brut. 31, 120 'nam ut Stoicorum ad-
strictior est oratio aliquantoque contrac-
tior quam aures populi requirunt, sic

15 utendum eorum potissimum qui maxime forti et, ut ita dicam,
uirili utuntur ratione atque sententia. nam Peripatetici, familiares nostri, quibus nihil est uberius, nihil eruditius, nihil grauius,
mediocritates uel perturbationum uel morborum animi mihi non
sane probant. omne enim malum, etiam mediocre, malum est;
20 nos autem id agimus ut id in sapiente nullum sit omnino. nam
ut corpus, etiamsi mediocriter aegrum est, sanum non est, sic in
animo ista mediocritas caret sanitate. itaque praeclare nostri, ut
alia multa, molestiam, sollicitudinem, angorem propter similitudinem corporum aegrorum aegritudinem nominauerunt. 23. hoc
25 propemodum uerbo Graeci omnem animi perturbationem appellant; uocant enim πάθος, id est morbum, quicumque est
motus in animo turbidus. nos melius; aegris enim corporibus

---

15. potissimum R V G B K L.   positissimum P. ‖ maxime R V P G L.

maxume B.   maxime K *atr. nigriore suppl.*   16. utuntur R V G K L.
utātur S. ‖ peripatetici R V P G K.   peripathetici B.   18. mediocritates G
B I 2 K W 2 D O I 7.   mediocritatē W I L.I.   19. mediocre magnum
est R I 6 7 17 V P I–4 G B I–3 K I 2 S E I–3 L I–5 W I M I 2 DC II
O I–3 7 8 ed. H.   et magnum est J.   ī magnum est W 2.   mediocre malum
est *corr. Bouhier.*
§ 23, 26. id̄ B. id ē L.

illorum (Peripateticorum et Academi-
corum) liberior et latior quam patitur
consuetudo iudiciorum et fori.' Cicero
generally uses *fuse* rather than *diffuse* in
the sense here found, cf. iv 26, 57 'quamuis
fuse lateque'; N.D. ii 7, 20 'uberius
disputantur et fusius)(breuius angustius-
que concluduntur'; Leg. i 13, 36.
eorum: sc. the Stoics.
familiares nostri: the expression no
doubt indicates Cicero's admiration for
the School as a whole, not his friendship
for individual Peripatetics. Cicero praises
these philosophers (as also those of the
nearly related Academy) not only for
their doctrine but also for their usefulness
to the orator. Cf. Fin. v 3, 7. Similarly
in i 32, 78 he refers to the Stoics, with
whom he agreed on many points, as
amici nostri.
nihil: often as here referring back to
persons, cf. i 2, 5; N.D. i 33, 93 'Phaedro
nihil elegantius.' Similarly the interrogative *quid* e.g. 12, 27.
mediocritates: μεσότητας, 'theory of
the mean as applied to emotions,' 'theory
of middle states.' Cf. Eth. Nic. ii 6, 10
οἷον καὶ φοβηθῆναι καὶ θαρρῆσαι καὶ ἐπιθυ-
μῆσαι καὶ ὀργισθῆναι καὶ ἐλεῆσαι...ἔστι καὶ
μᾶλλον καὶ ἧττον, καὶ ἀμφότερα οὐκ εὖ· τὸ
δὲ ὅτι δεῖ καὶ...ὡς δεῖ μέσον τε καὶ ἄριστον.
31, 74 'hic mihi adferunt mediocritates';
Ac. ii 44, 135. The doctrine of τὸ μέσον is

Aristotelian though the germ of it is to be
found in Plato's μέτριον, Politicus 283d, foll.
uel...uel, 'emotions or mental diseases,'
if you prefer the expression.'
omne enim malum: the introduction
of the word *malum* 'begs the question.'
The Stoic doctrine that all perturbations
are evils is assumed.
id agimus ut...sit: compressed for *ut
probemus id...esse.* Cf. Lucr. iii 765, 'in
tenero tenerascere corpore mentem confugient' = *eo confugient ut dicant...* Küh.
compares i 8, 16 'mors ut malum non sit
efficies' i.e. *ut mortem malum non esse
putem*; see also Madv. on Fin. i 5, 14 n.
on 'nam illud quidem adduci uix possum
ut...uideantur.'
§ 23. **hoc propemodum uerbo**, 'by a
very similar word.'
morbum: in 4, 7; iv 5, 10 and Fin.
iii 10, 35 Cicero prefers *perturbatio* as a
translation of πάθος and that is the word
that he usually employs. See Reid on
Ac. i 10, 38 n. on 'quasi morbis.'
nos melius: since we limit the word
which is similar to *morbis* to one of the
four πάθη, viz. to *aegritudo*, 'sickness of
soul.' For the four πάθη or irrational
emotions here mentioned, see n. on § 24,
below. For the Stoic parallel between
the state of health of the body and that
of the soul, see iv 10, 23 n.
aegris enim... = *animi aegritudo simil-*

simillima animi est aegritudo; at non similis aegrotationis est
libido, non inmoderata laetitia, quae est uoluptas animi elata et
30 gestiens. ipse etiam metus non est morbi admodum similis,
quamquam aegritudini est finitimus, sed proprie, ut aegrotatio in
corpore, sic aegritudo in animo nomen habet non seiunctum a
dolore. doloris huius igitur origo nobis explicanda est, id est
causa efficiens aegritudinem in animo tamquam aegrotationem
35 in corpore. nam ut medici causa morbi inuenta curationem esse
inuentam putant, sic nos causa aegritudinis reperta medendi
facultatem reperiemus.

XI. **24.** Est igitur causa omnis in opinione, nec uero aegritudinis solum, sed etiam reliquarum omnium perturbationum,
quae sunt genere quattuor, partibus plures. nam cum omnis
perturbatio sit animi motus uel rationis expers uel rationem

28. simillima R V P G B K L. ‖ animi est aegritudo R V G B 1 2 K 1 S
E 1 2 L 1 II O 7 8.   animi aegritudo est B 3 M 1 2 O 2.   est animi
aegritudo R 6 W 1 2 D C J O 1.   est *om.* O 3. ‖ similis G.   simil's R B
i *in e mut.*   sites B 2. ‖ aegrotationis E 2.   aegrotationes R V G B K E L.
29. inmoderata R V G K E.   immoderata B L.   31. egritudini W 1.
                                                                          i
egritudini O 1.   aegritudine R G K.   egritudine V B.   egritudine L 1.
egritudine B 2 E.   33. doloris huius igitur R V P G B K E O 3 7.   doloris
igitur huius R 6   B 2 3   L 1   W 1   M 1 2   D J   O 1 2 8.   igitur doloris huius S
E 2 II.   doloris igitur W 2 huius *om.*   37. reperiemus R V P G E 1 2.
repperiemus L.
XI. § **24,** 3. nam cum S *h. l. non in* quom *mut.*

lima est adfectioni corporis aegrotantis.
For the change from plural to singular
see i 17, 40 n.
gestiens, 'exultant,' 'boisterous'; lit. =
gestus faciens.
proprie, 'but with strict accuracy
annoyance in the case of the mind, just
as illness in the case of the body, bears a
name which contains the idea of pain.'
tamquam: here = *sicut*, cf. i 36, 88 n.
inuenta...reperta: to find here the
usual distinction, for which see i 47,
114 n., would involve a satire upon the
medical profession of the day which I
see no reason for expecting from Cicero.
inuento seems substituted merely for
variety in Fin. v 6, 17 'fons reperiendus
est, in quo sint prima inuitamenta naturae;
quo inuento...,' quoted by Mo.
XI. § **24. in opinione,** 'due to a mere
opinion,' cf. i 22, 53 n. and i 26, 63 n.
Virtue was based on accurate knowledge
(ἐπιστήμη), according to the Stoics (and
Socrates, Plato and others), e.g. courage
is based upon a knowledge of what is to
be feared and what not. Cf. iv 15, 34

'ipsa uirtus breuissime recta ratio dici
potest,' and Zeller, *Stoics, etc.*, p. 238.
genere quattuor, partibus plures: cf.
Fin. iii 10, 35. See the table, Introd.
p. xxxi.
The four *genera* are given within a
single verse by Virgil, Aen. vi 733 'hinc
metuunt cupiuntque, dolent gaudent-
que' and by Horace, Ep. i 6, 12 'gaudeat an doleat, cupiat metuatne, quid ad
rem?'
partibus: the sub-divisions of a *genus*
are usually called *partes* in Cicero, who
rejected *species*. Varro and Silver Age
writers have the latter term in this sense.
Cicero also employs the term *formae.*
Cf. v 25, 71 'genera partesque uirtutum';
de Inu. i 22, 32 'genus est quod plures
partes amplectitur, ut animal. pars est,
quae subest generi, ut equus'; Topica
6—7, 30—31 'nolim enim, ne si Latine
quidem possit dici, *specierum* et *speciebus*
dicere; ...*formis* et *formarum* uelim.'
cum omnis perturbatio sit: see Zeno's
definition in iv 6, 11 n. on 'haec definitio,
ut.'

5 aspernans uel rationi non oboediens, isque motus aut boni aut mali opinione citetur bifariam, quattuor perturbationes aequaliter distributae sunt. nam duae sunt ex opinione boni, quarum altera, u o l u p t a s g e s t i e n s, id est praeter modum elata laetitia, opinione praesentis magni alicuius boni, altera, quae est inmode-
10 rata adpetitio opinati magni boni rationi non obtemperans, uel c u p i d i t a s recte uel l i b i d o dici potest. **25.** ergo haec duo genera, uoluptas gestiens et libido, bonorum opinione turbantur, ut duo reliqua, metus et aegritudo, malorum. nam et m e t u s opinio magni mali inpendentis et a e g r i t u d o est opinio magni
15 mali praesentis, et quidem recens opinio talis mali ut in

5. aspernans R V G B K S E.   aspernens L.   ‖   oboediens R V G K. obędiens B.   6. citetur R 16 7 17 V P G   B 1 3   K 1   S   E 1 2   L 1   W 2 M 1 2   D C Π   O 1–3 7 8.   excitetur W 1.   7. nam duae sunt *om.* B 1.   ‖
o
expinione V.   9. alicuius boni rationi non obtemperans B 3   O 2.   alicuius boni rōē nō tēpans M 1.   altera cupiditas quae recte uel libido dici potest quae est inmoderata adpetitio opinati magni boni rationi non obtemperans uel cupiditas recte uel libido dici potest *hunc ordinem uerborum habent* R 1 2 10   V P G   B 1 2   K 1 2 S E 1–3   L 1 3 4   M 1 *et magna ex parte* R 6 16 17   B 3   L 2 6   W 1   M 2   C D J: *om.* O 2: Π *habet* uel cupiditas...dici potest *transuers. cal. notat.* : *post* opinati magni boni ⁀ *habet* V *et ad pedem paginae man. ant. sed atram. nigriore subscr.* et quidē magis significat nom̄ libidinis magnitudinem erroris. itaque in ea cupiditate q̄ flagrantissima⁀ppie plerūque nom̄ h' ponitur si omnis appetitio opinati boni: *textum restituit Dauisius.*   ‖   inmoderata R 1 2 17   V P.   immoderata G K L.
10. adpetitio R V G K E.   appetitio R 2 10 17   L. ‖ obtemperans R 1 2 10 17 B 3   W 1 *alii.*   obtemporans D C.   optemperans G.   tēpans M 1.
11. libido R V P G K L.
§ **25**, 12. libido R V P G K L.   13. ut duo G K L.   ūt V (ut *in* at *eod. atr.,*
i
ut uid., mut.).   14. inpendentis R V K E.   inpendentes G *alt. man. corr.* impendentis B L.

uel rationis...oboediens: Bouh. and others thought the first *uel*, and Ern. the clause *uel rationi non oboediens*, intrusive, but Nissen explains thus: 'Haec tria genera sunt motuum animi, quorum primo uoluptas comprehenditur, quae proprie eam partem hominis attingit, quae expers est rationis; alteri subiecta cupiditas est, quae praefracte rationem aspernatur; tertio denique metus et aegritudo, quibus uires hominis adeo extenuantur, ut obedire rationi nequeat. etenim duo haec genera animi motuum etsi sic conspirant, ut neutrum rationi obediat, ita tamen differunt, ut in altero contumacia, in altero imbecillitas inobedientiae sit causa.'
Zeno's definition of *perturbatio* is expanded to indicate the separate *perturbationes.*
citetur, 'is called forth,' 'is excited.' Usually *excitare, concitare.* The simple verb is elsewhere used by Cic. only of persons. *ciere motus* occurs i 10, 19;

N.D. ii 32, 81; cf. Ti. 7, 24 'eoque motu cuius orbis...ciebatur.'
praeter modum elata...: Diog. L. vii 114 ἡδονὴ δέ ἐστιν ἄλογος ἔπαρσις ἐφ' αἱρετῷ δοκοῦντι ὑπάρχειν.
opinati: in passive sense. Cf. 'meditata' iii 14, 30; Madv. § 153; Roby I § 734.
§ **25.** turbantur = *cum animi perturbatione mouentur,* 'are disturbing causes due to a mere opinion with regard to good things.' This compressed use of the verb is fully illustrated by Naegelsbach, *Stil.* § 102, who compares *turbare bellum* = *turbis concitandis efficere bellum.* Cf. iv 15, 34 'ex qua concitantur perturbationes'; Top. 26, 99 'huic generi, in quo et misericordia et iracundia et odium et inuidia et ceterae animi adfectiones perturbantur': iii 1, 1 n. on 'consecrata.'
recens opinio: cf. Stobaeus Ecl. ii 174 λύπην δ' εἶναι συστολὴν ψυχῆς ἀπειθῆ λόγῳ, αἴτιον δ' αὐτῆς τὸ δοξάζειν πρόσφατον κακὸν

eo rectum uideatur esse angi, id autem est, ut is qui doleat
oportere opinetur se dolere. his autem perturbationibus, quas in
uitam hominum stultitia quasi quasdam furias inmittit atque
incitat, omnibus uiribus atque opibus repugnandum est, si
20 uolumus hoc quod datum est uitae tranquille placideque traducere. sed cetera alias; nunc aegritudinem, si possumus,
depellamus. id enim sit propositum, quandoquidem eam tu
uideri tibi in sapientem cadere dixisti, quod ego nullo modo
existimo; taetra enim res est, misera, detestabilis, omni con-
25 tentione, uelis, ut ita dicam, remisque fugienda.

XII. **26.** Qualis enim tibi ille uidetur

Tántalo prognátus, Pelope nátus, qui quondam á socru
Oénomao rege Híppodameam ráptis nanctust núptiis?

16. uidetur L 1.   17. quas in uita B 3   K 2   S   W 1   D C Π   O 2 3 7 8.
quas in uita R *litt. post* s *eras.* V i *post* s *eras.*   quasi in uita P (*al. atr. corr.*)
E (*eod atr. fortasse corr.*).   quasi in uita G   B 1 2   K 1   W 2.   quas ī uīcta J.
quas O 1 in uita *om.*   in uita L 1 quas *om.*   in uitam *corr. Lambinus.*
18. inmittit R V P G B K E.   20. tranquille G.   tranquillę B K L.
tranquillae R.   21. cetera R V P G   B 2 3   K 1 2   S   E 1 2   W 2   D C Π J
O 1 3 7 8 Gr.   cętera B 1   W 1   L 1.   caetera M 2   O 2.   ceteras M 1.
22. id enim sit R P G   B 1 2   K 1   S   E 1 2   L 1   W 1 2   M 1 2   D C Π J   O 1 3 7 8.
id enim si² V.   24. existimo G K.   estimo L. ‖ taetra V G.   ta&ra R.
t&tra K 1.   tętra P.   tetra B L.   ‖   misera detestabilis R 1 10   P G   K 1
W 1   M 1 2 *alii.*   miser adetestabilis V *inter* 1 *et a latet ⸴ in ras.*   misera
                                                                                              i
& detestabilis L 1.   ‖   omni K 1.   om̄ī R 10   P B L.   oî R 16.   omne R V.
omne G.   om̄e B 2   E.
XII. § **26**, 2. a socro S   L 6.   a socero R 16 7 16 17   V   P 1–4   G   B 1–3
K 1   E 1–3   L 1–5   W 1   M 1 2   D C Π J   O 1–3 7 8   W 2 (*in marg. e cont. om.*).
          r
a foco K 2.   a socru *corr. Bentleius.*   3. oenomao regi G.   oęno mago regi L. ‖
                                                                                          i
hippodameam V G K.   hippoda meā B 2.   hippodamęam R 1 *atr. nigriore*
superscr.   ippodameā E B 1.   hippodemeā L 1.   hippodamiam W 1   M 2   O 2.
hippodomiam O 3.   ippodomiā S *in marg.* hippodamiam.   hiipadamiam M 1. ‖
                                                                     u
nanctus V G   B 2   L.   na⸴rctus R *eod. atr.*   nanctis E *eod. atr.*   nactus
P B 1 3 K 1 2   S   E 2   W 2   M 1 2   D J   O 1–3 7 8.   nactus ē W 1.   nactis R 7.
nanctust *corr. Tregder.*

παρεῖναι ἐφ᾽ ᾧ καθήκει συστέλλεσθαι, iii
31, 75 'additur ad hanc definitionem a
Zenone recte ut illa opinio praesentis
mali sit recens'; also 12, 26; iv 7, 14.

in eo, 'while it continues' lit. 'amid it.'
Mo. compares in Cat. ii 9, 20 'qui se
in...repentinis pecuniis...insolentius...iac-
tarunt.'

oportere opinetur: the importance of
this element in *aegritudo* was insisted on
by Chrysippus, see 31, 76 n. on 'Chrysippus autem...'

in uitam: the conj. of Lamb. is adopted
by most editors. Nothing is more common
than the loss of a final *m.* Küh. retains
in uita of the MSS in the sense of 'while

men live,' supplying *in eam* to *inmittit
atque incitat*, but the meaning so obtained
seems weak, nor are the words *in eam*
naturally supplied.

quasdam: intensifies, cf. ii 4, 11 n. on
'excelsum quendam.'

furias, 'hell-hounds.' *inmittere* involves a metaphor from slipping dogs
from a leash, cf. Verr. iv 21, 47 'inmitte-
bantur illi continuo Cibyratici canes.'

omnibus uiribus atque opibus: 3, 6 n.

uelis, ut ita dicam, remisque: a proverbial expression like *opibus uiribus* =
'with all our might' 'with might and
main.' Editors compare Plaut. Asin. i 3, 5
'remigio ueloque, quantum poteris, festina

Iouis iste quidem pronepos. tamne ergo abiectus tamque
5 fractus?

Nolíte, inquit, hospités ad me adíre! ilico ístic,
Ne cóntagió mea bonís umbraue óbsit.
.. tanta uís sceleris ín corpore haéret.

6. ilico R W 1 D Gr.   illico V.   illico G *alt. man. corr.*   illico K 1.
dico B 2.   *om.* L 1.   ‖ istic R 1 6 7 17   V   P 4   G B 1 2   K 1   S E 1 2   L W 1 2
D C   O 7 8.   istinc P 2.   istíc P *at al. atr. linea supra duct.*   isthinc O 3.
isti M 1.   ista B 3   O 1 2.   istane P 3   M 2.   istat J.   7. obsit tanta uis
R 1 6 7 10 16 17   V   P 1-4   G   B 1-3   K 1 2   S   E 1 2   L 2-6   W 1 2   M 1 2
D C Π J   O 1-3 7 8.   obstante uis L 1.   absit tanta uis ed. H.

et fuge,' and without metaphor Virg. Aen. iii 563; Sil. Ital. i 568 'remis uelisque impellite puppim'; Off. iii 33, 116 'uiris equisque, ut dicitur'; Ter. And. i 1, 134 'manibus pedibusque.'

XII. § 26. ílle: sc. Thyestes.

Tantalo prognatus... Bentley first saw that these lines were verse, viz. trochaic septenarii, and corrected the unmetrical *socero* of MSS to *socru* referring for *socrus* as masc. to Naeuius in Nonius and Accius in Priscian p. 698. Cf. Nonius 223 'socrus et masculino genere ueteres dici posse uoluerunt. Naeuius Pellice: desim socru tuo, fratri patrueli meo?' Priscian 1 p. 248 ed. Krehl. 'uetustissimi tamen communiter hic et haec socrus proferebant—"Accius in Atreo simul et Pisaea praemia arrepta a socru possedit suo."' Küh., Hei., Ml. and others accept the reading *socru*; Kl., followed by Bai. and T.S., reads *socro* having found that form as a dat. in an inscription (Muratori 532).

qui quondam: sc. Pelops, not Thyestes, cf. ii 27, 67 n.

Oenomao: *ao* are treated as one syllable by synizesis.

raptis...nuptiis: Hei. T.S. and Hasper refer *raptis* to the treachery by which Pelops gained his victory; but the word does not lend itself to this meaning nor was the story of treachery the only or, as it seems, the prevailing one with regard to the contest. Cf. ii 27, 67 n. In Pausanias v 17, 7 we read that on the front of the chest of Cypselus Oenomaus was represented pursuing Pelops who *had Hippodamia with him,* each hero having two horses and the horses of Pelops having wings. And Frazer there notes that 'on a terra-cotta relief, which was found at Velletri, Pelops *and Hippodamia* are apparently represented in a chariot drawn by winged horses' (O. Jahn, *Archäologische Aufsätze,* p. 6 n. 7). It seems to me that the idea of the artist in each case with regard to the race was that Pelops drove off with Hippodamia to take her

away if he could on the condition of being slain by Oenomaus if overtaken. Pelops not being overtaken gained H. *raptis nuptiis.* The lines *Tantalo prognatus... nuptiis* are referred by Vahlen (*Ennianae Poesis Reliquiae²,* p. 187) to Ennius' Thyestes (Fr. 357). Vahlen thinks with Bentley that the words *Iouis iste quidem pronepos* belong also to the poet, but most editors give them to Cicero, and they seem to lack the Ennian ring. Ribbeck (*Röm. Trag.,* p. 20) is pretty certainly right in thinking that these lines came soon after the lines 'pol mihi fortuna...' of 19, 44.

pronepos: the descent was Jove, Tantalus, Pelops, Thyestes. Cf. Quintil. ix 3, 57.

Nolíte hospites... Bentley first saw that these three lines were bacchiac tetrameters, as also the line 'quidnam est, obsecro? quid te adiri abnutas?' which is seen from Or. iii 41, 164 to have followed them. The three lines in the text are from the Thyestes of Ennius (Vahlen *op. cit.,* p. 186) and spoken by Thyestes to the chorus when he finds that he has eaten the flesh of his children; the line from the *de Oratore* was spoken in response by a member of the Chorus. Ribbeck, *Röm. Trag.,* p. 202.

istic: sc. *manete.* It is difficult to decide between this and *istinc* sc. *abite* or possibly *dicite.* Vahlen quotes Plaut. Merc. 912 'atque istic sta ilico'; Kl. Eur. Ph. 896.

The line 'tanta uis...haeret' is incomplete. Bentley inserted *meo* before *tanta*; Lachmann (on Lucr. iii 880) *stetis*; Sff. followed Küh. *uobis.* Sff. objects to *meo* that the adj. is not necessary since *contagio mea* precedes. Ribbeck in his first edition put in *meo* after *haberet* making four cretics, but in the second edition *Frag.,* 1 p. 59, writes 'sed fortasse nullo opus est additamento, siquidem post creticum dimetrum ditrochaeum posuit poeta.' But there is no trochaic rhythm in the line.

tu te, Thyesta, damnabis orbabisque luce propter uim sceleris
10 alieni? quid? illum filium Solis nonne patris ipsius luce indignum putas?

> Refúgere oculi, córpus macie extábuit,
> Lacrimaé peredere úmore exsanguís genas,
> Situm ínter oris bárba paedore hórrida atque
> 15   Intónsa infuscat péctus inluuié scabrum.

9. tu te B3 II (*at fuerat* tu ne).   tute V P G B2 K2 L1 W1 M1 2
D C O 1–3 8.   tute R *atr. nigr. mut.*   tu S *al. atr. suppl.*   tu & E 1.

tu ne E 2.   tu & hýesta B 1.   12. extabant G *alt. man. corr.*   13. lacrimae R.
lacrimę V L.   ‖ humore B 3.   umorē V *eod. atr.*   uṭmorem K 1 *atr. nigr.*
suppl. et corr.   humorē R 10 P 2 4 B 1 K 2 W 1 2 M 2 D J O 7 8.
umorem R 1.   humorem P 1 3 G B 2 S E 1 2 L 2–6 M 1 C O 1–3 ed. H.
hûorem R 16.   humor L 1 *om.* II.   ‖ exsanguis B E D C.   exanguis R V P G
B 2 K 1 W 2 M 1 J O 1.   exangues S E 2 W 1 M 2 O 2 3 8.   etiam
sanguis L 1 *om.* II.   ‖ gene sic C.   gene sit D.   14. situ nitoris R 7 10 16 17
P 1 2 G B 1 2 K 1 2 S L 1–5 W 2 M 1 J O 1 3 ed. H.   situ nitoris R 1
atr. nigriore suppl.   sitụ nitoris V *al. atr. mut.*   situ nidoris R 6 B 3 E 3
L 6 W 1 M 2 D C O 7.   si tu nidoris E 2.   sic unitoris E 1.   situ
mucoris O 8.   situ indecoris O 2 *om.* II.   situm inter oris *corr. Lachmannus.* ‖
pedore G B 1 2 K 1.   pendere L 1.   15. inluuie V E L.   inluuiae G.
inluuiae R.   illuuie B 1 2 K 1.

luce: by shrinking from the sight of
men he shrinks from the light of day.
Billerbeck compares Cato M. 4, 12 'nec
uero ille in luce modo atque in oculis
ciuium magnus, sed intus domique prae-
stantior.'

sceleris alieni: sc. of his brother
Atreus, who had murdered Thyestes'
children and served their flesh up to him.

filium Solis: Aeetes, king of Colchis,
son of Helios and Perseis (Homer's Perse,
Od. x 139). His brother Perses usurped
his throne. His daughter Medea, who
had left him with Jason when the latter
carried off the golden fleece, returned
after many years in a car drawn by winged
dragons. Medus, her son by Aegeus, had
a little earlier been shipwrecked on the
Colchian coast and, finding himself among
enemies, had pretended to be Hippotes
the son of Creon. Supposing him to be
really Hippotes Medea persuaded Perses
to hand him over to her for slaughter.
Then discovering him to be her own son
she hands him a sword wherewith to
avenge the wrongs of his grandfather
Aeetes by slaying Perses. The lines that
follow were no doubt part of the *Medus*
of Pacuuius, and were uttered by Aeetes
who appears upon the stage in woeful
plight while Medea is talking to Medus.

The line announcing his entry preserved
by Festus 'atque eccum in ipso tempore
ostentum senem' must have almost immediately preceded. Cf. Ribbeck's *Röm.
Trag.*, p. 323; *Frag.* 1² p. 263; Welcker,
Griech. Trag., p. 1215; Hyginus, *Fabulae*
27; Apollodorus i 9, 28, 4; Diodorus
iv 56.

refugere oculi, 'my eyes are sunken.'
The metre is iambic trimeter.

peredere, 'have furrowed.'

situm inter oris: this correction of
Lachmann is nearer to *situ nitoris* the
reading of the MSS than even *situ nidoris*
and yields a much better meaning. It
would probably be written in uncial
MSS SITVINTORIS with continuation
stroke to denote the last two letters of
inter. The error would then consist
merely in missing the two top-strokes
and writing NI for IN, an error of the
most common kind. *Situs* lit. 'a letting
alone' is used of the coating of dust that
comes over objects *lying by* neglected,
cf. Prop. iv 5, 72 'inmundo pallida mitra
situ'; or the scurf that comes over fields
left untilled, Virg. Geo. i 72 'segnem
patiere situ durescere campum'; Aen. vi
462 'per loca senta situ'; or of rust,
Tib. i 10, 50 'occupat arma situs.'

haec mala, o stultissime Aeeta, ipse tibi addidisti; non inerant
in iis quae tibi casus inuexerat, et quidem inueterato malo,
cum tumor animi resedisset (est autem aegritudo, ut docebo,
in opinione mali recenti); sed maeres uidelicet regni desiderio,
20 non filiae. illam enim oderas, et iure fortasse; regno non aequo
animo carebas. est autem inpudens luctus maerore se con-
ficientis, quod imperare non liceat liberis. 27. Dionysius quidem
tyrannus Syracusis expulsus Corinthi pueros docebat; usque eo
imperio carere non poterat. Tarquinio uero quid inpudentius,
25 qui bellum gereret cum iis qui eius non tulerant superbiam? is
cum restitui in regnum nec Veientium nec Latinorum armis

16. stultissime R V G B K L. || aeota V G. eota R 1 B 1 2 K 1.
eota P *at e in* t *al. man. mut.* oeta K 2 L 3–6 W 1 2 D O 1 3 8. tota
R 10 16 O 7. poeta L 2 *om.* L 1. Aeeta *corr. edd.* 17. in iis S. in hiis D.
in his R V P G B 1 2 K 1 E 1 2 L W 2 J. 19. recentis R 1 6 7 10 16 17 V
P 1–4 G B 1–3 K 1 2 S E 1–3 L 1–6 W 2 M 1 2 D C Π J O 1–3 7 8 ed. H.
p̄ntis W 1. recenti *corr. Bakius.* 21. inpudens V P G E. ipudens R.
impudens B K. || merore sed G *at punctis not. et conf. alt. man.*
§ 27, 22. dionysius G. dionisius R V K S E L. dẏonisius B.
23. tyrannus G K L. tyrrannus V. || syracuṣsis G *alt. man. corr.* || chorinthi G.
24. inpudentius G E. impudentius R V B K S L. 25. cum his G B. ||
tu̱lerant G *alt. man. corr.* 26. ueientium R 6 7 17 B 2 3 L 1 M 2 C O 1 2
G *at ientium in ras. alt. man. scr.* ueientiũ V D *at* ł uegentiũ *al. atr. suppl.*
ueṇientium O 3. uegentium R 1 *eod. atr.* uegentium P B 1 K 1 E 2 W 2
Π O 8. uegentiũ E S *at in marg.* uehietũ. uegencium K 2. uenientium O 7.
uehienciũ W 1. uegentiorum M 1. uehientium ed. H.

Beroaldus (in Mo.) seems to take *situ
nidoris* as meaning 'with *reek* of stench.'
Beroaldus quotes Donatus on Aeneid vii
440 'uicta situ uerique effeta senectus'
where he says that *situs* is *corruptio ex
umore et diuturnitate contracta* and that
the word was also applied to a musty
smell. But it is obvious that the action
of *umor* is not necessarily implied in the
word. *nidor* is used of various smells,
cf. Juv. v 162 'nidor culinae'; Lucr. vi
792 of a candle blown out; Livy xxxviii
7, 13 of burning feathers. The reading
situ liuentes had formerly some vogue
owing to Turnebus' assertion (*Adversaria*
xxvi, 6) that he found it in certain MSS.
atque: with hypermetric syllable, the
next line beginning regularly with a vowel
or h. *et quidem inueterato malo*, 'and this
you did at a time when the evil was
of long standing.' Many years elapsed
between the loss of Aeetes' throne and
the return of Medea and Medus. [Rib-
beck *loc. cit.* omits *atque*.]
tumor: cf. 31, 76; 'erat enim in tumore
animus.'
est autem...recenti: Ern. regarded
these words as intrusive but F.A.W. more
correctly notes that here, as in other
places, Cicero departs from the dialogue,

and speaks, as it were aside, to the
reader.
uidelicet: with some irony, as often.
liberis: the word can only mean 'the
free,' and we may perhaps see with T.S.
a veiled allusion to Caesar's ambition.
The Colchians were no more free under
Perses than they had been under Aeetes.
The word cannot mean 'men who ought
to be free.' Bouhier suspected that Cicero
wrote *Iberis*.
§ 27. **Dionysius** the younger. Dav.
notes that the same statement is made by
Val. Max. vi 9, 6 ext.; Lucian Gallus
c. 23 p. 737; Iustin xxi 5 and many
more. But Aelian, V.H. ix 8, says that
he ended by μητραγυρτῶν καὶ κρούων
τύμπανα καὶ καταυλούμενος and Athenaeus xii p. 541e agrees, neither writer
mentioning school teaching. Cic. makes
the same statement as here in Fam. ix
18, 1.
quidem: introducing an instance in
illustration, cf. i 48, 116 n.
usque eo...non, 'so little.'
imperio carere: cf. i 36, 88 n. on
'tamquam in febri.'
quid: 10, 22 n. on 'nihil.'
qui...gereret: causal subj.; cf. i 18,
41 n.; 32, 78 n.

H. 3

potuisset, Cumas contulisse se dicitur inque ea urbe senio et
aegritudine esse confectus.

XIII. Hoc tu igitur censes sapienti accidere posse ut aegritudine opprimatur, id est miseria? nam cum omnis perturbatio
miseria est, tum carnificina est aegritudo. habet ardorem libido,
leuitatem laetitia gestiens, humilitatem metus, sed aegritudo
5 maiora quaedam, tabem, cruciatum, adflictationem, foeditatem,
lacerat, exest animum planeque conficit. hanc nisi exuimus sic
ut abiciamus, miseria carere non possumus.

28. Atque hoc quidem perspicuum est, tum aegritudinem
existere, cum quid ita uisum sit ut magnum quoddam malum
10 adesse et urgere uideatur. Epicuro autem placet opinionem mali

latinorum R 6 7 B 3 K 2 W 1 M 2 Π O 1–3 8 ed. H. latiorum V.
latiorum W 2 E 2 *al. atr. linea supra duct.* latinorum C *man. ant. corr.*
latiorum R 1 17 G B 1 2 K 1 S E 1 L M 1 D O 7. 27. contulisse se R V P G
B 2 K 1 E 1 2 L 1 W 1 2 D C Π O 1 3 8. se contulisse B 1 3 M 2 J O 2.
cum tulisse O 7 *se om.* contulisse M 1 se *om.* ‖ se *superscr. eod. atr.* S. ‖
in qua urbe Π. 28. aegritudinem G *alt. man. corr.*
XIII. 3. tum G. tü W 1. tunc B. ‖ libido R G K L M 2. 4. genstiens
G *sed prius* n *conf. alt. man.* 5. adflictationem R V P G K. afflictationem L
R 1 6. afflictionem B R 10. 6. planeque G L. plęnaque K *i.e.* plena *in*
plane *atr. nigr. mut.*
§ **28**, 8. atque G. atq; R V P B 1 K 1 E 1 L W 1 O 1 3 8. atq3 B 2 3
S E 2 W 2 M 1 D C J Π. atq, M 2. at O 7. 9. existere R V G B K S E.
10. opinionem R V P G B 2 K 1 S M 1 2 C O 1 3 7 8. opinionē B 1 3
E 1 L W 2 D J O 2. opinione E 2 W 1 Π. oppini K 2 *eod. atr.*

Cumas contulisse se dicitur: Dav.
refers to Livy ii 21, 5; Dionys. Halic.
vi 21 and, for an opposite statement, to
Aug. Ciu. Dei iii 15 'in oppido Tus-
culo...quattuordecim annos priuatam
uitam quietus habuit, et cum uxore con-
senuit; optabiliore fortassis exitu quam
socer eius...exstinctus.' See also Mommsen, *R.H.* 1 p. 316.
inque ea urbe: the more usual order
in Cicero is *eaque in urbe.* For instances
of *que* attached to the prep., such as this
and p. Rosc. Amer. 39, 114 *inque eam
rem,* cf. Krebs, *Antibarbarus,* p. 406.
XIII. **cum...tum:** when each of these
particles has its own verb, *cum* has the
indicative when it merely introduces a
proposition parallel to and independent
of that contained in the *tum* clause; when
cum takes the subjunctive, the *cum*-clause
is subordinate to the *tum*-clause and serves
to explain it more clearly. Küh. *Gram.*
II pp. 895–6. The subjunctive in the
latter case is often concessive, e.g. v 39,
113. The verb in the *tum*-clause need
not be expressed, cf. p. r. Deiot. 4, 12.

habet ardorem, 'implies,' cf. i 49,
119 n. on 'leuationem habeant.'
aegritudo...foeditatem, 'annoyance...
disfigures a man.'
§ **28. atque...quidem:** here, as often,
introducing a more detailed treatment of
the subject, cf. 2, 4 n.
cum quid ita uisum sit ut...uideatur,
'when anything *presents itself* in such a
way that *we think* that we are in presence
of a great and oppressing evil.' Cf.
Pohlenz, *Hermes* XLI 3, p. 323, who
observes that the double use of *uideri* is
due to the following Gk form: ὅταν τι
οὕτω φαίνηται, ὥστε μέγα κακὸν παρεῖναι
δοκεῖ and that this again is due to the
necessity of distinguishing between φαν-
τασία and δόξα, the idea as presented
from without and the opinion formed
with ref. to it by the percipient subject.
[*quid*: for the indefinite *quid* after *cum*
see Kühner, *Gramm. d. Lat. Spr.* § 119,
iii.]
**opinionem mali aegritudinem esse
natura:** lit. 'that the belief that one is
in evil is an annoyance which is due to

aegritudinem esse natura, ut, quicumque intueatur in aliquod
maius malum, si id sibi accidisse opinetur, sit continuo in aegritudine. Cyrenaici non omni malo aegritudinem effici censent,
sed insperato et necopinato malo. est id quidem non mediocre
15 ad aegritudinem augendam; uidentur enim omnia repentina
grauiora. ex hoc et illa iure laudantur :

Égo cum genui, túm morituros scíui et ei rei
sú(stuli).

Praéterea ad Troiám cum misi ob défendendam
20   Graéciam,
Scíbam me in mortíferum bellum, nón in epulas
míttere.

ea
11. esse natura R 1 10   P G.   esse natura V.   esse non natura E 2.
esse natur⒜ R 16.   12. in egritudine R 7   P 2 3   B 3   E 2   W 1   M 2   D C Π
O 1 3.   in egritudinē P 4   B 1   S E 1   O 8.   in egritudinē L 1.   in aegritudinem
R 1 V P 1 G   K 1   M 1 ed. H.   in egritudinem B 2   O 7.   in egritudiē K 2.
i
ī egnē W 2.   13. malo aegritudine G.   ‖ effici G K L.   14. et necopinato
R V P G   B 1 2   K S   E 1 2   L 1   W 2   M 1   Π J   O 1 2 8 Gr. et *om.* B 3   W 1
M 2   D C   O 3 7.   16. et illa iure R V P G   B 1–3   K 1   S   E 1 2   L 1   W 1 2
M 1 2   D C Π J   O 1 2 7 8 et *om.* O 3.   17. morituros R 1 7 17   V   P 1–4   G
                                                                                          os
B 1–3   K 1 2   S   E 1 2   L 1   M 2   D C Π   O 2 3 7 8 Gr. ed. H.   moritur   W 2
eod. atr. ut uid.   moriturum R 6   W 1   M 1   J   O 1.   21. sciebam R V P G
B 1–3   K 1 2   S   E 1 2   L 1   W 1 2   M 1 2   D C Π J   O 1–3 7 8 Gr. ed. H.
scibam *corr.* *Lambinus.*   ‖ epulas G   B 1 2   K 1   E 2   W 2   O 1.   aepulas R
M 2.   ępulas V   L 1   W 1.

nature.' The same inaccuracy of expression is not uncommon, e.g. § 25 supr.
'metus opinio magni mali inpendentis...
est'; hence Küh. rightly rejects the conjecture of Sff. *ex opinione mali aeg. esse
natura* as unnecessary. *esse natura* here
=φύσει γίγνεσθαι, i.e. 'necessarily produced,' 'inevitable.'

The same view is stated in other words
in 15, 32 'Epicuri...qui censet necesse
esse omnis in aegritudine esse qui se in
malis esse arbitrentur.' Dav. compares
Diog. L. x 119 (where the view λυπηθή-
σεσθαι τὸν σοφόν is attributed to Epicurus)
and ii 91 where the same view is attributed
to the Cyrenaic Aristippus, καὶ λυπήσεσθαι
μέντοι καὶ φοβήσεσθαι· φυσικῶς γὰρ γί-
νεσθαι. The Stoics on the contrary held
that emotions are contrary to nature and
due to a man's own assent, and that they
can be controlled by an act of will. Cf.
33, 80 'quicquid esset in aegritudine
mali, id non naturale esse, sed uoluntario
iudicio et opinionis errore contractum';
34, 82 end; Fin. iii 10, 35 'perturbationes
autem nulla naturae ui commouentur, omniaque ea sunt opiniones ac iudicia leuitatis. itaque his sapiens semper uacabit.'

in aegritudine: Mo. reads *in aegritudinem.* Dav. while reading *in aegritudine*
refers to Gellius i 7, 16 where d. imp.
Cn. Pomp. 12, 33 is quoted for 'in prae-
donum potestatem fuisse' and Plaut.
Amph. 180 'numero mihi in mentem
fuit,' but that construction, though possibly
Plautine, is not likely to have been
employed sporadically by Cicero.

Cyrenaici: cf. 22, 52. For the relation
between the Epicureans and the Cyrenaics
see Zeller, *Stoics, etc.*, c. 21 pp. 489 foll.

necopinato: i 39, 94 n.

et illa: the use of *et* in the sense of a
weakened *etiam* is established in Cicero,
though rare. Editors compare iv 34, 73
'probe et ille'; Q. Fr. i 1, 34 'simul et
illud Asia cogitet'; i 1, 43 'simul et illud
cogita.' It occurs chiefly with pronouns.

ego cum genui...: these words are
spoken by Telamon on receiving the
news of the death of Ajax, cf. 24, 58;
Senec. Cons. ad Polyb. 30 quoted below;
Fronto, de Bell. Parth. p. 217 Nab.
quoted below. Vahlen, *Enn. Poes. Rel.*
p. 177, and Ribbeck, *Röm. Trag.* p. 133,
refer the lines to Ennius' Telamon. See
also Ribbeck, *Frag.* I p. 246.

XIV. 29. Haec igitur praemeditatio futurorum malorum lenit eorum aduentum quae uenientia longe ante uideris. itaque apud Euripiden a Theseo dicta laudantur; licet enim, ut saepe facimus, in Latinum illa conuertere:

5 Nam qui haéc audita a dócto meminissém uiro,
 Futúras mecum cómmentabar míserias,
 Aut mórtem acerbam aut éxsili maestám fugam
 Aut sémper aliquam mólem meditabár mali,
 Vt, sí qua inuecta díritas casú foret,
10 Ne me ínparatum cúra lacerarét repens.

XIV. § **29**, 3. euripiden R V P 4 G. euripidem P 1 2 B 1-3 S M 2
J O 2. euripidē K 1 E 1 2 W 2 O 7. euripedem K 2 M 1 D C Π.
eurypidē W 1. || theseo V S L. thesseo R G B 2 K 1 E. 6. commentabar
R V G B S E. cōmentabar K 1 L 1. 7. exilii R V P 1-4 G B 1 2 K 1
S E L 1 O 1 3 8. || *alterum* aut *in marg.* G *add. alt. man.* 9. inuenta B 3 L.
inuencta O 7. || duritas B 3 L. || casu R V G B 1 2 K S E 1 2 L W 1 2
M 1 2 C Π J O 1-3 8. caū B 3 O 7. 10. inparatum R V K E L.
inparatū G *at* atū *in ras. alt. man.* imparatum B.

morituros: the plur. is read by most editors with the best MSS. Dav. Bouh. and Mo. read *moriturum*. Ribbeck, *Röm. Trag.* p. 133, thinks that in the beginning of the play Telamon may have received a report that both Ajax and Teucer were slain. If this is correct, Seneca, quoted below, expresses himself inaccurately. Perhaps Telamon may be speaking of his sons in general terms, having heard of the death of Ajax and not as yet knowing anything as to the fate of Teucer. There seems room for a third view. *liberi* is used at times to refer to one child, e.g. Sall. Iug. c. 10 end. It is even possible that this word had been so used in the preceding context. Seneca, Cons. ad Polyb. c. 30, may be quoting from memory, as Klotz points out. He has 'quanto ille iustior, qui nuntiata filii morte, dignam magno uiro uocem emisit: ego cum genui tum *moriturum* sciui.' Cf. Fronto, de Bell. Parth. p. 199 *ed. Rom.* (105 Nieb. 217 Nab.) quoted by Ribbeck and Vahlen, 'an cunctetur de militibus nostris Mars pater illa dicere *ego cum genui tum morituros sciui et ei rei sustuli, praeterea cum...ob defendendum imperium scibam me in mortifera bella non...*'
el rei, 'to that end,' 'with that end in view.' Both words are here scanned as monosyllables.
sustuli: cf. 1, 2 n. on 'suscepti.'
ob, 'with a view to': this sense is rare. Küh. quotes as Ciceronian parallels Verr. ii 23, 78 'pecuniam ob absoluendum acceperis'; p. Mur. 1, 1 'ob...consulatum ... obtinendum.' '*ob* praepositione

antiquos usos esse pro *ad* testis est Festus' F.A.W.
scibam: it is not likely that Ennius used the form *sciebam* here with synizesis as Mo. supposes. Most modern editors follow Lamb. and Dav. in reading *scibam* for which Dav. refers to Festus p. 198 M. who quotes Ennius s.v. *obsidio* 'scibas natum ingenuum Aiacem cui tu obsidionem paras,' a line also from the Telamo. cf. Ribb. *Frag.* 1 p. 55; *Röm. Trag.* p. 135; Vahlen, *Enn. P.* p. 180. *scibam* also occurs in Accius' Clytemestra, cf. Nonius 226, 10 (i p. 340 ed. Müll.) Cf. also Plautus, Rudens 378, scibatis. There is no reason to suppose, with Küh., that Cic. substituted *sciebam* for Ennius' form, since he usually preserves the archaic forms.
XIV. § **29**. **longe**: not of time but = 'from afar.' So in Laelius 12, 40 'longe prospicere.'
uideris: i 6, 12 n. on 'cum fueris.'
apud Euripiden: in the Theseus, a lost play [quoted again in § 58]. The Greek is preserved in Plut. Cons. ad Apollon. pp. 443-4 and in Galen, de Plac. Hipp. et Plat. iv 7 p. 393 M. ἐγὼ δὲ τοῦτο παρὰ σοφοῦ τινος μαθών | εἰς φροντίδας νοῦν συμφοράς τ' ἐβαλλόμην | φυγάς τ' ἐμαυτῷ προστιθεὶς πάτρας ἐμῆς | θανάτους τ' ἀώρους καὶ κακῶν ἄλλας ὁδούς, | ἵν' εἴ τι πάσχοιμ' ὧν ἐδόξαζον φρενὶ | μή μοι νεωρὲς προσπεσὸν μᾶλλον δάκοι. Cic. as usual gives a free translation, cf. ii 8, 20 n. on 'o multa dictu grauia.' Leod. a Quercu in Mo. compares for the same *praemeditatio futurorum malorum* Virg. Aen. vi 103-5

30. quod autem Theseus a docto se audisse dicit, id de se ipso loquitur Euripides. fuerat enim auditor Anaxagorae, quem ferunt nuntiata morte filii dixisse: 'Sciebam me genuisse mortalem.' quae uox declarat iis esse haec acerba quibus non 15 fuerint cogitata. ergo id quidem non dubium, quin omnia, quae mala putentur, sint inprouisa grauiora. itaque quamquam non haec una res efficit maximam aegritudinem, tamen, quoniam multum potest prouisio animi et praeparatio ad minuendum dolorem, sint semper omnia homini humana meditata. et nimi- 20 rum haec est illa praestans et diuina sapientia, et perceptas penitus et pertractatas res humanas habere, nihil admirari,

§ 30, 11. theseus R V G   B 2   K L W.   theseius E.   ‖   de se ipso R 1 16
                                   ſe   ip̄o
G L W Π O 1 3 8.   de se ipso K.   de ipso V *eod. atr.* E *al. atr.*   de se B 2
eod. atr. ut uid.   de ipso R 10 B 1   S.   12. adiutor L 1.   13. filii R G S
L 1.   14. his G B L 1.   16. putantur L 1.   ‖   inprouisa R V G K L.
                                                                           v
improuisa B S.   17. maximam R V G.   maximam K *fort. eod. atr.*
                                                         t
magnam L 1.   19. et nimirum G K L.   enimirum V.   21. res humanas
R V̄ P G B 1–3   K S   E 1 2   L   W 2   M 1 2   D C J   O 1–3 7 8.   humanas
                                                                           d
res Π *alio atr.*   *om.* W 1. ‖ admirari K 1   E 1   L 1   O 1.   ammirari R *eod. atr.*
ut uid.   ammirari V G   B 1   E 2.   āmirari B 2.

'non ulla laborum, | o uirgo, noua mi facies inopinaue surgit; | omnia praecepi atque animo mecum ante peregi.' **licet enim**: Küh. thus explains the ellipse, so usual with *enim*: 'itaque apud Eur. a Theseo dicta laudantur, quae in Latinum sermonem conuersa sic se habent: licet enim.' Cf. i 6, 11 n.

qui: causal; cf. i 6, 12 n. on 'qui dimiserit.' **mortem acerbam**: = the Gk θάνατος ἀώρους; cf. i 39, 93 n. *acerbius.* **exsili...fugam**: cf. Or. iii 3, 9 'sibi exsilium et fugam deprecaretur.' Gen. of definition.

aliquam: not = *aliam quam* as many have supposed, though the etymology of the word, for which see Lindsay, *L.L.* p. 447, might seem to support this view. Better as Küh. explains = 'aut mortem aut exsilium *aut omnino aliquam* mali molem.'

repens: cf. 22, 52 'hostium repens aduentus.' Cicero's usual word is *repentinus.*

§ 30. **a docto...audisse**: Madv. on Fin. i 11, 39 'ut a patre audiebam' notes that Cicero more often wrote *audire ex* or *de aliquo.*

id de se ipso loquitur: Galen, de Plac. Hipp. et Plat. IV 7 p. 418, says that Posidonius, in criticising Chrysippus' definition of *aegritudo*, employs the story of what Anaxagoras said on hearing of the death of his son and said that it was

from this remark of Anaxagoras that Euripides got the idea of putting the sentiments translated in the text into the mouth of Theseus.

fuerat ... auditor Anaxagorae: cf. Strabo xiv 36 end; Diod. i 7 end; R. and P.[8] § 148 [Diog. Laert. ii 3, 5 [10]].

Anaxagorae: i 43, 104 n.

quem ferunt: a story like that here told of Anaxagoras was also told of Pericles and of Xenophon. All three instances are mentioned by Val. Max. v 10, 1 f. ext. and Plut. Cons. ad Apoll. p. 465 a. Diog. L. ii 13 tells the story of Anaxagoras and adds that some ascribe the remark to Solon and some to Xenophon. Diogenes there speaks of the death of *sons* and Aelian, V.H. iii 2, mentions two sons; but one son only is spoken of by Val. Max. *l.c.*, Plut. *l.c.*, and by other autho- rities cited here by Dav. [cf. Trebell. Pollio, uit. Gallien. c. 17, ubi de Valeriano patre comperit quod captus esset, id quod philosophorum optimus de filio amisso dixisse fertur, 'sciebam me genu- isse mortalem,' ille sic dixit 'sciebam patrem meum esse mortalem'].

haec una res: sc. the circumstance that they are unexpected.

meditata: with passive force, cf. 11, 24 n. on 'opinati.'

nimirum: i 22, 52 n.

res humanas, 'the vicissitudes of life.'

cum acciderit, nihil, ante quam euenerit, non euenire posse
arbitrari.

Quam ob rem ómnis, cum secúndae res sunt máx-

25   ime, tum máxime

Meditári secum opórtet, quo pacto áduersam ae-

rumnám ferant.

Perícla, damna péregre rediens sémper secum

cógitet

30 Aut fíli peccatum aút uxoris mórtem aut morbum

fíliae,

Commúnia esse haec, né quid horum umquam ácci-

dat animó nouom;

Quicquíd praeter spem euéniat, omne id députare

35   esse ín lucro.

XV. **31.** Ergo hoc Terentius a philosophia sumptum cum
tam commode dixerit, nos, e quorum fontibus id haustum est,
non et dicemus hoc melius et constantius sentiemus? hic est
enim ille uoltus semper idem, quem dicitur Xanthippe praedicare

---

24. omnis R V G K.   omis P B 1   E 1   W 2   D.   oms S L.   omēs J.
ōes B 2.   ‖   saecundae G.   ‖   maxume tum maxime R V P G.   maxume K
atr. nigr. tum maxuma *superscr.*   maxime tum maxime B S.   sunt tunc
maxime L.   26. aduersam V G B   E 1.   adu^rsam E 2.   aduersum R P K.
aduersus L.   28. pericula R V G B K S E.   30. filii G B K   L 1.
32. ne quot horum L 1.   34. p̄p̄t spem K.

        oc

XV. § **31**, 1. haec G *alt. man. superscr.*   ‖   sumptum cum R V P G E   O 3   S
h. l. non in quom *mut.*   2. ᵻe'quorum R *eod. atr.*   aequorum K.   equorum L.
4. uoltus R V G.   uultus P   B 1 2   S E L.   uᴜltus K *i.e.* u *in* o *al. atr. mut.*

---

nihil admirari: a principle prescribed
by many philosophers; e.g. the ἀθαμβία
or εὐθυμία of Democritus (R. and P.[8]
§ 205), the ἀταραξία of the Epicureans,
the ἀπάθεια of the Stoics. Cf. v 28, 81;
Hor. Epp. i 6, 1.

non euenire posse: not *non posse
euenire* because the negative goes with
euenire not with *posse*. *non euenire* is
contrasted with *euenerit*. Küh.

quam obrem omnis.... Iambic octonarii
from Terence, Phormio 241—246.

pericla, damna...: in Terence this line
runs thus 'pericla, damna, exsilia peregre
rediens semper cogitet' and the next line
but one thus 'communia esse haec fieri
posse, ut ne quid animo sit nouom.'
Faernus thought that Cicero might be
quoting from memory and Elmer, *App.*
to Phormio, adds that the copyists who
were professedly reproducing the text
before them, are more to be depended

upon. Bentley introduces into the text
of Terence the reading given here by
Cicero, applying to the reading supported
by the MSS of Terence the adverbs 'in-
sipienter, inepte ac stolide.' Fleckeisen
agrees with Bentley's view.

deputare: the infin. depends upon
oportet in spite of the intervention of
cogitet, which carries on *meditari oportet.*

XV. § 31. ergo...cum...dixerit: the
more usual form of the *argumentatio e
contrario* is seen in i 14, 31. Hence Dav.
in ed. 2 struck out *cum* and F.A.W. in
his notes took it to be spurious. But it is
similarly used elsewhere in Cicero and both
Dav. and F.A.W. subsequently retained
the word. Cf. ii 20, 46 n.

nos: sc. *philosophi.*

hic est enim: *enim* refers to *constantius
sentiemus,* 'this consistency is seen in
that unvarying equability of countenance
which....' [For *enim* introducing an ex-

5 solita in uiro suo fuisse Socrate, eodem semper se uidisse ex-
euntem illum domo et reuertentem. nec uero ea frons erat, quae
M. Crassi illius ueteris, quem semel ait in omni uita risisse
Lucilius, sed tranquilla et serena; sic enim accepimus. iure
autem erat semper idem uoltus, cum mentis, a qua is fingitur,
10 nulla fieret mutatio. quare accipio equidem a Cyrenaicis haec
arma contra casus et euentus quibus eorum aduenientes impetus
diuturna praemeditatione frangantur, simulque iudico malum
illud opinionis esse, non naturae; si enim in re esset, cur fierent

5. socrate R 6 P B 1 3 K 2 E 2 3 L 1 3 4 6 M 1 2 D C II O 1-3 7 8.
socratē R 10 W 2 J.   socratẹṁ V.   socratem R 1 16 B 2 K S L 5 ed. H.
socratam G *alt. man. superscr.*   6. quae · M· K 1 M 2.   quae m̅. R *in marg.*
al. atr.   marci quem V *atr. uirid. ut uid. punct. not.*   que. m. E 2 II.
que m̅ B 2 E 1.   que N M 1.   q̅ crassi S (q̅ *lineam claudit*; M *post* q̅ *extra
lineam excurrens erasum est*).   quẹ crassi B 1.   erat & M. illius crassi ueteris L 1.
q̅ ꝯ. W 2 D.   que G *at e in* ẹ *mut. et* M *add. alt. man. om.* W 1.   9. uoltus
R V G.   uultus B 1 2 S E L.   10. fieri G *alt. man. superscr.*   fieri B 1
eod. atr.   fieri K.   fuerit L.   11. impetus G K L.   12. frangatur R
eod. atr.   13. esset P 2 3 B 3 M 2 O 1-3 8.   essēt P 1 S.   essent R 1 6 7 17
V P 4 G K 1 E 1 2 D C II J.   ēent B 1 2 W 2 O 7.   iure essent L 1
in re mala essent M 1 ed. H. *om.* W 1.

ample, following a general statement,
cf. Draeger, *Synt. d. Lat. Spr.* § 350, 2 *d.*]
Dav. compares *Off.* i 26, 90 and quotes
Dionys. of Halic. in Stobaeus 108, 77
ἡ Ξανθίππη ἔφη μυρίων μεταβολῶν τὴν
πόλιν καὶ αὐτοὺς κατασχουσῶν ἐν πάσαις
ὅμοιον τὸ Σωκράτους πρόσωπον καὶ προϊόντος
ἐκ τῆς οἰκίας καὶ ἐπανιόντος θεάσασθαι·
ἥρμοστο γὰρ δηλονότι πρὸς πάντα ἐπιεικῶς·
τοιγάρτοι οὐδὲν πώποτε ἐλύπησεν αὐτόν.
Aelian, *V.H.* ix 7, has almost the very
same words.

Xanthippe: for the good and bad
qualities of this lady see note and reff. in
Zeller, *Socrates and the Socratic Schools*
E.T.[2] pp. 61–2.

Socrate: Bake (followed by Schiche)
ejected and Bai., Hei., T.S., Ml. bracket,
regarding *Socratem* of best MSS as a gloss
upon *illum.*

eodem semper se uidisse: *dicens* is
carried on from *praedicare.*

M. Crassi: cf. *Fin.* v 30, 92. Some
accounts represent him as having never
laughed, cf. Pliny, *N.H.* vii 18, 79 'ferunt
Crassum, auum Crassi in Parthis inter-
empti, numquam risisse; ob id Agelastum
uocatum'; also Solinus, *c.* 1, quoted by
Dav. who also refers to Joannes Sarisb.
Policr. viii 8 who quotes this statement
of Cicero [cf. Seneca, de ira ii 12, 4].

semel: the mirth-provoking words are
recorded by St. Jerome, epist. vii (ad

Chromatium Jouinum et Eusebium) 'similem habent labra lactucam asino carduos
comedente.'

Lucilius: cf. Marx' Lucilius, 1. 1299
and commentary.

a Cyrenaicis: 13, 28.

casus et euentus: ἐν διὰ δυοῖν.

quibus... diuturna praemeditatione:
it seems best, with T.S., Hei., and F.A.W.,
to regard *diuturna praemeditatione* as a
sort of apposition to *quibus*, the arms
consisting in *diuturna praemeditatio.*
Küh. follows Kl. in taking *quibus* as *abl.
instrumenti* and the second abl. as *abl.
modi.* If the arms are not the *praemeditatio* they must be the settled calm which
results from the latter.

malum illud: sc. *aegritudinis.* Wesenberg compares 11, 24 'est igitur causa
omnis (aegritudinis) in opinione'; 27, 65
'uides opinionis esse, non naturae malum';
28, 71 'non in natura, sed in opinione
esse aegritudinem'; 33, 80 quoted in
note on 13, 28; 34, 82 end.

opinionis...naturae: see ii 22, 53 n.
and cf. iii 13, 28 n. on 'opinionem mali
aegritudinem esse natura' and Fin. iii
10, 35 quoted there. On this point Cic.
adopts the Stoic view against that of the
Epicureans.

in re esset = *natura esset.* Cf. 30, 74
'cogitatio...nihil esse in re mali dolori
medetur.' The subject is *malum illud.*

prouisa leuiora? **32.** sed est isdem de rebus quod dici possit sub-
15 tilius, si prius Epicuri sententiam uiderimus, qui censet necesse
esse omnis in aegritudine esse qui se in malis esse arbitrentur,
siue illa ante prouisa et expectata sint siue inueterauerint. nam
neque uetustate minui mala nec fieri praemeditata leuiora, stultamque etiam esse meditationem futuri mali aut fortasse ne
20 futuri quidem; satis esse odiosum malum omne, cum uenisset; qui
autem semper cogitauisset accidere posse aliquid aduersi, ei fieri
illud sempiternum malum; si uero ne futurum quidem sit, frustra
suscipi miseriam uoluntariam; ita semper angi aut accipiendo
aut cogitando malo. **33.** leuationem autem aegritudinis in dua-
25 bus rebus ponit, auocatione a cogitanda molestia et reuocatione ad
contemplandas uoluptates. parere enim censet animum rationi
posse et quo illa ducat sequi. uetat igitur ratio intueri mo-

§ **32**, 14. isdem R V P 4 G B 1 2 K E 1 L W 2 J O 7.   iisdem S *at* ii
                                              i
al. atr.   hisdem M 1 O 1.   isdem P 1 (*sic*) *al. atr. superscr.*   iisdem B 3 E 2
M 2 C O 3.   hiisdem D Π O 8.   *om.* W 1.   16. omnis R V G B 1 E.
om̄s K W 2.   om̄s B 2 S L.   17. illa G *at* i *in ras. litterae* u. ‖ expectata
R V G B K S E L.   19. meditationem R V P 1 4 G B 1-3 K S E 1 2
L 2-5 W 2 M 1 2 D C Π J O 3 8 7.   praemeditationem O 2.   premeditationem
O 1 ed. H.   *om.* L 1 W 1.   23. uoluntariam G *addidit alt. man. in marg.*
extremo inf. ‖ semp pangi B.
    § **33**, 24. leuatitionem G.   25. reuocatione R O 1.   reuocatōē W 2.
reuocationē B 1 L.   reuocationem G K.   reuocationẹ V.   reuocatōm̄ B 2.
26. pareri G.

essent of most MSS is due to an attractive
influence exerted by the following *fierent
prouisa leuiora* on the mind of an early
copyist.
   prouisa: substantival = *ea quae prouisa
essent*. So Küh. who compares 13, 28
'uidentur enim omnia repentina grauiora';
14, 30; 22, 52 'quod prouisum ante non
sit, id ferire uehementius' and *ibid.* 'omnia
uideri subita maiora.'
   § **32. subtilius**, 'with more precision,'
cf. i 23, 55 n.
   qui se in malis esse arbitrentur: cf.
13, 28 'si id sibi accidisse opinetur.'
   siue...siue... i.e. neither accepting the
Cyrenaic remedy of *diuturna praemeditatio* nor Zeno's view that *aegritudo* consists in a *recens opinio.* For the latter see
11, 25 n. on 'recens opinio.'
   stultamque etiam esse... cf. *Fin.* i 17,
57 'stulti autem malorum memoria torquentur, sapientes bona praeterita grata
recordatione renouata delectant. est autem
situm in nobis, ut et aduersa quasi perpetua obliuione obruamus et secunda
iucunde ac suauiter meminerimus.'
   uenisset...cogitauisset...futurum sit:

as *censet*, used of an author who is dead
but lives on in his works (i 18, 42 n. on
'uolt'), involves a past idea we have it
here followed by secondary and primary
sequence in turn. Cf. *Fin.* iv 21, 58-9
'dicunt (Stoici)...uideatur...esset...uide-
antur...iudicaremus' and other exx. in
Küh. *Gram. d. Lat. Sprache* II p. 775.
   § **33.** in **duabus rebus ponit, auocatione...**: the prep. is usually omitted
before clauses in apposition owing to the
intimate connexion between such clauses
and the words which they explain. Cf.
iv 6, 11 'ex malis...metum futuris, aegr.
praesentibus'; de Inu. i 5, 7 'tribus in
generibus rerum uersari rhetoris officium
putauit, demonstratiuo etc.'
   auocatione: sc. *animi.*
   reuocatione: cf. i 16, 38 n. on 'seuo-
care.'
   animum)(**rationi**, 'feeling)(reason':
cf. i 18, 41 n. on 'animum.'
   ratio: sc. as Epicurus holds. The view
of Epicurus is being stated.
   abstrahit: absolutely used as in Cato
M. 6, 15 'a rebus gerendis senectus
abstrahit.'

lestias, abstrahit ab acerbis cogitationibus, hebetem <facit>
aciem ad miserias contemplandas; a quibus cum cecinit re-
30 ceptui, inpellit rursum et incitat ad conspiciendas totaque mente
contrectandas uarias uoluptates, quibus ille et praeteritarum
memoria et spe consequentium sapientis uitam refertam putat.
haec nostro more nos diximus, Epicurii dicunt suo. sed quae
dicant uideamus, quo modo neglegamus.

XVI. 34. Principio male reprehendunt praemeditationem
rerum futurarum. nihil est enim quod tam obtundat eleuetque

28. hebetat aciem E 2.   hebetem aciem R 1 6 7 17   P 2–4.   G   K 1   B 3
L 1–3   O 2.   hebetem aciē O 3.   hebetē aciem K 2   M 2   O 1.   hebetē aciē
                    e   ‡ habentē
B 2   W 2   J.   habetem aciem V *incert. an al. atr.*   hebetem aciem P 1 *al. atr.*
superscr.   hebetem atiem L 4 6.   ebetē aciem Π.   hebentem aciem S C.
hebentē atiam M 1.   hebentē aciem B 1 D   O 7.   hebētē aciem E 3.   habentē
aciem E 1.   habentem aciem L 5.   habentē aciē O 8.   *om.* W 1.   hebetem
                                                 facit
facit aciem *corr. Wesenbergius.*   29. contemplandas   V *man. ant. superscr.* ∥
                                                          nit
cecinit R 6   B 3   E 3   M 2   O 2.   cecinit Π *at fuerat* cecidit.   cecidit O 3.
cecidit R 1 7 10 16 17   V G   B 12   K 12   S   E 12   L   M 1   D C J   O 1 7 8.
cecidᵗ W 2.   *om.* W 1.   ∥   receptui B 3   E 3   M 2   O 2 3.   receptui Π
                           ti
at fuerat receptum.   receptu B 1 *leuiter superscr.*   receptu R 10 V   B 2   K 2   S E 1
L 1 5   W 2   D C   O 8.   receptū R 1   É 2   O 1 7.   receptum R 16   M 1 ed. H.
                                                            v
receptum pellit G *in* receptui inpellit *alt. man. mut.*   recepta K 1 *atr. nigr. superscr.*
om. W 1.   30. impellit R V B K S.   inpellit L   O 7   G *ut supr.*   33. epicurii
V   B 2   G L.   epicurei R 1 i *in* e *al. atr. ut uid. mut.*   epicurei R 6   P 1 2
                                                                 ~
B 1 K S   E 12   D C Π   O 1.   epicuri R 17   P 3   M 1 2   J   O 3 8 7.   epicui
W 2.   *om.* W 1.   ∥   quędicant V i *in* ę *eod. atr. mut.*   34. neglegamus
R V B 1 K E L J.   negglegamus G *at primum* g *exp. et conf. alt. man.*   negli-
gamus B 2.
    XVI. § 34, 1. repraehendunt praemeditationum G.   2. obtundat P 4   S   E 2
M 1 2   D C Π   O 1–3 7 8.   obtundet B 2   K   W 2   J.   optundat V B 1 E 1 L.
        a
optundā R *eod. atr. superscr.* P 1 *al. atr. superscr.*   optundet G.   ∥   eleuetque
                                                                l'eleuet
R V   P 1–4   G   B 12   K S E 1 L   W 2   M 2   D C J   O 3 7.   euellatq; O 8
al. atr.   leuetque E 2   Π   O 2.   releuetque M 1.

hebetem facit aciem: the reading of
most MSS cannot be right though Tr.
retained it and Kl., *Add.* p. 134, approved.
Sff.'s conj. *faciens* for *aciem* is untenable
since the object can neither be the indefinite pronoun nor *animum* carried on
from above. *hebetat* read by Man. 'e
uetere codice' and by Dav. from 'Eliens.
tert.' may possibly be right though not
found, as Wes. (*Em.* I p. 15) objected,
before the Augustan age (Aen. ii 605).
Wes. argues that Cic., who uses *hebescere*
several times (e.g. i 30, 73), says *obtun-
dere* or *praestringere* or even *hebetem
reddere* and he thinks that *reddit* or *facit*
has fallen out here. To Wes. Küh., who
reads *hebetat*, objects that there are many
ἅπαξ λεγόμενα in Cic. and that *hebetat*

may have been one. But one brought in
by emendation would be unconvincing
and it seems safer to adopt Wesenberg's
facit with most modern editors.
    cecinit: for the mood and tense see
ii 2, 5 n. on 'occurrit' and ii 24, 58 n. on
'aspeximus.'
    cecinit receptui = *auocauit*; a military
metaphor. Mo. compares Quint. xii 11, 4.
    rursum: i 17, 40 n.
    contrectandas: a bold metaphor, cf.
Tac. Ann. iii 12, 7, where Furneaux also
cites Lactantius, de Opif. Dei i.
    nostro more: sc. *eleganter* et *ornate*.
    suo: cf. ii 3, 7 n. on 'neque distincte...
scribere.'
    XVI. § 34. **male reprehendunt** = *male
faciunt, quod reprehendunt*, cf. v 37, 109

aegritudinem quam perpetua in omni uita cogitatio nihil esse
quod non accidere possit, quam meditatio condicionis humanae,
5 quam uitae lex commentatioque parendi, quae non hoc adfert,
ut semper maereamus, sed ut numquam. neque enim, qui rerum
naturam, qui uitae uarietatem, qui inbecillitatem generis humani
cogitat, maeret, cum haec cogitat, sed tum uel maxime sapientiae
fungitur munere. utrumque enim consequitur, ut et consider-
10 andis rebus humanis proprio philosophiae fruatur officio et

4. non accidere possit R V P G   B 1–3   K S   E 1 2   L   W 1 2   M 2   II J
O 1–3 7 8.   accidere non possit D C.   tam abscidere possit M 1. ‖ conditionis
                     r
G B L.   5. adfert R V G.   adfjet K *atr. nigr.*   affert B L.   7. inbecillitatem
V G B 1 2 E L.   ijbecillitatem R.   imbecillitatem K.   8. maxime
         v
R V G B S L.   maxime K *atr. nigriore.*   10. fruatur R 1 6 7 16   V   P 1 3 4
G   B 1–3   K 1 2   S   E 1–3   L 1 5 6   W 1 2   M 1 2   D C II J   O 2 7 8 ed. H.
frutatur L 3.   fungatur R 17   P 2   L 2 4   O 3.   fungantur O 1.

'stulte anteposuit': the adv. expresses a
judgment with regard to the action, not
the manner in which it is done. See
Madv. on Fin. iv 23, 63; Küh. *Gram.*
p. 597 Anm. 2.
eleuet=*extenuet.*
cogitatio: for the verbal with acc. and
infin. see Madv. § 395; Roby II §§ 1351–2.
non accidere possit: for the order of
words cf. 14, 30 n. on 'non euenire
posse.'
uitae lex: compressed for *uitae legis
meditatio*; nearly the same as *med. condicionis humanae*, further explained in
the next sentence 'neque enim, qui rerum
naturam...', cf. v 13, 38 'manet in lege
naturae'; Fam. vi 6, 12 'leuat enim
dolorem communis quasi legis et humanae
condicionis recordatio.' 'A consideration
of the human lot, of the general laws
under which men live, and a preparation
to obey those laws.' Virtue, according to
Chrysippus, consists in living in harmony
with oneself and with nature in general,
cf. Diog. L. vii 89 φύσιν δὲ Χρύσιππος
μὲν ἐξακούει, ᾗ ἀκολούθως δεῖ ζῆν, τήν τε
κοινὴν καὶ ἰδίως τὴν ἀνθρωπίνην. We must
be in harmony with the world in which
we live, and consequently know that
vicissitudes of fortune are inevitable. Cf.
25, 60 'necessitas ferendae condicionis
humanae quasi cum deo pugnare prohibet
admonetque esse hominem, quae cogitatio
magno opere luctum leuat.'
ut semper: as Epicurus maintained,
cf. § 32.
proprio: the Stoics held that 'the
proper study of mankind is man.' Of the
three main divisions of philosophy, δια-

λεκτική, φυσική and ἠθική, the last-men-
tioned was 'the central point towards
which all other inquiries converge. Even
natural science, although lauded as the
inmost shrine of philosophy, is, according
to Chrysippus, only necessary for the
philosopher to enable him to distinguish
between things good and evil, between
what should be done and what should be
left undone.' Zeller, *Stoics, etc.*, c. iv
p. 56 and Chrysippus in Plut. Stoic. Rep.
c. 9 p. 10, 35 d there quoted.
fruatur officio: Manutius and Lambinus, whether from MSS or their own
conjecture, substituted *fungatur* for *fruatur*, and Dav. Lall. Ern. and Küh. follow
them, but almost every other modern
editor retains *fruatur*. If, as Küh. supposes, *fruatur* has been substituted by
some one whose taste was offended by the
recurrence of *fungatur*, then, since all
the best MSS have *fruatur*, this must have
been done at least as early as the 6th
cent. A.D., a period when interpolation
was not in vogue and a period, too, when
such recurrences gave no offence. It is
more likely that *fungatur* is repeated
from two lines higher up, in the late MSS
in which it occurs. *fruatur officio*=*officio
fungendo delectetur*, cf. Hand on Wopkens
p. 112. Hand compares Senec. Ep. 93, 9
'omnium rerum cognitione fruiti sumus.'
There is also a contrast which would
be lost by the change from *fruatur* to
fungatur: the course prescribed gives
him before misfortune comes a congenial
occupation: after its arrival a three-fold
consolation.

aduersis casibus triplici consolatione sanetur, primum quod
posse accidere diu cogitauit, quae cogitatio una maxime molestias
omnis extenuat et diluit, deinde quod humana humane ferenda
intellegit, postremo quod uidet malum nullum esse nisi culpam,
15 culpam autem nullam esse, cum id quod ab homine non potuerit
praestari, euenerit. 35. nam reuocatio illa quam adfert, cum a

11. aduersis R V P 1 2 G B 1-3 K S E 2 L W 1 2 M 1 2 D C Π J
O 2 7 8.　　aduersus E 1 *eod. ut uid. atr.*　　auersis O 3.　　diuersis O 1. ||
casibus R V G B 1-3 K S E 1 2 L W 1 2 M 1 2 D C Π O 1-3 7 8. ||
sanetur W 1 2　　saneptur R V K.　　sanentur G B 2.　　sanatur L.
12. cogitauerit R V P 1-3 G B 1 3 K S E 1 2 L W 1 2 M 1 2 D Π O 1-3.
cogitau'it J O 7 8.　　cogitau̇t B 2 C.　　cogitauit *corr. Bentleius.*　|| maxime K
atr. nigriore.　maxime L.　13. omnis R V G B K E.　omis W 2.　omnes S L. ||
humana
humane ferenda V *man. ant. superscr.*　　humane ferenda R 7 P 4 B 1-3 K 1 2
E 2 3 L 3 5 6 W 2 M 2 D C Π J O 2 3 7 8 Gr.　　humana ferenda R 6 17
G S L 2 4 W 1 M 1.　　humanæ ferenda R *eod. ut uid. atr.*　humanæ ferenda
O 1.　　humanae ferenda P 3.　　humanę ferenda P 1 E 1 L 1.　　humana
ferendas P 2.　　14. intellegit R V P G B K.　　intelligit L.　　15. culpam R 6
V P 1-3 G B 1-3 K E 1 2 L 1 W 1 M 2 D C Π O 1 3 ed. H.　　culpā R
　　　　　　　　　　　　　　　　　　　　　　　　　　　uel p̄caueri
P 4 S W 2 M 1 J O 7 8.　　16. prestari R *atr. ant. superscr.*

§ 35. adfert R V G *at* ert *in ras. alt. man.*　　　adfet K r *eras. et al. atr. suppl.*
affert B L.　|| cum contuendis B a *om.*

aduersis casibus: abl. abs. giving the
circumstances, cf. i 5, 10 n. on 'maxima
corona.' Bentley's corr. *aduersus casus* is
unnecessary.

cogitauit: Bentley proposed *cogitauit*;
cogitauerit cannot be right. If it were
fut. perf. we should have had *consequetur*
above. The parallelism of the clauses
requires the indic. *cogitauit* in symmetry
with *intellegit* and *uidet*. Wopkens p. 108
thinks that Cicero forgot his constr. but
his exx. are not similar. Or. finds an
absurd meaning in *cogitauerit* 'since
perhaps, as we can easily imagine, he
had thought,' and Mo. imagines that
quod in the first clause means *quippe qui*
or *cum* and in the second and third
clauses *quia*, or *eo, quod.*

una maxime: i 9, 17 n.

humana humane ferenda, 'that the
incidents of the human lot must be borne
with resignation.' Cf. ii 27, 65 n. on
'humane' and exx. quoted there. Dav.
quotes here Plut. Cons. ad Apollon. 102 a
ἀνθρωπίνως φέρειν τὸ συμβεβηκός, 118 c
πείθοντες τὰ κοινὰ τοῦ βίου συμπτώματα
κοινῶς φέρειν καὶ τὰ ἀνθρώπινα ἀνθρωπίνως. Fam. vi 1, 4 'simus igitur ea
mente, quam ratio et ueritas praescribit,
ut nihil in uita nobis praestandum praeter
culpam putemus, eaque cum careamus,
omnia humana placate et moderate feramus.'

nisi culpam, 'that there is no evil

where there is no moral blame.' For
culpa cf. Fam. vi 1, 4 above. Camerarius
in Mo. quotes Fam. ix 16, 5 'nihil esse
sapientis praestare nisi culpam'; v 17, 5
'homines sapientes turpitudine, non casu
et delicto suo, non aliorum iniuria com-
moueri'; *ibid.* § 3 'ut et communem in-
certumque casum, quem neque uitare
quisquam nostrum nec praestare ullo
pacto potest, sapienter ferres et dolori
fortiter ac fortunae resisteres'; and he
defines *culpa* as ἁμάρτημα ἴδιον *seu malum
cuius sibi aliquis auctor ipse fuit,* comparing Plut. Cons. ad Apoll. 114 c τὸ
μὲν γὰρ μὴ δι' αὐτὸν κακῶς πράττειν ὁ μὲν
Κράντωρ φησὶν οὐ μικρὸν εἶναι κούφισμα
πρὸς τὰς τύχας, ἐγὼ δ' ἂν εἴποιμι φάρμακον
ἀλυπίας εἶναι μέγιστον. In law *culpa* =
'negligence' as contrasted with *dolus*
intentional 'wrong' and *praestare culpam*
was much used in this connexion also.
[Cf. Cic. de Or. i 24, 113 istam enim
cūlpam, quam uereris, ego praestabo.]

praestari: the word is much used in
law, e.g. Off. iii 16, 66 'emptori damnum
praestari' lit. 'to put oneself before something' hence 'to be responsible for something' whether for the occurrence or the
non-occurrence of an event.

§ 35. **nam**, 'but as for his proposed
remedy...' For *nam* in transition and
refutation see Hand, *Tursell.* III 147,
IV, 7.

quam adfert: sc. Epicurus, cf. § 33 init.

contuendis nos malis auocat, nulla est. non est enim in nostra
potestate fodicantibus iis rebus quas malas esse opinemur dissi-
mulatio uel obliuio; lacerant, uexant, stimulos admouent, ignis
20 adhibent, respirare non sinunt. et tu obliuisci iubes, quod contra
naturam est, qui, quod a natura datum est, auxilium extorqueas
inueterati doloris? est enim tarda illa quidem medicina, sed
tamen magna, quam adfert longinquitas et dies. iubes me bona
cogitare, obliuisci malorum. diceres aliquid, et magno quidem
25 philosopho dignum, si ea bona esse sentires quae essent homine
dignissima.

XVII. 36. Pythagoras mihi si diceret aut Socrates aut
Plato: 'Quid iaces aut quid maeres aut cur succumbis cedis-
que fortunae? quae peruellere te forsitan potuerit et pungere,

18. his rebus G B K.　　19. ignis R V G B 1 2 K.　　ignes S E L J.
i
igs W 2.　　21. est quod a natura R 6　W 1　D C.　　est qui a natura P G.
est quia natura R 1 10　V B K　E 1 2　L 1 5　Π J　O 1 7 8.　　est quod autem
a natura P 2　M 2.　　quod est autem a natura M 1.　　est quod quidem a
natura R 7　L 2.　　est q3 natura R 16 17　B 2　　S (*in marg.* quod āut a).
est Q 1 a nā W 2.　　est qd' natura E 3 (*in marg.* āut a).　　quod autem a (est *om.*)
L 3 6　O 2.　　est quod natura ed. H.　　est qui quod a natura *corr.* Tregder. ‖
datum est R V P G　K 2　E 1 3　L　W 1　Π O 2 3 7.　　est datum L 6.
elatum est B 2.　‖　extorqueas R V P G　B 1 3　K 1 2　S　E 1 2　L　W 1 2　M 2
Π J　O 1 2.　　extorqās B 2　O 8.　　extorques R 6 ed. H.　　extorqueris M 1.
　　　　　　　　　　　　　　　　　　　　　　　　　　　　　　e
extorquens O 3.　　extorquendi D C　O 7.　　22. illa quidam V.　　23. adfert
　　　　　　　fe
R V G E.　　adfr-t K *litt. post* r *eras.*　　affert B L.　‖　bona *om.* L 1.
25. esse sentires R V P G　B 1-3　K S　E 1 2　M 2　Π　O 2 3 7 8.　　sentires
esse R 6　L　W 1 2　M 1　J　O 1.　　esse *om.* D C.　　26. dignissima R V G B L.
　　　　　　　　　h
XVII. § 36, 1. pytagoras R *eod. atr.*　　pytagoras V G.　　Phȳtagoras B. ‖
si diceret R G　B 1 2　W 2.　　3. quae peruellere R V P G　B 1-3　K 1 2　S
E 2 3　L 1-6　W 2　M 1 2　D C Π J　O 1-3 7 8 ed. H.　　quae te peruellere W 1.

fodicantibus: the sentence is quoted
by Nonius p. 66 under this word.

et tu...iubes: '*et* eleganter ponitur cum
interrogatione in uehementioribus clau-
sulis, cum attulimus quae ualde com-
mouere possunt.' See Hand, *Tursell.*
II 492. Cf. i 38, 92.

qui, quod a...extorqueas: this reading,
which accounts for the variants, is to be
preferred to *qui a natura datum auxilium
extorqueas*, read by Or. and (with *extorques* instead of *extorqueas*) by Dav. The
subjunctive gives a reason for the surprise
and indignation implied in the question,
'though you deprive me of the aid...'

inueterati doloris: i 15, 34 n. on
'mercedem gloriae.'

tarda illa quidem...sed tamen: i 3,
6 n. on 'optimis.'

longinquitas et dies: ἐν διὰ δυοῖν =
longinquitas temporis.

aliquid: i 20, 45 n.

essent: Cic. might have written *sunt*
but *sentires* exerts attraction of tense and
mood, cf. i 5, 9 n. on 'moriendum esset...
uiuerent.'

XVII. § 36. Pythagoras...si diceret
...: the protasis includes all clauses down
to *expetenda uideatur*; the apodosis *pare-
rem et sequerer* should have followed
there; but Cicero, owing to the number
of the clauses to which the words *si diceret*
apply, breaks off the thread of the construction and sums up the protasis in
another form in the words *ad haec bona
me si reuocas*, upon which the apodosis,
pareo, sequor... follows. Cf. Küh., who
notes that, where the apodosis thus fails
but lurks in another form, we have the
figure ἀνανταπόδοτον of the grammarians,
a figure not uncommon in the letters and
philosophical works of Cicero, where the
strict rules of grammar are frequently
relaxed.

non potuit certe uires frangere. magna uis est in uirtutibus; eas
5 excita, si forte dormiunt; iam tibi aderit princeps fortitudo, quae
te animo tanto esse coget ut omnia quae possint homini euenire,
contemnas et pro nihilo putes; aderit temperantia, quae est
eadem moderatio, a me quidem paulo ante appellata frugalitas,
quae te turpiter et nequiter facere nihil patietur. quid est autem
10 nequius aut turpius ecfeminato uiro? ne iustitia quidem sinet te
ista facere, cui minimum esse uidetur in hac causa loci, quae
tamen ita dicet dupliciter esse te iniustum, cum et alienum
adpetas, qui mortalis natus condicionem postules inmortalium,
et grauiter feras te, quod utendum acceperis, reddidisse.
15 **37.** prudentiae uero quid respondebis docenti uirtutem sese

4. non potuit G K1 2 L1 W2 II O1 3 8.   non poterit W1.   non
potuerit D O7 *om.* C.   6. coget R V P1 3 4 G B1–3 K1 2 S E2
L3 4 6 W1 2 M1 2 D C II J O1–3 7 8.   cogit L2 5.   cogat L1.
cogitet E1 ed. H.   7. contemnas P.   contempnas V G E L.   contēpnas R K.
contem-nas S *litt. eras.*   9. patietur P2 G W1 O3.   patiatur R1 6 10 16
V P1 3 4 B1–3 K1 2 S E1–3 L2 3 4 6 W2 M1 2 D C II J O1 2 7 8.
                                                          f
10. ecfeminato B K.   eḟfeminato R1 *eod. atr.*   ecfeminato G *ead. man.*
effeminato R10 16 W1 D.   et feminato B2. ‖ nec iustitia B.   11. cui
nimium B. ‖ causa loci V *at ras. post* c.   causa loci II *at* ci *in ras.*   causa loci
O2.   causa loc s3 O7.   causa locus L4 M1 D C.   causa loqui R G
B1 2 K1 2 E1 2 L2 3 5 6 W1 2 M2 O1 3 8 ed. H.   causa loqui B3
                     loci
in marg. locus.   causa loqui E3.   13. adpetas R G K.   appetas V P B. ‖
condicionem R B2 E.   conditionem V G B1 K S W1. ‖ inmortalium
V G K.   immortalium R B E.
    § **37,** 15. quid R10 16 V P G B1 K2 L2 3 4 6 W1 2 D O18.   quǫd
R1 *eod. atr.*   qd' O7.   quidē B2. ‖ docenti R V G B1 2 K S E1 2
                                                          i
W2 M1 D C J O1 7 8.   docenti P *al. atr. superscr.*   dicenti R6 B3
W1 M2 O2 3.   dicenti II *at prius* i *in ras.*

peruellere: ii 20, 46.
    potuerit: potential, 'may have been
able.' Bent. and Dav. wrongly followed
Ascensius and Victorius in inserting *ut*
before *peruellere.*
    potuerit...non potuit: ii 17, 39 n.
    in uirtutibus: Cic. enforces his argu-
ment by reference to the four cardinal
virtues in turn, as in §§ 14—17 above, and
often.
    princeps, 'in the first place,' refers to
order of treatment not to order of importance.
    coget...patietur: Cic. would naturally
speak positively on both points and it
seems absurd to suppose with Mo. and
Küh. that he speaks 'magis dubitanter'
in the one place and 'confidentius' in the
other. Dav., Mo. and Küh. read *coget...
patiatur*; Bouh. and Ern. *cogat...patiatur*;
nearly all other modern editors read as
in the text. The confusion of *a* and *e* in
MSS is one of the most common.

    a me: Bent. followed by Dav. changed
to *a te* because Pythagoras or Socrates or
Plato is supposed to be speaking. But as
a parenthetic remark the words are quite
natural.
    paulo ante: 8, 16.
    nequiter, 'in an unprincipled manner.'
    cui minimum...: since justice was
concerned with our relations towards
others and this might seem to be a matter
personal to ourselves. Cf. Plut. de Stoic.
Rep. 7 p. 1034 c ὁ Ζήνων...φησί...τὴν...
δικαιοσύνην φρόνησιν ἐν ἀπονεμητέοις;
Stobaeus, Ecl. ii 59, 9 w.; Phil. Leg.
Alleg. i 87 p. 84, 2 ἡ δικαιοσύνη...
ἀπονέμει τὸ κατ' ἀξίαν ἐν ἑκάστῳ πράγ-
ματι.
    natus: θνητὸς ὤν. Cf. Fam. iv 5, 4 *ad
med.* 'uisne tu te, Serui, cohibere et
meminisse hominem te esse natum?' and
other exx. quoted by Dav.
    utendum: for the constr. cf. 7, 15 n.
on 'fungendum'; for the metaphor i 31,

esse contentam, quo modo ad bene uiuendum, sic etiam ad
beate? quae si extrinsecus religata pendeat et non et oriatur
a se et rursus ad se reuertatur et omnia sua complexa nihil
quaerat aliunde, non intellego cur aut uerbis tam uehementer
20 ornanda aut re tantopere expetenda uideatur.' ad haec bona me
si reuocas, Epicure, pareo, sequor, utor te ipso duce, obliuiscor
etiam malorum, ut iubes, eoque facilius, quod ea ne in malis
quidem ponenda censeo. sed traducis cogitationes meas ad uoluptates. quas? corporis, credo, aut quae propter corpus uel recorda-
25 tione uel spe cogitentur. num quid est aliud? rectene interpretor
sententiam tuam? solent enim isti negare nos intellegere quid
dicat Epicurus. **38.** hoc dicit, et hoc ille acriculus me audiente

16. contentam R V P K.   contemptam B.   ‖ sic etiam R V P G B 1–3
K S E 1 2 L 2–6 W 1 2 M 1 2 D C Π J O 1–3 7 8 ed. H.   17. beate
V G B K W 2 O 7.   beatǫe R.   beatę P.   beata B 2. ‖ extrinsecus G
at litt. inter n *et* s *eras.*   ‖ et non et oriatur V G B 1 2 E 1 2 Π Gr.   et non
oriatur R P 1 4 B 3 K 1 2 S L 6 W 1 2 M 2 D C J O 1–37.   et non
                      l' oriatur
orriatur M 1.   ut non hǫrreǫatur O 8 *al. atr. suppl.*   18. a se R V P G B 1–3
K 1 S E 1 2 W 1 M 2 D C Π O 2 3 7 8 Gr.   ex se K 2 W 2 J *om.* O 1. ‖
reuertatur et R V P G B 1–3 K 1 2 E 1 2 L 2–6 W 1 2 M 1 2 D C Π
O 1–3 7 8 ed. H.   19. intellego R V P G B K.   20. tantopere R V P G B K S E.
25. cogitemur G m *expunxit et* nt *superscr. alt. man.*   26. intellegere R V B G K.
§ **38,** 27. acriculus V c *post* a *paullo nigriore atr. scr., et ras. suspicari potest.*
 J   acriculus
acicul' W 2.   agriculus R P 1 4 G K 1 2.   agricolus J.   agricolus M 1
O 1 8 E 2 *in marg.* egriculus.   agriculus B 2 *i.e.* u *in o mut.*   egriculus S.
egriculus R 16 Π.   aegriculus B E.   egricolus R 7 O 7.   graeculus L 3
M 2 O 2.   grǫculus W 1.   greculus R 6 P 2 3 L 6 D C O 3.
ariolus R 17 L 2.   articulus L 5.   atthiculus L 4.

77 n. on 'usuram.' For the sentiment Mo.
compares Eurip. Phoen. 556, quoted in
Plut. Cons. ad Apoll. 116 a,

τὰ τῶν θεῶν δ' ἔχοντες ἐπιμελούμεθα,
ὅταν δὲ χρῇζωσ', αὖτ' ἀφαιροῦνται πάλιν.

§ **37.** **uirtutem...ad beate**: for the
Stoic doctrine τὴν ἀρετὴν αὐτάρκη εἶναι
πρὸς εὐδαιμονίαν cf. Diog. L. vii 127,
Fin. i 18, 61 and other authorities quoted
by von Arnim, *Stoic. Vet. Frag.* III pp.
13 foll.

quo modo...sic etiam: *etiam* with
intensive force, 'even.' Without this
intensive meaning *etiam* is not added in
such correlative expressions as *quo modo,
quem ad modum, ut* or *sicut...ita* or *sic.*
Cf. Küh. here.

si extrinsecus religata pendeat, 'if
she were dependent on externals.' Hei.
compares Fam. v 13, 1 'laudem sapientiae
statuo esse maximam non aliunde pendere
nec extrinsecus aut bene aut male uiuendi
suspensas habere rationes.'

et oriatur: *et* should not be omitted.
The correlatives *et...et* are often thus used
with contrasted expressions which are to

be taken together. Cf. i **20,** 45; iii 30,
74; Fin. i 17, 55 etc.

malorum...in malis, 'misfortunes...
evils,' i.e. evils as popularly understood)(
real evils.

quas: for the carrying on of the prep.
from the antecedent cf. i 39, 93 n. on
'quod tandem tempus?'

credo: i 38, 92 n. on 'opinor.'

aut quae...cogitentur, 'or pleasures
connected with the body, conjured up by
recollection or anticipation.'

propter corpus: Hand, *Tursell.* IV 613,
gives instances from Quintilian of *propter*
='in respect of' 'in relation to,' Quintil.
iii 8, 18; iv 3, 1; ix 4, 143.

rectene: ii 11, 26 n. on 'uidesne.'

solent enim isti negare...: cf. Fin. ii
4, 12.

§ **38.** **acriculus,** 'waspish'; cf. N.D.
i 34, 93 'Zeno quidem non eos solum qui
tum erant, Apollodorum, Silum, ceteros,
figebat maledictis, sed Socratem ipsum,
parentem philosophiae, Latino uerbo utens
scurram Atticum fuisse dicebat, Chrysippum numquam nisi Chrysippam uocabat.'

Athenis senex Zeno, istorum acutissimus, contendere et magna
uoce dicere solebat, eum esse beatum qui praesentibus uolupta-
30 tibus frueretur confideretque se fruiturum aut in omni aut in
magna parte uitae dolore non interueniente aut, si interueniret,
si summus foret, futurum breuem, sin productior, plus habiturum
iucundi quam mali ; haec cogitantem fore beatum, praesertim si
et ante perceptis bonis contentus esset <et> nec mortem nec
35 deos extimesceret. habes formam Epicuri uitae beatae uerbis
Zenonis expressam, nihil ut possit negari.

28. acutissimus R V P G B K.   32. sin R V P G B 1-3 K 1 S E 1 2
                                                 r
W 1 M 2 D C Π O 2 3 8.   si K 2 W 2 M 1 J O 1 ed. H.   si uo O 7.
33. iucundi R V G B K.   iocundi R 10 16. ‖ praesertim si et B 3 W 1 2 M 1 2
                                                                     fi
D Π O 3 7.   praesertim si̹ E 2.   praesertim & R *atr. nigr. superscr.*
  cū
prẹsertim & V *man. ant. superscr.*   praesertim cū ꞁ O 8.   praesertim si C.
praesertim et P G B 2 K 1 E.   praesertim cum O 1.   34. contemptus G
in contentus *alt. man. mut.*   ‖ esset nec R 1 6 7 10 16 17 V P 1-4 G B 1-3
K 1 2 S E L 2-6 W 1 2 M 1 2 D C Π J O 1-3 7 8 ed. H.   esset et nec
corr. Heinius.

me audiente Athenis: Cicero spent
79–77 B.C. in Greece, and the earlier part
of that period in Athens, and it was then
that he, along with Atticus, heard Zeno
and other philosophers.

Zeno: this was Zeno of Sidon, the
leading Epicurean philosopher of his day;
cf. N.D. i 21, 59 'principe Epicureorum'
and 'coryphaeum'; a man of clear and
polished style, cf. N.D. *ibid.* 'non igitur
ille, ut plerique, sed isto modo, ut tu,
distincte, grauiter, ornate'; and great
industry, cf. Diog. L. x 25 πολυγράφος
ἀνήρ. See also Zeller, *Ph. d. Griech.*[3]
III i, 373; *Stoics, etc.* p. 389.

[**eum esse beatum qui**...: cf. Epicur.
Epist. iii *ap.* Diog. Laert. x 133 (Usener,
Epicur. p. 65) ἐπεὶ τίνα νομίζεις εἶναι
κρείττονα τοῦ καὶ περὶ θεῶν ὅσια δοξάζοντος
καὶ περὶ θανάτου διὰ παντὸς ἀφόβως ἔχοντος
καὶ τὸ τῆς φύσεως ἐπιλελογισμένου τέλος
καὶ τὸ μὲν τῶν ἀγαθῶν πέρας ὡς ἔστιν
εὐσυμπλήρωτόν τε καὶ εὐπόριστον διαλαμ-
βάνοντος, τὸ δὲ τῶν κακῶν ὡς ἢ χρόνους ἢ
πόνους ἔχει βραχεῖς, τὴν δὲ ὑπό τινων
δεσπότιν εἰσαγομένην πάντων διαγελῶντος
εἱμαρμένην κ.τ.λ.]

aut in omni aut in magna parte:
i 1, 1 n.

si interueniret, si...foret...sin: *si
interueniret* is the protasis, the other
si clause and the *sin* clause respectively
modify the two limbs into which the
apodosis is divided. Küh. compares Fam.
xv 14, 4 'si quae sunt onera tuorum, si
tanta sunt, ut...possis, propera; ...sin
maiora, considera...'

cogitantem: for the participle with
general reference see exx. in n. on 'licet'
i 38, 91.

et nec: *et*, which is required to correspond to the *et* before *ante* and easily fell
out after *esset*, was restored by Hei.
Posen Progr. p. 8, who shows that Hand,
Tursell. IV 130, misunderstands Kritz on
Sall. Cat. 58, 1 and is not supported by
his exx. in his view that in *neque...neque*
the former often = *et neque*, the fact being
that in many instances the two words are
not correlatives but the former = *et non*,
connecting its clause with the preceding
context, and the latter only joins on a
negative clause to the clause so connected.
Hei. compares Sall. 2, 3 'quod si regum
...uirtus...ualeret, aequabilius...sese res
humanae haberent, neque aliud alio ferri,
neque mutari ac misceri omnia cerneres';
11, 3 'auaritia...semper infinita, insata-
bilis est, neque copia neque inopia min-
uitur.' The former ex. is good; in the
latter I think *neque...neque* are correlatives, with asyndeton.

habes...expressam, 'here you have
pourtrayed by Zeno the happy life as conceived by Epicurus.' *forma* often = 'outline,' 'sketch,' but *expressam*, ἐξηκασ-
μένην, makes it more substantial, cf. 2, 3
'solida quaedam res et expressa,' and
note there; also Off. i 5, 15 'formam
quidem ipsam...et tamquam faciem honesti
uides'; Fin. ii 15, 48 'habes undique
expletam et perfectam...formam honestatis.'

XVIII. **39.** Quid ergo? huiusne uitae propositio et cogitatio aut Thyestem leuare poterit aut Aeetam, de quo paulo ante dixi, aut Telamonem pulsum patria exsulantem atque egentem? in quo haec admiratio fiebat:

5   Hícine est ille Télamon, modo quem glória ad
                    caelum éxtulit,
   Quem áspectabant, cuíus ob os Graii óra obuerte-
                         bánt sua?

40. Quodsi cui, ut ait idem,

10   simul ánimus cum re cóncidit,

                   ne
XVIII. § **39**, 1. huius uitę V.   2. thyestem R V G K   B 2 3 *alii.* ‖
         oetä
aeetam G.   a&am R *ead. man. superscr. ut uid.*   a&am V.   aetä B 1.
o
aetam P *al. atr. superscr.* K *eod. atr. superscr.*   eetä S.   aetam II a *ex* o *mut.*
oetam R 6 16   E 2   L 2–6   M 1 2   O 7 8   W 1 (*marg.*).   ◇etä J.   eotam R 17.
          i
oetham R 7   O 3.   oętam R 10.   ęt,ā E.   etiam B 2   D.   3. exulantem
R V G   B 1 2   K E.   4. ammiratio B.   5. hicine B E.   hic inest B 2.
                                             ic
hiccine R 6 17   P 2   B 3   S   E 2   W 1   M 1 2   D C II   O 1–3 7 8.   haecine
R 1 *al. atr. suppl.*   haecine V G K.   heccine W 2   J.   ‖   Telamon R V G
B 1 2   K E   M 1   D C.   thelamon B 3   M 2   O 3 7.   7. aspectabant R V G
M 1–3   K   E 2   W 1 2   M 2   J   O 2.   exspectabant C.   expectabant S E
M 1   D II   O 1 3 7 8.   ‖ graii B 2   S   M 2   D II   O 2.   grai R V P G   B 1
E 1 2   W 2   J   O 1 3.   graï W 1 *alt.* i *eiecto.*   grauiora C   O 7.   gretia M 1.

§ **40**, 10. cum re concidit M 1   W 1   O 2   II *at* cum re *in ras.* V *at in ras.*: cū
in litura, re *fuerat* rem, c *post* n *in litura.*   re concidit R 6 (cum *om.*).
rē condidit R   K 2   E   W 2.   rem condidit S *at in marg.* re cōcidit.   rem
condidit R 7   P 1–4   G   B 1–3   K   E 3   L 2–4 6   M 2   D C   O 8 Gr.   rem
                                                 ut rem
condit O 1.   res condidit O 7.   simul rē condidit L 5   J *cett. om.*   idnem
condidit E 2 *al. atr. superscr.*   animus condidit R 17 *cett. om.*   simul rem
concidit O 3.

XVIII. § **39. quid ergo**: i 25, 60 n. on 'quid enim?'

propositio et cogitatio: ἐν διὰ δυοῖν, 'the mental realisation.'

de quo: as Cic. in c. 12, § 26 spoke of both Thyestes and Aeetes Bent., followed by Dav., read *de quibus*, but Cic. is not bound to maintain strict accuracy of detail in dialogues such as this.

Telamonem pulsum...egentem: after Telamon had lost his son Ajax in the Trojan war and banished his other son Teucer, he was deprived of his throne by a stranger and suffered great hardships in exile, but was ultimately restored by Teucer, who returned from Cyprus to prove to his father, by the testimony of Eurysaces, his innocence with regard to the death of Ajax. Cf. Ribbeck, *Röm. Trag.* pp. 420–1.

pulsum...exsulantem atque egentem: the three participles are not co-ordinate; *exsulantem atque egentem* give his position when *pulsus patria* and are in apposition to that expression, 'an exile and even in want.'

in quo: cf. v 9, 24 n. on 'in eo libro.'

hicine est ille: Ribbeck *l. c.* and *Scaen. Rom. Poes. Frag.* I² p. 248 believes that these lines belong to the Eurysaces of Accius. Cicero in *Fam.* ix 26, 2 applies to his own case the line 'quem aspectabant? ...sua.' Earlier editors (e.g. Dav.) thought that the lines belonged to the Telamo of Ennius.

For the spelling and pronunciation of *Graii* see Brambach, *Neugestalt.* pp. 184 foll.; Lindsay, *Lat. Lang.* p. 53. In *Fam.* ix 26, 2 the MS reading is *grai lora.*

§ **40. simul animus cum re concidit**: Ribbeck *ll. cc.* seems right in printing these words as part of the same extract

a grauibus illis antiquis philosophis petenda medicina est, non
ab his uoluptariis. quam enim isti bonorum copiam dicunt?
fac sane esse summum bonum non dolere (quamquam id non
uocatur uoluptas, sed non necesse est nunc omnia); idne est quo
15 traducti luctum leuemus? sit sane summum malum dolere; in
eo igitur qui non est, si malo careat, continuone fruitur summo
bono? **41.** quid tergiuersamur, Epicure, nec fatemur eam nos

11. medicina est non R 6 7   V W 1   O 1 8.   medicina est si non R P 1 2 4
G B K S   E 1 2   W 2   D C Π J   O 3 7.   medicina est sed non P 3   B 3   M 2   O 2.
medicina est et non M 1.   medicina est sm̄ B 2.   13.   non dolôre (*i.e.* o *in* e *mut.*)
V G K.   non dolere B 1   W 1   D   O 7.   non dolere B 2.   15. malum
dolôre (o *in* e *mut.*) V G K.   malum dolôre E *eod. atr.*   malum dolere B 1 3
E 2   W 1 2   D   O 7.   malum dolore B 2.

as the lines given above from the Eurysaces of Accius. For the expression Bent.
compares Ter. Eun. 241 'simul consilium
cum re amisti?'
antiquis: sc. Pythagoras, Socrates,
Plato ; compare § 36 above.
non: when the *non*-clause stands
merely in contrast to the preceding clause
non is not preceded by *et* or *ac*; compare
ii 12, 29 'quasi de uerbo non de re
laboretur.' With *et* or *ac* a correction is
introduced; compare i 7, 13 n. on 'et non
eos.' See Hand, *Tursell.* I 474. The
readings *et si* and *sed* arise by dittography
or quasi-dittography out of the preceding
est (*e*).
uoluptariis: compare ii 7, 18 'Epicurus homo...uoluptarius'; v 31, 88;
Fin. i 11, 37; iv 12, 31; v 25, 74; in
Pis. 18, 42.
bonorum copiam: compare v 33, 94;
N.D. i 40, 111 'suppeditatio, inquis,
bonorum nullo malorum interuentu.
quorum tandem bonorum? uoluptatum
credo...'
summum bonum non dolere: Epicurus recognised two divisions of pleasure,
pleasures of repose and pleasures of motion, Diog. L. x 136 ἡδονὴ ἡ κατὰ κίνησιν
καὶ ἡ καταστηματική; Fin. ii 10, 31
'stante...mouente,' *ibid.* § 32 'ea quae in
motu est...illa stabilis.' But he declared
the pleasure of repose of mind to be the
higher; Diog. L. x 139 ὅρος τοῦ μεγέθους
τῶν ἡδονῶν ἡ παντὸς τοῦ ἀλγοῦντος ὑπεξαί-
ρεσις; also x 121 τὴν εὐδαιμονίαν διχῇ
νοεῖσθαι, τήν τε ἀκροτάτην, οἵα ἐστὶ περὶ
τὸν θεόν, ἐπίτασιν οὐκ ἔχουσαν· καὶ τὴν
ἀνθρωπίνην, ἔχουσαν προσθήκην καὶ ἀφαί-
ρεσιν ἡδονῶν. Fin. ii 10, 30 'hanc in motu
uoluptatem...interdum ita extenuat, ut
M'. Curium putes loqui'; i 11, 37 (where
see Madv.'s n.) 'maximam uoluptatem
illam habemus, quae percipitur omni
dolore detracto'; Off. iii 33, 118 'dicunt

enim uoluptatis magnitudinem doloris
detractione finiri.' Compare iii 20, 47 n.
on 'non crescere uoluptatem dolore detracto'; Zeller, *Stoics, etc.* c. xix pp. 446
foll.; *Ph. d. Griechen* iii. 1² pp. 402 foll.
quamquam id non uocatur uoluptas:
Cic. in the beginning of Fin. ii maintains
that the word *uoluptas* (ἡδονή) is not used
by Epicurus in the ordinary sense of the
term when he applies it to the pleasure
of repose, Fin. ii 3, 7; 4, 11; 5, 16.
sed non necesse est nunc omnia: sc.
persequi. Verbs of saying are sometimes
omitted in short semi-parenthetic clauses.
idne est quo...leuemus, 'is it (i.e. *non
dolere*) a remedy to which we are to resort
in order to mitigate grief?'
in eo: *dolere* implies *dolor* and to
this *in eo* refers. Compare Anon. apud
Olivetum, quoted by Mo.
si malo careat: Mo. and Küh. take
these words as explanatory of *in eo...est*
but they are not necessary for that purpose; they may possibly be a gloss due
to an idea that they were so required. If
the words are sound the explanation of
Hei. seems best: from the Stoic standpoint Cicero could not admit that pain
was an evil but he allows the assumption
to pass for the sake of argument. Trans.
'supposing him to be free from evil.' It
is more likely that the words are sound
and that *fruatur* should be read; *a* and *i*
often interchange in MSS.
careat: compare i 36, 88 n. on 'dicitur
enim.'
§ 41. tergiuersamur: compare Off. iii
33, 118 (also of the Epicureans) 'non
incallide tergiuersantur,' where Beier
(quoted here by Küh.) derives the metaphor from those 'qui subinde terga dant
ante tubam, memores galeatum sero
duelli paenitere,' advancing in a hesitating
manner and shrinking from openly declaring themselves as enemies.

H.

4

dicere uoluptatem quam tu idem, cum os perfricuisti, soles
dicere? sunt haec tua uerba necne? in eo quidem libro qui
20 continet omnem disciplinam tuam (fungar enim iam interpretis
munere, ne quis me putet fingere), dicis haec: nec equidem
habeo quod intellegam bonum illud, detrahens eas
uoluptates quae sapore percipiuntur, detrahens eas
quae auditu et cantibus, detrahens eas etiam quae ex
25 formis percipiuntur oculis, suauis motiones, siue quae
aliae uoluptates in toto homine gignuntur quolibet
sensu; nec uero ita dici potest, mentis laetitiam solam
esse in bonis. laetantem enim mentem ita noui: spe

§ **41**, 18. cum os R V P G.   cū nos B O 7.   eam nos R 10 16.
22. intellegam R V G B K.   23. *post* detrahens *et ante* eas quę auditu *habet* V *in
marg. e regione contextus* eas q̄ reb; pcipiu N̄'uenereis detrahens *antiqui correctoris
man. script.*   24. et cantibus R V P G B 1-3 K 1 2 S E 1-3 W 1 2 M 1 2
D C Π J O 2 3 8 *om.* O 7.   25. suauis R V G B 1 2 K W 2.   26. quolibet
R 1 10 16 G B 1 2 E 2 M 1 W 1 O 3.   quo libet V *at* o *in ras.*   qd̄ libet E.
qd̄ K 1.   quol₃ W 2.   quolibet S.   quolibet e M 2 O 1.
tuo
e

os perfricuisti: compare Mart. xi 27, 7
'aut cum perfricuit frontem posuitque
pudorem.'

in eo quidem libro: sc. in the περὶ
τέλους, a work in 37 books on the *summum
bonum*. Compare Athenaeus vii 280 a
κἂν τῷ περὶ τέλους δέ φησιν οὕτω πως· οὐ
γὰρ ἔγωγε δύναμαι νοῆσαι τἀγαθὸν ἀφαιρῶν
μὲν τὰς διὰ χυλῶν ἡδονάς, ἀφαιρῶν δὲ τὰς
δι' ἀφροδισίων, ἀφαιρῶν δὲ τὰς δι' ἀκροαμάτων, ἀφαιρῶν δὲ τὰς διὰ μορφῆς κατ'
ὄψιν ἡδείας κινήσεις and xii 546 e; Diog.
L. x 6 ἐν δὲ τῷ περὶ τέλους γράφειν οὕτως·
οὐ γὰρ ἔγωγε ἔχω τί νοήσω τἀγαθὸν
ἀφαιρῶν...διὰ μορφῶν, almost as in Athen.
l. c. See Usener, *Epicurea* § 67.
The same passage is referred to in
Athenaeus vii 278 f.; Fin. ii 3, 7 'Epicurus
...quippe qui testificetur, ne intellegere
quidem se posse, ubi sit aut quod sit
ullum bonum praeter illud, quod cibo et
potione et aurium delectatione et obscena
uoluptate capiatur.'

nec...habeo quod=*mihi deest aliquid
quod* Küh.

bonum illud=τἀγαθόν, the subject of
Epicurus' enquiry. Sff. Schlenger's change
to *bonum ullum* 'from Eliens. 1' is unnecessary.

auditu et cantibus: a double translation of the Gk δι' ἀκροαμάτων. Nissen's
conj. *auditu e cantibus* is adopted by
T.S. Hei. and Schiche and noticed by
Ml. with the comment 'uerisimiliter.'

quae ex formis...motiones=τὰς διὰ
μορφῆς κατ' ὄψιν ἡδείας κινήσεις of Athe-

naeus *l. c.* Usener, *Epicurea* § 67, thinks
that the true reading here is 'detrahens
eas quae...*detrahens eas quae* auditu e
cantibus' comparing 20, 46 'saporem, inquit, et corporum complexum, et ludos
atque cantus...' and the aposiopesis in
18, 43 end; the lacuna is due to *librari-
orum culpa.*

nec uero ita: *ita* redundantly anticipates the clause *mentis...in bonis.* Hand,
Tursell. III p. 483.

laetantem enim: Sff. thought it necessary to alter *enim* to *etiam* but the
contrast is between pleasures of the intellect and pleasures of sense; in the
previous clause the emphasis is on *mentis.*
The argument seems a distortion of Epicurus' view. According to Epicurus the
highest pleasure consisted in ἀταραξία,
see above, § 40 n. on 'summum bonum
non dolere.' The pleasures of motion
were only pleasant because they gave rise
to a hope that, a disturbing cause being
removed by the motion, a state of repose
would ensue.

ita noui: another anticipatory *ita* but
with a restriction implied 'only if one
has a hope...' For the absence of a word
of limitation cf. ii 19, 44 n. on 'tantum
...quantum.'

fore ut...careat: explanatory expansion
of *spe eorum omnium, quae supra dixi.*

§ **42**. **norit**: cf. *noui* § 41 above; Fin.
ii 3, 8 'uerum hoc loco sumo uerbis his
eandem certe uim uoluptatis Epicurum
nosse quam ceteros,' and Madv.'s n.

eorum omnium, quae supra dixi, fore ut natura iis po-
30 tiens dolore careat. **42.** atque haec quidem his uerbis, quiuis
ut intellegat quam uoluptatem norit Epicurus. deinde paulo
infra: saepe quaesiui, inquit, ex iis, qui appellabantur
sapientes, quid haberent quod in bonis relinquerent,
si illa detraxissent, nisi si uellent uoces inanis fun-
35 dere; nihil ab iis potui cognoscere. qui si uirtutes
ebullire uolent et sapientias, nihil aliud dicent nisi
eam uiam, qua efficiantur eae uoluptates quas supra
dixi. quae sequuntur in eadem sententia sunt, totusque liber,

29. forte K. forte G *in* fore *mut. alt. man.* ‖ natura iis O 3. n̄a iis S.
natura hiis R 6. naturalis R V P 1 3 4 G B 2 3 K 1 E L 4 M 2.
naturalis̩ B 1. natu K 2. naturali R 17 P 2 L 3 5 6 W 1 2 D C J
O 1 2 7. naturali II *litt. post* i *eras.* naturalibus R 7 E 2 L 2 O 8.
uel natura uel M 1. ‖ potiens G L 2 5 W 2. patiens L 6. potens O 8.
potius R 17 P 2 M 1 D C J. pocius K 2 W 1.
§ 42, 31. intellegat R V G B K. 32. ex iis M 2. ex his R V P B K
W 1 2 O 3. ‖ appellabantur B 3 K D II O 3. apellabantur G *alt. man.*
superscr. appellantur K 2. 33. quod in bonis W 1 D C O 1 2. qd in
bonis II. quid in bonis B 1 K 2 S E 1 2 W 2 M 2 J O 3 8. quid bonis
K 1 *at in et* s *atr. nigr. script.* q, ĭ bonis M 1. quid in boni G B 2. quⓄd
in boni V *i.e.* i *in* o *mut.* quid ịn boni R *alio atr. corr.* quid in bono O 7.
ꟷbonis
quid bono B 3. quid homini P. ‖ relinquerint G i *in* e *alt. man. mut.*
34. detracxissent nisi si si G *tertium* si *expunx. et conf. alt. man.* ‖ uellent E 2
W 1 M 1 II O 7. uollent S. uolu̱nt E. uolent R V P G B 1 3 K
W 2 M 2 D (*non ut Küh.*) J O 1-3 8. uolunt B 2. nolent C. ‖ inanis
R V G B K E W 2. inanes B 2 3. 35. ab his R G B K. 37. uia̱m R 1 6
P 1-4 G B 1-3 S E 1 2 W 2 M 1 2 D C J O 1-3 8. uiā W 1 II.
uia̸m V. uia̱m K *litt. eras.* uitam O 7. ‖ qua̧e G *alt. man. corr.* ‖
efficiantur haec K 1.

uoces inanis fundere: cf. v 26, 73
'inanis sonos fundere.'

uirtutes…sapientias: the plur. disparages their endless harping upon the
words *uirtus* and *sapientia*. Cf. i 2, 3 n.
on ' poetas.'

ebullire, 'however pompously they
may persist in prating of virtue and
wisdom.' Nonius 26 s.v. *ebullire* quotes
this passage with the reading *uolens* and
lower down *nisi eam uim*…. Dav. proposed *nolent* for *uolent* and Bent. held
that either *si…nolent* or *nisi…uolent* must
be read. But *uolent* is sound. The meaning is much the same as if Cic. had
written *si maxime…uolent*. *ebullire* = ' to
talk pompously of,' lit. ' to bubble over
with,' ' to splutter about,' cf. Fin. v 27,
80 where Epicurus' word is turned against
himself. Bent. was sure that Cic. was

translating Gk παφλάζειν. Dav. remarks
that the Epicureans held that for all
other philosophers the virtues κόμποι
κενοὶ ψοφοῦσιν ἀντ' ὀνειράτων (Alexis ap.
Athen. viii p. 336) and compares Lucian,
Timon § 117 ἀρετήν τινα καὶ ἀσώματα καὶ
λήρους μεγάλῃ τῇ φωνῇ ξυνειρόντων and
Diog. L. x 7 where Epic. himself taunts
them with καύχησιν σοφιστικήν.

nisi eam uiam: Epicurus held that
virtue was not to be sought for its own
sake but only because it conducted to
happiness of life, cf. Diog. L. x 138;
Epicurus περὶ τέλους in Athenaeus xii
546 f. τιμητέον τὸ καλὸν καὶ τὰς ἀρετὰς καὶ
τὰ τοιουτότροπα ἐὰν ἡδονὴν παρασκευάζῃ·
ἐὰν δὲ μὴ παρασκευάζῃ, χαίρειν ἐατέον.
Fin. i 13, 42 foll. and Madvig's n.

in eadem sententia: *eiusdem sententiae,* cf. i 39, 94 n.

qui est de summo bono, refertus est et uerbis et sententiis
40 talibus. **43.** ad hancine igitur uitam Telamonem illum reuocabis
ut leues aegritudinem, et, si quem tuorum adflictum maerore
uideris, huic acupenserem potius quam aliquem Socraticum
libellum dabis? hydrauli hortabere ut audiat uoces potius quam
Platonis? expones, quae spectet, florida et uaria? fasciculum ad
45 naris admouebis? incendes odores et sertis redimiri iubebis et
rosa? si uero aliquid etiam—, tum plane luctum omnem absterseris.

39. refertus est et E 2 II O 8.   refertus ⁒ et V *atr. ant. suppl.*   refertus
est (et *om.*) S W 2 M 1   D C.   refertus et R 1 6   P 1 3 4   G B 2 3 K 1 2

E 3 L 4-6 W 1 M 2 J O 2.   refertur et E 1 L 3 R 7.   refert ͂ R 17.
refectus et O 7.   referctus et O 1 3.   ▪effectus ut L 2. ‖ et uerbis et sententiis
talibus R 17 V G B 1-3 K S E 1 2 W 1 2 J O 1 7 8.   talibus et uerbis
et sententiis C D.

§ **43**, 40. hancine R V G B K.   hanccine R 10 16 W 1   D C O 3 8 7.
h
anccine P.   hanc ne O 1.   hāc ne W 2.   hanc me B 2.   41. adflictum
R V P G K.   adfluctum E.   afflictum R 10 16 B 1 L 2-6 C.
42. accipenserem R P G B 1-3 K 1   E 2 W 1 2 M 2 D C Π J O 1-3.
pi
accipenserem V.   accipiensere͂ E.   accipiensere M 1.   accipiens rem O 7.
                                                                    v
accipienserem O 8 Nonius p. 550.   43. hydraliſ V d *fort. mut.* ſ *alio atr. inculc.*
hyΔραΛI R K E.   hTΔrali G.   hyÁPAΛI P.   hydrali B Gr.   hyarali R 17
S W 2 D C O 7.   hy arali B 2.   κυθάραϛ M 2 B 3.   αὐλῶν W 1.
aulon R 6. *om.* M 1.   44. expones R 6 W 1 O 1.   expones Π *at* s *in ras.*
exponet O 2.   exponens R 1 17 P 1-4 G B 1-3 K 1 2 S̄ E M 1 2 C O 3
ed. H.   exponēs R 7 E 2 D.   expone͂sq: V *al. atr. corr.*   exponensq;
R 10 16 O 7.   expōnes L 5.   expōnes ponēs O 8.   expoĩtioẽs W 2.
expositiones J B 3 *marg.* ‖ quae spectet R 6 17 V P 4 G.   quae spect & R 1
i.e. quae *in* q; *al. atr. corr.*   que spectat K 1 O 1.   quae expectat R 10 16
P 1 2 B 1 S D J O 3.   Q̄ expectat W 2.   que expetet O 8.   quae expetat P 3.
45. naris R V G B 1 2 K. ‖ et sertis R 1 10 16 V P G K 1 B 1-3 S W 1 2
D C Π O 2 7 8. ‖ iubebis R V P G.   uidebis R 16.   uidebus O 2.

liber qui est de: cf. i 11, 24 n.
§ **43. acupenserem**: this spelling
seems supported by the MSS in the extract from Lucilius Fin. ii 8, 24 *accubans
aere* A, *accubant aere* E. The readings
are similar in § 25, and in 28, 91 A has
accupem se re me non and BE have
accupenserem mene non. Cf. Kl. prooem.
xii. Ml. and Schiche here and Marx in
Lucilius 1240 'acupensere cum decimano'
adopt the same spelling. Athenaeus vii
294 f. has τὸν ἀκκιπήσιον. Keller and
Holder in Hor. Sat. ii 2, 47 have *acipen-
sere* supported by their MSS there. Pliny
N. H. ix 17, 27 says of this fish 'apud
antiquos piscium nobilissimus habitus...
nullo nunc in honore est.'
hydrauli: the water organ, invented
by Ctesibius of Alexandria, who lived
in the reign of the second Euergetes,
Ptolemy Physcon, 170—116 B.C. (Athen.

iv 174 d). It is described by his pupil
Hero of Alexandria, Pneumat. i 42 (vol. i
pp. 192 *sqq.* ed. Schmidt). Athen. iv
174 b—f; xi 497 d: Vitruvius x 8 p. 261.
We may probably, with Bouh., infer
from the use of Gk letters in several of
the best MSS that the word was not yet
established in Latin: in Athen. *l. c.* it is
ἡ ὑδραυλις.
et sertis: *et* can only be retained to
connect what follows with *incendes odores,*
as *et...et* cannot naturally be correlatives
here. Hei. brackets *et*, F.A.W. Bai. and
others eject, and they are very possibly
right, for the two short sentences *incendes
odores?* and *sertis ... rosa?* correspond
better to the short sentences that precede.
si uero aliquid etiam: Jeep, *Progr.
Guelf.* 1865 p. 13, conj. *etiam amorum
plane,* which Ml. thinks probable. But

XIX. **44.** Haec Epicuro confitenda sunt aut ea, quae modo expressa ad uerbum dixi, tollenda de libro uel totus liber potius abiciundus; est enim confertus uoluptatibus. quaerendum igitur, quem ad modum aegritudine priuemus eum qui ita dicat:

5　　...pol míhi fortuna mágis nunc defit quám genus. Námque regnum súppetebat mi, út scias, quanto é loco, Quántis opibus, quíbus de rebus lápsa fortuna óccidat.

XIX. § **44**, 1. aut ea R V P K.　　aꝰ ea R 16.　　ut ea G ut *in* aut *alt. man. mut.*　　aūt ea R 10.　　3. abiciundus R V G B 1 2 K E 1 3 J O 1. abiciundus R 7　P 1 4　B 3　S　E 2　L 2 6　W 2　M 1 2　D C　O 3 7 8 ed. H. abiiciundus R 6　L 4　W 1　Π　O 2.　‖ confertus R V P　B 1 2　K 1 2　W 1 2 D Π O 2 7 8.　confertis G *alt. man. superscr.*　conferctus O 3.　4. priuemus B 1 3　K 1　E 2　W 1 2　D C Π　O 1-3 7 8.　priuemꝰ K 2.　priuemur V *atr. uiridi superscr.* R *atr. nigro superscr.*　priuemur G　B 2.　5. mihi R V B. m R 10　P K 1.　mꝰ R 16.　‖ quam genus R V P　B 1 2　K 1　W 1　D O 1 3 7 8.　qꝙ genus G *at* qꝙ *in* quā *alt. man. mut.*　9. occidat R 6　B 3　W 1 M 2　O 1-3.　accidat R V　P 4　G　B 1 2　K 1　S　E 1 2　W 2　M 1　D C Π J O 7 8.　accidat P *al. atr. suppl.*

the aposiopesis seems natural; cf. Ursinus in Mo. 'Tullius uerecundissime...quae turpia erant, notauit, τὰ ἀφροδίσια, quo inuisiorem redderet Epicurum ob impudentiam.' Camerarius cft. Fin. ii 10, 29 'eam autem [uoluptatem] ita persequitur: quae palato percipiatur, quae auribus; cetera addit quae si appelles, honos praefandus sit.' Orelli (ed. Oxon.) compares Menander Κυβερνῆται: τἀργύριον εἶναι, μειράκιον, σοι φαίνεται οὐ τῶν ἀναγκαίων καθ' ἡμέραν μόνον τιμὴν παρασχεῖν δυνατόν, ἄρτων, ἀλφίτων, ὄξους, ἐλαίου, μείζονος δ' ἄλλου τινός. (Meineke *Fragg. Com. Gr.* iv 156.) The senses are being taken in turn: taste, hearing, sight, smell have been dealt with in succession; touch remains, cf. 20, 46 'corporum complexum.' [For *aliquid* as a euphemism for τὰ ἀφροδίσια see Friedrich's note on Catullus lxiv 145, who quotes, besides this passage, Juv. x 207, Prop. ii 22, 11, Ov. Her. xv 153, Cic. Fam. ix 22, 4.]

absterseris: i 13, 30 n. on 'sustuleris.' XIX. § **44. aut** contrasts *confitenda* and *tollenda*; **uel** corrects *tollenda*.

pol mihi fortuna: these lines are from the same poet as the lines *ex opibus s*... and *quid petam pr*.... below: Ribbeck and Vahlen believe them to belong to the Thyestes of Ennius: Ribb. *Röm. Trag.* p. 201; *Scaen. Poes. Frag.* i 69 Vahlen,

Ennian. Poes. Rell.[2] p. 186. The metre is trochaic tetram. catalectic.

magis: for *s* final in O.L. poetry cf. i 5, 10 n.: so *quibus* below.

defit = *deficit*, chiefly in O.L. poetry; once in Livy (ix 11, 6).

genus, 'birth' not 'my children' as Hei. takes it. Thyestes, returning from exile, appears in rags (cf. Arist. Ach. 433 τῶν Θυεστείων ῥακῶν) and reveals himself, as Ribb. conjectures, to some secret partisans, using the words in the text.

rebus, 'power.'

occidat: this must be read here instead of *accidat* of the best MSS. The two words frequently interchange. In i 35, 85 *occidisset* is plainly right against the best MSS, but there the reading of inferior MSS is reinforced by that of V[2], while here V[2] is silent. Passages cited by some edd. in support of *accidat* here are not parallel, e.g. 'quo accidam' below, and the opening lines of Ennius' Medea Exul 'utinam ne in nemore Pelio securibus | caesa accidisset abiegna ad terram trabes' quoted by Priscian vii 8, 41, Varro L.L. vii 33 and by Cic. in several places, for which see Mayor on N.D. iii 31, 75. In these passages that to which the fall takes place is denoted; *accido* means 'to fall to,' and no good instance of the word meaning merely 'to fall' has been put forward.

10 quid? huic calix mulsi impingendus est, ut plorare desinat, aut
aliquid eius modi? ecce tibi ex altera parte ab eodem poëta:

Ex ópibus summis ópis egens, Hectór, tuae.

huic subuenire debemus; quaerit enim auxilium:

Quíd petam praésidi aut éxsequar quóue nunc
15   Aúxilio exili aút fuga fréta sim?
Árce et urbe órba sum. quo áccidam? quo áp-
plicem?
Cuí nec arae pátriae domi stant, fráctae et dis-
iectaé iacent,
20   Fána flamma déflagrata, tósti alti stant párietes
Déformati atque ábiete crispa....

10. impingendus R P G B 2 K S.   inpingendus V B 1 E.   12. haector
tuae R V G K.   hectorne S.   hec tortue B 2.   hec tortue E.   13. quaerit
R G.   querit R 10 16 V B 2 K E.   14. praesidii R G.   presidii V B S.
p̄sidii B 3 E.   presidii B 2 K D O 1 3 7 8. ‖ exequar R V G K S E O 1.
exsequar B 1.   15. exilii R V P 1 4 G B 1-3 S E 1 L 2-6 W 1 2 D
O 1-3 7 8.   exiḷlii K. ‖ fuga R 1 6 V P 1-4 G B 1-3 K 1 2 S E 1 2
W 1 2 M 1 2 D Π J O 2 3 7 8 ed. H.   fuge R 17 O 1.   16. accidam S
at spatio post i *relicto et ras. fuisse uidetur.*   accedam R 1 6 17 V P 1-4 G
                                                                    ac
B 1-3 K 1 2 E 1 2 L 2-6 W 1 2 M 1 2 D C Π J O 2 3 7 8 ed. H.   cedam
O 1.   20. tosti alti Π L 4.   tosti alii R 1 6 7 10 17 V P G B 1-3 K 1 2 S
E 1-3 L 2 3 5 6 W 1 2 M 1 2 D O 1-3 7 8.   toti alii D C.   tosti allii R 16.
21. abiete R 1 V P K.   abiecte G *at* c *expunx. alt. man.*   abiecte R 10 16
L 6.   abiecta O 7.

In support of *fortuna occidat* Sff. well
quotes Hor. Carm. iv 4, 70 foll. 'occidit,
occidit | spes omnis et fortuna nostri |
nominis Hasdrubale interempto.'

impingendus, 'must we thrust a cup
of mead into his hands?'

Ex opibus....: an iambic trimeter. This
and the three extracts following are from
the Andromacha Aechmalotis of Ennius,
cf. Vahlen *Enn. Poes. Rell.*[2] pp. 131 ff.,
Ribb. *Röm. Trag.* p. 137, *Scaen. Rom.
Poes. Frag.* 1 pp. 24—6.

In her distress Andromache misses the
protection and help of Hector. Vahl.
l.c. quotes Eur. Andr. 523 ὦ πόσις πόσις
ἐλθὲ σὺν χεῖρα καὶ δόρυ σύμμαχον κτησαί-
μαν, Πριάμου παῖ and Tro. 587 μόλοις, ὦ
πόσις, μοι σᾶς δάμαρτος ἄλκαρ: see also
ibid. p. cciii.

The paronomasia *opibus...opis* is characteristic of O. L., cf. *urbe orba* below.

Quid petam praesidi: the first three
lines are cretic tetrameters as Bentley first
discovered. Cicero in Or. iii 47, 183
quotes 'quid petam praesidi, aut exsequar
quoue nunc' as examples of cretics.

In *auxilio* and *abiete* i is treated as a
consonant before the following vowel.

There is hiatus after *auxilio* and *exili*.
domi has the final syllable treated as
short. T.S. and Schiche read *auxiliod*
after Ribbeck. Ml. marks the passage as
corrupt.

accidam: as suppliant, Gk προσπίπτω,
προσπίτνω.

quo applicem = *quo me applicem*. This
intrans. use of transitive verbs is specially
common with verbs of motion, Küh.
Gram. II p. 67. Cf. i 44, 107 n. on
'recipiat.'

quo = *cui patrono*. This is better than
to see in the words a metaphor from
bringing a ship to land. The meaning
more naturally follows upon that of *quo
accidam*. For the *ius applicationis* see
Or. i 39, 177 'si se ad aliquem quasi
patronum applicauisset' and Wilkins'
notes and references.

cui nec arae...: the metre is trochaic
tetrameter catalectic.

deflagrata: the verb is usually intrans.
but cf. Cat. 4, 6, 12 'in cinere deflagrati
imperii.' See Naegelsb. § 97 new ed.

crispa, 'warped,' 'shrivelled,' by the
action of fire.

scitis quae sequantur, et illa in primis:

> O páter, o patria, o Príami domus,
> Saeptum áltisono cardíne templum!
> Vidi égo te astante ope bárbarica
> Tectís caelatis, láqueatis,
> Auro, ébore instructam régifice.

25

45. o poëtam egregium! quamquam ab his cantoribus Euphorionis contemnitur. sentit omnia repentina et necopinata

22. scitis R V P 1 4 G B 1 2 K 1 2 S E 1 2 W 1 2 M 1 Π J O 1 7 8.
          l' scitis
scis B 3 L 6 M 2 C O 2 3.   scis D *al. atr. superscr.* ‖ et illud in primis
                     in
R 6 7 17 B 3 E 2 3 L 2–46 W 1 M 1 D C Π O 1–3.   et illud primis
V *at* d *in ras. ut uid.* & illud imprimis M 2. et illū in primis K 2 W 2 ed. H.
et illū inprimis L 5 J.   et illū primis B 2 E.   et illum primis R P 1 4 G
              r   i
B K O 7.   et illum pmis S *at in marg.* illud impmis.   et illum u'sum in
primis O 8. et illa in primis *corr. Tregder.*   25. astante Π *at linea super*
e *erasa.* adstante V *ras. post* e. abstante M 1. adstantem R 1 P G B 3
K 1 O 2 3.   ad astante R 6. adstantē B 1 E 1 M 2. asstantē B 2.
astantem S E 2 L 5 6 C O 1 8.   astantē R 17 K 2 W 1 2 D J O 7.
27. regifice R 17 B 3 W 1 M 1 2 O 1 2. regifice S *at* m *eraso.* regifice Π
at fuerat regificem.   regificem B 1 K 1.   regificem R 7 G C O 3 7.
regificē R V B 2 K 2 E 1 W 2 D. regificam E 2.   regificā O 8.
regis sedem R 6.
§ **45.** 28. egregium R 10 16 V W 2. aegregium R 1 P. aegrium G
in aegregium *alt. man. mut.* ‖ euphorionis R G B 1–3 K 1 W 1 2 D O 2 3 7.
euphorioneis V *at* e *ante* i *ex* i *fort. mut.* euphrionis O 1. euforionis O 8.
29. contempnitur G. ‖ et necopinata R V P G B 1–3 K 1 S E 1 W 1 M 1 2
D C J O 1–3 7 8.   et ne opinata R 10 16 E 2. et inopinata Π.
ꝺ 1 f opīata W 2.

illa in: *illum* of RGPS[1] differs from
this reading only by *u* for *a*.
O pater: Andromache's father Eetion,
king of Thebe in Cilicia, slain by Achilles.
Il. vi 416. The metre of this and the
next four lines is anapaestic dimeter.
Virgil imitated this passage in Aen. ii 241
'O patria, o diuom domus Ilium, et
incluta bello | moenia Dardanidum,' where
Servius notes 'versus Ennianus.'
templum: cf. i 21, 48 n.; Varro L.L.
vii 2, 6—8 'templum tribus modis dicitur:
ab natura, ab auspiciendo, ab similitudine.
(ab) natura in caelo; ab auspiciis in terra;
ab similitudine sub terra...in terris dictum
templum locus augurii aut auspicii causa
quibusdam conceptis uerbis finitus.' The
home was consecrated to the worship of
the Lares and Penates. Cf. Plaut. Trin.
39 foll. and Brix' n.
astante...laqueatis: quoted also in
i 35, 85 where see notes.
regifice: cf. i 28, 69 n. on 'laetificae.'
§ **45. his cantoribus Euphorionis**, 'the
present-day writers of jingles in Euphorion's style.' Euphorion of Chalcis,

born about 274 B.C., became, late in life,
librarian to Antiochus the Great. Some
of his poems were translated into Latin
verse by Cornelius Gallus of Forum Julii
(69—26 B.C.); cf. edd. on Virg. Ecl.
10, 50. Cicero who preferred the national
and older writers of both Greece and
Rome disparages the Roman Alexandrianism which had come into fashion
within a few years of the date of the
Tusculan Disputations. Some of the
Greek Alexandrian poets tended to sacri-
fice clearness of thought to music of
expression, and this tendency in their
Roman imitators is referred to in *cantoribus* here. The obscurity of Euphorion's
style is noticed in Diu. ii 64, 132.
For the Roman Alexandrianism and
its causes see Mommsen *R.H.* vol. v
pp. 465 foll. (E.T.).
exaggeratis: cf. v 18, 51 *exaggerantem*) (*extenuantem*.
regis: rightly read by Dav. with
inferior MSS for *regis* of the rest. For the
confusion between *regiis* and *regis* cf. the
reading of V in iv 1, 1. Wes. *em.* II

30 esse grauiora. exaggeratis igitur regiis opibus, quae uidebantur
sempiternae fore, quid adiungit?

> Haec ómnia uidi inflámmari,
> Priamó ui uitam euítari,
> Iouis áram sanguine túrpari.

35 **46.** praeclarum carmen! est enim et rebus et uerbis et modis
lugubre. eripiamus huic aegritudinem. quo modo? conlocemus
in culcita plumea, psaltriam adducamus, hedychri incendamus
scutellam, dulciculae potionis aliquid uideamus et cibi. haec

30. regiis G K 2 W 1 2 J O 1.   regis R 1 6 7 17   V   P 1-4   B 1-3
K 1 S E 1 2 M 1 2 D C Π O 2 3 7 8.   34. sanguine R 6 7 17   P G   B 1 3
K 1 E 2 W 1 M 2 D C O 1-3.   sangūe M 1 W 2 Π O 8.   sanguinem
R 1 *eod. atr.*   sanguinē B 2 E 1.   sanguinem V.

§ **46,** 35. carmen R V P.   carnem G *in* carnem *alt. man. mut.*   36. lugubræ
P G (a *conf. alt. man.*)   ‖   conlocemus R V G B K E.   collocemus B 2 3   W 1

O 7.   37. culcita V G   B 1 2   K E.   culcita R *al. atr.* P *al. atr.*   culcita Π.
culcitra R 6   B 3   K 2   E 2   L 6   W 1   M 1 2   D   O 1-3 7 8.   culcit W 2   C.
culsita S. ‖ adducamus P   B 1-3   K   E 2   W 1   M 1 2   D C   O 2.   aducamus
R V G *alt. man. superscr.*   aducamus O 7.   ‖   *post* adducamus *habent* demus
R 6 7 17   P 2   B 3   K 2   E 2 3   L 2-4   M 1   D C   O 1 3 7 8.   damus R   P 4
G   B 1 2   K 1   S   E 1   L 5   W 2   M 2   J.   dcmus V a *in* e *mut.*   damus
P *al. atr. superscr.*   ‖   hedryçum R *eod. atr.*   hedryçum V.   hedrycrum
B K 1 E.   hedrycum P 1 4   C D.   hedricum K 2   E 2   W 1 2   Π   O 1 Gr.
hedricū B 2   J.   edricū S *eod. ut uid. atr.*   hedricrum O 8.   hediricum P 2.
edricum B 3   E 3   M 2 L 6   edricum P 3 e *post lacunam.*   aedricrum G.
herdricū O 7.   hedicum O 3.   hedericā M 1.   cedricum O 2.   hedricm
R 17 *om.* R 6.   hedychri *corr. Maduigius.*   ‖   incendamus R 1 6 7 17   V   P 1-4
G   B 1-3   K 1   E 1 2   L 6   W 2   M 2   D C J   O 1 3 7 8.   intendamus M 1.
intēdamus S.   ‖   *post* incendamus *habent* demus R 6   W 1   O 2 *et superscr.* P 3   Π.
incendamus dcmus L 6.   38. scutellam R V   P 1-3   G   B 1-3   K 1   S   E 1 2
W 1 2   M 2   D C J   O 1-3 7 8.   scutelam R 6.   scultellam P 4   M 1   Π. ‖
uideamus R 1 10 16 17   V   P 1-4   G   B 1-3   K 1 2   E 1 2   W 2   M 2   D C Π J
O 1-3 7.   puideamus S *at* p *extra lineam et atr. nigriore script.*   prouideamus
R 6   W 1   M 1.   addamus O 8 *al. atr. superscr.*   ‖   cibi R V P.   cybi G.
ubi R 10 16.

p. 54 compares variants in Rep. ii
§§ 29—31. It is more natural for Andromache to magnify the wealth of the
Kings of Troy than the wealth of the
King (Priam). If it seemed likely to last
for ever it must have been long established.
Haec omnia...turpari: cf. i 35, 85 and
notes there.

§ **46. modis,** 'melody,' refers to the
lyric parts of the play.

lugubre, 'tragic.' The Andromache
Aechmalotis presented a combination of
tragic incidents grouped round the central
point of the slaying of Astyanax, the last
male of Priam's line, by flinging him from
the walls of captured Troy in spite of

the passionate resistance of his mother
Andromache. See Ribbeck, *Röm. Trag.*
pp. 136 and 141.

huic: sc. *Andromachae.*

**hedychri incendamus scutellam, dulci-
culae potionis aliquid uideamus et cibi:**
this is the emendation of Madvig, adopted
by all recent editors. Beroaldus read
cedrum incendamus, quoting Aen. vii 13
and Od. v 60, and Camerarius, Man. and
Lamb. approved, though Pet. Victorius
had returned to *hedychrum* with some
misgiving 'quod inter unguenta potius
quam odoramenta *hedychrum* a medicis
recensetur.' Dioscorides i 58 καὶ τὸ
καλούμενον δὲ ἡδύχρουν, σκευαζόμενον δὲ

tandem bona sunt quibus aegritudines grauissimae detrahantur;
40 tu enim paulo ante ne intellegere quidem te alia ulla dicebas.
reuocari igitur oportere a maerore ad cogitationem bonorum
conueniret mihi cum Epicuro, si, quid esset bonum, conueniret.
XX. Dicet aliquis: quid ergo? tu Epicurum existimas ista
uoluisse, aut libidinosas eius fuisse sententias? ego uero
minime; uideo enim ab eo dici multa seuere, multa prae-

39. grauissumae G.　　grauissumę V.　　grauissume R K.　　grauissu̲me E. ‖
　　　　v
detrahamr V m *an* nr *incert.*　　　　40. intellegere R V G B K.　　　intellęgere P
e *in* i *mut.*　‖　te quidem R V　P 1 2　G　B 1-3　K 1 2　S　E 1 2　W 2　M 1 2
D C Π J　O 1 3 7 8.　‖　alia ulla D C.　　alia ulla V *at litt. ante* u *eras. et* l *ante*
a *mut.*　　　　alia multa R　P 2 4　G　B 1　K 1 2　E 1 2　L 2 5　J　O 1 8 ed. H.
　　　　r una　　　　　　　　　　　　　　　　　　bona
alia multa P *al. atr. superscr.*　alia mlta R 7 17　B 2　W 2　O 7.　　alia multa Π
al. atr. corr.　　　alia multa S *in marg.* bona alia.　　　bona R 6　P 3　B 3　E 3
L 3 6　W 1　M 1 2　O 2 3.　　　multa alia L 4.　　　41. oportere a Π *at* e *in ras.*

　　　　　　　　　　　　　　　　　　　　　　　　　　　v̄
et fuerat oportet ea.　　　oportet ea R 1 10　P 4　G　B 1 2　K 1.　　　oportet ea V
atr. uiridi suppl.　　　oport & | ęa P *al. atr. corr.*　　　oportet a E 1 3 *ras. inter* t *et* a.
oportet a P 2 3　B 3　L 3 6　M 2　D C　O 2 3.　　　oportet eum L 4　W 1　O 1.
oportet eū L 5　J ed. H.　　　opportet eū K 2　M 1.　　　　oportet eū a O 8.
oportet te a R 17　L 2.　　　oportet te ea E 2.　　　oportere cum R 6.　　　oportet R 7.
oppзta R 16.　　　a merore oportet ad O 7.　　‖　maerore R.　　　męrore V.
merore G E.　　　merorē J.　　　merorem K 2　M 1.　　　moerorem R 6.
morore R 10.　　morere R 16.　　　42. esset R V P K.　　　esse G *at* t *alt. man. add.*
　　XX. 1. dicit G i *in* e *mut. alt. man.*　‖　existimas L 3　O 1.　　　existimabis
R 7　L 2 6.　　　existimabas R 1 6 17　V　P 1-4　G　B 1-3　K 1 2　S　E 1-3
L 4 5　W 1 2　M 2　D C Π J　O 2 3 7 8 ed. H.　　　tu extima epicurum M 1.
2. libidinosas R V G B K.　　　libidinosas P.　　　3. minime R V G B K.

ἐν Κῷ, τῆς αὐτῆς ἔχεται δυνάμεως τε καὶ
σκευασίας τῷ ἀμαρακίνῳ· εὐωδέστερον δὲ
τυγχάνει. Dav. read *adducamus, hedychrum incendamus, demus scutellam dulciculae potionis*: Orelli *adducamus, hedychrum intendamus, scutellam dulciculae
potionis*: *intendamus* preserving both
accusatives; Mo. and Küh. *adducamus,
demus hedychrum, intendamus scutellam
dulciculae potionis*. But *scutella* is evidently not a cup but a shallow vessel
such as a censer, cf. *scutra*. It seems
necessary therefore to adopt the corr. of
Madv. and to assume that *damus* of MSS
(*demus* V²P²) arose by dittography from
the end of *incendamus*, and that, as the
word made no sense there, it was trans-
ferred to precede *hedychri* which was at
the same time altered to *hedychrum*.
aliquid uideamus=*prouideamus*. This
use is chiefly colloquial but well established. Editors compare iv 17, 38 'ut
semper uideat sedem sibi ac locum sine
molestia atque angore uiuendi'; Att. v
1, 3 'antecesserat Statius, ut prandium
nobis uideret'; xiv 21, 4 'talaria uideamus'; Fam. vii 20, 2 'ualebis meaque
negotia uidebis'; Priscian iii 5, 30 'Cic.

in iii Tusculanarum: *Dulciculae potionis
aliquid uideamus*' (an extract which lends
some support to Madvig's corr.). Similarly ὁρᾶν in Gk: Theocr. xv 2 ὅρη δίφρον,
Εὐνόα, αὐτᾷ· Soph. Ajax 1165 σπεῦσον
κοίλην κάπετόν τιν' ἰδεῖν τῷδ'.
ne intellegere quidem te: for the
order of words cf. § 47 'ne suspicari
quidem se.'
　XX. dicet aliquis: as often, introducing the supposed objection of an
opponent. For the mood see Roby
Gram. II Introd. CI foll.
　existimas: the fut. read by Küh. with
little MS support is very unnatural.
Nearly all modern editors adopt *existimas*. For the error in MSS cf. 31, 75
appellabatur *codd. opt. pro* appellatur;
ii 21, 49 dubitarunt *pro* dubitant.
　libidinosas, 'immoral.'
　uideo enim...praeclare: as instances
cf. Diog. L. x 140 οὐκ ἔστιν ἡδέως ζῆν
ἄνευ τοῦ φρονίμως καὶ καλῶς καὶ δικαίως,
οὐδὲ φρονίμως καὶ καλῶς καὶ δικαίως ἄνευ
τοῦ ἡδέως. ὅτῳ δὲ μὴ ὑπάρχει ζῆν φρονίμως
καὶ καλῶς καὶ δικαίως οὐκ ἔστι τοῦτον
ἡδέως ζῆν· Plutarch, Non posse suauiter
uiui secundum Epicurum 1097 a τὸ εὖ

clare. itaque, ut saepe dixi, de acumine agitur eius, non de
5 moribus; quamuis spernat uoluptates eas quas modo laudauit,
ego tamen meminero, quod uideatur ei summum bonum. non
enim uerbo solum posuit uoluptatem, sed explanauit quid diceret.
saporem, inquit, et corporum complexum et ludos
atque cantus et formas eas quibus oculi iucunde
10 moueantur. num fingo, num mentior? cupio refelli. quid enim
laboro, nisi ut ueritas in omni quaestione explicetur? **47.** at
idem ait non crescere uoluptatem dolore detracto, summamque uoluptatem \<esse\> nihil dolere. paucis uerbis tria magna

5. spernat W 1.   spernapt V.   sperna t B *litt. inter* a *et* t *eras.*   spernant
R B 2 K.   sperant G *alt. man. superscr.*   aspnant R 10.   aspernat R 16.
6. quid uideatur G S J.   7. quid diceret V S E 1.   qd diceret J.
8. complexum R V P G K E.   cōplexū R 16.   9. iucunde R V K.
iûcunde E u *in* o *al. atr. mut.*   iunde G *in* iocunde *alt. man. mut.*   iocūde S.
§ **47,** 11. ad idem V G ad *in* at *alt. man. mut.*   12. detractos G *alt. man. corr.* ||
summamque uoluptatem nihil dolere R V P 1 4 G B 1-3 K 1 2 S E 1 2 W 1 2
M 1 2   D C Π   O 2 3 7 8.   *pro* summamque *habent* summaque K 1 *et* summam
O 8: *pro* dolere *habent* dolore B 2 *et* dolore E 1.   summamque uoluptatem non
dolere O 1.   *post* summamque *habet* V *in marg.* ēē *man. ant. adscr.*   uoluptatem
esse *corr. Seyffertius.*

ποιεῖν ἡδιόν ἐστι τοῦ εὖ πάσχειν. Similar
instances are referred to in the ' Epicuri
et Metrodori honestas quasdam exclama-
tiones' of Tac. Dial. 31. Epicurus taught
that pain was to be endured for the sake
of greater pleasure and pleasure to be
foregone that greater pain might be
avoided, cf. v 33, 95. Wisdom, self-
control, justice and courage were all
recognised by him as contributing to
happiness of life. The virtues and pleasure
grow together inseparably, Diog. L. x
132 συμπεφύκασι...αl ἀρεταl τῷ ζῆν
ἡδέως; Fin. i 16, 50. Seneca, who is
much given to quoting the moral precepts
of Epicurus, declares his teaching to be
pure and severe but undeservedly mis-
understood, de Vit. Beat. 13, 1; cf. also
Ep. 33, 2. For the attitude of Epicurus
towards pleasure and pain see Usener's
Epicurea, §§ 440—449; Zeller, *Stoics,
etc.,* pp. 447 foll.
    de acumine: cf. ii 19, 44 'homo minime
malus uel potius uir optimus' and i 3, 6 n.
on 'optimis.'
    quamuis=*quantumuis*, F.A.W.
    non enim uerbo...diceret, 'for he did
not confine himself to the use of the word
pleasure (in stating what the chief good
was) but he also made clear what he
meant.'
    saporem...moueantur: cf. 18, 41 n.
and Athenaeus and other Gk sources
quoted there.

corporum complexum: τὰς δι' ἀφροδισίων ἡδονάς, cf. Athenaeus and Diog. L.
ll. cc.
    cupio refelli: cf. ii 2, 5 'nosque ipsos
redargui refellique patiamur' and the rest
of the section.
    § **47. non crescere uoluptatem dolore
detracto**: the essential cause of happiness,
according to Epicurus, is repose of mind,
ἀταραξία. Positive pleasure only increases
so long as it removes unsatisfied craving.
Beyond that point pleasure is not added
to but only varied. Fin. i 11, 38; ii 3,
10; cf. the 18th κυρία δόξα of Epicurus in
Diog. L. x 144 οὐκ ἐπαύξεται ἡ ἡδονὴ ἐν
τῇ σαρκί, ἐπειδὰν ἅπαξ τὸ κατ' ἔνδειαν
ἀλγοῦν ἐξαιρεθῇ, ἀλλὰ μόνον ποικίλλεται·
Plutarch, Non posse suau. uiui sec. Epic.
1088 c καὶ πέρας κοινὸν 'Επίκουρος τὴν
παντὸς τοῦ ἀλγοῦντος ὑπεξαίρεσιν ἐπιτέ-
θεικεν, ὡς τῆς φύσεως ἄχρι τοῦ λῦσαι τὸ
ἀλγεινὸν αὐξούσης τὸ ἡδὺ περαιτέρω δὲ
προελθεῖν οὐκ ἐώσης κατὰ μέγεθος, ἀλλὰ
ποικιλμούς τινας οὐκ ἀναγκαίους, ὅταν γοῦν
ἐν τῷ μὴ πονεῖν γένηται, δεχομένης. See
Usener, *Epicurea*, §§ 416 foll.
    summamque uoluptatem esse: Sff.
inserted *esse* here where it would be
more likely to fall out than after *summamque*: 'uerisimilius est *esse* post *uoluptatem* excidisse (eē post ē) quam post
summamque ubi inserunt V² Lamb. marg.
et nuper Hei. Saepissime fit ut id quod
excidit perperam a correctore restituatur.'

peccata. unum, quod secum ipse pugnat; modo enim ne su-
15 spicari quidem se quicquam bonum, nisi sensus quasi titillarentur
uoluptate; nunc autem summam uoluptatem esse dolore carere.
potestne magis secum ipse pugnare? alterum peccatum, quod,
cum in natura tria sint, unum gaudere, alterum dolere, tertium
nec gaudere nec dolere, hic primum et tertium putat idem esse
20 nec distinguit a non dolendo uoluptatem. tertium peccatum
commune cum quibusdam, quod, cum uirtus maxime expetatur
eiusque adipiscendae causa philosophia quaesita sit, ille a uirtute

15. titillarentur R 6 17 P B 3 K 12 E 12 W 12 M 12 D C Π J O 1-3 8.

titilarentur R 1. titilarentur V B 2. titularentur G *alt. man. superscr.*

tintillarentur O 7. nitillarentur B 1. tutarentur S *in marg.* titillarent. qua

sitit ilarent B 2. qua intitillarentur O 1. 16. carere *om.* E 1. calrere P.

18. tria sunt G *alt. man. mut.* 21. commune cum R 6 17 V P G B 1-3

K 12 E 12 W 12 M 12 D C O 1-3 7 8. commune cum S *fort. eod. atr.*
commune est J cum *om.* tertium peccatum commune *habet* Π *in marg. e contra om.*

maxime R V G B. maxime K *atr. nigriore superscr.* expetatur R V K 12
W 1 D O 8. expectatur G *at* c *expunx. et conf. alt. man.* expectatur

R 10 16 O 7. expectatur P *al. atr. superscr.* uerba maxime expetat *habet* V

multa in ras. scripta. 22. uirtute G *alt. man. superscr.*

summamque...nihil dolere: see 18,
40 n. on 'summum bonum non dolere.'
The passage in Diog. L. x. 139 does not
contain an assertion that the highest
pleasure consists in absence of pain and
Torquatus in Fin. i 17, 56, though he
emphasises the greatness of the pleasure
of non dolere, does not declare it to be
the greatest possible.

secum ipse pugnat: Madv. on Fin.
i 11, 37 admits that the doctrine of
Epicurus with regard to the two divisions
of pleasure is set forth in the sources
'breuiter nec constantissime, si cum
reliqua doctrina de origine uoluptatis
compares'; although Epic. says that
pleasures of mind spring from those of
the body, Fin. i 17, 55, and only makes
them 'greater than those of the body
because while the body perceives only
present pleasures the mind perceives past
and future as well, purely intellectual
pleasure seems to have been recognised
by him. Cf. his letter to Idomeneus
written on his deathbed, Diog. L. x 22.
The basis was materialistic rather than
corporeal.

modo enim: sc. *dicebat* §§ 41, 42, 46.
Hence the sequence *titillarentur* which
Dav. wrongly altered on Bentley's advice.

quasi marks *titillarentur* as a translation. Epicurus used the word γαργαλίζω.

Cf. i 12, 27 n., and for *titillare* Fin. i 11,
39; Lucr. ii 429.

a non dolendo, 'from insensibility,'
i 43, 102 n. on 'de nihil sentiendo.'

tertium peccatum: the third fault is
practically that he did not adopt the Stoic
definition of the chief good. The statement that Epicurus *a uirtute summum
bonum separauit* is not strictly correct,
cf. Diog. L. x 140 quoted above on § 46 n.
on 'uideo enim...praeclare,' where the
virtues are stated to be inseparably connected with pleasure. Cf. also Diog. L.
x 132 συμπεφύκασι γὰρ αἱ ἀρεταὶ τῷ ζῆν
ἡδέως καὶ τὸ ζῆν ἡδέως τούτων ἐστὶν ἀχώ-
ριστον. What he denies is that virtue is
the end of action. Happiness of life is
the end, virtue a means to that end. Cf.
Seneca, Ep. 85, 18 'Epicurus quoque
iudicat, cum uirtutem habeat, beatum
esse, sed ipsam uirtutem non satis esse
ad beatam uitam, quia beatum efficiat
uoluptas quae ex uirtute est, non ipsa
uirtus.'

separauit: on the sequence *expetatur,
quaesita sit, separauit* Küh. notes that
separauit is not historic perfect but
present perfect. But even so the historic
sequence is more usual in Cicero, cf.
i '1, 1 n. on 'pertinerent...continerentur.'
Cicero may have begun his sentence with
separat in view as the ending but on

summum bonum separauit. **48.** at laudat saepe uirtutem. et quidem C. Gracchus, cum largitiones maximas fecisset et effudisset
25 aerarium, uerbis tamen defendebat aerarium. quid uerba audiam,
cum facta uideam? Piso ille Frugi semper contra legem frumen-
tariam dixerat. is lege lata consularis ad frumentum accipiundum
uenerat. animum aduertit Gracchus in contione Pisonem stan-
tem; quaerit audiente populo Romano, qui sibi constet, cum ea
30 lege frumentum petat, quam dissuaserit. Nolim, inquit, mea

§ **48**, 23. at R 16   V P G   B 1–3   S   W 1 2   J   O 1 3 7 8 ed. H.   aṭ R
al. atr. corr.   ac R 10.   ad E 1.   ‖ laudat saepe R 1 10 16   V P G   B 1–3
K 1 2   S   E 2   W 1 2   M 1 2   D C J   O 1–3 7 8 ed. H.   adlaudat sepe E 1.
laudat ₍et₎ saepe II.   24. c. gracchus V R.   c. grachus E 1.   c. graccus S
fort. eod. atr.   c. grachus G *alt. man. superscr.*   ‖ maximas R V G B.

maximas K 1.   ‖ effudisset R 6   P   B 1 3   K 2   S   E 2   W 1 2   M 1 2   DC Π J
O 1–3 7 8.   effuṇdisset V.   effuṇdisset K 1.   effundisset R G   B 2   E 1
(et *om.*)   26. uideam? Piso G   K 2   W 2   D   O 1 3 8.   uideam Piso R P
K 1   B 1–3   S   E 1 2   W 1   M 1 2   C Π J   O 2 7.   uideā? . 1 . piso V *at* . 1 .
in marg. ad init. lineae, habet etiam in marg. al. atr. L. piso.   27. accipiundum
R V B.   accipiendum G *alt. man. superscr.*   accipiụndum E 1 *eod. ut uid. atr.*
accipiendum R 6 ₇   P   B 2 3   K 1   S   E 2   W 1 2   M 1 2   DC Π J   O 1–3 7 8.

28. animum aduertit B 1   E 1   C.   animam aduertit R *eod. atr.* K 1 *eod. atr.*
animam aduertit V P G.   animam aduerti B 2.   aīaduertit B 3   K 2   D Π.
aīadu'tit W 2   M 1   J   O 8.   animaduertit L 2 3 4 6   W 1   M 2   O 1–3.
animadu'tit S   E 2.   ‖ gracchus V.   graccₕus S.   grachus B G *alt. man.*
superscr.   grachus E 1.   ‖ in contione R G B.   in contentione E 1 *fort. eod. atr.*
29. p. r. *pro* populo romano G B.   30. dissuaserit R V P   K 1 2   L 2 5 6 ed. H.
dissuaʃɟit O 7.   disuaserit E 1.   dissuaserit L 4.   disuaserat G *in* disuaserit
alt. man. mut.   dissuaserat L 3   O 1 8.   ‖ inquid K 1.   inquid G d *in* t *mut.*

nearing the end found that that form
would give a very inferior rhythm. The
clausula *sum|mum bonum separauit* is
one of the best possible, Zielinski's 3 d;
sum|mum bonum separat would not have
the proper caesura to be a good instance
of 2.

§ **48. at laudat saepe**: *et saepe* of
earlier editors is not supported by the MSS.

et quidem: this expression admits the
fact but ironically refutes the inference
intended. See Madv. on Fin. i 10, 35 n.
on 'et quidem se texit, ne interiret.'
Also i 49, 119 n.

C. Gracchus: the argument is 'It may
be urged that Epic. often praises virtue.
True, but men's words are not always in
harmony with their deeds. C. Gracchus
praised economy while squandering the
public treasure.' The story of L. Piso
only bears upon the argument in so far as
it is meant to show on the evidence of a
uir grauis et sapiens that the statement

made with regard to Gracchus is correct.
Cic. brings him in in contrast to Epicurus
in Fin. ii 28, 90.

effudisset: of spending other money
than one's own, see Furneaux on Tac.
Ann. xiv 31, 6. For the historical refer-
ence cf. Off. ii 21, 72; p. Sestio 48, 103;
Mommsen *H.R.* III p. 344. [W. Warde
Fowler, *Social Life at Rome* p. 37.]

Piso ille Frugi: Kl. inserted *L.* before
Piso 'e cod. Vaticano' i.e. from V². For
this Piso cf. 8, 16 n.

accipiundum: on the fluctuation between *e* and *u* in the gerund and gerundive
see Brambach, *Neugestalt.* pp. 106—7;
Fleckeisen, *Fünfzig Artikeln* p. 16; Neue,
Formenlehre iii³ 332 foll.

animum aduertit: for the full form cf.
v. 23, 65.

sibi constet: i 5, 9 n. on 'tibi constare.'

nolim: present because it is still in
Gracchus' power to do otherwise if he
chooses.

bona, Gracche, tibi uiritim diuidere libeat, sed, si
facias, partem petam. parumne declarauit uir grauis et
sapiens lege Sempronia patrimonium publicum dissupari? lege
orationes Gracchi, patronum aerarii esse dices. **49.** negat Epi-
35 curus iucunde posse uiui, nisi cum uirtute uiuatur, negat ullam
in sapientem uim esse fortunae, tenuem uictum antefert copioso,
negat ullum esse tempus quo sapiens non beatus sit. omnia
philosopho digna, sed cum uoluptate pugnantia.—non istam
dicit uoluptatem.—dicat quamlibet; nempe eam dicit, in qua
40 uirtutis nulla pars insit. age, si uoluptatem non intellegimus, ne
dolorem quidem? nego igitur eius esse, qui dolore summum
malum metiatur, mentionem facere uirtutis.

31. bona R V P G K 1 W 1 2 O 1 3 7.　　　bone\ B 1 *i.e. e in a mut.*
　　　　　　　　　　　　　　　　　　　　　　　　c
bone D Gr.　　gracche V E 1 D.　　grache G. ‖ uiritim V G.　uirium E 1. ‖
libeat R V P G B K 1 O 8.　　liceat B 3 W 1 O 1 3.　32. parumne R G.
　　　　　l' satis
parū ne P.　　parum ne V.　　33. publicum R V P.　　puplicum G. ‖
dissupari R V B.　　dissuparę K 1 *atr. nigr. mut.*　dissupari E 1.　dissipari P
ras. et spat. post si.　dissipari G R 6 S J.　34. gracchi V G.　grachi E 1.
§ **49,** 35. iucunde R V G B.　　iūcunde E 1 u *in o mut.*　　iocunde S. ‖
negat illum G illum *in* ullam *alt. man. mut.*　　38. philosophię G i *exp. et lineam
duxit alt. man.*　　39. quamlibet R V P G K 1.　　quanlibet B O 7.
　　　　　　　　　　　　　　　　　　　　　　　　　　　　e
quam lubet O 1.　　quē libet R 16.　‖　nempeam G *alt. man. superscr.*
40. intellegimus R V G B K.　intelligimus E 1 S.　41. qui dolore B 3 M 2.
qui dolorem S.　　qui dolorē Π *at linea magna ex parte eras.*　qui dolorē W 1 2
J O 7.　　qui dolorem V K 2 E 2 M 1 D C O 1-3 8.　qui dolorem B 1
at d *post* i *eras.*　　quid dolorē E 1.　quid dolorem R 1.　quid dolorem G
B 2 K 1.　‖　summum malum *om.* O 2.　　42. metiatur R 1 10 16 V P B 1 3
K 1 2 E 2 W 1 M 2 Π O 1-3.　　meciatur G *at c in t alt. man. mut.*

mentiatur B 2 M 1 D C O 7.　　mētiat~ O 8.

mea bona : the state property in which
Piso as a citizen had a share.
　lege...dices: i 13, 30 n. on 'tolle...
sustuleris.'
　orationes Gracchi : these were read in
Cicero's day; Brut. 33, 125. Several
fragments survive; among these an important fragment (translated in Momms.
H.R. III p. 343 n.) is preserved by the
Ambrosian scholiast on Cicero.
　§ **49. negat Epicurus...uiuatur** : cf.
v 9, 26; Fin. i 16, 50; 18, 57; Diog. L.
x 140 quoted on § 46; *ibid.* § 132 partly
quoted in the same place. Usener, *Epicurea* §§ 504 foll.
　negat ullam...fortunae: cf. v 9, 26;
26, 73; Fin. i 19, 63; ii 27, 89; Diog. L.
x 144 (the 15th κυρία δόξα) βραχέα σοφῷ
τύχη παρεμπίπτει, τὰ δὲ μέγιστα καὶ
κυριώτατα ὁ λογισμὸς διῴκηκε καὶ κατὰ
τὸν συνεχῆ χρόνον τοῦ βίου διοικεῖ καὶ
διοικήσει. Usener §§ 584 foll.
　tenuem uictum : cf. v 9, 26; 32, 89;

Fin. ii 28, 90; Diog. L. x 130 τὸ μὲν
φυσικὸν πᾶν εὐπόριστόν ἐστι, τὸ δὲ κενὸν
δυσπόριστον. οἵ τε λιτοὶ χυλοὶ ἴσην πολυ-
τελεῖ διαίτῃ τὴν ἡδονὴν προσφέρουσιν ὅταν
ἅπαν τὸ ἀλγοῦν κατ' ἔνδειαν ἐξαιρεθῇ· καὶ
μάζα καὶ ὕδωρ τὴν ἀκροτάτην ἡδονὴν
ἐπειδὰν ἐνδέων τις αὐτὰ προσενέγκηται...
Usener, *op. cit.* § 469 foll.
　negat...beatus sit: cf. Diog. L. x 118
quoted in n. on ii 7, 17. Usener § 601.
　omnia philosopho digna: i 43, 102 n.
on 'rem non difficilem.' Hei. takes the
constr. to be the same as in i 26, 65 'non
iusta causa cur Laomedonti tanta fieret
iniuria,' where see n.
　non istam...: 'he does not understand
pleasure in the sense to which you refer.'
The argument that follows is more fully
stated in Fin. ii 4, 12 foll.; 23, 75 foll.
　age, si uoluptatem...: the line of
thought is this: 'Epicureans say that we
(i.e. non-Epicureans) do not understand
what Epicurus means by pleasure; but

XXI. **50.** Et queruntur quidam Epicurei, uiri optimi (nam nullum genus est minus malitiosum), me studiose dicere contra Epicurum. ita, credo, de honore aut de dignitate contendimus. mihi summum in animo bonum uidetur, illi autem in corpore, 5 mihi in uirtute, illi in uoluptate. et illi pugnant, et quidem uicinorum fidem inplorant; multi autem sunt qui statim conuolent. ego sum is qui dicam me non laborare; actum habiturum, quod egerint. **51.** quid enim? de bello Punico agitur? de quo ipso cum aliud M. Catoni, aliud L. Lentulo uideretur, nulla inter eos con-

XXI. § **50,** 1. et queruntur V B 1 2 K 2 W 1 D C O 1 3 7 8.   et q̄runtur
E 2 W 2.   et queruntur K 1.   et quaeruntur R 1 G O 2.   et querentur P
al. atr. superscr.   et 9queruntur B 3.   et conqueruntur M 2.   et con queruntur
II con *in marg. excurrente.*   ‖   quidam R 1 6 7 V P 1 3 G B 1-3 K 1 E 1
W 1 2 M 2 D C J O 1-3 7 Gr.   qdā M 1.   quidem R 17 P 2 S E 2
II O 8.   quid P 4. ‖ epicure G *alt. man. superscr.*   epicurhei W 1. ‖
optimi G K 1.   5. uicinorum R.   uicinor m V *charta inter* r *et* m *perforata.*
ut inorum E 1.   6. inplorant G.   implorant R V B K.   7. ego sum his K 1. ‖
actum habiturum R V P G.   actum abiturum E 1.   acnō habiturum J. ‖
quod egerint R G.   quid egerint J.

they must at least admit that he means the same thing by pain as we do. Since then he makes pain the measure of the chief evil we must conclude that pleasure not virtue is his chief good.' Neide. Epicureans would no more have admitted that their opponents used the word pain than that they used the word pleasure in their sense of the term. The argument is stated from a narrow Stoic point of view and Cic. tacitly brushes aside Epicurus' known assertions with regard to the intimate connexion between virtue and pleasure, for which see reff. in 20, 46 n. on 'uideo enim praeclare.'

XXI. § **50. et queruntur**: *et* marks indignant surprise, cf. 16, 35 n. on 'et tu...iubes.' Schlenger's alteration to *sed* is uncalled for.

quidam Epicurei, 'certain Roman Epicureans.' But *quidem* of inferior MSS may be right.

uiri optimi: i 3, 6 n. on 'optimis.'

malitiosum, 'crafty,' cf. ii 19, 44 'uenit Epicurus, homo minime malus, uel potius uir optimus.'

studiose, 'in the spirit of a partisan.'

ita, credo, 'Ha! One would suppose...' Ironical. F.A.W. There is no need for heat where truth is the object of search. For *credo* cf. i 38, 92 n. on 'opinor.'

et illi pugnant, 'and they actually fight' i.e. although they accuse me of being contentious, they are so themselves. For *et* cf. *et queruntur* above.

uicinorum fidem inplorant: Mo. compares the extract from Statius' Synephebi metaphorically applied in N.D. i 6, 13 'pro deum, popularium omnium, omnium adulescentium clamo, postulo, obsecro, oro, ploro atque inploro fidem.'

multi autem sunt: all dogmatic schools would be more or less hostile to the New Academy.

me non laborare, 'that I do not trouble myself.'

actum habiturum, quod egerint, 'that I will acquiesce in any arrangement they may make.' Cf. the proverbial *actum ne agas* which forbids the opposite course. Att. ix 18, 3, Laelius 22, 85; Ter. Phormio 419; Adelphi 232, where Donatus explains it as a metaphor from the law-courts applied where a case once decided is opened up again.

§ **51. quid enim?** The argument is 'Excitement is out of place in a philosophic discussion. This is not a question about war, though even such a question can be argued without animosity, as the case of Cato and Lentulus shows.'

de bello Punico: sc. *tertio.*

M. Catoni: see Mommsen, *H.R.* III pp. 238 foll.

L. Lentulo: L. Cornelius Lentulus Lupus, consul 156 B.C., evidently acted along with Scipio Nasica in opposing Cato's agitation for the destruction of Carthage.

10 certatio umquam fuit. hi nimis iracunde agunt, praesertim cum
ab iis non sane animosa defendatur sententia, pro qua non in
senatu, non in contione, non apud exercitum neque ad censores
dicere audeant. sed cum istis alias, et eo quidem animo, nullum
ut certamen instituam, uerum dicentibus facile cedam; tantum
15 admonebo, si maxime uerum sit ad corpus omnia referre sapientem siue, ut honestius dicam, nihil facere, nisi quod expediat,
siue omnia referre ad utilitatem suam, quoniam haec plausibilia
non sunt, ut in sinu gaudeant, gloriose loqui desinant.

XXII. **52.** Cyrenaicorum restat sententia; qui tum aegritudinem censent exsistere, si necopinato quid euenerit. est id

§ **51**, 10. umquam R V E 1. unq̇ S. 11. ab his G B K. ‖ non satis S.
12. in contione V G B 3 K 1 E 2 W 2 M 1 2 Π O 1 3. contione O 7 in *om.*
in concione W 1 C. in con̄t̆ĕn̄tione R 1. in contentione P *al. atr. superscr.*
in contentione B 2 E 1. ‖ neque ad R 1 7 P 1-4 B 1 3 K 1 2 S E 1 2 L 4-6
W 2 M 1 2 Π J O 2 3 8 7. nequae ad G *in* neque ad *alt. man. mut.*
neque ạd V *man. ant. mut.* neque apud R 6 L 2 3 D C O 1. neque āp W 1. ‖
neque accensores B 2. 15. admonebo R V G K W 2. ammonebo B S.
āmonebo B 2. ‖ maxime R V G B S E. maxime K 1 *atr. nigriore superscr.*
17. siue omnia referre ad utilitatem suam *habent* R V P G B 1-3 K 1 S E 1 W 1 2
M 1 2 D C J O 1 7 Π *habet* facere *pro* referre. 18. in sinu R 6 B 3 E 1
W 1 M 2 D C Π O 2 3. in sinū B 2 O 8. in signuṃ P. in siġnum K 1.
in sinum R 1 7 V B 1 E 2. in signum G g *expunx. alt. man.* in signū
K 2 M 1. in signu E 3. in signum R 1 7 J O 1. insignē O 7.
in sig W 2. ‖ gloriose V P K G. gloriosẹ R. ‖ designant P.
XXII. § **52**, 1. cirenaicorum V. ‖ qui tum R 1 6 7 V P G B 1-3 K 1 S
E 1 2 W 1 M 2 D Π J O 2 3 7 8 ed. H. que tum K 2 M 1 O 1.
q̇ tum C. q̄ tum W 2. 2. censent R 1 6 7 V P G B 1 S E 1 2 M 2
C O 7. censet K 2 W 2 M 1 J O 1. cessent R 1 7. ‖ existere R V G
B 1 2 K 1 S E 1 2 W 1. ‖ sineopinato G *alt. man. superscr.*

praesertim cum, 'and that though,'
Madv. on Fin. ii 8, 25; Mayor on Phil.
ii 24, 60.
animosa, 'spirited.' Cf. Fin. ii 22,
74.
ad censores: although Küh. endeavours
to draw a distinction it seems to me that
apud could also have been used here
before *censores* cf. p. Cluentio 47, 131
'quod si hanc apud eosdem ipsos censores
mihi aut alii causam agere licuisset.' Also
that *ad* might have been used before
exercitum just as it is before *populum* in
Brut. 20, 80 'cum quidem eo ipso anno
contra Ser. Galbam ad populum summa
contentione dixisset.'
uerum dicentibus facile cedam: for
this attitude of Academic philosophers
towards opponents cf. ii 2, 5 n. on 're-
fellere sine pertinacia.' Cicero was *nullius addictus iurare in uerba magistri.*

[Cf. de Off. iii 4, 20 nobis enim nostra
Academia magnam licentiam dat, ut
quodcunque maxime probabile occurrat,
id nostro iure liceat defendere.]
siue omnia referre ad utilitatem suam.
Bouh. and F.A.W. suspected a gloss.
Hei. *Posen Progr.* p. 2 more correctly
notes 'inanem tautologiam habent, quam
tamen ipsi Ciceroni tribuere non dubito.'
in sinu gaudeant: a proverbial expression, 'let them disguise their joy';
cf. our phrase 'to laugh in one's sleeve.'
Mo. compares Tibull. iv 13, 8 'procul
absit gloria uolgi: | qui sapit, in tacito
gaudeat ille sinu'; Prop. ii 25, 30 'in
tacito cohibe gaudia clausa sinu'; Senec.
Ep. 105, 3 'si bona tua non iactaueris, si
scieris in sinu gaudere.'
XX. § 52. Cyrenaicorum...sententia:
the treatment of the Cyrenaic view, post-
poned in 15, 32, is here resumed.

quidem magnum, ut supra dixi; etiam Chrysippo ita uideri
scio, quod prouisum ante non sit, id ferire uehementius; sed non
5 sunt in hoc omnia. quamquam hostium repens aduentus magis
aliquanto conturbat quam exspectatus, et maris subita tempestas
quam ante prouisa terret nauigantes uehementius, et eius modi
sunt pleraque. sed, cum diligenter necopinatorum naturam con-
sideres, nihil aliud reperias nisi omnia uideri subita maiora, et
10 quidem ob duas causas, primum quod, quanta sint, quae accidunt, considerandi spatium non datur, deinde, cum uidetur
praecaueri potuisse, si prouisum esset, quasi culpa contractum

3. ut supra dixi R V G.   ut sup̄ dixi J.   ut pr̥edixi S.   ut p̄dixi B E. ‖

etiam *om.* B E. ‖ crysippo G E.   4. ſr̥eirt V i *post* ſ *et* i *post* r *in* e *mut.*, i *ante* r
in ras.   fieri R 1 6 7 17 P 1–3 G B 1–3 K 1 S E 1 2 L 2–6 W 1 M 2
D C Π J O 1–3 7 8 ed. H.   fſ P 4.   fſ⁴ W 2.   fſ⁹ K 2.   fieí M 1.

5. aduentus K 1.   aduetⁿus R V G *alt. man. superscr.*   ad uetus B 2.

6. aliquanďo V.   aliquando R P G K 1 S E 1   aliqnᵃdo B 1. ‖ expectatus
R V P G B 1 2 K 1 S.   exspectatus E 1.   7. nauigantes R V G B 1 2
K 1 S E 1.   9. rep̣perias R *eod. atr.*   reperias P B 1 K 1 E 1.
repias E 2.   repperias V G.   10. accidunt R G B 1 2 K 1 O 1 3.
accidant V u *in* a *mut. eod. ut uid. atr.*   11. deinde cum R V P B 1–3 K 1 2

E 1 2 W 1 2 M 1 2 D C Π J O 1 2 7 8.   deinde qᵒum S cum *in* quom *mut.*

deinde tum G.   12. contraᶜtum V.

ut supra dixi: 13, 28; 14, 30.
etiam Chrysippo: the main point, in
Chrysippus' eyes, was that the cause
should be *recens* (πρόσφατος); cf. Galen,
l.c. iv p. 391 M., where the definition
of annoyance given by Zeno and Chrysippus is stated shortly thus 'λύπη ἐστὶ
δόξα πρόσφατος κακοῦ παρουσίας.' See
also 23, 55 and 31, 75. For Chrysippus'
recommendation of *praemeditatio* cf.
Galen *l.c.* p. 392 M. where in the words
'διὸ καὶ προενθυμεῖν δεῖν φησι τοῖς πράγμασι μήπω τε παροῦσιν οἷον παροῦσι χρῆσθαι' the subject to φησι is ὁ Χρύσιππος.
Cf. Bake, *Posid. Rell.* p. 204. The objection of v. Arnim, who after printing
the passage as Chrysippean in *Stoica* III
482 (p. 131 ll. 26–7) changed his mind
when he came to write his preface (1 p.
xxii), seems met by A. C. Pearson,
Class. Rev. XIX 456 b. See also Pohlenz,
Hermes XLI 334.
ferire: Dav. compares 23, 55 'feriunt
enim fortasse grauius'; Seneca, Consol.
ad Marciam c. 9 'necesse est itaque
magis corruamus, qui quasi ex inopinato
ferimur'; Ep. 57, 3 'huius quoque
ferietur animus, mutabitur color'; also
Ep. 108, 11.

non sunt in hoc omnia: cf. Cato M.
3, 8 and often.
aliquanto: the vulgate *aliquando* is
obviously wrong. The effect of the unexpected is *always* more severe than that
of the expected, as Dav. notes. Cf. ii 27,
66 n.
quam ante prouisa terret: Mo. compares Hor. Epist. i 6, 11 'improuisa
simul species exterret utrumque.'
et...pleraque, 'and this principle applies in most cases.'
cum...consideres: a conditional relative clause, hence the subjunctive; cf. i
41, 98 n.; 49, 118. The correspondence
between the conditional relative forms
and those of ordinary protasis, worked
out for Greek by Goodwin, *Gk Moods
and Tenses*, §§ 524 foll., applies to Latin
also.
deinde, cum: Kl. follows Lamb. in
reading *quod* after *deinde* but the transition
to a main clause is not unusual; cf. ii 26,
64 n. on 'non quo...sed tamen...est.'
deinde...acriorem facit: Cicero does
not deal with this second cause in detail.
potuisse, si prouisum esset: in or.
recta *potuit, si prouisum esset.* Madv.
348 e.

malum aegritudinem acriorem facit. **53.** quod ita esse dies declarat, quae procedens ita mitigat ut isdem malis manentibus
15 non modo leniatur aegritudo, sed in plerisque tollatur. Karthaginienses multi Romae seruierunt, Macedones rege Perse capto;
uidi etiam in Peloponneso, cum essem adulescens, quosdam
Corinthios. hi poterant omnes eadem illa de Andromacha
deplorare:

20   Haec ómnia uidi....,

sed iam decantauerant fortasse. eo enim erant uoltu, oratione,
omni reliquo motu et statu ut eos Argiuos aut Sicyonios jiceres,
magisque me mouerant Corinthi subito aspectae parietinae
quam ipsos Corinthios, quorum animis diuturna cogitatio callum

---

§ **53,** 14. mittigat G *priore* t *expuncto et confosso.* ‖ isdem V G K.
15. implerisque G E 1. ‖ Karthaginienses B 1.   Kartaginienses R V G B 2 K.

Cartaginenses S.   Kartaginenses E 1.   Cartaginenses W 1.   16. maçidones
E 1 *fort. eod. atr.* ‖ perse R G.   pse V S E 1.   17. pelo ponneso V *eod. ut*
uid. atr., *litt. ante* po *eras.* ‖ adulescens R V P G   B 2 K 1.   adolescens
B 1 S E 1.   18. corinthios V P G B 1 2.   chorinthios R K 1. ‖
de andromacha O 1.   . deandromacha B 1.   deantromacha R V G.
deandramacha B 2.   deanthromacha K 1.   19. deplorasse S.   21. sed iam G.
sed etiam R K. ‖   uoltu R V K.   uultu B 1 2.   uolutu G u *prius expunx.*
et conf. alt. man.   22. argiuos R S.   argyuos E 1. ‖   sicyonios G E 1.
sycionios R V B S.   sicionios K. ‖ diceres V R 10.   diceref P *al. atr.*
superscr.   dɩ̃es R 16.   dicere R 1 G K E 1.   dicerē B 1.   23. corinthi R.
chorinti G. ‖ aspectae V.   aspecta R 1 10 16 P G B 1 2 K 1 S E1 O 7.
aspecte R 17 S *marg.*   aspecti L 2.   aspectu B 3 K 2 E 2 L 3-6 W 1 2
M 1 D C O 1 3. ‖ pari—&inequam V *duarum litt. spatio relicto.*   pari & inequā
B 1.   pari & in æ quam P 1.   parietine quam R 17 G B 3 Π O 3.
pariet–inequā E 1.   pari–& i naǵ quam R 1 *ante* n *apparet* i *uix erasum.*
                                                                      r
pari & inequā K 1 *eod. atr. suppl.*   parique et inequā O 7.   pai 〗 inequā W 2.
parique et inechā R 16.   pari g̃ & in ęquā R 10.   pari: & inquā M 2 L 5 6.
pari equam M 1.   parietū ruinae q̄ O 2.   parietes q̄ R 7.   et in equam B 2
pari *om.*   aspectu tunc quequam E 2 tunc *multa in rasura.*   parti ne quam C.
ꝉ pari
parti qm̃ D.   aspectum pati et me ed. H.   24. corinthios K 1.   chorinthios R.
chorintios G.

---

§ **53. dies:** cf. 16, 35 'longinquitas et
dies.'

quae: for the gender where *dies* denotes
'period of time' see Küh. *Gram.* I p. 254;
Roby I § 337.

Perse capto: by L. Aemilius Paulus
after Pydna in 168 B.C. For the form
Perses and its declension in Cicero see
Neue, *Formenlehre* I³ p. 517.

uidi...Corinthios: Corinth was taken
by Mummius in July 146 B.C. Cicero,
born in 106, was in Greece and Asia
Minor in 79—77 B.C.; he would thus be
able as a young man to see some still

surviving Corinthians who had witnessed
the capture of the city.

cum essem, 'being a young man at the
time.' *Cum* with the subjunctive here
characterises the temporal circumstances
under which the action took place. See
Gildersleeve and Lodge § 585. Cf. p.
Sest. 57, 122 'cum...demonstraret'; 59,
126 'numquam est conspectus, cum ue-
niret.'

de Andromacha: Dobree proposed
quae for *de* but Or. compares Off. iii 21,
82; Rep. i 18, 30.

haec omnia: cf. 19, 45.

25 uetustatis obduxerat. **54.** legimus librum Clitomachi, quem ille euersa Karthagine misit consolandi causa ad captiuos ciues suos; in eo est disputatio scripta Carneadis, quam se ait in commentarium rettulisse. cum ita positum esset, uideri fore in aegritudine sapientem patria capta, quae Carneades contra 30 dixerit scripta sunt. tanta igitur calamitatis praesentis adhibetur a philosopho medicina, quanta inueteratae ne desideratur quidem, nec, si aliquot annis post idem ille liber captiuis missus

§ **54**, 26. Karthagine R.   Kartagine V G B 2 K.   carthagine E 1.
cartagine S. ‖ consolandi R V P G.   inconsolandi B 1. ‖ ciues R V G B 1 2 K 1.
27. carneadis R V P G B 1 2 S E 1 W 1.   28. commentarium R V G B S.
                                                                                    t
cōmentarium K 1.   ‖   r & tulisse R.   rettulisse W 1.   retulisse G.
retulisse V P 1 4 B 1 2 S E 1 M 1 J O 1 3 7 8.   retuḷlisse K 1. ‖ uidi
G *alterum* i *expunx. et* eri *superscr. altera fort. man.*   ‖   forte E 1.
30. conduxerit S *at* u *ex* i *mut. atr. nigr. et in marg.* coñ dixerit.   31. quanta
inueterate Π.   quanta inueterata R 16 17 V P 1–4 G B 1–3 K 1 2 S
E 1 2 L 2–6 W 1 2 M 1 2 J O 1–3 7 8 ed. H.   quanta in inueterata D C. ‖
ne desideratur R P G   B 2 3 K 1 E 2 W 1 2 M 1 2   D C O 1 8.   ne desi-
                                                                                    re
deretur O 2.   ne desideratur V *al. atr. superscr.*.   ne desideraretur O 3.
                                                                     r
nec desideratur B 1   E 1 Π.   nec dexiderat O 7.   neẹ desideratus S.
                                                                                    c
32. quidem R V G   B 1 K 1 E 1 W 1 2 M 1. ‖ nec si aliquod G.   ne si
aliquod E 1.

decantauerant: here in the sense of *cantare destiterant.*

oratione: Man. unnecessarily proposed *ornatu*; cf. Off. i 29, 102 'quorum omnium uoltus, uoces, motus statusque mutantur.'

Argiuos aut Sicyonios: whose cities no misfortune had befallen.

me: contrasted with *ipsos Corinthios.*

parietinae: Dav. quotes Isid. Orig. xv 8 'parietinas dicimus quasi parietum ruinas. sunt enim parietes stantes sine tecto et sine habitantibus.'

Dav. notes 'pari modo Iulius Caesar, Corinthi uisis ruderibus εἰς τοιαύτην ἦλθε συμπάθειαν καὶ φιλοδοξίαν ὥστε μετὰ πολλῆς σπουδῆς πάλιν αὐτὴν ἀναστῆσαι. Verba sunt Diodori Siculi in Excerpt. Peiresc. pag. 345, ed. Par.'

callum...obduxerat: ii 15, 36. **uetustatis**, subjective gen.

§ **54.** Clitomachus, whose real name was Hasdrubal, came to Athens from Carthage, his native city, and there studied under Carneades whom he succeeded as head of the Academy in 129 B.C. Diog. L. iv 67. The present passage shows that he must have left Carthage before its fall in 146 B.C.

For this Consolatio of Clitomachus which is also cited by Hieronymus, ep. 60,

c. 5 (ad Heliodorum), 'Platonis, Diogenis, Clitomachi, Carneadis, Posidonii ad sedandos luctus opuscula percurrimus,' see Buresch, *Leipziger Studien* IX 47 and 58. **commentarium**, 'note-book,' ὑπομνήματα. Cf. Diog. L. *l.c.* διεδέξατο τὸν Καρνεάδην καὶ τὰ αὐτοῦ μάλιστα διὰ τῶν συγγραμμάτων ἐφώτισεν.

cum ita positum esset, 'the subject of discussion being thus stated.' Hirzel, *Untersuchungen* III 380 n., observes that the method styled 'uetus et Socratica' in i 4, 8 is shown by this passage and Fin. ii 1, 2 'quod quidem iam fit etiam in Academia. ubi enim is, qui audire uolt, ita dixit *uoluptas mihi uidetur esse summum bonum, perpetua oratione contra disputatur*, etc.' to be the method usually followed in the Sceptic Academy. Cf. also N.D. i 5, 11 quoted in i 4, 8 n.

quae Carneades...: Zeller, *Stoics*, etc. c. xxiii p. 527.

calamitatis ... adhibetur ... medicina: see v 1, 1 n. on 'finem faciet...disputationum.'

a philosopho: sc. *a Clitomacho.*

inueteratae: most MSS have *inueterata*: the choice lies between inserting *in* and reading with Sff. *inueteratae*. Küh. thinks it also possible to take *inueterata* as abl. abs., supplying *calamitate*,

esset, uolneribus mederetur, sed cicatricibus. sensim enim et
pedetemptim progrediens extenuatur dolor, non quo ipsa res
35 immutari soleat aut possit, sed id quod ratio debuerat usus
docet, minora esse ea quae sint uisa maiora.

XXIII. 55. Quid ergo opus est, dicet aliquis, ratione aut
omnino consolatione illa, qua solemus uti, cum leuare dolorem
maerentium uolumus? hoc enim fere tum habemus in promptu,
nihil oportere inopinatum uideri; aut qui tolerabilius feret in-
5 commodum, qui cognouerit necesse esse homini tale aliquid
accidere? haec enim oratio de ipsa summa mali nihil detrahit,
tantum modo adfert, nihil euenisse quod non opinandum fuisset.
neque tamen genus id orationis in consolando non ualet, sed id

33. uolneribus R V G B K.   uulneribus S E.   34. pedetemptim R V P G B K.
pedetemptü B 2.   pedetemtim E 1. ‖ non quo R 1 6 V P G B 1-3 K 1 2
S E 1 2 M 1 2 D C II O 2 3 7 8.   non qd O 1.   non qd' J.   non q' W 1 2.
35. immutari R V G B S E.   immitari K.   36. sint R V G S.   sunt E 1.
XXIII. § 55, 1. ratione R V P G B 1-3 K 1 S E 1 2 W 1 2 M 1 2
D C II J O 1-3 7 8.   2. consolatione illa L 4 5 C O 8.   consolatione
 illa L 2.   consolatione ulla R 1 6 7 17 V P 1 4 G B 1-3 K 1 2 S E 1 2
L 3 6 W 1 2 M 1 2 D II J O 1-3 7.   3. hoc enim R V P G B 1-3 K 1 S
E 1 2 W 1 M 1 2 D C J O 2 3 8.   hec enim II O 1 7.   h' enim K 2.
h̄ enim W 2. ‖ ferre G *in* fere *alt. man. mut.* ‖ in promtu R G.   4. aut qui
R V P G B 1-3 K 1 E 1 2 W 1 2 M 1 2 II J O 1-3 8.   atqui D C.
aut quid S.   aut q̃, O 7.   5. cognouerit E 2 W 1 M 1 II J O 1 2 7.

cognouit C.   cognoũit O 8.   cognoũit K 2 W 2.   cognouerint R V B.
cognouerint E.   cognouerint G B 2 3 K 1 M 2 O 3.   cognoũit D.
7. adfert R V G K.   affert B S E.   8. sed id R V P G B 1-3 K 1 2 S
E 1 2 W 1 2 D II J O 1-3 7 8.   set id C.

comparing 16, 34 *aduersis casibus* but
inueterata in pointed contrast to *praesentis* would not present the symmetry
which we expect from Cicero and which
inueteratae gives.

mederetur, 'its relief would have been
applied.' The act involves duration, cf.
i 12, 27 n. on 'haereret.'

cicatricibus: cf. Sen. de Ira i 16, 7
'nam, ut dicit Zenon, in sapientis quoque
animo etiam cum uulnus sanatum est,
cicatrix manet. sentiet itaque suspiciones
quasdam et umbras affectuum, ipsis quidem carebit.'

non quo...sed...docet: for the transition to a main clause cf. 22, 52 n. on
'deinde cum' and ii 26, 64 n. on 'non
quo.'

debuerat: i 49, 116 n. on 'magnum est.'

usus docet...maiora: when an evil is
fresh it appears exaggerated to our eyes.
Time shows it in its true proportions.
The same effect is produced by consolation
(§ 55) and by philosophic reflexion (*praemeditatio* § 34).

XXIII. § 55. **ergo**: sc. if time removes
all annoyance.

ratione: 'ratio est i. q. rationum enumeratio' Nissen. A statement of philosophic considerations, such as Clitomachus
had put forward, is referred to. Dav.
(ed. 2) and Ernesti needlessly substituted
oratione.

tolerabilius, 'enduringly.' The adj. has
here an active force, = *tolerantius*, cf.
Munro on Lucr. i 11. Dav. compares
Fam. xv 20 2 'quo tolerabilius feramus
igniculum desiderii tui,' Fin. iii 13, 42
'dolores eosdem tolerabilius patiuntur.'

adfert: Mo. thinks *tantum modo* = *id
modo*; but if *tantum* were the object of
adfert, *modo* would be unnecessary, the
limitation being implied (ii 19, 44 n. on
'tantum...quantum'). *Adferre* can be used
absolutely, cf. i 29, 70 n., but here it has
an acc. and inf. clause as object.

sed id: Sff. changed *sed* to *et* thinking
that after *neque...non* there was nothing
for *sed* to correct; but *neque...genus id...
non ualet* = *neque genus id ui caret* and

haud sciam an plurimum. ergo ista necopinata non habent tantam
10 uim ut aegritudo ex iis omnis oriatur; feriunt enim fortasse
grauius, non id efficiunt, ut ea quae accidant maiora uideantur;

h
9. aut sciam G aut *in* haud *alt. man. mut.*   aud sciam E *al. atr. superscr.* ‖
plurimum R V P G B K.   10. ex iis M 2.   ex iis S *linea ante* i *eras.*
ex hiis D C Π O 8.   ex his R V G B 1 3 K 1 E 1 2 W 1 2 M 1 O 1-3 7. ‖
                              i
feriunt R V P J.   ferunt G *alt. man. superscr.*   ferunt S E R 17.

sed id=immo id naturally follows, cf.
Küh. here. The emphatic repetition of
id within such a brief space has led some,
unnecessarily, to suspect the word. Wes.
Em. 1 p. 6 thought that it arose out of
sed.

haud sciam an plurimum=*fortasse
plurimum. Haud sciam an* affects a little
more diffidence than *haud scio an,* for
which see ii 17, 41 n.

ergo: with *ergo* Cicero evidently draws
together his argument against the Cyrenaics begun in § 52. Compare 'est id
quidem *magnum...quod prouisum ante
non sit* id *ferire* uehementius; sed non
sunt in hoc omnia...quanta* sint *quae
accidunt* considerandi *spatium non datur'*
of § 52 with 'ista *necopinata* non habent
tantam uim...omnis...feriunt enim...*ea
quae accidant...quia recentia sunt maiora
uidentur'* of our present passage.
The passage 'ergo ista...repentina'
would come quite naturally immediately
after § 52 and the context in §§ 53 foll.
would flow naturally from it. The arguments summed up by *ergo* are all to be
found in § 52. The *ergo* clause, where it
stands, is not in connexion with the preceding context, a fact noted by Heine,
and it interrupts the argument found in
that context. For in that context Cic.
asks what is the use of *ratio* and *consolatio*
and decides that these have their use.
After the interrupting clause *ergo...re-
pentina* he proceeds to state two ways
of ascertaining the real dimensions of a
seeming evil, with a view, as the context
shows, to reasoning with and consoling
those suffering from such seeming evils.
The clause *ergo...repentina* may have
originally stood after *acriorem facit* of
§ 52; may have dropped out of the
archetype, where it should have stood
near the head of a page, and been written
in the margin at the foot of the page;
and thence it may have got into the text
where it now stands.

enim: the argument is 'annoyance is
not *wholly* caused by the unexpected:
the unexpected has some effect in its
production, *feriunt enim,* etc.'

non id efficiunt...: this passage is
rendered difficult by the fact that Cicero
has already said that all seeming evils
are more severe when *repentina* (§ 28) or
inprouisa (§ 30) and repeats the assertion
with reference to the *necopinatum* in § 59.
Hence Bentley conjectured and Dav. read
'*nam* id efficiunt...'; and Wes. *Em.* 1
p. 16 adopting Bentley's *nam* read 'uideantur; *sed* maiora uidentur, quia recentia
sunt, non quia repentina,' comparing
variants in iv 26, 56 for *non* as a v.l. for
nam; and Hei. thought it not improbable
that Cic. wrote 'non id efficiunt ut ea
quae accidant *mala* uideantur,' the rest
being gloss; and Schiche adopts this
reading from Hei., but keeps the rest as
in the text and adds a second *mala* after
repentina, an addition which seems to
give a very questionable *clausula.* Turnebus conjectured 'non id efficiunt ut ea
quae accidant maiora *sint*; quia recentia
sunt maiora uidentur non quia repentina,'
but this reading, though palaeographically
probable, yields a defective sense. *uidentur* might have been substituted by
haplography for *sint* and changed of
necessity to *uideantur,* and *quia recentia
sunt* might have got into the margin, and
in replacing it in the text inversion, such
as we find in R, might have occurred.
But this would give a contrast between
sint and *uidentur* which is nowhere an
element in the discussion while the real
contrast between *recentia* and *repentina*
would be less forcibly expressed.
Bouhier adopted the reading which is
now seen to be that of some of the best
MSS, including V, 'non id efficiunt ut ea
quae accidant maiora uideantur; quia
recentia sunt maiora uidentur, non quia
repentina,' and he is followed by Sff. Or.
Bai. T.S. and Ml. Küh. follows Mo.
in placing *maiora uidentur* immediately
after *maiora uideantur,* agreeing in the
rest with Bouhier.
The meaning is 'the *necopinata* do not
by reason of their being *necopinata* make
the evil seem greater but by reason of
their being *recentia.*' Here and in § 52
Cicero is in harmony with the Stoic

quia recentia sunt, maiora uidentur, non quia repentina. **56.** duplex
est igitur ratio ueri reperiendi non in iis solum quae mala, sed in
iis etiam quae bona uidentur. nam aut ipsius rei natura qualis
15 et quanta sit, quaerimus, ut de paupertate non numquam, cuius
onus disputando leuamus docentes quam parua et quam pauca
sint quae natura desideret, aut a disputandi subtilitate orationem
ad exempla traducimus. hic Socrates commemoratur, hic Diogenes, hic Caecilianum illud :

20 Saépe est etiam súb palliolo sórdido sapiéntia.

12. quia recentia sunt maiora uidentur non quia repentina R 2 6 7 10 16 17
V (ſ *habet pro* sunt) P 2–4   B 1–3   K 1 (*eod. atr. suppl.*) S E (*habet* uidentur *al. atr.*
superscr.) L 2 4 6   M 2   O 2 3 7.   maiora uidentur *e contextu om. in marg. habent*
P   W 2   quia recentia sunt maiora uidentur *e contextu om. in marg. habet* G.
maiora uidentur *om.* R 1   K 2   E 2   L 3 5   M 1   D C J   O 1 8.   quia recentia
sunt uidentur non quia repentina Π.   qui recentia sunt maiora non quod repentina
W 1   R 1 *habet* non quia repentina quia recentia sunt *et in marg.* ſq̅, *non ut Sff.*
somniauit.
§ **56**, 13. est igitur ratio R V P G   B 1–3   K 1   S   E 1 2   M 2   C Π O 1–3 8.
igitur est ratio W 2   M 1   D J   O 7.   igitur ratio est W 1. ‖ repperiendi K 1. ‖
non inhis B 1.   non his V K.   non his R *alio atr. superscr.*   non is G
alt. man. superscr. ‖ sed in his G.   14. nam aut B 3   E 2   W 1   M 1 2   D C Π
O 1 3   W 2 *in marg. e cont. om.*   .ut B 1 *eod. atr. ut uid.*   ut R V P G   B 2
K 1   E 1   O 8.   ut S *in marg.* aut de. *om.* J. ‖ naturā E 1.   15. cuius onus
R V P G J.   cuius honus K 1.   cui onus B 1   E 1   O 7   S *marg.* cuiǫ.
17. suptilitate G.   18. commemoratur R V P G.   cōmemoratur B K.
19. cecilianum G K.   20. suppalliolo G.

definition laid down in § 25, 'aegritudo
est opinio magni mali praesentis, et quidem
recens opinio...' But in §§ 28, 30, and 59
he is not drawing from the same source
but probably *de suo*. [**ergo ista**: these
words seem to me to be not, like the
preceding sentence, a comment of Cicero's
in reply to the objection, but a continuation of the objector's remarks after the
interjection of the comment 'neque tamen
...plurimum.' Translate '"What then," I
shall be asked, "is the use of appealing
to reason or in fact to the style of consolation which we employ when we desire
to comfort the sorrows of the mourner?
An argument we generally have ready
is—nothing ought to take us by surprise.
Or, again, how will one bear misfortune
in a more reasonable spirit from knowing
that something of the kind is the necessary
fate of a mortal? Talk like this does not
diminish in the least the magnitude of
the misfortune: it merely proves that
nothing has happened which might not
have been expected to happen" (yet for
all that this kind of talk *has* weight in
bringing comfort—in fact I am inclined

to believe it has very great weight indeed).
"I conclude that what takes us by surprise,
as you say, is not of such importance as
to be the source of all annoyance ; surprises do perhaps come with greater force
—they do not make our misfortunes seem
greater : they seem greater because they
are recent, not because they take us by
surprise."' For this interjecting of a comment or objection in the middle of the
statement cf. iv 17, 40; iv 24, 54.]

quia recentia sunt = *quod, quanta sint,
quae accidunt, considerandi spatium non
datur* (§ 52).

§ **56. ipsius rei...quanta sit,** 'the
actual character and magnitude of the
affair.'

a disputandi subtilitate, 'from abstract discussion.' Hei. compares N.D.
ii 38, 98 'licet enim iam remota subtilitate
disputandi oculis...contemplari pulchritudinem.'

Socrates...Diogenes : both examples
are cited in v 32, 91–2. Diogenes the
Cynic is referred to.

Caecilianum : Caecilius Statius, by
birth an Insubrian Gaul, was brought to

cum enim paupertatis una eademque sit uis, quidnam dici potest, quam ob rem C. Fabricio tolerabilis ea fuerit, alii negent se ferre posse? **57.** huic igitur alteri generi similis est ea ratio consolandi, quae docet humana esse quae acciderint. non enim id solum

25 continet ea disputatio ut cognitionem adferat generis humani, sed significat tolerabilia esse quae et tulerint et ferant ceteri.

XXIV. De paupertate agitur, multi patientes pauperes commemorantur; de contemnendo honore, multi inhonorati proferuntur, et quidem propter id ipsum beatiores, eorumque qui priuatum otium negotiis publicis antetulerunt nominatim uita

5 laudatur, nec siletur illud potentissimi regis anapaestum, qui laudat senem et fortunatum esse dicit quod inglorius sit atque

§ **57, 24.** id solum R V P G B 1-3 K 1 2 S E 1 2 W 1 2 M 2 D C Π J
O 1-3 7 8. solum M 1 id *om.* 25. cognitionem R V P. cogĭtationem
G *alt. man.* ita *expunct.* cogitationem E 1. ‖ adferat R V G K. afferat
B P S E. 26. tollerabilia R V G K. ‖ quae tulerint B 1 et *om.*
XXIV. 2. commemorantur R V G. cõmemorantur K. ‖ contemnendo R G.
contēnendo B. contempnendo V E. contēpnendo K. 3. eorumque V P E.
eorum que B. eorumqu͡e͞s K. eorumqu͡se R *eod. atr.* eorum quae G.
4. nominatim R 6. nominatĭ V P R. nominati B *eod. atr.* nominati G K E.
5. potentissimi R V G B K. ‖ regis Alexandri O 2. ‖ anapaestum R.
anapestum V P 1-4 G B 1-3 K 1 2 E 1 2 W 1 2 M 1 2 D C Π J O 1-3 7.
anapest͡ic͡um S *fort. eod. atr.* anapestam O 8. qui laudat R V P 1-4 G
B 1-3 K 1 2 S E 1 2 W 1 2 M 1 2 D C Π J O 1-3 7. ‖ q̂ laudat O 8.
6. inglorius R 6 17 P 3 B 1 2 K 2 S E 2 W 1 II. inglori͡us V *duarum*
litt. spat. relicto. inglorious G o *ante* u *ead. man. expunx.* inglorioṣus M 2.
inglorioṣus K 1. ingloriosus R 1 7 P 1 2 4 B 3 E 1 W 2 D C O 1-3 8.
inglliosus O 7. ingl'osus M 1 J.

Rome between 200 and 194 B.C. probably as a prisoner of war, and began life there as a slave. He wrote numerous comedies, many of which were adapted from Menander, cf. i 14, 31; iv 32, 68; hence the reference to the Greek garb (*palliolo*) in the text. 'Saepe est...' Ribbeck, *Scaen. Rom. Poes. Frag.* II² p. 77.

§ **57. huic alteri generi** : sc. *docendi ipsius rei naturam.*

humana, 'incident to the human lot' ii 27, 65 n.; iii 16, 34 n.

ut cognitionem...humani : 'humanum genus fluxum esse, caducum, inbecillum, quassum, malis obnoxium' Beroaldus.

XXIV. de paupertate agitur : for the ellipse of *si* cf. ii 12, 28 n. on 'rogo.'

inhonorati, 'who never gained office.'

potentissimi regis : Agamemnon.

anapaestum, 'anapaestic lines,' cf. Fin. ii 6, 18; 'reliquique Graeci, qui hoc anapaesto citantur.' Cf. the use of

iambus in N.D. iii 38, 91 'quem Hipponactis iambus laeserat'; Att. xvi 11, 2 'ut Aristophani Archilochi iambus, sic epistula tua longissima quaeque optima uidetur.' Lamb. wished to read *anapaesticum*, a form which Dav. rejected, comparing ii 16, 37 'anapaestis pedibus' and Or. notes that that form seldom, if ever, occurs in Latin writers before Servius and Sidonius Apollinaris.

The reference is to Eur. Iph. in Aulis 16 foll. ΑΓ. ζηλῶ σὲ, γέρον, | ζηλῶ δ' ἀνδρῶν ὃς ἀκίνδυνον | βίον ἐξεπέρασ' ἀγνώς, ἀκλεής.

regis anapaestum qui : for the relative referring to a dependent genitive, and not to the noun on which that gen. depends, as its antecedent cf. 22, 52 'Cyrenaicorum...sententia qui...'; iv 5, 10 'Platonis discriptionem...qui...'; v 14, 40 'Laconis illud dictum...qui....' Hence Bentley's emendation *quo* was unnecessary.

ignobilis ad supremum diem peruenturus. **58.** similiter commemorandis exemplis orbitates quoque liberum praedicantur,
eorumque qui grauius ferunt luctus aliorum exemplis leniuntur;
10 sic perpessio ceterorum facit, ut ea quae acciderint multo
minora quam quanta sint existimata uideantur. ita fit sensim
cogitantibus ut, quantum sit ementita opinio, appareat. atque
hoc idem et Telamo ille declarat:

Égo cum genui......

15 et Theseus:

Futúras mecum cómmentabar míserias

et Anaxagoras: 'Sciebam me genuisse mortalem.' hi
enim omnes diu cogitantes de rebus humanis intellegebant eas

---

7. ad supremum G *alt. man. superscr.*   et sup̄mū E.   & supremum B. ||
p̄reuenturus G *ead. man.*
   § **58**, 7. commemorandis R V P G.   cōmemorandis K.   8. liberum R   P 1 4
G B 1 2   K 1   E 1 2   S *at in marg.* liberorū.   libe2̸4̸ W 2 *alio atr. superscr.*
libe_Λrū K 2 *atr. ant. superscr.*   libero2̸4̸ V *at* 2̸4̸ *in ras. neque satis spatii habet.*   libe_Λrū II *alio atr.*
superscr.   libero2̸4̸ V *at* 2̸4̸ *in ras. neque satis spatii habet.*   liberorum R 6 7
P 2 3   B 3   W 1   M 1 2   D C   O 1-3 7.   lib'o2̸4̸ R 17 J.   11. minora quam
R G.   m_Λora quam V 𝛥 *in ras.*   minora quanta E 1.   12. appareat
R V G B K S E.   13. telamo R V G K E.   telamon P.   thelamo S *eod. atr.*
thelamo B *fort. eod. atr.*   Thelamon W 1.   14. qum genui S.   genui
et theseus V P G   B 1 2   K 1   O 3.   genuisset theseus E 1.   genui et has eius
S *in marg.* theseus: *post* genui *habet* R tū morituros sciui et ei rei sustuli *manu
minore sed antiqua: idem habet* O 7: genui moriturū sciui et ei rei sustuli C.
genui moriturū sciui *cett. om.* K 2   E 2   W 1 2   M 1   D II J   O 1 2 8. *idem habet* S
in marg.   genui moriturum *cett. om.* R 7   B 3   M 2.   16. commentabar
R V G B S.   cōmentabar K.

---

§ **58. liberum**: both this form and
liberorum are found in Cicero's prose.
See especially Neue, *Formenlehre* I³
pp. 166–7, 177–8. Many instances of
liberum in the Verrines are supported by
the MS authority.

praedicantur = *commemorantur*, cf. 33,
79 'ut enim tulerit quisque eorum...
praedicandum est.'

sensim; the punctuation depends upon
whether we take *sensim* with *fit* or with
appareat. Either view seems possible.

opinio: since *aegritudo* arises *cum
quid ita uisum sit ut magnum quoddam
malum adesse et urgere uideatur*, 13,
28.

These references to Telamon, Theseus
and Anaxagoras have already been given

in §§ 28—30, where see notes. The reff.
to Telamon and Anaxagoras are shown by
Buresch, *Leipziger Studien* IX 47—49, to
have been employed by Crantor in his
περὶ πένθους, and no doubt the ref. to
Theseus was also there. Buresch cites
Hieronymus, Ep. lx 5 'ubi illud ab in-
fantia studium litterarum, et Anaxagorae
ac Telamonis semper laudata sententia:
"sciebam me genuisse mortalem?" Legimus Crantorem cuius uolumen ad con-
fouendum dolorem secutus est Cicero.'
Owing to the cognate character of the
subject Cicero, in several places in the Tusculans, has worked in matter which he had
previously made use of in the Consolatio.

rebus humanis, 'the incidents of the
human lot.'

nequaquam pro opinione uolgi esse extimescendas. et mihi
20 quidem uidetur idem fere accidere iis, qui ante meditantur, quod
iis, quibus medetur dies, nisi quod ratio quaedam sanat illos,
hos ipsa natura intellecto eo, quod rem continet, illud malum
quod opinatum sit esse maximum nequaquam esse tantum ut
uitam beatam possit euertere. 59. hoc igitur efficitur ut ex illo
25 necopinato plaga maior sit, non, ut illi putant, ut, cum duobus
pares casus euenerint, is modo aegritudine adficiatur cui ille
necopinato casus euenerit. itaque dicuntur non nulli in maerore,
cum de hac communi hominum condicione audiuissent, ea lege
esse nos natos ut nemo in perpetuum esse posset expers mali,
30 grauius etiam tulisse.

XXV. Quocirca Carneades, ut uideo nostrum scribere

19. uolgi R V G B K.   uulgi S E. ‖ extimescendas K 1 W 1 M 1 2 O 2 3.
if
extimescendas R *al. man. superscr. atr. ant.*   existimescendas V G *at mes in mis*
ead. man. mut.*   estimen·cendas E 1 *al. atr. mut.*   extumescendas O 7.
ł extimescendas
estimandas C.   estimandas D *al. atr. superscr.*   existi miscendas B 2.
extimandas O 8.   20. his R 1 (*bis*).   21. ratione E 1 *fort. eod. atr.*   ratio V
at duarum litt. spatio relicto in ras.   ratione quaedam G K.   ratione quaedam R.
ratione quaedam B ę *in a mut.*   22. quod rem continet malum L 3 (illud *om.*).
quod rem continet illud O 1 (malum *om.*).   quod rem illud continet malum R 1 17
P 1 4 G B 1 2 K 1 E 1 L 2 5 W 2 O 8 S *at in marg.* remedium.   quod
remedium illud continet malum R 6 O 2.   quod remedium continet malum P 2 3
B 3 E 3 L 6 M 2 O 3.   quod rem illam continet malum E 2 Π.   quod res
illud continet malum W 1 J.   quod re illud continet malum R 7.   quod řo
illud continet malum M 1.   quā rem illud continet malum O 7.   quod omne
illud continet malum L 4.   quod illud continet malum D C.   quod remon3 illud
malum K 2 (on3 *extra lineam,* continet *om.*).   quod rem continet illud malum
                                                                                    v
corr. Bentleius.   23. maxumum R V G B.   maximum K.   maximum S.
§ 59, 26. adficiatur V G.   afficiatur R B K.   27. necopinato R V G K.
nec opinato R 17 B 1 2 E 2 W 2 M 1 2 D C Π J O 1 3 8.   nec oppinato R 7.
nec opinatus R 6 W 1.   ne oppinato O 7.   *om.* E 1.   28. condicione G
in conditione *alt. man. mut.*   conditione B K.   29. esse possit B 1.
                                                                    ades
XXV. 1. carne ades V.   carne E 1 *al. atr. superscr.*

qui ante meditantur: for Chrysippus'
recommendation of *praemeditatio* cf.
20, 52 n.

quod iis sc. *accidere solet.*

intellecto ... continet ..., 'since they
realize that which is the important point,
viz. that...'

opinatum sit: here in passive sense,
cf. 11, 24 n. on 'opinati.' *opino* is frequent in O.L.

§ 59. efficitur ut: i 8, 16 n. 'From
all this it follows'...

ut ex illo necopinato.... The point all
along here is that the *necopinatum* is
subjective not objective. The cause of

annoyance is not the *necopinatum* but the
supposed magnitude of the evil. The
evil is supposed to be greater where it is
necopinatum, but this is not the only case
in which the dimensions of an evil are
over-estimated.

illi: sc. *Cyrenaici.*

itaque dicuntur...: see M. Pohlenz in
Hermes XLI p. 326.

XXV. **Carneades**: Zeller, *Stoics*, etc.
XXIII pp. 506 foll.

nostrum...Antiochum: When Cicero
withdrew to Athens and the East for two
years, commencing with 79 B.C., he
attended the lectures of various philo-

Antiochum, reprendere Chrysippum solebat laudantem Euripideum carmen illud:

Mortális nemo est quém non attingát dolor
5　Morbúsque; multis súnt humandi líberi,
Rursúm creandi, mórsque est finita ómnibus,
Quae géneri humano angórem nequicquam ád-
ferunt.

2. anthiochum R. ‖ reprendere R G.　　rep̄hendere V *i.e.* r *in* h *mut. et linea*
supra p *ducta.*　　rep̄hendere B 1 3　S　W 2　D J　O 7.　　rep̄henđe E 1.
reprehenđe E 2.　　reprehendere B 2　K 1　C　O 1 3 8.　　‖　crysippum R G.
crypsippum E 1.　　4. non attingat R 6 17　L 3 4　W 1　D.　　non ac tingat C.
non attingit R 10 16　B 1–3　E 2 3　L 6　M 1 2　Π　O 2 8.　　non ut adtingit E 1.
　　　　　　　　　　　　　　　　　　　　　　　　　　　　　　non　　　　　ᴺ
non attigit R 7　L 2.　　non atingit O 7.　　attigit K 1 *eod. atr.*　　a ttingit V
　　　　　　　non
ras. inter a *et* t.　　adtingit P *al. atr. superscr.*　　attingit (non *om.*) R G　K 2　S
L 5　W 2　J. ‖ *post* attigit *habet* R 7 morbusque dolorque.　　5. multi sunt
humandi R 1 6 7 10 16 17　V　P 1–4　G　B 1–3　K 1 2　S　E 1–3　L 2–6　W 1 2
M 1 2　D C Π J　O 1–3 7 8 ed. H.　　multis *corr. Lambinus.*　　6. morsquæeest R
eod. atr.　　morſ quę ᵉˢᵗ V (ſ *in ras.*).　　morsquę est P.　　mors quae est G. ‖
finita V P G　B 2 3　K 1　W 2　M 1 2　O 8 Gr.　W 1 s *post* a *eras.*　　finitas O 1 3.
　　　　ˢ　　　　　　　　　ˢ
finita R 1.　　finita E 1　　finis E 2　C Π.　　7. generi E 2　W 2　M 2
　　　　　　　　　　　　　　　　　　　　　　　i
D C　O 1 3.　　gn̄ī B 3　W 1　M 1　O 7　gn'i O 8.　　genere V *atr. uiridi*
superscr.　　geneṛ E 1.　　genere R G　B 1 2　K 1 2　S J. ‖　nequicquam
　　　　　　　　　　　　　　　　　　　　　　　　　　　　　　a
R V G B K S E D J. ‖ adferunt R G K E.　　adferunt V.　　afferunt B D S　E 2.

sophers and at Athens was specially influenced by those of Antiochus of Ascalon, the founder of the fifth Academy, as it is sometimes called; hence *nostrum* in the text. Cf. Brut. 91, 315. Cicero possibly had a work of Antiochus open before him at this point. Carneades' criticism of the view of Chrysippus is rejected with the words 'mihi uero longe uidetur secus. nam...,' in § 60 below, and Pohlenz acutely conjectures in *Hermes* XLI p. 338 that the refutation also is taken from Antiochus so that *mihi uero* practically means *Antiocho uero*.

Euripideum carmen: from Euripides' Hypsipyle, cf. Dind. *Poet. Scaen. Graec. Frag.* 757. Amphiaraus endeavours to console the mother of Archemorus on the premature death of her son. The Greek words are preserved in Stobaeus Ecl. IV 44, 12 (ed. Hense); Plut. Cons. ad Apollon. 110 F.; the first three lines (with one earlier and three later) by Clemens Alex. Strom. iv p. 495 C (ed. Sylb.); the last line by Marcus Anton. vii 40. They run as follows: ἔφυ μὲν οὐδεὶς ὅστις οὐκ ἀεὶ πονεῖ. | θάπτειν τε τέκνα χἄτερα κτᾶσθαι πάλιν | αὐτούς τε θνήσκειν· καὶ τάδ' ἄχθονται βροτοὶ | εἰς γῆν φέροντες γῆν· ἀναγκαίως δ' ἔχει | βίον θερίζειν ὥστε κάρπιμον στάχυν.

For a theory to account for the fact that these lines, which as we see were quoted by Chrysippus, occur also in Plutarch's Cons. ad Apollon. and therefore no doubt formed part of Crantor's περὶ πένθους, and to account for the use by Chrysippus and Crantor of much other matter in common see Pohlenz, *Hermes* XLI p. 354 n.

carmen: i 16, 37 n.

attingat: F.A.W. thinks *attingit* of MSS old Latin for *attingat*, but if this were a Latin version of Euripides' words by an early Latin author Cicero would have named him instead of calling it *Euripideum carmen*. The version is by Cicero himself. Cf. ii 11, 26 for his practice in this matter.

finita = *definita, constituta*, cf. Leg. ii 26, 66 'sepulcris nouis finiuit modum'; Caes. B.G. vi 18 'spatia omnis temporis non numero dierum, sed noctium finiunt.' T.S.

quae generi... lit. 'facts which...'

nequicquam: F.A.W. notes that this word is properly used in the sense of *frustra* only by poets; Or. cites p. Quinct. 25, 79 'et sero et nequicquam pudet' but thinks those words may perhaps be taken from some unknown comic poet or from Ter. Heaut. ii 2, 104 'hodie sero ac nequicquam.'

Reddénda terrae est térra, tum uita ómnibus
Meténda, ut fruges. síc iubet Necéssitas.

10 **60.** negabat genus hoc orationis quicquam omnino ad leuandam
aegritudinem pertinere. id enim ipsum dolendum esse dicebat,
quod in tam crudelem necessitatem incidissemus; nam illam
quidem orationem ex commemoratione alienorum malorum ad
maliuolos consolandos esse accommodatam. mihi uero longe
15 uidetur secus. nam et necessitas ferendae condicionis humanae
quasi cum deo pugnare prohibet admonetque esse hominem,
quae cogitatio magno opere luctum leuat, et enumeratio exemplorum, non ut animum maliuolorum oblectet, adfertur, sed ut
ille qui maeret ferundum sibi id censeat quod uideat multos
20 moderate et tranquille tulisse. **61.** omnibus enim modis fulciendi

---

8. terrae est terra R 11 10 16 V P 14 G B 12 K 1 S E 12 Π O 2.
est terrae terra B 3 K 2 E 3 L 2–6 M 2 D C J O 1.   est terra terrae W 1 2
M 1 O 7.   terra terrae est O 8.   terra est terrae O 3. ‖ tum R V P G *plerique*.
cum L 3 M 1.   tam K 2.

§ **60**, 10. negabat R G B K.   negĕbat V.   13. ex commemoratione V

com *in ras*.   ex cōmemoratione E 12 O 1.   ex quomemoratione P.
cō
ex quomemoratione K 1.   exquomemoratione R 1.   ex quo nemo ratione G.
14. maliuolos R V G B K E.   malīuolos S i *in e mut*. ‖ accomodatam G.
accomōdatam K.   accōdatā E 1.   15. condicionis E.   conditionis
R V P G B K.   16. prohibet L 6.   ᵽhibet E 3 ᵽ *eod. atr. at in ras. esse uidetur*.
                                                                          ᵽ
ᵽhib3 W 2 *at ante* ᵽ *indistincte* c *uideri potest*.   ᵽhibet ed. H.   çohibet V.
cohibet R 67 17 P 1–4 G B 1–3 K 12 S E 12 L 2–5 W 1 M 12 D C Π J
          c
O 1–3 7 8.   quohibet R 1. ‖ admonet G K.   ammonet B 1.   āmonet B 2.
                                                                       o
17. magno opere G B 2.   magnoopere R V.   magnopere K *eod. atr*.
magnopere B S E.   18. maliuolorum R V G B K S E W D. ‖ adfertur
R V G K E.   affertur B S.   19. ferundum R V G B 1 K 1
W 2 O 1.   ferendum R 67 P 1 2 4 B 2 3 K 2 S E 12 W 1 M 1 2
D C Π J O 2 3 7 8.

---

tum: Sff. conjectured *tam* and Küh.
nam. But by *tum* 'further' 'moreover'
Cic. is probably, as suggested by T.S.,
giving an awkward rendering of δέ of the
original.
Necessitas: Ἀνάγκη.
§ **60**. **negabat**: sc. *Carneades*.
mihi: see n. on 'nostrum...Antiochum'
§ 59 above.
**necessitas ferendae condicionis hu-
manae**: cf. 16, 34 'meditatio condicionis
humanae' and *ibid*. 'humana humane
ferenda.'
quasi cum deo pugnare: cf. Cato M.
2, 5 'quid est enim aliud Gigantum modo
bellare cum diis nisi naturae repugnare?'
prohibet: Wes. *Em*. II p. 55 points

out that while *prohibere* (=*procul habere*)
naturally takes the simple abl. and the
simple inf., *cohibere* (=*continere, coercere*)
cannot take either constr. to express that
from which one is restrained, but it has
such constructions as *manus ab auro,
hostem a praedandi licentia cohibere* or
(Tac. A. ii 24) *quem...uix cohibuere
quominus...oppeteret*, and with the inf.
the verb would rather express that which
one was constrained to do, than that
from which one was restrained.
admonetque esse hominem=*ad. nos
esse homines*. The subject accusative
(understood) to *esse* is indefinite. For
the omission of the accus. cf. i 25, 60 n.
'nec me pudet...fateri nescire.'

sunt qui ruunt nec cohaerere possunt propter magnitudinem
aegritudinis. ex quo ipsam aegritudinem λύπην Chrysippus
quasi solutionem totius hominis appellatam putat; quae tota
poterit euelli explicata, ut principio dixi, causa aegritudinis; est
25 enim nulla alia nisi opinio et iudicium magni praesentis atque
urgentis mali. itaque et dolor corporis, cuius est morsus acerrimus, perfertur spe proposita boni, et acta aetas honeste ac
splendide tantam adfert consolationem, ut eos qui ita uixerint
aut non attingat aegritudo aut perleuiter pungat animi dolor.

XXVI. Sed ad hanc opinionem magni mali cum illa etiam
opinio accessit, oportere, rectum esse, ad officium pertinere
ferre illud aegre quod acciderit, tum denique efficitur illa grauis
aegritudinis perturbatio. 62. ex hac opinione sunt illa uaria
5 et detestabilia genera lugendi, paedores, muliebres lacerationes

§ 61, 22. aΫΠHN R 1.　　AΥΠHN G.　　ΔyΠHN R 2 10.　　λyΠHN P. ||
chrysippus R V G.　　chrisippus K 1　R 10 16.　　crisippus S E.　　dirisipus R 2.
23. quasi solutionem R V G　B 1 3　K 1 2　S　E 1 2　W 1 2　M 1 2　D C Π J
O 1 3 8.　　quasi et solutioni O 2.　　quasi solicitudie O 7.　　om. P. || appellatam
putat G E.　　appellat am|putat R V.　　appellat amputat K 1.　　appellat
amputa B 2.　om. P at in marg. appellat amputatq3 in appellatis putat quae mut.
24. ut principio R G B　W 2.　　ut in principio W 1.　　aut principio V.
25. nulla nisi B E alia om.　　26. acerrimus S　R 10 16.　　acerri mus R u in i
ras. mut.　　acerrumus G.　　accerrumus V B K.　　acerrimus E.
27. perfertur R 6　B 3　W 1　O 1–3 7.　　perfer&ur V eod. atr. punctis appositis.
perfer&ur R 1.　　perferetur P G　B 1　K 1 2　S　E 1 2　W 2　M 1　D C Π J　O 8.
preferetur B 2.　　praefertur M 2.　　28. adfert R V G K.　　affert B S E.
29. attingat R V G　B 1 3　K S　E 2　M 2　D Π　O 3 8.　　adtingat E.
atingat O 7.　　tangat K 2　W 1 2　M 1　J.
XXVI. 2. accessit R V P G　B 1–3　K 1 2　S　E 1 2　W 2　M 1 2　Π J
O 2 3 7 8.　　accessit C.　　accesserit R 6　W 1　D　O 1.

§ 62, 5. genera V G　B 2.　　genere R eod. atr.　　generi P ras. post i. ||

paedores R V G.　　pedores R 6　P 1 3　B K S.　　pectores E 1.
pudores P 2　J.

§ 61. fulciendi...ruunt...cohaerere,
'we must prop the resolution of those
who are sinking and cannot hold together....' The metaphors are taken from
building and are in harmony with the
derivation of λύπη that follows. Cf. v
28, 80 'nec enim uirtutes sine beata uita
cohaerere possunt'; de Harusp. Resp.
27, 60 'uix haec si undique fulciamus,
iam labefacta,...cohaerebunt.'
　λύπην...quasi solutionem: the same
derivation is found in Plato, Crat. p. 419C,
ἤ τε λύπη ἀπὸ τῆς διαλύσεως τοῦ σώματος
ἔοικεν ἐπονομασθῆναι.
　Similarly Cleanthes, cf. Stobaeus, Ecl.
iv 44, 59 (ed. Hense) ὁ δὲ Κλεάνθης ἔλεγε
τὴν λύπην ψυχῆς παράλυσιν. [According
to Vaniček (Etym. Wört. pp. 789 sq.)
λύπη is derived from a root RAP or RUP

(seen in rapio and strengthened in rumpo)
meaning 'to break' or 'to tear.']
　ut principio dixi: 10, 23.
　aegritudo...animi dolor : Bent. wrote
'quid aliud est aegritudo nisi animi
dolor? frustra igitur sententia oneratur et
ultra perfectum trahitur.' He therefore
proposed 'aut non attingat omnino aut...'
and Dav. admitted this to the text.
Ernesti omitted aegritudo.
　XXVI. accessit: for the perf. indic.
cf. ii 2, 5 n. on 'occurrit'; ii 23, 54 n. on
'restiterunt'; ii 24, 58 n. on 'aspeximus.'
　ad officium pertinere : this view was
specially refuted by Chrysippus, cf. 31,
76.
　§ 62. paedores : e.g. putting ashes on
one's head.
　muliebres: cf. the provision of the

genarum, pectoris, feminum, capitis percussiones; hinc ille Agamemno Homericus et idem Accianus

    Scindéns dolore idéntidem intonsám comam,

in quo facetum illud Bionis, perinde stultissimum regem in luctu
10 capillum sibi euellere, quasi caluitio maeror leuaretur. 63. sed
haec omnia faciunt opinantes ita fieri oportere. itaque et Aeschines in Demosthenem inuehitur quod is septimo die post filiae
mortem hostias immolauisset. at quam rhetorice, quam copiose,

---

6. genarum G K.   gene|Narum V *at* N *in ras.* ‖ feminum R V P 1 3 G
B 1 3 K S E 1 2 M 2 D C Π O 1 2 7 8.   femorum P 2 W 1 O 3.
femīni W 2.   femurum M 1.   feīnei J. ‖ agamemno R V G K E.
agamemnŏ S.   agamemnon W 1 M 2.   agamenno B 1.   agamemnon P
ras. post en *fort. ex* em *mut.*   agamenon E 2 M 1 O 3.   agamēon W 2.

7. accianus R V P G B K S J.   accidē E *eod. atr. ut uid.*   8. identidem R G B K.
idemtidem V.   9. stultissimum R V G B K.
§ 63, 11. aescīnes V *i.e.* cin *in* chi *al. atr. mut.*   escīnes P *al. atr. mut.*

aescinnes R G K.   eschines S.   escines E *al. atr. superscr.*   esci nes B.
12. Demosthenē J.   demosthenem W 1 O 1 3.   demostenem R V P G B 2.

demostenē B 3 K 2 E 1 W 2.   demonstenem S.   demonstenem K 1.
demostenen B 1 D.   demosten O 7. ‖ quod his V.   13. immolauisset
R V G K S E. ‖ rhetorice K S.   r&horice V.   rethorice G B 1 2.
rethorice R E. ‖ quam copiose R 6 P 3 B 3 S L 2 4 6 W 1 M 1 2 DC
O 1–3 7 8 ed. H.   quam copiose W 2 *spat. et ras. ante* c.   quam 2 copiose R 7.
quam ex copiose P 2 4 J.   quam excopiose V *eod. ut uid. atr.* E *eod. ut uid. atr.*
quam excopiose R 1 G B 2 K 1 2 E 2 L 3 5 Π.   quas excopiose B τ *fort.*
mut.   et quam copiose R 17.   & quam copiose E 3.   *Fortasse* quam etiam copiose.

XII Tables quoted on ii 23, 55 'mulieres
genas ne radunto.'

feminum : for the form cf. Giles'
Manual of Comp. Phil. § 354.

Homericus : Il. x 14—15 Aὐτὰρ ὅτ'
ἐς νῆάς τε ἴδοι καὶ λαὸν Ἀχαιῶν, | Πολλὰς
ἐκ κεφαλῆς προθελύμνους ἕλκετο χαίτας.

et idem Accianus : probably in the
Nyctegresia of Accius, which was founded
upon the tenth book of the Iliad. Ribbeck,
R. Trag. p. 364, conjectures that this line
was spoken in the prologue by a follower of the king or perhaps by Minerva,
in describing the situation and the distress
of Agamemnon.

Bionis : Bion the Borysthenite (a pupil
of Crates, Theodorus the Cyrenaic (ὁ ἄθεος)
and Theophrastus) was celebrated for his
biting wit, of which specimens are given
by Diog. L. iv 46—57. Cf. Hor. Epp.
ii 2, 60 'ille Bioneis sermonibus et sale
nigro.'

perinde : i 36, 86 n. on 'proinde.'

§ 63. **et Aeschines** : a second *et*-clause
should have corresponded. *et alii solitudines captant,* but instead we have a

separate sentence, *ex quo euenit...,* and
owing to the detail with which the first
clause is expanded, *et* is left pendens.
F.A.W. thinks *et* intensive here.

Aeschines : in his speech against Ctesiphon, § 77 ἑβδόμην δ' ἡμέραν τῆς θυγατρὸς
αὐτῷ τετελευτηκυίας πρὶν πενθῆσαι καὶ τὰ
νομιζόμενα ποιῆσαι, στεφανωσάμενος καὶ
λευκὴν ἐσθῆτα λαβὼν ἐβουθύτει καὶ
παρενόμει, τὴν μόνην ὁ δείλαιος καὶ
πρώτην αὐτὸν πατέρα προσειποῦσαν ἀπολέσας, a passage which is quoted by
Plut. Cons. ad. Apollon. 119 B—C. Dav.
also compares Plut. *Vita Demosth.* c. xxii
where it is stated that Demosthenes'
rejoicing was caused by the death of
Philip of Macedon.

inuehitur : the pres. because the speech
was extant, cf. i 18, 42 n. on 'uolt.' The
secondary sequence **immolauisset** can
follow, cf. iii 15, 32 n. on 'uenisset...'

quam copiose : this is not satisfactory
for *quam excopiose* of the best MSS. Sff.
reads *quam ingeniose* referring this adverb
by chiasmus to *sententias colligit* and
rhetorice to *uerba contorquet.*

quas sententias colligit, quae uerba contorquet! ut licere
15 quiduis rhetori intellegas. quae nemo probaret, nisi insitum
illud in animis haberemus, omnis bonos interitu suorum quam
grauissime maerere oportere. ex hoc euenit ut in animi doloribus alii solitudines captent, ut ait Homerus de Bellerophonte:

Qui miser in campis maerens errabat Aleis
20 Ipse suum cor edens, hominum uestigia uitans.

et Nioba fingitur lapidea propter aeternum, credo, in luctu
silentium. Hecubam autem putant propter animi acerbitatem

---

14. colligit R V G B K S E.   15. rhetori K.   r&hori R *eod. atr.*   rethori
G B S E. ‖ intellegas R V G B K.   intelligas S E.   16. omnis R V G
B 1 2 K.   omis E.   omnes S.   17. grauissime R V P G B K. ‖
ex hoc uenit B.   19. aleis Π *at* eis *in ras. et fuerat* alienis.   alienis R 1 6 7
V P 1-4 G B 1-3 K 1 2 S E 1-3 L 2-6 W 1 2 M 1 2 D C J O 1-3 7 8
ed. H.   habenis R 17.   20. edens R 17 P 2 B 3 E 3 M 1 2 D C Π
O 1-3 8.   edens W 2 *spat. et ras. ante* ed.   edens uḷ' euịdẹṇṣ P (*sic*).

ẹdens W 1.   edans P 3.   euịdens S.   euịdens V *al. atr. corr.*   euidens
R 17 P 4 G B 1 2 K 1 2 E 2 L 5 J O 7.   eudens E 1. ‖ uitans R 6
B 3 K 2 E 2 W 1 M 1 2 Π O 1-3.   uitãs R 7 17 E 3 W 2 O 8.
uitaɴт V.   uitas R 1 P G B 1 2 K 1 S E 1 D C O 7.   uetans J.

21. nioba R G.   nioba S.   22. haecubam R G K.   hẹc uerbã E 1.

---

uerba contorquet, 'hurls' (as missiles).
For the metaphor Küh. compares iv
36, 77 'intorquentur'; Or. i 57, 242 'a
quo cum *amentatas hastas* acceperit, ipse
eas oratoris lacertis uiribusque torquebit';
Brut. 78, 271; Or. 70, 234.
rhetori: F.A.W. says 'significatione
Graeca pro oratori' and Hei. takes a
similar view. But I know no parallel in
Cicero. Küh. seems more correct in
explaining the word as emphatic and
= *dicendi artifici*.
de Bellerophonte: Bellerophon grieved
thus when he lost the favour of heaven
and his children were slain.
Qui miser in campis: Homer, Il. vi
201-2:
ἤτοι ὁ κὰπ πεδίον τὸ Ἀλήϊον οἶος ἀλᾶτο,
ὃν θυμὸν κατέδων, πάτον ἀνθρώπων ἀλεείνων
where a Scholiast notes Ἀλήϊον πεδίον
τῆς Κιλικίας καλούμενον ἀπὸ τῆς τοῦ
Βελλεροφόντου ἄλης, τουτέστι πλάνης. Cf.
Herod. vi 95; Strabo xiv p. 676; Etym.
Magn. s.v. Ἀλήϊον. Dav.
et Nioba: since *alii...captent* preceded
we should strictly have had *alii aeternum
silentium seruent, ut Nioba, quae...* in the
corresponding clause.
For Niobe, turned into a stone from
which tears ever flowed, cf. Scholiast A
on Hom. Il. xxiv 602; Pausan. i 21, 5,
who says that he himself saw the famous

Niobe rock on Mt Sipylus, in Phrygia,
which, when one approached it nearly,
resembled a woman weeping and bowed
down; Soph. Elect. 150 foll.; Ov. Met.
vi 310 foll. In this instance also the
grief was for children slain.
Niobe, daughter of Tantalus and wife
of Amphion, king of Thebes, proud of
her six sons and six daughters, declared
herself superior to Latona, who had only
one son and one daughter. Thereupon
Apollo slew all her sons and Diana all
her daughters. Dav. notes that Lucian
also, de Saltat. § 41, mentions τὴν ἐπὶ τῷ
πένθει σιγήν of Niobe.
propter aeternum: F.A.W. thinks
this theory probably due to the Stoic
tendency to apply allegory to myths; for
this tendency see Zeller, *Stoics*, etc.,
c. xiii pp. 346-7.
Hecubam: when her daughter Polyxena
was sacrificed by Neoptolemus and her
youngest son Polydorus murdered by
Polymestor, king of Thrace, Hecuba is
said to have torn out the eyes of Polymestor and slain his two sons and then,
or subsequently, to have been changed
into a dog. Ov. Met. xiii 423-575; Eur.
Hec. 1265 (Polymestor speaks) κύων
γενήσει πύρσ' ἔχουσα δέργματα. Strabo
xiii p. 595; Juvenal x 271-2 with Mayor's
references.

quandam et rabiem fingi in canem esse conuersam. sunt autem
alii quos in luctu cum ipsa solitudine loqui saepe delectat, ut
25 illa apud Ennium nutrix:

> Cupído cepit míseram nunc me próloqui
> Caclo átque terrac Médeai míserias.

XXVII. 64. Haec omnia recta, uera, debita putantes faciunt
in dolore, maximeque declaratur hoc quasi officii iudicio fieri,

23. quandam R V *hoc loco* G K E.   24. alii quos V E 2 W 1 M 2 D II

O 3 8.   alii autem quos M 1.   alii quo B *eod. atr.* R *al. atr.* P *al. atr.*
alii quo G B 2 K 1 E 1. ‖ delectat R 1 6 7 17 V P B 1 3 K 1 2 S E 1–3
L 2 3 5 6 W 1 2 M 1 2 II J O 1 2 7 8 ed. H.   delectät B 2.   delectet G L 4
D C O 3.   27. medeae R V P G K 1 M 2 O 2.   medee B 1 S L 4
W 1 O 3.   medee R 7 17 P 2 B 2 3 K 2 E 2 L 2 3 6 W 2 M 1 D C II J

O 1 7 ed H.   medę E 1.   medae R 6.   medete L 5.   medere O 8.
Medeai *corr. Turnebus.*

XXVII. § 64, 2. maximeque V G B.   maximeque K.   maximįeque
R *eod. atr.* ‖ declaratur R 1 7 17 V P 1–4 G B 1–3 K 1 S E 2 3 M 1 2

D C II O 1–3 8.   declarat͂ E W 1 2 O 7.   declatur K 2.   decl'at͡r J.
delectantur R 6. ‖ hoc R V P 1–4 G B 1–3 K 1 S E 1–3 L 2–4 6 W 1

M 1 2 D C II O 1–3 7 8 ed. H.   h J.   ħ K 2.   ħ R 17.   ħ L 5 W 2. ‖
officii R V P G B 2 K.

acerbitatem quandam: *quandam* intensifies, cf. i 12, 27 *n.* on 'quandam
quasi.'

delectat: although a definite instance
is immediately cited the reference here is
to a class *alii* and we should expect the
class-subj. to follow. Either Cic. has
inaccurately accommodated the constr.
to the definite instance that follows or we
should read *delectet* against most (and the
best) MSS. For the difference between
sunt qui, est qui with the subj. and with
the indic. cf. Hor. Epp. ii 2, 182 'sunt
qui non habeant, est qui non curat
habere.'

apud Ennium: in the Medea Exul cf.
Ribb. *Scaen. Rom. Poes. Frag.* I² p. 46,
ll. 216–7; *Röm. Trag.* p. 150.
In Euripides' Medea which Ennius
follows the words are (ll. 56—58):
ἐγὼ γὰρ ἐς τοῦτ' ἐκβέβηκ' ἀλγηδόνος
ὥσθ' ἵμερός μ' ὑπῆλθε γῇ τε κοὐρανῷ
λέξαι μολούσῃ δεῦρο δεσπoίνης τύχας.
XXVII. § 64. **uera**=*iusta*, cf. 29,
73 'rectum quoque et uerum'; Caes.
B.G. iv 8, 2 'neque uerum esse, qui suos
fines tueri non potuerint, alienos occu-
pare'; Hor. Epp. i 7, 98; i 12, 23.
declaratur hoc: Ml. takes the meaning to be *officii iudicio hoc fieri eo*

declaratur quod... and he explains *hoc*
as=*ut haec omnia recta, uera, debita
putantes faciant in dolore.* As the MS
reading thus yields a good sense it
does not seem well to depart from it.
hoc after *haec omnia...* is hardly what we
should expect from Cicero. Wes. proposed *haec* and the confusion between
hoc and *haec* in MSS is very common.
Ml. thinks *hoc* no more to be changed
into *haec* than *utraque in re* into *utrisque
in rebus* in Lael. 17, 64 ex. where in
bonis rebus aut in malis preceded. Hei.,
followed by T.S., reads *declaratur haec.*
For *eo* supplied in thought before *quod*
Hei. compares Off. i 18, 61 'declaratur
autem studium bellicae gloriae, quod
statuas quoque uidemus ornatu fere mili-
tari.' Or. Kl. Bai. and Sff. read *declarat
hoc*, Bai. noting that *hoc* is to be taken as
nom. and that the subj. acc. to *fieri* is
haec omnia. The symbol for *ur* has been
sometimes erroneously inserted in MSS.,
a good instance being *suscitabitur* for
suscitabit in ii 22, 51; it is still more
easily omitted as it seems to have been in
cod. Rehdigerianus, a fact upon which
Or. lays too much stress.

quasi officii iudicio, 'under the idea
that duty demands it.'

quod, si qui forte, cum se in luctu esse uellent, aliquid fecerunt
humanius, aut si hilarius locuti sunt, reuocant se rursus ad
5 maestitiam peccatique se insimulant quod dolere intermiserint.
puros uero matres et magistri castigare etiam solent, nec uerbis
solum, sed etiam uerberibus, si quid in domestico luctu hilarius
ab iis factum est aut dictum, plorare cogunt. quid? ipsa remissio
luctus cum est consecuta intellectumque est nihil profici mae-
10 rendo, nonne res declarat fuisse totum illud uoluntarium?
65. quid ille Terentianus 'ipse se poeniens,' id est ἑαυτὸν τιμωρούμενος?

> Decréui tantispér me minus iniúriae,
> Chremés, meo gnato fácere, dum fiám miser.

3. cum se in luctu R V P G   B 1 2   S   E 1 2   W 1 2   M 1   D C Π J   O 1–3 7 8.

cum in luctu B 3   M 2.   cum se in lectu K 1 *eod. atr.*   8. ab his R G B.

9. intellectûque est V.   intellectū est Π *al. atr. superscr.*   intellectū est E 2.

intellectaque est R 1 6   G   B 1 2   K 1   D C   O 7.   intellecta quę ÷ E 1 *al. atr.*
superscr.   intellectaque (est *om.*) R 7 1 7   P   B 3   K 2   S   E 3   L 3–6   W 1 2
M 1 2   J   O 1–3 8.   intellectâque (est *om.*) L 2.   10. nonne res R V P G *plerique.*
nō eres B 2.
§ 65, 11. terjentianus V.   terrentianus R G K.   ‖ puniens R 6   P 3   B 3   L 6
M 1 2   Π ed. H.   poenitens R V G O 2.   penitens R 10   P 1   B 1.
penitens R 17   P 2   B 2   K 1 2   S E 1   L 2–5   D C J   O 1 3 7 8.   penitens
E 2 *at* p *eraso.*   penitēs R 7.   p̄nitens P 4.   pēitēs W 2.   crucians W 1.
poeniens *corr.* Gulielmius.   ‖ ΕΑΥΤΟΝ ΤΕΙΜΩΡΟΫΜΕΝΟC R E.   ΕΑΥΤΟΝΤΕ
ιμωρο|υμΕΝΟC V.   ΕΑΥΤΟΝΤΕΙΜΩΡΟΫ ΜΕΝΟC G.   ΕΑΥ ΤΟΝ
ΤΡΜΩΡ|ΟΙΜΕΝΟC K 1.   14. Chremes R G   B 1 2   K E D C   O 2.   chremef V
ſ *al. man. add.*   chremeſs P *eod. atr.*   chremens O 7.   cremes M 1 2.

creme S ſ *post* me *eras.* W 1.   chreme O 3.   omes W 2 *al. atr. superscr.*

humanius: most editors take this to
mean 'with moderation,' cf. ii 27, 65, but
I think the idea is rather 'naturally' i.e.
in accordance with their feelings. F.A.W.
explains 'genio indulgentes.'
castigare: usually of verbal reproof,
though not limited to that meaning, cf.
Livy xxvi 27, 8 'pridie eum uerberibus
castigatum.'
uerbis...uerberibus: for the *anno-*
minatio, cf. Ter. Heaut. 356 'tibi erunt
parata uerba, huic homini uerbera' and
i 40, 95 n. on 'leuius...leuitati.'
consecuta: 'h.e. ipsa remissio luctus
cum est *secuta, ita quidem, ut simul*
intellegatur.' Küh. Cf. i 16, 36 n.
res, 'the fact itself.' The fact that we
can abandon grief when we realise that it
does no good shows that we had it in our
power to avoid giving way to it. This
topic is further dealt with in c. 28 init.
§ 65. Terentianus... τιμωρούμενος: as
the Greek name was given to the play by
Terence himself and therefore generally

known, Bouh. thinks that it should have
come first. He suggests that it was omitted by some copyists who did not know
Greek and afterwards inserted by others
in the wrong place, and he believes that
Cic. wrote *ille Terentianus ἑαυτὸν τιμωρού-*
μενος, id est ipse se poeniens. P. Manutius
thought that one or other of the two titles
should be cut out as a gloss and Fabricius
would read *ille Ter. ἑαυτὸν τιμωρούμενος.*
Or. thinks that Cic. placed the words in
the order of the text to indicate that in
his opinion Terence would have done
better to choose the Latin title. Dav. defends the text with the following parallels
v 3, 9 'hos se appellare sapientiae studiosos, id est enim philosophos'; Ac. ii 29,
93 'placet enim Chrysippo...quiescere, id
est, quod ab his dicitur, ἡσυχάζειν'; Quint.
ii 15, 4 'dicens esse rhetoricen persuadendi
opificem, id est πειθοῦς δημιουργόν'; iii
11, 6 'causa quoque ex causa, id est
αἴτιον ἐξ αἰτίου, nasci uidetur.' Cf. Madv.
on Fin. i 10, 33 n.

15 hic decernit ut miser sit. num quis igitur quicquam decernit inuitus?

Maló quidem me quóuis dignum députem.

malo se dignum deputat, nisi miser sit. uides ergo opinionis esse, non naturae malum. quid, quos res ipsa lugere prohibet?
20 ut apud Homerum cotidianae neces interitusque multorum sedationem maerendi adferunt, apud quem ita dicitur:

Namque nimis multos atque omni luce cadentis
Cernimus, ut nemo possit maerore uacare.
Quo magis est aequum tumulis mandare peremptos
25 Firmo animo et luctum lacrimis finire diurnis.

66. ergo in potestate est abicere dolorem, cum uelis, tempori seruientem. an est ullum tempus, quoniam quidem res in nostra

15. numquiơ K 1 d *in* [*mut.*   17. deputem R 1 6 7   V   P 1 2   G   B 1–3
K 1 2   S   W 2   M 1 2   D C   O 1–3 7 8.   depute W 1 *om.* E 2   Π.   18. deputat
R 1 6 7   V   P 2   G   B 1–3   K 1 2   S   E   L 3 4 6   W 1 2   M 1 2   D C Π J
e
O 1–3 7 8.   deputat P *al. atr. superscr.*   deputet L 2 5.   19. quid quos R V G
B 2   K 1   E 1 2   W 2   Π J   O 1 2.   quid quod S *at* quod *in* quos *mut.*
o   o   l' d
quid qd quos P (*sic*) qd *in ras. et al. atr. script. at in spatio suo.*   quid quos B 1.
quid quod L 5   M 2   D C   O 7.   quid qd O 3.   quid q' B 3   W 1   M 1   O 8.
quid q K 2.   20. cotidianae G.   cotidiane R V.   cotidiᾳne E 1 e *in a mut.*
o
cotidiᾳnae B 1 e *in a mut. eod. atr.*   qtidiane S *at* q *in ras.*   21. adferunt
R V G K.   afferunt B E S.   22. carentis R 1 2   V   P 4   G   B 1   K 1   W 2
e
O 1 Gr.   carentis P *al. atr.* O 8 *al. atr.*   carentes R 6 7 10 16 17   P 2 3   B 2 3
K 2   S   E 1–3   L 2–6   W 1   M 1 2   D C Π J   O 2 3 7 ed. H.   cadentis *corr.*
Manutius.   25. lacrimis R V P G B K E.

§ 66, 26. abicere R V P G   B 1 2   K 1   E   W 2   D J   O 7 8.   abᵢcere S
man. ant. superscr.

decreui... Ter. Heaut. ll. 147–8. The speaker is Menedemus who reproaches himself for having driven his son away to foreign service by his harsh treatment.
Chremes: both this form and *Chreme* are found in Terence. Masc. nouns in -*es* with gen. in -*is* usually make vocative in -*es* in old poetry. Neue, *Formenlehre* 1³ pp. 447–9.
meo: monosyllabic.
deputat: not in prose use. Cicero merely echoes the Terentian word, and this makes it the more strange that he has not retained the construction which Terence used. Probably we have here another instance of the interchange of *a* and *e* in MSS.
apud Homerum: Iliad xix 226—229:
λίην γὰρ πολλοὶ καὶ ἐπήτριμοι ἤματα

πάντα | πίπτουσιν· πότε κέν τις αναπνεύσειε πόνοιο; | ἀλλὰ χρὴ τὸν μὲν καταθάπτειν ὅς κε θάνῃσι | νηλέα θυμὸν ἔχοντας, ἐπ' ἤματι δακρύσαντας. With these words Ulysses seeks to calm the grief of Achilles for the death of Patroclus. Dav. notes that Seneca has the same passage in mind in Ep. 63, 2 'duram tibi legem uideor ponere, cum poetarum Graecorum maximus ius flendi dederit in unum dumtaxat diem.'
[cadentis, the conjecture of P. Manutius, is based on the Homeric πίπτουσιν.]
diurnis, 'to limit our grief to the tears of a day,' cf. ἐπ' ἤματι δακρύσαντας in the Greek.
§ 66. curae et aegritudinis: as *et* is not in most MSS A. Manutius proposed to eject *curae* and H. Wolf bracketed the

potestate est, cui non ponendae curae et aegritudinis causa serui-
amus? constabat eos qui concidentem uolneribus Cn. Pompeium
30 uidissent, cum in illo ipso acerbissimo miserrimoque spectaculo
sibi timerent, quod se classe hostium circumfusos uiderent, nihil
aliud tum egisse, nisi ut remiges hortarentur et ut salutem adipiscerentur fuga; posteaquam Tyrum uenissent, tum adflictari
lamentarique coepisse. timor igitur ab his aegritudinem potuit
35 repellere, ratio ab sapienti uiro non poterit?

　　XXVIII. Quid est autem quod plus ualeat ad ponendum
dolorem, quam cum est intellectum nil profici et frustra esse
susceptum? si igitur deponi potest, etiam non suscipi potest;

28. cui non R G K J.　　cum non V. ‖　curae & aegritudinis M 1　D C.
curae aegritudinis R 1 6 7 17　V　P 1–4　G　B 1–3　K 1 2　S　E 1 2　L 2–4 6
W 1 2　M 2　Π J　O 1–3 7 8.　　curae et *om.* L 5.　　29. uolneribus R V G B K.
uulneribus E 1.　　mulieribus S *marg.* uulneribus. ‖　GN R P K G. GN V G *ex* C
mut. al. atr. ut uid. Gn. B 3　W 1　O 3. ·CN· M 1 2　O 1. C.N. B 2　E.
c͞n S *at fort. mut. est.* . G . H . W 2.　　gneū E 2.　　Gneium O 7.　　30. acerbissimo
miserrimoque R V G B K.　　　32. aliud tum R V P G　B 1–3　K 1　S E 1 2
W 1　M 1 2　C Π　O 2 3 8.　　tum aliud R 6　W 2　J　O 1.　　aliud cum O 7.
aliud tamen D.　　　33. adflictari R V G K E.　　afflictari B S.　　　34. ab his
R V P G　B 1 3　K 1　E 1 2　W 1 2　M 1　J　O 17.　　　　　　ab iis M 2　O 3.
ab iis S *at ras. ante* i.　　ab hiis D C Π　O 8.　　　35. ac sapientia uera
R V P G S E　L 2–5　J *alii.*　　et sapientia uera L 6.　　　ab sapienti uiro
corr. Bentleius.
　XXVIII. 2. nil profici R V P G　B 1 3　E 1　W 2　M 2　J　O 3 7 8.　　nihil
K 1　W 1　M 1　O 1 2.　　　nihil S *litt. ante* h *eras.*　　nichil B 2　D C Π.
nich' E 2.

word, while Bai. suspects *aegritudinis* as
a gloss. But the redundancy is natural in
Cicero and *et* (*ē*) would easily fall out, *ae*
preceding and following.
　　constabat: imperf. because at the
time when Pompey died this was in the
mouth of the people. (F.A.W.) [Plutarch,
Pomp. 80 says οἱ δ' ἀπὸ τῶν νεῶν ὡς
ἐθεάσαντο τὸν φόνον, οἰμωγὴν ἐξάκουστον
ἄχρι γῆς ἐκχέαντες ἔφυγον ἀράμενοι τὰς
ἀγκύρας κατὰ τάχος].
　　acerbissimo: i 39, 93 n. on 'acerbius.'
　　adipiscerentur: with conative force,
cf. iv 6, 12.
　　Tyrum: other accounts make those
with Pompey flee to Cyprus: thus Livy,
Epit. cxii 'Cornelia uxor et Sex. Pompeius
filius Cypron refugerunt'; Lucan, Phars.
ix 117 'prima ratem Cypros spumantibus
accipit undis.' Hence Wesseling, *Var.
Obs.* I 13, p. 44, proposed *Cyprum*, an
emendation which he afterwards withdrew in his notes on Herodotus, p. 724.
And the text is supported by Dio Cassius
xlii 49 τά τε ἀναθήματα τοῦ ἐν τῇ Τύρῳ
Ἡρακλέους πάντα ἀνείλετο ὅτι τὴν τε γυν-
αῖκα καὶ τὸν παῖδα τοῦ Πομπηίου ὑπεδέξαντο
ὅτε ἔφυγον.
　　timor igitur potuit...non poterit: the

form is more commonly *ergo timor*...: cf. i
14, 31 n. on 'ergo arbores seret...rem
publicam non seret.'
　　ab sapienti uiro: *ac sapientia uera* of
the MSS is retained by Mo. and Küh.
Orelli proposed to cut these words out.
Almost all other recent editors adopt
Bentley's conj. *ab sapienti uiro.* Sapientia uera is an odd expression and with
that reading we should have *ab his* (or
something awkwardly supplied from *ab
his*) carried on to the second clause,
whereas *ab sapienti uiro* gives a natural
antithesis to *ab his.* An emendation in
the margin of the edition of Lambinus
and Gothofredus, *ratio uera ac sapientia*,
may be noticed.
　　XXVIII. **nil profici**...i.e. *eo nil profici
et frustra eum esse susceptum.* The discovery would indicate that earlier they
had thought that something would be
gained, and therefore that their grief was
voluntary.
　　si igitur...: if it can be laid aside by an
act of will it can be avoided by an act of
will.
　　non suscipi = *uitari.* F.A.W. notes that
non belongs to *suscipi* and that *ne suscipi
quidem* could not be used here.

H.　　　　　　　　　　　　　　　　　　　　　　　　6

uoluntate igitur et iudicio suscipi aegritudinem confitendum est.
5 **67.** idque indicatur eorum patientia qui, cum multa sint saepe
perpessi, facilius ferunt quicquid accidit, obduruisseque iam
sese contra fortunam arbitrantur, ut ille apud Euripidem:

> Si míhi nunc tristis prímum inluxissét dies,
> Nec tam aérumnoso náuigauissém salo,
> 10 Essét dolendi caúsa, ut iniecto éculei
> Frenó repente táctu exagitantúr nouo;
> Sed iám subactus míseriis obtórpui.

defetigatio igitur miseriarum aegritudines cum faciat leniores,
intellegi necesse est non rem ipsam causam atque fontem esse

---

           idq;   u

§ **67**, 5. itaq; K 1 *eod. atr.*   6. ferunt R 6.   ferant L 4.   ferant R 1 7 17
V P 1–4 G B 1–3 K 1 2 S E 1 2 L 2 3 5 6 W 1 2 M 1 2 D C Π J

O 1–3 7 8 ed. H. ‖ obduruisse quam R 1 P 1 4 G B K.   obduruisse q̃ 3 B 2.

                                                               q;

obduruisse q,iā B 1 *at inter* q *et* ā *fuerat* u *ut uid.*   obduruisse quā E 1 *al. atr.*

                                        quum l tō

superscr.   obduruisse q̃ S *marg.* q3ₐ.   obduruisse q̃ L 5 W 2 J.
obduruisse q̃ q; R 17 L 4.   obduruisse q̃ q; O 2.   obduruisse que R 6 V
e *post* qu *in ras.*   obduruisse q; P 2 3 B 3.   obduruisse q3 K 2 E 3 D C O 3.
obduruisse quoniam O 1.   obduruisse quidem O 7. ‖ sese R 16 7 17 P 1–4 G
B 1–3 K 1 2 E 2 3 L 2–4 6 W 1 M 1 2 Π J O 1 3 7 8 ed. H.   sẹse V.
se D C O 2.   obduruisseque iam *corr. Tregder.*   7. euripidem R P G B 1–3
K M 1 2 D O 2 3 7.   euripidē E 1 W 1 2.   eurupidem V.   euripedem S.
8. inluxisset R V G K E.   illuxisset S.   9. nauigassem R V G B 1–3 K
L 2–6 W 1 2 M 1 2 D O 2 8.   nauigasse O 3.   legauisset O 7.
10. eculei R V G B 1 2 K 1 E 1 O 7.   equlei W 2.   equulo E 2.
equis B 3.   12. subactus M 1 D C ed. H.   subiactus V B 1.   subiactus
G S E.   subiectus R 16 7 17 P B 3 K 1 2 E 2 L 2–6 W 1 2 M 2 Π
O 1–3 7 8.   subiactis B 2. ‖ optorpui G B 1.   oﬄtorpui R p *in* b *mut.*
13. def&igatio R *marg.* defetigatio.   defetigatio V G B 1 2 K 1 W 2 J.
defetigratio E 1.   defatigatio P S W 1 M 1.   14. intellegi R V G B K.

                                                                atq;

intelligi S E. ‖ ipsam causam atque fontem R 6.   ipsam ~~atque~~ causam ₐ fontem
Π *al. atr. corr. et superscr.*   ipsam atque causam fontem R 1 7 17 V (*at fon in ras.*)
P 1–4 G B 1–3 K 1 2 S E 1 2 L 3–6 W 2 M 1 2 D C J O 1 3.   ipsam

                                                             ~
fontem atque causam W 1.   ipsam atque cam forte O 7.   ipsam neque
cãm fontē O 8.   ipsam neque causam fontem L 2.   ipsam neque cãm
frontem O 2.

---

§ **67. apud Euripidem**: the original
lines are preserved in Galen, de plac.
Hipp. et Plat. iv p. 394 M., where they
immediately follow upon the lines ἐγὼ
δὲ τοῦτο... of Euripides' Theseus translated in iii 14, 29. Their source is indicated by a fragment of Tzetzes, quoted
by Dindorf, *Poet. Scen. Graec., Eurip.
Frag.* 818, from an article by Keil in *Rh.*

Mus. vi p. 616, to have been Euripides'
Phrixus. The Greek lines are εἰ μὲν τόδ'
ἦμαρ πρῶτον ἦν κακουμένῳ | καὶ μὴ μακρὰν
δὴ διὰ πόνων ἐναυστόλουν | εἰκὸς σφαδᾷειν
ἦν ἂν ὡς νεόζυγα | πῶλον χαλινὸν ἀρτίως
δεδεγμένον· | νῦν δ' ἀμβλύς εἰμι καὶ κατ-
ηρτυκὼς κακῶν.

defetigatio miseriarum: subjective
gen. 'the weariness which miseries bring.'

₁₅ maeroris. **68.** philosophi summi nequedum tamen sapientiam consecuti nonne intellegunt in summo se malo esse? sunt enim insipientes, neque insipientia ullum maius malum est; neque tamen lugent. quid ita? quia huic generi malorum non adfingitur illa opinio, rectum esse et aequum et ad officium pertinere
₂₀ aegre ferre quod sapiens non sis, quod idem adfingimus huic aegritudini in qua luctus inest, quae omnium maxima est. **69.** itaque Aristoteles ueteres philosophos accusans, qui existimauissent philosophiam suis ingeniis esse perfectam, ait eos aut

§ 68, 15. neque dum P 2.   neq; nondum V P.   neque nondum R 1 (*sic*).
nec dū II *at ras. inter* c *et* d.   nec dum P 3 B 3 L 6 W 1.   necdum R 6 M 2.
neque nondum R 17 P 4 G B 1 K 1 S L 3 D J O 1 3.   neq; ñdū E 1
linea eod. atr. duct.   neque ñ dū C.   neque nōꝗ· nō B 2.   neque ñ̄ꝗ·K 2.
neque nūdū E 2 ūdū *in ras. et al. atr. ut uid.*   neque nundum O 2.
neque mūdū L 2.   ñdū W 2 *at duar. litt. spat. cum rasura praecedente.*
atque nōdū O 7 ed. H.   nec tñ M 1.   16. intellegunt R̄ V P G B.
                                                   na
intellegunt K.   intelligunt S E.   18. non adfingitur G K E.   nodfingitur
R *eod. atr.*   N̄ af fingitur V *at* N̄ *extra lineam al. atr. et* af *multa in rasura.*
non affingitur B S.   20. adfingimus R V G K E.   affingimus B.   affingimus S.
21. maxuma R V G B K.   maxima S E J.
    § 69, 22. existumauissent R V G B K.

§ 68. philosophi summi nequedum tamen sapientiam consecuti: a rendering of the Gk οἱ προκόπτοντες, cf. Galen *l.c.* iv p. 370 M. ὁμοίως δὲ καὶ τοὺς προ-κόπτοντας μεγάλας βλάβας ὑπὸ τῆς κακίας ὑπολαμβάνοντας παρεῖναι ἔδει καὶ ὑπο-φέρεσθαι φόβοις καὶ λύπαις περιπίπτειν μὴ μετρίαις, ὅπερ οὐδὲ αὐτὸ συμβαίνει; *ibid.* p. 392 M. ἀναμιμνήσκων τῶν τε σοφῶν καὶ τῶν προκοπτόντων...οἱ μὲν γὰρ ἐν μεγίστοις ἀγαθοῖς, οἱ δὲ ἐν μεγίστοις κακοῖς ἑαυτοὺς ὑπολαμβάνοντες εἶναι ὅμως οὐ γίνονται διὰ τοῦτο ἐν πάθει. The reference is therefore only to Stoic philosophers and, as the wise man was with the Stoics an ideal person never found on earth, their highest philosophers, Zeno, Cleanthes, Chrysippus, were only in a state of progress (προκοπή) towards wisdom. Cf. Zeller, *Stoics, etc.* xi p. 276. 'Dogma Stoicorum est eos, qui natura doctrinaque longe ad uirtutem processissent, nisi eam plene consecuti essent, summe esse miseros, neque inter eorum uitam et improbissi-morum quicquam omnino interesse.' Be-roaldus. For a somewhat similar line of thought cf. ii 12, 28 'quis igitur Epicurum sequitur dolor...?'
    quia huic generi: it is indicated in Galen *l.c.* iv p. 371 M. that Chrysippus said that the σοφοί were free from emotions because they did not suffer from ἀσθένεια τῆς ψυχῆς, where Posidonius in quoting Chrysippus' view for refutation has used σοφοί loosely so as to include the προκόπ-

τοντες. Pohlenz *l.c.* p. 334 shows that the ἀσθένεια τῆς ψυχῆς referred to is the result of liability to the opinion that it is a duty to give way to grief or other emotion. Posidonius himself gives a different reason in Galen v p. 454 M. καὶ μὴν οἱ προκόπ-τοντες μεγάλα κακὰ δοκοῦντες ἑαυτοῖς παρ-εῖναι ἢ ἐπιφέρεσθαι οὐ λυποῦνται· φέρονται γὰρ οὐ κατὰ τὸ ἄλογον τῆς ψυχῆς οὕτως, ἀλλὰ κατὰ τὸ λογικόν.
    adfingitur: cf. 33, 80 'qui nihil opini-one adfingit.'
    huic aegritudini in qua luctus inest: cf. 26, 62.
    quae omnium maxima est: cf. Plut. Cons. ad Apollon. 102 C πολλῶν γὰρ ὄντων ψυχικῶν παθῶν ἡ λύπη τὸ χαλεπώτατον πέφυκεν εἶναι πάντων. Cicero, in his pre-sent mood, regards mourning for the dead as the severest form of *aegritudo*. It was grief for his daughter that specially im-pelled him to write. Introd. to vol. I p. xv.
    § 69. itaque Aristoteles: Posidonius, who made the emotions movements of the irrational parts of the soul, criticises Chrysippus, who made them judgments or opinions of the rational soul (ἡγεμονι-κόν), asserting (in Galen, quoted above on § 68) that if it were true that the greatness of an evil or good produced an opinion that one ought to be excited by annoyance or joy, we should expect to see the wise rejoicing with special vehemence because they possess wisdom, a priceless treasure, and the προκόπτοντες grieving

stultissimos aut gloriosissimos fuisse; sed se uidere, quod paucis
25 annis magna accessio facta esset, breui tempore philosophiam
plane absolutam fore. Theophrastus autem moriens accusasse
naturam dicitur, quod ceruis et cornicibus uitam diuturnam,
quorum id nihil interesset, hominibus, quorum maxime inter-
fuisset, tam exiguam uitam dedisset; quorum si aetas potuisset
30 esse longinquior, futurum fuisse ut omnibus perfectis artibus
omni doctrina hominum uita erudiretur. querebatur igitur se
tum, cum illa uidere coepisset, exstingui. quid? ex ceteris philosophis nonne optimus et grauissimus quisque confitetur multa

24. stultissimos aut gloriosissimos R V G B K.   26. Theophrastus V S.

Teophrastus E.   28. maxime R V G B.   maxime K.   31. querebatur M 1.

querebat B 1 W 1.   querebat⁾ V.   quaerebatur M 2.   quaerebat R P'G.
querebat K.   32. extingui R V G B K S E.   ‖   caeteris G hoc loco.

33. optumus et grauissumus R V G B.   optumus et grauissimus E.   optimus et

grauissimus K.   optimus et grauissimus S.

most deeply because they lack it. And
Hirzel, *Untersuchungen*, III p. 437, is
undoubtedly right in thinking that, in defending the Stoic view, Cicero is answer-
ing, not Posidonius, but early opponents
of the Stoics, and that the mention of Aristotle and Theophrastus and the polemic
directed against the Peripatetics in § 71
indicate that these early opponents were
Peripatetics. We may go further. As we
see from § 76, 'Chrysippus...debito,' that
the refutation 'quid ita? quia huic generi
...' was introduced by Chrysippus, we may
infer that the Peripatetic criticism, which
Posidonius reproduced, was developed in
the time of Zeno or Cleanthes.

We may perhaps suppose that these
Peripatetic critics, in stating the Stoic
view that lack of perfect wisdom is the
greatest of evils, brought in a reference
to the statements of Aristotle and Theophrastus contained in the text. An extract
from the opinion of these critics was
probably stated and refuted by Cicero's
source (?Chrysippus) and *itaque*, which
yields no satisfactory meaning in the text,
would have been natural if Cicero had
given the entire passage upon which he
is drawing.

Dav. points out that Lactantius, Diu.
Inst. iii 28, had our passage in view. But
Lactantius places the words *ait eos...fuisse*
before the words *qui...perfectam.*

[Hartlich in *Leipziger Studien* xi 2
p. 267 (1889) gives satisfactory reasons
for assuming that the quotation from
Aristotle comes from his Προτρεπτικός.]

ueteres philosophos: especially Heraclitus and the Eleatics. Hei.

paucis annis: since Socrates began to
teach.

Theophrastus: contrast Sall. Jug. 1, 1
'falso queritur de natura sua genus hominum, quod inbecilla atque aeui breuis...'
[Seneca de breu. uit. 1, 2 attributes this
saying to Aristotle: 'inde Aristotelis
cum rerum natura exigentis minime con-
ueniens sapienti uiro lis: aetatis illam
animalibus tantum indulsisse ut quina
aut dena saecula educerent, homini in
tam multa et magna genito tanto citeri-
orèm terminum stare'.]

ceruis: Dav. defends this reading
against *coruis* which had hardly any MS
support. He cites an old poet in Stob.
Serm. x p. 127 εἰ μὲν ἦς ἐλάφου ταναὸν
χρόνον ἠὲ κορώνης, | συγγνώμη πλεῖστον
πλοῦτον ἀγειρομένῳ; Ov. Met. vii 273;
Pedo Albinouanus, Eleg. ii 115 [i.e. Eleg.
in Maec. i 115 Bähr. PLM. i p. 132];
Auson. Id. xi 12, xviii 3 [i.e. xxvi 2, 14:
xxxii 4 ed. Schenkl]. For *ceruis, coruis*
and *cornici* see Pliny N.H. vii 48, 153
quoted on i 31, 77.

querebatur igitur: Diog. L. v 2, 41
says that he said, when dying at the age
of eighty-five, ἡμεῖς γὰρ ὁπότ᾽ ἀρχόμεθα
ζῆν, τότ᾽ ἀποθνήσκομεν. Dav. compares
Hieronymus ad Nepotianum 52, 3 'sapiens ille uir Graeciae Theophrastus (MSS
Themistocles) cum expletis centum et septem annis se mori cerneret, dixisse fertur
se dolere, quod tunc egrederetur e uita,
quando sapere coepisset.'

se ignorare, et multa sibi etiam atque etiam esse discenda?
35 70. neque tamen, cum se in media stultitia, qua nihil est peius,
haerere intellegant, aegritudine premuntur; nulla enim admis-
cetur opinio officiosi doloris. quid, qui non putant lugendum
uiris? qualis fuit Q. Maximus efferens filium consularem, qualis
L. Paulus duobus paucis diebus amissis filiis, qualis M. Cato

34. multa sibi R P 1–4 B 2 3 E 2 W 1 2 D C J O 1 3 7 8.   multa sibi
V *at* a *ex* i *mut.*   multa sibi II *at ras. post* a.   multa sibi E 1 i *in a mut.*

multi̧ sibi B 1 *eod. atr.*   multi sibi G K. ‖ discenda R V P G B 1–3 K S E 1
W 1 2 M 2 D O 1–3 7 8.   dicenda J *eod. atr.*   dicenda E 2 M 1 C II.
§ 70, 35. qua nihil R V P G K 1 W 1.   qua nil O 7.   quia nihil B S.
36. intellegant R V P G B K.   intelligant S E.   37. lugendum R 6 7 17 B 3
K 2 E 2 W 1 M 1 2 D II O 1–3 8.   lugend' C.   lu gendum V *litt. eras.*
lugendum W 2 *at ras. praeced. et fuerat ut uid.* iüged'.   iungendum S *marg.*
lugendum   iungendum R 1_ B 1 K 1 E 1 J.   lungendum G.   lugentum O 7.
vugeng̦. B 2.   38. fuit Q̣ maximus R.   fuit Q. maximus W 1 D C O 2 7.
                                                                          .Q.
fuit q. maximus II.   fuit.q· maxumus V.   fuit q̧uq̧ maximus E 1 *al. atr.*

fuitq; maximus K.   fuit qu̧e maxumus G. ‖ efferens B 1 K 1 E 2 W 1 M 2.
                                                                          f
efferēs B 2 W 2.   effe rens R r *eras.*   efferren V f *post* e *fort. mut.*
efferrens G.   afferens M 1.   39. lucius paulus P 1 4 K 1 S E 1 2 II.
l. paulus W 1 2 D C O 7.   L. Paulus J.   lucius pau lus V l *eras.*
                                        l
lucius Paullus R.   lucius paulus G. ‖ amissis B 1 K 1 E 2 M 1 2.
f
amisis R V G.   amisis B 2 E. ‖ marcus cato G E S.

etiam atque etiam: not in the ordinary
sense of 'again and again' but = 'ever
more and more.' Hei. compares Fam. vi
22, 1 'haec quamquam nihilo meliora
sunt, nunc etiam atque etiam multo des-
peratiora tamen inanis esse meas litteras
quam nullas malui.' Emendation is therefore uncalled for and in Sff.'s *multi...disten-
dum, multi*, though supported by MSS, is
awkward and unsymmetrical. Sff. compares Solon's γηράσκω δ' αἰεὶ πολλὰ
διδασκόμενος.

§ 70. **cum**, 'although' i 17, 39 n.

intellegant: the subject is the collective 'optimus...quisque' carried on, but it
has been separated into its individual
components by the intervention of the
word *se*, cf. Fin. ii 1, 1 'cum *uterque* me
intueretur seseque ad audiendum *signifi-
carent paratos*'; p. Flacco 41, 104 '*quo-
tus* enim *quisque* est qui...*sequatur?* qui
...*putet*, cum illam uiam *sibi uideant* ex-
peditiorem ad honores et ad omnia quae
concupiuerunt?'

officiosi, 'demanded by duty' cf. § 68
'ad officium pertinere'; p. Mil. 5, 12
'hos officiosos labores.'

Q. Maximus: Q. Fabius Maximus
Cunctator, who recovered Tarentum from
Hannibal in 209 B.C., bore with great

calmness the loss of his son, who had
been consul in 213 B.C.

efferens: Maximus himself pronounced
in the forum the *laudatio funebris* upon
his son, cf. Plut. Fab. 24 τὸ δ' ἐγκώμιον...
αὐτὸς εἶπε καταστὰς ἐν ἀγορᾷ καὶ γράψας
τὸν λόγον ἐξέδωκεν. This *laudatio* was
extant in Cicero's time, cf. Cato M. 4,
12 'est in manibus laudatio, quam cum
legimus, quem philosophum non con-
temnimus?'

Cicero, Fam. iv 6, in acknowledging
Sulpicius' letter of condolence upon the
death of Tullia, cites the instances of
Maximus, Paulus, Gallus and Cato, all
of which he also used in his Consolatio;
see below.

L. Paulus: L. Aemilius Paulus, con-
queror of Perseus, had given two of his
four sons in adoption and, of the two that
remained, lost one five days before his
triumph and the other three days after
that event, 168 B.C.: Livy xlv 40, 7.
Cf. Val. Max. v 10, 2; Vell. Paterc. i 10;
Plut. Paulus 35; Senec. Cons. ad Marc.
13.

M. Cato: M. Porcius Cato Censorius
lost a son who was already grown-up and
distinguished, cf. Lael. 2, 9 'perfecto et
spectato uiro'; Cato M. 23, 84 'pro-

40 praetore designato mortuo filio, quales reliqui quos in Consolatione conlegimus. 71. quid hos aliud placauit, nisi quod luctum
et maerorem esse non putabant uiri? ergo id quod alii rectum
opinantes aegritudini se solent dedere, id hi turpe putantes
aegritudinem reppulerunt. ex quo intellegitur non in natura,
45 sed in opinione esse aegritudinem.

XXIX. Contra dicuntur haec: quis tam demens ut sua
uoluntate maereat? natura adfert dolorem, cui quidem Crantor,
inquiunt, uester cedendum putat; premit enim atque instat, nec
resisti potest. itaque Oïleus ille apud Sophoclem, qui Telamonem
5 antea de Aiacis morte consolatus esset, is cum audiuisset de suo
fractus est. de cuius commutata mente sic dicitur:

41. conlegimus R G B K E.   co̜nlegimus V.   collegimus S.

§ 71. hos V S.   his J.   hos E *al. atr.* ‖ placauit V S.   plac‸uit K 1
eod. atr. W 1 *fort. eod. atr.*   placuit E J.   42. esse non putabant R 1 6 V P G
B 1-3 K E 1 2 M 2 Π O 2 3 7 8.   non putabant W 1 2 J O 1.   non
putabant esse M 1 D C.   44. reppulerunt R V P G B K E.   repulerunt S
M 1 J. ‖ intellegitur R V G B K.   intelligitur S E.
XXIX. 2. adfert R V G K E (*hoc loco*).   affert B S.   3. uester R P 2 4
G B 2 K 1 E W 1 D O 3.   u̅r R 7 P B 1 K 2 E 2 W 2 M 1 Π J
O 7.   u̅r̅t V.   noster R 6 P 3 S M 2 O 2.   n̅r̅ B 3 C O 1 8 *om.* R 17. ‖
p̅mit enim R B K.   4. itaque oileus V *spatio relicto*. ‖ sophoclem R G B K S.
sophocle̅ V.   5. is cum R V P G B 2 3 K 1 E 1 2 W 1 M 1 2 D C Π J
O 1-3 8.   is ꞔum S.   his cum O 7. ‖ audiuisset R V G B 1-3 S E 1 2
M 2 O 7.   audisset K 1 *eod. atr.*   audiisset O 2.   audisset P W 1 2 M 1
D C J O 3 8. ‖ de suo R V P G B 1 2 K 1 2 S E 1 2 Π O 2 3 7.   de suo
filio R 6 M 1 D C O 8.   de filio R 7 B 3 W 1 2 M 2 J O 1.

ficiscar...ad Catonem meum...cuius a me
corpus est crematum...quem ego meum
casum fortiter ferre uisus sum, non quo...'
    reliqui quos...: Dav. quotes Hierony-
mus in Epitaph. Nepotiani p. 21 (ad
Heliodorum 60, 5). L. Paulus 'septem
diebus inter duorum exsequias filiorum
triumphans urbem ingressus est. praeter-
mitto Maximos, Catones, Gallos, Pisones,
Brutos, Scaeuolas, Metellos, Scauros,
Marios, Crassos, Marcellos atque Au-
fidios quorum non minor in luctu quam in
bellis uirtus fuit et quorum orbitates in
Consolationis libro Tullius explicauit.'
    in Consolatione: i 26, 65 n.
    § 71. id...id: cf. 8, 18 n. on 'ab eo...ab
eo.'
    XXIX. dicuntur: by the Peripatetics.
    natura adfert...: cf. Plut. Cons. ad
Apollon. c. 3, 102 C τὸ μὲν οὖν ἀλγεῖν
καὶ δάκνεσθαι τελευτήσαντος υἱοῦ φυσικὴν
ἔχει τὴν ἀρχὴν τῆς λύπης, καὶ οὐχ ἐφ' ἡμῖν.
The words οὐ γὰρ ἔγωγε συμφέρομαι...
quoted on 6, 12 follow and Buresch notes

l.c. p. 46 'Ciceronis autem proprium
uidetur esse auctoris membra passim
disicere, cum Plutarchus contra continuo
ordine soleat exscribere.'
    Crantor uester, 'of you Academicians.'
Bentley rightly rejected *noster* noting that
the Peripatetics here reproach Cicero,
who professed to belong to the Academy,
with dissenting from the Academician
Crantor.
    Oïleus: father of the Locrian Ajax.
    is: the repetition tends to clearness
and emphasises the contrast, cf. 8, 18 n.
on 'ab eo...ab eo.' Bake unnecessarily
conjectured *idem.*
    de suo: sc. *Aiace.*
    Nec uero: the verses are preserved in
Stob. Ecl. iv 49, 7 (ed. Hense) where
they are referred to Σοφοκλέους Οἰδίποδι.
Grotius thought Οἰδίποδι an error for 'Οἰλεῖ.
Küh. Hei. T.S. follow Brunck, *Frag.
Soph.* p. 588 (II p. 180 ed. Lond. 1819)
in referring the passage to the Αἴας
Λοκρός, but Welcker *Gr. Trag.* pp. 162

Nec uéro tanta praéditus sapiéntia
Quisquámst, qui aliorum aerúmnam dictis ádleuans
Non ídem, cum fortúna mutata ímpetum
10 Conuértat, clade súbita frangatúr sua,
Vt ílla ad alios dícta et praecepta éxcidant.

haec cum disputant, hoc student efficere, naturae obsisti nullo modo posse, et tamen fatentur grauiores aegritudines suscipi quam natura cogat. quae est igitur amentia? ut nos quoque 15 idem ab illis requiramus. **72.** sed plures sunt causae suscipiendi doloris. primum illa opinio mali, quo uiso atque persuaso aegritudo insequitur necessario; deinde etiam gratum mortuis se

8. aerumnam R G. erumnam V. erūnā S. erūpnā E 1. ǁ adleuans R V G B K. alleuans S E. 9. impetum R V G B K S E. 10. conuertat R V P G B K S E W 2 D O 38. conuertat & W 1. ǁ clade subita E 1. clade subita ut R 6. clade ut subita R 1 7 17 V P 1–4 G B 1–3 K 1 2 E 2 W 1 2 M 1 2 D C Π J O 1–3 7 8. 13. hi tamen R V P 2 G B 1 3 K 1 h

E 2 3 L 4 W 1 2 J O 1–3 7 ed. H. i tamen P *al. atr. superscr.* ii tamen R 6 P 3 L 3 6 M 2. ii tamen S *at ras. ante prius* i. hii tamen R 7 10 16 P 4 K 2 L 2 5 D C Π O 8. intamen E 1. tñ hii B 2. et tamen *corr.* *Seyffertius.* 15. ab aliis R 1 6 7 10 16 17 V P G B 1–3 K 1 2 S E 1–3 L 2–6 W 1 2 M 1 2 D C Π J O 1–3 8 ed H. *om.* O 7. ab illis *corr. Vrsinus.*

and 193 gives the lines to Teucer, 'probabiliter' as Dindorf says. The Greek is τοὺς δ' αὖ μεγίστους καὶ σοφωτάτους φρενὶ | τοιουσδ' ἴδοις ἂν οἷός ἐστι νῦν ὅδε | καλῶς κακῶς πράσσοντι συμπεραινέσαι· | ὅταν δὲ δαίμων ἀνδρὸς εὐτυχοῦς τὸ πρὶν | πλάστιγγ' ἐρείσῃ τοῦ βίου παλίντροπον | τὰ πολλὰ φροῦδα καὶ καλῶς εἰρημένα.

conuertat: Sff. against the mss altered to *conuertit* but the subjunctive is due to an attraction, quite common in similar relative clauses, exercised by the subj. 'frangatur' of the main clause, cf. v 37, 108 'ut, quocunque haec loco suppeditetur, ibi beate queant uiuere'; i 5, 9 n. on 'moriendum esset...uiuerent.'

clade subita: *ut* before *subita* in the mss must have arisen, as Küh. suggests, through the eye of a copyist wandering to the following *ut*.

excidant: sc. *de memoria.*

efficere: i 8, 16 n. on 'efficies ut.'

et tamen: Seyffert's convincing emendation implies the corruption of *et* into *ei* and thence into *ii* and *hi*. This lends support to the spelling *eiȳii.* For *et tamen* and *ac tamen* joining on something opposed to what preceded Sff. compares Madv. on Fin. ii 27, 85.

idem: since they were represented above as asking *quis tam demens...*

§ 72. sed plures...: Cicero continues the argument against the Peripatetic view that grief was due to nature by stating three forms of wrong opinion which lead people to grieve.

quo uiso atque persuaso, 'upon the sight of which and conviction with regard to which annoyance necessarily follows.' From a desire for a concise and symmetrical expression *persuaso* has been attracted to the preceding *uiso*; strictly Cic. should have written *quod cum uisum est* (passive), *cumque de eo persuasum est* (impersonal).

Pohlenz *l.c.* pp. 332–3 throws light on this passage by showing that Chrysippus made the idea of the magnitude of the evil a necessary element in inducing the *insipientes* to think that it was a duty to grieve. He quotes Galen, de plac. Hipp. et Plat. p. 370 M. εἰ γὰρ τὸ μέγεθος τῶν φαινομένων ἀγαθῶν ἢ κακῶν κινεῖ τὸ νομίζειν καθῆκον καὶ κατὰ ἀξίαν εἶναι παρόντων αὐτῶν ἢ παραγινομένων μηδένα λόγον προσίεσθαι, and *ibid.* p. 392 M. κατὰ γὰρ τὴν γνώμην αὐτοῦ (sc. Χρυσίππου) μᾶλλον μεγάλου κακοῦ...τὴν λύπην εἰρῆσθαι ἔδει δόξαν.

gratum mortuis se facere: Beroaldus quotes Seneca [Consol. ad Polyb. 9, 3] 'aut beatus aut nullus est (sc. mortuus); beatum deflere inuidia est; nullum dementia.'

facere, si grauiter eos lugeant, arbitrantur. accedit superstitio
muliebris quaedam; existumant enim dis inmortalibus se facilius
20 satis facturos, si eorum plaga perculsi adflictos se et stratos esse
fateantur. sed haec inter se quam repugnent plerique non
uident. laudant enim eos qui aequo animo moriantur; qui
alterius mortem aequo animo ferant eos putant uituperandos.
quasi fieri ullo modo possit, quod in amatorio sermone dici solet,
25 ut quisquam plus alterum diligat quam se. 73. praeclarum illud
est et, si quaeris, rectum quoque et uerum, ut eos qui nobis car-
issimi esse debeant aeque ac nosmet ipsos amemus; ut uero
plus, fieri nullo pacto potest. ne optandum quidem est in amicitia,
ut me ille plus quam se, ego illum plus quam me; perturbatio
30 uitae, si ita sit, atque officiorum omnium consequatur.

§ 72, 19. existumant R V G B K E.   existimant P S. ‖ diis R V P G B K E
W 1 J O 7.   di s S *spatio relicto*.   ‖   inmortalibus R V P G K.
immortalibus B S.   20. perculsi R 1 6   V P G   B 1–3   K 1   S   E 1 2   W 1 2
                                                                pculsi
M 1 2 II O 2 3 7.   percussi R 7   K 2   D C J.   pcussi O 8 *al. atr. superscr.*
pertusi O 1. ‖   adflictos R V P G K.   afflictos S E. ‖   stratos R 1 10
V P G   E 1 2.
    § 73, 26. carissimi R V G B K.   27. at uero plus R 1 6 7 10 16 17   V P 1–4
G B 1–3 S E 1–3 L 2–6 W 1 2   M 1 2   D C II J O 1–3 7 8 ed. H.   ad uero
plus K 1.   at uero fi plus K 2.   ut uero plus *corr. ed. Iuntina.*   29. plus quam
se ego R V P G   B 1–3   K 1   S   E 1 2   L 2 3 4 6   W 2   M 2   D C J   O 1–3 7 8.
                                                                         amet
plus quam se amet ego R 6   W 1   M 1.   plus quam se˄ego II *al. atr. superscr.* ‖
illum R G B K   M 1 2.   ullum V.   30. consequatur R V P G   B 1–3   K S
                                                                         a r
E 2   W 2   M 2   II   O 2 3 7 8.   conseqt E 1 *fort. eod. atr.*   consequetur W 1
M 1   D C J.   consequitur O 1.

muliebris: cf. *N.D.* ii 28, 70 ' super-
stitiones paene aniles.'
perculsi: besides being the reading of
the best MSS this, and not *percussi*, is in
harmony with *adflictos* and *stratos*, as
Nissen notes.
stratos: Hei. thinks the idea is of
persons *ad pedes strati* 'humbled,' 'self-
abased.' The word does not seem to be
used metaphorically elsewhere in Cicero
and very possibly *prostratos* of Tischer
may be right, the abbreviated suffix being
lost, or *fractos* of Sff., the error being
due to confusion of *f* with *s*. Ti. compares Or. ii 52, 211 'adflicta et prostrata
uirtus maxime luctuosa est'; and Sff. *Att.*
xii 21 extr. 'adflicti et fracti animi'; p.
domo 36, 97 'animo nimis fracto esse
atque adflicto.'
moriantur...ferant: reported speech or
thought.
quasi...solet: ' as if that assertion, so
usual in the conversation of lovers,

could possibly be true,' cf. Hor. Odes iii
9, 12 and 15.
plus: both *plus diligere* and *magis
diligere* can be said. The former denotes
measure, corresponding to the positive
multum; the latter degree, corresponding
to the positive *ualde*. Cf. Madv. on Fin.
i 2, 5 n. on 'a quibus tantum.'
    § 73. **uerum** = *iustum*: 27, 64 n. on
'uera.' For the constr. *uerum est, ut* in
the sense of *fieri debet, ut* cf. i 19, 43 n.
on 'accedit ut...euadat' and Küh. on v 21,
62 'ei ne integrum quidem erat, ut.'
[**ut uero plus**: this correction of the
MSS *at uero plus* is now accepted by all
edd. Kl. (as Küh. notes), reading *at*,
printed the sentence as an interrogative.]
plus quam se: sc. *amet*, from preceding *amemus*. The insertion of *amet* by
some early editors has little MS authority
to support it.
consequatur: i 16, 36 n. on 'consecuti
sunt.'

XXX. Sed de hoc alias; nunc illud satis est, non attribuere
ad amissionem amicorum miseriam nostram, ne illos plus quam
ipsi uelint, si sentiant, plus certe quam nosmet ipsos diligamus.
nam quod aiunt plerosque consolationibus nihil leuari adiun-
5 guntque consolatores ipsos confiteri se miseros, cum ad eos
impetum suum fortuna conuerterit, utrumque dissoluitur. sunt
enim ista non naturae uitia, sed culpae. stultitiam autem
accusare quamuis copiose licet. nam et qui non leuantur,
ipsi ad se miseriam inuitant, et qui suos casus aliter ferunt
10 atque ut auctores aliis ipsi fuerunt, non sunt uitiosiores

XXX. 1. attribuere S J. attribuere R *eod. atr.* V *al. atr.* G *alt. man.*
atribuere B E. adtribuere P K. 3. ipsi uelint R V G. ipsɇ uelint P
e *in* i *mut.* ipse uelint K. ‖ plus certequam V *spat. et ras.* 6. impetum
R V P G B K. ‖ suum *om.* D C. ‖ fortuna E 3 L 2 4 W 1 D C O 7 8
V *ant. man. superscr.* S *marg. ant. man. script.* II *al. atr. superscr.* E 2 *al. atr.*
superscr. om. R P 1-4 G B 1-3 K 1 2 E L 3 5 6 W 2 M 1 2 J O 1-3 ed. H.
pro fortuna *habet* casus R 7. ‖ conuerterit R 7 G K E 2 L 2-4 W 1 D O 3 8.
conuerterint B 3 K 2 L 6 O 1 2. qᵉutūt W 2 *marg.* conuerterit. conuertit O 7.
9. ad se miseriam inuitant M 1. ad miserias inuitant O 2. ad miseriam
inuitant R 1 7 1 7 V P 1 2 4 G B 1-3 K 1 2 S E 1-3 L 2-6 W 2 M 2
D C II J O 1 3 7 8. alios ad miseriam inuitant R 6 W 1. 10. ut auctores aliis
R V P 1-4 B 1 3 K 1 2 E 1 2 M 1 2 O 1-3 8. ut auctores aliiˢ II *al. atr.*
ut actores aliis W 2. ut autores aliis B 2 W 1. ad auctores aliis G ad *expunx.*
et ut *superscr. alt. man.* ut actores aliis J. ut aₐctores alii S. ut auctores
ipsi fere non sunt uitiosiores D C. ut auctore ipsi ferant O 7.

XXX. **non attribuere** = *non addere.*
nam quod aiunt: for *nam* in refutation
cf. 16, 35 n. The constr. is (*id*) *quod
aiunt*...(*id*)*que quod adiungunt*... for
which *adiunguntque* (*hoc*) is substituted
on the principle stated in ii 25, 61 n. on
'quem...uidi et id dicam.' These ante-
cedents *id...id* are accusatives of respect
and are taken up in *utrumque.*
Cic. here replies to the Peripatetic
objections of § 71.
cum...conuerterit: the case of Oïleus
is referred to, cf. § 71 'cum fortuna mutata
impetum conuertat.'
fortuna: absent from the best MSS (except V²) but cannot be omitted though
Dav. supposed that *miseria* could be
carried on 'ἀπὸ κοινοῦ.' Or. suggests
that it was omitted by an early Christian
copyist who was unwilling to give *fortuna*
the rank of a goddess.
dissoluitur: for *dissoluere* = *refutare* or
rather *argumenti uim infirmare atque
infringere* = διαλύειν cf. Diu. ii 4, 11; Or.
ii 38, 159 Mo.
non naturae uitia, sed culpae: cf. iv
37, 81 'qui autem non natura, sed culpa
uitiosi esse dicuntur.' Trans. 'for the

fault of the individual, not the nature of
the case, is to blame for these results.'
The following word *stultitiam* shows in
what *culpa*, in this case, consists. See
16, 34 n. on 'nisi culpam.'
quamuis copiose = *tam copiose, quam
uis*, cf. i 21, 47 n.
ipsi ad se miseriam inuitant: *se* is
inserted after *ipsi* by the most recent
editors, who quote in support of the
constr. 34, 82 'quod non natura exoriatur, sed iudicio, sed opinione, sed
quadam inuitatione (sc. *sui*) ad dolendum.'
Küh. following Dav. (ed. 2) reads as in
the text.
aliter...atque ut: 'otherwise than as
they had themselves advised others' = *alio
modo, atque eo modo, quo*....Nissen compares Verr. i 46, 119 'quod iste aliter,
atque ut edixerat, decreuisset.' Wopkens,
Lectt. Tull. p. 118, notes that *ut* is usually
omitted in this expression but that it can
be inserted where it does not interfere
with clearness of construction. Hand in
a note there compares Att. xvi 13 c 'de
Antonii itineribus nescio quid aliter audio
atque ut ad te scribebam.'
non sunt ... plerique, 'only display

quam fere plerique qui auari auaros, gloriae cupidos gloriosi
reprehendunt. est enim proprium stultitiae aliorum uitia cernere,
obliuisci suorum. **74.** sed nimirum hoc maximum est experimentum, cum constet aegritudinem uetustate tolli, hanc uim non
15 esse in die positam, sed in cogitatione diuturna. nam si et eadem
res est et idem est homo, qui potest quicquam de dolore mutari,
si neque de eo propter quod dolet quicquam est mutatum neque
de eo qui dolet? cogitatio igitur diuturna nihil esse in re mali
dolori medetur, non ipsa diuturnitas.

XXXI. Hic mihi adferunt mediocritates. quae si naturales

12. repraehendunt G K.

　　　　　　　　　　　† me
§ **74**, 13. maxumum R V G.　　maxumū B *eod. ut uid. atr.*　　maximum K E. ‖
experimentum R 6 7 17　W 1　M 1　O 8.　　　　　exprimendum R V G　B 1–3　K 1

　　　　　　　　　　　　　　　　　　　　　　　i
E 2 3　W 2　M 2　C Π　O 1–3 7.　　expmendū E 1.　　　　exꝑmēdum K 2.
expri mendū D *ras. interueniente.*　　exprimentum ed. H.　　14. aegritudinem V.
egritudinem M 1.　　egritudinē P　W 1.　　egritudinē M 2.　　aegritudine R G K.
egritudine B 2　E.　‖ tolli R 6　S　W 1　M 1　D C　O 1 3 7 8 V *at litt. post* i *eras.*
tolli et M 2　J.　　tollit R G　B 2　K 1 2　E 1　W 2.　　15. diuturna R 6　P 2 3

　　　　　　　　　　　　　　　　　　　　　　　r
B 1–3　E 2　W 1　M 1 2　C Π　O 1–3.　　diutina S D.　　diurna R 1 7 17　V
P 4　G　K 1 2　E 1　W 2　J　O 7 8.　　　diurna P *marg.* diut'na *al. atr.* ‖
si et eadem R V　P 1–3　G　B 1–3　K 1　S　E 1　W 1　M 2　D C　O 7.
et si eadem P 4　K 2　W 2　J　O 3 ed. H.　　et *om.* E 2　M 1　Π.　　18. diuturna

　　　　　　　　　　　　　　　　　　　　　　　　tu
R 6 7　P 2　B 3　S　E 1 2　W 1　M 1　D C Π　O 1–3 7.　　　diurna B 1
P *al. atr.*　　diutina P 3.　　diurina M 2.　　diurna R 1 17　V　P 4　G　K 1 2
W 2　J　O 8.
XXXI. 1. adferunt R V G K.　　afferunt B S E. ‖ mediocritates V　W 1.
　† tes
mediocritᚗs P.　　mediocritas R G K.

weakness similar to that commonly displayed by so many....' The implication
is that as misers and men of ambition,
who can rebuke avarice and ambition in
others, are not miserly or ambitious by
natural necessity but by their own choice,
so those who give way to grief, though
able to console others in grief, grieve not
natura sed iudicio.

§ **74.** **hoc**: defined by *cum constet aeg.
uet. tolli.*

experimentum: though this word, in
the sense of *documentum,*'proof,' is chiefly
post-Augustan, it seems the only possible
reading here. *exprimendum,* of most
MSS, would seem to involve, as Or. says,
the reading *maxime,* and the meaning
hoc maxime cogendi sunt, ut fateantur
would not be naturally expressed. Mo.
thinks that *maximum* is not impossible
in the sense of *hoc quod maximum est*
with *exprimendum* explained as above.

hanc uim, 'this effect,' the power of
making people forget.

in die: i.e. *in longa die, in longin-*

quitate temporis as Bent. notes. Cf. 16,
35 'longinquitas et dies'; 22, 53 'dies
declarat, quae procedens ita mitigat...';
24, 58; iv 17, 39. Hence *diuturna,* not
diurna is the only possible reading; cf.
diuturnitas below.

si et...et...: expanded below in *si
neque de eo, propter quod dolet, quicquam
est mutatum, neque de eo, qui dolet.* Cf.
17, 37 n. on 'et oriatur.'

in re: instead of being *opinionis.* See
15, 31 n. 'iudico malum illud *opinionis* esse,
non *naturae*; si enim *in re* esset, cur...?'

XXXI. **adferunt**: sc. *Peripatetici,* cf.
10, 22 n. on 'mediocritates.' Nonius
p. 29 quotes this passage inaccurately
thus *ad haec mihi adferuntur mediocritates,
quae si...consolatione.* With the Peripatetics the proper degree of grief would
mark an intermediate state between excessive emotion on the one hand and
apathy on the other.

quae si naturales...: Hei. notes that
Cicero's criticism is unsatisfactory for it
is by their consolation that they seek to

sunt, quid opus est consolatione? natura enim ipsa terminabit
modum ; sin opinabiles, opinio tota tollatur. satis dictum esse
arbitror aegritudinem esse opinionem mali praesentis, in qua opin-
5 ione illud insit ut aegritudinem suscipere oporteat. **75.** additur
ad hanc definitionem a Zenone recte ut illa opinio praesentis
mali sit recens. hoc autem uerbum sic interpretantur ut non
tantum illud recens esse uelint quod paulo ante acciderit, sed
quam diu in illo opinato malo uis quaedam insit, ut uigeat
10 et habeat quandam uiriditatem, tam diu appelletur recens. ut
Artemisia illa, Mausoli, Cariae regis, uxor, quae nobile illud

3. sin opinabiles R G K   O 7.   si/nopinabiles V *ras. inter* i *et* n.   sim
opinabiles E 1.
§ 75, 7. interpretantur R V P G   B 1 2   S E   M 1 2   D C J   O 1 3.   inter·
praetantur K 1.   inter$\bar{p}$ra͟nt W 2.   interpretâtur O 8.   interpretatur E 2

W 1   Π   O 2.   int'petrat O 7.   int'p̄lant' J.   *om.* B 3.   8. uelint R V P G
B 1–3   K 1   S   M 2   J   O 1–3 8.   uelĭt W 2   O 7.   uelit E 2   W 1   M 1
D C Π.   ‖ paulo R V G.   9. insit ut uigeat R 10 16.   insit & uigeat R 1 6 7 17
V   P 1–4   G   B 1–3   K 1 2   E 1 2   L 2–5   W 1 2   M 1 2   D C Π J   O 1–3 8.
insistat uigeat O 7.   10. appelletur R V G   B 2   O 1.   appellatur K 1

E 1   W 1   D.   appellat S *at a post* 1 *mut. ut uid.*   ‖   ut artemisia G.
                                                                              misia
ut art$\bar{f}$misia V i *in* e *mut.*   utarde misia R.   ut artē is̶ai̶ E 1 *al. atr.*
       e   v
ut artemisia S.   11. mausoli G.   ma͞isoli E 1.

bring people back from the extreme to
the proper mean.
terminabit modum = *ponet modum.*
The tendency to combine a verb with an
object cognate in meaning is illustrated
by Naegelsbach, *Stil.* § 105, 2, from iv
10, 23 'morbis corporum comparatur
(instead of *adcommodatur*) morborum
animi similitudo'; Or. 35, 122 'perora-
tionem concludere' (=*facere*); d. Part.
Orat. 32, 110, ' partitio...distributa est '
(=*facta est*).
aegritudinem esse opinionem...: cf.
11, 25.
§ 75. **additur...ut**: in a few instances,
where a condition, proviso or command,
and not a mere statement of fact is appended, *addo* is followed by *ut* and the
subj., not by the acc. and inf., cf. Laelius
18, 65 'addendum eodem est, ut ne crimi-
nibus aut inferendis delectetur aut credat
oblatis'; Livy xxvi 24, 9 'additumque
ut...eodem iure amicitiae Elei...essent';
Caes. Bell. Ciu. i 87, 1 'addit ut...resti-
tuatur.'
a Zenone: Cf. Galen, de plac. Hipp.
et Plat. p. 391 M. ὁ γοῦν ὅρος οὗτός φησι
[sc. ὁ Ποσειδώνιος], ὁ τῆς λύπης, ὥσπερ
οὖν καὶ ἄλλοι πολλοὶ τῶν παθῶν ὑπό τε
Ζήνωνος εἰρημένοι καὶ πρὸς τοῦ Χρυσίππου

γεγραμμένοι, σαφῶς ἐξελέγχουσι τὴν γνώμην αὐτοῦ. δόξαν γὰρ εἶναι πρόσφατον τοῦ
κακὸν αὐτῷ παρεῖναί φησι τὴν λύπην.
recens : = πρόσφατος, cf. Galen *l. c.*,
where it is stated that Chrysippus defined
τὸ πρόσφατον as τὸ ὑπόγυον κατὰ τὸν χρόνον.
hoc autem uerbum sic interpretantur :
Galen *l.c.* gives Posidonius' criticism of
Zeno's use of the word πρόσφατος (*recens*)
in this special sense, saying that Chrysippus, on his own view, ought to have
defined λύπη as an idea of a great or
unbearable evil, not an idea of a recent
one. Cf. Stob. Ecl. ii 7, 10 (ed. Wachs.)
τὸ δὲ πρόσφατον ἀντὶ τοῦ κινητικοῦ συστο-
λῆς ἀλόγου ἢ ἐπάρσεως.
interpretantur: sc. *Zeno et Chrysippus*,
or *Stoici.*
opinato: 11, 24 n. on 'opinati.'
quandam uiriditatem: for *quidam*
with metaphors cf. i 12, 27 n. For the
metaphor here Lael. 3, 11 'senectus...
aufert eam uiriditatem in qua etiam nunc
erat Scipio'; Hor. Epod. 13, 4 'dumque
uirent genua.'
[**Mausoli, Cariae regis**: though Strabo
xiv p. 656 agrees with Cicero here in
calling him king, inscriptions prove that
not even during his rebellion against the
king of Persia did he bear this title, cf.

Halicarnasi fecit sepulcrum, quam diu uixit, uixit in luctu
eodemque etiam confecta contabuit. huic erat illa opinio cotidie
recens; quae tum denique non appellatur recens cum uetustate
15 exaruit.

Haec igitur officia sunt consolantium, tollere aegritudinem
funditus aut sedare aut detrahere quam plurimum aut suppri-
mere nec pati manare longius aut ad alia traducere. **76.** sunt
qui unum officium consolantis putent \<docere\> malum illud

12. alicarnasi R V P G B K S E W D. ‖ sepulcrum G E 1.   sepulcrum^h P.
sepultᶜʰrum R 1 *in* c *mut. et linea ducta eod. ut uid. atr.*   sepulcʰrum V K.
13. cotidie R V P G K E.   q̊tidie S.   quottidie J.   14. appellatur B 2
L 2 3 5 J.   appellabatur R 1 6 7 17 V P 1-4 G B 1 3 K 1 2 S E 1 2
L 4 6 M 2 D C II *marg. e cont. om.* O 2 3 7 8.   appellaretur O 1.   appll'at'
W 2.   appellabant M 1.   reputatur W 1.   17. autdetrahere V (*sic*). ‖
plurumum R V G.   plurimum P K E.   18. manare V G S.   manere E. ‖
ad alia R V P G E J Gr.
§ **76,** 19. consolantis B 1 W 1 2 D II O 3 7.   consolantis V *at* o *post* s *mut.*
consolantis R *eod. atr.*   consûlantis K 1 u *in* o *mut.*   consulantis G B 2.
consulaⱱ̅ïſ E 1 i.e. t *in* nt *mut. et* is *add.*   consolationis O 1 2. ‖ putent malum
R 1 7 V P 1-3 G B 2 3 K 1 2 E 2 3 L 3-6 W 2 M 2 D C II J O 1 3 8.
putant malum P 4 S L 2 W 1 M 2 O 7.   putent malum B 1.   putāt
consolantis malum M 1.   putent docere malum *corr. Lambinus.*

Dittenberger, *Sylloge Inscr. Graec.* I³
pp. 226 ff. The testimony of the inscrr.
is borne out by Aul. Gell. x 18, 2 'Mausolus
autem fuit, ut M. Tullius ait, rex terrae
Cariae, ut quidam Graecarum historiarum
scriptores, prouinciae praefectus, σατρά-
πην Graeci uocant.' In inscrr. the name
is spelled Μαύσσωλλος. For an account
of his career see Curtius, *Griech. Gesch.* III³
pp. 466 sqq.]

nobile...sepulcrum: the ruins of this
famous tomb, erected on a magnificent
scale by Artemisia to the memory of her
husband, were discovered by Sir Chas.
Newton in 1857, and considerable fragments are now in the British Museum.
Cf. Mart. Epigrammaton Liber (Lib.
Spect.) 1, 5—6 where it is coupled with
other wonders of the world. [See also
Michaelis, *A Century of Archaeological
Discoveries* (E.T.) pp. 99 ff.]

[**contabuit**: cf. Strabo *l.c.* τὴν ἀρχὴν
κατέλιπε τῇ γυναικί...φθίσει δ' ἀποθανούσης
διὰ πένθος Ἰδριεὺς ἦρξε.]

exaruit: the reflexion is general. 'And
this opinion (i.e. an opinion like this)....'
appellabitur, which Dav. proposed, and
Küh. and some others adopted, would
require *exaruerit* to follow.

haec igitur...: with these words Cicero

commences to deal with the remedial
treatment of *aegritudo*.

§ **76. putent:** the very fact that
Cleanthes is cited as an instance shows
that a class is referred to here, not certain definite individuals. It is therefore
necessary to alter the following verbs
abducunt, putant, colligunt, to the subjunctive, not to alter this verb, with Dav.
and Küh., to the indicative. Cf. i 9, 18
where MSS have *putant...censeant* though
there is nothing to differentiate the constr.
of the one verb from that of the other.
Sff. in our passage seeks to justify *abducunt*, holding that with *ut Epicurus*
the ref., although *sunt qui* preceded, is
limited to Epicurus individually, while *ut
Epicuro placet* would have included the
school. He thinks that the mood of *abducunt* caused the copyists to alter the
following verbs *putent* and *colligant*.

docere: the insertion, with Lamb. and
Dav., of *docere*, against the MSS (or *dicere*,
but the former is better) is necessary.
Most editors follow Or. in imagining that
it is not so. Schiche inserts *docere* after
non esse, perhaps rightly, and Ml., though
he does not insert the word in his text,
has the crit. note 'putent docere Lamb.,
Bait. ed. Tauchn., fortasse uere.' Or.

20 omnino non esse, ut Cleanthi placet; sunt qui non magnum
malum, ut Peripatetici; sunt qui abducant a malis ad bona, ut
Epicurus; sunt qui satis putent ostendere nihil inopinati accidisse, <ut Aristippus.> Chrysippus autem caput esse censet in

20. cleanti G.   de auti E 1.   21. abducunt R V P G   B 1–3   K 1 2   S
E 1 2   L 5   W 1 2   M 1 2   J   O 2 3 8.   adducunt D C.   ducunt O 7 om. O 1.
22. putant R V G   B 1–3   K 1 2   W 1 2   M 1   O 7.   ‖ inopinati P   B 3   W 2
M 1 2   D C   O 1 3 7.   inopinaṇti V.   inopinanti R G   B 1   S E.
inopinant B 2.   opinanti K 1   E 2   W 1   Π.   ostendere opinanti accidisse
O 2 cett. om.   ‖ accidisse nihil mali R 1 6 7 17   P 1–4   G   B 1–3   K 1 2   S   E 1 2
L 2–6   W 2   M 1 2   D C Π J   O 1–3 8 Gr. ed. H.   accidisse nihil aṃali V.
accidisse nil mali O 7.   accidisse mali W 1.   accidisse, ut Aristippus
corr. Orellius.

writes 'sane necessarium non est, cum
eius significatio insit in ipso v. consolantis,
consolatio enim sine doctrina aliqua prae-
beri nequit.' The fact is that any idea
that is to be carried on to the clause
malum illud omnino non esse must be
found in officium, not in consolantis. If
we had had sunt qui unam consolationem
putent the ellipse would have been possible with the verbal but, even where we
actually have the verbal in 32, 77 erit
igitur in consolationibus prima medicina,
we have docere expressed in the text. No
real parallel for such an ellipse as the
MS reading presents can be found. Those
put forward by Küh. are inadequate:
docere is not supplied to the third clause
in 32, 77, but is carried on from the first
clause, just quoted above. In 15, 31
dicens is easily supplied from praedicare
and in iv 38, 83, sed et aegritudinis et
reliquorum animi morborum una sanatio
est, omnes opinabiles esse..., una sanatio
est is nearly = una sanandi doctrina est
and the idea required flows smoothly
from the verbal. Dav. wrongly altered ut
Peripatetici of the MSS to ut Peripaticis
below, but his suggestion that the true
reading may be sunt qui unum officium
consolantis putant malum illud omnino
non esse, ut Cleanthes, persuadere is worth
recording.

ut Cleanthi placet: we have no ref. to
show why this view is specially attributed
to Cleanthes. This passage is not illustrated by ii 25, 60 to which Hei. and T.S.
refer, for there the view of Cleanthes is
that held by Zeno before him. Cleanthes
must have specially employed this view
for consolation or some similar purpose
and hence been quoted by Cicero's source.
He wrote a Προτρεπτικός Diog. L. vii 5,
175 which is probably referred to in Diog.
L. vii 1, 91 διδακτήν τ' εἶναι αὐτήν, λέγω
δὲ τὴν ἀρετήν, καὶ Χρύσιππος ἐν τῷ πρώτῳ

περὶ τέλους φησὶ καὶ Κλεάνθης καὶ Ποσειδώνιος ἐν τοῖς προτρεπτικοῖς.

ut Peripatetici: sc. putant. For the
change from ut Cleanthi placet cf. Ac. ii
39, 124 'ut Platoni placuit...ut Xenocrates.' For the Peripatetic view cf. ii 27,
66 n. on 'aut...tantulum.'

ut Epicurus: cf. 15, 33.

nihil inopinati: for this Cyrenaic view
cf. 13, 28; 22, 52.

ut Aristippus: nihil mali must be a
gloss upon nihil inopinati, cf. Wes. Em.
1 p. 10. Dav. rightly argues that, as we
have an authority cited for each of the
preceding three views, we must have an
authority mentioned for this view and he
inserts ut Cyrenaici. Or., in notes to
F.A.W.'s notes, suggested ut Aristippus
which seems better, as Aristippus might
easily be missed by a copyist before
Chrysippus.

Chrysippus autem...: this passage
shows that in the Stoic definition of
aegritudo we have an addition introduced
by Chrysippus in the words in 11, 25
'talis mali, ut in eo rectum uideatur esse
angi'; 26, 62 'oportere, rectum esse, ad
officium pertinere'; ut 7, 14 'in quo
demitti contrahique animo rectum esse
uideatur.' This is also indicated by the
words with which Posidonius assails
Chrysippus' view in Galen op. cit. iv p.370
M. εἰ γὰρ τὸ μέγεθος τῶν φαινομένων ἀγαθῶν
ἢ κακῶν κινεῖ τὸ νομίζειν καθῆκον καὶ κατὰ
ἀξίαν εἶναι παρόντων αὐτῶν ἢ παραγενομέ-
νων μηδένα λόγον προσίεσθαι περὶ τοῦ
ἄλλως δεῖν ὑπ' αὐτῶν κινεῖσθαι. Cf. v.
Arnim, Stoica, Introd. p. xxiii; Pohlenz
l.c. p. 332.

opinionem...si se...putet: for the
constr., which Bent. suspected, Hei.
compares i 47, 111 'illa suspicio...si
opinamur.'

in Consolatione: Tregder, against the
best MSS, omitted these words but Wes.

consolando detrahere illam opinionem maerenti, si se officio
25 fungi putet iusto atque debito. sunt etiam qui haec omnia
genera consolandi colligant (alius enim alio modo mouetur), ut
fere nos in Consolatione omnia in consolationem unam coniecimus; erat enim in tumore animus, et omnis in eo temptabatur
curatio. sed sumendum tempus est non minus in animorum
30 morbis quam in corporum; ut Prometheus ille Aeschyli, cui
cum dictum esset:

> Atquí, Prometheu, te hóc tenere exístimo,
> Medéri posse rátionem iracúndiae,

24. moerenti sise W 1.   merenti si se II *at litura post* ti.   maerentis se G.
maerentis‸se V *man. ant. superscr.*   moerentis se O 2.   merentis se R P 4
B 1 2 K 1 2 E 1 2 L 2 5 D C J O 7 8 ed. H.   merentisse P.   merenti se
O 3 S *at marg.* ne se W 2 *at* s *post* ti *eras. et marg.* ne *alio atr.*   moerentis
ne se L 3.   merentis se E 3 *al. atr. superscr.*   merenti ne se P 2 3 B 3 L 6 M 2.
merentis ut se M 1.   merentis quod se O 1.   merentis *ỿ* se L 4.   26. colligunt
R V P G B 1–3 K 1 2 S E 1 2 L 2–6 W 1 2 M 1 2 D C II J O 1–3 7 8.
27. nos in consolatione omnia R P G B 1–3 K 1 2 S E 2 M 1 2 O 2 3.
nos in consolatione omnia V.   nos ~~in consolatione~~ omnia II.   nos in consolationem
unam *cett. om.* W 1 J O 1 8.   ‖ nos omnia in consolationem D C.   nos in
consolationem omnia coniecimus W 1 *marg.* unā.   nos in consolationem omnia unā
cett. om. O 7.   30. aeschyli R V G K.   aeschili E 1.   eschili B 1 S.
32. existimo R V G B K S.   33. posse rationem B 3 S E 1 2 L 4 M 2 C
O 2 3 7.   posse ratione B 1 D II.   posse ratione R 6 7 17 L 2 3 J O 1.
posse rōne L 5 W 1.   posse rōē K 2 M 1 O 8.   posse rōni B 2.   posse
ratione ratione P *alio atr.*   posse ratione ratione V.   posse ratione ratione G
alterum expunx. alt. man.   posse ratione ratione R.   posse rōē rọe W 2.
posse ratione ratione K 1.   *om.* L 6.

Em. II p. 58 points out that they are
necessary to mark the time referred to in
the following words *erat enim in tumore
animus*.

in tumore: cf. 12, 26 'cum tumor
animi resedisset'; and iv 29, 63 where
the word is used in the same connection
as here.

in eo: sc. *in tumore*.

sumendum tempus est: *tempus* here =
'the right time,' cf. *tempestiuam* (ἐν καιρῷ
γε) below. For the connection of this
point with Chrysippus' teaching see iv 29,
63 n. on 'quodque uetat Chrysippus...'

Aeschyli: Prom. Vinct. 377 foll. Oce-
anus speaks: οὔκουν, Προμηθεῦ, τοῦτο γιγ-
νώσκεις, ὅτι | ὀργῆς νοσούσης εἰσὶν ἰατροὶ
λόγοι; | to which Prometheus replies ἐάν
τις ἐν καιρῷ γε μαλθάσσῃ κέαρ | καὶ μὴ
σφριγῶντα θυμὸν ἰσχναίνῃ βίᾳ. Dav.
compares Hieron. Ep. 39 (ad Paulam
super obitu Blaesillae filiae) 'recens uolnus est, et tactus iste, quo blandior, non
tam curat quam exasperat. Attamen
quod tempore mitigandum est cur ratione
non uincitur?' a passage no doubt derived

from Cicero's *Consolatio*. The extract
from the Prom. Vinct. may have been
quoted there by Cicero; Hieron. Ep. 66,
1 (ad Pammachium) 'uereor ne...attrec-
tans uolnus pectoris tui, quod tempore et
ratione curatum est, commemoratione ex-
ulcerem.'

cui: cf. v 10, 30 n. on *quos*.

rationem: H. Stephanus and Lamb.
(in ed. 2) proposed *mederi posse orationem iracundiae*, with synizesis in
orationem. But it is not necessary to
depart from the MSS.; *rationem* is more
applicable to consolation than *oratio* and,
though the Gk has λόγοι, the sing. λόγος
would mean *rationem* as well as *orationem*,
and Cic. gives a free translation.

respondit: as the pres. is usual in
quoting from still extant writings (i 18,
42 n.) F.A.W. thought *respondet* a better
reading here. But the words *cum dictum
esset* above show that this constr. has not
been adopted here. *respondet* would be
impossible unless *cui cum dicitur* preceded. Or. compares 18, 39 'in quo haec
admiratio fiebat.'

respondit:

35   Siquidém qui tempestíuam medicinam ádmouens
Non ádgrauescens uólnus inlidát manu.

XXXII. 77. Erit igitur in consolationibus prima medicina
docere aut nullum malum esse aut admodum paruum, altera
et de communi condicione uitae et proprie, si quid sit de ipsius
qui maereat disputandum, tertia summam esse stultitiam frustra
5 confici maerore, cum intellegas nil posse profici. nam Cleanthes
quidem sapientem consolatur, qui consolatione non eget. nihil
enim esse malum quod turpe non sit, si lugenti persuaseris, non
tu illi luctum, sed stultitiam detraxeris; alienum autem tempus
docendi. et tamen non satis mihi uidetur uidisse hoc Cleanthes,

34. respondit R V P G   B 1-3   K 1 2   E 2   M 1 2   D C Π J   O 3 8 7.

Rñdit W 1.   Pfnd. W 2.   dixit O 2.   35. siquidem qui R P G S E.

siquidem qui V.   si quidem W 2 q *eraso*.   si quis est qui R 7.

36. adgrauescens R G K.   adgrauescens V.   aggrauescens B.   ‖   uolnus

R V P (*hoc loco*) G B.   uolnos K 1.   uulnus S E.   ‖   inlidat R V P G   B 1
K E 1.   illidat R 2   S   E 2.   inclinat B 2.   ‖   manu O 3.   manus R 1 6 7
V P G   B 1 3   S   E 1 2   L 2 3 5 6   W 1   M 1 2   D C J   O 1 2 7 8 ed. H.
man₊ K 1.   man⁹ R 2 10 K 2   W 2   Π.   mai⁹ R 17.   māǫ B 2.   maius L 4.
XXXII. § **77**, 2.   aut multum malum B 1.   3. condicione R G S.
conditione V B K E.   ‖   proprie R V   E 2.   propriae G a *conf. alt. man.*
propriae K.   ♭pǫ E 1.   propriae P.   5. intellegas R V G B K.
intelligas S E.   ‖   cleantes quidem R V P G K S E.   6. nihil R V P.
nichil R 10 16   E 1 2.   nil G.   9. cleanthes R V G.

siquidem qui: *qui=quis* (τις in the Gk)
is archaic and it is strange to find it here
as the Latin verses must be by Cicero.

XXXII. § 77. erit igitur...: the constr.
is best explained thus: from *docere* of the
first clause, *disserere* or *disputare* is carried
on (Hei.) by zeugma to the *altera* clause
and *docere* (or *disserere, disputare*) to the
tertia clause. Ernesti wrongly bracketed
disputandum; if this were ejected or, as
F.A. W. suggested, altered to *disputare*,
sit would be in no satisfactory constr.

proprie, contrasted with *communi*, but
formally *de ipsius* corresponds to *de communi condicione* and hence *condicione*
is easily carried on. Sff. among other
changes, which do not seem necessary,
inserted *fortuna* after *maereat*, comparing
vv. ll. § 73 and suggesting that an abbreviation may have caused the loss of
that word.

nam: 'I need not mention Cleanthes'
method as a fourth remedy, for...' Cleanthes' view is given in § 76 *init*.

non...luctum sed stultitiam: i.e. you
will make him a Stoic philosopher, for no
other would recognise the force of that

argument. Cicero does not use *sapientem*
in its strictest sense. See note on 'et
tamen' below.

detraxeris: i 30, 74 n. on 'excesserit.'

alienum autem tempus docendi, 'the
occasion is not favourable for imparting
instruction,' because those in grief are not
inclined to listen to philosophic lore.

et tamen...: the argument is—and indeed Cleanthes does not even console
philosophers in all cases, for they may
well be in grief at times because they
have not yet attained to perfect wisdom
and, as Cleanthes would admit that this
is a real evil (since the assertion that it is
so is one of his leading doctrines), his
consolation, which consists in denying
that the thing grieved about is an evil,
cannot be applied. In 28, 68 it is said
that philosophers do not grieve on this
point, but Cic. is there thinking of Stoics,
and here he is speaking more generally,
as the ref. to Alcibiades shows; there, too,
he speaks of *philosophi summi*, while those
here referred to might have made but
slight progress.

10 suscipi aliquando aegritudinem posse ex eo ipso quod esse summum malum Cleanthes ipse fateatur. quid enim dicemus, cum
Socrates Alcibiadi persuasisset, ut accepimus, eum nihil hominis
esse, nec quicquam inter Alcibiadem summo loco natum et
quemuis baiolum interesse, cum se Alcibiades adflictaret lacri-
15 mansque Socrati supplex esset ut sibi uirtutem traderet turpi-
tudinemque depelleret, quid dicemus, Cleanthe? num in illa
re quae aegritudine Alcibiadem adficiebat mali nihil fuisse?
78. quid? illa Lyconis qualia sunt? qui aegritudinem extenuans
paruis ait eam rebus moueri, fortunae et corporis incommodis,
20 non animi malis. quid ergo? illud quod Alcibiades dolebat

11. cleanthes R V E.   cleantes P G S.   ‖   ipse *habent*
R V P G B 1–3 K S E 1 2 W 1 2 M 1 2 D C Π O 1 7 8 *om.* O 3. ‖ fateatur
R 1 6 7 V P 3 4 G B 1–3 E 1 W 1 M 1 2 D C O 2 7.   fatetur R 17
                                                                                          r
P 1 2 E 2 Π O 3.   fatebatur W 2 J O 1.   fatebat *in* fatetur *mut. ut uid.* O 8.
12. persuasisset R G B K.   psuasiset V E.   13. alcibiadem R V P G K 1
B 1 3 S W 1 M 1.   alcibiaden B 2 E D.   alcibiadē W 2 M 2.
14. baiolum R V P G B 1 2 K S E O 7.   baiulum B 3 W 1.   buolū W 2. ‖
adflictaret R V P G K E.   afflictaret B S.   16. cleanthe R P 1 4 G
B 1 2 K 1.   ạcleanthe V.   cleante R 6 P 3 B 3 S E 2 W 2 M 2
                                                            cl
D Π O 2 3.   o cleante R 17 W 1 O 8.   deante E 1 *alio ut uid. atr.*
              o
cleante R 7 *al. atr. superscr. rasura post* te.   cleantes P 2 M 1.   cleantem O 1.
om. E 2 O 7. ‖   num R 6 7 P 3 B 3 W 2 M 2 O 8 Π *at fuerat* tum.
tum R 1 1 7 V P 1 2 G B 1 2 E 1 2 L 5 W 1 M 1 C O 1–3 Gr.
tū D.   tum S *marg.* num.   cum P 4.   17. aegritudine P.   egritudine
D O 1.   aegritudinẹm R *al. atr. corr.*   aegritudineṃ V K.   aegritudinem G.
egritudinem E 2.   egritudinē R 10 16 B 2. ‖   alcibiadem R V P G B 2
K S W 1.   alcibiaden B.   alcibiadē B 3 E W 2 D O 8. ‖ adficiebat
              ci
R V G.   adfiebat K E.   afficiebat P B.

§ 78, 18. lyconis R V K S.   liconis P B E.   lyanis G. ‖ sunt? qui P E 2
W 1 Π O 7 V *at ras. post* i.   sunt? quia R G.   sunt? que O 1.
                                                                                          c
20. non animi malis E 1 2.   non animi mali R 1 10 16 G B K. ‖ dolebat
R G K J.   dofebat V (*sic*).   doleat S.

Cleanthes ipse fateatur: *Cleanthes* has
been suspected by many editors and could
well be spared, but the repetition has a
certain emphasis which may have been
intended. *fateatur* has been changed to
fatebatur by Bai. but the conditional
seems quite natural.

cum Socrates Alcibiadi persuasisset:
Dav. quotes Augustin. C.D. xiv 8 ' Alcibiadem ferunt, si me de nomine hominis
memoria non fallit, cum sibi beatus uideretur, Socrate disputante et ei quam miser
esset, quoniam stultus esset, demonstrante,
fleuisse.' This is the only other place
where this statement directly occurs and
St Augustine very probably took his account from our passage. F.A.W. thinks
that the passage is probably taken from
some (lost) Socratic dialogue. In Plato,

he adds, e.g. in Alcib. 1, Alcibiades is
indeed humbled, but not to such a degree
as to shed tears. Or., accepting this, adds
that our passage cannot refer to any expressions of Alcibiades in the Symposium
(215 E) since the words *quemuis baiolum*
give a strong individual character to the
narrative, which appears to have been
literally translated from some Gk original.

hominis: the contrast here is between
homo and the lower animals; he had no
true reason, no wisdom.

Cleanthe: ii 21, 49 n. on 'Vlixes';
Neue, *Formenlehre* I³ 447.

§ **78. Lyconis:** a Peripatetic philosopher from Troas who succeeded Straton
as head of the school about 270 B.C. He
died in 225 B.C. Cf. Diog. L. v 4, 65.

quid ergo: i 25, 60 n. on 'quid enim?'

non ex animi malis uitiisque constabat? ad Epicuri consolationem satis est ante dictum.

XXXIII. 79. Ne illa quidem firmissima consolatio est, quamquam et usitata est et saepe prodest : 'Non tibi hoc soli.' prodest haec quidem, ut dixi, sed nec semper nec omnibus; sunt enim qui respuant; sed refert quo modo adhibeatur. ut enim
5 tulerit quisque eorum, qui sapienter tulerunt, non quo quisque incommodo adfectus sit, praedicandum est. Chrysippi ad ueritatem firmissima est, ad tempus aegritudinis difficilis. magnum opus est probare maerenti illum suo iudicio et quod se ita putet oportere facere maerere. nimirum igitur, ut in causis non sem-
10 per utimur eodem statu (sic enim appellamus controuersiarum genera), sed ad tempus, ad controuersiae naturam, ad personam accommodamus, sic in aegritudine lenienda quam quisque curationem recipere possit uidendum est.

XXXIII. § 79, 1. ne illa R G B 2 3 W 1 O 1. nec illa B E. ṇǫṇne illa K.
ne ulla R 10 16 S. nulla O 7. ‖ firmissima R V P G B K. 6. adfectus
R V G K. affectus B S. ‖ chryppi V. chrisippi G. crysippi R K E.
7. firmissima R V P G B K. 8. opus R 6 7 P 4 K 2 E 3 W 1 2 M 1 J
O 1 7 8. opus S i.e. n *in* p *mut.* opus Π *at fuerat* onus. onus R 1 17 V
P 1-3 G B 1 K 1 E 1 2 M 2 D C O 2 3 Gr. onus B 3 *marg.* opus.
opp B 2 *ead. fort. manu.* ‖ et quá [ę V. 12. accōmodamus B *linea eod. atr. ducta*
R 1 *al. atr.* accomodamus V G K S. ‖ quam quisque K 2 W 2 D C J O 1 8.
nam quam quisque R 1 10 17 V P 1-3 G B 1 3 K S E 1 2 M 2 Π O 2 3 7.
nāq quisque W 1 *al. atr. superscr.* nam quisque B 2. eam quam M 1.

ad: i 4, 7 n. on 'ad id.'
XXXIII. § 79. **ne...quidem,** 'not... either.'

non tibi hoc soli : this consolation was so ancient and so hackneyed as almost to have become proverbial ; hence the jest of Theocritus recorded in Stobaeus, Floril. 124, 34 Θεόκριτος, ἐν περιδείπνῳ τοῦ πενθοῦντος λαιμάργως ἐσθίοντος, θάρρει, βέλτιστε, εἶπεν, οὐ σοὶ μόνῳ ταῦτα γέγονεν. Dav. quotes lines of Timocles, preserved in Athenaeus vi 223c and in Stob. Floril. 124, 19 concluding
ἅπαντα γὰρ τὰ μείζον' ἢ πέπονθέ τις
ἀτυχήματ' ἄλλοις γεγονότ' ἐννοούμενος
τὰς αὑτὸς αὑτοῦ συμφορὰς ῥᾷον φέρει.
ut dixi : 23, 57 ; 24, 58 and especially 25, 60.
sunt enim qui respuant: cf. 25, 59—60.
Chrysippi: 31, 76. The nom. *consolatio* is carried on from above.
ad ueritatem, 'in theory, *in abstracto*' F. A. W. *ad* = ' in respect of,' as often with adjectives.
suo iudicio, 'by deliberate choice,' 'by an act of his own will.'

[**et** : for the copula, which Bent. wished to delete, see iv 27, 59 n.]
statu: cf. Topica 25, 93 foll. where status, Gk στάσις, is defined as 'refutatio accusationis, in qua est depulsio criminis ...in quo primum insistit quasi ad repugnandum congressa defensio.' Part. Orat. 29, 102; Quintil. iii 6, 1 foll. In § 21 he says 'nostra opinio semper haec fuit...in eo credere statum causae...in quo maxime res uerteretur'; Cornificius ad Herenn. i 11, 18 foll. makes three *constitutiones causae (status)* (a) *coniecturalis,* where the case is a question of fact, e.g. did the accused do the deed with which he is charged? (b) *legitima,* where the case is one of interpretation, e.g. of the terms of a law or of an ambiguously-worded will, or between conflicting laws. (c) *iuridicialis,* where the fact is admitted and the question is whether it was right or wrong, e.g. was the act murder or justifiable homicide? Trans. 'we do not always take the same standpoint.'
quam quisque...: many editors, including Küh. and Mo., retain *nam,* of best

H.   7

80. Sed nescio quo pacto ab eo quod erat a te propositum
15 aberrauit oratio. tu enim de sapiente quaesieras, cui aut malum
uideri nullum potest quod uacet turpitudine aut ita paruum
malum ut id obruatur sapientia uixque appareat, qui nihil opinione adfingat adsumatque ad aegritudinem, nec id putet esse
rectum, se quam maxime excruciari luctuque confici, quo prauius
20 nihil esse possit. edocuit tamen ratio, ut mihi quidem uidetur,
cum hoc ipsum proprie non quaereretur hoc tempore, num quid

---

§ 80, 17. obruatur R V P G L 2 3 4 6.   obseruatur R 10 16 Gr.   obp̊uatur
S *marg.* obruat͏ʳ. ‖ appareat R V G B K S E.   18. adfingat R V P G K E.

affingat B S. ‖ adsumatque R V G K E.   adsumatq; P.   assumatque B S.

19. rectum se R G K.   rectum se V *man. ant. superscr.*   rectum si R 10. ‖

maxume R V G B.   maxime K. ‖ prauis V *atr. ant. superscr.*   21. nū quid
K 2 L 2 W 1.   nūqd R 7.   num qd' O 8.   nūnç quod V *atr. ant. corr.*

nunc quđ P.   nunc quid O 2.   nūc đ W 2.   nunc ꝙ B 2.   nunc qđ R
G B 1 K 1 E J.   nunc qd' L 3 5.   nunc quod P 2 4 S O 3 7.   ne quod
P 3 B 3 *at* aliqd' *superscr.* L 6 M 2.   non quod L 4.   non q, M 1.
ne quidem ullum esset R 6.   proprie hoc non turpe quod esset malum D C.
tempore quod nichil esset E 2 II.

MSS, before *quam,* placing a semicolon
after *lenienda, facimus* or *faciendum*
being understood. This reading is possible but not nearly so natural, and there
is some MS authority for omitting *nam*
while it seems possible to account for its
intrusion. See crit. n.

§ 80. **nescio quo pacto**: i 11, 24 n. on
'nescio quo modo.' In 4, 7 A. had put
forward for discussion the assertion 'uidetur mihi cadere in sapientem aegritudo,'
but after section 21 this question is
dropped, and Cicero divides his subject
into two parts, the setting forth of the cause
of annoyance, and the discovery of its
cure.

cui aut malum...turpitudine: this is
the well-known strict Stoic doctrine. In
the qualifying clause *aut ita paruum...
appareat* Cic. is thinking specially of grief
for the dead, and his thought is illustrated
by Sen. de Ira i 16, 7 quoted in 22, 54 n.
on 'cicatricibus.'

adfingat adsumatque...putet: these
subjunctives are very difficult. Bake proposed to change all three (and *possit* also)
into indicatives, but it is hardly likely
that, apart from interpolation in the
archetype, which there is little reason
to suspect, all three words would have
been corrupted. The two clauses *cui aut
malum uideri...* and *qui nihil opinione...*
read to me like coordinate clauses, and
the theory which makes *qui=quippe qui,*

adopted by editors here, is only a make-
shift device. Draeger, *H.S.* § 151, 5 a
(1 p. 292), rejecting the *qui=quippe qui*
theory, places these subjunctives under
instances of attraction in relative clauses.
And I think that the preceding subjunctives *obruatur* and *appareat* probably are
the cause of the error; but if so we have
here no ordinary instances of attraction in
rel. clauses, for that takes place when the
rel. clause is *dependent* upon the clause
containing the verb which is the cause of
the attraction, whereas the verbs in the
text are in a clause independent of the *ut-*
clause which contains the verbs which
exercise the attraction. As an alternative
to this theory it might be suggested that
Cic. *wrote quippe qui,* as he would not
have expressed himself so ambiguously as
the text would make him do, if he meant
the *qui*-clause to depend upon the *cui-*
clause. But if we read *quippe qui* or take
qui as =*quippe qui* the meaning is unsatisfactory, for that would make this clause
give a reason for the *sapiens* thinking that
nothing can be an evil which is free from
baseness or that, if anything can, the evil
would be slight. It is obvious that if *qui=*
quippe qui it must refer to *cui* above and
could not refer to the *ut id obruatur*
clause alone. I believe that *qui* is a corruption for *quoniam* (=q̄m̄), a very slight
change, in which case we have a legitimate attraction of the verbs that follow to

esset malum, nisi quod idem dici turpe posset, tamen ut uideremus, quicquid esset in aegritudine mali, id non naturale esse,
sed uoluntario iudicio et opinionis errore contractum. 81. trac-
25 tatum est autem a nobis id genus aegritudinis, quod unum est
omnium maximum, ut ·eo sublato reliquorum remedia ne magnopere quaerenda arbitraremur.

XXXIV. Sunt enim certa, quae de paupertate, certa, quae
de uita inhonorata et ingloria dici soleant; separatim certae
scholae sunt de exsilio, de interitu patriae, de seruitute, de debilitate, de caecitate, de omni casu in quo nomen poni solet
5 calamitatis. haec Graeci in singulas scholas et in singulos libros
dispertiunt; opus enim quaerunt; quamquam plenae disputa-

§ 81, 24. tractatum R B 1–3 K 1 O 1 7 8. tractum $\overset{\text{ta}}{\text{tractum V S.}}$ tractum
R 10 16 G O 3. 26. maxumum R V G B. maximum K S. ‖ nemagnopere
R (*hoc loco*) V (*hoc loco*) G B K S E. nec magno opere O 7. 27. arbitraremur
R V P G B 1–3 K 1 2 S E 1 2 L 6 W 1 M 1 2 D C Π J O 3 8 7.
arbitremur L 2–4 W 2 O 1 2.
XXXIV. 3. scolae R G. ‖ exilio R V G B K S E. ‖ dedī̄bilitate R *et* V
i *in* e *mut.* 4. de caecitate de omni R 1 7 V P 1 2 G B 1 2 K 1 2 E 1 2
W 2 M 1 D C J O.1–3 7 8. de cecitate de debilitate de omni W 1.
de caecitate de ommo $\overline{\text{cau}}$ S. $\overset{\text{et}}{\text{de caecitate}_\wedge \text{de omni Π.}}$ de caecitate et de
omni R 6. de caecitate & omni B 3 M 2. 6. plene L 4. planae G.
planę R V P B 1 E 1 W 1. plane R 6 7 10 16 17 P 2–4 B 2 3 K 1 2 S
E 2 L 3 5 6 W 2 M 1 2 D C Π J O 1–3 7 8 Gr. ed. H. *om.* L 2. ‖ disputationes
R 7 P 2 3 B 3 E 3 L 2 4 W 1 M 2 C O 3 8. disputationis P *al. atr.*
superscr. $\overset{\text{ϝ i}}{\text{disputationes D }\textit{al. atr. superscr.}}$ disputationis R 1 6 V P 4 G
B 1 2 K 1 S E 1 2 L 3 5 6 M 1 Π J O 1 2 7. disputationisq3 W 2.
$\overset{\text{is}}{\text{disputa}}$ K 2 *eod. atr.*

the verbs *obruatur* and *appareat* on which
they depend. *qui* might also have arisen
from *cum = quom (quō).*
For the matter cf. the definition of
aegritudo in 11, 25 and nn. there.
num quid: Wes. *Em.* 1 p. 19 seems
right in reading *num quid* against nearly
all MSS and Bai. and Sff. follow him; but
quod can be adjectival 'whether there
was any evil...'
tamen ut uideremus: *tamen* repeats
the previous *tamen* for the sake of clearness after the preceding clauses. *ut uideremus* could have been omitted, the acc.
and infin. following upon *edocuit*; the
constr. is as though *effecit* had preceded.
uoluntario...errore, 'a deliberate act
of will and a mistaken idea.'
opinionis errore: gen. of definition.
Hei. notes that the same meaning is
given in Diu. ii 69, 143 by 'opinio
erroris.'
§ 81. **id genus aegritudinis**: sc. grief

for the death of relatives. See also Pohlenz
in *Hermes* XLI p. 327 n. 3.
ut...ne: see i 32, 78 n. on 'illud...non
dant ut...ne intereat.'
XXXIV. **inhonorata**, 'unambitious,'
a life that avoids the *cursus honorum.*
certae scholae...: see Buresch, *Leipz.
Stud.* IX p. 77, where he compares Seneca,
de remediis fortuitorum. [Musonius Rufus
wrote a treatise ὅτι οὐ κακὸν ἡ φυγή.]
scholae: i 4, 7 n.
opus enim quaerunt, 'they make work
for themselves.' Editors have found different meanings in this expression, but Livy
v 3, 6, quoted by Menkius, seems fairly
parallel, 'sic hercule tamquam artifices
improbi opus quaerunt; quippe semper
aegri aliquid esse in republica uolunt, ut
sit ad cuius curationem a uobis adhibeantur.' This somewhat depreciatory remark
is qualified by the following clause.
plenae...delectationis, 'very interesting.'

tiones delectationis sunt. **82.** et tamen, ut medici toto corpore
curando minimae etiam parti, si condoluit, medentur, sic philosophia cum uniuersam aegritudinem sustulit, <sustulit> etiam,
10 si quis error alicunde exstitit, si paupertas momordit, si ignominia
pupugit, si quid tenebrarum obfudit exsilium, aut eorum, quae

7. delectationis R V G B 3 K 1 L 4 E 3 O 3 7 8 E 2 *marg.* W 2 *marg.*
X dilectionis
a‌ls delectationis Π.   delectationis D *al. atr. superscr.*   delectationisq; K 2 L 3
J O 1.   delectationes L 2 6 ed. H.   delectationi W 1.   dilectionis B 2.
om. O 2. ‖ sunt P 1 4 G B 1 2 K 1 S E 2 W 2 M 1 2 C Π J O 1 2 8 Gr.
sint W 1.   summae V *at* mae *in ras. et al. atr.*
§ 82. Ta | m̅ ut medici V *at* Ta *et* m̅ *extra lineam al. atr. script.*   9. aegritudinem
sustulit tamen si quis R 1 7 1 7 V(sustu]lit *habet*) P 1-4 G B 1-3 K 1 2 S E
L 3–6 W 1 (substulit *habet*) W 2 M 1 D O 2 3 7 8.   aegritudinem sustulerit
tamen si quis R 6 M 2 J O 1.   aegritudinem sustulit tum si quis E 2 L 2 C Π.
aegritudinem sustulit, sustulit etiam *corr. Keilius.*   10. aliunde R 1 2 6 7 10 16 17
V P G B 1–3 K 1 2 S E 1 2 L 2–6 W 1 2 M 1 2 D C Π J O 1-3 7 8.
alicunde *corr. Ernestius.* ‖ extitit R V G B K S.   11. pupugit P B 1 3 K 1
                                                v
E 2 W 2 M 1 2 Π O 1–3 8.   pupv̥git V i *in* u *mut.*   pupigit R *atr. ant.*
G *alt. man. suppl.*   pupuᵃgit E 1.   pupigit B 2.   pungit W 1.   pupugnit O 7. ‖
                                                v
obfudit R G B E S.   obfodit K.   offudit M 1 2 O 7.   obtudit J.
effudit W 1 O 1. ‖ exsilium V *h. l.* G *h. l.*   exilium R B K E S. ‖
eorum quae M 2.   eorum que B 3 M 1 D C O 1 7 8 W 2 *at cum ras. et spatio
post* que.   eorum q̄ K 2.   eorum quaeque R K.   eorum quaequ̥e G.   eorum
                                                                                                q̄
quȩ que V B.   eorum queque B 2 E 1 2 Π.   eorum quoq; ˄ S.   eorum
q̄q̄q̣̄O 2.   eorum quō W 1.

§ 82. et tamen: Bouh. suspected *tamen*
and conj. *etenim*, but the line of thought
is 'I have dealt with the most vehement
form of annoyance in order that when it is
removed we might not think that there
is much need to seek out remedies for the
remaining forms. For there are remedies
put forward for all the different forms of
misfortune. But, just as physicians...'
si condoluit: ii 24, 58 n. on 'aspeximus.'
sic philosophia... : the emendation of
Keil, *sustulit, sustulit etiam* for 'sustulit
tamen' gives the required antithesis to *ut
medici...medentur* and has been deser-
vedly accepted by recent editors. For
the omission of one of the two, where the
same word occurs twice in succession, cf.
Introd. to vol. 1 p. xlviii; Madv. on Fin.
ii 10 30 'appellauit, appellat'; Ac. ii 3,
9 'potuerint, potuerunt.' *et* easily fell out
after -*it* in *sustulit* and *iam* was easily
corrupted into *tam̅*=*tamen*.
Klotz, *Quaest. Tull.* I 109–113, retains
the MS reading. He thinks that the
parallel instituted in the previous clause
between the physician and the philosopher
prepares the reader for carrying on *medentur*, so that after *sustulit* we supply
medicinam tamen adfert, and he understands the clause *et si singularum* as a

sort of etcetera clause, equivalent to *et si
singulis rebus opus est singulis consolationibus*, but in this we should hardly
recognise 'Ciceronem optimum orationis
artificem' as Kl., in criticising Orelli, has
just declared him to be.
Keil was the first to explain that we
have *etsi* here not *et si*. Or. retained the
reading of the MSS with the exception of
etsi which is struck out without accounting for its intrusion. He punctuated as
follows: *sic, philosophia cum...sustulit,
tamen, si...si...si quid exstitit, singularum
rerum sunt propriae consolationes.* Dav.
suggested *ei* for *et*, rejecting *si* as due to
dittography from *si* in *singularum*. Ern.
read *sic philosophiae...* and *ei* for *etsi*,
Nissen *sic in philosophia.* F. A. W.
thought that Cic. intended to add *similiter medetur*, but forgetting this says
*singularum rerum sunt propriae conso-
lationes.* He would omit *et si*.
uniuersam: ii 1, 4 n. on 'uniuersam.'
alicunde is a necessary emendation for
aliunde, the meaning 'from another source'
being impossible. In i 23, 53 MSS presented the converse error. *alicunde=ex
aliqua una re=ex singulis rebus* and
corresponds, as Wes. notes, to *minimae
etiam parti, si condoluit*, above.
quae modo dixi: in § 81.

modo dixi, si quid exstitit; etsi singularum rerum sunt propriae
consolationes, de quibus audies tu quidem, cum uoles. sed ad
eundem fontem reuertendum est, aegritudinem omnem procul
15 abesse a sapiente, quod inanis sit, quod frustra suscipiatur, quod
non natura exoriatur, sed iudicio, sed opinione, sed quadam
inuitatione ad dolendum, cum id decreuerimus ita fieri oportere.
83. hoc detracto, quod totum est uoluntarium, aegritudo erit
sublata illa maerens, morsus tamen et contractiuncula quaedam
20 animi relinquetur. hanc dicant sane naturalem, dum aegritudinis
nomen absit grave, taetrum, funestum, quod cum sapientia esse
atque, ut ita dicam, habitare nullo modo possit. at quae stirpes

---

12. siquid extitit R V G B S E.   sicut extitit K.   ‖   2 si singularum O 7.
7 si singularum W 2   D   O 8.   &si singularum O 1 3.   et si singularum R 7
G B 2 3   K 2   S W 1   C Π J.   & si singularum R 1 6 17   P B 1   K 1   E 2
M 2.   & sic singularum M 1.   et singularum V S   E 1   O 2.

§ 83, 18. erit *om.* B E. S *marg.*   19. ita maerens G *al. man. superscr.* ‖
morsus tamen V P G K S M 2 D C O 12.   morsus tam R   E 1   O 1.

morsus tñ B 3 E 2 W 1 2 Π.   morsus O 8.   morsus & tñ M 1. ‖
contractiunculae R 6 P 1 3 G K 1 M 2 O 2.   contractiuncle R 1 10   V E
W 1 O 3.   contractiuncule R 7 17   B 3 K 2 S E 2 L 2-6 W 2 D C Π J
O 7 8.   contratiuncle P 4 B 1.   contratiuncle P 2 O 1.   contracluℓ0cle⟩
R 16.   confracti uncule B 2 *al. atr. superscr.*   contractiuncula *corr.* Bentleius. ‖
quaedam R 10 V P E.   quaedam R a *in* ae *mut.*   quaedam G.   q̄dam E 2.
quodɷ R 16.   21. tetrum G *h. l.*   22. atque stirpes R G.   atq; stirpes R 7 10
V P 1 2 4 K 1 2 S E 1-3 L 3 5 W 2 M 1 D C Π J O 7 8 ed. H.
atq stirpes B 3 L 4.   atq, stirpes W 1.   atqui stirpes R 6 P 3 M 2 O 1 3.
at qui stirpes L 6 O 2.   at quae stirpes *corr.* Bentleius.

---

etsi: not uncommon in introducing a
correction (καίτοι) but *quamquam* is
more usual, i 42, 99.
    audies: sc. in book iv.
    ad eundem fontem: sc. *in singulis
rebus tractandis*. The general principles
here cited are the *source* from which the
arguments are to be drawn for each particular case.
    [**sed...sed...sed**: for the anaphora of
sed, rare in Cicero but common in later
writers, cf. Fin. ii 14, 45 'non sibi se
soli natum meminerit, sed patriae, sed
suis' with Madv.'s note.]
    inuitatione: sc. *sui*, cf. 30, 73 n. on
'ipsi ad se miseriam inuitant.'
    § 83. **morsus**: may be plur. here as in
Off. ii 7, 24 'acriores morsus sunt inter-
missae libertatis quam retentae.'
    contractiuncula, 'dejection.' Against
the MSS and Nonius the sing. is rendered
necessary by the following *hanc*, as Bent.
rightly held. *hanc* cannot refer to *aegritudo* above, as Hand and Wopkens, *Lectt.
Tull.* p. 119, suppose. The examples
which they cite do not refute the objec-

tion, which they anticipate, that this
would make Cicero say that they may
pronounce *aegritudo* natural provided
they do not call it *aegritudo*. Of Bentley's
further emendations *tantum* for *tamen* is
unnecessary, and *relinquetur* for *relinquentur*, though very possibly right, is
not essential. Sff., thinking that *morsus*
must have something to define it, reads
*morsus tamen ex contractione quadam
animi relinquentur* (*quadam* with some
MS support); but Küh. points out that
et often has an explanatory force. *contractiuncula* is only a depreciatory diminutive of *contractio*, which occurs several
times in the sing. in this sense, i 37, 90;
iv 6, 14; 31, 66, 67. For the opinion
here asserted cf. 22, 54 n. on 'cicatricibus.'
    hanc dicant...naturalem: cf. the Peri-
patetic view 10, 22 n. on 'mediocritates.'
The singulars *hanc...naturalem* are ac-
counted for by Küh. on the ground that
contractiuncula is more important than
morsus, as the latter are transient while
the former is deep-rooted.
    atque...habitare: v 24, 69 'sapientis

sunt aegritudinis, quam multae, quam amarae! quae ipso trunco
euerso omnes eligendae sunt et, si necesse erit, singulis disputa-
25 tionibus. superest enim nobis hoc, cuicuimodi est, otium. sed
ratio una omnium est aegritudinum, plura nomina. nam et
inuidere aegritudinis est et aemulari et obtrectare et misereri

23. quae trunco V ipso *om.*   24. eligendae R G L 4.   eligende̢ R 10
                                                              de
B K E.   eligende R 7 16 17 P 4 B 2 L 5 W 2 J O 7 8.   elig K 2.
              ci   d
eligendi D C.   eligendae V *eod. atr.*   eligende P.   elidendae R 6   P 3
M 2 O 2.   elidende P 2 B 3 S E 2 3 L 2 6 M 1 II O 1 3 ed. H.
eliendae L 3.   euellende̢ W 1.   25. cuicuimodi R 1 G.   cui cuimodi P 4 K 1.
cuicui modi B 2 L 5.   cuimodi B 1.   çui cuĩmodi V P *al. atr. superscr.*
et punctis appositis.   cuĩmodi P 2 K 2 E 2 D J E 1 *al. atr. suppl.*   cuĩmōi
W 2 *eod. atr. ut uid.*   cuiusmodi P 3 S L 3 6 M 2 C II O 1–3.   cuiusmodo
R 6.   cuieiusmodi L 4.   cuĩ3mōi R 17.   huiuscemodi R 7 L 2.
huiusmodi O 7 8.   eiusmodi B 3 W 1 M 1 ed. H.

animum cum his habitantem pernoctantemque curis.' F. A. W. compares συνοι-
κεῖν, συνεῖναι.
at quae : Wopkens, *Lectt. Tull.* I p.
115, reads 'atqui stirpes sunt aegritudinis
quam multae! quam amarae!' which is
Latin but *atque* of the MSS points to *at
quae* not *atqui* as the true reading and
the expression so obtained is better. The
variant is very common.
eligendae: Nonius 290 M. has 'diligit,
diuidit. Plautus in Curculione [1. 453]:
clipeatus, elephantum ubi machaera diligit. Titinius Proelia: pernam totam diligit.'
MSS in Curculio 453 read *dessicit* and
Goetz and Schoell (after Gronov.) *dissicit.*
But Paulus ex Fest. iv 52 (Müller, p. 69)
has 'dirigere apud Plautum inuenitur
pro discidere (discindere corr. Scal.).'
Ribbeck, *Scaen. Rom. Poes. Frag.* II²
LIX—LXI, thinks *diligit* may have its
ordinary sense in the passage of Titinius
and suggests *eiciendae* as the correct reading here as in the MSS in Diu. ii 72, 149
'superstitionis stirpes omnes eiciendae.'
The MS reading *eligendae* in our passage
is supported by C. F. W. Müller, *Prosod.*
490 and Madv. *Em. Liv.* 155 and *Advers.*
ii 205. Madv. would read *eligendae* in
Diu. ii 72, 149 (after Manutius) ; *electos* in
Liv. vii 39, 6 with Gronov. and Gebh.;
electis in de leg. agr. ii 33, 91 'neruis
urbis omnibus electis' where MSS read
eiectis.
Nonius 278 M. quotes from Lucilius,
Bk xxix 'concedat homini id quod uelit,
deleniat, | corrumpat prorsum ac neruos
omnis eligat' and Non. p. 301 says
eligere=*defetigare,* quoting the same line.
It is very possible that 'neruos omnis
uirtuti *eligunt*' should be read in ii 11, 27

where *elidunt* of the MSS is rather strangely
used.
Against Ribbeck's statement that *legere*
and *sublegere* are used without any idea of
violence Ml. *Ann. crit.* to our passage
cites Senec. Cons. ad Marc. 22, 3 'lacerationes medicorum ossa uinis legentium';
de prouid. 3, 2 ; de benef. v 24, 3. All
these are cases of the removal of bones by
surgeons. We may add Quintil. vi 1, 30
'lecta e uolneribus ossa.' The surgeon
would hardly be *violent,* it may be remarked, but neither need the philosopher.
But *euellere,* the word used in the same
connexion in 6, 13, implies violence.
Dav. refers to Varro, R.R. i 47. Ml.
would read in N.D. ii 60, 151 'nos e
terrae cauernis ferrum *eligimus*' for MSS
elicimus (where see Mayor's n.), and
would follow the MSS in N.D. ii 64, 161
'multa ex earum corporibus remedia
morbis et uolneribus eligamus,' and he
thinks that in Fin. ii 35, 119 *eligerem* of
MSS may be right as against Gruter's
elicerem. The evidence seems to indicate
uses of *lego, eligo,* etc., from a root
different from that found in the sense of
'gather,' though the latter meaning would
suit our present passage, where we may
translate 'The roots must be weeded out,'
i.e. 'picked out.' The surgeon also picks
out the bones that he extracts.
hoc...otium=*huius rei otium,* 'the
necessary leisure' i 19, 45 n. on 'haec
pulchritudo.' [But see v 41, 121 n.]
cuicuimodi : this form, which was
always used instead of the cumbrous
cuiuscuiusmodi, is recognised by Priscian
and is common in Cicero. Neue cites
thirteen instances, the word going in
every case with *esse. Formenlehre* II² 513.

et angi, lugere, maerere, aerumna adfici, lamentari, sollicitari,
dolere, in molestia esse, adflictari, desperare. **84.** haec omnia
30 definiunt Stoici, eaque uerba, quae dixi, singularum rerum sunt,
non, ut uidentur, easdem res significant, sed aliquid differunt,
quod alio loco fortasse tractabimus. haec sunt illae fibrae stirpium, quas initio dixi, persequendae et omnes eligendae, ne
umquam ulla possit exsistere. magnum opus et difficile, quis
35 negat? quid autem praeclarum non idem arduum? sed tamen
id se effecturam philosophia profitetur, nos modo curationem
eius recipiamus. uerum haec quidem hactenus, cetera, quotiens-
cumque uoletis, et hoc loco et aliis parata uobis erunt.

28. et angi R V P G B 1–3 K 1 2 S E 1 2 W 1 2 M 1 2 D C Π J O 1–3 8.
om. O 7. ‖ adfici R V P G K E.   affici B S.   29. adflictari R V P G K E.
afflictari B S.

§ **84,** 32. haec sunt R 1 6 P G K.   hẹc V B E.   hec R 7 P 2 4 B 2 K 2
W 2 D C Π J O 7 8.   hec S *marg.* hẹ.   heẹ O 3.   he E 2 *at c eras.*
hae P 3 W 1 M 2 O 2.   he B 3 M 1 O 1 ed. H.   33. quas initio R G.
ae
qs ininitio E 1 *eod. atr.*   quas inicio V. ‖ eligendae G L 3.   eligendẹ B 1 K 1.

eligende B 2 D C J O 7 W 2 *at marg.* d *alio atr.*   eligendẹ V *eod. atr.*

elegendẹ E 1.   elegande K 2.   eligendae R *al. atr. superscr.*   elidendae R 6
P 3 M 2 O 2.   elidendẹ R 10 S O 3.   elidende R 7 P 2 4 B 3 E 2 3
L 6 M 1 Π O 1 ed. H.   ẹllidendẹ W 1.   eligạnde P *al. atr. corr.*
eligendas *superscr.* O 8.   erudiendas L 2.   exstirpandas L 4.   eruendas R 17.
34. umquam ulla R V P G B K S E D Π J O 1 7 8.   ulla unquam O 2 3 ed. H.
umquam C ulla *om.*   ne ulla possit unquam W 1. ‖ existere R V G B K S E.
37. quidem haec R V P G E 1 2 L 3–6. ‖ haec *om.* L 2. ‖ hactenus R 6
G E 2.   actenus R K.   actenus R 2 E 1. ‖ caetera G *h. l.*

§ **84.** alio loco: iv c. 8.
haec: for this fem. form cf. i 11, 22 n.
and Neue, *Formenl.* II³ 417–8.
initio dixi: 6, 13.
persequendae et...: cf. Hieronymus,
Ep. 132 (133) (ad Ctesiphontem), *init.*
'omnium haereticorum uenena complecti,
quae de philosophorum et maxime Pythagorae et Zenonis principis Stoicorum fonte
manarunt. illi enim quae Graeci appellant πάθη, nos perturbationes possumus
dicere: aegritudinem uidelicet et gaudium,
spem et metum, quorum duo praesentia,
duo futura sunt, asserunt exstirpari posse
de mentibus et nullam fibram radicem-
que uitiorum in homine omnino residere,
meditatione et assidua exercitatione uirtutum,' quoted by v. Arnim, *Stoica* III § 447,

who adds 'cf. dial. adu. Pelag. ii 6 (ubi
Chrysippum quoque nominat).'
quid autem...arduum: proverbial, cf.
Plato, Rep. iv 435 c ἴσως γάρ, ὦ Σώκρατες,
τὸ λεγόμενον ἀληθές, ὅτι χαλεπὰ τὰ καλά.
Camerarius quotes Hesiod, Works and
Days 288 μακρὸς δὲ καὶ ὄρθιος οἶμος ἐς
αὐτήν (sc. τὴν ἀρετήν).
haec quidem: Küh. endeavours to
justify *uerum quidem haec* of the MSS,
taking *uerum quidem* as = ἀλλά γε and
comparing *quamquam quidem* and καίτοι
γε, but it would be hard to illustrate this
use of *uerum quidem*. For the formula
F.A.W. compares καὶ ταῦτα μὲν τοιαῦτα,
and Mo. καὶ ταῦτα μὲν δὴ ταῦτα.
hoc loco: sc. *in Academia*, 3, 7; ii 3,
9 n.

M. TVLLI CICERONIS

TVSCVLANARVM DISPVTATIONVM

LIBER QVARTVS

I. 1. Cum multis locis nostrorum hominum ingenia uirtutes-
que, Brute, soleo mirari, tum maxime in iis studiis quae sero
admodum expetita in hanc ciuitatem e Graecia transtulerunt.
nam cum a primo urbis ortu regiis institutis, partim etiam
5 legibus auspicia, caerimoniae, comitia, prouocationes, patrum
consilium, equitum peditumque discriptio, tota res militaris diuinitus esset constituta, tum progressio admirabilis incredibilisque
cursus ad omnem excellentiam factus est dominatu regio re
publica liberata. nec uero hic locus est, ut de moribus institutis-

I. §1, 2. mirari R 1 6 7 V P 1 4 G B 1–3 K 1 S E 1 2 W 1 2 M 1 2
D C Π J O 1 2 7 8.   admirari O 3. ‖ maxime R V G B K. ‖ in iis S *ras. inter*
n *et* i.   in his R V P G B E.   4. regiis G B 1 K 1 2 W 1 2 O 1–3 7 8.
grạegiis R.   regis V.   5. caerimoniae R G.   caerimoniẹ V.   cẹrimoniẹ S.
cerimoniẹ E.   6. discriptio R V G K E.   descriptio P B 1 2 S W 1.
8. re p. B 3 W 1 M 2 Π O 1 3 W 2 *at* s *eraso* E 2 *at* re *in ras. spatio unius*
litt. relicto.   re pu O 7.   r. p. K 2 M 1.   resp. R V P G B 1 2 K 1 E J
O 2 8.   R. p. D C.

multis locis: 'in many respects,' cf.
Lael. 13, 47 'specie quidem blanda, sed
reapse multis locis repudianda,' where
Sff., who deduces this use from that of
locus as a verbum proprium in rhetoric
(τόπος), quotes Cat. iv 10, 22 and other
exx. See i 24, 57 n.

iis: Sff. notes that *his* of MSS would
refer to philosophy, the subject of the
Tusculans, whereas 2 § 5 shows that that
is not the ref. here. Cf. i 3, 5 n. on 'qui
his' for the confusion between *his* and *iis*
in MSS.

prouocationes: appeal to the people
existed under the kings: but the king
might grant or refuse it as he pleased.
This continued to be the rule under the
republic, as against dictators, but the *lex
Valeria de prouocatione* of 509 B.C. made
the right absolute as against the ordinary
magistrates. Mommsen, *H.R.* 1 82, 95,
192, 320 (E.T.). Dav. compares Sen. Ep.
108, 31 where Cic. Rep. [ii 31, 54] is
referred to; Livy viii 33; Val. Max. viii
1, 1.
Instances were rare under the kings

and Hei. is probably right in referring
the plural here to separate decisions upon
questions of *prouocatio*.

consilium: a term often applied to the
senate which was originally the board of
advisers of the early kings. [Liv. xxvi
16, 10; Cic. Diuin. i 2, 4; Sen. de Ira iii
2, 4.]

equitum peditumque discriptio: the
Servian constitution, which was in origin
a *military* reform.

diuinitus: not *sensu stricto* but = 'ex-
cellently,' cf. Fam. i 9, 12 'quae sunt
apud Platonem nostrum scripta diuinitus';
'multa a Crasso diuinitus dicta ferebantur,'
Or. iii 1, 4.

disciplina ac temperatione, 'constitution and organization,' i 10, 21 n.

sex libris...de re publica: part of
the sixth book, the Somnium Scipionis,
has been preserved in Macrobius' Commentarium in Somn. Scip. in two books.
What we have of the remainder of the
work was discovered by Mai in a Vatican
palimpsest and published at Rome in
1822.

10 que maiorum et disciplina ac temperatione ciuitatis loquamur;
aliis haec locis satis adcurate a nobis dicta sunt maximeque in
iis sex libris, quos de re publica scripsimus. 2. hoc autem loco
consideranti mihi studia doctrinae multa sane occurrunt cur ea
quoque arcessita aliunde neque solum expetita, sed etiam con-
15 seruata et culta, uideantur. erat enim illis paene in conspectu
praestanti sapientia et nobilitate Pythagoras, qui fuit in Italia
temporibus isdem quibus L. Brutus patriam liberauit, praeclarus
auctor nobilitatis tuae. Pythagorae autem doctrina cum longe
lateque flueret, permanauisse mihi uidetur in hanc ciuitatem,
20 idque cum coniectura probabile est, tum quibusdam etiam uesti-
giis indicatur. quis enim est qui putet, cum floreret in Italia
Graecia potentissimis et maximis urbibus, ea quae magna dicta

11. accurate R V G B K S. ‖ maximeque V G B K. maximaeque R *eod. atr.* ‖
in his sex R G B K.   12. puplica G p *in* b *mut. alt. man.*
§ 2, 14. arcessita R V P G B 1 2 K E J Gr. S *at in* accersita *mut.*
accersita B 3 E 2 W 1 M 1 2 D II O 1–3 8. acersita O 7. accessita W 2.
ex'cita C.   16. et nobilitate R V P G K S E J. ‖ pythagoras B K.
 h   i
pytagoras G *eod. atr.*   17. isdem R V G B 1 2 K E J.   isdem P *al. atr.*
superscr.   iisdem W 1 M 2 C O 3 S *at ras. antecedente.*   eisdem O 8.
hisdem E 2 M 1 O 2.   hiisdem II.   18. pythagorae G.   pythagore B S.
Pythagore R V.   Phitagore E.   21. quis enim est R V P G B 1 2 K 1 S
E 1 2 W 1 2 M 1 D C II O 3.   quis est enim B 3 M 2 J O 1 2 7 8.
22. Graeciae G K.   graecie R.   grecie V B S.   gretie E. ‖ potentissumis
et maximis R V.   potentissumis et maxumis G.   potentissumis et maximis
P *al. atr. corr.*   potentissimis et maximis B K.

§ 2. **multa sane occurrunt cur**: cf.
i 21, 49 'nec tamen mihi sane quicquam
occurrit cur....' The arguments with which
Cicero supports his view are neither
forcible nor forcibly expressed.

nobilitate: *non generis sed famae ac
nominis*, Sff., who compares i 16, 38,
where *auctoritate* bears much the same
force. The conjecture of Madv. 'praestanti *sapientiae* nobilitate' is therefore
rightly rejected.

temporibus isdem quibus...: cf. i 16,
38 n. on 'Superbo regnante' and following note. Also Zeller, *Pre-Soc. Phil.* I
325 n. 1 'The usual opinion now is that
Pythagoras was born about the 49th
Olympiad, that he came to Italy about
the 59th or 60th, and died in the 69th.
This is no doubt approximately correct...'

auctor, 'founder of your illustrious
family.' For this statement cf. Brut.
14, 53; Phil. ii 11, 26. Niebuhr, *R.H.*
i pp. 522 foll. (E.T.) conjectures that the
early Brutus, the *exactor regum*, was a
plebeian; but, even if he was a patrician,
that circumstance would not in itself
refute the assertion in the text. Dionys.
Halic. v 18, if correct, would decide the

matter, as he asserts that Brutus left
γενεὰν οὔτ' ἄρρενα οὔτε θήλειαν. This
statement, however, was not unchal-
lenged in antiquity: thus Plut. Brut. i
says that Posidonius asserted that a son
under age survived. On the other hand
false genealogies and accounts of *ad
plebem transitiones* were rife, cf. Brut.
16, 62; Dion. Halic. vi 70; the Bruti had
many motives for claiming this descent;
and the opponents of Caesar were very
ready to accept the theory, as is shown
by the writing on walls and on the base
of the early Brutus' statue during the
conspiracy a little later on.

nobilitatis: sc. *generis*. For the repetition of the word in a different sense
within a very short interval Küh. refers to
Sff. on Laelius 12, 40 p. 268 (*turpis...
turpis*) where many exx. are collected.

longe lateque flueret: according to
Diog. L. viii 14 pupils flocked to him not
only from the Gk cities of Italy but also
from native communities, including even
Romans.

Graecia...magna: for Magna Graecia
cf. i 16, 38 n. on 'magnam illam Graeciam.'

est, in iisque primum ipsius Pythagorae, deinde postea Pythagoreorum, tantum nomen esset, nostrorum hominum ad eorum
25 doctissimas uoces aures clausas fuisse? 3. quin etiam arbitror
propter Pythagoreorum admirationem Numam quoque regem
Pythagoreum a posterioribus existimatum. nam cum Pythagorae
disciplinam et instituta cognoscerent regisque eius aequitatem
et sapientiam a maioribus suis accepissent, aetates autem et
30 tempora ignorarent propter uetustatem, eum, qui sapientia ex-
celleret, Pythagorae auditorem crediderunt fuisse.

II. Et de coniectura quidem hactenus. uestigia autem Pythagoreorum quamquam multa colligi possunt, paucis tamen utemur,

23. in hisque R G J. ‖ pythagoraeorum V.   pytagorae eorum G e *conf. et
punctis not. alt. man.*   25. doctissimas R V P G B K. ‖ aures R V G B 1 2
K S E W 1.
§ 3, 26. admirationem G B 2 K 1 W 1.   ammirationem B 1.
27. Pythagoreum R G J V *at spat. et ras. post* m.   pythagerorum K.
28. instituta W 1 D C O 2 ed. H.   constituta R V P G B 1-3 K 1 2 S
E 1 3 L 2 3 4 6 W 2 M 1 2 Π J O 1 3 7 8.   cōstituta E 2 *at cō in ras.*
                              te   æ
29. aetates V P G.   aetas E 1.   λ & af R 1.   etates B 2.
31. crediderunt fuisse R V P G B 1-3 K 1 S E 1 2 M 1 2 DC Π O 2 3 ed. H.
fuisse crediderunt R 6 K 2 W 1 J O 1 8.   fuisse credunt W 2. *om.* O 7.
II. 2. colligi R V G B K S E.

ea quae...dicta est = *eam dico, quae
dicta est.*
§ 3. Pythagoreorum: objective genitive.
Numam...Pythagoreum: the theory
that Numa was either a pupil or at least
a follower of Pythagoras (Schwegler,
Rom. Hist. 1 560–4; Plut. Q. Rom. 10) is
put forward in de R.P. ii 15, 28 and
refuted by a reference to chronology, in
which we find a translation of a reflexion of
Polybius (vi 59, 2) and in the immediately
preceding context Cicero has the words
'sequamur enim potissimum Polybium
nostrum, quo nemo fuit in exquirendis
temporibus diligentior.' Hence Niebuhr,
H.R. 1 238, rightly observes that 'The
discourse on the early history of Rome
which Cicero puts in the mouth of Scipio
is entirely taken from Polybius.' Polybius' criticism has been repeated by many
subsequent writers, e.g. Cic. de R.P., *l.c.*;
Or. ii 37, 154; Livy i 18, 2; xl 29, 8;
Dionys. Halic. ii 59, 1.
Rejecting the story, Mo. on de R.P.
l.c. traces the error to the following
causes: (*a*) one Pythagoras of Sparta was
victor in the Olympiad in which Numa
gained the throne; (*b*) Pythagoras settled
in Italy, where Numa reigned; (*c*) there
seemed to be a parallel between the
wisdom and legislation of the two leaders;

and Seeley, Livy i, Introd. p. 40, accounts
for its origin by the theory that, when
Numa's intercourse with Egeria ceased to
be believed, some other explanation of
his wisdom was sought and hence arose
the theory of his being a pupil of Pythagoras, the only Gk philosopher who was
well-known to the Italians. See also
Momms. *R.H.* II 91.
instituta: Klotz in *Add.* p. 152 points
out that *constituta* cannot be defended by
such passages as Att. vi 1, 2 'quod
quaedam a se constituta rescinderem,' and
ibid. 'cogitabam eius multa inique constituta et acta tollere' for *constituta* is a
participle in those places. Klotz is probably right in thinking that the error is
due to an abbreviation *īstituta*) (*ǭstituta.*
aetates...et tempora, 'their periods
and dates.'
II. uestigia...Pythagoreorum: the first
sure indication of knowledge of Pythagoras at Rome is found in the setting up
of statues to that philosopher and Alcibiades *in cornibus comitii* at Rome by
order of the senate in obedience to the
Delphic oracle in the time of the Samnite
wars, cf. Pliny, N.H. xxxiv 12, 2–6;
Plut. Numa 8; another is afforded by
the story of the Gk books said to have
been found in 181 B.C. on the Janiculum
in a box labelled as containing writings

quoniam non id agitur hoc tempore. nam cum carminibus soliti
illi esse dicantur et praecepta quaedam occultius tradere et
5 mentes suas a cogitationum intentione cantu fidibusque ad tranquillitatem traducere, grauissimus auctor in Originibus dixit
Cato morem apud maiores hunc epularum fuisse ut deinceps,
qui accubarent, canerent ad tibiam clarorum uirorum laudes
atque uirtutes. ex quo perspicuum est et cantus tum fuisse di-
10 scriptos uocum sonis et carmina. 4. quamquam id quidem etiam

6. grauissumus R V P G B.   grauissimus K.   8. ad tibiam R V G S.
                                                      de
a tibia E.   tibia B.   9. descriptos uocum L 2.   rescripto ·ſ·uo cum V.
rescriptos R 1 6 7 17 P 1 2 4   G B 1–3 K 1 2   S E 1 2 L 3–6 W 1 2 M 2
D C Π J   O 1–3 8 ed. H.   resscriptos O 7.   perscriptos M 1.   discriptos
corr. Seyffertus.

of Numa, these writings being referred to
by Piso Censorius and Valerius Antias as
Pythagorean, cf. Livy xl 29; Pliny N.H.
xiii 13, 85–7; the criticism of Polybius,
referred to in the n. on 'Numam...Pytha-
goreum,' above, shows that the story was
current in the time of the younger Scipio
and this is also indicated by the statement
of Plutarch, Quaest. Rom. 10, 76, that
Castor referred Roman customs to Pythagoras τὰ 'Ρωμαϊκὰ τοῖς Πυθαγορικοῖς
συνοικειῶν. Cf. Dav. here and *Rh. Mus.*
LVII p. 236. Mommsen I p. 271 finds
indications of Pythagorean influence in
the Roman calendar.

carminibus: 'By applying mathematics to music the Pythagoreans became
the founders of the scientific theory of
sound... The practical importance of
music, however, was quite as great among
them; it was cultivated partly as a means
of moral education, partly in connexion
with the art of medicine.' Zeller, *Pre-
Soc. Phil.* I 348. And *ibid.* n. 2, 'The
Harmony of the Pythagoreans presupposes
a diligent study of music,' cf. p. 431. For
the χρυσᾶ ἔπη formerly ascribed with
little reason to Pythagoras and the ἱερὸς
λόγος, both mentioned here by Hei. in
his n., see Zeller, *l. c.* p. 311 n. 2.

occultius: cf. Porphyr. Vit. Pyth. 41
ἔλεγε δέ τινα καὶ μυστικῷ τρόπῳ συμ-
βολικῶς, ἃ δὴ ἐπιπλέον 'Αριστοτέλης ἀνέ-
γραψεν and Zeller, *l. c.* p. 351 and n. 2.
Also Diog. L. viii 15 ἔλεγόν τε καὶ οἱ
ἄλλοι Πυθαγόρειοι μὴ εἶναι πρὸς πάντας
πάντα ῥητά, ὥς φησιν 'Αριστόξενος ἐν δεκάτῃ
παιδευτικῶν νόμων. The Pythagorean
silence became proverbial. R. and P.[8]
§ 55 a distinguish between the disciplinary
test of silence imposed on learners in
their first five years and the mysterious
silence observed by all throughout their

life with regard to certain observances
and doctrines. For the question of
esoteric and exoteric doctrines see Zeller,
l. c. pp. 342, 356.

mentes suas...traducere: so Porph.
Vit. Pyth. 32 says that Pythagoras began
the day by calming his mind with the
strains of the lyre and singing paeans.
See also Quintil. ix 4, 12.

in Originibus: cf. i 2, 3 n. Brutus
19, 75; Hor. Odes iv 15, 29 foll.; Val.
Max. ii 1, 10; Varro de uita pop. Rom.
in Nonius, s.u. *assa* p. 76 M. See also
Sellar, *Rom. Poets of the Republic*,
pp. 37–8. [Ribbeck, *Gesch. der Röm.
Dicht.* I 8.] The reasoning, as Hei.
observes, is remarkable: the Pythagoreans
had maxims in metrical form and calmed
their minds by singing to the lyre; the
early Romans sang in turn at banquets
the deeds of heroes to the flute; therefore
the early Romans were acquainted with
the Pythagorean doctrine.

discriptos: Turnebus, *Advers.* vii c. 17,
defends *rescriptos* of the MSS, comparing
ἀναγράφειν, and Dav. takes the same
view. Küh. says 'cantus uocum sonis
rescribere est cantus scribendo (h.e. notis
signisue) reuocare uel redigere ad aptos
(acutos et graues) uocum sonos, quod
nos uocamus *komponiren*, *tonsetzen*.'
But illustrations of this use are wanting.
J. Fr. Gronovius, on Livy vii 2, and
other early scholars conjectured *descriptos*,
which Wes. *Em.* III 1 supports and Bai.
adopts. But Sff. points out that the
meaning is not *cantus ex uocum sonis
signatos* or *notatos* but *c. ex u. s. dispositos.*
discripto is the better reading in Liv. vii
2, 7 and no substitution is more common
in MSS than that of *describere* for *di-
scribere*; see variants in i 17, 38 and
numerous exx. collected by Bücheler in

duodecim tabulae declarant, condi iam tum solitum esse carmen; quod ne liceret fieri ad alterius iniuriam lege sanxerunt. nec uero illud non eruditorum temporum argumentum est, quod et deorum puluinaribus et epulis magistratuum fides praecinunt, 15 quod proprium eius fuit, de qua loquor, disciplinae. mihi quidem etiam Appii Caeci carmen, quod ualde Panaetius laudat epistula quadam, quae est ad Q. Tuberonem, Pythagoreum uidetur.

§ 4, 11. duodecim R V P G   B 1–3   K   E 1 2   W 1   O 1 3.   XII   S D   O 7 8 ed. H.   12. longe sanxerunt K.   14. praecinunt G.   prȩcinu nt V *litt. eras.*

p̄cinunt R.   p̄ciunt E.   16. appii R V G B K S.   apii E. ‖ epistola V P G. aepistola R.   ‖ in *non habent* R V P G   B 1–3   K   S   E 2   W 1 2   II J   O 2 3 7.

in epistola O 1.   in epl'a C   O 8.   ep̄a E 1.   17. ad Q. W 1 2   M 1 2 d. Q.

D C   O 1 2 7.   Q *superscr.* B 3   II.   Q *om.* S   E 2   O 3.   atquȩ V. ad Q.

atq; E 1.   atq; B 1 2   K *marg.*   atque R G.   ‖ pythagoreum W 1   O 1.

pythagareorum P *al. atr. superscr.*   pythagoreorum R V P 4 G S J.   phitagoreo2̣4 E 1.   pytagoreo2̣4 E 2 *similiter desinentia habent* K 1 2   B 2 3   W 2   M 1 2

D C II   O 3 7.   pictagoreū O 8.   pythagore eorum B 1 *at* e *ante* o *ex parte eras.*

Rh. Mus. xiii pp. 598 foll. 'Melodies composed in accordance with the notes of the voice and poetry existed even in that day.'

sonis : Pantagathus proposed *notis* but Or., against F.A.W., who quoted this corr. with approval, points out that *sonis* denotes the higher and lower *notae*, with their appropriate signs, comparing *comporre, cantare un suono* of early Italian writers. For the abl. see Madv. *Gram.* § 254 obs. 5.

§ 4. duodecim tabulae : cf. de R.P. iv 10, 12 preserved in Augustin. Ciu. Dei ii 9 ' *Cicero...in libris quos de re publica scripsit, ubi Scipio disputans ait*..."nostrae...contra XII tabulae, cum perpaucas res capite sanxissent, in his hanc quoque sanciendam putauerunt, si quis occentauisset siue carmen condidisset, quod infamiam faceret flagitiumue alteri."' Hor. Sat. ii 1, 80 foll. and probably Ep. ii 1, 152. Küh. and some others claim to give the exact words of the fragment, but these can only be inferred by conjecture from the reff. found in Latin writers. Cf. for this and for the remaining authorities Dirksen, *Zwölf-Tafel Fragmente*, on table VIII fr. 1.

iam tum : there is an interval of more than 220 years between the death of Numa and the decemviral legislation, though ballad poetry, which is no doubt the kind referred to in the law, may well have existed in the time of the early kings.

nec uero..., 'and indeed we are not without a proof of the culture of those times in the fact that...'

deorum puluinaribus : i.e. at the feasts of the gods on the occasion of a *lectisternium*, for which see Livy v 13, 6; Fowler, *Roman Festivals* 180 f. *puluinaribus* and *epulis* are ablatives of time like *comitiis, ludis, gladiatoribus*. See Madv. *Gr.* § 276 obs. 2.

[**fides** Gk. σφίδη 'gut' : for the employment of the lyre in ritual see Mommsen's note *R.H.* i 293 (E.T.).]

proprium : Zeller, *Pre-Soc. Phil.* i 348 n. 2.

Appii Caeci carmen : a poem which evidently consisted of oracular maxims of practical wisdom, a specimen of which is preserved in the *de re publica oratio* i, 1 formerly attributed to Sallust 'fabrum esse suae quemque fortunae'; another is given by Priscian viii 4, 18 (Krehl), another by Festus in *stuprum* p. 317 Ml. Goettling on Hesiod p. xxxi ed. 2 compares the style to that of Hesiod and finds Pythagoras indebted to the latter poet, cf. Mommsen, *R.H.* II 100. [Ribbeck, *Gesch. der Röm. Dicht.* i 14.]

Appius Claudius, censor 312 B.C., lived at a time when Pythagoras was known at Rome; he was a man of original genius and open mind and might have taken an interest in Pythagorean views; but the three maxims preserved from him seem to be just what one might expect a Roman of his day to develope.

multa etiam sunt in nostris institutis ducta ab illis; quae praetereo
ne ea quae peperisse ipsi putamur aliunde didicisse uideamur.
20 **5.** sed ut ad propositum redeat oratio, quam breui tempore quot et
quanti poëtae, qui autem oratores exstiterunt! facile ut appareat
nostros omnia consequi potuisse, simul ut uelle coepissent.

III. Sed de ceteris studiis alio loco et dicemus, si usus
fuerit, et saepe diximus. sapientiae studium uetus id quidem
in nostris, sed tamen ante Laelii aetatem et Scipionis non re-
perio quos appellare possim nominatim. quibus adulescentibus
5 Stoicum Diogenen et Academicum Carneadem uideo ad sena-

18. multa R 10 16 E 2.　　　multaę R 1.　　　multae G.　　　multę E 1.
multe R 2.　　　19. peperisse R 10 S E 2 W 1 O 2.　　　peᵣperisse E 1.
perperisse·P *al. atr. corr.* pperisse V G K. perperisse R B 2. ppeperisse B 1. ‖
putamur R V P G B 1 2 S E 1 W 1 O 2 3.　　　putemur R 6 P 4 B 3
K 2 E 2 W 2 M 2 D Ⅱ J O 18. ‖ aliunde didicisse uideamur *post* putamur
uel putemur *habent* R 2 6 10 16 P 2 S W 1 M 1 O 1–3 V *manu antiqua
superscr.*

§ **5,** 20.　ᵈᵖ positum G *alt. man. superscr.*　　　21. extiterunt R V G B K S E. ‖
appareat R V G B K S E D.　　22. nostros omnia consequi potuisse R 2 6 10 16 P 2
S W 1 O 3 7.　　*post* nostros *habent* aliunde didicisse uideamur *uel* uideantur
omnia R 1 17 P 1 4 G B 1–3 K 2 E 2 3 W 2 Ⅱ J O 8.　licet *ante* aliunde
habent Ⅱ E 2.　　*pro* uideantur *habent* uideanturq; R 7 M 1.　　ut appareant
nostros aliud didicisse uideantur M 2.　　nostros et aliunde didicisse et omnia O 1.

nostros a‖liun‖de dᴚd‖iᴚis‖se uᴚdᴚa‖m‖ur omnia V. ‖ ᵗ&ᵉ simul ut uelle V.
III. 3. laelii R G.　　　lelii V S E.　　　5. diogenen R V P G B 2 K.
diogenē R 10 16 B 3 K 2 S E W 1 2 M 2 D O 2 7.　　　diogenem R 2 B
E 2 C O 3.　　dyogenem M 1.　　dyogenē Ⅱ. ‖　achademicum G. ‖
carneadem R V P G K S.　　carneadē B 2 E W 1 2 O 7.

Panaetius : i 18, 42 n.
epistula...ad Q. Tuberonem: cf. Fin. iv
9, 23 'Panaetius, cum ad Q. Tuberonem
de dolore patiendo scriberet'; Ac. ii
44, 135.
Q. Tubero, son of the sister of Africanus
the younger, was a Stoic in theory and
practice [see the story of his *peruersa
sapientia* in p. Mur. 36, 75].
Pythagoreum: Küh. endeavours to
defend *Pythagoreorum* of most MSS,
imagining the genitive to denote 'derived
from Pythagoreans.'
peperisse: most editors read *repperisse*
but Or. Mo. Hei. and Sff. seem justified
in reading *peperisse* which is nearer the
MSS and justified by numerous examples.
Dav. compares Or. 32, 114; Wopkens,
ed. Hand, p. 121 Fin. iii 1, 3; Or. ii
34, 146; N.D. ii 29, 74; Leg. ii 14, 36;
Fam. iv 13, 7; Sff. adds Off. ii 2, 8.
repperisse ipsi would be a more complete
contrast to *aliunde didicisse* but *peperisse
ipsi* gives a very good contrast too.
§ **5. autem**: continues, with intensive
force; cf. v 20, 57 'qua pulchritudine
urbem, quibus autem opibus praeditam

seruitute oppressam tenuit ciuitatem!'
Hand, *Tursell.* 1 p. 568.
simul ut: much rarer than *simul ac*
but supported by the MSS here and in
Ac. ii 16, 51 ; 2 in Verr. i 26, 67 ; Or.
ii 5, 21 ; Phil. iii 1, 2 ; Fin. ii 11, 33
where see Madvig's n. Reid in a good
note on Ac. ii 16, 51 adds Planc. 6, 14
where Madv. suspected the reading.
III. **uetus id quidem...sed tamen**...
i 3, 6 n.
adulescentibus: Cic. uses the same
expression with ref. to Laelius in Fin. ii
8, 24, where Madv. shews that the word
is not to be taken strictly, as Africanus
Minor was born in 185 or 184 B.C. and
Laelius was older still.
Stoicum Diogenen: Diogenes Babylonius, born at Seleucia in Babylonia,
pupil of Chrysippus and teacher of
Antipater of Tarsus. For the form
Diogenen see Neue, *Formenl.* I³ 474
(where there is a misprint in the citation
of this passage).
Carneades, born at Cyrene in 215 B.C.,
founder of the New Academy. The
third member of this famous legation, the

tum ab Atheniensibus missos esse legatos, qui cum rei publicae
nullam umquam partem attigissent essetque eorum alter Cyren-
aeus, alter Babylonius, numquam profecto scholis essent excitati
neque ad illud· munus electi, nisi in quibusdam principibus tem-
10 poribus illis fuissent studia doctrinae. qui cum cetera litteris
mandarent, alii ius ciuile, alii orationes suas, alii monumenta
maiorum, hanc amplissimam omnium artium, bene uiuendi disciplinam, uita magis quam litteris persecuti sunt. **6.** itaque illius
uerae elegantisque philosophiae, quae ducta a Socrate in Peri-
15 pateticis adhuc permansit et idem alio modo dicentibus Stoicis,

6. misos K.   7. attigissent R V P G B 1 2 K S E J.   ‖ cyreneus R.
cyreneus G B K.   cireneus R 2.   8. babylonius R V G.   babyllonius K.
                                                                    legatōis
babilonius B E.   ‖   scolis R V G B K S E.   9. munus R G K.   munus V
                          u
al. atr. superscr.   minus B *eod. atr.*   11. monumenta B 2 K S.
                                      v
moni menta B E u *in* i *ras. mut.*   monomenta R *eod. atr.*   mo nōm ta V.
monomenta G.   12. amplissimam R V P G B K.
    § **6,** 14. Socratae G.

Peripatetic Critolaus, is left unmentioned
here and in Plutarch, Cato M. **22,** 1.
The date, 155 B.C., marks an epoch in
the attitude of the Roman nobility towards
Greek philosophy. An earlier trace of the
new influence is indicated by the S.C.
of 161 B.C., which banished Gk philosophy and teachers of rhetoric from Rome.
The residence of the thousand Achaeans
in Italy, from 168 B.C. onwards, no
doubt helped to prepare the way for the
effect produced by the embassy. For the
circumstances that gave occasion for the
sending of the legation see Momms.
H.R. iv 199. The Athenians had plun-
dered Oropus and, when condemned by
the Sicyonians, whom the Romans had
appointed arbitrators, to pay a fine of
500 talents, appealed to Rome. The
senate reduced the fine to 100 talents.
    uideo : of a fact learned from history,
cf. 37, 79 and 22, 50 with Kühner's n.
    numquam profecto...nisi...: the argu-
ment is inconclusive. The Athenians had
at that time no statesmen properly so
called. The sending of philosophers and
rhetoricians as envoys even in the earlier
period is illustrated by T.S.
    scholis...excitati=*e scholis, in quibus
uitam umbratilem agebant, protracti.*
Küh.
    temporibus illis : abl. of time. Küh.
thinks that the words have the meaning
of *ut temporibus illis,* comparing Or. ii
23, 98. But this meaning is not required
here, while the ref. to the date is natural.

    ius ciuile : e.g. Sex. Aelius Paetus
Catus, for whom see i 9, 18 n. ; also
Appius Claudius Caecus, of § 4 (cf.
Teuffel 1 § 90) and others in Teuffel 1
§ 125.
    orationes suas : e.g. Cato the Censor,
who was the first Roman who wrote
out and published his speeches. Cf. i, 2
3 n.
    monumenta maiorum : especially Cato's
Origines.
    bene uiuendi disciplinam..., 'they set
forth in their lives rather than in
their writings a correct system of moral
philosophy.'
    § **6. elegantis,** 'logically precise,'
'thorough.' A contrast to that of the
Epicureans, cf. i 22, 55 n. on 'tam eleganter.'
    idem alio modo dicentibus Stoicis :
cf. Leg. i 13, 38 'eis omnibus, siue in
Academia uetere cum Speusippo, Xenocrate, Polemone manserunt, siue Aris-
totelem et Theophrastum, cum illis congruentes re, genere docendi paulum
differentes, secuti sunt, siue, ut Zenoni
uisum est, *rebus non commutatis in-
mutauerunt uocabula...*' See also v 12,
34 n. on 'ignobilis uerborum opifex.'
The assertion involved in the text is
strictly true with reference to the department of logic alone. For this see Zeller,
Stoics, etc., p. 118. For Stoic obligations
and differences in physics and ethics see
ibid. pp. 374 foll.

cum Academici eorum controuersias disceptarent, nulla fere sunt
aut pauca admodum Latina monumenta siue propter magnitudinem rerum occupationemque hominum, siue etiam quod
imperitis ea probari posse non arbitrabantur, cum interim illis
20 silentibus C. Amafinius exstitit dicens, cuius libris editis commota
multitudo contulit se ad eam potissimum disciplinam, siue quod
erat cognitu perfacilis, siue quod inuitabantur inlecebris blandis
uoluptatis, siue etiam, quia nihil erat prolatum melius, illud,
quod erat, tenebant. 7. post Amafinium autem multi eiusdem
25 aemuli rationis multa cum scripsissent, Italiam totam occu-

16. academici R G K. academici V. 17. aut pauca R 6 7 K 2 W 1.
āt pauca O 8. ac pauca R 1 17 V P 4 G B 13 K S E 1 2 W 2 M 1 2
D C Π J O 1-3. apauca P *eod. atr. ut uid.* ex pauca B 2. ‖ monumenta G K.
monūta R V. monimenta B S E. 18. hominum W 1 O 2. omnium
R V G B 1 3 K 1 2 S E 1-3 L 2 3 5 W 2 M 1 2 D C Π O 1 3 ed. H.
oūm L 4 6 O 7. oīm B 2 O 8. 19. imperitis R V G K. 20. c. amafinius
B 1 2 S E 1 2 M 1 D Π O 8. Π *at* a *post* m *ex* i *al. atr. mut.*
c̄ amifinius R *eod. atr.* c. amifinius V G K. amifinius W 2. amifinius J.
.c. amafanius M 2. c. anafinius W 1. amaffinius O 7. c. amaphanius O 3.
c. amacinius O 1. ‖ extitit R V G B K S E. ‖ dicens R V G. docens S *at* o
ex i *al. atr. mut.* 21. ad eam V G B 1 2 E 2 Π O 2. S *marg.* eandem.
ad eandem P B 3 K W 1 2 M 2 D C J O 1 3. adeadem R *al. atr. superscr.*
adeadem M 1 O 7. ad eandāe E. ‖ potissimum R V G B K.
22. inuitabantur R 17 W 1. inuitabatur R 1 6 7 V P G B 1-3 K 1 S
E 1-3 L 2-6 M 2 D C Π O 1 3 7 8 ed. H. inuitebatur M 1. imitabatur
W 2 O 2. mutabatur K 2. nuitabatur J. ‖ inlecebris R V P G K.
illecebris S E. ‖ blandis R V P G B 1-3 K 1 2 S E 1 L 3-6 W 2 M 2
C Π O 2 3 8. blandę W 1. blande E 2 L 2 M 1 O 1 7 ed. H.
et blandis D. blandiciis J. 23. erat prolatum R V P G B K *plerique.*
erat probatū B 2.
§ 7, 24. amafinium R V P G B K S E 1 2 M 2 D C Π O 8. amifinium
W 2 J O 1. amaffinium O 7. anafinium W 1. amaphanium O 3.

cum Academici ... disceptarent: the reference is to the philosophers of the new Academy, who, being committed to no positive doctrines, could act impartially as arbitrators, cf. v 41, 120 'quorum (sc. Peripateticorum et Stoicorum) contro-uersiam solebat *tamquam honorarius arbiter* iudicare Carneades. nam....'

C. Amafinius: what is known about this writer, who first introduced the Epicurean philosophy to Latin readers, is found here and in Ac. i 2, 5—6 and Fam. xv 19. See Reid, *Introd. to Ac.* p. 21.

dicens, 'with plenty to say'; contrasted with *illis silentibus.*

ad eam...disciplinam sc. *Epicuream,* that being the system which Amafinius adopted. *eam,* which will be seen from the vv. ll. above to have more MS support than it was previously known to have, is

rightly regarded by Sff. as demanded by *potissimum.*

cognitu perfacilis: Fin. i 8, 27.

inuitabantur ... tenebant: collective substantives in the singular, when they refer to persons, seldom take a plural verb in Cicero or Caesar, frequently in Livy. *contulit,* the verb in *direct* connexion with the collective noun, is in the singular, and this is always so in Cicero. Küh. *Gr. d. Lat. Spr.* ii p. 17.

blandis: *blandae* would be more strictly correct but such use of hypallage is not limited to poetry. Wes. illustrates from Cic. N.D. ii 39, 98 'fontium gelidas perennitates...speluncarum concauas ampli-tudines'; iii 27, 69 'spe dubiae salutis.'

§ 7. **multi:** Rabirius (Ac. i 2, 5) and Catius the Insubrian (Fam. xv 16, 1; 19, 1) seem the only other Latin writers known of.

pauerunt, quodque maximum argumentum est non dici illa subtiliter, quod et tam facile ediscantur et ab indoctis proben tur, id illi firmamentum esse disciplinae putant.

IV. Sed defendat quod quisque sentit; sunt enim iudicia libera; nos institutum tenebimus nullisque unius disciplinae legibus adstricti, quibus in philosophia necessario pareamus, quid sit in quaque re maxime probabile, semper requiremus. 5 quod cum saepe alias tum nuper in Tusculano studiose egimus. itaque expositis tridui disputationibus quartus dies hoc libro concluditur. ut enim in inferiorem ambulationem descendimus, quod feceramus idem superioribus diebus, acta res est sic:

8. Dicat, si quis uolt, qua de re disputari uelit.

26. maxumum R V P G.   maximum B K.   27. sumtiliter G. ‖ quod & tam W 1.   quod etiam R 1 6 7 17   V P G   B 1-3   K 1   E   L 2 3 5 W 2   M 2   D C J   O 1 3 7 8 ed. H.   quod et S *marg.* iam.   quod ēt L 4 6. q̣ etiam O 2.   q∂'x facile etiam K 2.   quod et E 2   M 1   Π.

IV. 1. quod quisque E 2   W 1 2   D Π   O 1-3 7 8.   quoquisq; V B E. quoquisque R G K   S *marg.* quid́ quod.   quidem quod quisque M 2. q̣,q̣ quisque M 1.   2. nullisque R 1 6 7 10 16 17   V   P 1 4   G   B 1-3   K 1   S E 1-3   L 2-6   W 1   M 1 2   D C Π J   O 1-3 7 8 ed. H.   nll'is W 2. nłłq3 K 2.   3. adstricti R V G K.   astricti B S.   4. maxime R V G K.   5. saepe alias R V P G B K S E *plerique.*   alias sepe D C. 6. disciplationibus G *in* disputationibus *alt. man. mut.*   7. concluditur R V P G S J.

§ 8. *Personarum indicia non habent* R G   B 1 2   E   O 7 : S *non habebat* : M *et* A *in marg.* habet V *sed semel tantum,* M *ante* dicat *et* A *ante* non mihi : M *ante* dicat *et* aegritudine *et* D *ante* non mihi *habet* P *atr. nigro scripta* : M *et* A habent B 3   W 1 O 3 : M *et* D habent W 2 D C : T *et* D *habet* Π : B *et* T *habet* O 8 : Dis. *uel* Di *et* M habet O 1 : J *habet* Magister *ante* egritudine *et* Discipulus *ante* minime, *postea* M *et* D.

9. uolt R V G B K.   uolt P *al. atr. superscr.*

aemuli : 'partisans'; cf. p. Mur. 29, 61 'Zeno cuius inuentorum aemuli Stoici nominantur'; Livy i 18, 2 ; Tac. Hist. iii 81 init.

non...subtiliter, 'of the superficial character of those utterances,' i 17, 41 n.

IV. quod quisque : for the order of words cf. i 4, 7 n. on 'de quo quis.'

nos...tenebimus : on the nature of Cicero's scepticism see Zeller III² 1, p. 581.

nullisque : it seems best, with the most recent editors, to retain the ms reading, with which Ml. compares v, 29, 82 'quoniam te nulla uincula impediunt ullius certae disciplinae' : 'nam unus per se est *unus aliquis* aut *ullus certus,* recteque et usitate dicitur *non unus (nec, nullis,* etc.) ita, ut contrarium sit *sed plures* aut *uniuersi,*' Ml. Bentley supported his conj. *nulliusque* by ref. to Brutus 59, 216 'nulla re una magis

oratorem commendari' to which Sff. adds Rep. ii 39, 65 'nullumque ex eis (ciuitatum generibus) unum esse optimum'; T.D. v 36, 105 'nemo de nobis unus excellat'; Livy ii 6, 3 'eos inter se, quia nemo unus satis dignus regno uisus sit, partes regni rapuisse.'

requiremus : Küh. explains as = '*rursus,* non semel, sed *iterum et saepius* uel *etiam atque etiam* quaerere.' Perhaps we have rather an instance of the intensive use of *re-.* That emendation is not required seems evident from N.D. ii 38, 96 ' sed adsiduitate cotidiana et consuetudine oculorum adsuescunt animi neque admirantur neque requirunt rationes earum rerum, quas semper uident.'

quartus dies : i.e. *quarti diei disputationes.*

in inferiorem ambulationem : i.e. *in Academiam,* cf. ii 3, 9. For *ambulationem* cf. Or. i 7, 28.

10 Non mihi uidetur omni animi perturbatione posse
sapiens uacare.

Aegritudine quidem hesterna disputatione uidebatur, nisi
forte temporis causa nobis adsentiebare.

Minime uero; nam mihi egregie probata est oratio tua.

1 Non igitur existimas cadere in sapientem aegritudinem?

Prorsus non arbitror.

Atqui, si ista perturbare animum sapientis non potest, nulla
poterit. quid enim? metusne conturbet? at earum rerum est
absentium metus, quarum praesentium est aegritudo. sublata
20 igitur aegritudine sublatus est metus. restant duae perturbationes, laetitia gestiens et libido; quae si non cadent in sapientem, semper mens erit tranquilla sapientis.

9. Sic prorsus intellego.

Vtrum igitur mauis? statimne nos uela facere an quasi e
25 portu egredientis paululum remigare?

Quidnam est istuc? non enim intellego.

10. omni animi E 2 W 1 M 1 2 Π O 1–3 8.   omni perturbatione animi
D C.   omī animi B.   omī aī B 3 O 7.   oī aī W 2.   omni animi V
litt. inter i *et a* eras.   omnią animi R K.   omnia animi G.   oīa aī B 2.
13. nobis R 6 L 2 W 1 O 8 L 5 *at* bis *in ras.*   nobis non M 1.   noui
R 1 17 P 4 G B 1–3 K 1 2 E 1 3 L 3 6 W 2 M 2 Π J O 1 2 S *marg.*
nobis.   nōui V *atr. uiridi linea ducta* E 2.   non ui L 4.   nō R 7 O 7.
non D C.   nouis Gr.   noui nobis non ed. H. ‖ assentiebare R 2 10 16 B 3
K 1 S W 1 2 D C Π O 1 3 8.   asentiebare B 1 *at spatio inter* i *et* e *relicto*
et e *ex* i (*fuerat* a) *mut.*   asentibare E 1.   asentiabare R 1 *eod. atr.*
aseṇti aḅere V *i.e.* abaere *in* ebare *mut. al. atr.*   assentêtiabare P.   asentiabare
B 2.   aḅsenti⊃abare G.   absentiabare O 7.   14. minime R V P G B K. ‖
egregie B.   aegregie G.   aegregię R.   aegregiae V K.   15. existumas
R V B G K.   18. et earum R 10 16 P G K 1 2 E 1 3 L 3–6 M 2 C J O 2.
& earum R V B 1–3 W 1 2 D O 1 3 7 8.   et earum S *marg.* etenim.
sed earum E 2 L 2 Π.   non quia earum M 1.   at eąrum *corr. edd.*
20. aegritudine sublatus R 6 7 V P 4 G B 1 S E 1 2 D C Π O 2 7 8 ed. H.
aegritudine et sublatus R 1 17 P B 3 K 1 2 W 1 2 M 1 2 J O 1 3.
aegritudine sublata B 2.   21. libido R V P G B K.
§ 9, 23. intellego (*bis*) R V G B K.   intelligo (*bis*) S E.   25. egredientis R 1 2
G B 1 2 K 1 O 7.   egredientes R 10 16.   aegriḍientis V. ‖ paululum
R V P G S E.

§ 8. **aegritudine**: for this and the
other three irrational emotions (πάθη) see
iii 10, 23–4 and Introd. p. xxxi.

temporis causa: 'under the pressure
of the moment,' 'to suit the occasion.'
'temporibus inseruiens, motus auctoritate
mea, ne dubiis tuis taedium mihi ex-
hiberes,' Neide. So Sff. on Lael. 8, 26
explains as = *tempori cedens*, comparing
Fam. iv 9 *init.* 'tempori cedere, id est
necessitati parere'; Ac. ii 35, 113. Cf.

also Mur. 30, 62 'at temporis causa';
p. Flacc. 15, 36: 16, 37.

ista: sc. *perturbatio.*

quid enim? 'for, I would ask;' i 25,
60 n.

absentium: cf. iii 11, 25 'metus opinio
magni mali inpendentis.'

gestiens: iii 10, 23 n.

§ 9. **utrum**: the neuter pronoun, the
alternative clauses marked by *-ne* and *an*
following in a separate sentence as in

V. Quia Chrysippus et Stoici cum de animi perturbationibus disputant magnam partem in his partiendis et definiendis occupati sunt, illa eorum perexigua oratio est qua medeantur animis nec eos turbulentos esse patiantur, Peripatetici autem ad pla-
5 candos animos multa adferunt, spinas partiendi et definiendi praetermittunt. quaerebam igitur, utrum panderem uela orationis statim an eam ante paululum dialecticorum remis propellerem.

Isto modo uero; erit enim hoc totum quod quaero ex utroque perfectius.

10   **10.** Est id quidem rectius; sed post requires, si quid fuerit obscurius.

Faciam equidem; tu tamen, ut soles, dices ista ipsa obscura planius quam dicuntur a Graecis.

Enitar equidem, sed intento opus est animo, ne omnia dila-
15 bantur, si unum aliquid effugerit. quoniam, quae Graeci πάθη

Fin. ii 19, 60; Diu. ii 58, 120; 63, 129; Ac. ii. 22, 71 and Reid's n. there. Another use, common in Plautus (e.g. Capt. 268, Trin. 306), in which *-ne* is appended to the first emphatic word after *utrum* in the question, is also found in Cicero, e.g. iv 27, 59; p. Quint. 30, 92.

uela facere = *uela pandere*, cf. Verr. ii 5, 34; 88 'uela fieri imperauit.'

remigare: cf. *dialecticorum remis* below. The metaphor contrasts the smooth and free movement of continuous discourse with the jerky and slower process of dialectic argument.

V. quia: elliptic = *haec dixi quia*, cf. iii 7, 14 n. on 'quoniam.'

Chrysippus et Stoici = *et ceteri Stoici*, the views of Chrysippus being far the most influential among the Stoics of Cicero's day. This mode of expression, which is common in Gk and Lat., is illustrated by Dav., who compares Diu. i 53, 121 Dareus et Persae ab Alexandro et Macedonibus; Homer, Il. xix 63

"Εκτορι μὲν καὶ Τρωσὶ τὸ κέρδιον, etc., Petron. 2 Pindarus nouemque lyrici.

spinas: cf. *spinosum* applied to the Stoic style in Fin. iii 1, 3 quoted in n. on i 8, 16; also Fin. iv 3, 6; *dumeta* Ac. ii 35, 112; N.D. i 24, 68.

dialecticorum remis: 'h.e. an orationem exordirer more dialecticorum a subtiliore disputatione, quae lentius progreditur' Küh. Cf. iii 6, 13 'primo... Stoicorum more agamus.'

isto modo uero: 'As you suggest, by all means.' *isto* does not express the *latter* alternative but the method suggested by the person addressed, the mention of alternatives being taken to imply a recommendation of their acceptance. For the affirmative use of *uero*, not uncommon in replies, cf. ii 11, 26.

ex utroque, 'by an application of both methods.'

§ 10. animo sc. *tuo*, cf. ii 5, 15.

ne...dilabantur, 'lest the whole argument be lost if a single stage is missed.' Editors compare Fin. iii 22, 74 where

uocant, nobis perturbationes appellari magis placet quam morbos, in his explicandis ueterem illam equidem Pythagorae primum, dein Platonis discriptionem sequar, qui animum in duas partes diuidunt, alteram rationis participem faciunt, alteram expertem; 20 in participe rationis ponunt tranquillitatem, id est placidam quietamque constantiam, in illa altera motus turbidos cum irae, tum cupiditatis, contrarios inimicosque rationi. 11. sit igitur hic fons; utamur tamen in his perturbationibus discribendis Stoicorum definitionibus et partitionibus, qui mihi uidentur in hac quaes-25 tione uersari acutissime.

18. dein R V G B 2 K E 2 O 7.   deiñ P W 2 J.   deinde B 3
                                                                              inc
S W 1 M 1 2 Π O 1 3.   dehinc C O 8.   dehoc in platonis E 1.

de hoc in B 1 *al. atr. superscr.* ‖ discriptionem R V P G K.   discriptione E.
descriptionem B 1–3 S E 2 W 1 2 M 1 2 Π J O 1 3 7. ‖ partes R V P G B K S.
19. participem faciunt R 1 10 16 V G B 1–3 S E L 2–6 W 1 2 C J O 1–3 7.

participem facint K *eod. atr.*   20. ponunt B 3 K 2 S E 2 W 1 2 M 1 2
                                                                    v
C Π J O 1 3 7 8.   ponunt B u *ex a mut.*   ponant V.   ponant E 1.
ponant R G B 2 K.   ‖   id ÷ K.   idē B 1 *pro* id est.   .i. W 2.
21. turbidos cum P 2 L 4 O 1 3.   turbidos cum E 2 *at* c *al. atr.*   turbidos tum
R 17 V P 14 G B 1–3 K 1 2   S   E L 2 3 5 6 W 1 2   M 1 2   C Π J
                                                         motus
O 7 8 ed. H. *om.* D.   22. cupiditatis contra V *atr. uiridi.* ‖   rationi G K.
rationi R.   rationis B.
§ 11, 24. partitionibus K 1.   parti(*corrupt*)tionibus R 1.   particionibus V G.
partionibus R 2 10 16.   25. acutissime R V G B K.

Cato thus refers to the Stoic system: 'admirabilis compositio disciplinae incredibilisque rerum traxit ordo....quid non sic aliud ex alio nectitur, ut si ullam litteram moueris, *labent* omnia? nec tamen quicquam est, quod moueri possit.'

morbos: cf. iii 4, 7 n. on 'ego poteram morbos.'

Pythagorae primum: this division of the soul seems to have been first attributed to Pythagoras by writers such as Posidonius, cf. Galen, de Plac. Hipp. et Plat. iv p. 425; v p. 478; Plutarch, Plac. Phil. iv 4. A more correct statement of the Pythagorean view is no doubt that of Diog. L. viii 30 τὴν ἀνθρώπου ψυχὴν διῃρῆσθαι τριχῇ, εἴς τε νοῦν καὶ φρένας καὶ θυμόν. νοῦν μὲν οὖν καὶ θυμὸν εἶναι καὶ ἐν τοῖς ἄλλοις ζῴοις, φρένας δὲ μόνον ἐν ἀνθρώπῳ.

For the Platonic division of the soul into two parts, τὸ λογιστικόν and τὸ ἄλογον, the latter being subdivided into τὸ θυμοειδές and τὸ ἐπιθυμητικόν, see n. on i 10, 20 'Plato triplicem.' The Stoics on the other hand derived all faculties of the soul from the ἡγεμονικόν. Plut. Plac. Phil. iv 21; i 33, 80 n. on 'is, contra quem.'

It is observed by editors that Cicero does not make any use of this division in the details that follow, §§ 11—33. For a suggested explanation of the significance of this fact see Introd. pp. xliii ff.

in participe rationis...turbidos: this of course applies only to those (including Posidonius) who adopted the Platonic division of the soul. With the Stoics *tranquillitas* was a calm state of the ἡγεμονικόν due to the obedience of the passions and desires to reason; *perturbatio* was a disordered state of the same ἡγεμονικόν due to a false judgment (κρίσις). Cf. Off. i 29, 102 'efficiendum autem est, ut adpetitus rationi oboediant ...sintque tranquilli atque omni animi perturbatione careant; ex quo elucebit omnis constantia, omnisque moderatio' (quoted by Hei.).

cum: Küh. would approve of this reading if it had more MS support but thinks *tum...tum...* may be defended in the usual sense of *modo...modo...*, but 'both...and' is the natural meaning here and most editors read *cum...tum*, nothing being more frequent in MSS than the confusion of these two words.

§ 11. **fons:** the *pars rationis expers* is then the source of the *perturbationes*.

VI. Est igitur Zenonis haec definitio, ut perturbatio sit, quod πάθος ille dicit, auersa a recta ratione contra naturam animi commotio. quidam breuius perturbationem esse adpetitum uehementiorem, sed uehementiorem eum uolunt esse qui longius 5 discesserit a naturae constantia. partes autem perturbationum uolunt ex duobus opinatis bonis nasci et ex duobus opinatis malis; ita esse quattuor, ex bonis libidinem et laetitiam, ut sit laetitia praesentium bonorum, libido futurorum, ex malis metum et aegritudinem nasci censent, metum futuris, aegri-10 tudinem praesentibus; quae enim uenientia metuuntur, eadem adficiunt aegritudine instantia. 12. laetitia autem et libido in bonorum opinione uersantur, cum libido ad id quod uidetur bonum inlecta et inflammata rapiatur, laetitia ut adepta iam aliquid concupitum ecferatur et gestiat. natura enim omnes ea quae

VI. 2. παθos G.   πατοϲ R K. ‖ auersa a recta R G B 1–3 K 1 W 2 O 2.
                                          a
auersa recta V.   auersa a ratione O 1 recta om.   auersa a rōne recta W 1.
auersa recta O 7.   3. commotio R V G.   cōmotio K. ‖ adpetitum G.
appetitum K.   5. partes R V G B 1 2 K S E.   6. opinatis G prius i in ras.
8. libido R V G B K.   11. adficiunt R V G K E.
                e
O 2 3 8 7.   afficiunt M 2.   efficiunt W 1 2 M 1 Π J O 1. om. D.‖
aegritudine V G O 2.   aegritudineṁ K eod. atr.   egritudine B 1–3 E 1 2 M 2
O 3 8.   egritudinem P.   aegritudinē R 1.   egritudinē W 1.   egritudinē S J.
egritudinem W 2 M 1 C Π O 1 7. om. D.
§ 12, 11. libido (bis) R V P G B K.   13. illecta R 6 B 3 E 3 L 6 M 1 2
O 2 3.   iniecta R 1 7 17 V P 1 2 4 G B 1 2 K 1 2 S E 1 2 L 2–5 C Π
O 1 8 ed. H.   iniecta W 1 marg. illecta.   ī recta O 7. om. W 2 D J.
14. ecferatur R V G K.   hec fe/ Ratur E 1.   et feratur B 2.   efferatur P
B 1 3 S W 1 2 J O 3 7 8. ‖ natura K 2 S W 1 M 2 O 1–3 8 ed. H.
  ∨   nā M 1.   a   a
nata W 2.   nat
nature B E.   nature K E 2 C O 7.   natê B 2.   nature R 17.   naturae R G.
                                          nature V.
natate B 2.

VI. haec definitio, ut..., 'Zeno's definition then makes emotion to be...'
Zeno in Diog. L. vii 110 defines πάθος
(perturbatio) as ἄλογος καὶ παρὰ φύσιν
ψυχῆς κίνησις ἢ ὁρμὴ πλεονάζουσα (adpetitus uehementior). Cf. Stobaeus, Ecl. Eth.
ii 166; and other exx. in Dav. Hence
Salmasius conjectured et contra naturam:
but contra naturam = auersa a recta
ratione and the definition is repeated in
the same words in 21, 47. For the attri-
butive use of the prep. with its case see
i 22, 51 n. on 'animum sine corpore.'
uehementiorem ...: Hei. compares
Chrysippus in Galen, Hipp. et Plat. iv
369 κατὰ τοῦτο δὲ καὶ ὁ πλεονασμὸς τῆς
ὁρμῆς εἴρηται διὰ τὸ τὴν καθ' αὐτοὺς καὶ
φυσικὴν τῶν ὁρμῶν συμμετρίαν ὑπερ-
βαίνειν.
partes: here used of main divisions
(genera). See iii 11, 24 n. on 'genere

quattuor, partibus plures.' pars more
often denotes a subdivision, cf. 7, 16;
9, 20.
uolunt, 'they maintain,' 'hold,' i 18, 42.
opinatis: iii 11, 24 n.
libidinem = cupiditatem (ἐπιθυμίαν).
futuris...praesentibus: for the non-
repetition of the preposition see iii 15,
33 n. on 'in duabus rebus ponit, auocatione...'
uenientia...instantia = futura...prae-
sentia. Mo. compares Or. ii 25, 105;
Auct. ad Herenn. ii 5; Quintil. v 10, 42
'praeteritum, instans, futurum.' For the
thought Dav. compares Arrian, Epict.
iii 26 p. 360 ὧν γὰρ προσδοκωμένων
φόβος γίνεται καὶ λύπη παρόντων. [For
the partitio cf. S. Paul. Nol. Epp. 39, 6
sunt enim in corpore nostro principalia
totidem incentiua uitiorum spes metus
gaudium dolor quibus maxime genus

15 bona uidentur sequuntur fugiuntque contraria. quam ob rem simul obiecta species est cuiuspiam quod bonum uideatur ad id adipiscendum inpellit ipsa natura. id cum constanter prudenterque fit, eius modi adpetitionem Stoici βούλησιν appellant, nos appellemus u o l u n t a t e m. eam illi putant in solo esse sapiente, 20 quam sic definiunt : uoluntas est, quae quid cum ratione desiderat. quae autem a ratione auersa incitata est uehementius, ea libido est uel cupiditas effrenata, quae in omnibus stultis inuenitur. **13.** itemque cum ita mouemur ut in bono simus aliquo, dupliciter id contingit. nam cum ratione animus mouetur placide 25 atque constanter, tum illud g a u d i u m dicitur; cum autem in-

15. sequuntur B 1   S E W 1   M 1   J   O 3 8.   secuntur R V P G   B 2 3
                                                          es
K E 2   W 2   M 2.   16. species est E 2   C.   speci est R *eod. atr. superscr.*
spês est O 7 8.   species B E 1 est *omisso.*   speciest V t *extra lineam excurr.* G.
specie est B 2.   speci ē K 1.   species cuiuspiam est B 3   M 2.   species iam M 1.
                                                          ē
speties est O 3.   spes ē W 1 2.   est species O 1.   ᴧspecies S *fort. ead. man.*
superscr. om. D.   17. impellit R V G B K.   18. adpetitionem R V G K.
appetitionem S. ‖ BOYΛHCIN K.   boYΛHCin G.   19. appellamus R V P
B 1-3   K 1 2   S   E 1 2   W 1 2   M 1 2   C Π J   O 1 2 7 8.   apellamus G *om.* D.
appellemus *corr. Wesenbergius.*   20. daefiniunt G.   21. a ratione aduersa S.
ratione auersa R 1 6   L 4 5   W 1.   ratione aduersa R 1 7   V P G   B 1-3   K 1
E 1 2   L 2 6   W 2   M 1 2   Π J   O 1-3 7 8.   rationi aduersa C.   aduersus
rationem R 6.   *om.* D.   a ratione auersa *corr. Orellius.*   22. effrenata R V G
B 1-3   K 1   S E   W 2   O 1 3 8.

turbatur humanum, duobus praesentibus et duobus futuris ; praesentibus aegritudine animi uel gaudio, futuris metu uel spe. unde cauendum est ne dum aliud ex his uitium fugimus, incurramus contrarium.]
  12. simul=*simul atque,* cf. Fin. iii 6, 21 ; Ac. ii 27, 86.
  adpiscendum : iii 27, 66 n.
  βούλησιν : with specialised force, = '*reasonable* wish.' βούλησις is one of the three εὐπάθειαι (*constantiae*) treated of in this chapter. Cf. Diog. L. vii 116 εἶναι δὲ καὶ εὐπαθείας φασὶ τρεῖς, χαράν, εὐλάβειαν, βούλησιν· καὶ τὴν μὲν χαρὰν ἐναντίαν εἶναι τῇ ἡδονῇ, οὖσαν εὔλογον ἔπαρσιν· τὴν δ' εὐλάβειαν τῷ φόβῳ, οὖσαν εὔλογον ἔκκλισιν· φοβηθήσεσθαι μὲν γὰρ τὸν σοφὸν οὐδαμῶς, εὐλαβηθήσεσθαι δέ· τῇ δ'ἐπιθυμίᾳ ἐναντίαν φασὶν εἶναι τὴν βούλησιν, οὖσαν εὔλογον ὄρεξιν.
  appellemus : the necessary em. of Wes. *Em.* I p. 18, who supports the subj. by a long list of parallel passages, e.g. § 13 below, *appelletur, nominetur* ; 12, 28 *dicatur,* Bentley's corr., supported by the following *nominetur* and *habeat. appellemus* is also read in Fin. iii 6, 20, after Bentley, where see Madvig's n. Meaning as well as usage condemn *appellamus* in our passage, as the indic. would mean

that the word *uoluntas* was commonly used in Latin in the sense expressed by the Stoic technical term βούλησιν. Where we have *gaudium dicitur* in § 13 below the expression is compressed for (*a Stoicis*) χαρά, *id est, gaudium dicitur.*
  a ratione auersa : *ratione aduersa* of the MSS may be good Latin, though Wes. thinks Cic. would rather have written *aduersante, inuita* or *repugnante*; but we must take this passage along with § 13 ' metus ⟨a⟩ ratione auersa cautio ' where the insertion of *a* is the natural emendation, supported by 9, 22 'auersa a praescriptione rationis'; 15, 34 'motus auersi a ratione'; 6, 11 and 21, 47 'auersa a ratione...commotio,' instances cited by Orelli.
  § 13. nam cum ratione : Dav. on Bentley's conj. read *nam cum cum ratione*; Sff. shows that Cic. avoided this combination and reads *nam cum ratione animus cum mouetur....* But Küh. notes that with passives the simple abl. is perfectly correct, comparing 38, 83, 'a te ratione propositum'; Off. i 2, 7 ' omnis quae ratione suscipitur de aliqua re institutio.'
  gaudium : χαρά ; see notes above on βούλησιν and 'appellemus.'

aniter et effuse animus exsultat, tum illa laetitia gestiens uel nimia dici potest, quam ita definiunt: sine ratione animi elationem. quoniamque, ut bona natura adpetimus, sic a malis natura declinamus, quae declinatio cum ratione fiet, cautio ap-
30 pelletur, eaque intellegatur in solo esse sapiente; quae autem sine ratione et cum exanimatione humili atque fracta, nominetur metus; est igitur metus a ratione auersa cautio. 14. Praesentis autem mali sapientis adfectio nulla est, stulti autem aegri-

§ 13, 26. exultat R V P G B 1 2 K S E.   28. quoniamq3 C.   quŏque K 1
(*i.e.* quoniamque *cf. infra* § 14 *ubi* K 1 *habet* quŏ aegritudini nulla).   qm̄que K 2
W 2 J O 7 8.   qm̄ *om.* que II O 1.   quoniam quę E 1 *al. atr. superscr.*
quoniam (qm̄) quae R G E 2 M 2 O 2.   quoniam quę B 1 W 1.   Qm̄ quę V
atr. nigro punctis appos.   quāq; B 2.   quomodoq; O 3.   qmodoque P.
qm̄ₐqueₐut S.   ‖   adpetimus V G.   aₚlp&imus R *eod. atr.* d *in* p *mut.*
appetimus R 2 B K.   29. declinatio si cum ratione R V P G B 1 3 K 1 S
E 1 2 W 1 2 M 1 2 C II J O 1–3 7 8.   declinatio fiet *cett. om.* B 2.   *om.* D.
declinatio cum ratione *corr. Bentleius.*   ‖   appelletur R G B 1 2 K 2 C II
O 2 3 7 8.   appelletur V.   appellatur B 3 K 1 W 1 2 O 1.   30. intellegatur
R G B K.   intellegatur V.   intellegatur S.   32. metus ratione auersa
R V P G B 1–3 K 1 2 E 1 M 2 J W 1 *marg. e contextu om.*   metus ratione
aduersa R 6 7 S E 2 W 2 II O 3 7 8.   metus auersa ratione O 2.   metus
rationi aduersa C O 1.   metus aduersa ratione M 1.   metus a ratione auersa
Gr. ed. H.   *om.* D.
§ 14, 33. adfectio R V G K E.   affectio P B S.   ‖   stulti autem R 6 O 1.
stulta S *i.e.* a *in* i *man. recenti mut.*   stulta autem R V P 1 2 4 G B 1–3
K 1 2 E 1 2 L 2–6 W 1 2 M 1 2 C J O 2 3 8 7.   stulti. II.   *om.* D.

quae declinatio cum … : editors generally, except Mo. and Küh., follow Bentley in ejecting *si* before *cum*. This gives a straightforward constr. if *quae declinatio* be taken in the sense of *ea declinatio, quae....* Küh., retaining *si*, finds here an instance of the figure *anantapodoton*, as in iii 17, 36 (n. on 'Pythagoras...si diceret') 'qua apodosis cum parenthesi coaluit.'
cautio : εὐλάβεια, see note above on βούλησιν.
quae autem=*ea autem quae...*
§ 14. praesentis...aegritudo est : exception has been taken (*a*) to the double genitive *mali sapientis adfectio* ; (*b*) to the change of number *stulti aegritudo est...adficiuntur* ; (*c*) to the repetition of *autem.* Hence the following conjectures : *praesentibus autem malis,* Dav. in ed. 2 and Sff.; *sapienti...stultis autem* Bent. followed by Dav. and Lall. ; *stultorum* omitting *autem* Dav. in ed. 2 ; *stultorum tum* Sff.
Wopkens, *Lectt. Tull.* I 122, finds all three objections groundless. Instances of

such double genitives are not uncommon, cf. ii 15 35 functio quaedam uel animi uel corporis grauioris operis ; iv 17, 40, etc. The transition from singular to plural, or plural to singular, provided it does not take place within a single clause, is Ciceronian, cf. 31, 65 'perturbationem... omnes eas...'; *Fin.* ii 19, 61 with Madvig's n. ; Ac. ii 7, 22; N.D. i 38, 106 ; Diu. i 33, 72. See 3, 6 n. on 'inuitabantur...tenebant.'
The repetition of *autem* within such short space would not necessarily condemn the word here but the contrast between the *sapiens* and the *stultus* requires asyndeton, as pointed out by T.S. *autem* may possibly be a copyist's repetition of the preceding *autem* and *stulti* (MSS *stulta*) may be the correct reading. But it is more likely to have arisen from the end of *stultorum,* perhaps contracted, *stultorū* becoming *stulta āu.*
eaque : Bake's corr. for *ea qua* of the MSS, which would seem to distinguish this *aegritudo* from some other species of *aegritudo.* Interchanges of *que quae* and

tudo est, eaque adficiuntur in malis opinatis animosque demittunt
35 et contrahunt rationi non obtemperantes. itaque haec prima definitio est, ut aegritudo sit animi adversante ratione contractio.
sic quattuor perturbationes sunt, tres constantiae, quoniam aegri-
tudini nulla constantia opponitur. VII. Sed omnes perturbationes iudicio censent fieri et opinione. itaque eas definiunt pressius, ut intellegatur non modo
quam uitiosae, sed etiam quam in nostra sint potestate. est ergo
aegritudo opinio recens mali praesentis, in quo demitti contra-
5 hique animo rectum esse uideatur, laetitia opinio recens boni
praesentis, in quo ecferri rectum esse uideatur, metus opinio
inpendentis mali, quod intolerabile esse uideatur, libido opinio

34. eaq3 O 7.   ea quę E 1.   ea quae G.   ea qua R 1 6 16   V   P 1 4
B 1-3   K 1 2   S   E 2   L 2-6   W 1   M 1 2   C Π J   O 1-3 8 ed. H.   ea q E 3.
ea q W 2.   *om.* D.   eaque *corr. Bakius.*   ‖ adficiuntur R V G K E.
afficiuntur B S.   35. obtemperantes G K.   optemperantes B 1. ‖ definitio
                                              ut gaudium uoluntas cautio
G K.   difinitio V.   37. tres constantię V *atr. uiridi superscr.*
VII. 2. intellegatur R V G B K.   3. ergo R V G   B 1 2   J   O 1 8.
r   o
ęgro E 1.   g W 2   O 7.   igitur W 1   O 3.   5. animo B 1. ‖
laetitia......intolerabile esse uidetur *e contextu om.* G *in marg. inferiore add. alt. man.*
                                                          h c
6. ecferri R G.   etferri E.   hęc ferri V.   et ferri K *atr. nigro mut.*
efferri B 1-3   K 2   S   W 1 2   J   O 7 8.   7. impendentis R V G S.
inpendentis E.   ‖ lubido *hic et infra* B 1.   lubido G *at* u *in* i *mut. ead. man.*
                          v
lubido K 1 *at infra* libido *atr. nigro superscr.*   libido *hic et infra* R 1 *at* i *ex* u
ras. mut.   libido V P.

qua are very common in MSS. Cf. variants
in iv 13, 31 (*ea quae* for *eaque*) ; iv 18, 41
omnino quaeque for *omninoque quae*.
aegritudo...contractio: Dav. gives the
Greek definition from Stobaeus, Ecl. Eth.
ii 90, 14 W. λύπην δ᾽ εἶναι συστολὴν ψυχῆς
ἀπειθῆ λόγῳ, upon which follow the
words αἴτιον δ᾽ αὐτῆς τὸ δοξάζειν πρόσφατον κακὸν παρεῖναι, ἐφ᾽ ᾧ καθήκει
συστέλλεσθαι, which serve to illustrate the
beginning of c. 7. Diog. L. vii 111 and
Andronicus Rhodius περὶ παθῶν p. 523 1
p. 11 (Kreuttner) pronounce λύπη to be
συστολὴ ἄλογος. Cf. i 37, 90 n. on 'animi
contractio'; iii 34, 83 n. on 'contractiuncula.'
constantiae: εὐπάθειαι, cf. 6, 12 n. on
βούλησιν.
VII. iudicio: Zeller, *Stoics, etc.*, c. x
pp. 228 foll. ; iii 13, 28 n. on ' opinionem
mali aegritudinem esse natura.'
pressius, ' more exactly.' Fin. iv 10,
24 ; Ac. ii 9, 29 and Reid's n.
est ergo aegritudo...: see n. on 'aegritudo...contractio' above.

in quo...rectum esse uideatur: iii 31,
76 n. on ' Chrysippus autem.'
laetitia: cf. Andronicus, περὶ παθῶν
1 p. 11 (Kreuttner) p. 523 ἡδονὴ δὲ ἄλογος
ἔπαρσις, ἢ δόξα πρόσφατος ἀγαθοῦ παρουσίας, ἐφ᾽ ᾧ οἴονται δεῖν ἐπαίρεσθαι.
metus: Andronicus, *l.c.* φόβος δὲ ἄλογος
ἔκκλισις, ἢ φυγὴ ἀπὸ προσδοκωμένου
δεινοῦ· Stobaeus, Ecl. Eth. II 90, 11 W.
φόβον δ᾽ εἶναι ἔκκλισιν ἀπειθῆ λόγῳ, αἴτιον
δὲ αὐτοῦ τὸ δοξάζειν κακὸν ἐπιφέρεσθαι τῆς
δόξης τὸ κινητικὸν πρόσφατον ἐχούσης τοῦ
ὄντως αὐτὸ φευκτὸν εἶναι.
libido: Andronicus, *l.c.* ἐπιθυμία δὲ
ἄλογος ὄρεξις, ἢ δίωξις προσδοκωμένου
ἀγαθοῦ.
On comparing Galen, Hipp. et Plat.
iv p. 366, where Chrysippus is represented as departing from the view of the
παλαιοί, τὴν λύπην ὁριζόμενος δόξαν πρόσφατον κακοῦ παρουσίας, τὸν δὲ φόβον
προσδοκίαν κακοῦ, τὴν δ᾽ ἡδονὴν δόξαν
πρόσφατον ἀγαθοῦ παρουσίας, we see that
all the definitions given here by Cicero
are Chrysippean.

uenturi boni, quod sit ex usu iam praesens esse atque adesse.

15. sed quae iudicia quasque opiniones perturbationum esse
10 dixi, non in eis perturbationes solum positas esse dicunt, uerum
illa etiam quae efficiuntur perturbationibus, ut aegritudo quasi
morsum aliquem doloris efficiat, metus recessum quendam animi
et fugam, laetitia profusam hilaritatem, libido effrenatam adpetentiam. opinationem autem, quam in omnis definitiones
15 superiores inclusimus, uolunt esse inbecillam adsensionem.

§ 15, 10. eis R V G B 1 2 K W 1 Π O 1 2 7.   11. efficiuntur R V G B K S. ‖
quas|i inmorsum V i *extra lineam et al. atr. script.*   13. effrenatam R 6 7 P B S
W 1 O 1 8.   effrenatā R 1 K 1.   effrenata V G B 2.   effrena E. ‖
adpetentiam R G B 2 K E.   appetentiam R 2 16 V P B 1 S.   appententiā
R 10.   14. opinationem R V G B 1-3 K S E 1 2 L 3-6 W 1 2 M 2
D C Π J O 1 2 7 8 Gr. ed. H.   oppinationem M 1.   opinionem L 2 O 3.
oppinionem K 2.   ‖   omnis R V G K E.   omīs B 1   W 2.   omnes P.
15. inbecillam R V G B 1 2 K 1 E 1 M 1 O 7.   ibecillā J.
inbecillem S.   imbecillam R 2 10 16 P B 3 K 2 E 2 W 2 M 2 D C O 1 3 8.
ibecillem Π.   ibecillē W 1.   ‖   adsensionem R V P G K E.   assensionem R 2
B 1 S W 1.

[**praesens...adesse**: cf. Fin. i 17, 55
'nam corpore nihil nisi praesens et quod
adest sentire possumus,' where Madv.
notes that *adesse* is temporal not local in
its signification as here and that the combination of *praesens* and *adesse* is for the
sake of emphasis.]

§ **15. sed quae iudicia...**: in Galen,
Hipp. et Plat. v 1 p. 429, we read that
Χρύσιππος μὲν οὖν ἐν τῷ πρώτῳ περὶ
παθῶν ἀποδεικνύναι πειρᾶται κρίσεις τινὰς
εἶναι τοῦ λογιστικοῦ τὰ πάθη, Ζήνων δὲ οὐ
τὰς κρίσεις αὐτὰς ἀλλὰ τὰς ἐπιγινομένας
αὐταῖς συστολὰς καὶ διαχύσεις ἐπάρσεις τε
καὶ πτώσεις τῆς ψυχῆς ἐνόμιζεν εἶναι τὰ
πάθη. The difference here indicated was
really less than it would at first appear to
be. Chrysippus, in asserting that the
πάθη were decisions of the reason, did not
exclude the elation or dejection or other
excitement that follow upon such decisions.
This is clear from Galen, *l.c.* iv p. 367,
where we find that Chrysippus made
λύπη a μείωσις and ἡδονή an ἔπαρσις and
from the same work iv 5 p. 392,
whence we see that the maxim that every
πάθος is πτοία and every πτοία πάθος
(Stob. Ecl. Eth. ii 88 W.) belonged to
Chrysippus. It was no doubt with a
view to strengthening, against opponents
who maintained the triple division of the
soul, the Stoic doctrine, which made
emotion due to a change taking place in
the ἡγεμονικόν, that Chrysippus insisted
on giving prominence to the intellectual

origin of emotion. Conversely, Posidonius,
later on, made the πάθη neither judgments nor consequences of judgments but
movements of the irrational parts of the
soul, i.e. of Plato's ἐπιθυμητικόν and
θυμοειδές.

The source, which Cicero followed in
our passage, evidently set forth views
derived from Chrysippus and contained
a definite statement of the qualification of
Chrysippus' dogmatic assertion, a qualification which, as may be seen above, can
be inferred from other statements which
he is known to have made.

We might have expected *sed non in eis
iudiciis eisque opinionibus....* For the
attraction of *iudicia* from the main clause
into the body and construction of the
subordinate clause cf. Off. iii 22, 87
'quas ciuitates L. Sulla...liberauisset, ut
eae rursus uectigales essent.' The converse attraction from the subord. to
the main clause, for which cf. i 24, 56 n.
on 'nam sanguinem,' is more common.

opinationem: a word coined by Cic. to
express the act of opining.

inbecillam adsensionem: for *adsensio*
=συγκατάθεσις see Reid on Ac. ii 12, 37
'de adsensione atque adprobatione, quam
Graeci συγκατάθεσιν uocant.' Cf. also
Ac. i 11, 42 'errorem autem...et opinationem et suspicionem et uno nomine
omnia, quae essent aliena firmae et con-
stantis adsensionis, a uirtute sapientiaque
remouebat (Zeno).'

16. Sed singulis perturbationibus partes eiusdem generis plures subiciuntur, ut aegritudini inuidentia (utendum est enim docendi causa uerbo minus usitato, quoniam inuidia non in eo qui inuidet solum dicitur, sed etiam in eo cui inuidetur), aemu-
20 latio, obtrectatio, misericordia, angor, luctus, maeror, aerumna, dolor, lamentatio, sollicitudo, molestia, adflictatio, desperatio, et si quae sunt de genere eodem. sub metum autem subiecta sunt pigritia, pudor, terror, timor, pauor, exanimatio, conturbatio, formido, uoluptati maleuolentia laetans malo alieno, delectatio,
25 iactatio et similia, libidini ira, excandescentia, odium, inimicitia, discordia, indigentia, desiderium et cetera eius modi.

Haec autem definiunt hoc modo: inuidentiam esse dicunt aegritudinem susceptam propter alterius res secundas, quae nihil noceant inuidenti.

VIII. **17.** Nam si qui doleat eius rebus secundis a quo ipse

§ 16, 17. subiciuntur R V G　B 1 2　K E　W 2　D J　O 3 7 8.　　subiiciuntur
S *i.e.* i *in* ij *mut.*　　21. adflictatio V G E.　　adflectatio R *eod. atr.* K *eod. atr.*
afflictatio B S.　　22. sub metum R G B K S　M 2　Π　O 8.　　sub metū R 7 17
P　B 2 3　E 1 2　M 1　D C.　　submetu *linea supra* u *ut uid. eras.* V　W 2.
sub metu K 2　W 1　J　O 1-3 7.　　24. uoluptati E 2　W 1　M 2　D C Π　O 2 3 7 8.
uolup K 2.　　uoluptati W 2 *at* s *eras.*　　uoluptati B 3 *al. atr. superscr.*
uoluptatis R V P G　B 1 2　K E 1　O 1.　*om.* M 1. ‖ maleuolentia R V G B K.
maliuolentia S E. ‖ la&ans R.　　letans V P G.　　25. libidini R　B 1-3　K 1 2
W 1　M 1　D O 1 3 7 8.　　libidini W 2 *at* s *eras.*　　libini G.　　libidini V
atr. uiridi superscr.
　　VIII. § 17, 1. si qui V P G B E.　　si quis B 3　K 2　S　E 2　W 1 2　M 1 2
D C Π J　O 1-3 7 8 ed. H.　　si quid R.　　si qui K 1 d *eras. om.* B 2.

§ 16. **inuidentia :** iii 9, 20 n. *ut aegritudini ... inuidetur* quoted by Nonius, s.uu. *inuidia* et *inuidentia* p. 443, M.
　　sub metum...subiecta sunt : but above *perturbationibus...subiciuntur* and below *uoluptati...libidini.* Both constructions are used with *subicere*, see Madvig's full n. on Fin. ii 15, 48 ; the abl. *sub metu*, only found here in inferior MSS, is not used. The departure from symmetry of constr. led Lamb. to alter *sub metum* to *metui*, but Cicero's rule is not so rigid, cf. Wopkens, *Lectt. Tull.* II 226 ed. Hand, where among other instances is quoted T. D. iv 11, 25 'ut odium mulierum...ut in hominum uniuersum genus.'
　　maleuolentia laetans malo alieno : Bent. and Dav. bracketed *laetans malo alieno* as an unnecessary gloss and have been followed by T.S. Hei. Bai. and Wes. *Em.* I 23. But the passage is cited in Nonius (who read *lactans* not *laetans*)

p. 16 M. and the objection that an explanatory addition is out of place in an enumeration of subdivisions does not seem fatal, or this may rather be a circumlocutory rendering of the Gk ἐπιχαιρεκακία. The added words are necessary to express the idea of ἐπιχαιρεκακία and they also, as Nissen observes, serve to show why *maleuolentia* is placed under *uoluptas* rather than under *libido.*
　　et similia : and below *et cetera. similia* and *cetera*, not being units in the series, are sometimes tacked on by *et*, as summing up the series (iii 2, 3 n. on ' et inhaerescunt'), cf. iv 31, 66 'honores, diuitiae, uoluptates, cetera'; Fin. v 12, 35 'et reliquae'; v 13, 36 'et reliquas'; but even with these words asyndeton is more usual. See Madv. on Fin. iv 20, 56; Küh. on T.D. v 14, 41.
　　indigentia, 'insatiate desire,' a meaning specially given to the word by Cic., its usual meaning being 'need.'

laedatur, non recte dicatur inuidere, ut si Hectori Agamemno;
qui autem, cui alterius commoda nihil noceant, tamen eum doleat
iis frui, is inuideat profecto. aemulatio autem dupliciter illa
5 quidem dicitur, ut et in laude et in uitio nomen hoc sit ; nam et
imitatio uirtutis aemulatio dicitur (sed ea nihil hoc loco utimur ;
est enim laudis), et est aemulatio aegritudo, si eo quod concupierit alius potiatur, ipse careat. 18. obtrectatio autem est, ea
quam intellegi ζηλοτυπίαν uolo, aegritudo ex eo, quod alter
10 quoque potiatur eo quod ipse concupiuerit. misericordia
est aegritudo ex miseria alterius iniuria laborantis; nemo enim

2. dicatur R V P G B I 3 K I S E I 2 W I M I 2 D C O 2 3 7 8.
dicetur W 2 J O I.   dī K 2.   ‖   haectori R G K.   hęctori B. ‖
agamemno R V G K.   agamemno P B E.   agamemnō S *at linea supra* o
al. atr. duct.   agamemnon W I M 2.   agamennon E 2.   agamenon M I
D C II O 3.   3. comoda R G.   4. frui is R 6 P 2 B 3 M I 2 O 2 3.
frui s/e is R I *al. atr. se expunct. et* is *add.*   frui se P *marg.* is frui is W 2 se *post*
frui *eras. et* is *al. atr. script.*   frui sę V B I.   frui se R 2 17 P 4 G B 2
K 2 W I J O I 8.   fruisse R 10 16 S *marg.* is *man. ant. adscript.*   fuisse K I
E I.   frui se hiis R 7.   frui hic E 2 II.   frui si O 7.   hiis dōleat is C.
hiis doleat hiis D.   ‖   inuideat R V P G K S E I 2 M I 2 D C.   inuidet
P 2 O 3.   nichil uideat J.   7. laudis est aemulatio G et *om.*   8. obtrectatio
R V G K S.   optrectatio B E.   9. intellegi R V G B.   intellėgi K.
intelligi S E. ‖ zeloptypian R V P G B I.   zelotipian B 2.   zeletipian E.
zelotypiam K.   zelotipiam S.   zelotippiam M I.   10. quod ipse R V P G
B I-3 K I S E 2 W I M I 2 D C II J O I-3.   q'ipse W 2 O 7.
d
q, O 8. ‖ concupiuerit R V.   concupierit G S.   cupiuerit J.

quae nihil noceant inuidenti: an addition to the definition made by Cicero, cf. Diog. L. vii 111 φθόνον δὲ λύπην ἐπ' ἀλλοτρίοις ἀγαθοῖς. [Cicero's 'addition' is really implied (by exclusion) in the form of the definition quoted from Chrysippus by Plut. de St. repug. 25 p. 1046 B λύπη ἐστὶν ἐπ' ἀλλοτρίοις ἀγαθοῖς ὡς δήποτε βουλομένων ταπεινοῦν τοὺς πλησίον, ὅπως ὑπερέχωσιν αὐτοί.]

VIII. § 17. **ut si Hectori Agamemno** sc. *inuidere dicatur.* For the form *Agamemno* see Neue I³ pp. 246—250.

in laude...in uitio: for this use of the prepositional clause cf. i 39, 94 n. on 'in eadem breuitate.'

est aemulatio: cf. Stobaeus, Ecl. Eth. ii p. 92 W. ζῆλος δὲ λύπη ἐπὶ τῷ ἕτερον ἐπιτυγχάνειν, ὧν αὐτὸς ἐπιθυμεῖ, αὐτὸν δὲ μή· λέγεσθαι δὲ καὶ ἑτέρως ζῆλον μακαρισμὸν ἐνδεοῦς καὶ ἔτι ἄλλως μίμησιν ὡς ἂν κρείττονος. Diog. L. vii 111 ζῆλον λύπην ἐπὶ τῷ ἄλλῳ παρεῖναι ὧν αὐτὸς ἐπιθυμεῖ. Cf. 26, 56 below.

concupierit: the subject is *aemulans* implied in *aemulatio.* Küh. compares § 18 'quod ipse concupierit' sc. *obtrectans* implied in *obtrectatio*; 9, 20 'sine

emolumento suo' where *suo* is to be referred to *alicuius gaudentis* implied in *uoluptas*; 11, 26 'iudicatio se scire quod nesciat,' where *iudicatio* implies an *aliquis iudicans*; 20, 46 'ipsum illud aemulari, obtrectare non esse inutile, cum aut se non uidet uideat consecutum...'

§ 18. obtrectatio, 'jealous detraction.' Cf. below 26, 56 'obtrectantis autem angi alieno bono, quod id etiam alius habeat'; Diog. L. vii 111 ζηλοτυπίαν δὲ λύπην ἐπὶ τῷ καὶ ἄλλῳ παρεῖναι, ἃ καὶ αὐτὸς ἔχει. Stob. Ecl. Eth. ii 92 W.; Andronicus Rhodius, p. 524, as quoted and emended by Dav., ζηλοτυπία δέ ἐστι λύπη ἐπὶ τῷ καὶ ἄλλοις ὑπάρχειν, ἃ καὶ ἡμῖν ὑπάρχει. *quoque* and *etiam* in Cicero's definitions represent ἃ καὶ αὐτὸς ἔχει in the Greek. [The repetition of *concupierit*, if sound, goes a long way towards abolishing the distinction between *aemulatio* and *obtrectatio*: for the second *concupierit* Cic. should have written *habeat*, ἔχει of the Gk.]

ipse: for the ref. cf. § 17 n. on 'concupierit.'

misericordia: Diog. L. *l.c.* ἔλεον μὲν οὖν εἶναι λύπην ὡς ἐπὶ ἀναξίως κακοπαθοῦντι.

parricidae aut proditoris supplicio misericordia commouetur; angor aegritudo premens, luctus aegritudo ex eius qui carus fuerit interitu acerbo, maeror aegritudo flebilis, aerumna 15 aegritudo laboriosa, dolor aegritudo crucians, lamentatio aegritudo cum eiulatu, sollicitudo aegritudo cum cogitatione, molestia aegritudo permanens, adflictatio aegritudo cum uexatione corporis, desperatio aegritudo sine ulla rerum expectatione meliorum. quae autem subiecta sunt sub metum, ea sic 20 definiunt: pigritiam metum consequentis laboris, 19 ...... terrorem metum concutientem, ex quo fit ut pudorem rubor,

§ 18, 12. ut proditoris B.   ut proditoris E.   13. angor aegritudo
R V P G B K *plerique.*   angor est aegritudo W 1.   angor ∧ egritudo Π. ‖

premens V B 2 K O 3.   praemens R G.   pmens P.   p̄mens B 1 W 2.
14. maeror R G.   meror R 2 10 16 V B.   15. crutians G.   17. adflictatio
R P G K.   afflictatio B 1-3 S E 2 W 1 M 1 2 D C Π J O 2 8.
afflic₁tio E 1 *al. atr. superscr.*   afflictatio W 2 (*sic*).   a₫flictio V.   afflictio O 1.
afflitio O 7.   applicatio O 3.   18. expectatione R V P G B K.
19. sub metum R V G K 1 E 1 L 2 5 O 1 2.   sub metū P 1 4 B 1 2 S
E 2 M 1 D C Π O 7 8.   sub metu R 17 B 3 K 2 L 3 4 6 W 2 M 2
J O 3.   metui W 1 sub *om.*

parricidae: for the spelling see Fleckeisen, *Fünfzig Artikeln*, sub uoce [*parricida* is contracted for *patricida*: until the time of Ennius it was spelled *paricida*, v. Lindsay, *Latin Language*, pp. 371, 3. Walde, *Latein. etymol. Wörterb.* s.u., derives *parri-* not from *pater* but from the root *pasos* seen in Gk πηός 'kinsman'].

angor...premens: cf. Diog. L. vii 112 ἄχθος δὲ λύπην βαρύνουσαν.

luctus: the definitions of *luctus, maeror, lamentatio* and *desperatio* are omitted by Diog. L. vii 111-2; those of *lamentatio* and *desperatio* by Stobaeus, Ecl. Eth. ii 91 W.; on the other hand Diog. L. has σύγχυσιν, λύπην ἄλογον, ἀποκναίουσαν καὶ κωλύουσαν τὰ παρόντα συνορᾶν, which is wanting in Stobaeus and Cicero. The list of Andronicus Rhodius is much fuller, containing twenty-five species: cf. Stob. *l.c.* πένθος δὲ λύπην ἐπὶ θανάτῳ ἀώρῳ. Andron. περὶ παθῶν 2 (p. 12 Kr.) πένθος δὲ λύπην ἐπὶ ἀώρῳ τελευτῇ.

acerbo: i 39, 93 n. on 'acerbius.'

maeror is represented in Stobaeus and Andron. by ἄχος δὲ λύπην ἀφωνίαν ἐμποιοῦσαν.

aerumna and **dolor** may both be found in ὀδύνη, cf. Diog. L. *l.c.* ὀδύνην λύπην ἐπίπονον.

dolor: Andron. *l.c.* σφακελισμὸς δὲ λύπη σφοδρά.

lamentatio: Andron. has γόος and κλαῦσις.

sollicitudo: cf. Andron. *l.c.* φροντὶς δὲ λογισμὸς λυπουμένου.

molestia: ἀνία, cf. Diog. L. *l.c.* ἀνίαν λύπην ἐκ διαλογισμῶν μένουσαν ἢ ἐπιτεινομένην.

adflictatio: Diog. L. *l.c.* ἐνόχλησιν λύπην στενοχωροῦσαν καὶ δυσχωρίαν παρασκευάζουσαν. Stob. *l.c.* and Andron. *l.c.* ἄσην δὲ λύπην μετὰ ῥιπτασμοῦ.

desperatio: cf. Andron. *l.c.* ἀθυμία δὲ λύπη ἀπελπίζοντος ὧν ἐπιθυμεῖ τυχεῖν.

subiecta sunt sub metum: 7, 16 n.

pigritiam: Diog. L. *l.c.* and Stobaeus *l.c.* ὄκνος δὲ φόβος μελλούσης ἐνεργείας.

§ 19. terrorem: before this word the definition of *pudor* (αἰσχύνη) given as a subdivision of φόβος by Diog. L. and Stobaeus must have fallen out, as the words *ex quo fit, ut pudorem rubor...consequatur* also serve to indicate. Cf. Stob. *l.c.* ἔκπληξις δὲ φόβος ἐξ ἀσυνήθους φαντασίας· αἰσχύνη δὲ φόβος ἀδοξίας, and similarly Diog. L. *l.c.* and Andron *l.c.* Hence Sff. conjectures *pudorem metum dedecoris* accounting for the error on the theory that the copyist's eye strayed from the ending of *laboris* to that of *dedecoris.* Wes. *Em.* III p. 3 sought a participle ending like the following *concutientem,* e.g. *calefacientem*: similarly Bai., ed. Tauchn., conj. *pudorem metum sanguinem* terrorem pallor et tremor et dentium crepitus consequatur, **timorem** metum mali adpropinquantis, **pauorem** metum mentem loco mouentem, ex quo illud Ennius:

25   Túm pauor sapiéntiam omnem mi éxanimato ex-
péctorat,

exanimationem metum subsequentem et quasi comitem pauoris, **conturbationem** metum excutientem cogitata, **formidinem** metum permanentem.

IX. **20.** Voluptatis autem partes hoc modo discribunt, ut

§ **19, 23.** adpropinquantis R V K.   appropinquantis G B S.   ‖   pauorem metum K 2   M 2   O 2.   pauorem metū P B 1 3   E 2   M 1   Π   O 7. pauorem metu R V G   B 2   K.   24. loc o K c *ex* qu *ras. mut.*   ‖   ennius R V P G   B 1 2   K   E 1   J Gr.   ēnī W 2.   ennius S.   * ennii Π ii *ex* ius *ras. mut.*   ennii B 3   W 1   M 1 2   D   O 1 7 8.   25. ex anima R V G   B 1 3 K 1   E 1   L 6   O 3 7 8.   ex animo O 1.   ex aīo W 1   J.   exaiq P a *ex* o *mut.* exanimato Non. 1 p. 16 M.   ‖ expectorat R 6   L 4   W 1   O 1 ed. H.   expectoret B 1 Π.   expect⊕ret S.   expectoret O 8.   exspect or⅄t K 1 *fuerat* exspectaret. expectaret E 2 *marg.* expectorar&. expectaret R   P 1 4   G   B 2   K 2   L 5   M 1   D O 7.   exspectaret E 1   C.   expectar& V *atr. uiridi superscr.*   expelleret R 7 17 L 2   W 2.   expelletur J.   expulerat B 3   L 3 6   M 2   O 2 3. IX. § **20,** 1.   partes R V P G B K.

diffundentem. This line of emendation is supported by the following *ex quo fit.*

consequatur: i 16 36 n. on 'consecuti sunt.'

timorem: Cic. gives to the species practically the same definition as he gave to the genus, cf. 7, 14 'metus opinio inpendentis mali.' Diog. L. *l.c.* has δεῖμα μὲν οὖν ἐστι φόβος δέος ἐμποιῶν· Stob. *l.c.* δεῖμα δὲ φόβος ἐκ λόγου.

pauorem, 'consternation.' In Diog. L. there is only one word, ἔκπληξις, to correspond to *terror* and *pauor.* Andron. and Stob. *l.c.* have δέος.

tum pauor...expectorat: from the Alcumeo of Ennius, cf. Ribbeck, *Scaen. Rom. Poes. Frag.* I² p. 17; *Röm. Trag.* p. 197. The passage is quoted in Or. iii 38, 154, where *expectorat* is cited as a coined word, and, more fully, *ibid.* 58, 218.

exanimato: ' non conuenit inter uiros doctos utrum *exanimo* coniunctim an *ex animo* separatim legi debeat: illud Turnebo lib. vii *Aduers.* c. 17, hoc Lambino in Annot. in lib. iii de Oratore probatur' (Fabricius). Dav. defended *ex animo expectorare* by ref. to Accius' Phoenissae quoted by Nonius 1 p. 16 M. but Ribbeck there adopts (I² p. 213) N. Faber's conj. *exanimum.* All recent editors adopt in our passage the reading

exanimato from Nonius, *l.c.*, and Or. iii 38, 154.

expectorat: see Wilkins on Or. iii 38, 154.

exanimationem: does not correspond very closely to ἀγωνία, which Diog. L. *l.c.* defines as φόβος ἀδήλου πράγματος, while Stob. *l.c.* defines it thus—ἀγωνία δὲ φόβος διαπτώσεως, καὶ ἑτέρως, φόβος ἥττης.

conturbationem, 'agitation,' not a very lucid term to denote a subdivision of *perturbatio.* Cf. Diog. L. vii 113 θόρυβος δὲ φόβος μετὰ κατεπείξεως φωνῆς· similarly Stob. *l.c.*

excutientem: cf. Pliny, Epp. i 18, 3 'quae singula excutere mentem mihi post tam triste somnium poterant.'

formidinem: here = 'dread'; cf. Andron. ὀρρωδία δὲ φόβος ἐννοηθέντος, but more usual in the sense of an intense rather than an enduring fear; this word is not represented in the list of Diog. L. nor in that of Stobaeus. The latter and Andronicus have δεισιδαιμονία, which is not represented in the lists of Cic. or Diogenes.

IX. § **20. uoluptatis**: cf. iii 10, 23 ' laetitia, quae est uoluptas animi elata et gestiens'; *ibid.* § 24 'uoluptas gestiens'; 13, 27 'laetitia gestiens'; iv 6, 11 'ex bonis libidinem et laetitiam'; 7, 14 'laetitia.'

maleuolentia sit uoluptas ex malo alterius sine emolumento
suo, delectatio uoluptas suauitate auditus animum deleniens;
et qualis est haec aurium, tales sunt et oculorum et tactionum
5 et odorationum et saporum, quae sunt omnes unius generis ad perfundendum animum tamquam inliquefactae uoluptates. iactatio
est uoluptas gestiens et se ecferens insolentius. 21. quae autem
libidini subiecta sunt, ea sic definiuntur, ut ira sit libido poeniendi
eius qui uideatur laesisse iniuria, excandescentia autem
10 sit ira nascens et modo exsistens, quae θύμωσις Graece dicitur,

2. maleuolentia V G B K.　　　malẹuolentia R *eod. atr.*　　　maliuolentia S E. ‖
emolumento R G B.　　　emulumento V.　　　emolomento K *atr. ant.*
4. sunt oculorum et R V P 1 4　G　B 1-3　K 1　S　E 1 2　W 1 2　M 1 2　D C Π J
O 1-3 7 8: *lectio* sunt et oculorum et *ex Nonio uidetur esse eruenda s. u.* tactus 1
227 M.　　5. perfundendum R G B K.　　perfudendum V.　　6. inliquefactae
R V G B E.　　inli que factẹ K.　　illi quẹ factẹ S.　　illi que fcte B 2.
7. efferens R V B K S.　　efferrens G.
§ 21, 8. libidini R V P G B K.　‖ definiuntur R V G　B 1 2　K 1　E 2　Π.
definiunt　P E 1.　diffiniuntur B 3　W 2　M 1 2　D C J　O 1 2.　definūtur O 7.
definiūt W 1.　　diffiniunt O 3.　‖ libido R G K.　　lubido B.　　‖ poeniendi
R G　B 1 2　K 1.　peniendi V o *eod. atr.* u *atr. uiridi superscr.*　　puniendi B 3
E 1 2　W 1　M 1 2　C Π J　O 1 7 8.　　peïtendi S *marg.* puonēdi *ut vid.*
peniēndi P 1 *sic.*　pariendi O 3.　　10. existens R G B K E.　　existens S *marg.*
desistens.　　existens V *atr. uiridi superscr.*　　‖ ΘΥΜѠCIC R V B E.

maleuolentia: Diog. L. vii 114 and
Stobaeus, *l.c.* ἐπιχαιρεκακία δὲ ἡδονὴ ἐπ'
ἀλλοτρίοις κακοῖς. Similarly Andron. *l.c.*
[With regard to *maleuol.* cf. the curious
statement attributed to Chrysippus by
Plut. de St. repug. 25 p. 1046 B τὴν ἐπιχαιρεκακίαν...ἀνύπαρκτον εἶναί φησιν· ἐπεὶ
τῶν μὲν ἀστείων οὐδεὶς ἐπ' ἀλλοτρίοις κακοῖς
χαίρει, τῶν δὲ φαύλων οὐδεὶς χαίρει τὸ
παράπαν.]
　suo: cf. 8, 17 n. on 'concupierit.'
　delectatio: cf. Diog. L. *l.c.* κήλησις
μὲν οὖν ἐστιν ἡδονὴ δι' ὤτων κατακηλοῦσα·
Andron. περὶ παθῶν 5, p. 19 Kr. κήλησις
δὲ ἡδονὴ δι' ἀκοῆς κατακηλοῦσα· ἢ ἡδονὴ
ἐκ λόγου τε καὶ μουσικῆς ἢ δι' ἀπάτης
γινομένη. Stobaeus has not κήλησις but
has γοητεία δὲ ἡδονὴ δι' ὄψεως κατ' ἀπάτην
for which Andron. *l.c.* has γοητεία δὲ
ἡδονὴ κατ' ἀπάτην ἢ διὰ μαγείας. Cic. has
selected a word which is too wide for
κήλησις and then extended it to apply
to the other senses, for which the Stoics
probably employed separate expressions.
　ad perfundendum..., ' to steal over the
mind.'
　iactatio: this word is not represented
in the lists of Diog. L., Stobaeus or
Andronicus. Unrepresented in Cic. are

τέρψις and διάχυσις of Diog. L., τέρψις in
Andron. and ἀσμενισμός in Stob. and
Andron.
　§ 21. definiuntur: it is not necessary
to read *definiunt* with many early editors
and some moderns, e.g. Kl. T.S. The
transition from active to passive or vice
versa (*discribunt* above, *distinguunt*
below) is not uncommon. Sff. compares
11, 26-27 below 'definiunt...definiunt...
definitur.' The termination *-ur* could of
course come in by quasi-haplography
before *ut*, but see iii 27, 64 n. on 'declaratur hoc.'
　ira: Diog. L. *l.c.* § 113 ὀργὴ δ'
ἐπιθυμία τιμωρίας τοῦ δοκοῦντος ἠδικηκέναι
οὐ προσηκόντως; Stob. *l.c.* and Andron. 4
p. 16 Kr. almost the same [cf. Sen. de
Ira i 2, 4 'ira est...ut ait Posidonius,
cupiditas puniendi eius a quo te inique
putes laesum '].
　excandescentia...: Nonius p. 103 M.
quotes this passage thus : ' excandescentia
autem est ira nascens et sine modo
exsistens' for which Mueller reads ' et sine
modo aestuans.'
　exsistens: not the same as *nascens* but
='apparens et semet ostendens' Dav.
　θύμωσις: the Gk sources have θυμός,

odium ira inueterata, inimicitia ira ulciscendi tempus ob-
seruans, discordia ira acerbior intimo animo et corde concepta,
indigentia libido inexplebilis, desiderium libido eius qui
nondum adsit uidendi. distinguunt illud etiam, ut libido sit
15 earum rerum quae dicuntur de quodam aut quibusdam, quae
κατηγορήματα dialectici appellant, ut habere diuitias, capere

12. intimo odio et corde R 16 7 17 V P 14 B 1–3 K 1 2 S E 1 2 L 2–6
W 1 2 M 1 D Π J O 1–3 7 8.   intimo corde et odio G.   et intimo corde M 2
marg. odio.   intimo ore et corde C.   intimo animo et corde *corr. Lambinus.*
13. libido (*ter*) R G B K.   14. distinguunt B 1 2 W 1 M 2.   distingunt
R V P G K 1 S E 1 W 2 D Π J O 2 3.   disiūgūt O 8.   ‖ etiam illud
W 2 J.   15. earum rerum R V P 14 G B 1–3 K 1 E 2 W 1 2 M 1 2
D C Π J O 2 3 7.   earum S E 1 rerum *om.*   eorum O 8 rerum *om.*
16. κατηγορημΑτΑ R V G.   κατΜϲορηΜΛΑτΑ B E.   ‖ dialectici R G B K.
dialetici V E.   dyaletici R 16.   dialecti R 2.

ὀργὴ ἐναρχομένη Stob. and Andron. ὀργὴ
ἀρχομένη Diog. L. Or. thinks θύμωσις
a Chrysippean word 'ideo nouatum, ne
confunderetur haec *excandescentiae* notio
cum θυμῷ Platonis.'
   odium: Diog. L. *l.c.* § 114 μῆνις δέ
ἐστιν ὀργή τις πεπαλαιωμένη καὶ ἐπίκοτος,
ἐπιτηρητικὴ δέ ... : Stob. *l.c.* μῆνις δὲ ὀργὴ
εἰς παλαίωσιν ἀποτεθειμένη ἢ ἐναποκειμένη :
Andron. *l.c.* almost the same.
   inimicitia: Diog. L. has μῖσος as well
as μῆνις. Stob. *l.c.* κότος δὲ ὀργὴ ἐπιτη-
ροῦσα καιρὸν εἰς τιμωρίαν· Andron. *l.c.*
almost the same.
   [**tempus**, 'opportunity' as in iii 31, 76.]
   discordia: no exact equivalent is given
by Diog. L., Stob. or Andron.
   intimo animo et corde: *animo* abbreviated into *aio* probably combined
with the *o* at the end of *intimo* to produce the variant *odio*. The expression
intimo odio is impossible and cannot be
defended by *odio penitus insito* de Leg.
Agr. ii 6, 14 quoted by Kl.
   indigentia: 7, 16 n. Andron. *l.c.*
σπάνις δὲ ἐπιθυμία ἀτελής. Diog. L. *l.c.*
§ 113 ; Stob. *l.c.* omits.
   desiderium: cf. Andron. *l.c.* πόθος δὲ
ἐπιθυμία κατὰ ἔρωτα ἀπόντος ; Stob. *l.c.*
ἵμερος δὲ ἐπιθυμία φίλου ἀπόντος ὁμιλίας·
Diog. L. omits the equivalent for *desiderium*. The meaning of *desiderium* is
narrowed by Cicero's definition.
   illud, 'they draw the following distinction also...'
   ut libido sit... : there are two views
with regard to this passage. According
to the first view we have a distinction
drawn between *desiderium* and *indigentia, ut lib. sit...* being = ut *desiderium
libido sit...* This view was supported by
P. Manutius, who remarked that distinc-

tions are drawn not between a genus and
one of its subordinate species, as between
animal and *man*, but between two species
within a genus, as between *man* and
wolf. The view is that Cic. here asserts
that the Stoics used *desiderium* in connexion with a predicate ; *indigentia* with
a direct object: e.g. *desidero habere
pecuniam, desidero capere honores*, not
desidero pecuniam, honores ; and on the
other hand *indigeo pecuniae, honorum*, not
indigeo habere pecuniam, honores ; *desiderium habendi pecuniam* but *indigentia
pecuniae.* Cf. Bentley, who adds ' vides
ineptias Stoicorum, quos saepe incusat
ipse Cicero, tamquam qui usitatum
loquendi morem inmutarent et corrum-
perent. Nam ut uerum sit hoc de *indigentia*, siue τῇ σπάνει, at certe alterum
illud desiderium siue πόθος apud optimos
utriusque linguae auctores non minus,
immo saepius, ad res ipsas refertur quam
ad κατηγορήματα.'
   According to the second view (Hei.
T.S.) *libido* and *indigentia* are contrasted,
but the latter word is taken in its usual
sense, for which see 7, 16 n., and is not
a subordinate species of *libido*.
   A further distinction between *desiderium* and *indigentia* is more naturally
to be expected here, immediately after
the definitions of these words, than a
distinction between *libido* and *indigentia*,
and if Cic. really meant to note that
indigentia has an ordinary use in which it
is not subordinate to *libido* he has taken
a very obscure way of expressing his
meaning.
   rerum ipsarum sit: *ut* must naturally
be carried on to this clause. *est* and *sit*
are often confused in MSS, cf. i 17, 41 n.
on ' est.' For the repetition of *sit* cf. i

honores, indigentia rerum ipsarum sit, ut honorum, ut pecuniae.
22. omnium autem perturbationum fontem esse dicunt intemperantiam, quae est a tota mente et a recta ratione defectio,
20 sic auersa a praescriptione rationis ut nullo modo adpetitiones
animi nec regi nec contineri queant. quemadmodum igitur
temperantia sedat adpetitiones et efficit ut eae rectae rationi
pareant, conseruatque considerata iudicia mentis, sic huic inimica
intemperantia omnem animi statum inflammat, conturbat, incitat,
25 itaque et aegritudines et metus et reliquae perturbationes omnes
gignuntur ex ea.

X. **23.** Quemadmodum, cum sanguis corruptus est aut
pituita redundat aut bilis, in corpore morbi aegrotationesque
nascuntur, sic prauarum opinionum conturbatio et ipsarum inter
se repugnantia sanitate spoliat animum morbisque perturbat.

---

17. indigentia R 7 L 2 W 1 D C ed. H.   Jndigentia E 2 *at* Jnd *multa in
litura et al. atr. script.*   diligentia V *marg.* indigentia *atr. uiridi.*   diligentia
R 1 17 P 1 4 G B 1–3 K 1 2 S E 13 L 3–6 W 2 M 2 Π J O 1–3 7 8.
diligentiam R 6. ‖ ipsarum est R V G *plerique.*   ipsarum sit *corr. P. Manutius.*
  § **22,** 18. perturbationum fomitem J.   19. mente et a recta B 3 W 1 M 2
J O 2 7.   mente a recta R 1 17 V P 1 4 G B 1 2 K 1 S E 1 2 W 2
M 1 D C O 1 3 8.   et *al. atr. superscr.* habet Π.   mente ac recta R 7.
mente etiam recta R 6.   20. aperte scriptione V. ‖ adpetitiones R V G E.
appetitiones B S.   apetitiones K.   21. animi nec regi nec R 1 2 10 16 G.
    c
animi regi ne V *atr. uiridi superscr.*   22. adpetitiones R G K.   appetitiones
V B.   adpeticiones E. ‖ efficit R V G B K. ‖ ut eae V G M 2.
ut ee R 2 10 S.   ut aeae R 1.   utae ae K 1.   ut rectae eae O 2.
ut ea B 2.   ut hee D Π O 8.   ut he E 2 *at litt. post* e *eras.*   ut he B 3 W 2
M 1 J O 1 7.   ut he B 1 W 1 O 3.   ut hec E 1.   ut esse R 16. ‖
      ae per
recte V B 3 O 1 7.   25. reliq; conturbationes G *ead. man. superscr.*
26. ex aea G.

X. § **23,** 4. morbisque R V G S.   morbique E *al. atr. superscr.*

25, 60 'quae sit illa uis et unde sit'
where Bai. quotes reff. from Wesenberg.
  § **22. intemperantiam** : see Zeller,
Stoics, etc., c. x p. 232.
  a tota mente : the words *a recta ratione*
are redundant and somewhat awkward
with *a praescriptione rationis* following,
and the fact that *et* after *mente* is absent
from all the best MSS lends great support
to the theory that they are a gloss on *a
tota mente.*
  considerata iudicia mentis as opposed
to the *inbecilla adsensio* upon which the
irrational emotions rest, cf. 7, 15.
  X. § **23. quemadmodum, cum** ... : the
parallel between the state of the body
and that of the soul as regards health and
disease was worked out in great detail

by the Stoics and especially by Chrysippus. Cf. Cicero's statement below;
Diog. L. vii 115; Stob. Ecl. Eth. ii 93 W.;
Galen, de Plac. Hipp. et Plat. v p. 432 foll.;
Sen. Epp. 75, 11; Zeller, *Stoics, etc.*
c. x p. 235 n. 2. [Cf. also Hartlich,
Leipziger Studien XI 2 p. 330.]
  pituita : the phlegmatic humour, φλέγ
μα; cf. Galen περὶ διαφ. πυρ. ii 6 (vii
p. 348 ed. Kühn) ὅστις ἂν ἐν τῷ σώματι
χυμὸς ὑγρὸς ᾖ καὶ ψυχρὸς ἡμεῖς μὲν τοῦτον
ὀνομάζομεν φλέγμα, σὺ δ' εἰ βούλει κάλει
σκινδαψόν; de Plac. Hipp. et Plat. viii
pp. 686 ff. ed. Müller; Hippocrates περὶ
φύσιος ἀνθρ. 116 (ii p. 357 ed. Kühn).
  morbi aegrotationesque : for the distinction between these see 13, 28.

5 ex perturbationibus autem primum morbi conficiuntur, quae
uocant illi νοσήματα, eaque quae sunt eis morbis contraria, quae
habent ad res certas uitiosam offensionem atque fastidium,
deinde aegrotationes, quae appellantur a Stoicis ἀρρωστήματα,
hisque item oppositae contrariae offensiones. hoc loco nimium
10 operae consumitur a Stoicis, maxime a Chrysippo, dum morbis
corporum comparatur morborum animi similitudo. qua oratione
praetermissa minime necessaria, ea quae rem continent pertrac-
temus. 24. intellegatur igitur perturbationem iactantibus se
opinionibus inconstanter et turbide in motu esse semper; cum
15 autem hic feruor concitatioque animi inueterauit et tamquam

6. nosemata G.   nōsemāta V.   ‖   eis morbis R V P G   B 1-3   K 1   E 2
M 1 2   C Π   O 2.   his morbis W 1.   7. uitiosam offensionem R 6   M 1 2
C O 3 7 8.   uiciosam offensionem R 17   B 3   D.   uitiosā offensionē B
at lineis al. atr. supra duct.   uiciosā offensionē Π.   uitiosa offensione R G

B 2 K.   uitiosa offensione V *atr. uiridi superscr.*   uiciosa offensione E 2.
uitiosas offensiones R 7   W 2.   uiciosas offensiones W 1.   officiosas offensiones

O 1 2.   9. hisque item R V   B 2   K   E 2   O 1 3.   hisque idem B S.

hisque idem G *at* d *in* t *alt. man. mut.*   hisque idem E 1.   hisq item P
al. atr. superscr.   hiisque item D.   his item B 3   W 1 2   J.   hiis item O 8.

hisque irem O 7.   isque item O 2.   ‖   appositae G *alt. man. superscr.*
10. maxime R V P B K.   maximae G a *ante* e *expunx. alt. man.* ‖ a chrysippo R.

a crysippo G.   acrisippo E.   11. qua oratione R G.   quaratione V
atr. ant. superscr.   12. minime R V B.   minimae G a *expunx. alt. man.*
§ 24, 13. intellegatur R V G B K.   intelligatur S E.   14. in motu W 1
M 1 2   D   O 1 3 7 8.   inmotu S *litt. post* u *eras.*   ī motu W 2 s *post* u *eras.*

inmotus B 1.   immotus V.   immotus R G.   immotos K 1 *atr. nigriore*

superscr.   immotu E 1.   ī mot9 E 2.   15. inueterauerit R V G   B 1-3   K 1
E 1 2   W 2   M 1 2   C Π J   O 1 3 7 8.   inuet'au'it S D.   inueterauerint
W 1   O 2.   inueterauit *corr. Seyffertus.*

quae: for the attraction of the gender
of the relative cf i 1, 1 n.
νοσήματα: cf. Galen, de Plac. Hipp.
et Plat. v p. 439 ἐναργῶς γάρ...ὁ Χρύσιππος
ἀναλογίαν τινὰ βούλεται σώζεσθαι τῶν ἐν
τῇ ψυχῇ τοῖς κατὰ τὸ σῶμα καὶ παθῶν
πρὸς πάθη καὶ ἀρρωστημάτων πρὸς ἀρρωστήματα καὶ νοσημάτων πρὸς νοσήματα.. καὶ
γὰρ τοὔνομα καὶ τὸν λόγον αὐτῶν βούλεται
εἶναι τὸν αὐτόν, εἴ γε δὴ συνώνυμά φησιν
ὑπάρχειν αὐτά.
uitiosam offensionem, 'diseased aversion,' as opposed to the εὔλογος ἔκκλισις
of Diog. L. vii 116.
aegrotationes...ἀρρωστήματα, chronic
ailments of the mind, due to weakness of
the will, which cannot resist the attraction of unworthy objects.
comparatur...similitudo = 'adcommo-

datur morborum animi similitudo,' cf. iii
31, 74 n. on 'terminabit modum.'
oratione, 'a speech on this point,'
ironically referring to 'operae nimium
consumitur' above: *qua=de eo habita*.
§ 24. **perturbationem...in motu esse
semper**. Dav. who thought this statement too obvious to be worth making
proposed to read *perturbationum...in
animo motus e.s.*: or (in ed. 2) to omit
perturbationem and read *inconstantes et
turbidos in animo motus esse semper*.
Wopkens, *op. cit.* p. 124, defends the
reading in the text and he is followed by
all recent edd.
inueterauit...insedit. Sff.'s conjecture
for the reading of the MSS *inueterauerit...
insederit.* Küh. who keeps the MSS reading here changes *exsistit* of the MSS below

in uenis medullisque insedit, tum exsistit et morbus et aegrotatio et offensiones eae quae sunt iis morbis aegrotationibusque
contrariae.

XI.	Haec, quae dico, cogitatione inter se differunt, re quidem
copulata sunt, eaque oriuntur ex libidine et ex laetitia. nam
cum est concupita pecunia nec adhibita continuo ratio quasi
quaedam Socratica medicina, quae sanaret eam cupiditatem,
5 permanat in uenas et inhaeret in uisceribus illud malum, exsistit-
que morbus et aegrotatio, quae auelli inueterata non possunt,
eique morbo nomen est a u a r i t i a; **25** similiterque ceteri morbi,

16. insederit R V G   B 1–3   K 1   E 1 2   W 2   M 1 2   Π J   O 1 3 7 8.
insed'it P S D C.   insedit R 10.   insederint W 1   O 2.   insedit
corr. Seyffertus.   ‖   existit R 1 6 7   V   P 1 4   B 1–3   K S   E 1 2   W 1 2   M 1 2
D C Π J   O 1–3 7 8.   exsistit G.   existat R 17.   17. eae quae G.
⊦   ɪ
eae quę V K.   ęiquę B *al. atr. superscr.*   eiquę E 1 *al. atr. superscr.*
hęq; W 1.   he q̄ W 2.   hę quae O 3.   hee que O 8.   he que O 17. ‖
eis morbis R V G   B 1–3   K S   E 1 2   W 1 2   M 1 2   D C Π J   O 1 3 7 8.
                                                                                      q̣
XI.   2. eaque B 1 3   M 1   O 1.   eaquę E 1 *al. atr. superscr.*   eaquę V.
ea quae R G   M 2   O 2.   eaq, W 1 D.   ea q3 O 7 8. ‖ libidine R V P B K.
            dī
libine G *alt. man. superscr.*   ‖   ex laetitia R V P G   B 1–3   K   E 1   W 2   M 2
D J   O 1 3 7.   laetitia (ex *omisso*) S   E 2   W 1   M 1   Π   O 2 8.   4. quae
sanaret R V P G   B 1–3   K S   E 2   W 1 2   M 1 2   D C Π J   O 1–3 7 8 *om.* E 1.
5. existitque R 6   B 1   W 2.   existit qui R V E.   exsistit qui G K.
                                                                                      u
pro que *habent* qui B 2   Π D C   O 3 7.   q M 2.   q, O 8.

to *exsistet.* Confusion between -*it* (indic.)
and -*īt* (subj. = -*erit*) is, as Sff. points out,
very common in MSS. For the construc-
tion cf. ii 24, 58 n. on 'aspeximus' and
for the thought Amm. Marc. xxvii 7, 4
'hanc (sc. iram) enim ulcus esse animi
diuturnum interdumque perpetuum pru-
dentes definiunt.'
   uenis medullisque: for the metaphor
cf. v 9, 27, Cat. i 13, 31 'periculum...
residebit et erit inclusum penitus in uenis
atque in uisceribus rei publicae.' Lucan
ix 741, Sil. Ital. i 59.
   XI.   **Haec**: sc. *morbi et aegrotationes.*
   cogitatione: 'though theoretically distinct are yet in reality inseparable': for
the contrast implied in *quidem* cf. i 41,
99 n.
   quae sanaret = *quae, si adhiberetur,*
sanaret: the fact that the condition is
unreal is implied in the preceding negative. Bentl. conjectured *sanet* and he is
followed by Dav. Bouh. Or. (ed. 1),
F.A.W. and Sff. who believe 'imperfecto
sanaret contra temporum rationem misere
peccatum esse.' The passage in v 13, 39

quoted by Küh. is not parallel: see n.
there.
   permanat in uenas like a poison: cf.
Cluent. 62, 173 'celerius potuit [sc.
uenenum] comestum quam epotum in uenas
atque in omnis partis corporis permanare';
Epist. Vindiciani ap. Marcell. de medi-
camentis § 6 (p. 23 ed. Helmr.) 'cum
ergo peruenerit ad ea loca uenarum, in
quae pocula hausta descendunt'; Lucan
ix 614 'noxia serpentum est admixto
sanguine pestis.'
   auelli: Wopkens (*op. cit.* p. 125) conj.
euelli comparing 26, 57 'sunt enim omnia
ista ex errorum orta radicibus, quae
euellenda et extrahenda penitus...sunt.'
Hand in his note to Wopkens, however,
points out by a comparison of Fam. v
12, 5 'qui tum denique sibi auelli iubet
spiculum' with Fin. ii 30, 97 'euelli
iussit eam, qua erat transfixus, hastam,'
that both *auelli* and *euelli* can be used in
this connection.
   morbo: sing. because for practical purposes *morbus* and *aegrotatio* are not two
affections but one.

H.

ut gloriae cupiditas, ut mulierositas, ut ita appellem eam
quae Graece φιλογυνία dicitur, ceterique similiter morbi aegro-
10 tationesque nascuntur. quae autem sunt his contraria, ea nasci
putantur a metu, ut odium mulierum, quale in μισογύνῳ Atili
est, ut in hominum uniuersum genus, quod accepimus de
Timone qui μισάνθρωπος appellatur, ut inhospitalitas est,

§ 25, 8. eam quae M 1   D C   O 2 3 8.   eā quae B E *linea al. atr. supraduct.*
ea quae R V P G   B 2   K S   E 2   W 2   J   O 1.   eaq3 B 3.   eaq, M 2.
9. ΦΙΛΟΓΥΝΙΔ R V.   ΦΙΛΟΓΥnia G.   φιλογυγιαν W 1.   φυλογυνια B 1.
                                                                                                                                v
ΦΙΛΟΤΫnia B 2.   Φυλοτιμα E 1.   11. molierum R *eod. atr.* ‖ in μισογυνια
W 1.   in missogyno G.   in missogino K 2   C.   in missogine B 3   E 3   M 2.
in missoginio O 3.   in missogynia O 1.   inmisso guno V.   inmisso gÿno R 1.
inmisso gino D.   inmisso gino S o *in a mut.*   in misso gyno P 4.   in misso
gino B 1   O 8.   imisso gyno R 17.   imisso gino W 2   J.   inmissogino P 1.
                                                                                                                                v̄
inmissogφno E 1.   inmissio gino B 2.   immisso gÿNo K 1 *eod. atr.*   imissum
gyno E 2   II.   innuscagyno O 7.   gyno M 1 *cett. om.* ‖ atili R 1 7 17   V   P 4
                                                                                                                                a
G B 12 K 12 S E 12 L 5 W 2 Π O 8.   a tili C.   atili P 1
al. atr. superscr. marg. atiliē.   a tili E 3.   atilia B 3 L 3.   atilia M 2 *marg.*
at hipolito.   atiliē D.   atilie M 1.   atiliem O 7.   atile L 2 *om.* L 4 6
W 1   O 1.   13. qui μισαθρωποσ W 1.   quimisanepωττος V *litt. post* c *eras.*
quimisanepωιτοcα R. quimis ΔΝΕΡωΠωεα quę P (*sic*).   qui misane ΡΩΙΤΟCa
G.   qui misaNepωιτοcA K 1.   qui misaNPωΙΤΟCΔ B 1.   quimisa
NθΡΟΙΤωcΔ E 1.   qui misanepaitca W 2.   qui msane paitoca K 2. ‖
appellatur W 1   O 17.   appellaptur S.   appellantur R 1 17   V   P 14   G
B 1-3 K 12 E 12 W 2 M 12 D C Π J O 2 38.

ceterique similiter morbi: Bentl.
conj. *ceteri, inquam, similiter morbi,*
offended by the carelessness of the repetition after *similiterque ceteri morbi* above:
but this is not the only sign of carelessness and hurry in the passage.

in μισογύνῳ Atili: this play of Atilius
was perhaps an imitation of Menander:
it is not referred to elsewhere; Ribbeck,
Scaen. Rom. Poes. II² 32. Cic. calls
Atilius in Att. xiv 20, 3 *poeta durissimus*
and quotes in Fin. i 2, 5 the epithet of
ferreus scriptor applied to him by
Licinius. Volcacius Sedigitus in his 'liber
de poetis' quoted by Aul. Gell. xv 24
placed him fifth on his list of comic
poets, immediately preceding Terence.
Bentl., however, asserting that Cic., who
seems to have thought little of him,
would have preferred to quote the Gk
original, expunges his name here and
reads *quale μισογόνου Hippolyti est.* He
finds further confirmation of his view in
the fact that in the résumé at the end of
§ 27 Hippolytus' name is introduced with
Timon's in such a way as to suggest that
it has occurred before.

in hominum uniuersum genus: Lamb.
with an excessive zeal for grammatical
symmetry reads *hominum uniuersi generis*

to correspond with *odium mulierum*
above: but see 7, 16 n. on 'sub metum.'

Timone: Timon, son of Echecratides
(Lucian, Tim. 50) lived about the time
of the Peloponnesian war (Plut. Ant. 70).
He is mentioned by Aristophanes (e.g.
Av. 1549, Lysistr. 808) and other comic
poets who represent him as δυσμενὴς καὶ
μισάνθρωπος, ἐκκλίνων δὲ καὶ διωθούμενος
ἅπασαν ἔντευξιν (Plut. *l.c.*). An epitaph
on him, quoted by Plutarch, was attributed to Callimachus: Τίμων μισάνθρωπος
ἐνοικέω. ἀλλὰ πάρελθε | οἰμώξειν εἶπας
πολλὰ πάρελθε μόνον.

qui μισάνθρωπος appellatur: the
balance of MSS evidence seems in favour
of the singular here; Tr. Kühn. who
read μισάνθρωποι *appellantur* ('men like
him being called misanthropes') defend
the transition from pl. to sing. by passages
like Fin. v 31, 94 'hic si Peripateticus
fuisset, permansisset, credo, in sententia,
qui dolorem malum dicunt esse': but
neither this passage nor that quoted by
Madv. *ad. loc.* 'L. Cantilius, scriba
pontificius, quos nunc minores pontifices
appellant' Liv. xxii 57, 3 is precisely
parallel, as in both cases a word (*Peripateticus, scriba*) precedes which can be
predicated of a number of persons,

quae omnes aegrotationes animi ex quodam metu nascuntur
15 earum rerum quas fugiunt et oderunt. **26.** definiunt autem
animi a e g r o t a t i o n e m opinationem uehementem de re non
expetenda, tamquam ualde expetenda sit, inhaerentem et penitus
insitam. quod autem nascitur ex offensione, ita definiunt: opinionem uehementem de re non fugienda inhaerentem et penitus
20 insitam tamquam fugienda; haec autem opinatio est iudicatio se
scire quod nesciat. aegrotationi autem talia quaedam subiecta
sunt: a u a r i t i a, a m b i t i o, m u l i e r o s i t a s, p e r v i c a c i a, l i g u r-
r i t i o, u i n u l e n t i a, c u p p e d i a, et si qua similia. est autem
a u a r i t i a opinatio uehemens de pecunia, quasi ualde expetenda
25 sit, inhaerens et penitus insita, similisque est eiusdem generis definitio reliquarum. **27.** offensionum autem definitiones sunt eius
modi, ut i n h o s p i t a l i t a s sit opinio uehemens ualde fugiendum
esse hospitem, eaque inhaerens et penitus insita, similiterque
definitur et m u l i e r u m o d i u m, ut Hippolyti, et, ut Timonis,
30 g e n e r i s h u m a n i.

§ **26,** 20. iudicatio R V G B 1 2 E 1 O 2 Gr.   iuditio K 1   iudicare R 17
P 1 4 B 3 S E 2 W 1 2 M 1 2 D C Π J O 1 3 7 8 ed. H.   iudi^{re} K 2
eod. atr. et ead. manu.   23. cuppedia R V B 1 2 K E.   cup⏝edia S
litt. post p *eras.*   cu pedia G p *eras.*
§ **27,** 29. hippolyti R K.   hyppolyti B 2.   hippoliti B 3 G.   hyppoliti S
eod. atr.   hyppoliti V B 1 E 1 W 1.

whereas here the only antecedent is the
proper name ; unless one should assume
(for which there seems no evidence) a
use of the word *Timon* in Latin such as
one finds in Arist. Av. *l.c.* III. νὴ τὸν Δι'
ἀεὶ δῆτα θεομισὴς ἔφυς. ΠΡ. Τίμων καθαρός
'a Timon,' pure and simple.
aegrotationes carelessly put for *offensiones.*
§ **26. definiunt...insitam.** This is the
definition not of *aegrotatio* (ἀρρώστημα)
but of *morbus* (νόσημα): cf. Diog. L.
vii 115 τὸ γὰρ ἀρρώστημά ἐστι νόσημα μετ'
ἀσθενείας, τὸ δὲ νόσημα οἴησις σφόδρα
δοκοῦντος αἱρετοῦ : Stob. Ecl. ii 93, 6 W.
νόσημα δ' εἶναι δόξαν ἐπιθυμίας ἐρρυηκυῖαν
εἰς ἕξιν καὶ ἐνεσκιρωμένην, καθ' ἣν ὑπολαμβά-
νουσι τὰ μὴ αἱρετὰ σφόδρα αἱρετὰ εἶναι...τὰ
δὲ νοσήματα μετ' ἀσθενείας συμβαίνοντα
ἀρρωστήματα καλεῖσθαι. Sen. Epp. 75, 11
'morbus est iudicium in prauo pertinax,
tamquam ualde expetenda sint, quae
leuiter expetenda sunt.' Cicero has forgotten for the moment the ἀσθένεια which
is the distinguishing mark of *aegrotatio.*
quod...offensione: another instance of
careless expression ; the definition which
follows is that of *offensio* itself, not of the

result of it, cf. Stob. *l.c.* εἶναι δέ τινα καὶ
ἐναντία τούτοις τοῖς νοσήμασι κατὰ προσ-
κοπὴν γιγνόμενα, οἷον μισογυνίαν, μισ-
οινίαν, μισανθρωπίαν.
opinatio: cf. 7, 15 n.
iudicatio: 'an act of judgment,' a word
coined by Cicero, like *opinatio.*
se: as if *iudicantis* not *iudicatio* had
preceded: see Madvig's note to Fin. i 20, 67.
auaritia ... uinulentia: φιλοχρηματία,
φιλοτιμία, λαγνεία, προσπάθεια, γαστρι-
μαργία, οἰνοφλυγία,—all in the list given
by Andronicus περὶ παθῶν 4 (p. 16
Kreutter) of the ἐπιθυμίας εἴδη.
cuppedia: another coinage of Cicero's :
perh., as Dav. suggests, a transl. of
φιλοψία.
§ **27. offensionum.** The *offensiones*
come under the definition of φόβος: cf.
Stob. Ecl. ii 90, 7 W. φόβον δ' εἶναι
ἔκκλισιν ἀπειθῆ λόγῳ, αἴτιον δ' αὐτοῦ τὸ
δοξάζειν κακὸν ἐπιφέρεσθαι, τῆς δόξης τὸ
κινητικὸν πρόσφατον ἐχούσης τοῦ ὄντως
αὐτὸ φευκτὸν εἶναι : an *offensio* is a φόβος
inseparably attached in the mind to a
certain class of objects.
Hippolyti: the son of Theseus, who fell
a victim to the wrath of Aphrodite for his

XII.   Atque ut ad ualetudinis similitudinem ueniamus eaque
conlatione utamur aliquando, sed parcius quam solent Stoici :
ut sunt alii ad alios morbos procliuiores (itaque dicimus grauedinosos quosdam, quosdam torminosos, non quia iam sint, sed
5 quia saepe), sic alii ad metum, alii ad aliam perturbationem; ex
quo in aliis anxietas, unde anxii, in aliis iracundia dicitur,
quae ab ira differt, estque aliud iracundum esse, aliud iratum, ut
differt anxietas ab angore; neque enim omnes anxii qui anguntur aliquando, nec, qui anxii, semper anguntur, ut inter

XII. 1. ualetudinis R 1 2 V G B 3 K M 2. ualitudinis P B 1 S E M 1. ||
ueniamus L 4 M 1 D C O 8.   ueniā   E 1 al. atr. superscr.   ueniam : R 6
W 1 M 2.   ueniam· R 1 2 16 B 3 E 2 3.   ueniam. O 3.   ueīam/ W 2.
ueniam V G K L 2 3 5 6 Π O 1 2 7.   ueniā R 7 10 17 P 1 4 B 1 2 K 2 S J.
2. conlatione R G B K E.   collatione P B 2 3 S C Π J O 2.   consolatione V.
3. dicimus R V G B 2 K 1 S W 1 2 O 1 2.   diximus B 1 E 1.   dominis J. ||
grauedinosos W 1.   grauidinosos R V G B 1-3 S E W 2 M 1 2 C J O 8.
                                                                      quosdam
grauidnosos K.   grandissonos O 2.   4. quosdam   Π al. atr. superscr.
quosdam (semel tantum) R 1 6 7 17 V P 1 4 G B 1-3 K 1 2 S E 1-3 W 2
M 1 2 D C J O 1-3 7 8.   quosdam alios W 1. || torminosos V P G B 2 W 1
D O 3 8.   torminosos B 1 o in e mut.   terminosos R 1 B 3 K 1 E 3 L 6
M 1 Π O 1 2.   t'minosos E 2 C.   t'mīosos K 2.   terminiosos M 2.
tminos W 3.   om. O 7.   5. saepe sint R 1 67 10 16 17   V P 1 4 G B 1-3
K 1 marg.   K 2 S E 1-3 L 2-6 M 1 2 M 1 2 D C Π J O 1-3 7 8 ed. H.
saepe sic Gr.   9. aliquando nec R 7 B 3 K 2 E 2 M 1 2 D C Π O 1-3 7.
aliquando neque R 6.   aliquando nec B 1 (sic) n fortasse ex h mut.   aliquando
        n
hec E 1.   aliquando hec B 2.   aliquando haec R V G K̦.   aliquando h' J.
aliquando hii R 17.   aliquando W 1 nec om.   nec W 2 aliquando om.

persistent neglect of her rites; ἀναίνεται δὲ
λέκτρα, κοὐ ψαύει γάμων Eur. Hipp. 14.
Aphrodite inspired his stepmother Phaedra
with a passion for him; as he was deaf to
all her solicitations she denounced him
to his father Theseus who prayed for
vengeance to Poseidon ; as Hippolytus
drove along the shore his horses took
fright at a bull sent by Poseidon and
running off tore him to pieces along the
ground.
  XII. atque marking a transition as in
13, 30, iii 13, 28.
  parcius...Stoici : cf. 10, 23 'hoc loco
nimium operae consumitur a Stoicis.'
  procliuiores : cf. Diog. L. vii 115 καὶ
ὡς ἐπὶ τοῦ σώματος εὐεμπτωσίαι τινὲς
λέγονται οἷον κατάρρους καὶ διάρροια, οὕτω
κἀπὶ τῆς ψυχῆς εἰσὶν εὐκαταφορίαι οἷον
φθονερία, ἐλεημοσύνη, ἔριδες καὶ τὰ παρα-
πλήσια. Cf. Stob. Ecl. ii 93, 1.
  grauedinosos : καταρρώδεις ' subject to
catarrh' (κατάρρους, destillatio).
  quosdam, quosdam : the second quosdam is omitted by nearly all MSS and
Dav. defends their reading by ref. to such
passages as Liv. iii 37, 8 'et iam ne tergo

quidem abstinebatur : uirgis caedi, alii
securi subici' Curt. vii 4, 11 ; but, as Kl.
points out, the parallels are not to the
point; since words like alii, interdum,
etc. are repeated where (as here) par est
orationis membrorum ratio, whereas they
are used once only when to the general
statement is added a clause expressing
another fact.
  torminosos : δυσεντερικούς 'subject to
dysentery' Celsus, de medic. iv 22.
  saepe : sc. sint; the subj. is due to the
orat. obl. ; the sint which follows saepe
in so many MSS is due to confusion with sic.
  dicitur : Dav. conjectured efficitur ;
but as Wopkens (op. cit., p. 125) points
out dicitur is due to the βραχυλογία so
frequent in Cic. He compares N.D. ii
20, 51 'quarum ex disparibus motionibus
magnum annum mathematici nominauerunt; i.e. 'q. e. d. m. conficitur quem
mathematici magnum annum nominauerunt'; so here iracundia dicitur is
equivalent to motus animi efficitur quae
iracundia dicitur.
  quae ab ira differt : ira (ὀργή) is a
πάθος whereas iracundia (ὀργιλότης) is

10 ebrietatem et ebriositatem interest, aliudque est amatorem esse, aliud amantem. atque haec aliorum ad alios morbos procliuitas late patet; nam pertinet ad omnes perturbationes; in multis etiam uitiis apparet, **28** sed nomen res non habet. ergo et inuidi et maliuoli [et liuidi] et timidi et misericordes, quia procliuius 15 ad eas perturbationes, non quia semper, feruntur. haec igitur procliuitas ad suum quodque genus a similitudine corporis aegrotatio dicatur, dum ea intellegatur ad aegrotandum procliuitas. sed haec in bonis rebus, quod alii ad alia bona sunt

---

10. et ebriositatem interest R 6 B 3 L 6 M 2 D C O 1 S *marg.* W 2 *marg.* et ebrium interest M 1.　　interest et ebriositatem Π E 2.　　interest et ebriosum W 1.　　*uerba* et ebriositatem *omittunt* R 1 17 V P 1 4 G B 1 2 K 1 2 E 1 3 L 2-5 J O 2 3 7 8 ed. H.　　12. omnes R V G.　　oms B 2.　　13. apparet R V G B K S.

§ **28.** ergo et inuidi et maliuoli R V G B 2 W 1 O 2 7.　　ergo et maliuoli et inuidi K 2 O 1.　　ergo inuidi et maliuoli P B 3 S E M 2 Π O 3 8. ergo dicuntur inuidi et maliuoli D C.　　ergo maliuoli et inuidi J.　　14. et liuidi R V G B 1-3 K 1 2 S E 1 2 W 1 2 M 1 2 D C Π J O 1-3 7 8 E 3 *al. atr. superscr.*　　15. perturbationes non R 1 7 17 V P 1 4 G B 1 2 K 1 2 S E 1 2 L 2-5 D C J O 1-3 7 8.　　perturbationes non W 2 *marg.* ſt¹ *al. atr. inculc.*
perturbationes non Π *al. atr. superscr.*　　perturbationes sunt non R 6 B 3 L 6 W 1 M 1 2. ‖ feruntur R 1 17 V P G B 1 2 K 1 2 E W 1 2 M 1 D C J O 1-3 7 8.　ₚ feruntur S.　　ferantur R 6 7 B 3 M 2.　　perferuntur E 2 Π. 17. dicitur R 1 6 16 G B 1 2 K 1 S L 2-4 W 2 M 1 2 C Π J O 1-3 7 8. dr̄ R 7 10 17 V P 1 4 B 3 K 2 E 1-3 L 5 6 W 1 D.　　dicatur *corr. Bentleius.* ‖ intellegatur R V G B K.　　intelligatur S E M 1.

---

reckoned as a εὐεμπτωσία, a constant predisposition to *ira*.

estque aliud…iratum: cf. Sen. de Ira i 4 'quid esset ira satis explicitum est. quo distet ab iracundia adparet: quo ebrius ab ebrioso et timens a timido. iratus potest non esse iracundus; iracundus potest aliquando iratus non esse.'

amatorem: almost equivalent to *scortatorem*: cf. Donat. ad Ter. Andr. iv 3, 3 'amicus animi est, amator corporis' and Isid. Hispal. Orig. x *ad init.* (p. 1067 Gothofred.) 'amicus…quasi animi custos …amator turpitudinis quia amore torquentur libidinis.'

§ **28**. The words *et liuidi* found in the MSS after *maliuoli* are probably due to a mistake on the part of the copyist who 'quom pro *ettimidi* praue *etliuidi* scripsisset, ipse statim correxit' (Küh.). Heine (*Pos. Progr.* p. 11) quotes with approval Wesenberg's dictum 'Ciceronem *liuendi* uerbum et quae inde deriuata sunt de inuidia nunquam usurpare.'

procliuius. Sff.'s correction for *procliues* of the MSS, which can hardly be defended, either by understanding *sunt*, which is very doubtful Ciceronian Latin (*sunt* after *perturbationes* in many MSS is evidently a correction), or by taking *procliues* with *feruntur* on the analogy of phrases like *praeceps ferri* which, as Sff. points out, are not really parallel. Bent. conjectured *procliue*.

suum quodque genus, i.e. *procliuitas cuiusque ad suum genus*: for this attraction of *quisque* to the case and gender of *suus* cf. Liu. xxv 17, 5 'cum tripudiis Hispanorum motibusque armorum et corporum suae cuique genti'adsuetis,' Cic. N.D. iii 34, 84 'edixisse ut quod quisque ex sacris haberet id ante diem certam in suum quidque fanum referret.' Fin. v. 17, 46 'sed quia cuiusque partis naturae et in corpore et in animo sua quaeque uis sit' with Madv.'s note.

dicatur. Bent.'s correction accepted by all edd. for the MSS *dicitur*; the subj. is required here, as is shown by *nominetur* below.

aptiores, facilitas nominetur, in malis procliuitas, ut sig-
20 nificet lapsionem, in neutris habeat superius nomen.

XIII. Quo modo autem in corpore est morbus, est aegrotatio, est uitium, sic in animo. morbum appellant totius
corporis corruptionem, aegrotationem morbum cum inbecillitate, uitium, **29** cum partes corporis inter se dissident, ex quo
5 prauitas membrorum, distortio, deformitas. itaque illa duo, morbus et aegrotatio, ex totius ualetudinis corporis conquassatione
et perturbatione gignuntur, uitium autem integra ualetudine
ipsum ex se cernitur. sed in animo tantum modo cogitatione
possumus morbum ab aegrotatione seiungere; uitiositas au-
10 tem est habitus aut adfectio in tota uita inconstans et a se ipsa
dissentiens. ita fit, ut in altera corruptione opinionum morbus
efficiatur et aegrotatio, in altera inconstantia et repugnantia.

XIII. 2. est uitium R 16 Gr.　　　et uitium R 1 6 7 10 17　V　P 1 4　G
B 1–3　K 1 2　S　E 1–3　L 2–6　W 1 2　M 1 2　D C Π J　O 1–3 7 8 ed. H.
3. imbecillitate R　B 1　K S.　　imbecilitate G.　　inbecillitate V　B 2　E.
　　　　　　　　　　　　　　　l'　i
§ **29**, 8. sed in animo B *al. atr. superscr.*　　　10. adfectio R V G K.
affectio B S.

procliuitas: εὐκαταφορία or εὐεμπτωσία,
cf. Diog. L. vii 115 quoted in 12, 27 n.
lapsionem: a coinage of Cicero's.
neutris, i.e. τοῖς ἀδιαφόροις.
superius nomen, i.e. *aegrotatio*, not
facilitas as some edd. take it. Cic. wishes
to keep a distinctive word *facilitas* to
denote the propensity to virtue, and to
employ *lapsio* (εὐεμπτωσία) only of a
tendency to what is distinctly vicious: as
a *procliuitas* towards *res indifferentes*
was reprehensible though the objects
might be in themselves indifferent he
falls back upon the word *aegrotatio* to
express it.
XIII. § **29**. **morbus...aegrotatio**: cf.
the definitions of Diog. L. and Stob.
quoted in 11, 26 n.
uitium: the distinction drawn by Cic.
between *morbus* and *uitium* involves a
narrower meaning of *uitium* than the
definitions of the jurists quoted by Aulus
Gellius iv 2. Labeo there defines *morbus*
as *habitus cuiusque corporis contra
naturam qui usum eius facit deteriorem*,
and proceeds *balbus autem et atypus
uitiosi magis quam morbosi sunt, et equus
mordax aut calcitro uitiosus non morbosus
est*. In the *libri ueterum iurisperitorum*
the distinction was laid down that
uitium was *perpetuum* whereas *morbus
eum accessu decessuque sit*.

ualetudinis corporis: for the double
genitive cf. ii 15, 35 n.
uitiositas, a translation of κακία in the
wider meaning in which it was used
(e.g.) by Posidonius (Diog. L. vii 91)
as the opposite of ἀρετή: to keep the
parallelism which he has set out to estab-
lish between the *uitia corporis* and the
uitia animi Cic. should have used *uitium*
as the Stoics did κακία in the narrower
meaning which we find (e.g.) in Diog. L.
vii 95 ὡσαύτως δὲ καὶ τῶν κακιῶν τὸ μὲν
εἶναι ἀφροσύνην δειλίαν ἀδικίαν καὶ τὰ παρα-
πλήσια. But he wished to insist upon the
essential unity of vice as upon the essential unity of virtue, and, this being so,
the references to bodily disease serve only
to point an interesting contrast, somewhat
at the expense of the lucidity of the argument.
habitus aut adfectio: these two words
correspond to ἕξις and διάθεσις without,
however, preserving the distinction maintained by the Stoics Diog. L. vii 98 ἔτι
τῶν περὶ ψυχὴν ἀγαθῶν τὰ μέν εἰσιν ἕξεις,
τὰ δὲ διαθέσεις...διαθέσεις μὲν αἱ ἀρεταὶ
ἕξεις δὲ τὰ ἐπιτηδεύματα.
paris...dissensiones. Bentley's emendation adopted by Müller, Sff., Hei.,
T.S., Schiche, for the MSS *partes...dis-
sentientes*: those edd. such as Mo. and
Hasper who keep *partes* must, as Küh.

non enim omne uitium paris habet dissensiones, ut eorum qui
non longe a sapientia absunt adfectio est illa quidem discrepans
15 sibi ipsa, dum est insipiens, sed non distorta nec praua. morbi
autem et aegrotationes partes sunt uitiositatis, sed perturbationes
sintne eiusdem partes quaestio est. 30. uitia enim adfectiones
sunt manentes, perturbationes autem mouentes, ut non possint
adfectionum manentium partes esse. atque ut in malis attingit
20 animi naturam corporis similitudo, sic in bonis. sunt enim in
corpore praecipua, ualetudo, uires, pulchritudo, firmitas, uelocitas,
sunt item in animo. ut enim corporis temperatio, cum ea con-
gruunt inter se e quibus constamus, sanitas, sic animi dicitur,
cum eius iudicia opinionesque concordant, eaque animi est uirtus,
25 quam alii ipsam temperantiam dicunt esse, alii obtemperantem

13. non enim omne uitium R V P G B K *plerique*. non enim uitium R 7 E 3.
habet enim omne uicium ed. H. ‖ partis habet dissentientis R P G B 1 2 K 1 2
E 1 2 D C J O 7.   partis habet dissentieN^{is} V *at* N^{is} *eod. atr. in ras. et in*
duarum litt. spatio script.   partes habet dissentientes B 3 S M 1.   partis habet
dissentiens W 2.   paris habet dissensiones *corr. Bentleius*.   16. aegrotationès
K i *in e mut.*   egrotationes B.   egrotationes D.   aegrotationis R G.
egrotationis V.   egrotationis S.
   § 30, 22. sicut enim corporis C ed. H.   sic enim corporis M 1 D.   est enim
corporis R 7 L 2 3 J O 18.   ē. n. corporis W 1.   est enim corporis V *at* est
in marg. ad initium lineae atr. uiridi script.   enim corporis R P 1 4 G B 1 2
K 1 S E 1 2 Π O 7 Gr.   corporis *cett. om.* R 6 17 K 2 E 3 L 4-6 W 2
M 2 O 2 3.   ut enim corporis *corr. Camerarius*.   25. alii ipsam V K 1
E 1 2 W 1 2 ed. H.   aliam ipsam S.   aliam ipsam R P G. ‖ obtemperantem V.
optemperantem R 1 2 P G B.

says, interpret *partes habet dissentientes*
in a pregnant sense as equivalent to
*singulas inter se animi partes habet dis-
sentientes* or, with Küh., insert *omnes*
before *omne*.
   illa quidem: i 3, 6 n.
   § 30. **uitia**, i.e. κακίαι in the narrower
sense as contrasted with κακία (*uitiositas*)
the root principle of evil.
   mouentes, 'transitory': for the intran-
sitive use of *mouere* cf. Finn. ii 10, 31,
Liu. v 25, 6 *praeda quae rerum mouentium
sit*.
   attingit ... similitudo, i.e. *corporis
natura similis est naturae animi*: for the
expression cf. 10, 23 'morbis corporum
comparatur morborum animi similitudo,'
ii Verr. v 36, 94 'ut ei Lampsaceni
periculi similitudo uersaretur ante oculos.'
   praecipua. Cic. preferred *praepositus*
or *praecipuus* to *productus* as a translation of προηγμένος (Finn. iv 26, 72).
Chrysippus and his school classed these
bodily advantages under the head of
ἀδιάφορα κατ' εἶδος προηγμένα: Posidonius καὶ ταῦτά φησι τῶν ἀγαθῶν εἶναι

(Diog. L. vii 103): Cicero's language
here, however, cannot be taken as proving his indebtedness to Posidonius or
even sympathy with his views. He
merely says, as Chrysippus might have
said, that health and strength of body
were *to the body* what *sanitas* and consistency were to the mind. The difference
between Chrysippus and Posidonius
turned on the value to be assigned to
physical qualities *in relation to the mind*.
   ut enim corporis temperatio: Dav.
quotes Stobaeus, Ecl. Eth. p. 168 (ii 7, 5)
ὥσπερ γὰρ τὴν τοῦ σώματος ὑγίειαν εὐκρασίαν εἶναι τῶν ἐν τῷ σώματι θερμῶν καὶ
ψυχρῶν καὶ ξηρῶν καὶ ὑγρῶν οὕτω καὶ τὴν
τῆς ψυχῆς ὑγίειαν εὐκρασίαν εἶναι τῶν ἐν
τῇ ψυχῇ δογμάτων.
   sic animi, sc. *sanitas*.
   ipsam temperantiam, 'nothing more
nor less than self control,' i.e. these
authorities considered that *temperantia*,
usually regarded as one of the four
cardinal virtues, was simply that *sanitas
animi* which was the necessary presup-
position in all virtue.

temperantiae praeceptis, et eam subsequentem nec habentem
ullam speciem suam, sed, siue hoc siue illud sit, in solo esse
sapiente. est autem quaedam animi sanitas quae in insipientem
etiam cadat, cum curatione medicorum conturbatio mentis au-
30 fertur. **31.** et ut corporis est quaedam apta figura membrorum
cum coloris quadam suauitate, eaque dicitur pulchritudo, sic in
animo opinionum iudiciorumque aequabilitas et constantia cum
firmitate quadam et stabilitate uirtutem subsequens aut uirtutis
uim ipsam continens pulchritudo uocatur. itemque uiribus
35 corporis et neruis et efficacitati similes similibus quoque uerbis
animi uires nominantur. uelocitas autem corporis celeritas

28. quę insápientem V *h. e.* i *in* a *ut uid. mut.*   29. cum curatione et
perturbatione R 1 2 10 16 17 V P 14 G B 1 2 K 1 2 S E 1-3 L 2 5 6 W 2
                                                    l' pturbatione
M 2 Π J O 7 8 Gr.   cum curatione et pcuratione D *al. atr. superscr.*
cum curatione et procuratione C.   cum curatione et prouisione M 1.   cum
                                                                 l.
curatione et gubernatione L 4 O 1.   cum curatione W 1 *et in marg. inf.*
      /.   ua   cat
eod. atr. et ptractatione.   cum curatione et pturbatione R 7.   cum curatione
cett. om. R 6 L 3 O 2 3.   cum curatione et tractatione ed. H.   et perturbatione
om. Victorius.   et pertractatione *coni. I. M. Brutus.* ‖ conturbatio R 1 2 10 16 17
V P 4 G B 1 2 K 1 S W 2 M 1 O 1 2 7 8.   perturbatio R 6 7 P 1 E 2
W 1 M 2 D C Π O 3.
    § **31**, 31. eaq; B 1 2 E 1 W 1 2 M 2 D O 1 3 8.   eaque O 7.   ea q3 S
at q3 *in lit.*   ea q3 J.   eaquę R V.   eaq̄ P.   eaquæ K 1.   ea quae G.
35. similes similibus quoque M 1.   similes similibusque R V P G B 1 3 K 1 2
L 2-6 W 1 2 M 2 D C Π J O 1-3 7 8.   sites|q3 siłibo uîs B 2.   similibusque
similes *om.* S E 1 2 3.   similes similibusq3 quoque ed. H.

speciem, 'never appearing independently,' i.e. it was not an independent
virtue but the quality of mind which
underlay all virtue, 'without constituting
any peculiar kind of itself' (Wolf).

est autem quaedam: the 'soundness
of mind' resulting from the harmony of
all its parts belongs only to the *sapiens*;
but a special kind of it, though of a
lower order, may be seen even in one
who is not *sapiens* when, after a fit of
insanity, the faculties are restored to
their normal state by medical treatment:
the health of mind which the *sapiens*
enjoys is as far above the state of mind of
the *insipiens* as sanity in the ordinary use
of the word is above insanity. Sff.,
through failure to follow the connection,
follows Turnebus (*Adu.* vii 17) in changing *sanitas* to *insanitas* and *insipientem*
to *sapientem*.

§ **31. et ut corporis.** Dav. quotes
Stob. Ecl. Eth. p. 168 [ii 63, 1 W.]
ὥσπερ τε τὸ κάλλος τοῦ σώματός ἐστι

συμμετρία τῶν μελῶν καθεστώτων αὐτῷ
πρὸς ἄλληλά τε καὶ πρὸς τὸ ὅλον, οὕτω καὶ
τὸ τῆς ψυχῆς κάλλος ἐστὶ συμμετρία τοῦ
λόγου καὶ τῶν μερῶν αὐτοῦ πρὸς τὸ ὅλον τε
αὐτῆς καὶ πρὸς ἄλληλα : for the addition of
colour to the conception of beauty cf.
Seneca, de Ira ii 1, 2 'post haec omnia,
qui maxime oculos rapit, color ultimus
perfecto iam corpore adfunditur.' Maximus Tyrius xxv 3 p. 300 H. τὴν χρωμάτων
τε καὶ σχημάτων καὶ τῆς ἐν τούτοις ἡδο-
νῆς καὶ ἀηδίας ὁμιλίαν.

uim ipsam, 'the very essence'; there
is the same difference of view in the case
of *pulchritudo animi* as in the case of
sanitas animi (§ 30): some held that
pulchr. animi was a concomitant of
virtue, others that virtue and it were one
and the same thing. Bent.'s change of
ipsam to *ipsa* is unnecessary.

animi multarum rerum: for the double
genitive see ii 15, 35 n. on *functio...
animi...muneris.*

appellatur, quae eadem ingenii etiam laus habetur propter animi multarum rerum breui tempore percursionem.

XIV. Illud animorum corporumque dissimile, quod animi ualentes morbo temptari non possunt, corpora·possunt; et corporum offensiones sine culpa accidere possunt, animorum non item, quorum omnes morbi et perturbationes ex aspernatione rationis 5 eueniunt; itaque in hominibus solum existunt; nam bestiae simile quiddam faciunt, sed in perturbationes non incidunt. 32. inter acutos autem et inter hebetes interest, quod ingeniosi, ut aes Corinthium in aeruginem, sic illi in morbum et incidunt tardius et recreantur ocius, hebetes non item. nec uero in omnem morbum ac

---

38. percursionem R 6 B 3 J D C O 1 8.   percu͜ssionem V *atr. uir.*
S *eod. atr.*   percussionem R 1 7 1 7 G B 1 2 K 2 E 1 2 W 1 2 Π O 3 7.
percursionem M 2.   per͜jussionem K 1 *atr. nigriore.*
    XIV. 2. corpora autem G.   corpora-possunt K 2. ‖ sed corporum R 1 6
V G B 1 2 K 1 S E 2 L 3 4 W 1 M 1 2 Π J O 1 3 8 ed. H.   s͜3 corporum
R 7 10 16 17 P 1 4 B 3 K 2 E 1 3 L 2 5 6 W 2 D O 2.   set corporum C.
et corporum *corr. Seyffertus.*   5. simile quidam R V.   simile quidam G.
    § 32, 7. inter *ante* hebetes *omittunt* R 6 P 1 B 3 W 1 M 1 2 O 1–3. ‖
hebetis R 6 P 1 4 B 1 2.   8. in aerugine G.   inerugine V.

breui tempore: for a temporal ablative qualifying a verbal substantive cf. Liv. xxi 16, 2 *tot uno tempore motibus animi.*
XIV. **animi ualentes…possunt ; et** : the mind of the philosopher which has been strengthened and perfected by virtue is superior to the assaults of evil (cf. iii 5, 11 'eos enim sanos quoniam intellegi necesse est, quorum mens motu quasi morbo perturbata nullo sit'), since evil can attack the soul only from within, but the body is always open to attacks of disease which come from without and from sources not under its control. *et* is Sff.'s correction of the mss *sed*; Madv. and Tregd. omit the words *non possunt, corpora* and credit Cicero with the inconsistent statement that the philosophic mind is subject to mental disturbance. Bent. inserted *ut* before *corpora.* Sff. is evidently right in reading *et*: the statement in the second sentence is not a correction of, nor in contrast to, the statement in the first : it is the statement of the essential difference between mental and bodily *morbi* which is the justification for the statement in the first clause. *Sed* is retained by Heine (*Posen Progr.* p. 6) who regards it as marking a transition from one idea to another.
bestiae. Dav. quotes Sen. de Ira i 3, 4 'dicendum est feras ira carere et omnia praeter hominem. nam cum sit inimica rationi nusquam tamen nascitur, nisi ubi

rationi locus est…§ 6 muta animalia humanis adfectibus carent, habent autem similes illis quosdam impulsus.' Stob. Ecl. Eth. p. 175 [ii 6, 9] κατὰ τὸ γένος δὲ ταύτην διττῶς θεωρεῖσθαι τήν τε ἐν τοῖς λογικοῖς γιγνομένην ὁρμὴν καὶ τὴν ἐν τοῖς ἀλόγοις ζῴοις and Galen, de Plac. Hipp. et Plat. iv p. 371 διὰ μὲν οὖν τοῦ ἀπεστράφθαι φάναι τὸν λόγον ἐχώρισε [sc. ὁ Χρύσιππος] τὴν κατὰ τὸ πάθος ἄλογον κίνησιν τῆς τῶν ἀψύχων τε καὶ τῶν ἀλόγων ζῴων: id. v p. 431 τῶν ἄλλων Στωικῶν οἵ γε μέχρι τοσούτου φιλονεικίας ἤκουσιν, ὥστ' ἐπειδὴ τῆς λογικῆς δυνάμεως ἔφασαν εἶναι τὰ πάθη, τοῖς ἀλόγοις ζῴοις μὴ μετέχειν αὐτῶν συγχωρεῖν.
faciunt, i.e. *patiuntur* or *habent* : for this use of *facio* to supply the place of another verb, cf. v 32, 90 'an Scythes Anacharsis potuit pro nihilo pecuniam ducere, nostrates philosophi facere non poterunt' and i 11, 24 n.
§ 32. **aes Corinthium**, a mixture of gold, silver and copper: Plin. H. N. xxxiv 2, 3 § 6 refutes the vulgar idea that the mixture was first discovered by accident at the burning of Corinth by Mummius in 146 B.C. as statues of *aes Corinthium* were known from before that date. Connoisseurs claimed to be able to recognize the true Corinthian bronze by the smell. Mart. ix 59, 11.
illi: cf. 30, 61 n. on *ille.*

10 perturbationem animus ingeniosi cadit; † non enim multa ecferata
et immania: quaedam autem humanitatis quoque habent primam
speciem, ut misericordia, aegritudo, metus. aegrotationes autem
morbique animorum difficilius euelli posse putantur quam summa
illa uitia, quae uirtutibus sunt contraria. morbis enim manentibus
15 uitia sublata esse possunt, quia non tam celeriter sanantur, quam
illa tolluntur. **33.** habes ea quae de perturbationibus enucleate
disputant Stoici, quae λογικά appellant, quia disseruntur subtilius. ex quibus quoniam tamquam ex scrupulosis cotibus
enauigauit oratio, reliquae disputationis cursum teneamus, modo
20 satis illa dilucide dixerimus pro rerum obscuritate.

A. Prorsus satis; sed si quae diligentius erunt cognoscenda,
quaeremus alias, nunc uela quae modo dicebas exspectamus et
cursum.

10. non enim multa R 1 6 7 17 V P 1 4 G B 1–3 K 1 2 S E 1 2 L 2–6
W 1 2 M 1 2 D C Π J O 1–3 7 8.   non enim in multa ed. H.   non enim
cadit ĭ
multa E 3 *al. atr. superscr.* ‖ ecferata R G.   efferata V B K 1 W 1 2 D
O 1 3 7. ⟅ ferata P *at* ef *in marg. adscr.* et nec ferata B 2. hec efferata ed. H.
11. immania R V P B K S E.   inmania G.   in mania B 2 O 7.
15. sublata esse non possunt R 1 7 17 V P 1 4 G B 1–3 K 1 2 S E 1 2
W 1 2 M 2 D C Π J O 1–3 7 8.   sublata est non possunt M 1.   esse uitia
sublata non possunt R 6.   sublata esse possunt *corr. Lambinus.* ‖ quia non tam
R V P G B K *plerique.*   qui non tam W 1.   quare non tam O 1.
§ **33**, 17. logica R V G S D *alii.*   lo_ica *unius litt. spat. rel.* K 1.
            g
loica E 1 *al. atr. superscr.*   18. ex scrupulosis R 2 10 16 B 1–3 S E 1 2
                                v
D C Π O 1 3 8.   ex scruplosis G *ead. man.*   excrupulosis P *atr. ant. superscr.*
ex⸀crupuloſ, K 2.   ex scrosolis K 1 *at in marg.* scrupulosis.   ex scrupolosis R 1.
excrupulosis V W 1.   ex scrupolosis O 7.   ex scopulosis O 2.   21. si quae
                                                t a
G K 1 M 2 O 2 3.   si que R V S E.   si que B 1.   si que R 16 B 2 3
                        si   l' si aliqua
K 2 E 2 D O 7.   que Π.   siq̄ P C.   si que O 8 *al atr. superscr.*
si qua W 1 2 J O 1.   quia M 1 si *om.*   22. expectamus R V G.
ex pectamus K 1 *litt. ante* p *eras.*   expetamus B 1.

non enim multa ecferata: this, which
is the MSS. reading, is obviously corrupt.
Bentl. proposed *in ulla* and he is followed
by Küh. Hei. Schiche, Sff. Mo. etc.
Madv. proposed *sunt enim multa*. It
seems more probable that *multa* is a corruption of *in uitia* sc. cadit 'he does not
fall into gross and outrageous faults':
some noun like *uitia* seems to be required to which *quaedam* may be referred.
The danger to the *ingeniosus* proceeds
from the more insidious *perturbationes*
which appear as amiable weaknesses.

primam speciem, 'a superficial resemblance to,' lit. 'the beginning of a
resemblance.'

putantur: sc. *a philosophis*.

quia: if this, which is the MSS. reading,

be retained, the subject to *sanantur* is
morbi, to be supplied out of *morbis*,
which, though awkward, is not impossible, *morbis* being by its position the
most emphatic word in the sentence.
Küh. follows Lamb. in inserting *hi*, with
the same distinction between *hic* and *ille*
as in i 49, 117: Dav. proposed *qui* and
he is followed by Or. Bai. and Sff.

§ **33. enucleate**: 'concisely,' see San-
dys' n. on Cic. Or. § 28. Conciseness
(συντομία), the λέξις αὐτὰ τὰ ἀναγκαῖα
περιέχουσα πρὸς δήλωσιν τοῦ πράγματος,
was, acc. to the Stoics, one of the virtues
of speech. Diog. L. vii 59.

cursum: 'a straight run,' cf. Att. v
8, 1 'cursum exspectabamus.' For the
metaphor cf. Quint. vi 1, 52 'e confrag-

XV. 34. *M.* Quando, ut aliis locis de uirtute et diximus et saepe dicendum erit (pleraeque enim quaestiones quae ad uitam moresque pertinent a uirtutis fonte ducuntur), quando igitur uirtus est adfectio animi constans conueniensque, laudabiles 5 efficiens eos in quibus est, et ipsa per se sua sponte separata etiam utilitate laudabilis, ex ea proficiscuntur honestae uoluntates, sententiae, actiones omnisque recta ratio, quamquam ipsa uirtus breuissime recta ratio dici potest. huius igitur uirtutis contraria est uitiositas (sic enim malo quam malitiam appellare 10 eam quam Graeci κακίαν appellant; nam malitia certi cuiusdam uitii nomen est, uitiositas omnium); ex qua concitantur perturbationes, quae sunt, ut paulo ante diximus, turbidi animorum concitatique motus, auersi a ratione et inimicissimi mentis

XV. § **34**, 1. et *ante* aliis *habent* R V P G B K *plerique.* om. R 7. ut aliis *corr. Manutius.* ‖ et *ante* diximus *omittunt* R 6 K 2 E 3 L 2 6 O 3 7
superscr. *eod. atr. habet* W 1. 3. ducuntur R V G M 1 2 O 2. ducut B 2.
d̆cuntur B 1 *al. atr. superscr.* dĭ∧cuntur S. dicuntur E 1 J.
8. breuissume R K E. breuissumme V. breuissumme G *prius* m *expunx.*
alt. man. breuis summę B 1. 11. cōcitantur W 1. cogitantur R 1 6 7 17
V P 1 2 4 G B 1–3 K 1 2 S E 1–3 L 2–6 W 2 M 1 2 D C Π J
O 1–3 7 8 ed. H.

osis atque asperis euecti tota pandere possumus uela'—no doubt a direct imitation of this passage.

XV. § **34**. **Quando**: for *quoniam*, rare in Cicero: see Mdv.'s n. to Fin. v 8, 21; Charisius p. 86 says '*quando* acuta prima syllaba interrogationem temporis significat, sed posteriore acuta *quoniam* uel *quandoquidem*.'

ut, Manutius' emendation for the MSS. *et*, has been accepted by Dav. Wes. Kl. Sff. in view of the awkwardness of three *et*'s in close succession. Or., who will not accept this emendation, omits the *et* before *diximus*.

uirtutis fonte: 'virtue as their source'; gen. of definition, cf. 'mercedem gloriae' i 15, 34.

igitur, like *ergo*, often resumes after a digression, cf. i 7, 14 n.

adfectio animi: *adfectio* is used here, as in Fin. iii 20, 65, as equivalent to the Gk διάθεσις. The definition of virtue here is the same as that quoted in Stob. Ecl. Eth. p. 167 (ii 60, 5) κοινότερον δὲ τὴν ἀρετὴν διάθεσιν εἶναι ψυχῆς σύμφωνον αὐτῇ περὶ ὅλον τὸν βίον combined with that of Cleanthes as given by Diog. L. vii 89 τήν τ' ἀρετὴν διάθεσιν εἶναι ὁμολογουμένην καὶ αὐτὴν δι' αὑτὴν αἱρετήν, οὐ διά τινα φόβον ἢ ἐλπίδα ἤ τι τῶν ἔξωθεν·

ἐν αὑτῇ τ' εἶναι τὴν εὐδαιμονίαν, ἅτ' οὔσῃ ψυχῇ πεποιημένῃ πρὸς τὴν ὁμολογίαν παντὸς τοῦ βίου.

omnisque recta ratio, 'and right reason in general': *recta ratio* or *absoluta ratio* (v 13, 39) is the ὀρθὸς λόγος of the Stoics which objectively is ὁ νόμος ὁ κοινός and subjectively is the state of mind which is in harmony with the law of the universe: this state of mind is essentially virtue itself as Cicero says in the next sentence: cf. Sen. Epp. 113, 2 'uirtus autem nihil aliud est quam animus quodammodo se habens.' For *omnis* in the sense of *omnino* cf. i 40, 95 'in omni uirtute'; Stat. Theb. v 364 'raptus ab omni sole dies.'

uirtutis contraria: for the gen. cf. Fin. iv 24, 67, Inu. ii 54, 165.

malitia: so in Fin. iii 11, 39 'quas enim Graeci κακίας appellant uitia malo quam malitias nominare': Cic. defines *malitia* in N. D. iii 30, 75 to be 'uersuta et fallax nocendi ratio' and this def. agrees with the general use of the word (e.g. Ter. Andr. iv 3, 8): Sall. Iug. 22 'uirtute non malitia P. Scipioni, summo uiro, placuisse' (quoted by TS.) is an instance of the use disowned by Cic.

concitantur = *concitando efficiuntur*, cf. iii 11, 25 n. on *turbantur*.

uitaeque tranquillae. inportant enim aegritudines anxias atque
15 acerbas animosque adfligunt et debilitant metu; iidem inflam-
mant adpetitione nimia, quam tum cupiditatem, tum libidinem
dicimus, inpotentiam quandam animi a temperantia et moderatione plurimum dissidentem. **35.** quae si quando adepta erit
id quod ei fuerit concupitum tum ecferetur alacritate, ut 'nihil
20 ei constet quod agat,' ut ille, qui 'uoluptatem animi
nimiam summum esse errorem' arbitratur. eorum igitur
malorum in una uirtute posita sanatio est.

15. idem R V P G B 1 2 K E 2 M 1 O 7.　　　iidem W 1 D O 3 8.
idē S *marg.* item.　　id ē E 1.　　idest J.　　'i· (*i.e.* id est) W 2.　　unde O 1.
16. quam tum R B 1 3 S E W 2 M 1 2 D C O 1-3 7 8.　　quātū P.
quā
　tum W 1 *fort. eod. atr.*　　quarntum K 1 n *in* m *mut.*　　quantum V G B 2.
quamcum E 2.　　17. animi a W 2 M 1 2 D C O 1-3 II (*marg.*).　　aī a B 3
　　　　　　　　　　　　　　　　　　　　　　　　ia　　　　　　　　i
W 1 O 7 8.　　aīa B 2.　　a nimia E 3.　　anima E 1.　　anima V B 1.
anima R G K.　　animi E 2.
§ **35,** 18. adepta ē R 6.　　adeptaret¹ J S *marg.*　　adeptaretur L 3 O 1.
ea adeptā retur E 3 *at litterae post* d *al. atr. script.*　　ea demptaretur B 1 K 2 S
　　　　　　　　　　　　　　　　　　　　　　　　　　　　　　　　r
M 1 D C O 7.　　eademptaretur R V P G K E.　　ea d'ptaret W 2.
　　　　　　　　　r
ei adeptaretur O 3.　　ei demptaret P 4.　　ea temparetur B 2.　　ea tēptaretur R 7.
　　　　　　　　　　　　　　　　　　　　　　　　oti
ea dēpdaretur L 2.　　eadem piaretur B 3 L 6.　　eadem piạretur M 2 *al. atr. corr.*
eadem putaretur R 17 O 8.　　cadere putaretur O 2.　　adipisceretur W 1.
ea adipiscitur L 4.　　ea depredarentur L 5.　　*om.* II *at marg.* adepta est.
piaret ed. H.　　adepta erit *corr. Lambinus.*　　19. tum fertur alacritate W 1 Gr.
tum fert alacritate R V P 1 2 4 G B 1 2 K 1 O 3 8.　　tum fert alacritatē B 3
E 2 3 M 1 ed. H.　　tum fert alacritatem R 6 7 1 7 L 3 4 M 2 O 1.　　tūc fert
te
alacri K 2.　　tum affert alacritatem O 7.　　fert alacritate E 1 cum *om.*
fert alacritatē S W 2 II *marg.* O 2 cum *om.*　　affert alacritate D C cum *om.*
tum fert cum alacritate L 2 5.　　feret alacritatem L 6 cum *om.*　　tum ecferetur
alacritate *corr. Baiter praeeunte Dauisio.*　　||　　nihil ei R 7 L 2 O 8.
　　ei
nihil ē E 1 *al. atr. superscr.*　　nihil ei B 1 *at* i *postea inculc. et linea super* e
　　　　　　　　　　　　　　　　　　　　se
ex parte eras.　　nihil ē K 1.　　nihil est V *atram. uiridi.*　　nihil est R 1 G B 2.
nihil ēē R 17 P B 3 E 2 3 L 4 5 W 1 2 O 1 7.　　nihil esse R 6 P 2 4 K 2
L 3 6 M 1 2 D C II *marg.* J O 3 ed. H.　　nihil eius O 2.　　20. quod R 6
L 2 4.　　q∂ II *marg.*　　qđ W 1.　　qd R 7 P.　　quid R V G
B 1-3 K 1 2 S E 1 2 L 3 5 6 W 2 M 2 D C J O 1-3 8 ed. H.　　q' R 17
M 1 O 7.

§ **35. ecferetur**: the future (as against
the pres. *ecfertur* of Küh. and others) is
required here by the preceding future
perf. *adepta erit.* Most edd. adopt the
compound, as against the simple verb
feretur read by Sff. *feretur* is undoubtedly
nearer the best MSS, but on the other
hand the meaning required here seems to
be not 'will be impelled by,' which Sff.
argues for, but 'will be carried away by,'
to which 17, 39 'quod aut cupias ardenter
aut adeptus ecferas te insolenter' furnishes

a close parallel. The MSS often confuse
ecfe-(effe-) and *fe-*.
ille, qui uoluptatem: a quotation from
the comic poet Trabea (Ribbeck, *Sc.
Rom. Poes. Frag.* II² 32), which occurs
again Fin. ii 4, 13, Fam. ii 9, 2. Bentley
shewed that the line was a trochaic tetram.
'*ego uoluptatem animi nimiam summum
esse errorem arbitror,*' though he chose to
alter *errorem* to *aegrorem,* which would,
however, spoil the quotation in Fam. ii
9, 2.

XVI. Quid autem est non miserius solum, sed foedius etiam
et deformius quam aegritudine quis adflictus, debilitatus, iacens?
cui miseriae proximus est is, qui adpropinquans aliquod malum
metuit exanimatusque pendet animi. quam uim mali signifi-
5 cantes poëtae impendere apud inferos saxum Tantalo faciunt
    Ób scelera animique ínpotentiam ét superbilo-
                                        quéntiam.
ea communis poena stultitiae est. omnibus enim quorum mens
abhorret a ratione semper aliqui talis terror inpendet. **36.** atque
10 ut haec tabificae mentis perturbationes sunt, aegritudinem dico
et metum, sic hilariores illae, cupiditas auide semper aliquid expetens et inanis alacritas, id est laetitia gestiens, non multum
differunt ab amentia. ex quo intellegitur, qualis ille sit quem

XVI. 2. debilitatus iacens R V P G B 1 2 K 1 S E 1 2 D C O 3 7 Gr.
debilitatusque iacens B 3 K 2 L 5 W 1 2 M 1 2 Π O 1 8 ed. H.   et debilitatus
iacens C.   debilitateque iacens J O 2.   3. is qui R G K *alii*.   isq; V.
9. aliquid aliis R V P 1 4 G B 1–3 K 1 2 E 1 L 3 5 6 W 2 M 2 J O 1 3 Gr.
S *at in* aliquis aliis *mut. et marg.* dolor aliis.   aliquis aliis O 7.   aliquis alius L 4.
aliquis illis W 1 ed. H.   aliquis *om.* aliis R 7 E 2 L 2 M 1 D C Π O 8.
aliquid aliis dolor aliis M 2.   aliquis aliis dolor aliis R 6   O 2.   aliqui talis
corr. Gronouius.
§ 36, 10. haec R G K.   h̨c V B E.   hec D C Π O 1 7 8 ed. H.
h̨ᶜᶜ P *al. atr. superscr.*   hᶜ B 2.   h' W 2 J.   ħ K 2.   h̨ S *at ras. post* ȩ.
hae M 2 O 2.   h̨ W 1 O 3.   he B 3 E 2 M 1.   11. illae G.
illȩ V P K.   ille R. ‖ auide V P K.   auidȩ R.   auidȩe G.

XVI. **quid**: the use of the neuter in
place of the masculine is very common;
it makes the question more emphatic by
extending the range of comparison to
things as well as persons : *nihil* is used
instead of *nemo* in the same way, e.g. in
N.D. i 33, 93 ; so *quicquid* for *quisquis*
in Ovid, Rem. Am. 247.
quis, indefinite: for this use of *quis*,
common after *si, ne, nisi, num*, etc. see
Draeger, *Syntax d. Lat. Spr.* I § 44.
animi, locative. In Cic. *animi* is always
used with verbs (*pendere, angi*), never
with adjectives. The plural *animis* is
found in the best MSS in i 40, 96 though
Ursinus and Bentley alter it to *animi*.
Cf. Draeger, *op. cit.* I § 206, 5: there seems
to have been in early Latin some confusion between the gen. and the locative
in such phrases, e.g. *desipiebam mentis*
in Plaut. Epid. 138.
Tantalo: here and in Fin. i 18, 60 Cic.
follows, as does Lucretius (iii 980) the
version of the punishment of Tantalus
adopted by Pind. Ol. i, 90 and Eur.
Orest. 5: in i 5, 10 he follows the alternative version of Od. xi 582.

faciunt, 'tell of ': for the use of *facio*
with acc. and inf. cf. v 39, 115; N.D. iii
16,41 'quem Homerus...conueniri facit ab
Ulixe,' Virg. Aen. viii 630 ' fecerat et uiridi
fetam Mauortis in antro | procubuisse
lupam ': the use of *facio* (*efficio*) with this
constr. in the sense of ' cause' is very rare
in Classical Latin, e.g. Cic. Brut. 38,
142 'tales oratores uideri facit, quales ipsi
se uideri uolunt': Draeger, *op. cit.* I,
§ 442.
ob scelera: the words are, as Turn.
(*Adv.* vii 18) saw, a quotation from some
unknown poet: *superbiloquentiam* is perhaps a translation of the ἀκόλαστος γλῶσσα
of Eur. Or. 10. The line is a trochaic
tetrameter catalectic.
§ 36. id est: an instance of the explanatory use of the phrase, for which see
Reid's n. to Ac. i 2, 8.
tum moderatum...alias constantem:
the reading in the text has been shown
by Wopkens, *Lect. Tull.* p. 128, to be
quite sound. The reading adopted by Or.,
modestum et temperantem, is shown to be
unsound by a comparison of iii 8, 16 where
a clear distinction is drawn between the

tum moderatum, alias modestum, <tum> temperantem, alias
15 constantem continentemque dicimus; non numquam haec eadem uocabula ad frugalitatis nomen tamquam ad caput referre
uolumus. quodnisi eo nomine uirtutes continerentur, numquam
ita peruolgatum illud esset ut iam prouerbii locum obtineret,
'hominem frugi omnia recte facere.' quod idem cum Stoici de
20 sapiente dicunt, nimis admirabiliter nimisque magnifice dicere
uidentur.

XVII. **37.** Ergo hic, quisquis est, qui moderatione et constantia quietus animo est sibique ipse placatus, ut nec tabescat
molestiis nec frangatur timore nec sitienter quid expetens ardeat
desiderio nec alacritate futtili gestiens deliquescat, is est sapiens
5 quem quaerimus, is est beatus cui nihil humanarum rerum aut

14. modestum temperantem R 1 7 17 V P 1 4 G B 1–3 K 1 2 E 1
L 2–6 W 2 M 1 2 D C J O 1–3 7 8.   modestum et temperantem R 6.

moderatum $_\wedge$ temperantem II *cett. om.*   moderatum temperantem E 2 *cett. om.*
tum modestum alias moderatum temperantem W 1.   modestum tum temperantem
corr. Handius.   18. ita peruolgatum illud esset R V P G B 1–3 S E M 2 C.
ita peruolgatum esset illud K 2 W 1 2 M 1 J O 1 2.   illud ita promulgatum
esset O 3. ‖ obtineret V.   optineret R P G B K.   19. omnia recte R 6 P
B 1 3 E 1 2 W 1 M 1 2 O 1 3 8.   recte omnia S.   omnia recta R V G K 1
W 2 D C 11 J O 2.   omnia rectæ B 2.   20. nimis R 6 7 17 G B 3 K 2
E 2 W 1 2 M 1 2 D C 11 J O 1–3 8.   animis V B 1.   nimis S *at a ante*
n *eras.*   animis R 1 2 P 1 4 B 2 K 1 E.   āīs O 7.
XVII. § **37,** 1. hic R V P G B 1 2 K 2 S E 1 2 W 2 M 1 D C 11 J
O 7 8.   is B 3 W 1 M 2 O 1–3.   his K 1.   3. expetens B 1–3 W 2
M 1 2 D C O 1 2 8.   expe xens V *litt. ut uid. eras.*   ex pectens K 1.
expectens R G.   expectans P S E 2 11 O 3 7.   exspectans E.
$\overset{\text{eat}}{}$
appetens W 1. ‖ ardeat S W 1 D J O 1 3 7 8.   ard& V *atr. uiridi superscr.*
ardet B 1 *marg.* ardeat.   ardet R G B 2 K 1 2 E 1 2.   arderet W 2.
4. futili R 2 6 10 16 B 1 3 K 2 E 2 W 1 2 M 1 2 D C 11 J O 1 2 8.
futtuli V.   futtili B 2 E 1.   futtuli R G K 1.   futuli P.   facili O 3.

two words, which Or.'s reading makes
practically synonymous: the *et* arose from
a desire to supply the lacuna caused by
the accidental omission of *tum* after *modestum. Tum...alias*, more usually *tum
...tum* or *alias.. alias*, is found only here.
ad frugalitatis nomen...referre, 'bring
under the category of': this wide sense of
frugalitas has already been expounded
in iii 8, 16. For *nomen* (apparently a
metaphor from book-keeping, originally
meaning an 'account') cf. Verr. 11 2, 57,
141: 3, 91, 212, pro Planc. 15, 36.
quodnisi: in this phrase (cf. *quod si*)
quod, originally an adverbial relative, has
become a mere connecting particle; cf.
Att. xiii 10, 1 'quod nisi mihi hoc
uenisset in mentem.' The phrase is not
found in Caesar or Sallust, and very

seldom in Livy. Draeger, *op. cit.* 1
§ 484*a.*
Stoici: e.g. Chrysippus, who, acc. to
Diog. L. vii 122, held that the wise were
ἔτι καὶ ἀναμαρτήτους, τῷ ἀπεριπτώτους
εἶναι ἀμαρτήματι· ἀβλαβεῖς τ' εἶναι, οὐ
γὰρ ἄλλους βλάπτειν οὔθ' αὑτούς. Arche-
demus (Diog. L. vii 88) gave it as his
definition of virtue πάντα τὰ καθήκοντα
ἐπιτελοῦντα ζῆν.
nimis admirabiliter: cf. Chrysippus,
ap. Plut. de Stoic. repug. p. 1041 F
διὸ καὶ διὰ τὴν ὑπερβολὴν τοῦ τε μεγέθους
καὶ τοῦ κάλλους πλάσμασι δοκοῦμεν ὅμοια
λέγειν καὶ οὐ κατὰ τὸν ἄνθρωπον καὶ τὴν
ἀνθρωπίνην φύσιν.
XVII. 37. **tabescat...frangatur...
ardeat...deliquescat:** for the metaphors
cf. Nägelsbach, *Lat. Stil.* §§ 129 sqq.

intolerabile ad demittendum animum aut nimis laetabile ad
ecferendum uideri potest. quid enim uideatur ei magnum in
rebus humanis cui aeternitas omnis totiusque mundi nota sit
magnitudo? nam quid aut in studiis humanis aut in tam exigua
10 breuitate uitae magnum sapienti uideri potest, qui semper animo
sic excubat ut ei nihil inprouisum accidere possit, nihil inopinatum, nihil omnino nouum? **38.** atque idem ita acrem in omnis
partis aciem intendit ut semper uideat sedem sibi ac locum sine
molestia atque angore uiuendi, ut, quemcumque casum for-
15 tuna inuexerit, hunc apte et quiete ferat; quod qui faciet, non
aegritudine solum uacabit sed etiam perturbationibus reliquis
omnibus. his autem uacuus animus perfecte atque absolute beatos
efficit, idemque concitatus et abstractus ab integra certaque ratione non constantiam solum amittit uerum etiam sanitatem.

---

6. into lerabile V *litt. post* o *eras.*　　　7. adferendum V *atr. uiridi superscr.*
adferendum R B K E.　　ad ferendum G　B 2　K 2　J　O 1 ed. H.　　ad efferendum
E 2　L 2–4 6　W 1　D　O 3 7.　　ad efferendum S *at* ef *extr. marg. alio ut uid. atr.*
ad ^{de} eferendum O 8 *al. atr. superscr.*　　afferendum W 2 ad *om.*　　ad deferendum L 5.
9. nam quid R 1 7　V　P 4　G　B 1–3　K 1　S　E 1–3　L 5　W 1 2　M 1 2
D C Π J　O 1 2 7 ed. H.　　　num quid P 1.　　　nunquid O 3　K 2 *om.*
10. animo sic B 3　K 2　M 1 2　Π J　O 1–3 7.　　aīo sic W 1 2　D.　　　animo sic
R *et* B s *post* o *eras.*　　　animos sic V E.　　　animos sic G K　O 8.
aīos sic P　B 2.
§ **38,** 12. idem B 1 3　K 1　E 1 2　W 1 2　M 1 2　D C Π J　O 1–3 7 8.
ęidem V.　　　eidem R G　B 2.　　‖ omnis partis R V G K E.　　omnis partes B.
oīs partes S.　　17. absolute K 1 o *in a mut. atr. ant.*

---

ad demittendum = *ita ut demittat animum:* cf. 38, 82 ' dolore ad patiendum
leuato'; Part. Or. 29, 102 'tertius (sc.
status) aequi et ueri et recti et humani
ad ignoscendum disputatione tractandus
est'; pro Font. 18, 40 'meliore fortuna
ad probra non audienda' (= *ita ut probra
non audiat*): see Küh. *Lat. Gr.* I p. 134.
　quid enim uideatur ei magnum: for
the thought cf. v 25, 71.
　nam quid, which is the MSS reading, is
defended by Wopkens, *Lect. Tull.* p. 90,
against Bentley's conjecture *num quid*:
Wopkens regards *nam* as a mere variant of
enim in the preceding question: but Cic.
has no objection to repeating *enim* in
consecutive clauses, e.g. Ac. ii 33, 108,
and Küh.'s explanation seems preferable:
'*enim* antecedentis enuntiationis causam
notat; *nam* habet explicandi uim.'
　excubat: the same metaphor is found
in Phil. vi 7, 18 'consilio quantum potero,
labore plus paene quam potero excubabo
uigilaboque pro uobis.' For the whole

passage cf. Virg. Aen. vi 103 quoted by
Seneca, Ep. 76, 33.
　§ **38. acrem**: 'so keen an eye,' the
adj. being not proleptic (TS. and Hei.)
but descriptive of a permanent characteristic of the *sapiens*, who is 'sure in all
his ways,' ἀλλ' οὐδὲ παρορᾶν [ἀλλ'] οὐδὲ
παρακούειν νομίζουσι τὸν σοφὸν οὐδὲ τὸ
σύνολον παραπαίειν κατά τι τῶν αἰσθητη-
ρίων, Stob. Ecl. Eth. p. 183 (ii 6, 6): for
the expression cf. Fin. i 17, 57 'acri
animo et attento intuemur.'
　uideat: not = *prouideat* 'is ever on the
look out for' as Küh. and TS. take it,
comparing iii 19, 46, but 'has ever in
view,' almost = *uideat paratam sibi* (Or.):
Cic. wishes to emphasize the confidence
and assurance, not the mere hope and
expectation, of the Stoic: for the attribu-
tive use of the phrase *sine...uiuendi* cf.
Nägelsb. *Stil.* § 75, 2.
　certaque ratione: cf. ii 27, 65 'nihil
enim potest esse aequabile quod non a
certa ratione proficiscatur.'

20   Quocirca mollis et eneruata putanda est Peripateticorum ratio
et oratio, qui perturbari animos necesse dicunt esse, sed adhibent
modum quendam quem ultra progredi non oporteat. **39.** modum
tu adhibes uitio? an uitium nullum est non parere rationi? an
ratio parum praecipit nec bonum illud esse quod aut cupias
25 ardenter aut adeptus ecferas te insolenter, nec porro malum quo
aut oppressus iaceas aut, ne opprimare, mente uix constes? eaque
omnia aut nimis tristia aut nimis laeta errore fieri, qui error
stultis extenuetur die, ut cum res eaedem maneant, aliter ferant
inueterata, aliter recentia, sapientis ne attingat quidem omnino?
30 **40.** etenim quis erit tandem modus iste? quaeramus enim modum aegritudinis, in qua operae plurimum ponitur. aegre tulisse

20. enaruata V.   21. adhibea*N* V a*N* *al. atr. script.*

§ **39, 24.** aut B 3   W 1   J.   ut V *atr. uiridi superscr.*   ut R G K E.
25. ecferas R V G K.   efferas B 1 3   S   E 2   W 1 2   M 1   D J   O 1 3 8.
et feras P E   B 2 *at incertum utrum* et *an* ec.   afferas O 7.   27. tristitia V
om. E 1.   28. stultis R V G   B 2 3   K 1 2   E 3   W 1 2   M 2   J   O 1 2 8 ed. H.
stultus B 1   S   E 1 2   M 1   D C   O 3 7. || extenuetur R V P G B K *plerique.*
extenuatur M 1   O 1. || eaedem M 2   O 2.   eg̣dem P   O 3.   eedem R 7   B 3
S   E 3   M 1.   eadem R 1 6   V   P 4   G   B 1 2   K 1 2   S   E 1   W 1 2   D C J
O 1 7 8 ed. H.   eodem Π O *in e al. atr. mut.*   eodem E 2. || maneant R 1 7
V   P 1 4   G   B 2 3   K 1   E 1–3   M 2   Π   O 2.   maneāt S   M 1   O 3.
maneạnt B 1.   maneat R 6   K 2   S   W 1 2   D C J   O 1 7 8 ed. H. || ferat
R G S.   29. sapientis S.

§ **40, 31.** in qua R G   K 1   W 1   M 1   J   O 1 8.   in quo R 6   V   P 1 4
B 1 3   S   E 2   M 2   D C Π   O 2 3 7.   in quo E 1 *ut uid. at in litura.*

in q K 2.   inq B 2   W 2. || operae R 6   M 2.   operẹ B 1   W 1   O 3.

opere R V   P 1 4   G   K 1   B 3   E 1 2   W 2   D C Π   O 1 2 7 8.   opē B 2.

Peripateticorum: cf. iii 10, 22, Ac. i
10, 30: 'cumque perturbationes illi (sc.
Peripatetici) ex homine non tollerent
naturaque et condolescere et concupiscere
et extimescere et efferri laetitia dicerent,
sed eas contraherent in angustumque de-
ducerent....'
    ratio et oratio, 'view and assertion':
Cic. is fond of this phrase; cf. 28, 60;
Off. i 16, 50; Inu. i *s*, 2.
    quendam : in a disparaging sense, cf.
'opinio quaedam' ii 22, 52; 'magnis quibusdam bonis' i 40, 95 and nn. there.
    § **39. modum tu adhibes uitio?:** once
a *perturbatio* is recognized to be a *uitium*
the impossibility of speaking of degrees
of mental disturbance follows as a matter
of course; cf. Diog. L. vii 120 ἀρέσκει
τ' αὐτοῖς ἴσα ἡγεῖσθαι τὰ ἁμαρτήματα...*el*
γὰρ ἀληθὲς ἀληθοῦς μᾶλλον οὐκ ἐστι...οὐδ'
ἁμάρτημα ἁμαρτήματος, and 127 ὡς γὰρ
δεῖν φασιν ἢ ὀρθὸν εἶναι ξύλον ἢ στρεβλόν,
οὕτως ἢ δίκαιον ἢ ἄδικον οὔτε δὲ δικαιότερον
οὔτ' ἀδικώτερον, καὶ ἐπὶ τῶν ἄλλων ὁμοίως.

    The argument is one of the usual Stoic
'chain-arguments': (*a*) a *perturbatio* consists in the thought that certain things
are evil, (*b*) reason tells us that these
things are not evil, (*c*) it is a *uitium* to
disobey reason, (*d*) there are no degrees
in *uitium*; therefore, there are no degrees
possible in *perturbatio.*
    an...parum, nearly equivalent to *an...
non,* expecting an affirmative answer, for
which see Draeger, *Syntax* 1 § 158 B (*a*).
    porro=*rursus, ex altera parte*: cf. Fin.
i 10, 32 'nemo enim ipsam uoluptatem,
quia uoluptas sit, aspernatur...neque porro
quisquam est qui dolorem ipsum, quia
dolor sit, amet.'
    ne opprimare, depending upon the idea
of *fear* implied in *mente uix constes.*
    die=*longinquitate temporis,* cf. iii 16,
35 'longinquitas et dies.'
    § **40. etenim,** introducing a further
argument; not only is moderation in
perturbationes philosophically absurd, but
can be shown to be impossible in practice,

P. Rupilium fratris repulsam consulatus scriptum apud Fannium
est. sed tamen transisse uidetur modum, quippe qui ob eam
causam a uita recesserit; moderatius igitur ferre debuit. quid, si,
35 cum id ferret modice, mors liberorum accessisset? nata esset
aegritudo noua. sed ea modica. magna tamen facta esset accessio. quid, si deinde dolores graues corporis, si bonorum amissio,
si caecitas, si exsilium? si pro singulis malis aegritudines acce-
derent, summa ea fieret quae non sustineretur.

XVIII. **41.** Qui modum igitur uitio quaerit, similiter facit,
ut si posse putet eum qui se e Leucata praecipitauerit sustinere

32. p. rutilium R 1 7   V P   K 2   S   E 1 2   L 3-6   W 2   M 1 2   D C II J
O 1-3 7 ed. H.   prutilium G K.   prutiliũ B 2.   prutulium B 1.
P. Rutilum R 6.   P. Ruttiliũ W 1.   p. rutillum O 8.   p. ruptiliũ L 2.
Rupilium *corr. Manutius.*
XVIII. § **41**, 2. leucata R V P G   B 3   K S   E 2   W 2   M 1 2   II J   O 1 2.
leucate R 7.   leucada O 3 7.   leucade R 6.   leuchata B 1.   leuticata B 2.
leuata E 1   O 8.   λευκοτὰ W 1.   rupe D C.

as may be seen in the case of one of them,
aegritudo: *enim* after *quaeramus* introduces the example, as in iii 15, 31.
   P. Rupilium: i.e. P. Rupilius Lupus,
cons. 132 B.C.; Plin. N.H. vii 36 'P.
Rupilius morbo leui impeditus nuntiata
fratris repulsa in consulatus petitione ilico
exspirauit.' The date of his death falls
between 132 and 129, the date of the
death of Scipio, who assisted his brother's
candidature. His brother was Lucius Rupilius, praetor in 147 B.C. The brothers
were both protégés of Scipio Aemilianus,
Lael. 20, 73.
   Fannium: i.e. C. Fannius, the historian, son-in-law of C. Laelius and
pupil of Panaetius; he was trib. pleb.
in 142, praetor between 129 and 125 and
consul in 122. Cic. makes the curious
mistake in Brut. 26, 99 of supposing that
the consul of 122 and the historian were
two different people, a mistake perhaps
corrected at the time by Atticus (Att. xii
5, 3) and demonstrated by Mommsen
(*C.I.L.* i p. 158). The fragments of his
history are collected by Peter (*Hist. Rom.
rell.* i pp. 138—140).
   uidetur: the sarcastic tone of this
passage is further heightened by the suggestion of a dialogue between Cicero and
a Peripatetic which seems to underlie it.
   id = *fratris repulsam.*
   sed ea modica: the supposed retort of
the Peripatetic, with whom the question
is being argued: for the rare use of *sed*
in place of *at* in a retort see Draeger,
Syntax II § 333, 3; Bentley's conj. *sit*
for *sed* has been adopted by Dav. Hei.
T.S.

accessio, 'a serious aggravation of his
trouble'; cf. Fin. i 17, 55 'ut enim
aeque doleamus, cum corpore dolemus,
fieri tamen permagna accessio potest si...':
accessio is a word much used by medical
writers to denote the onset of a disease
e.g. fever; cf. Seneca, de benef. ii 14, 3
'cum accessio illa quae animum inflam-
mabat remiserit.'
   summa, 'the final result would be
such as to be intolerable'; for *summa* cf.
Off. i 18, 59 'uidere quae reliqui summa
fiat'; Fin. ii 24, 67 'ad uirtutis autem
summam accedere nihil potest.'
   XVIII. § **41**. **uitio**: Reid (Ac. ii 7,
19 n.) thinks that *uiti* should be read
here as 'with *fidem facere*, *modum f.*,
finem f. and many similar expressions,
the overwhelmingly prevalent construction in the best writers is *alicuius rei* not
alicui rei': he cites also 38, 82 'sit iam
huius disputationis modus.' A much
closer apparent parallel is to be found in
§ 40 'quaeramus enim modum aegritudinis.' But there seems to be a clear distinction between the two uses: *quaerere
m. aegritudinis* means 'to be in quest of
the mean in *aegritudo*': a purely theoretical search, whereas *qu. m. aegritudini* =
'a practical endeavour to regulate feeling.'
The latter seems to be required by the
context here, the former in § 40.
   similiter...ut si: this use of *ut si* is
rare before Cicero: it is found after
similiter (Off. i 25, 87), *similis* (Senect.
6, 17), *idem* (Off. i 14, 42); in Fin. ii 7,
21; iv 12, 31 Madv. reads *et si* after
similiter and *similem* respectively. For
further exx. see Draeger, *Synt.* II § 518, 2.

se, cum uelit. ut enim id non potest, sic animus perturbatus et
incitatus nec cohibere se potest nec, quo loco uult, insistere,
5 omninoque quae crescentia perniciosa sunt, eadem sunt uitiosa
nascentia; **42** aegritudo autem ceteraeque perturbationes, ampli-
ficatae certe, pestiferae sunt; igitur etiam susceptae continuo in
magna pestis parte uersantur. etenim ipsae se inpellunt, ubi
semel a ratione discessum est, ipsaque sibi imbecillitas indulget
10 in altumque prouehitur inprudens nec reperit locum consistendi.
quam ob rem nihil interest utrum moderatas perturbationes
adprobent an moderatam iniustitiam, moderatam ignauiam, moderatam intemperantiam; qui enim uitiis modum apponit, is
partem suscipit uitiorum; quod cum ipsum per se odiosum est,

---

4. nec quo loco V P.   necqu*o*loco R 1 *eod. atr.*   neqoloco G.   nec coloco
K 1.   ‖ uult R *h. l.*   V *h. l.*   G *h. l.*   B *h. l.*   K S E.   5. omninoque quae L 3.
omninoq; que R 7   J   O 1.   oīoq; qu*e* W 1.   ōīoq₃ que O 8.   omnino
quaeque R 1 6   G L 2   M 2.   omnino qu*e*que V S E.   omnino qu*e*qu*e* B 1.
omnino qu*e*q; P   L 4.   omnino quaeq; O 2.   omnino queq; B 2 3
E 2   L 5 6   D C Π   O 3 7 ed. H.   omnino quaequae K 1.   omnino
quecūq; K 2   M 1.
§ **42,** 8. ipse se G.   se ip̄s̄ S.   9. inbecillitas G E.   imbecillitas R *h. l.*
V *h. l.*   B 1 2.   imbeccillitas K 1.   10. imprudens R V G B K.   ‖ reperit B 3
E 2   W 1 2   Π J   O 1 8.   repit S.   repperit B 1.   repperit R V P G   B 2
K 1 2   E 1   D   O 3 7.   12. adprobent R V G K E.   approbent B S.
13. apponit R V G B K S E.

Leucata: mod. Capo Ducato, the promontory to the extreme S. of Leucas
(mod. Santa Maura), famous as the spot
whence Sappho leaped into the sea
when her love had been rejected by
Phaon. The comparison is probably
suggested here, however, by the renown
of Leucata on the stage. There was a
temple of Aphrodite on the promontory,
said to have been founded by Aeneas.

sustinere se, 'check his fall': for
sustinere cf. Ac. ii 29, 94 'ego enim ut
agitator callidus priusquam ad finem
ueniam equos sustinebo, eoque magis, si
locus is quo ferentur equi praeceps erit.'

potest: sc. *fieri* i 11, 23 n. The passage closely resembles Seneca's argument
de Ira I 7, 4 'ut in praeceps datis corporibus nullum sui arbitrium est nec
resistere morariue derecta potuerunt…et
non licet eo non peruenire quo non ire
licuisset, ita animus si in iram, amorem
aliosque se proiecit adfectus, non per-
mittitur reprimere impetum.' Pohlenz,
Hermes XLI, pp. 339 sqq. makes it probable that Cicero and Seneca followed in
this line of argument some common
source, possibly Chrysippus.

nascentia: Sen. de Ira i 13, 2 'non
est bonum quod incremento malum fit'
(quoted by Pohlenz, *l.c.*).

§ 42. in magna pestis parte uersantur,
'partake largely of the nature of disease':
for the expression cf. v 38, 111 'non
uersari in oculorum ulla iucunditate' and
Nägelsbach, *Stil.* § 109; cf. also Madvig's
n. to Fin. ii 14, 47 'in eadem pulchritudine,' and Quintil. ii 10, 11 'in aliqua
sine dubio ueritate uersantur.'

prouehitur, a change of metaphor,
'rashly puts farther and farther out to
sea': for this force of *pro* in *prouehitur*
cf. Off. ii 6, 19 'cum prospero flatu
fortunae utimur, ad exitus prouehimur
optatos.'

adprobent: sc. 'Peripatetici'; cf. Ac.
ii 44, 135 'mediocritates illi probabant et
in omni permotione naturalem uolebant
esse quendam modum.'

partem suscipit, 'espouses the cause
of'; cf. Mil. 15, 40 'adulescens nobilissimus rei publicae partem fortissime
suscepisset.'

procliui: this and not *procliue* is the
reading of the best MSS here and in Fin. v
28, 84, where see Madv.'s note: the

15 tum eo molestius quia sunt in lubrico incitataque semel procliui labuntur sustinerique nullo modo possunt.

XIX. **43.** Quid, quod iidem Peripatetici perturbationes istas, quas nos exstirpandas putamus, non modo naturalis esse dicunt, sed etiam utiliter a natura datas; quorum est talis oratio. primum multis uerbis iracundiam laudant, cotem fortitudinis esse dicunt, 5 multoque et in hostem et in inprobum ciuem uehementiores iratorum impetus esse, leuis autem ratiunculas eorum qui ita cogitarent: 'Proelium rectum est hoc fieri, conuenit dimicare pro

15. incitataque R V P G B 3. incitata q3 B 2 S J. incitata quę E 1.
concitata quę B 1. ‖ procliui R V P G B 1 2 K 1 E D O 7 Gr. procliue R 7 B 3 W 2 M 1 2 J O 1 2 8. in procliui C O 3. in procliue R 6. procliua W 1. proclimi S *marg*. ī. ꝑcliue procliuis II. procliuius E 2. 16. sustinerique V P D O 3. substinerique W 1. sustineri que B 2. sustineri quę R. sustineri quae G K. sustinereque se S O 1. XIX. § **43**, 1. idem R V P G B 1–3 K E 1 2 M 1 D C II J O 2 7. id' W 2. iidem *ex* idem *mut*. S. iidem M 2 O 1 3 8. *om*. W 1. 2. nos extirpandas V P K S. nos exstirpandas B E. non extirpandas R G. ‖
naturalis R V P G B K E. nāles S. 4. cotem R V P G. quotem E
al. atr. superscr. quotem B. 5. et in improbum B 3 K 2 S W 2 M 2 D C J O 1–3 8. & inprobum V *al. atr. superscr*. et inprobum G B 1 W 1 M 1. et improbum R 1 6 P K E O 7 ed. H. et i̱ꝑbū B 2. et in probū II. et in probum E 2. ‖ uehementioręs V i *in* e *mut*. uehementioris R P G B K S E. 6. leuis R V P B K E. laeuis G. leues B 3 S. 7. praelium G.

---

same variation between -*i* and -*e* is seen in other words : cf. Aul. Gell. x 24, 8 'sane quam consuetum is ueteribus fuerit litteris is plerumque uti indifferenter, sicuti "praefiscine" et "praefiscini," "procliui" et "procliue" atque alia item multa hoc genus uarie dixerunt.' On the other hand Lachm. prefers the form *procliue* in Lucr. ii. 455.

XIX. § 43. **Quid, quod** : Draeger, *Synt*. II § 378, 7.

naturalis=*a natura datas* : cf. Off. i 25, 89 'iracundiam...utiliter a natura datam' ; Ac. ii, 44, 135 'atque illi quidem etiam utiliter a natura dicebant: permotiones istas animis nostris datas, metum cauendi causa, misericordiam aegritudinemque clementiae,' where, as here, *utiliter*='for a useful purpose.' In holding this view the Peripatetics merely continued the tradition of the Old Academy.

iracundiam : strictly speaking Cicero should have (as Dav. notes) used *ira* here in place of *iracundia*, in accordance with the distinction he has himself drawn in 12, 27 : but writing from the Stoic point

of view Cicero is entitled as a contro versialist to hold that the Peripatetics, in praising *ira* (θυμός), were logically compelled to praise *iracundia* (ὀργιλότης), the one necessarily involving the other and all degrees of any vice being equal to each other.

laudant : Arist. Eth. Nic. iv 5 ὁ μὲν οὖν ἐφ᾽ οἷς δεῖ καὶ οἷς δεῖ ὀργιζόμενος ἔτι δὲ καὶ ὡς δεῖ καὶ ὅτε καὶ ὅσον χρόνον ἐπαινεῖται.

cotem fortitudinis : cf. Ac. ii 44, 135 'ipsam iracundiam fortitudinis quasi cotem esse dicebant, recte secusne alias uiderimus,' where Reid quotes Sen. de Ira iii 3, 1 'stat Aristoteles defensor irae et uetat illam nobis exsecari ; calcar ait esse uirtutis,' and Philod. περὶ ὀργῆς (ap. Bonitz, *Fragm. Arist*. 95) ἔνιοι τῶν περιπατητικῶν...ἐκτέμνειν τὰ νεῦρα τῆς ψυχῆς φασὶ τοὺς τὴν ὀργὴν καὶ τὸν θυμὸν αὐτῆς ἐξαιροῦντας ; Dav. quotes Lactant. Div. Inst. vi 19 'Peripatetici...iram cotem dicunt esse uirtutis, tanquam nemo possit aduersus hostes fortiter dimicare nisi fuerit ira concitatus.'

cogitarent : for the sequence of tenses cf. iii 16, 32 n.

legibus, pro libertate, pro patria.' haec nullam habent uim nisi ira
excanduit fortitudo. nec uero de bellatoribus solum disputant; im-
10 peria seueriora nulla esse putant sine aliqua acerbitate iracundiae;
oratorem denique non modo accusantem, sed ne defendentem
quidem probant sine aculeis iracundiae, quae etiamsi non adsit,
tamen uerbis atque motu simulandam arbitrantur, ut auditoris
iram oratoris incendat actio. uirum denique uideri negant qui
15 irasci nesciat, eamque, quam lenitatem nos dicimus, uitioso leni-
tudinis nomine appellant. 44. nec uero solum hanc libidinem
laudant (est enim ira, ut modo definiui, ulciscendi libido), sed
ipsum illud genus uel libidinis uel cupiditatis ad summam utili-

8. nullam R G K.   nullûm V u *in a mut.*   15. nesciat R 6 B 3 S M 1 2
D C   O 7.   nesciet R 1 7 17 V P 1 4 G B 1 2 K 1 2 E 1 2 L 5 W 1 2
Π J   O 1–3 8.   nesciant ed. H.
   § **44**, 18. libidinis uel R 7 17 V P G B 1–3 S E 1 2 W 1 2 M 1 2 D C Π J
O 1–3 7 8. ‖ uel *om.* R 1 K 1.

habent : for the transition from *orat.
obl.* to *orat. rect.* cf. ii 26, 62 n. Bentley
followed by Dav. changed *habent* to *habere*
without noticing that the change involved
reading *excanduerit* with some inferior
MSS in the next line.

excanduit, 'has the glow of passion':
cf. *Fam.* viii 12, 2 'id postquam resciit,
excanduit, et me causam inimicitiarum
quaerere clamitauit.' For the perf. in the
protasis to denote an antecedent condition
cf. Draeger, *Synt.* II § 548 B.

oratorem : cf. Sen. de Ira ii 17, 1
'"Orator," inquit "iratus aliquando melior est," immo imitatus iratum. Nam et
histriones in pronuntiando non irati populum mouent, sed iratum bene agentes :
et apud iudices itaque et in contione et
ubicumque alieni animi ad nostrum arbitrium agendi sunt, modo iram, modo
metum, modo misericordiam ut aliis in-
cutiamus, ipsi simulabimus.'

non modo...sed ne...quidem : cf. i 36,
87 n.

quae : for the case of the relative cf. v
10, 30 n. on *quos.*

actio : Or. 17, 55 'est enim actio quasi
corporis quaedam eloquentia cum constet
et uoce atque motu '; *ib.* 25, 86 'modica
iactatione corporis, uultu tamen multa
conficiens.'

uirum, 'a man at all': *uir* is generally
a term of praise, cf. ii 22, 53 'C. Marius,
rusticanus uir, sed plane uir.'

lenitatem ..lentitudinis : to the Stoic
πραότης (*lenitas*) meant ἀρετὴ καθ' ἥν
πρὸς ὀργὰς γίνονται ἀκίνητοι (Andron.
Rhod. περὶ παθ. 526), cf. Stob. Ecl. ii 7,
p. 184 c.; to the Peripatetic it meant the
golden mean between an excessive ten-

dency to anger and the apathy which
refused to be roused by anything. Arist.
Eth. Nic. ii 7, 10 ἔστι δὲ καὶ περὶ ὀργὴν
ὑπερβολὴ καὶ ἔλλειψις καὶ μεσότης· σχεδὸν
δὲ ἀνωνύμων ὄντων αὐτῶν τὸν μέσον πρᾷον
λέγοντες τὴν μεσότητα πρᾳότητα καλέ-
σωμεν : for the Stoic ideal quality the
Peripatetic had a name ἀοργησία (Arist.
l.c. ὁ δὲ ἐλλείπων ἀοργητός τις, ἣ δὲ
ἔλλειψις ἀοργησία) or ἀναλγησία in Theophrastus (ap. Stob. *l.c.*): either school
gave the name πρᾳότης to the state of
mind which it considered the ideal, but
the feelings which the Stoic considered
to be right, the Peripatetics considered
to be wrong and gave them a *uitiosum
nomen* accordingly. TS. strangely think
that Cic. is unfair to the Peripatetics and
attributes to them a contempt for πρᾳότης
which they did not feel.

uitioso=*uitium indicanti.*

lentitudinis : Q. Fr. i 1, 38 'te illud
admoneo...tibi esse diligentissime lin-
guam continendam, quae quidem mihi
uirtus interdum non minor uidetur quam
omnino non irasci: nam illud est non
solum grauitatis sed nonnunquam etiam
lentitudinis.'

§ **44. modo** : 12, 27.

uel libidinis uel cupiditatis : since the
second *uel* is omitted in R1, Tregd.
bracketed the words *uel libidinis uel* :
their genuineness is defended by Wesenb.
Em. ii, 10 who notes that *libidinis* is
required here after *libidinem* above, and
that in § 55 where the Stoic reply to these
statements is given, the word occurs twice.
The genitives are gen. of definition,
i 15, 34 n.

tatem esse dicunt a natura datum: nihil enim quemquam, nisi
20 quod lubeat, praeclare facere posse. noctu ambulabat in publico
Themistocles cum somnum capere non posset, quaerentibusque
respondebat Miltiadis tropaeis se e somno suscitari. cui non sunt
auditae Demosthenis uigiliae? qui dolere se aiebat si quando
opificum antelucana uictus esset industria. philosophiae denique
25 ipsius principes numquam in suis studiis tantos progressus sine
flagranti cupiditate facere potuissent. ultimas terras lustrasse

20. lubeat R 1 7 G B 1 K 1 W 1 J O 1.   lubeat V *at fuerat ut uid.*
       u eat
iubeat.   lib P *al. atr. superscr.*   libeat R 6 17 B 3 K 2 E 2 L 5 W 2
M 1 2 Π O 2 3 7 8.   iubeat S *marg.* libeat.   iubeat P 4 B 2 E 1 D C.
21. quod somnum R V P B K S E *alii.*   quod sonum G.   cum *corr. Seyffertus.*
                                                                           it
22. respondebat R V P G B 2 K 1 E 2 W 1 2 O 1–3 7 8.   respondeat E 1.
                                                                            i
respondit D C. ‖ Miltiadis M 1 J O 2.   militia dis V.   mil⌃tiadis B 3
eod. ut uid. atr.   militiadis G D.   militia dis R B 1 2 E W 2 *marg.* miltiadis.
milciadis R 6 M 2 O 3.   miliciadis R 17.   melchiadis W 1.   meltiadis O 1.
mitiadis O 8.   miltiātis O 7.   miliadi f K 2.   miliciam dis E 2.
militia ads K 1. ‖ tropḥaeis R.   trophaeis V G.   tropheis B 1 K 1 E 1 D.
tropeis K 2.   trope isse W 2 *marg.* tropheis.   tro phacis E 2. ‖ suscitari B 3
                                                           i
W 1 2 D O 1 7.   suscitare V *atr. uiridi superscr.* P *alio atr. superscr.*
B *eod. ut. uid. atr.*   suscitarẹ E 1.   suscitar ꝑ O 8 e *in* i *mut.*   suscitare R G
B 2 K 1 E 2.   suscitare S *marg.* excitari.   excitari O 3.   23. demosthenis B.
                h
demostenis S.   demostenis R V G K. ‖ dolere V P K 1 W 1 2 D.
                                                                                             e
dol&re K o *in* e *mut.*   dolore G B 2 E 1. ‖ agebat K.   25. princ e̅ps K
eod. ut. uid. atr. ‖ progressus   sine V us *in lit. et spatio relicto.*

nisi **quod lubeat**=*nisi id ad quod
faciendum libidine incitetur.*
   Themistocles : Plut. Them. c. 3, 4
σύννους ὁρᾶσθαι τὰ πολλὰ πρὸς ἑαυτῷ καὶ
τὰς νύκτας ἀγρυπνεῖν καὶ τοὺς πότους
παραιτεῖσθαι τοὺς συνήθεις καὶ λέγειν πρὸς
τοὺς ἐρωτῶντας καὶ θαυμάζοντας τὴν περὶ
τὸν βίον μεταβολὴν ὡς καθεύδειν αὐτὸν
οὐκ ἐῴη τὸ τοῦ Μιλτιάδου τρόπαιον. Cf.
also Val. Max. viii 14, 1 ext.
   cum : Sff.'s emendation for the MSS
quod which probably arose out of *quom*
(for *quom* omitted after *quod* cf. Fin ii 26,
82 ; *ib.* 31, 101). The subj. after *quod*
can be defended (with Küh.) only on the
ground that *sententia ex Themistoclis
mente profertur* : but Döderl.'s objection
to this holds good that, if this be so, the
words ought to have formed part of
Themistocles' reply: he accordingly trans-
poses them to stand after *respondebat* :
Baiter brackets the clause.
   cui : for the dat. of the agent cf. ii 1, 2 ;
Madv. *Gr.* 250 *a* ; Gildersleeve and Lodge
§ 354.
   Demosthenis : cf. Plut. Demosth. c 7;
Stob. Ecl. iii 29, 60 Δημοσθένης ὁ Δη-

μοσθένους εἰ ἔμελλε τῆς ὑστεραίας ἔσεσθαι
ἐκκλησία, ἀλλὰ ἐκεῖνός γε διὰ τῆς νυκτὸς
ἠγρύπνει πάσης διαφροντίζων δηλονότι καὶ
ἐκμανθάνων ταῦτα ἃ ἔμελλεν ἐρεῖν : Hieron.
Ruf. i 4 p. 495.
   dolere : Bentley preferred a reading
which he found in a MS of Dav.'s *dolore
se angebat* on the ground that *maius est re
ipsa dolere quam id prae se ferre*.
   potuissent : the protasis is contained
in *sine flagranti studio* : cf. i 15, 32
'nemo unquam sine magna spe inmor-
talitatis se pro patria offerret ad mortem ';
i 25, 63 n. ; v 2, 5.
   ultimas terras : Fin. v 19, 50 'quid de
Pythagora? quid de Platone aut Demo-
crito loquar? a quibus propter discendi
cupiditatem uidemus ultimas terras esse
peragratas'; *ib.* 29, 87 where Plato is
said to have visited Egypt to learn
numeros et caelestia from the priests and
Pythagoras to have visited the Magi in
Persia; Plin. N.H. xxx 1, 2 says that
Pythagoras, Democritus and Plato went
to foreign countries to learn the secrets of
the magicians.
   Iamblichus, Pythag. uit. iii 13 sqq.,

Pythagoran, Democritum, Platonem accepimus. ubi enim quicquid esset quod disci posset, eo ueniendum iudicauerunt. num putamus haec fieri sine summo cupiditatis ardore potuisse? XX. 45. Ipsam aegritudinem, quam nos ut taetram et inmanem beluam fugiendam diximus, non sine magna utilitate a natura dicunt constitutam, ut homines castigationibus, reprehensionibus, ignominiis adfici se in delicto dolerent. inpunitas

27. pythagoran R V K. Pÿtagoran P. pytagoran B 2. phytagoran G. phithagoran E. pytagorā B 1. ǁ quicquid R V P 1 2 B 1 3 K S E 1 2 M 2 O 2 3. quiquid G *alt. man. superscr.* quidquid II. q̇dq̇d W 2. quicqt O 7 quicquam B 2 M 1 C O 1. quicq̃, D O 8. quid R 6 W 1. 28. esset quid B 1 *al. atr. corr.* ǁ disci E 2 W 1 D O 1 3 8. dici V *atr. ant. superscr.* R *eod. atr.* B *al. atr. superscr.* dici R 2 10 16 P G K 1 O 7. XX. § 45, 1. tetram R V P G *h. l.* ǁ inmanem R V G E. in manē B 2. immanem B 1 S. 2. fugienda G. 3. omnes R 16 V G S L 3-5 M 1 2 C II O 1-37. om̄s R 10 16 P B 1 2 K 1 E 1 L 2 W 1 D O 8. om̄es R 17 B 3 L 6 J. ois W 2. ōs E 2. homines *corr. Manutius.* 4. affici se R 6 7 17 B 3 K 2 W 1 2 M 1 2 D C J O 1-3 8. adficisse V E. adficisse R G K. afficisse B 2. affecisse B 1 S II. *om.* O 7. ǁ inpunitas G E. impunitas R V B 1 2 K S.

says that Pythagoras visited Syria and Egypt ἔρωτι καὶ ὀρέξει θεωρίας and that after twenty years spent in Egypt he was taken as a prisoner to Babylon by Cambyses where he spent twelve years with the Magi: cf. Porph. Vit. Pyth. 6. For his journey into Egypt both Porphyry and Diog. L. viii 3 rely upon the authority of Antiphon who wrote περὶ τῶν ἐν ἀρετῇ πρωτευσάντων: the story is also told by Isocr. Bus. 11, 28 and probably is an invention to account for the similarity in many points between Egyptian and Pythagorean beliefs (Herod. ii 81, 123).

The evidence for Democritus' travels is his own statement quoted by Clem. Alex. Strom. i 69 p. 357: ἐγὼ δὲ τῶν κατ' ἐμεωυτὸν ἀνθρώπων γῆν πλείστην ἐπεπλανησάμην ἱστορέων τὰ μήκιστα...οὐδείς κώ με παρήλλαξεν οὐδ' οἱ Αἰγυπτίων καλεόμενοι Ἁρπεδονάπται, σὺν τοῖς δ' ἐπὶ πᾶσιν ἐπ' ἔτεα πέντε ἐπὶ ξείνης ἐγενήθην. Later writers (*ap.* Diog. L. ix 35) make his travels extend to Ethiopia, Persia and India.

Plato's journeys to Italy, Sicily and Cyrene seem well established and his journey to Egypt is not improbable. Cf. Ritter and Preller § 308 and Gomperz, *Greek Thinkers* II pp. 254 ff.

quicquid: Dav. Or. and Bouh. with some MSS and most ancient edd. before Gr. read *quid*. The use of *quicquid* for *quidque*, a survival of the older usage of Plautine Latin, is well attested for Cicero, cf. v 34, 98; Fin. v 9, 24 with Madv.'s

note. Küh. denies that the relative force of *quicquid* is ever wholly obscured in Cic. and explains *ubi quicquid esset* as equivalent to *ubi aliquid esset, quicquid esset*, but such an explanation seems rather forced in a passage like Fam. vi 1, 1 'quocunque in loco quisquis est,' and the tradition of the use of *quidquid* for *quidque* from Plautus to Lucretius renders any other explanation unlikely.

XX. § 45. **beluam**: cf. Ac. ii 34, 108 'credoque Clitomacho ita scribenti Herculi quendam laborem exanclatum a Carneade quod ut feram et immanem beluam sic ex animis nostris adsensionem, id est opinationem et temeritatem, extraxisset'; Rep. ii 40, 67; Stob. Ecl. Eth. II p. 175 [ii 6, 6] ὑπὸ τῆς σφοδρότητος ἐκφερομένους καθάπερ ὑπό τινος ἀπειθοῦς ἵππου. But what is metaphor here was in Stoic theory almost sober earnest: acc. to Chrysippus the passions were not merely σώματα but ζῷα and Plut. sarcastically says that if the Stoic theory is right one might ἀποφαίνειν ἕκαστον ἡμῶν παράδεισον ἢ μάνδραν ἢ δούρειον ἵππον. Plut. de comm. not. c. 45 p. 1084 B.

The comparison of the passions to wild animals becomes a commonplace in later writers; cf. Galen περὶ ψυχῆς παθῶν 5, 26; Maximus Tyrius xxxiv fin. Heins. p. 343; Chariton, Aprodis. vi. 9, 4; S. Basil, *de leg. libr. gent.* p. 182 D.

ut homines...dolerent = *ut homines, castigationibus...adfecti, se in delicto esse dolerent*—an illogical brachylogy.

5 enim peccatorum data uidetur iis qui ignominiam et infamiam
ferunt sine dolore; morderi est melius conscientia. ex quo est
illud e uita ductum ab Afranio. nam cum dissolutus filius :

    Heú me miserum!

tum seuerus pater :

10   Dúm modo doleat áliquid, doleat quídlubet.

46. reliquas quoque partis aegritudinis utilis esse dicunt, misericordiam ad opem ferendam et hominum indignorum calamitates
subleuandas; ipsum illud aemulari, obtrectare non esse inutile,
cum aut se non idem uideat consecutum quod alium, aut alium
15 idem quod se; metum uero si qui sustulisset, omnem uitae diligentiam sublatam fore, quae summa esset in iis qui leges, qui

7. euicta V.   8. heu me *om.* B 1.   10. doleat *post* aliquid *om.* B 1. ‖
quidlubet R V G B E 3 M 2 J.   quidlibet R 17 P 1 2 B 3 M 1 D C
Ó 2 3 7.   quod lubet R 6 7 W 1 O 1.   quodlibet R 2 10 16 S E 2 L 5 Π
O 8.   qad lībet W 2.   quid lubet K *at fuerat* iubet.   quid iubet B 2 E.
§ **46,** 11. partis R V G B 1 2 K.   partes S E. ‖ utilis R V G B 1 2 K E.
utiles S.   12. calamitates hominum indignorum R 6 7 17 P B 3 S W 1
M 1 2 D J O 1–3 7 8 ed. H.   calamitates hominum indignorum calamitate W 2.
cal. hom. indign. calamitates R G B 2 K 1 E 1 2 V *sed linea subter uerb. ult.*
ducta. B *sed* s *in loco ult. eras.* Π *sed ult. uerb. transuerso calamo not.*   calam.
hom. indign. hominum calami K 2.   13. obtrectare G *h. l.*   15. si qui
R B K E D C.   si qui V *atr. uiridi superscr.*   si quis R 6 P G B 3 S E 2
W 1 2 M 1 2 Π J O 2 3 7 8.

Afranio: L. Afranius, the principal
author of *fabulae togatae*, whose comedies
were considered by enthusiasts to equal
those of Menander, 'dicitur Afrani toga
conuenisse Menandro,' Hor. Epp. ii 1
57 ; Quintilian (x 1, 100) says ' togatis
excellit Afranius : utinam non inquinasset
argumenta puerorum foedis amoribus,
mores suos fassus.'

filius : sc. *dixisset,* which early editions
before Victorius actually insert in the text
after *miserum.*

Heu me miserum : quoted also in
Att. xvi 2, 3 from an unidentified play ;
the two sentences form a trochaic tetrameter catalectic. For the antithesis between *aliquid* and *quidlubet* cf. Ov. Epp.
ex Pont. i 1, 4 'excipe, dumque aliquo,
quolibet abde loco.'

§ **46. misericordiam :** cf. Arist. Rhet.
ii 8, 2 with Cope's n.

indignorum : sc. *calamitatibus* to be
supplied out of *calamitates.* The ellipse of
the abl. after *indignus* is not uncommon.
Dav. quotes Plaut. Curc. iv 2, 27; Ov.
Met. i 631; iv 138; A.A. iii 708; F. ii
780 etc. : *indignus* is sometimes equiva-

lent to *innocens* e.g. in Lucr. ii 1104
' exanimatque indignos inque merentes.'
Erasm. Bouh. Niss. with some MSS read
indigorum, and Sff. who asserts that
indignorum here can only mean ' persons
unworthy of pity ' reads *calamitates hominum indignorum calamitate* which, though
awkward, comes very near the reading of
some of the best MSS.

ipsum illud aemulari : Arist. Rhet. ii
9, 2 καὶ ἄμφω τὰ πάθη [sc. ἔλεος καὶ
νέμεσις] ἤθους χρηστοῦ· δεῖ γὰρ ἐπὶ μὲν
τοῖς ἀναξίως πράττουσι κακῶς συνάχθεσθαι
καὶ ἐλεεῖν, τοῖς δὲ εὖ νεμεσᾶν; Eth. Nic. ii
7, 15 νέμεσις δὲ μεσότης φθόνου καὶ ἐπι-
χαιρεκακίας...ὁ μὲν γὰρ νεμεσητικὸς λυπεῖ-
ται ἐπὶ τοῖς ἀναξίως εὖ πράττουσι.

uideat, sc. *aliquis :* for the ellipse of an
indefinite subj. see 8, 17 n. on *concupierit.*

alium...se : sc. *uideat consecutum :* cf. i
17, 39 n. on *quod Pythagoram.*

metum : Arist. Eth. Nic. iii 6, 3 ἔνια γὰρ
καὶ δεῖ φοβεῖσθαι καὶ καλόν, τὸ δὲ μὴ
αἰσχρόν, οἷον ἀδοξίαν. ὁ μὲν γὰρ φοβούμενος
ἐπιεικὴς καὶ αἰδήμων, ὁ δὲ μὴ φοβούμενος
ἀναίσχυντος.

magistratus, qui paupertatem, qui ignominiam, qui mortem, qui dolorem timerent. haec tamen ita disputant ut resecanda esse fateantur, euelli penitus dicant nec posse nec opus esse, et in 20 omnibus fere rebus mediocritatem esse optimam existiment. quae cum exponunt, nihilne tibi uidentur an aliquid dicere? *A.* Mihi uero dicere aliquid, itaque exspecto, quid ad ista. XXI. **47.** *M.* Reperiam fortasse, sed illud ante: uidesne quanta fuerit apud Academicos uerecundia? plane enim dicunt quod ad rem pertineat. Peripateticis respondetur a Stoicis. digladientur illi per me licet, cui nihil est necesse nisi, ubi sit illud 5 quod ueri simillimum uideatur, anquirere. quid est igitur quod occurrat in hac quaestione, e quo possit attingi aliquid ueri

18. tenerent K 1.   19. discant G *at* s *expunx. et conf. ead. ut uid. man.* ‖ et in omnibus R V P G K S E *plerique.*   ut in omnibus Π *at* u *ante* t *in ras.* ut Eit in omnibus B 1 *al. atr. superscr.* XXI. § **47**, 1. reperiam R V P G K.   repperiam B.   reppiam R 2. 2. achademicos R V G B K S E.   5. anquirere R V P G B 1 2 K E Gr. inquirere R 6 W 1 2 M 1 2 D C O 1–3 7 8.   inquerere J *at ras. ad init. fuisse* ac *uidetur.*   inquirere S *unius litt. spatio relicto post* n.   inquirere B 3 *eod. ut* l o *uid. atr.*   acquirere Π E 2.   6. ex quo M 1.   e qua B 1 *al. atr. superscr.* e qua R 6 P 4 K 2 S E 2 3 L 2 3 5 6 W 1 2 M 2 Π J O 1–3 8.   de qua D C.   4e¦qua V.   equa R 17 B 2 3 E 1.   e͞q P 1.   aequa R G K L 4. est qua O 7 ed. H. ‖ attingi R V G B K S E.

mortem...dolorem: this is hardly an anti-climax: *dolor* and *mors* are the two things *quae maxime metuuntur* (30, 64), and Cic. adopts, sometimes the order used here (e.g. ii 18, 43 *mortis dolorisque contemptio*), sometimes the opposite (e.g. ii 17, 41 *contra dolorem et mortem disciplina*).

haec is to be taken with *resecanda esse*: for the order of the words cf. Ac. i 2, 8 'ea, quantum potui...feci ut essent nota nostris'; for the tendency in Latin to put a pronoun at the beginning of the clause see Nägelsbach, *Stil.* § 189, 1.

et has overwhelming MSS authority. Wopkens (*op. cit.* p. 132) defends *ut*, the reading of the old edd. and inferior MSS (which is grammatically faultless) by citing instances of the repetition of consecutive *ut*, e.g. Ac. i 6, 24; 12, 45 etc.

aliquid: cf. i 20, 45 n.

ad ista: sc. *habeas* or *dicturus sis*, cf. ii 18, 42 'nisi quid uis ad haec'; Nägelsbach, *Stil.* § 183, 1.

XXI. § 47. **Reperiam:** sc. *quid dicam.*

illud: sc. *dicendum est*, cf. Fin. iv 1, 2 'quare ad ea primum, si uidetur.'

uerecundia: 'moderation' in speech: Beroald. compares Fam. ix 22, 5 'ego

seruo et seruabo (sic enim assuewi) Platonis uerecundiam'; cf. also Off. i 28, 99 'iustitiae partes sunt non uiolare homines, uerecundiae non offendere'; Q. Fr. iii 1, 3 'Caesar...meam in rogando uerecundiam obiurgauit.'

digladientur: 'fence' διαξιφίζεσθαι; cf. Off. i 9, 28 'de quibus inter se digladiari soleant' and Reid's note to Acad. frag. i 1 (p. 161).

cui: Cicero, as an adherent of the New Academy, held that there was no absolute criterion of truth; the utmost to be attained was the probable; cf. v 11, 33 'quodcunque nostros animos probabilitate percussit, id dicimus'—a point of view which is expounded at length in the *Academics*: the *probabile* or *ueri simile* corresponds to the τὸ εὔλογον of Arcesilaus; cf. Sext. Emp. Math. vii 158 φησὶν ὁ Ἀρκεσίλαος ὅτι ὁ περὶ πάντων ἐπέχων κανονιεῖ τὰς αἱρέσεις καὶ φυγὰς καὶ κοινῶς τὰς πράξεις τῷ εὐλόγῳ, κατὰ τοῦτό τε προερχόμενος τὸ κριτήριον κατορθώσει.

anquirere: ii 10, 25 n.

e quo: either this, the reading of some MSS, accepted by Küh. Kl. Hei. TS. Sff. or *quo* Bouh.'s conjecture accepted by Ern. Or. W. Mo. must be read in pre-

simile? quo longius mens humana progredi non potest. definitio
perturbationis, qua recte Zenonem usum puto. ita enim definit
ut perturbatio sit auersa a ratione contra naturam animi
10 commotio, uel breuius, ut perturbatio sit adpetitus uehementior, uehementior autem intellegatur is qui procul absit
a naturae constantia. **48.** quid ad has definitiones possint dicere?
atque haec pleraque sunt prudenter acuteque disserentium, illa

7. qua R P G *alii.* quȩ V. quae K. 9. a ratione R 7 P 4 B 3 E 2
M 1 2 D C II O 2 8 Gr. ed H.   ratione B 1 *al. atr. superscr.* S *eod. atr.*
ratione R 1 6 1 7 V P G B 2 K 1 2 E L 5 W 1 2 J O 1 3 7. 10. adpetitus
R V G K E. appetitus B S. ‖ uehementior uehementior R 6 7 B 3 E 2
W 1 M 1 2 II O 1-3 8. uehementior *semel tantum habent* R 1 17 V P G
B 1 2 K 1 2 S E 1 W 2 D C J. 11. is R V P G. his B 1. his E 1.
§ **48,** 12. possim R 1 6 7 17 V G B 1-3 K 1 2 S E 1-3 L 4 6 M 1 2
D C O 3 8. possum L 3 5 W 1 2 II J O 1 2 7 ed. H. possem L 2.
possint *corr. Bentleius.* 13. atque E 2 II. atqui R V P G B 1-3 K 1 S
E 1 W 1 2 M 1 2 D C J O 1-3 7 8.

ference to Bentley's *qua* accepted by Dav.,
the antecedent being obviously *quid* not
quaestione: Sff. *probante Küh.* notes in
favour of *e quo*, as against *quo*: 'ipsum
attingendi uerbum ductum a cursu mari-
timo definitionem Zenonis tamquam locum
intellegi uult, e quo egressa disputatio ad
id, quod uelit (ueri simile), peruenire
possit.'

Zenonem: cf. 6, 11 where the same
definition (with the addition of *recta*
before *ratione*) is given, and n. there.

definit ut...sit: 'for by the terms of
his definition a *perturbatio* is....' It is
hardly correct to say, as do Küh. TS.
Hei., that this expression is a contraction
for *definit ut dicat...esse...*, and the parallels quoted by Küh. are not to the point.
Cic. uses both constructions in speaking
of a *definitio uerbi*; cf. with the constr.
here Fin. v 26, 76 'percipiendi uis ita
definitur a Stoicis ut negent quidquam
posse percipi nisi tale uerum quale falsum
esse non possit.' In the former case the
word is regarded (quite logically) as being
made to mean a certain thing by being
defined to mean it : this is the idea under-
lying the expression of Or. i 15, 64 'si
quis uniuersam et propriam oratoris uim
definire complectique uult, is orator erit
qui...'; in the latter case the insertion of
dicere etc. or the use of the acc. and inf.
(e.g. in Off. i 27, 96) lays stress upon the
fact that the *definitio* is an *assertion* which
may or may not be accepted universally.

§ **48. possint**: sc. *Peripatetici*: *possint*
is Bentley's emendation accepted by Dav.
F.A.W. Or. Sff. and most recent editors.
Or. says it is the reading of the *prima*

manus in S; Bouh. Ern. and (formerly)
Kl. retained *possim* which, as Bouh. puts
it, must imply 'Quid, etiam si contra
dicere liberet, aduersus istas definitiones
ego possim dicere ? prorsus enim sunt
rectae.' But the question is (not what
reply an Academic like Cicero could give
if he wished, but) what reply a Peripatetic
could make to the Stoic definition.

atque: Tregd.'s emendation for the
reading of the best MSS *atqui* has been
accepted by Wes. Bait. Ml. TS. Hei. Sff.
and is actually found in two MSS. The
reading *atqui* is kept by Or. and Küh.
Atque is required by the sense : Cic. is
adding a general consideration in favour
of the Stoic definition : for the use of
atqui see Madv.'s note on Fin. i 18, 58.

disserentium : the Stoics, upon whose
dialectical superiority Cic. continually
lays stress, sometimes rather grudgingly ;
e.g. Fin. iii 12, 41 'magna contentio quam
tractabat a Peripateticis mollius (est enim
eorum consuetudo dicendi non satis acuta
propter ignorationem dialecticae) Carneades tuus egregia quadam exercitatione
in dialecticis summaque eloquentia rem
in summum discrimen duxit'; *ib.* iii, 1, 3
'Stoicorum autem non ignoras quam sit
subtile uel spinosum potius disserendi
genus'; Brut. 31, 118 'omnes fere Stoici
prudentissimi in disserendo'; cf. also
Diog. L. vii 47 sq. ; *ib.* 83 καὶ τοιοῦτοι
μὲν ἐν τοῖς λογικοῖς οἱ Στωϊκοί, ἵνα μάλιστα
κρατύνουσι διαλεκτικὸν μόνον εἶναι τὸν
σοφόν.

illa : the rhetorical statements of the
Peripatetics. In Fin. iv 3, 5 sqq. Cicero
enlarges with enthusiasm upon the 'oratio

quidem ex rhetorum pompa: 'ardores animorum cotesque
15 uirtutum.' an uero uir fortis, nisi stomachari coepit, non potest
fortis esse? gladiatorium id quidem; quamquam in iis ipsis
uidemus saepe constantiam:

> Cónloquuntur, cóngrediuntur, quaérunt aliquid, póstulant,

20 ut magis placati quam irati esse uideantur. sed in illo genere sit
sane Pacideianus aliquis hoc animo, ut narrat Lucilius:

> Occidam illum equidem et uincam, si id quaeritis, inquit.

14. rh&orum K 1. r&ħorum R *eod. atr.* rethorum V G B S E.
15. coepit R V K 1 W 1. coeperit O 2. caepit G. cẹpit B 1 S.

caeperit M 2. cepit B 2 E 1 2 C J O 3. cep K 2. ceperit B 3 W 2
M 1 D O 18. 16. gladiatorium R V P G B K E 1 M 2 Gr. gladiatorum
B 23 K 2 S E 2 L 5 W 1 2 M 1 D C Π J O 1–3 7 8. 18. conloquuntur
G B. cōloquuntur E 1. colloquuntur S. conlocuntur R V. ||
quaeruntur V G M 2. q̄rūt B 2 W 2. q̄runt R 7 P 1 L 2. q̄runtur P 4.
quẹrunt W 1. quæeruntur R *eod. atr.* queruntur R 6 17 B 1 3 K 1 2 S
E 1 2 L 3–6 M 1 D C Π J O 2 3 7 8. cōqueruntur O 1. quaerunt
corr. Schlenger. 21. pacideianus R 6. pacidianus R V P G K 1 2 S E 1 2
W 1 D C J O 2 3 7 8. pacidiamus M 1. pacidiarius Π. pacidianus W 2.
placidianus B 1 M 2 O 1. placidanus B 2. 23. inquit R G K.
inquid V.

ornata et grauis' which the Peripatetics owed to their study of rhetoric. For *rhetorum pompa* Ern. compares Or. 13, 42 'uerum haec [eloquentia] ludorum atque pompae' and de Or. ii 22,'94 'sed eorum [oratorum]partim in pompa partim in acie illustres esse uoluerunt,' where, as here, the ref. is to the γένος ἐπιδεικτικόν.

The *pompa* was the procession which preceded the displays of athletic prowess witnessed at the games and serves as an appropriate metaphor for the mere display of rhetorical power as opposed to its actual exercise in the γένος δικανικόν. For this and similar metaphors see Nägelsbach, *Stil.* § 136, 4.

iis ipsis: sc. *gladiatoribus* to be supplied from *gladiatorium* above: Hei. compares Liv. ii 53, 1 'Veiens bellum exortum, quibus (sc. Veientibus) Sabini arma coniunxerant'; cf. also 33, 70 n. on *qui*, v 27, 77 *in ea gente* n.

conloquuntur...postulant: recognized as a trochaic septenarius by Schlenger (*Philol.* xii p. 288): his view has been accepted by Bait. TS. Ml. Sff. Küh.: edd. before Schlenger regarded the words as Cicero's own, reading *queruntur* with

the majority of the MSS. Bentley proposed *expostulant*, referring to v 5, 14.

The line (from an unidentified poet) describes the parade of indifference and bonhomie which professional etiquette sometimes imposed upon gladiators— *non protinus ira nec ictus.*

in illo genere, 'in that profession' sc. *gladiatorum*: cf. Verr. ii 2, 61, 149 *genus hoc aratorum.*

sane: for *sane* 'of course,' 'assuredly,' with concessive subj. cf. Fin. ii 23, 76 'sit sane ista uoluptas'; de rep. i 19, 32; Att. vi 1, 7; Amic. 5, 18 with Sff.'s n.

Pacideianus: 'optimus longe | post homines natos gladiator qui fuit unus,' Lucil. *ap.* Non. iv 64: his great rival was the *Samnis*, Aeserninus. The spelling in the text adopted by Or. Kl. Ml. Sff. as against 'Pacidianus' (Tr. Ba. Küh.) is confirmed by the Medicean MS of Q. Fr. iii 4, 2 and by Hor. Sat. ii 7, 97.

Lucilius: in book iv, ll. 153 ff. of Marx's edition 1 p. 12.

si id quaeritis, 'if you want to know'; this meaning seems more in accordance with Ciceronian usage (e.g. Off. iii 20,

Verum illud credo fore: in os prius accipiaʳ ipse,
25　Quam gladium in stomacho spurci ac pulmonibus
　　　　　　　　　　　　　　　　sisto.
　Odi hominem, iratus pugno, nec longius quicquam
　Nobis, quam dextrae gladium dum accommodet
　　　　　　　　　　　　　　　　alter;
30　Vsque adeo studio atque odio illius ecferor ira.

XXII. **49.** At sine hac gladiatoria iracundia uidemus pro-
gredientem apud Homerum Aiacem multa cum hilaritate, cum
depugnaturus esset cum Hectore; cuius, ut arma sumpsit,
ingressio laetitiam attulit sociis, terrorem autem hostibus, ut

25. insthomacho G.　‖　furia ac R V　P 1 4　G　B 1 2.　　suria a E 1.
fura ac S.　　　fura ac R 6 7　P 2 5　K 1 2　E 2　L 3 4 5　Π　O 1–3 8.
fi ira ac J.　　sura ac Urs. 3240 *marg.* l' una.　　sura et L 2.　　fupac R 17.
furia ac P 6 *incert. an* s.　　furia atque O 7.　furia a D C.　　una ac P 3　W 1 2
M 1 2　L 6.　　stomacos una ac E 3.　　unam B 3.　　spurci *corr. Seyffertus.* ‖
pulmonibusisto G *in* pulmonibus sisto *alt. man. corr.*　　pulmonibus isto V.
27. ne longius B 1.　　28. nobis R 7　B 2　E 3　L 2 5 6　W 1　D　O 1 7 ed. H.
uobis R 6 17　V P G　B 3　K 1　E 1 2　L 3 4　W 2　M 1 2　C Π J　O 2 3 8.
ɖobis R 1 (*sic*).　*om.* B 1.　　30. ecferor R V G.　　ęcferor K 1 *ex* ecferor
nigriore atr. mut.　　aecferor B 2.　　efferor P　B 1 3　S J.　*om.* E 1.
XXII. § 49, 1. at sine R 6　V　B 3　S　E 2　W 1　M 1 2　C Π　O 2 8 ed. H.
ac sine R P G　B 1 2　K 1　W 2　J　O 1 7.　　ac sine D.　　ut sine O 3.
3. hectore B *h. l. et infra* hectorem.　　haectore G.　　4. attulit R V G B S E.
attollit K 1.

80; de Or. ii 62, 254) than Küh.'s explanation, ' si id uultis, optatis, flagitatis.'
　accipiam: sc. *plagam.*
　spurci: Sff.'s emendation adopted by
Küh.: the word is applied in Lucil. *ap.*
Non. p. 393 to Aeserninus: Bentley conjectured *furiae* and Dav. *Furi* (i.e. Furi
Aesernini, though he offers no proof that
Aeserninus was called Furius). Tischer
proposed *furi* (dat.) 'the thief,' a frequent
term of general abuse in Comedy; Marx
reads *furia*; other conjectures are *fibra*
(Turn.), *hira* (Douza), *sicam* (om. *ac* Scal.).
Or. keeps the *sura*, which is de-
fended by Rossbach, *Phil.* lxiii (1904)
p. 100. Further conjectures in Mo. iii
exc. xiv pp. 390 ff.
　sisto: Küh. compares Virg. Aen. x
323 'intorquens iaculum clamanti sistit
in ore.'
　nec longius...quam...dum, 'nor can
we (i.e. either of us) bear to wait till the
other etc.': for the phrase *longum est
dum* 'it is tiresome waiting until,' cf.
Fam. xi 27, 1; Verr. ii 4, 18, 39; pro
Rab. Post. 12, 35; cf. also Sil. Ital. Pun.
xii 381 'longumque coire uidetur | et con-
ferre gradum'; Ter. Andr. 977. This

interpretation is better than Küh.'s 'nec
diutius pugnam morabimur quam uterque
nostrum gladium dextrae adaptauerit'—a
meaning which the Latin will hardly bear.
　For the scansion of *longius* and *pulmonibus* cf. i 5, 10 n.
　alter = *uterque.*
　odio: cf. Lucan, Phars. iv 708 'ueluti
fatalis arenae | muneribus non ira uetus
concurrere cogit | productos; odere pares.'
　XXII. § 49. **apud Homerum**: Il. vii
211 sq. where the phrase μειδιόων βλοσυ-
ροῖσι προσώπασι is Cicero's warrant for
the *multa cum hilaritate* of the text.
　esset, impft. since *uidemus progredi-
entem* is equivalent to *progressus est, ut
uidemus apud H.*
　cuius: i.e *Aiacis*, the more prominent,
though not the nearer, of the two names:
for the relative referring to the more re-
mote noun cf. Amicit. 21, 78 'cauendum
uero ne etiam in graues inimicitias conuertant se amicitiae, ex quibus iurgia,
maledicta, contumeliae gignuntur.'
　laetitiam: τὸν δὲ καὶ Ἀργεῖοι μέγ'
ἐγήθεον εἰσορόωντες, Hom. *l.c.*
　terrorem: Τρῶας δὲ τρόμος αἰνὸς ὑπή-
λυθε γυῖα ἕκαστον, *ibid.*

5 ipsum Hectorem, quem ad modum est apud Homerum, toto
pectore trementem prouocasse ad pugnam paeniteret. atque hi
conlocuti inter se, prius quam manum consererent, leniter et
quiete nihil ne in ipsa quidem pugna iracunde rabioseue fecerunt.
ego ne Torquatum quidem illum qui hoc cognomen inuenit
10 iratum existimo Gallo torquem detraxisse, nec Marcellum apud
Clastidium ideo fortem fuisse quia fuerit iratus. 50. de Africano
quidem, quia notior est nobis propter recentem memoriam, uel
iurare possum non illum iracundia tum inflammatum fuisse, cum
in acie M. Allienium Paelignum scuto protexerit gladiumque

6. paeniteret R G K.   pęniteret B S.   peniteret V P E. ‖ atque hi R G.
q;
athi V *atr. ant. superscr.*   7. conlocuti R V G B K E.   collocuti S.
                        ne a
9. ne torquatum R V G.   retorqtū E 1.   re tor quatū B 1.   nec torquatum R 7. ‖
qui hoc cognomen inuenit R 2 6 7 10 17   P   B 3   K 2   E 2 3   L 5   W 1 2   M 1 2
D C Π J   Ó 1–3 7 8 ed. H.   qui hoc cog-nouit nom̄ inuenit E 1.   qui hoc
cognouịt ṇomen inuenit V qui hoc cog   nom̄ inuenit B 1 *ras. ante* nom̄.
                                                    o
qui hoc cognouit nomen inuenit R G B 2 K 1.   10. galla,torquē uedetraxisse E 1.
cl
11. dastidium G *ead. man. superscr.*
§ 50, 14. in acie R 6 7   V   B 3   S   E 2   W 1   M 1 2   D Π   O 1 3.   acie O 7.
in aịaçe acie C.   in aciē R P   B 2   J ed. H.   in aciem G B   K 1 2   E 1   O 8.
fuisse W 2 *marg.* cū ī acie. ‖ M. alliennium D C M.   Haliēnum R 6.
M. Alliēniū W 1.   malliennium V.   malienium O 2.   maltienium R 7.
mascellum B 1.   alieniū S *marg.* M.   alliennium R P B K.   alli enniū B 2.
                                                    l
Alliēnniū J W 2 *marg.* alienū.   aliennium G *ead. man. superscr.*   allienium O 3.
allienum B 3 E 2 Π.   aliennium E 1   O 8.   aliēniū K 2.   allicnum M 2.
alienum M 1   O 1 7.   ad Enniū ed. H. ‖ paelignum R G.   pae lignū B 2.
pe lignū V.   pelignum P B K S E   W 1   D *alii.*

ipsum Hectorem: Cic. gives what
F.A.W. calls 'a somewhat strong version'
of Homer's lines "Εκτορί τ' αὐτῷ θυμὸς ἐνὶ
στήθεσσι τάτασσεν | ἀλλ' οὕτως ἔτι εἶχεν
ὑποτρέσαι οὐδ' ἀναδῦναι. Ern.'s remark
'hoc non est apud Homerum, nec ibi
reppererunt ueteres' goes rather far.

prouocasse, 'issued a challenge'; Hom.
Il. vii 66 ff. where Hector challenges any
of the ἀριστῆες Παναχαιῶν who might care
to fight in single combat.

nihil ne…quidem: for *ne…quidem*
with preceding negative cf. i 23, 53; ii
23, 56; Amic. 2, 10; Draeger, *Synt.* I
§ 82. It is not easy to see much justification for Cicero's statement that the duel was
conducted without heat and anger: Homer
(*l.c.* 256) says σύν ῥ' ἔπεσον, λείουσιν ἐοικό-
τες ὠμοφάγοισιν ἢ συσὶ κάπροισιν, though
they separate in a courteous fashion.

Torquatum: T. Manlius Torquatus;
the story is told in Liv. vii 9 and 10.
Aulus Gellius ix 13, 7 sqq. quotes the
account given by Claudius Quadrigarius
in the first book of his *Annals.*

inuenit: cf. Fin. i 7, 23 'ita prorsus
existimo neque eum Torquatum qui hoc
primus cognomen inuenit, aut torquem
illum hosti detraxisse'; Off. iii 31, 112,
where Beier explains *cognomen inuenit*
as = 'data hac occasione appellatus est.'
For the insertion of the defining or explanatory rel. clause *illum qui…inuenit,*
independent of the oratio obl., see
Draeger, *Synt.* II § 456, 2.

torquem: 'ubi eum euertit, caput prae-
cidit, torquem detraxit eamque sanguinu-
lentam sibi in collum imponit.' Claud.
Quadr. *ap.* Gell. *l.c.*

Marcellum, who won the *spolia opima*
from Viridomarus at Clastidium in 222 B.C.
Plut. Marc. 6; Polyb. ii 34.

apud: exx. of *apud* with geographical
names are not uncommon in Cicero. Mo.
quotes i 39, 94; Cluent. 7, 21; Diu. i
54, 123; N.D. iii 5, 11; Fin. ii 22, 73:
30, 97; Off. iii 30, 109; Fam. ii 10, 3;
Draeger, *Synt.* I § 253, 5, who notes
that this constr. is found only once in
Livy (xlii 12), regards it as a colloquial

15 hosti in pectus infixerit. de L. Bruto fortasse dubitarim an
propter infinitum odium tyranni ecfrenatius in Arruntem in-
uaserit; uideo enim utrumque comminus ictu cecidisse contrario.
quid igitur huc adhibetis iram? an fortitudo, nisi insanire coepit,
impetus suos non habet? quid? Herculem, quem in caelum ista
20 ipsa, quam uos iracundiam esse uultis, sustulit fortitudo, iratumne
censes conflixisse cum Erymanthio apro aut leone Nemeaeo?

16. ecfrenatius R G. efrenatius V *atr. ant. superscr.* c̄ frenati⁹ P.
h & frenatius K 1 h *atr. nigriore add.* effrenatius B 1 K 2 E 2 W 1 2 D
O 1 7 8. effrenatus O 3. effrenatius S. ‖ arruntem M 1 C O 3.
arruntē R 17 P S E 2 D. arrunte R V G B 1 2 K 1 E 1 J.
arrontem B 3 K 2 M 2. aruntem R 6 O 1. aruntē W 1 II. arūtē O 8.
arūte W 2. arontem R 7 O 2. marunte O 7 in *om.* 17. comminus
R V G B. cōminus K E. cominus S. 18. adhuc G *ead. man.* ‖
coepit R 1 6 V G B K O 2. cẹpit S. cepit K 2 Ė 2 L 5 D O 1.
cep C. cep̄ W 2. coepit W 1. cepit P O 7. ceperit B 3 O 3 8.

caeperit M 2. 19. herculem R V G. herculē B 1. erculē E *al. atr. superscr.*
20. uultis R V G K S E. ‖ iratum R 6 7 17 B 2 3 W 1 2 M 1 2 D C II J
O 1–3 7 8. ratum V. ratum R G K. fratrum E 1. Frm̄ B 1
marg. furentem. 21. erymanthio B. esymanthio E 1. erymathio R
eod. ut uid. atr. erymathio G K. erimanthio R 2 W 2 D. erimantho W 1.
erimathio V. herimathio P. ‖ apro aut V P G E 2 W 1 2 M 1 2 D
O 1 3 7 8. apro/a ut R 1 a *in marg. scr.* apaut B 2. ap | ut B 1 *al. atr. mut.*
E 1 *al. atr. mut.* ‖ nemaeo R V G K E O 8. nemẹo B 1. nemeo R 2 10 16
P S E 2 W 1 2 D O 1 ed. H. ne meo B 2.

usage which found its way into literary Latin.

Clastidium : a κώμη (Plut. *l.c.*) in Cisalpine Gaul, south of the Po (Liv. xxi 48, 9; xxix 11, 14).

§ 50. quidem, like γε, lends emphasis to the word preceding : the emphasis here serves to contrast the necessarily conjectural statement (*existimo*) about Torquatus, with the vigorous certainty (*uel iurare possum*) of the expression about Scipio, cf. ii 17, 41 n. For the constr. *de Africano...iurare possum...illum...fuisse*, Hei. compares v 20, 57; Or. ii 1, 3, and *de L. Bruto...inuaserit* below: see also Fin. iii 17, 57 'de bona autem fama... Chrysippus quidem et Diogenes ... ne digitum quidem eius causa porrigendum esse dicebant,' quoted by Nägelsbach, *Stil.* § 100, 2 *b*.

M. Allienium Paelignum : the fact is otherwise unknown. It is the younger Africanus who is referred to; the *memoria* of the elder would be no more *recens* than that of Marcellus.

L. Bruto : Liv. ii 6.

dubitarim an : 'I should be inclined to suspect that,' a polite form of assertion, nearly equivalent to *fortasse* : *haud scio* (*sciam*) *an* and *nescio an* which are more usual in Cicero have the same force : see Draeger, *Synt.* II § 467, 2 *d* (8), and for the potential perfect subj. *ib.* § 148 A.

uideo=*scriptum uideo*, cf. 3, 5 : 37, 79; v 33, 93; Ac. ii 5, 13.

comminus...contrario : the expression *contrario ictu* occurs in Liv. ii 6, 9 and it is possible that Cic. is quoting the actual words of some of the annalists, perhaps Tubero or Piso who seem, according to Soltau's analysis (*Livius' Geschichtswerk*, pp. 140 ff.), to have been Livy's principal authorities here.

Erymanthio apro, the *Erymanthia belua* of ii 9, 22, the boar which descending from Erymanthus in Arcadia ravaged Psophis till it was killed by Hercules, Diod. Sic. iv 12, 1.

leone Nemeaeo, the lion sprung from Typhon and Echidna, which inhabited Nemea and was strangled by Hercules, ii 9, 22; Diod. Sic. iv 11, 3.

an etiam Theseus Marathonii tauri cornua conprehendit iratus?
uide ne fortitudo minime sit rabiosa sitque iracundia tota leuitatis. neque enim est ulla fortitudo quae rationis est expers.
XXIII. 51. Contemnendae res humanae sunt, neglegenda
mors est, patibiles et dolores et labores putandi. haec cum
constituta sunt iudicio atque sententia, tum est robusta illa et
stabilis fortitudo, nisi forte, quae uehementer, acriter, animose
5 fiunt, iracunde fieri suspicamur. mihi ne Scipio quidem ille
pontifex maximus, qui hoc Stoicorum uerum esse declarauit,
nunquam priuatum esse sapientem, iratus uidetur fuisse Ti.
Graccho tum cum consulem languentem reliquit atque ipse

22. marathonii R V G   B 1 3   E 1.   ‖   tauri R 6   P   B 1 3   E 2   W 1 2
                                                    t
M 1 2   D J   O 1 3 7.   auri R *eod. atr.*   V *eod. atr.*   E *al. atr. superscr.*
auri G.   ‖   marathonḥt auri K *atr. nigriore mut.*   ‖   conprehendit V G *h. l.*   E.
comprehendit R B K S.   24. ulla R V P G B K S *plerique.*   illa W 2.
XXIII. § 51, 1. neglegenda R V G B K E.   negligenda P S.   3. sunt B 1
K 2   S   E 1   W 1   M 2   D C   O 7 8.   sint R V P G   B 2 3   K 1   E 2   L 5
W 2   M 1   Π J   O 2 3.   *om.* O 1.   ‖   iuditio R.   ‖   sentia K 1.   5. mihine B 1 3
W 2   M 1 2   D C J   O 1 3 8.   mihi ɱe E 1.   mihi me R G K.   michi me
B 2.   minime V S   O 7.   mimine E 2.   uōne W 1.   6. pontufex maxumus
R V K G.   pontīfex maximus B.   pontifex maximus P S E.   ‖   stoicorum R P
                                                                              l' stoicorum
B 2   K 1   W 1   M 2   D C Π   O 1 3 8.   stoicicorum V G.   stoici quorum B 1
al. atr. superscr.   stoici quorum E.   stoicum M 1.   stoycorum B 3   W 2   O 7.
                                                                              tro
7. tigracho R V G   W 2.   tygracho B.   tygracho E *al. atr. superscr.*
                                                                              i
τ‌ⅎhgrac cho K 1 i *post* t *ex parte amoto.*   8. reliquit R G K.   reliqd V.
reliqd P.

Marathonii tauri: ' Theseus taurum,
qui fuit Marathone, quem Hercules a
Creta ad Eurystheum adduxerat, occidit,
ut ait Hyg. Fab. 38 ' Dav. who refers
also to Ov. Met. vii 433 ; Diod. Sic. iv
13, 4 ; Plut. Thes. 14.
   conprehendit, ' seized and held '; Cat.
iii 7, 16 'belli duces captos iam et com-
prehensos tenetis.'
   uide ne : i 34, 83 ; ii 18, 43 ; v 36, 103 :
the polite expression of a strong probability, generally (as here) in the imper.
but *uideamus* and *uidendum est* are also
found (iii 6, 13 ; Off. i 9, 28) ; Draeger,
Synt. II § 410, 10.
   XXIII. § **51.** *patibiles* = *tolerabiles*,
only here in Cic. in this sense ; the only
other occurrence of the word in Cic. is
N.D. iii 12, 29 'omne animal patibilem
naturam habeat ' where *pat.* = *in quem
perpessio cadere potest* (Ern. *Clav. s.v.*).
The negative *impetibilis* is found, Fin. ii
17, 57, contrasted with *tolerabilis*.
   haec cum constituta sunt…tum : ' No
sooner are these convictions firmly established than ' : the indic. *sunt*, as Ern.

(followed by most edd.) saw, is required
here as against *sint* of the majority of
mss which cannot be defended (with Kl.)
as involving a future reference. On *cum…
tum* with ind. in this sense see Draeger,
Synt. II § 496 A (1 a).
   animose: ' courageously ' ; see Küh.'s
note to iii 21, 51.
   Scipio : P.Corn. Scipio Nasica Serapio,
continually spoken of by Cicero with
praise for his action against Tib. Gracchus,
Cat. i 1, 3 ; Off. i 22, 76. His philosophy
did not prevent him from dying of vexation at his virtual exile to Pergamum
(Plut. Tib. Gr. 21 ; Val. Max. v 3, 2).
   uerum…declarauit, 'showed the truth
of' by his action : Off. i 8, 26 ; pro Domo
37, 98.
   nunquam priuatum esse sapientem :
Stob. Ecl. Eth. II 6, 6 (ii p. 594 Gaisf.)
ἀστείοις δὲ ἔτι καὶ τὴν ἀρχὴν (leg. ἀρχικὴν)
κατανέμουσι [ἦ] ἐπιστασίαν καὶ τὰ ταύτης
εἴδη…κατὰ τοῦτο δὴ καὶ μόνος ὁ σπουδαῖος
ἄρχει καὶ εἰ μὴ πάντως κατ' ἐνέργειαν, κατὰ
διάθεσιν δὲ καὶ πάντως…τῶν δ' ἀφρόνων
οὐδεὶς τοιοῦτος· οὔτε γὰρ ἄρχειν οὔτε

priuatus, ut si consul esset, qui rem publicam saluam esse
10 uellent, se sequi iussit. **52**. nescio, ecquid ipsi nos fortiter in re
publica fecerimus; si quid fecimus, certe irati non fecimus. an
est quicquam similius insaniae quam ira? quam bene Ennius
'initium,' dixit, 'insaniae.' color, uox, oculi, spiritus, inpotentia
dictorum ac factorum quam partem habent sanitatis? quid

9. saluam R 6　E 3　L 5　W 1　D　O 1 3 ed. H.　　saluā E 2　W 2　O 7 8.
salua R V G.　　　10. uellent B 3　M 2　O 2.　　uellet R 1 6 7 17　V P G　B 1 2
K 1 2　S　E 1–3　L 5　W 1 2　M 1　D C Π J　O 1 3 8.　　uelet O 7.

§ **52**. ecquid R 6　G　B 1.　　et͜-quid R 1.　　~~ee~~ quid$_\wedge$ S *alia man. mut.*
etquid B 2 3　E 2　L 3–6　M 2　C Π J　O 7.　　et quid W 1　D　O 1 3.
7̄ quid R 7　W 2.　　hẹcquid K 1 *atr. nigriore* ec *in* hẹc *mut.*　　hẹc quid V E.
π̄ quid P *marg.* ecq̣d.　　et si quid R 17　M 1.　　etiam quid L 2　O 8.

quid O 2.　　11. non fecimus R G　B 1　K 1　E 2 *alii.*　　fecimus V.
12. insaniæ B 1.　　insaniẹ R 6.　　insania R V G K E.　　13. inicium V. ‖
inpotentia R V G B K E.　　impotentia B 2　S.　　14. ac R V P G　B 1 2　K 1
S　E 1 2　W 1 2　D C Π J　O 1 7 8.　　atque B 3　M 2.　　et M 1.
aut O 2 3.

ἄρχεσθαι οἷός τ᾽ ἐστιν ὁ ἄφρων ; *ibid.* p. 586
ἐπόμενον δὲ τούτοις ὑπάρχειν καὶ τὸ πολιτεύεσθαι τὸν σοφόν. Fin. iii 20, 68 ' consentaneum est huic naturae ut sapiens
uelit gerere et administrare rem publicam.'
Plut. de repugn. St. 1 p. 1033 has some
caustic remarks on the difference between
Stoic principle and Stoic practice in this
respect.
　　consulem : P. Mucius Scaeuola.
　　languentem, 'lacking in energy' :
Scipio (according to Plut. Tib. Gr. 19)
asked the consul to take measures to
ensure the public safety, ἀποκριναμένου
δὲ πράως ἐκείνου, βίας μὲν οὐδεμίας ὑπάρξειν
οὐδ᾽ ἀναιρήσειν οὐδένα τῶν πολιτῶν ἄκριτον
...ἀναπηδήσας ὁ Νασικᾶς κ.τ.λ. Scipio's
action was in harmony with the most
advanced Stoic principles as expounded
in Stob. Ecl. Eth. II 6, 6 (p. 588 Gaisf.)
οὐκ ἐπιεικῆ δέ φασιν εἶναι τὸν ἀγαθὸν ἄνδρα,
τὸν γὰρ ἐπιεικῆ παραιτητικὸν εἶναι τῆς κατ᾽
ἀξίαν κολάσεως, καὶ τοῦ αὐτοῦ εἶναι
ἐπιεικῆ τε εἶναι καὶ ὑπολαμβάνειν τὰς ἐκ
τοῦ νόμου τεταγμένας κολάσεις τοῖς ἀδι-
κοῦσι σκληροτέρας εἶναι.
　　uellent : Wesenberg's correction (*Em.*
I p. 24) (confirmed by three MSS) of the
reading *uellet* of most MSS, which arose
probably from a misreading of *uellēt,* and
the idea that the relative clause refers to
consul immediately preceding. Dav. compares Appian, Bell. Ciu. 1, 16 Κορνήλιος
Σκιπίων ὁ Νασικᾶς ἐβόα μέγιστον ἔπεσθαι
οἱ τοὺς ἐθέλοντας σώζεσθαι τὴν πατρίδα, and
Servius on Aen. vii 614, viii 1, who
shows that this was the standing formula
for appealing for the assistance of the
citizens in a crisis.

§ **52. nescio, ecquid,** 'We have, perhaps,
shown some courage '—an affirmative
formula; for *ecquid* used as an interrogative particle see Plaut. Men. 163 ; Mil.
Gl. 1106 'ecquid fortis uisa est' ; Trin.
717 ; Hand, *Tursell.* ii 352.
　　an...quicquam : Hand, *Tursell.* I p.
347, explains the connection to be ' Con-
cedisne me, si quid fortiter fecerim,
iratum non fecisse, an putas quicquam
similius insaniae esse ira?'
　　For the thought cf. Sen. de Ira i 1, 2
'quidam itaque ex sapientibus uiris iram
dixerunt breuem insaniam' ; *ib.* ii 36, 4
' nulla celerior ad insaniam uia est ' ; Hor.
Epp. i 2, 62 'ira furor breuis est' ;
Macrobius, Sat. iv 2 fin.; Themistius,
Or. i p. 7 Β ἐγὼ μὲν οἶμαι τὴν ὀργὴν
μανίαν ὀλιγοχρόνιον εἶναι.
　　Ennius : see Vahlen, *Enn. Poes. Rell.*
p. 233; it is not certain from which work
of Ennius the quotation is taken.
　　color : Seneca lays great stress upon
the disturbing physical effects of anger as
an argument against indulging the passion;
de Ira i 1, 3 ; ii 35, 3 sq.; iii 4, 2 ; cf. also
Plut. περὶ ἀοργ. 6 p. 455 F οὕτως ὁρῶν
ὑπ᾽ ὀργῆς ἐξιισταμένους μάλιστα καὶ μετα-
βάλλοντας ὄψιν χρόαν βάδισμα φωνήν ;
Galen περὶ ψυχῆς παθῶν iv 16.
　　quam partem, 'how little do they
comport with sanity': *quam* almost =
quantulam.
　　quid...foedius : more universal and
emphatic than *quis...foedior,* cf. v 2, 5 ;
de Rep. iii 3, 5 'quid P. Scipione, quid C.
Laelio, quid L. Philo perfectius cogitari
potest?'

15 Achille Homerico foedius, quid Agamemnone in iurgio? nam
Aiacem quidem ira ad furorem mortemque perduxit. non igitur
desiderat fortitudo aduocatam iracundiam; satis est instructa,
parata, armata per sese. nam isto modo quidem licet dicere
utilem uinulentiam ad fortitudinem, utilem etiam dementiam,
20 quod et insani et ebrii multa faciunt saepe uehementius. semper
Aiax fortis, fortissimus tamen in furore.

Nam fácinus fecit máximum, cum Dánais incli-
                              nántibus
Summám rem perfecít, manu suá restituit proélium
25 Insániens.

XXIV. **53.** Dicamus igitur utilem insaniam? tracta definitiones fortitudinis, intelleges eam stomacho non egere. fortitudo

18. parata armata R V G B 1 2 K 1 2 S E 1 2 W 2 M 1 Π J O 1 2 7 8.
armata parata P B 3 W 1 M 2 D C O 3. ‖ isto modo quidem licet R V P G B.
isto modo licet quidem D C. 19. uinulentiam R G K. uinolentiam P B.
V *om. uerba inter* dicere utilem *et* etiam. 21. aiax R V P G B 1 K W 2 J.
alax B 2 E 1. 22. cum in acie facit fecit maximum nam danais M 1.
24. rem perfecit R 6 7 P 2 B 3 K 2 E 2 3 L 2–6 W 1 2 M J 2 D C Π J
O 1–3 7 8 ed. H. rem perficit R 1 10 16 17 V P 1 4 G B 1 2 K 1 S E 1. ‖
manu ed. H. manu maius E 2 Π. manus R 1 6 7 16 V P 2 G B 1 3
K 1 S L 3–6 W 1 M 1 2 D C J O 1–3 7 8. man⁹ R 10 17 P 1 4 K 2
E 1 W 2. mn⁹ B 2. monus L 2. ‖ restituit insaniens R V P 1 4
G B 1–3 K 1 2 S E 1 2 W 1 2 M 1 2 D C Π J O 1–3 8. restituit insanies
P 2 O 7. manu sua restituit proelium *corr. G. Hermannus.* ‖ proelium R 1 6
V G B K. praelium M 2 O 2. p̄lium (p̄liū) R 7 P 1 4 B 2 3 K 2 S E 1 2
W 2 C J O 8. prelium P 2 M 1 Π.
XXIV. § 53, 1. definitiones R V G K S *at* s *al. atr. scr.* diffinitiones B 2.
definitionem E 1 W 1 2. deffinitionem D. definitione B P. diffinitione
C Π O 2 3. difinitione E 2 *at litt. post* e *eras.* O 7.

Achille...Agamemnone: Hom. Il. i
122 sqq.
nam...quidem: a form of *praeteritio*
very common in Cic.; Küh. paraphrases
thus 'de Aiacis ira nihil dicam; quam
foeda illa fuerit constat inter omnes; nam
ira eum ad furorem mortemque conduxit';
cf. 33, 71; v 7, 20; Off. iii 6, 28 'nam
illud quidem absurdum est'; Draeger,
Syntax II § 347, 4 (a).
For the thought Bouh. compares Sen.
de Ira ii 36, 5 'Aiacem in mortem egit furor,
in furorem ira.'
aduocatam: a legal metaphor 'craves
the assistance of'; cf. v 38, 111 'adhibet
oculos aduocatos'; Ac. ii 27, 86 'adhibes
artem aduocatam.'
isto modo quidem: so Or. Küh. with
the best MSS, *isto modo* being practically
equivalent to a single word: Wes. reads
isto quidem modo and he is followed by
Bait. Sff. Ml. Hei. TS.
Nam facinus: the lines are iambic
tetrameters acatalectic: Bentley sup-

poses them to be *ex comico quodam
producti*: they are classed by Ribbeck,
Scaen. Rom. Poes. Frag. I² p. 243, among
the *incertae incertorum fabulae* as a fragment of a tragedy. Küh. suggests that they
may come from a tragedy of Pacuvius.
manu sua: practically equivalent to
'unaided.' Sff., by omitting *sua* and
making *insaniens* the last word in the
line, renders *manu* almost otiose.
XXIV. § 53. **tracta**: sc. *animo=con-
sidera*; cf. v. 25, 70 'haec tractanti animo
et noctes et dies cogitanti exsistit.'
stomacho: the word is metaphorically
employed to denote 'ingenium hominis
cuiusque aut animus in rebus aut pro-
bandis aut fastidiendis' (Ern.) and then
by a process of 'deterioration' to denote
'anger'; Dav. quotes Hor. C. i 6, 6;
Quint. x 1, 117; Sen. Epp. 112, 3. For
the thought Cam. compares Plut. περὶ
ὀργῆ. 10 p. 458 E ἡ δ' ἀνδρεία χολῆς οὐ
δεῖται.

est igitur adfectio animi legi summae in perpetiendis rebus
obtemperans uel conseruatio stabilis iudicii in eis rebus, quae
5 formidolosae uidentur, subeundis et repellendis uel scientia rerum formidolosarum contrariarumque aut omnino neglegendarum
conseruans earum rerum stabile iudicium uel breuius, ut Chrysippus (nam superiores definitiones erant Sphaeri, hominis in
primis bene definientis, ut putant Stoici; sunt enim omnino
10 omnes fere similes, sed declarant communis notiones, alia magis

3. est igitur R V P G B 1–3 K S E 1 2 W 1 2 M 1 2 D C Π J O 1 3 7 8.
igitur est O 2. ‖ adfectio R V G K E. affectio B S. 4. iudicii R V P G B K.
6. contrariarumque aut R V P 1 4 G B 1–3 S E 2 W 2 M 1 2 D C Π J
O 1–3 7 8. contrariorumque aut E 1. contrariarumque a͞t R 16.
contrariarumque haud W 1. contrarirumque aut K 1. ‖ neglegendarum

R V G B K E. negligendarum P S. 7. conseruans G K. conseru^ans V

atr. uiridiore mut. et superscr. ‖ chrysippus R G W 1 O 1 2. chrysipus K.
chrisippus V B. crisippus S E 1 2. 8. diffinitiones B 1. ‖ spheri
R V G B K S O 1. pheri E 1. speri B 2 E 2. supbi P 1. superbi O 3.
℘ phetici M 1. asperi W 1 O 8. 9. sunt enim R V P G B 1–3 K 1 S
E 1 2 L 5 W 1 2 M 1 2 D C J O 1–3 7 8. 10. o͞mis sil'is W 2. ‖ declarant
R V P G B 1–3 K 1 S E 1 2 L 5 W 1 2 M 1 2 D C J O 1–3 7 8. ‖

communis notiones R V B 1 3 K E M 2 O 2. communis n^otiones G *ead. man.*

superscr. communes notiones S M 1. homines communis n^eotiones P 1.
· · · · · ·

adfectio: 13, 29 n.
legi summae: the ὀρθὸς λόγος. Cf.
Diog. L. vii 88 διόπερ τέλος γίνεται τὸ
ἀκολούθως τῇ φύσει ζῆν, ὅπερ ἐστὶ κατά τε
τὴν αὑτοῦ καὶ κατὰ τὴν τῶν ὅλων, οὐδὲν
ἐνεργοῦντας ὧν ἀπαγορεύειν εἴωθεν ὁ νόμος ὁ
κοινὸς ὅσπερ ἐστὶν ὁ ὀρθὸς λόγος διὰ πάντων
ἐρχόμενος ὁ αὐτὸς ὢν τῷ Διὶ καθηγεμόνι
τούτῳ τῆς τῶν ὅλων διοικήσεως ὄντι. This
first definition of *fortitudo*, then, is but
the definition of virtue in general with
the addition of the differentiating words
in perpetiendis rebus (περὶ τὰς ὑπομονάς).
Lambinus conjectured *laboribus* for *rebus*.
scientia: Stob. Ecl. II 59 10 W ἀνδρείαν
δὲ [sc. εἶναι] ἐπιστήμην δεινῶν καὶ οὐ
δεινῶν καὶ οὐδετέρων: the same definition
occurs in Andron. περὶ παθῶν p. 19
Schuch. In Sext. Emp. adu. math. ix
158 τῶν μεταξύ is substituted for οὐδετέρων, a variant which is found also in
Clem. Alex. Strom. ii p. 394 D ed. Sylb.
This definition of courage goes back to the
Platonic school; Laches, 195 A ταύτην
[sc. ἀνδρείαν] ἔγωγε [sc. φημὶ] τὴν τῶν
δεινῶν καὶ θαρραλέων ἐπιστήμην.
Or. follows a few mss in inserting *perferendarum* before *aut*: the word has
evidently crept in from Chrysippus' definition lower down. Hei. reads *et* for *aut*
to bring the translation into more exact

correspondence with the original: but
Cic. is making two divisions where the
Gk makes three, as the difference for
practical purposes between οὐ δεινά and
οὐδέτερα is infinitesimal.
Sphaeri, a native of the Bosporus, who
after studying under Zeno and Cleanthes,
at Athens, went to teach in Alexandria at
the invitation of Ptolemy Philopator. He
was a great admirer of Heraclitus and left
an exposition of his poem. Diogenes L.
credits him with the authorship of a large
number of treatises. Diog. L. vii 6; ix
1, 15.
sunt: sc. *definitiones Stoicorum.*
enim: Dav. objected to *enim* here on
the ground that the clause furnished no
sufficient reason for the Stoic estimate of
Sphaerus and proposed *autem.* The fact is
that the clause does not refer to the definitions of Sphaerus, as all editors assume;
it is a second parenthesis, and the *enim*
is explanatory. Cicero has quoted three
definitions and is about to add a fourth by
Chrysippus: he remarks first that the three
preceding defs. were due to Sphaerus, and
secondly that while the four definitions
were all very much alike yet they brought
into relief, in various ways, the *communes
notiones* with regard to courage: the last
parenthesis, since it contains Cicero's

alia) — quo modo igitur Chrysippus? 'Fortitudo est,' inquit, 'scientia rerum perferendarum uel adfectio animi in patiendo ac perferendo summae legi parens sine timore.' quamuis licet insectemur istos, ut Carneades solebat, metuo ne soli philosophi sint.

15 quae enim istarum definitionum non aperit notionem nostram, quam habemus omnes de fortitudine tectam atque inuolutam? qua aperta quis est qui aut bellatori aut imperatori aut oratori quaerat aliquid neque eos existimet sine rabie quicquam fortiter facere posse? **54.** quid? Stoici, qui omnis insipientes insanos

11. chrysippus R G K W 1 O 1. chrisippus V B. crisippus E.
12. adfectio R V G K E. affectio B S. 14. phylosophi G.
15. diffinitionum B 1. 17. qui aut R V P G B 2 3 K S E 2·W 1 2 D J
O 1–3 7 8. ut E qui *om.* 18. existumet R *h. l.* V *h. l.* G B K.
§ **54**, 19. omnes R V G K.

reason for piling up similar definitions, is appropriately introduced by *enim*: 'now they are all, as a general rule, pretty much alike, but they, etc.'

declarant: Lamb. conjectured *declarat* which Tr. adopts; Wes. (*Em.* iii p. 10 sq.) shows that the conjecture is 'non modo inutilis sed praua': 'Quoniam per *omnino ...sed* duo illa quae de Sphaeri definitionibus enuntiantur (*sunt* quidem. fere similes, sed communes notiones non aeque bene *declarant*), inter se opponuntur, necesse est, ut *omnes* appositio est subiecti in *sunt* latentis, sic *alia* non per se ipsum subiectum alterius uerbi esse sed communis subiecti appositionem.'

communes notiones, the ἔννοιαι or προλήψεις possessed by the ordinary person, Top. 7, 31: cf. Diog. L. vii 54 ἔστι δ' ἡ πρόληψις ἔννοια φυσικὴ τῶν καθόλου. The Stoics drew a distinction between ἔννοιαι and προλήψεις, acc. to which ἔννοιαι came δι' ἡμετέρας διδασκαλίας καὶ ἐπιμελείας, while the latter φυσικαὶ γίγνονται (Plut. Plac. iv 11, 1); on Cicero's alleged carelessness (Madv. Fin. iii 6, 21) in the use of these terms see the excellent remarks of Reid, Ac. ii 10, 30 n.

igitur: resuming after a parenthesis: the parenthesis is complicated by an anacoluthon, after which sometimes, as here, an interrogative resumes the construction, e.g. iii 3, 5; Fin. i 7, 23.

quamuis licet, 'carp at them as much as we like, yet....' For the construction cf. N.D. iii 36, 88 'quamuis licet Menti delubra...consecremus' (quoted by Dav.); Lael. 20, 73 'quamuis licet excellas'; Legg. iii 10, 24 and Lucr. vi 601, 620.

Carneades: cf. v 29, 83; N.D. ii 65, 162 'Carneades lubenter in Stoicos inuehebatur'; Diog. L. iv 9, 62. Carneades

as an adherent of the New Academy naturally objected to the Stoic dogmatism : he fell foul of the Stoic ethics, especially with regard to their doctrine of the *summum bonum*, and its necessity for purposes of happiness.

aperit notionem...inuolutam : the ἔννοιαι or προλήψεις are formed in the mind by a gradual, obscure and incomplete process of analogical reasoning upon the premisses supplied by the senses : Ac. ii 10, 30 'mens enim ipsa quae sensuum fons est atque etiam ipse sensus est naturalem uim habet quam intendit ad ea, quibus mouetur. itaque alia uisa sic adripit ut iis statim utatur, alia quasi recondit e quibus memoria oritur : cetera autem similitudinibus construit ex quibus efficiuntur notitiae rerum quas Graeci tum ἔννοιας tum ˌπρολήψεις uocant.' When reason examines these notions and tests them the ἔννοια becomes a κατάληψις, or assured conviction : the statement of this is then a *definitio*. For *inuolutam* Küh. compares Or. 33, 116 'inuolutae rei notitia definiendo aperienda est.'

quaerat aliquid, 'supposes anything to be wanting to': *aliquid*=anything other than the qualities comprised in the definition of *imperator, bellator* or *orator*; *ira* is not included in these, and is therefore not necessary either to make up the character or contribute to the resolution with which its duties are performed. For the expression cf. Brut. 38, 143 'neminem esse qui, horum altero utro patrono, cuiusquam ingenium requireret' ('would feel that any other talent was required').

§ **54. Quid? Stoici...colligunt?** Ern., quoted by Küh. with approval, explains this sentence thus : 'esse autem uidetur : hoc efficiunt conclusionibus per induc-

20 esse dicunt, nonne ista colligunt? remoue perturbationes maximeque iracundiam, iam uidebuntur monstra dicere. nunc autem
ita disserunt, sic se dicere omnes stultos insanire, ut male olere
omne caenum. at non semper. commoue, senties. sic iracundus
non semper iratus est; lacesse, iam uidebis furentem. quid? ista
25 bellatrix iracundia, cum domum rediit, qualis est cum uxore,
cum liberis, cum familia? an tum quoque est utilis? est igitur
aliquid quod perturbata mens melius possit facere quam constans? an quisquam potest sine perturbatione mentis irasci? bene
igitur nostri, cum omnia essent in m o r i b u s uitia, quod nullum
30 erat iracundia foedius, iracundos solos m o r o s o s nominauerunt.

---

20. conligunt R B E.   conligunt K *atr. nigr. superscr.*   colligunt G *in* conl.

ead. man. mut.   coligunt V *atr. uiridi superscr.*   colligunt S C. ‖
maxumeque V K.   maxumeq; B.   maxume quae R G *at* quae *in* que
ead. man. mut.   maximeque S E.   21. nostra G.   22. omnes R V G.
oms B K.   23. caenum V G.   cęnum R B K S E.   27. aliquid quod G K.
aliquid qđ R B.   aliquid qđ V *eod. ut uid. atr.*   29. morib; B 1.   morbus V
atr. ant. superscr.   mobis S *al. atr. superscr.*   morbus R G B 2.
morbis R 6 7 17 P 1 B 3 K 1 2 E 1-3 L 2-6 W 2 M 1 2 D C Π J O 1-3 7 8.
mobis W 1.   30. solus V.   ‖   morosos R V G B 1 2 K 1 D C O 7.
morosos S *al. atr.* E 2 *al. atr.* II *al. atr. superscr.*   molosos E 1.
morbosos R 6 7 17 P B 3 E 3 L 2-4 6 W 1 2 M 1 2 J O 1-3 8.   morbos
L 5 ed. H.

tionem ut de singulis adscendant ad
genus. Huic conueniunt sequentia. Si e
numero insanorum eximuntur iracundi,
insanire ipsi et monstra dicere uidebuntur,
quod pars ea exempta sit, quae foedior
etiam ceteris est.' F.A.W. who rightly
calls this 'very forced' assumes the loss
of a whole clause after *colligunt*.

No explanation which regards the
sentence *Stoici...colligunt* as designed to
carry on Cicero's argument is satisfactory: the remainder of the paragraph
down to *uidebis furentem* is entirely taken
up with an attempt to justify and explain
the paradox *omnes insipientes esse insanos*, which must therefore have been
introduced as a difficulty or objection.
The sentence, then, is to be regarded as
the interruption of a supposed antagonist
who tries to weaken the argument by a
reminder that it proceeds from the school
of philosophy which had framed the most
absurd of all paradoxes. Cicero proceeds
then to reply first by defining *insanos* to
include *iracundos* and secondly by pointing out that both words are used to
denote not an actual but a potential state.
monstra dicere: Mo. quotes Att. iv

7, 1; ix 11, 4 : Q. Fr. ii 4, 5, 'qui de
Caesare monstra promulgarunt.'

at non semper: *at* marks an objection,
Draeger, *Synt.* II § 334 (9). Heine wished
to transfer *at* to stand before *commoue*,
unnecessarily since it makes quite good
sense and grammar where it is and gives
more vigour to the style.

commoue, senties: i 13, 30 n. on *tolle*.

sic iracundus: a point insisted upon
by Chrysippus, Plut. de St. repug. c. 27,
p. 1046 F.

Quid? ista bellatrix iracundia... The
argument is resumed here after the
digression on the Stoic paradox.

For the thought, cf. Sen. de Ira iii 35, 1 sq.:
Plut. περὶ ἀοργ. 13, p. 462 B οὕτως οὕτε
γάμος οὕτε φιλία μετ' ὀργῆς ἀνεκτόν.

utilis: Sen. de Ira iii 5, 4 'iracundus
dominus quot in fugam seruos egit? quot
in mortem? quanto plus irascendo quam
id erat propter quod irascebatur amisit?'

Bake proposed to delete *an...utilis* but
the words are strictly relevant, as the
whole discussion has turned on the point
urged by the Peripatetics that the emotions *utiliter a natura datas esse*.

morosos, 'peevish': Dav. quotes Sen.

XXV. 55. Oratorem uero irasci minime decet, simulare non dedecet. an tibi irasci tum uidemur, cum quid in causis acrius et uehementius dicimus? quid? cum iam rebus transactis et praeteritis orationes scribimus, num irati scribimus?

5   Ecquis hoc animaduértit? uincite!

num aut egisse umquam iratum Aesopum aut scripsisse existimas iratum Accium? aguntur ista praeclare, et ab oratore quidem

---

XXV. § 55, 1. minime R V P G K.   ‖   non dedecet R 6 7 17   B 3   W 2   M 2
                          de   de
II *marg.* J O 1–3 8.   non decet S.   non decet E 2 *al. atr. superscr.*
non decet R P G B 1 K 1 2 E 1 W 1 M 1 D C O 7.   non dicet B 2.
minime decet an tibi irasci V *cett. om., non ut Küh.*   5. et quis R 1 6 10 16 17
V P G B 1–3 K S E 1–3 L 2–6 W 1 2 M 1 2 D C II J O 1–3 7 8.   ecquis
corr. Victorius.   6. aesopum R V G.   hẹsopum S.   esopū B 1.
esoppū E 1.   ‖   existimas R 10 V P G B 1–3 S E 2 L 6 M 2 D C II
O 3 8 ed. H.   existimụs E u *ex a mut.*   estimas E 3.   existimamus R 1 6 17
K 1 2 L 3–5 W 1 2 M 1 J O 1 2 7.   extimamus R 7 L 2.   7. accium
R V G K 1 W 1 J O 1.   actium P   B 1 3 S O 2.   actiū E 1.

---

de Ira i 4, 2 'inter hos (sc. iracundos) morosum ponas licet, delicatum iracundiae genus' and Don. in Ter. Hec. iv 2, 2 'mores proprie senum dicuntur, unde senectus morosa et morosi homines qui sui cuiusdam moris sunt.' Curt. *Gr. Etym.* 340 connects *morosus* with the root found in μῶρος: Vaniček, *Etym. Wört.* p. 654, adopts the derivation from *mores*.

XXV. § 55. **Oratorem** : cf. Sen. de Ira ii 17, 1 '"Orator" inquit "iratus aliquando melior est." immo imitatus iratum. nam et histriones in pronuntiando non irati populum mouent, sed iratum bene agentes. et apud iudices itaque et in contione et ubicumque alieni animi ad nostrum arbitrium agendi sunt, modo iram, modo metum...ipsi simulabimus et saepe id quod ueri adfectus non effecissent, efficit imitatio adfectuum.' In de Or. ii 45, 189 Cic. puts the very opposite opinion into the mouth of Antonius: 'non me hercule umquam apud iudices aut dolorem aut misericordiam aut inuidiam aut odium excitare dicendo uolui, quin ipse in commouendis iudicibus iis ipsis sensibus ad quos illos adducere uellem permouerer': cf. also Or. 38, 132.

simulare, sc. *se irasci*.

orationes scribimus : speeches were not as a general rule, as this passage shows, written out in the form in which they were published until after their delivery : cf. de Sen. 11, 38 where Cato is represented saying 'causarum inlustrium, quascumque defendi, nunc cum maxime conficio orationes.' Occasionally

a speech was delivered from manuscript, Planc. 30, 74 'recitetur oratio quae propter rei magnitudinem dicta de scripto est.' The practice enabled the orator to deal in his published speech with arguments which he heard for the first time when he came into court, or to embody points which occurred to him during delivery. Sometimes as in the case of the pro Milone a speech was published which had never been delivered at all. The Romans borrowed this practice from the Greeks.

animaduertit? 'Will no one inflict punishment for this?' *Ecquis* with the present indic. is quite common with this meaning in Plautus.

This, as Or. and F.A.W. saw, is the right interpretation. Küh. Hei. T.S. follow Neid. in interpreting 'quis hoc facinus uidit.'

The words are taken from the Atreus of Accius (Ribbeck, *Sc. Poes. Rom. Frag.* I², p. 166); cf. de Or. iii 58, 217. They form a composite object to *egisse*.

Aesopum : ii 17, 39: his acting is often referred to by Cicero who seems to have admired it : but his criticisms in other places imply that his method was conspicuous for his abandonment of himself to the feelings of the character he impersonated : Diu. i 37, 80 'uidi in Aesopo ...tantum ardorem uoltuum atque motuum ut eum uis quaedam abstraxisse a sensu mentis uideretur,' p. Sest. 56, 120 '[Aesopus] summi poetae ingenium non solum arte sua sed etiam dolore exprimebat.'

melius, si modo est orator, quam ab ullo histrione, sed aguntur
leniter et mente tranquilla. libidinem uero laudare cuius est
10 libidinis? Themistoclen mihi et Demosthenen profertis, additis
Pythagoran, Democritum, Platonem. quid? uos studia libidinem
uocatis? quae uel optimarum rerum, ut ea sunt, quae profertis,
sedata tamen et tranquilla esse debent. iam aegritudinem laudare, unam rem maxime detestabilem, quorum est tandem
15 philosophorum? at commode dixit Afranius:

　　Dúm modo doleat áliquid, doleat quídlubet.

dixit enim de adulescente perdito ac dissoluto, nos autem de
constanti uiro ac sapienti quaerimus. et quidem ipsam illam iram
centurio habeat aut signifer uel ceteri, de quibus dici non necesse
20 est, ne rhetorum aperiamus mysteria. utile est enim uti motu
animi, qui uti ratione non potest; nos autem, ut testificor saepe,
de sapiente quaerimus.

8. si modo est melius G *ead. man. corr.*　‖　histrione B 1.　　istrione S

eod. atr. superscr.　　istrione R V　B 2　K 1　E 1.　　strione G *ead. man. superscr.*

9. libidinem R P G K.　　libidem V (*sic*) *fort. eod. atr.*　　lubidinem B 1.

10. libidinis V P.　　libidinis K 1 *atr. nigr. superscr.*　　lubidinis R G　B 1. ‖
themistoclen D J.　　themistoden C.　　themistoclem R V G K S　L 6
W 1　O 2.　　themisthoclem E 1　B 3.　　temistoïcem S 1 *eod. atr. inculc.*
themistoclē B 1.　　themistodē B 2　W 2.　‖　demosthenen E 1　J.　　demostenen
R V P G K D C.　　demosthenē B 3　O 2.　　demostenē S.　　themostenē B 2. ‖
proferri G r *post. expunx. et* t *superscr. alt. man.*　　11. pythagoran R V G
B 1　K 1.　　pithagoran J.　　phitagoran E 1.　　pitagoran B 2.　‖　libidinem
R V P B *h. l.*　　libidine G K.　　12. optimarum R G B K E.　　obtimarum V.

14. maxime R V G B.　　maxime K *atr. nigr. superscr.*　　15. at commode V G.
accommode S *marg.* at B.　　ad commode R E K.　　16. lateat G *in* doleat
alt. man. corr.　‖　quidlubet B 3　E 3.　　quodlubet R 6　K 2　W 1　M 2　J　O 1 2.
quidlibet R V P G　B 1 2　K 1　S　E 2　M 1　II　O 3 7.　　quodlibet R 17　L 5
W 2　D　O 8 ed. H.　　quilibet E 1.　　quislibet C.　　17. adulescente R V G
K 1.　　adolescente P　B 1　S　E 1　J.　　20. rh&orum K 1.　　r&horum R
eod. atr. corr.　　rethorum G B.

si modo est orator, 'that is, a real
orator,' cf. Or. iii 56, 213 'sed haec
omnia perinde sunt ut aguntur: actio,
inquam, in dicendo una dominatur; sine
hac summus orator esse in numero nullo
potest.'

Themistoclen : for this and the following names see 19, 44.

unam, cf. i 9, 17 n.

at, 24, 54 n. Cic. had previously
(20, 45) quoted this line with approbation as *e uita ductum*, and he now
supposes an objector to retort with it.

enim, 'Yes, for,' admitting and explaining an objection.

et quidem : cf. iii 20, 48 ; Finn. i 10,
35 ; Draeger, *Synt.* II §311, 13.

habeat here has almost the sense of
sibi habeat, 'he is welcome to.'

ceteri, 'others of the same class,' 'the
rest of their kind,' the *infima plebs*,
whose feelings the orator was justified in
arousing.

mysteria, 'the secrets,' Ac. ii 18, 60.
The *rhetores* are represented as possessing
secrets of their craft by which they were
able to play upon the passions of an
audience.

utile...potest : not=*utile est eum uti*,
etc. (as Küh.) but *utile est ei, qui*...

XXVI. **56.** At etiam aemulari utile est, obtrectare, misereri. cur misereare potius quam feras opem, si id facere possis? an sine misericordia liberales esse non possumus? non enim suscipere ipsi aegritudines propter alios debemus, sed alios, si possumus, 5 leuare aegritudine. obtrectare uero alteri aut illa uitiosa aemulatione, quae riualitati similis est, aemulari quid habet utilitatis, cum sit aemulantis angi alieno bono, quod ipse non habeat, obtrectantis autem angi alieno bono, quod id etiam alius habeat? qui id adprobari possit, aegritudinem suscipere pro experientia, 10 si quid habere uelis? nàm solum habere uelle summa dementia est. **57.** mediocritates autem malorum quis laudare recte possit?

XXVI. § **56**, 1. obtrectare R 6 17   K 2   D C   O 2 ed. H.   obtrectate M 1. obtrectari R 1 7   V P G   B 1–3   K 1   S   E 1 2   W 1   M 2   Π   O 1 3 8. abtrectari W 2   J.   obtractari O 7.   3. possumus R V P G   B 1–3   K 1 2   S W 1 2   M 1 2   D Π J   O 1–3 7 8.   possimus C.   5. obtrectare R 16 7 17   V P G   B 1 3   K 1 2   S   E 1 2   W 1 2   M 2   D C Π J   O 1 2 7 8 ed. H.

optrectare B 2.   7. habeat R G B.   abeat V *atr. ant. superscr.*   9. qui id L 3   O 3   S *litt. post* qui *eras.*   quid id O 1 7.   quid B 3   L 6   M 2. quis id R V P G   B 1 2   E 1 2   W 1   M 1   D C Π   O 2 ed. H.   quidid K 1 i.e. d *in* s *mut.*   quid ul' L 5.   quid uel id O 8.   quis qui J.   quis uel K 2 L 2   W 2.   ‖ adprobari R G K.   approbari V P   B 2 3   S   E 1 2   W 2   M 2 Π J   O 3 8.   approbare W 1   M 1   D C   O 2 7.   approbarè B 1 i.e. i *in* e *mut.* 10. nam solum R 10   P G   B 1–3   E 1 2   W 1   M 1 2.   non solum R 1   V K.

potest, uti motu animi: the whole discussion has turned upon the utility of emotion to the person who feels it.

XXVI. § **56. at etiam**: referring to and developing the objections to the statements of the Peripatetics already mentioned in 20, 46.

At here has, as often, the force of *at enim* introducing an objection (Draeger, *Synt.* II § 334, 10): *etiam* emphasises *aemulari* and corresponds to the *id ipsum* of § 46. Sff.'s conjecture *at enim* (adopted by Ml. T.S.) proceeds from a failure to notice the force of *etiam*: Bake's *at tamen* (as Sff. points out, with a ref. to Madv.'s nn. on Finn. ii 27, 86; iii 15, 48) is not even good Latin.

cur misereare: cf. Sen. Clem. ii 6, 3 sq. 'ergo non miserebitur sapiens sed succurret, sed proderit...misericordia uicina est miseriae; habet enim aliquid trahitque ex ea...misericordia uitium est animorum nimis miseria pauentium.'

aemulatione: see 8, 17 for the two meanings of the word, and i 19, 44 n.

riualitati: only here in Cic.; in class. Lat. the word always means 'jealousy,' 'rivalry in love;' *riualis* occurs in Cicero only in Q. Fr. iii 8, 4.

obtrectantis: see 8, 17 n.

qui id adprobari: so Dav. Or. Küh. Sff. Ml. Sch. TS. Hei. Bait. reads *quis id*

adprobare with B 2. It is more likely, as Sorof notes, that *qui* was corrupted to *quis* than that *adprobare* was corrupted to *adprobari*.

pro experientia, 'instead of making an attempt' (sc. to gain what you want): so Küh. TS. Hei. Mo. F.A.W. Nissen: Ern. explains 'ut intelligas te habere uelle, ut ea sit argumento cupiditatis tuae.' For *experientia* cf. ad Fam. x 18, 3 'agam gratias fortunae constantiaeque meae, quae me ad hanc experientiam excitauit.'

nam solum...est: not 'for merely to *wish* to possess' (sc. instead of making an attempt to get it) 'is the height of madness' which would require *nam solum uelle habere*, but 'to wish to be the sole possessor of anything is the height of madness': the sentence refers not to *aemulatio*, but to *obtrectatio*, which has been defined as the feeling of vexation at seeing someone else enjoy what one has oneself: the *nam* is elliptic, 'I need not argue the case of *obtrectatio*, for....'

§ **57. mediocritates**: τὰς μεσότητας of the Peripatetics. The addition of *malorum* begs the question at issue. The Peripatetics did not admit that the πάθη became evil until they had passed the mean.

quis enim potest, in quo libido cupiditasue sit, non libidinosus
et cupidus esse? in quo ira, non iracundus? in quo angor, non
anxius? in quo timor, non timidus? libidinosum igitur et ira-
15 cundum et anxium et timidum censemus esse sapientem? de
cuius excellentia multa quidem dici quamuis fuse lateque possunt, sed breuissime illo modo, sapientiam esse rerum diuinarum
et humanarum scientiam cognitionemque quae cuiusque rei
causa sit. ex quo efficitur ut diuina imitetur, humana omnia

§ **57**, 12. libido *et infra* libidinosus, libidinosum R V P G B K.   14. lubidi-
nosum J.   ‖ igitur et iracundum R V P G   B 1 3   K S   E 1 2   W 1   M 1 2   Π
O 2 3 7 8.   et iracundum B 2 igitur *om.*   igitur et cupidum W 2   J   O 1.
igitur et anxium et iracundum et tumidum C.   igitur et anx. et irac. et timidum D.

post iracundum *habet* et cupidum W 1.   16. excelentia V *eod. atr.*   R *fort. eod. atr.* ‖

fuse *om.* V.   ‖ possunt O 3 7.   possint L 4 *eod. atr.*   possịt B 1 *eod. fort. atr.*
possint R 6 7 17   B 3   L 2 3 5 6   W 1   M 1 2   D C J   O 1 2 8.   possĭt W 2   Π.
possit R V P G   B 2   K 1 2   S   E 1–3.   17. breuissime R V G B K. ‖

sapientiā R B.   sapientia V *atr. uiridi superscr.*   sapiente\m K 1.
sapientia G.

cupiditasue...et cupidus. There is no
necessity to alter the reading either to
cupiditasque with Bouh. or to *aut cupidus*
with Dav., as there is no difference
between *libido* and *cupiditas*: to be
possessed by either is to be possessed by
both.

libidinosum igitur: the words *et
cupidum* which follow in some MSS. are
evidently a mistaken attempt to complete
the list of adjectives.

quamuis=*quantumuis* as in 24, 53 ;
the reading *possint* of many MSS. is
perhaps due partly to the influence of the
supposed meaning of *quamuis* 'although'
as well as to the misreading of the contraction for *possunt.* For *fuse lateque*
cf. Or. 32, 113 'facultatem...fuse lateque
dicendi.'

sapientiam...causa sit: for this definition Dav. compares v 3, 7 : Off. ii 2, 5
'sapientia autem est...rerum diuinarum et
humanarum causarumque quibus eae res
continentur scientia'; Orig. in Celsum iii
p. 494 ἡ σοφία ἐπιστήμη θείων ἐστὶ καὶ
ἀνθρωπίνων πραγμάτων καὶ τῶν τούτων
αἰτίων and Sen. Epp. 89, 5 who objects
to the last clause in the definition as
superfluous, 'quia causae diuinorum hu-
manorumque pars diuinorum sunt.' Cic.
employs this shorter form himself in Off. i
43, 153. The definition seems to be due
to Pythagoras ; see Hobein's n. to
Maximus of Tyre, xxvi 1 (p. 308), where
many other quotations of it are referred
to.

    Ern. *Clau. Cic.* s.v. *diuinus* points out

that of the three divisions of philosophy,
dialectics, physics and ethics, *res diuinae*
correspond to physics including natural
theology, while under *res humanae* he
classes ethics and dialectics. But why
should dialectics be a sub-division of *res
humanae* any more than of *res diuinae*?
Undoubtedly the *scientia quae cuiusque
rei causa sit* is τὸ λογικόν, which including,
as it did, the discussion of τὰ κριτήρια
τῆς ἀληθείας was necessarily concerned
with first causes. Seneca's objection to
its being included in the definition of
philosophy may be explained partly by
his contempt for dialectics, partly by the
fact that the *causae cuiusque rei* though
really the province of τὸ λογικόν might
very naturally be regarded as falling
equally within the province of τὸ φυσικόν
and τὸ ἠθικόν respectively. This indeed
would seem to have been a view recognized generally by the Stoics for the
purposes of instruction ; cf. Diog. L.
vii 40, who speaking of the threefold
division says καὶ οὐθὲν μέρος τοῦ ἑτέρου
ἀποκεκρίσθαι, καθά τινες αὐτῶν φασιν,
ἀλλὰ μεμίχθαι αὐτά· καὶ τὴν παράδοσιν
μικτὴν ἐποίουν : and Chrysippus quoted
by Plut. de Stoic. rep. 9, p. 1035 E οὐ
καθάπαξ ἀφεκτέον ἐστὶ τῶν ἄλλων τῷ τὴν
λογικὴν ἀναλαμβάνοντι πρῶτην ἀλλὰ
κἀκείνων μεταληπτέον κατὰ τὸ διδόμενον.

    quae...sit: the verbal noun *cognitio*
takes the construction of *cognoscere* ; cf.
pro Sull. 1, 3 'iudicium qui...uideatur'
with Reid's n.

20 inferiora uirtute ducat. in hanc tu igitur tamquam in mare quod est uentis subiectum perturbationem cadere tibi dixisti uideri? quid est quod tantam grauitatem constantiamque perturbet? an inprouisum aliquid aut repentinum? quid potest accidere tale ei, cui nihil quod homini euenire possit non praemeditatum sit?
25 nam quod aiunt nimia resecari oportere, naturalia relinqui, quid tandem potest esse naturale, quod idem nimium esse possit? sunt enim omnia ista ex errorum orta radicibus, quae euellenda et extrahenda penitus, non circumcidenda nec amputanda sunt.

XXVII. **58.** Sed quoniam suspicor te non tam de sapiente quam de te ipso quaerere (illum enim putas omni perturbatione

20. in hanc R V P G B 1 3 K 1 E 2 W 1 2.   hanc in B 2.
21. cadere *ante* tibi *e contextu om.* R *in spat. sub linea eod. atr. inserit.*
23. inprouisum R V G B K E.   improuisum S.   ‖   aliquid aut R P G B 1-3
                                                                                                ei
K 1 2 S E 1 2 W 1 2 M 1 2 D C Π J O 1-3 7 8. ‖ tale cui Π *al. atr. superscr.*
tale et cui P 1-5 G B 2 3 S E 1 L 3 4 6 W 1 M 2 J O 7 Urs. 3240.
tale & R 1 6 17 V B 1 K 1 2 E 3 L 5 W 2 D O 1-3.   tali cui M 1.
tali 4 cui C.   tale cui R 7 E 2 L 2 O 8 ed. H.   24. cui quod euenire possit
non praemeditatum sit O 2.   cui nihil quod homini euenire possit ne praemeditatum
sit P 2 5 L 3 4 O 3.   non (ne) praemeditatum sit *om.* R 1 6 17 V P 1 3 4 6
G B 1-3 K 1 2 E 1-3 L 6 W 1 2 M 1 2 D C Π J O 1 7: *e contextu om. in*
marg. habet S: *pro* non praem. sit *habent* R 7 L 2 O 8 nouum sit.   cui nihil
subitum est quod homini euenire possit ed. H.   quod homini euenire possit potest
                                                                                          i
esse improuisum aut repentinum L 5.   25. aiunt R G.   agunt K.
                                        e
27. euellenda R V G K.   auellenda B 1 *al. atr. superscr.*   uellenda P.
28. et extrahenda *om.* V.

in hanc: this which is the MSS. reading was altered by Bent. and Dav. (following Manut. Lamb. and others) to *hunc*: wrongly, for *sapientia* is the subject of *imitetur* and *ducat* and is to be understood in the acc. with *hanc*. Wopkens, *op. cit.* p. 92, points out instances of similar quasi-personifications of abstract ideas, e.g. ii 26, 64; v 14, 41; Finn. iv 13, 32.

quid potest accidere......praemeditatum sit? Many editors rejecting the last three words mark this sentence as corrupt: but the reading in the text is accepted by Küh., Wesenberg and Schiche on adequate MSS. authority: Sff. reads *praemeditatum non sit*. The MS. variations point to the three words in question having been omitted at an early period, and Küh. is perhaps right in his conjecture that the omission was due to the similarity of ending *possit...sit*.

nam quod aiunt, iii 30, 73 n.: for the statement cf. 20, 46.

quid tandem, etc. The argument here

is like the better known Stoic argument to prove that pleasure was not to be regarded as a good: εἶναι γὰρ καὶ αἰσχρὰς ἡδονάς, μηδὲν δ' αἰσχρὸν εἶναι ἀγαθόν Diog. L. vii 103.

enim: cf. ii 26, 62 n. on *itaque*.

errorum: gen. of definition; *ex errorum radicibus=ex erroribus qui quasi radices sunt.*

euellenda: Bake altered this and the following gerundives to the feminine, taking them to refer to *radices*; but as Sff. points out *quae* here, as often, is merely connective and=*et ea*.

circumcidenda...amputanda: the same combination is found in Ac. ii 45, 138; Finn. i 13, 44, v 14, 39; Or. i 15, 65.

XXVII. In this chapter Cicero begins his discussion of the *remedia perturbationum* which extends to c. 37: the first three chapters are taken up with the method of treating *perturbationes* in general: cc. 30—37 deal with the special cases of *metus, laetitia, cupiditas* and *ira*.

esse liberum, te uis), uideamus, quanta sint quae a philosophia
remedia morbis animorum adhibeantur. est enim quaedam medi-
5 cina certe, nec tam fuit hominum generi infensa atque inimica
natura ut corporibus tot res salutaris, animis nullam inuenerit;
de quibus hoc etiam est merita melius, quod corporum adiumenta
adhibentur extrinsecus, animorum salus inclusa in his ipsis est.
sed quo maior est in iis praestantia et diuinior, eo maiore indigent
10 diligentia. itaque bene adhibita ratio cernit quid optimum sit,
neglecta multis inplicatur erroribus. **59.** ad te igitur mihi iam
conuertenda omnis oratio est; simulas enim quaerere te de sapiente, quaeris autem fortasse de te.

Earum igitur perturbationum quas exposui uariae sunt
15 curationes. nam neque omnis aegritudo una ratione sedatur;

§ **58**. **te uis** : sc. *perturbatione esse
liberum.*

quanta sint, quae ... remedia, i.e.
quanta sint ea remedia, quae, etc. For
the constr. Wopkens on N.D. ii 24, 62
(*op. cit.* p. 218) compares Ac. ii 14, 45 ;
31, 99 : Legg. ii 12, 29.

est enim quaedam medicina : for the
thought cf. iii 3, 5 sq.

his ipsis : Bake read *in ipsis* and he is
followed by Bait. and Hei. ; *his* is altered
to *iis* by Mo. Tr. Kl. ; Sff. who rightly
keeps the MS. reading remarks ' neque
enim animorum adiumenta adiumentis
corporum, sed ipsi animi, de quibus cum
maxime agitur itaque *hi* uocantur, corporibus...oppositi sunt.'

bene adhibita ratio : cf. 11, 24 'adhibita continuo ratio quasi quaedam
Socratica medicina.' Brut. 75, 261 :
adhibita is appropriate here, being the
usual word for *applying* remedies as in

Off. i 24, 83 '(medici) grauioribus morbis
periculosas curationes et ancipites adhibere coguntur' and often. Turn. and
Bent. read *habita*, and Turn. remarks
(*Adu.* vii 18) '*bene haberi* dicitur quod
diligenter seduloque curatur et colitur,
neque neglegitur'—which is true ; but
Cic. wishing to emphasise the fact that
ratio is at once the patient, the physician
and the remedy in diseases of the soul
says " Reason, properly applied, discerns
the best course ; deprived of proper
attention, it becomes involved in mis-
takes."

§ **59. curationes** =*rationes medendi*: cf.
iii 10, 23 where *morbi curatio* is paralleled
by *aegritudinis medendi facultas*. On the
force of verbals in *-io* see Nagelsb. *Stil.*
§ 58.

neque : a clause beginning with *neque*
or *et* might have been expected in place
of the clause beginning *est etiam in*

alia est enim lugenti, alia miseranti aut inuidenti adhibenda
medicina. est etiam in omnibus quattuor perturbationibus illa
distinctio, utrum ad uniuersam perturbationem, quae est aspernatio rationis aut adpetitus uehementior, an ad singulas, ut ad
20 metum, libidinem, reliquas, melius adhibeatur oratio, et utrum
illudne non uideatur aegre ferundum ex quo suscepta sit aegri-

16. miseranti aut inuidenti R P G   B 1–3   K 1 2   E 1 2   W 1 2   M 1 2   D C Π J
O 2 3 7 8.   miseranti alia inuidenti S   O 1.   miseranti aut inuidentiạ V.
17. quattuor R V G B E.   18. distintio G.   ‖   aspernatio R G B K S E.
a spernatio V *litt. inter* a *et* s *eras.*   19. adpetitus R V G K E.   appetitus B S.

                                    v
20. lubidinem R G B J.   libidinem K.   libidinem V P E.   ‖   reliquas R 17
                                    i
P B 2   E 2   L 2   O 7.   reliqas E 1.   reliquias R G K.   reliquasq; V
                                            q;   i   q;
at q; *atr. uiridiore scr.*   reliquas∧ II *al. atr. superscr.*   reliquas B 1 i *eod. atr.*
q; *al. atr. superscr.*   reliquasq; R 6 7   B 3   K 2   S   L 3–6   W 1 2   M 2   J
O 1–3 8.   et reliquas M 1   D C.   ‖   oratio R 1 2 10 16   V P G   B 2   K S   E 1 2
W 2   D J   O 1.   21. illudne non R V P G   B 1 3   K 1   S   E 1 2   M 2   Π J
O 1–3 8.   illudne M 1 non *om.*   illudnē nō B 2 (*sic*).   illud nō ne W 1.
                            an
illud nec ne D C.   illud ne nō W 2 *al. atr. superscr.*   illud uideatur ne non O 7. ‖
ferundum R V G   B 1   K.   ferūndum B 2.   ferendum R 6 7 17   P   B 3   S
E 1 2   W 1 2   M 1 2   D C Π J   O 1–3 7 8.

omnibus : for the anacoluthon cf. iii 3, 5
(where, as here, it is due to an inter-
jected explanation) and Finn. ii 22, 71
with Madv.'s note and his Excursus to
Finn. i 7, 23.

miseranti : Cic. has used *misereri* in
§ 56 and Lamb. conjectured *miserenti*
here. Fest. p. 123 Müll. lays down the
distinction : '*miseratur* is qui conqueritur
aliena incommoda ; *miseretur* is, qui
miserum subleuat,' a distinction which is
in flat contradiction to Cicero's usage in
§ 56. Nonius Marcellus, p. 445 M, says
'*miserari et misereri* ueteres his sensibus
esse uoluerunt ut sit *miserari* flere et
lamentari, *misereri* miserationem alienis
casibus exhibere.' Servius, however (on
Aen. i 597) declares 'et *miseror* et
misereor unum significat' quoting in support of his view Aen. ii 144 and iv 370.

in omnibus, 'in dealing with': for this
use see Sff.'s note to Lael. 2, 9, who
compares Gk ἐπί and quotes Off. ii 18,61 ;
Phil. xiv 3, 9 ; Or. ii 61, 248 ; Finn.
v 11, 30 *hoc cum in amicitiis...dicitur.*

quattuor, i.e. *aegritudo, laetitia, metus,
lubido* (7, 14).

illa, 'the following,' as often.

uniuersam, 'as a whole,' cf. *uniuersa
philosophia* ii 2, 4 ; iii 3, 6.

oratio. Bent. followed by Dav. read
curatio, and Bouh. comparing *bene adhibita ratio* above and *edocuit tamen ratio*

in iii 33, 80 conjectured *ratio. Oratio* is
defended by F.A.W. and Or. who compare § 62 and Phil. xiv 13, 34 'atque
utinam...aliqua talis iis adhiberi publice
posset oratio qua deponerent maerorem'
and is kept by all recent edd.

utrum illudne : cf. 4, 9 n. and Draeger,
Synt. I § 158 A (c).

The clause (though connected by *et*
with the preceding) merely restates the
same alternative as before in a reverse
order, *illud...ferundum* corresponding to
an ad singulas...oratio and *an omnium
...aegritudo* to *utrum ad uniuersam...
uehementior* ; the following clause *ut...
oportere* gives an instance of the alternative (following the order of the clause
immediately preceding) as applied to a
special case.

For *illudne non* Bentl. read *illud
necne* (comparing 29, 62) which by
making *illud...aegritudo* a disjunctive
question destroys the balance of the
clauses.

For *et* connecting two phrases of
practically identical meaning Wopkens
(*op. cit.* p. 136) compares Finn. iii 21, 71
'nunquam aequitatem ab utilitate posse
seiungi *et* quidquid aequum iustumque
esset id etiam honestum.' Ac. i 4, 17 ;
T.D. iii 33, 79 'suo iudicio et quod se
ita putet oportere facere' where Bentl.
wished to delete the *et*.

tudo, an omnium rerum tollenda omnino aegritudo, ut, si quis
aegre ferat se pauperem esse, idne disputes, paupertatem malum
non esse, an hominem aegre ferre nihil oportere. nimirum hoc
25 melius, ne, si forte de paupertate non persuaseris, sit aegritudini
concedendum; aegritudine autem sublata propriis rationibus,
quibus heri usi sumus, quodam modo etiam paupertatis malum
tollitur.

XXVIII. 60. Sed omnis eius modi perturbatio animi pla-

22. tollenda R 6   P 2 3 6   E 2   M 1 2   Π   O 2 3   B 3 *marg.* toleranda.
Urs. 3240 *marg., e cont. om.*   toll'anda R 17   J.   tol'anda P 1   W 2.
tolleranda R 7   P 4 5   K 2   C   O 7 ed. H.   tolleranda O 8.   toleranda R V G
B 1 2   K 1   S   E 1   W 1   D   O 1 Gr. *Vict.*
XXVIII. § 60, 1. perturbatio enim V *marg.* āı *atr. uiridi adscr.*

tollenda : this reading, which was also
a conjecture of Lambinus, is to be preferred
to *toleranda* of the best MSS. *toleranda* is
impossible in view of the corresponding
phrase in the example taken up in the
next clause 'hominem aegre ferre nihil
oportere.'
    ut, 'for example' as in 28, 61 ; v 24, 69 ;
Diu. ii 69, 142.
    concedendum, ' we may have to leave
the field free to'; if an unsuccessful
attempt be made to prove that *paupertas*
is not an evil, the failure renders it impossible to proceed further and argue that
there is nothing which can properly be
described as an evil ; for *concedere = cedere*,
cf. 29, 63 and the line from Cicero's poem
de suis temporibus quoted in Off. i 22, 77
' cedant arma togae concedat laurea laudi.'
    heri : in the discussion reported in
Book iii.
    malum : the phrase *paupertatis malum*
is in the context an easily understood
brachylogy for *cogitatio paupertatem esse
malum*. Bent. proposed to read (with
Gebh.'s Palatine codex) *nomen* and in
this he is followed by Bouh. : he gives as
his reasons 'quippe alienum est ab hac
disputatione concedere paupertatem esse
malum : deinde si *aegritudo omnino
sublata* sit, non *quodammodo* sed prorsus
omnino paupertatis malum tollitur' and
he explains his own reading, ' nam qui
nihil desiderat…cur pauper est uocandus?'
With regard to the first point Bent. is
quite right in his assertion ; the only
logical conclusion to be drawn with
regard to poverty from proving 'hominem
aegre ferre nihil oportere' is, not 'paupertatem malum non esse' but, 'hominem
aegre ferre paupertatem non oportere';
and this very fact is, *pace Bentleii*, the
justification for *quodam modo* ; once the
assertion 'hominem aegre ferre pauper-

tatem non oportere ' is established, it
becomes increasingly difficult (not logically impossible, but *quodam modo* impossible) to argue that *paupertas* is in
any real sense *malum*.
    XXVIII. § 60. **Sed omnis…** ' But
granting that all disturbances of this kind
may be cleared away by that process of
soothing the mind which consists in
proving that, etc.'; *abluatur* is concessive
subjunctive ; for the concessive use of
quidem after *ille* and *is* cf. i 3 6 n. : for
the metaphor in *abluatur* cf. iii 18, 43
' tum plane luctum omnem absterseris ' ;
de Sen. i 2 'omnis absterserit senectutis
molestias.'
    Bent. attacks the reading with his
usual vigour ' uix crediderim occultius aut
sanatu difficilius mendum in toto Cicerone
latitare' ; he objects to *placatione* on the
grounds that ; first, the phrase *perturbatio
…abluatur* is absurd ; one might as well
say *morbum leuari sanitate*: and, secondly,
that the word *placatio* cannot properly be
used where *res externae* are in question :
' placatio enim potius fit cum ipsa intus
aegritudo leniatur, utcumque se habeant
res externae.' He objects also to the
subj. *abluatur*: his proposed reading is
*sed cum omnis eiusmodi perturbatio
duplici ratione abluatur*; he claims for
duplici ratione that it gives a proper reference for *illa* and *haec* which follow : the
emendation is adopted by Lall. and (with
hac for *duplici*) by Nissen. The proposal
involves an anacoluthon, *illa quidem*
having no *hac* to correspond ; it is palaeographically highly improbable that *duplici
ratione* should have been corrupted into
animi placatione ; and the objection to
placatio animi is unsound, the phrase
being = *ratio placandi animi*, surely a
legitimate description of an argument
addressed to an *animus perturbatus*.

catione abluatur illa quidem, cum doceas nec bonum illud esse,
ex quo laetitia aut libido oriatur, nec malum, ex quo aut metus
aut aegritudo; uerum tamen haec est certa et propria sanatio, si
5 doceas ipsas perturbationes per se esse uitiosas nec habere quicquam aut naturale aut necessarium, ut ipsam aegritudinem leniri
uidemus cum obicimus maerentibus inbecillitatem animi ecfeminati, cumque eorum grauitatem constantiamque laudamus qui
non turbulente humana patiantur. quod quidem solet iis etiam
10 accidere qui illa mala esse censent, ferenda tamen aequo animo
arbitrantur. putat aliquis esse uoluptatem bonum, alius autem
pecuniam; tamen et ille ab intemperantia et hic ab auaritia
auocari potest. illa autem altera ratio et oratio, quae simul et

2. nec bonum B 3 K 2 W 1 M 1 2 O 1–3 8.   nec et bonum V *atr. uiridi*

nec   nec
superscr.   7 bonum W 2 *al. atr. superscr.*   bonum E 3 *al. atr. superscr.*

c
neque bonum ed. H.   n et bonum J.   et bonum R P G B 1 2 K 1 S E 1 2
D C II O 7.   3. libido R V G B K.   6. aut ipsam V.   ꝗut ipsa R *eod. atr.*
ut ipsa G.   7. obicimus V B 3 K 2 W 1 2 M 2 D C II J O 3 7 8.

cim'
obicim⁹ E 2 *at* m⁹ *al. atr. script.*   obicib; E 1.   obicib̨ M 1 *h.e.* obicibus
in obicimus *mut.*   obicibus R P G B 1 2 K 1.   obiicimus S O 1 2.
obncimus R 6.   ‖   merentibus R G B 1 3 E 1.   ‖   inbecillitatem E 1.

l
inbecilitatem G *ead. man. superscr.*   imbecillitatem R V B 1 2 K S. ‖
ecfeminati R G B.   h,ecfeminati K 1 h, *atr. nigriore script.*   etfeminati B 2.

ef
& feminati V *atr. uiridi superscr.*   ef feminati E 1.   effeminati P B 3 S W 1
M 2 C J O 3 7.   8. grauitatem constantiamque V P K.   grauite
constantiaque R G.   10. ferenda R V P G B 1 2 S E 1 2 W 1 J.
ferendam O 2.   ferendum K 1.   11. arbitratur G.   ‖ putat K.

t   ab
puta V *atr. uiridi superscr.*   puta R G.   12. ab auaritia R P G.   auaritia V
eod. ut uid. atr.   13. et oratio R P G *om.* V.

cum doceas: cf. for these methods iii
31, 76 sqq.

haec est...si doceas: cf. Draeger,
Synt. II § 549 b (α), to whose list of
instances this should be added.

**qui illa...censent, ferenda...arbitran-
tur**, the Peripatetics and the Cyrenaics.

aliquis...alius: Madv. on Finn. iii
19, 63 shows that *aliquis...alius* is never
used in classical Lat. as the equivalent of
alius...alius; in this case *putat aliquis*
gives one instance out of many which
might be given, and to it another (*alius...
pecuniam*) is added.

illa altera, i.e. 'cum doceas nec
bonum illud esse ex quo laetitia aut
libido oriatur, nec malum ex quo aut
metus aut aegritudo'; though the 'certa
et propria sanatio' for *perturbationes*
from the philosophical standpoint is to
show that a *perturbatio* is in itself un-

natural and unnecessary, yet the method
which, dealing with a particular case,
tries to show that the object which gave
rise to the *perturbatio* is not *malum* or
bonum as the case may be, is more
useful, since in addition to getting rid of
the *perturbatio* it establishes right views
of the object which caused it, a result
which the 'certa et propria sanatio' does
not aim at. The drawback to the method
is that it is seldom successful, and can
only be applied in the case of persons of
a philosophic mind (*uulgus* = οἱ πολλοί, a
Stoic synonym for οἱ φαῦλοι, the non-
philosophic).

For *ratio et oratio* cf. 17, 38 n.

Bent. objected strongly to *utilior*
('nihil uidi tetrius foediusue hac lectione...
qui, malum, si non proficit, utilis esse
poterit?') and proposed *subtilior* which
has been accepted by Dav. Bouh. Lall.

opinionem falsam tollit et aegritudinem detrahit, est ea quidem
15 utilior, sed raro proficit neque est ad uolgus adhibenda. **61**. quaedam autem sunt aegritudines quas leuare illa medicina nullo
modo possit, ut, si quis aegre ferat nihil in se esse uirtutis, nihil
animi, nihil officii, nihil honestatis, propter mala is quidem angatur, sed alia quaedam sit ad eum admouenda curatio, et talis
20 quidem, quae possit esse omnium etiam de ceteris rebus discrepantium philosophorum. inter omnis enim conuenire oportet
commotiones animorum a recta ratione auersas esse uitiosas, ut,
etiamsi †nec mala sint illa, quae metum aegritudinemue, nec bona,

14. falsam R 2 10 16   P K.   falsa R 1   V G.   ‖   aegritudinem V K.
aegritudine R G.   15. utilior R V P G   B 1–3   K 1 2   S   E 1 2   W 1 2   M 1 2
D C II J   O 1–3 7 8.   ‖   uolgus R V G B K.   uulgus S E.
§ 61, 16. ulla V *fuerat* illa, i *extra lineam atr. uiridi adscr.*   18. officii
R V G B S E.   officiii K 1.   ‖   si quidem agatur G *in* is q. angatur *alt. man. mut.*
20. omnium etiam R 1 6   P G   B 1–3   K 1 2   E 2   W 1 2   M 2   D II J   O 1 2 7.
etiam omnium V E   O 8.   omnium esse etiam C.   etiam esse omnium M 1.
esse omnium de ceteris rebus etiam O 3.   21. omnis R V G B K.
23. nec mala...nec bona R 1 2 6 7 10 16 17   V   P 1–5   G   B 2 3   K 1 2   S E 2
L 2–4   6   W 1 2   M 1 2   D C II   O 1–3 7 8 Urs. 3240.   nec macula E 1.
nec ma la B 1 *duabus litt. eras.*   etiamsi nec *om.* L 5.   etiamsi nec letitiamue J
cett. om.   ‖   quae metum R G.   quęmmetum V.

Ern. Sff. ; the MSS. reading is followed
by Mo. Or. F.A.W. Küh. Ml. T.S. Hei.
Utilior is (it must be granted) ambiguous
and may mean either ' productive of
benefit to a greater number' (sc. than the
rival method) or ' productive of a greater
benefit' (sc. than the rival method, to the
person with whom both might be successful) ; the latter is Cicero's meaning
here ; and though it might have been
expressed with less possibility of misunderstanding, the phrase cannot be said
to be inaccurate or absurd. *Subtilior*, at
any rate, could not have been used here ;
Cicero's whole contention has been that
the rival method, the *certa et propria
sanatio*, is the more logical method, the
one most in accordance with sound
philosophy ; *subtilis* as applied to an argument means in Cic. ' precise,' ' accurate,'
' careful' and would not be applied to
one which sacrificed logical precision to
anything else.

proficit, a medical term. Küh. quotes
Cels. v 28, 2 ' neque ulla umquam
medicina proficit' ; Plin. N.H. xxvii 72
' radix aduersatur omnium serpentium
generibus....nec alia res celerius proficit.'

§ 61. **illa medicina**, the argument that
the disturbing cause was not *malum*,
since the absence of virtue was the only
malum. This is another argument in
favour of the *certa et propria curatio*, the
only method which could possibly afford

relief in such a case. This particular kind
of *aegritudo* was first it seems brought
prominently forward by Posidonius in
his criticism of Chrysippus' doctrine of the
πάθη, cf. Galen, de Plat. et Hippocr.
plac. iv p. 370 M.

ut, ' for example,' 27, 59 n.

nihil in se esse uirtutis: cf. iii 28, 68.

officii, i.e. τοῦ καθήκοντος.

etiam...discrepantium=*etiam si...dis-
crepent*, ' even while differing on other
points.'

ut etiamsi nec. The MSS. read *nec
mala sint...nec bona*, which is defended
by Wopkens, *op. cit.* p. 138, who notes
' sensus est constare inter omnes, tametsi
res illas quae perturbationes et commotiones in nobis concitent esse indifferentes concedatur, ipsas tamen commotiones a rebus illis indifferentibus
concitatas uitiosas esse.' Hand in his
note to Wopkens takes a different view,
explaining the passage thus : ' etiamsi
perturbationes animi ab ea parte quod
nec mala sint quae metum aegritudinemue
nec bona quae cupiditatem laetitiamue
moueant improbari debeant, tamen ipsa
adeo commotio uitiosa sit.' Or. in his
notes to F.A.W. and Mo. agree with
Hand ; but it is difficult to see how either
this or Wopkens' meaning can be got
without violence out of Cicero's Latin.

Küh. who also reads *nec...nec* translates
' so dass, selbst in dem Falle, dass

quae cupiditatem laetitiamue moueant, tamen sit uitiosa ipsa
25 commotio. constantem enim quendam uolumus, sedatum, grauem,
humana omnia spernentem illum esse quem magnanimum et

26. prementem *uel* praementem *codd. omnes.*   spernentem *corr. uir doctus*
apud Lambinum. ‖ illum esse quem R V G K E 2 W 1 2 O 1 7 8.   illum esse

quam R 2 B E D.   illum esse q̇ P.   illum esse Φ S *ras. post* Φ *et marg.* quē.

einerseits die Dinge, welche Furcht oder
Kummer einflössen, keine Uebel, anderer-
seits die Dinge, welche Begierde oder
Fröhlichkeit erregen, keine Güter sind,
dennoch die Gemüthsbewegung an und
für sich fehlerhaft ist' ; i.e. even supposing the Stoic view to be true yet perturbation is undesirable. As this, the only
natural meaning of the Latin words, is
the precise opposite of what Cicero
might be expected to say in the context,
most edd. follow Bent. and Lamb. in
altering the negative to the positive: Bent.
followed by Ml. Sff. Hei. T.S. Schiche
reading *uel...uel* in place of *nec...nec*,
and Lamb. followed by Fabr. F.A.W.
Schz. *et...et* : the meaning will then be
'even if the objects which give rise to fear
or vexation are evils and those which
arouse desire or delight are goods yet
mental perturbation is in itself undesirable,' i.e. even adopting a view which at
first sight might seem to justify *perturbatio* if anything could, philosophers
would yet be agreed that it was in itself
vicious. A superficial support is lent to
this view by the fact that Cic. has himself earlier in the § adduced a case of
aegritudo which required to be cured
although the *aegritudo* was *propter mala.*
The objection which may be made to
all the explanations proposed above is
that they do not take sufficiently into
account first, that the clause *ut, etiamsi...
...ipsa commotio* is the statement (not of
a fact or a conclusion but) of a point of
view to be adopted by agreement among
all philosophers ; and secondly that the
parties to the agreement adopt a common
attitude upon one point, *etiam de ceteris
rebus discrepantes.* This point of agreement is *uitiosam esse ipsam commotionem* ;
differences are allowed upon the questions to which the words *etiamsi...moueant*
refer. Yet both those who read *et...et* (or
uel...uel) and those who read *nec...nec*
make the sentence contemplate some one
definite point of view (whether that of the
Stoics or their opponents) as adopted on
these other points as a part of the general
agreement.
The clause beginning *inter omnes enim
conuenire oportet* is, as *enim* shows, ex-

planatory of the preceding *talis quidem...
philosophorum* and Cicero's habit of taking
up and developing his own statements in
detail makes one expect some clause
explanatory of, or expanding, the phrase
etiam de ceteris rebus discrepantium ; this
clause can only be *etiamsi...moueant* and
must of course not contradict *de ceteris
rebus discrepantium* in meaning.
These conditions are satisfied by reading *etiam si nec malane sint illa...nec
bona quae...moueant,* understanding *conueniat* from *conuenire* in the preceding
clause. Trans. ' There should be, I mean,
a general agreement that emotions opposed
to right reason are morbid states, so that
if there should not be any agreement
whether those things which excite fear
and vexation are evils or not, or those
things good which excite desire and
delight, still perturbation is in itself a
morbid state.' This is supported by the
résumé in the next paragraph, where *ut
nihil quale sit illud quod perturbet
animum [docendum sit]* answers to the
clause *etiamsi...moueant* here.
quendam : cf. i 12, 27 n. ; Nägelsbach,
Stil. 82, 3.
spernentem, an anonymous conjecture
for the MSS *prementem* mentioned (to
be rejected) by Lamb. but approved by
Bent. and adopted by Mo. Bai. Wes.
Ml. TS. Hei. The MSS reading is kept
by Lamb. Dav. Or. Küh. Kl. and defended by Wopkens (*op. cit.* p. 138) and
Hand. Bouh. conjectured *ferentem.*
Dav. wished to give to *prementem* the
sense of *calcantem,* a meaning which Bent.
showed was only possible if *pedibus* or
some similar word was expressed. *Premere* can be used with words denoting
feeling, in the sense of 'repress', 'control'
(Seneca, de Ira iii 6, 1 (quoted by Wopkens) ; Stat. Theb. 9, 546; Val. Fl. iii
370 etc.), a meaning which is impossible
here as *humana* cannot mean 'human
feelings' ; nor is it possible to get a
satisfactory meaning out of the sense
noted by Hand '*premere* dicitur de omnibus rebus quae ne exsurgant aut euagentur
moderatione et temperatione cohibentur,'
since the wise man has no control over
the accidents of fortune. In silver age

fortem uirum dicimus. talis autem nec maerens nec timens nec
cupiens nec gestiens esse quisquam potest. eorum enim haec
sunt, qui euentus humanos superiores quam suos animos esse
30 ducunt.

XXIX. 62. Quare omnium philosophorum, ut ante dixi,
una ratio est medendi, ut nihil, quale sit illud, quod perturbet
animum, sed de ipsa sit perturbatione dicendum. itaque primum
in ipsa cupiditate, cum id solum agitur ut ea tollatur, non est
5 quaerendum, bonum illud necne sit, quod libidinem moueat, sed
libido ipsa tollenda est, ut, siue, quod honestum est, id sit summum bonum, siue uoluptas siue horum utrumque coniunctum
siue tria illa genera bonorum, tamen, etiamsi uirtutis ipsius
uehementior adpetitus sit, eadem sit omnibus ad deterrendum
10 adhibenda oratio. continet autem omnem sedationem animi

29. qui euentus R 1 2 10 16. quæ ᵢuentus V *atr. uiridi mut.*　　quae uentus G
in qui euentus *ead. man. mut.*　　30. ducunt R 6 L₄ 6 M 1 2 O 1 2.

dicunt S *eod. atr.* B 3 *fort. eod. atr.*　　dicunt R 1 7 1 7 V P 1 2 4 G B 1 2
K 1 2 E 1–3 L 2 3 5 W 1 D C Π J O 3 7 8 ed. H.　　dñt W 2.
XXIX. § **62**, 1. ut ante R 1 2 10 16 G.　　ạut ante V.　　3. in *ante* ipsa
addidit G *prima manu.*　　5. nece G *ead. man.* ‖ lubidinem R V G B.
libidinem K 1.　　lubidinem J *marg. e contextu om.*　　6. lubido R V B K
J *marg. e cont. om.*　　lubidio G i *ante* o *expunx. alt. man.* ‖ ut siue R G K.
ut siṇe V *atr. uiridi superscr.*　　8. tria illa R 1 17 V G B 1 2 K 1 E 1 2
Π O 2.　　illa tria R 6 P B 3 K 2 S W 1 2 M 1 2 D C J O 1 3.
ulla tria O 7. ‖ bonarum G.　　9. adpetitus R V G K.　　10. adhibenda R V P G
B 2 3 K 1 S E 1 2 W 2 M 1 2 D C Π O 1–3 7.　　adhibita W 1.
adhib ꝺa B 1 *litt. post* b *eras. et* t *in* d *mut. eod. ut uid. atr.*

Latin *premere* bears the sense of ' be
superior to,' ' surpass ' e.g. Stat. Silu. i 2,
115 ' quantum Latonia nymphas uirgo
premit,' but there is no evidence, unless
the present passage be such, for this
meaning in Cicero.

haec : *maerere, timere, cupere, gestire.*
XXIX. § **62**. **ante** in § 61.

nihil, ' never a word '; like *nullus*,
often used as an emphatic substitute for
non.

primum : the parenthesis beginning
continet autem disarranges the intended
order ; the ideas awakened by his quotation lead Cicero on to think first of
aegritudo and then of its congener *metus*
and he does not return to *cupiditas* before
§ 65.

horum utrumque coniunctum : cf. v
30, 85 ' uoluptatem cum honestate Dinomachus et Callipho copulauit '; Off. iii
33, 119 ' quo magis reprehendendos

Calliphontem et Dinomachum iudico qui
se dirempturos controuersiam putauerunt
si cum honestate uoluptatem tamquam
cum homine pecudem copulauissent ; '
Fin. ii 11, 34 ; Ac. ii 42, 131.

tria illa genera : sc. *animi, corporis,
externa,* the view of the Peripatetics and
the old Academy ; v 30, 85 ; Fin. *l.c.*;
Ac. *l.c.*

uirtutis ipsius, ' if even virtue itself
should be the object of an immoderate
yearning,' as in the case instanced in 28,
61.

deterrendum : not *ab iis quae perturbent animum* (Küh. Mo.), since to induce
terror is hardly a philosophic means of
banishing *perturbationes,* but sc. *adpetitum uehementiorem,* which is quasi-personi-
fied and represented as being frightened
away by the calmness of the mind it was
about to invade. Unless, indeed, we
should read *detergendum.*

humana in conspectu posita natura; quae quo facilius expressa
cernatur, explicanda est oratione communis condicio lexque
uitae. 63. itaque non sine causa, cum Orestem fabulam doceret
Euripides, primos tris uersus reuocasse dicitur Socrates:

15 Neque tám terribilis úlla fando orátio est
Nec sórs nec ira caélitum inuectúm malum,
Quod nón natura humána patiendo écferat.

est autem utilis ad persuadendum ea quae acciderint ferri et

---

12. conditio R V G B K S.
§ 63, 13. orestem R V G K C.   orestē P E 1 J.   horestem B 3.
h r
horestē B 1.   o‸restem S *marg.* horestis.   horestis W 1. ‖ dĩcēt Π i *in* o *mut.*
diceret R 1 6 7 10 16 17   V P 2 G B 1-3   K 1 2 S E 1 3 L 2-6 W 1 M 1 2
D C J O 1-3 7 ed. H.   dr̄et P 1 E 2. *om.* W 2.   14. tris R V G B K̃ E
W 1 2 J O 7.   tres P B 3 S.   15. fando R 1 2 7 10 16 V P G B 2 K 1
                                                                           i
S O 1 3 7 ed. H.   fando Π *at* o *ex* i *mut. ut uid.*   fando B 3.   fandi R 6
K 2 E 2 3 W 1 2 M 1 O 2.   fanda E 1 D.   fraudi R 17. ‖ oratio E 1
D C.   ratio R 1 6 7 16 17   V P G B 1-3   K 1 2   S E 2 3 W 1 2 M 1 Π J
O 1-3 7 ed. H.   16. sors R 6 17   P 1 4 B 3   K 2 E 3 W 2 *marg. e cont. om.*
M 2 O 1 ed. H.   fors R 1 7 V B 1 K 1 E 2 W 1 D C Π O 2 3 7
Gr. *Vict.*   fons E 1.   fortis S *marg.* sors.   fors *an* sors *incert.* B 2 M 1.
sor *in* fors *mut. alt. man.* G. *om.* J. ‖ inuectum O 1.   inuēctum O 7.
inuentum R 1 2 6 7 10 16 17   V P G B 1-3   K 1 2   S E 1-3 L 2-6 W 1 2 M 1 2
D C J O 2 3 ed. H.   17. ecferat R V G K.   hęc ferat B 1 E 1.
ef
hec ferat S *al. atr. superscr.*   et ferat B 2.   efferat P B 3 W 1 M 2 Π J
O 2 3 Gr.   eferat M 1.   ferat O 1.   18. autem R V P G B 1-3 K *plerique.*
aūt D.   āt W 2. ‖ eaque G. ‖ acciderint R V P G B K *plerique.*
acciderit O 7.   accidunt O 3.

---

expressa: cf. iii 2, 3 n. on *eminentem
effigiem.*
condicio lexque uitae: cf. iii 16, 34 ;
24, 59.
§ 63. **doceret**: the usual phrase for
producing a play (lit. instructing the
actors in the play), cf. Brut. 18, 72 ; Hor.
A.P. 288.
reuocasse, 'encored': 'proprie dicitur
actor reuocari: sed quia id fit ut repetat
quae dixerat etiam *uersus reuocari* dici
potest.' Ern.; Boettiger (quoted by Mo.)
thinks this could not have occurred at a
public performance of the play and must
have taken place at the rehearsal.
Neque tam: οὐκ ἔστιν οὐδὲν δεινὸν ὦδ'
εἰπεῖν ἔπος | οὐδὲ πάθος, οὐδὲ συμφορὰ
θεήλατος | ἧς οὐκ ἂν ἄραιτ' ἄχθος ἀνθρώπου
φύσις. Eur. Or. 1—3.
fando: a kind of modal abl. 'terrible
in the speaking' i.e. 'terrible to speak
of.' Draeger, *Synt.* II § 599 (1); cf. N.D.
i 29, 82 'ne fando quidem auditum est';
Pacuuius, Teucer (Ribbeck *Scaen. poes.
Rom. frag.* I² p. 117 IV) 'nihilne a Troia
adportat fando'; Val. Flacc. iv 170 'his
fando si nuntius exstitit oris' and Sil.

Ital. x 483 'si Porsena fando | auditus
tibi.'
Cicero has (as Fabr. Dav. and Mur.
pointed out) mistaken the meaning of the
Gk. He seems to have construed the first
line οὐκ ἔστιν ἔπος οὐδὲν ὦδε δεινὸν εἰπεῖν,
whereas in the Schol. ὦδ' ἔπος εἰπεῖν is
paraphrased by ἐν συντόμῳ εἰπεῖν (*ut uno
uerbo complectar*): and the meaning of the
last line evidently is 'nihil tam taetrum
esse cuius grauitati natura humana non
sit exposita ' (Fabr.)
ecferat: Beroald. explains the word as
equivalent to *uincere,* 'do away with,'
' efferre enim est ad sepulturam ferre :
unde *efferri* dicuntur mala quae patiendo
uincimus et quasi tumulamus.' Mo. is,
however, undoubtedly correct in explaining it by *perferre*; he quotes in support
the words of the *uetus poeta* (i.e. Attius) in
Cic. p. Sest. 48, 102 'nisi laborem summa
cum cura ecferas' (Ribbeck, *Scaen. Rom.
Poes. Frag.* i² p. 164) and Lucr. i 141.
autem: Dav. conjectured *etiam,* which
was at one time accepted by Or. Wopkens
(*op. cit.* pp. 10 sq.), who compares i 33, 80
hominum autem (where Lamb. proposed

posse et oportere enumeratio eorum qui tulerunt.
etsi aegri-
20 tudinis sedatio et hesterna disputatione explicata est et in Consolationis libro, quem in medio (non enim sapientes eramus)
maerore et dolore conscripsimus; quodque uetat Chrysippus, ad
recentis quasi tumores animi remedium adhibere, id nos fecimus
naturaeque uim attulimus ut magnitudini medicinae doloris
25 magnitudo concederet.

XXX. 64. Sed aegritudini, de qua satis est disputatum,
finitimus est metus, de quo pauca dicenda sunt. est enim metus,
ut aegritudo praesentis, sic ille futuri mali. itaque non nulli
aegritudinis partem quandam metum esse dicebant, alii autem
5 metum praemolestiam appellabant, quod est quasi dux conse-

19. *post* oportere *habet* V *trium litt. spat. in ras.* ‖ tulerunt K O 1. tuꞎlerunt R *eod. atr.* tuꞎlerunt V. tullerunt G. 22. uetat R 1 2 10 16 G B. uertat V. ‖ chrysippus R V G W 1. chrisippus B 1. crisippus E 1. 23. recentis R V G B K E. recentes B 2 S. 24. uim R G B 1–3 K W 1. çum V. ‖ attulimus R B S E. attullimus G K. adtullimus V. XXX. § 64, 3. ille B 3 K 2 W 1 2 D J O 1 3 7 B 1 *at* e *ex* i *mut.* illi V. illi R G B 2 K 1 E 1. 5. praemolestiam R 2. praemolestiā R 10 P. premolestiā V. premolestia R G B 1 2 K. pmoleticia E 1 (*sic*). ‖ appellabant R V G K. ‖ quod est R V G B 3 S L 2–6 W 2 M 2 D C II O 1 3 ed. H. quod ē R 6 7 17 P B E 1–3 W 1 M 1 (*non ut Küh.*) J O 7. quod ⌖ B 2. quod÷ K 1 2. qui ē O 2.

item); N.D. ii 23, 60; Off. i 4, 11, shows
that *autem* often means much the same
as *etiam* with a slight notion of contrast
in addition. Cf. Küh.'s n. on i 18, 42.
etsi : 'still,' cf. i 42, 99 n.
in Consolationis libro : i 26, 65 n.
non enim sapientes eramus. 'Diese
leise mit der innigsten Trauer um die
geliebte Tochter verbundene Ironie liess
sich nicht anmuthiger ausdrücken als
durch eine solche, sonst bei Cic. unge-
wöhnliche, Parenthese zwischen d. Adject.
und Subst.' F.A.W.
quodque uetat Chrysippus : cf. Chrysippus' words, quoted by Galen, de plac.
Hipp. iv 7 (152) p. 398 Mü. καθ' ὃν
λόγον οὐκ ἂν ἀπελπίσαι τις οὕτως τῶν
πραγμάτων ἐγχρονιζομένων καὶ τῆς παθητικῆς φλεγμονῆς ἀνιεμένης τὸν λόγον παρεισδυόμενον καὶ οἱονεὶ χώραν λαμβάνοντα
παριστάναι τὴν τοῦ πάθους ἀλογίαν; cf.
also Hieron. Epp. 39, 4 'recens uulnus
est et tactus iste quo blandior non tam
curat quam exasperat : attamen quod
tempore mitigandum est, cur ratione non
uincitur?'; Ov. Epp. ex P. i 3, 15 f.
tempore ducetur longo fortasse cicatrix |
horrent admotas uulnera cruda manus :
Seneca, Cons. ad Helu. i 2 ; de Ira iii 39,
2 ; Plin. Epp. v. 16, 11 ; Plut. Consol.

ad Apoll. 1. Chrysippus, carrying out his
idea of the close analogy between mind
and body, by which πάθη are regarded
as diseases, employs the word φλεγμονή
(which Cic. seems to replace by *tumor*)
to denote the inflamed and swollen condition of the mind under the influence of
grief.
Pohlenz (*Hermes* XLI p. 336) thinks
that the idea was due originally to
Krantor, since it is found in the beginning of Plutarch's Consol. ad Apoll.,
which was closely modelled upon Krantor's περὶ πένθους. He compares also
Seneca, Cons. ad Helu. i 2 ; Cons. ad
Marc. 4, 2 ; de Ira iii 39, 2.
Cicero's grief was so violent that he felt
justified in attempting a violent remedy.
XXX. § 64. **metus** : 7, 16 n.
ille : for the redundant pronoun, used
to point the distinction between the *ut*
and the *sic* clause, cf. 30, 61 ; de Or. ii
30, 130 'qui, ut litterae sed uerbum scri-
bendum sic illi ad causam explicandam
statim occurrant' and Reid on Ac. ii 5,
13 ; Draeger, *Synt. d. Lat. Sp.* § 37.
praemolestiam : a word apparently
coined by Cicero, as it occurs nowhere
else. It is perhaps a translation of Plato's
προλύπησις ; Rep. ix 584 C οὐκοῦν καὶ αἱ

H. 12

quentis molestiae. quibus igitur rationibus instantia feruntur,
eisdem contemnuntur sequentia. nam uidendum est in utrisque
ne quid humile, summissum, molle, ecfeminatum, fractum ab-
iectumque faciamus. sed quamquam de ipsius metus inconstantia,
10 inbecillitate, leuitate dicendum est, tamen multum prodest ea
quae metuuntur ipsa contemnere. itaque siue casu accidit siue
consilio, percommode factum est quod eis de rebus quae maxime
metuuntur, de morte et de dolore, primo et proximo die disputatum est. quae si probata sunt metu magna ex parte liberati
15 sumus.

XXXI. 65. Ac de malorum opinione hactenus; uideamus
nunc de bonorum, id est de laetitia et de cupiditate. mihi quidem in tota ratione ea quae pertinet ad animi perturbationem
una res uidetur causam continere, omnis eas esse in nostra
5 potestate, omnis iudicio susceptas, omnis uoluntarias. hic igitur
error est eripiendus, haec detrahenda opinio atque, ut in malis

---

7. contempnuntur *et infra* contempnere G.   8. ecfeminatum R V G B K.
et feminatum B 2 E 1.   effeminatum P B 3 K 2 S W 1 J.   10. inbecillitate
R V G B 2 K E.   imbecillitate B 1.   ībecillitate S.   11. siue casu
R P G B K   E 2   W 2   M 1 2   D J   O 1-3.   siue causa V.   siue caũ B 2
W 1   O 7.   12. maxime R V G B K S E.   13. proxumo R G B K.
             i
proximo V S E.   ‖   de G *alt. man. superscr.*
XXXI. § 65, 1. actenus G.   3. pertinet B 3   K 2   W 1   M 2   O 1-3.
   ¹ net
pertineꞂ B 1.   ptinēt B 2   W 2   M 1   D J   O 7 ed. H.   pertinent R V P G
K 1   E 1 2   C II.   ‖   perturbationem G   B 2 3   K 1   E 2   W 2   M 1 2   D C
O 1 7.   perturbatione V P B S   E 1   W 1   Π J   O 2 3 ed. H.   4. omnis (*ter*)
R V G   B 1 3   K.   oms̄ (*ter*) S   B 2.   om̄s...omīs...om̄s E 1.

πρὸ μελλόντων τούτων ἐκ προσδοκίας γιγνό-
μεναι προησθήσεις τε καὶ προλυπήσεις κατὰ
ταὐτὰ ἔχουσι;
    est : the MSS reading is retained by
Schiche alone among recent edd. : Dav.
Ern. Küh. TS. Sff. F.A.W. Hei. Or.
follow Bentley in altering to *esset*; but
there is no reason to assume that Cic. is
borrowing the explanation (*quod...moles-
tiae*) along with the term; *quasi* does
not mark out *dux* as a translation of an
original Gk word, but softens the metaphorical explanation of *praemolestia* by
dux molestiae.
    instantia : τὰ ἐνεστῶτα, cf. 6, 11 n.
    consilio : sc. *factum est* to be supplied
out of *accidit.*
    quae : i.e. *ea quae primo et proximo die
dicta sunt* ; the plural is implied in *disputatum est.*
    XXXI. § 65. **ac...hactenus** : cf. 2, 3
'et de coniectura quidem hactenus,' a
formula of transition.

ratione : 'process of reasoning,' 'enquiry,' μέθοδος.
    perturbationem : this, which is the
MSS reading, was altered unnecessarily
by Bentley, followed by Dav. Ern. Or.
Tr., to the plural on account of *eas* following : but the change from singular to
plural (from the general to particular
cases) is quite common; edd. quote Fin.
v 23, 66; Leg. i 14, 40: N.D. i 38, 106
'hoc idem fieri in *deo...ex quo esse beati*
atque *aeterni intellegantur*' : the opposite
change is seen in Fin. ii 19, 61 'aliquid de
uoluptatibus suis cogitabat? ubi ut *eam* cap-
eret aut quando,' where see Madv.'s note.
    continere : cf. 10, 24; iii 24, 58.
    hic...error : 'this then is the mistake
which must be eradicated,' the mistake
being the denial of the truth of the preceding statement 'omnes perturbationes
esse in nostra potestate.' It is better to
assume here that Cic. has expressed himself loosely than to explain *hic error* as

opinatis tolerabilia, sic in bonis sedatiora sunt efficienda ea quae
magna et laetabilia ducuntur. atque hoc quidem commune
malorum et bonorum, ut, si iam difficile sit persuadere nihil
10 earum rerum quae perturbent animum aut in bonis aut in malis
esse habendum, tamen alia ad alium motum curatio sit adhibenda aliaque ratione maleuolus, alia amator, alia rursus anxius,
alia timidus corrigendus. **66**. atque erat facile sequentem eam
rationem quae maxime probatur de bonis et malis negare
15 umquam laetitia adfici posse insipientem, quod nihil umquam
haberet boni. sed loquimur nunc more communi. sint sane ista
bona quae putantur, honores, diuitiae, uoluptates, cetera, tamen

7. tolerabilia P B 1 3 K 1 S E 1 2 W 1 2 D C O 1-3. tollerabilia
or
R *eod. atr.* tollerabilia R 7 V G B 2 J O 7. tolerabili͈a II *al. atr. mut.*
tolerabiliora M 2. tolleranda M 1. 8. dicuntur R 1 6 7 10 16 17 V G B 1-3
K 1 2 S E 1-3 L 2-6 W 1 2 M 1 2 II O 1-3 ed. H. dic̄r P 1. dn̄r J.
dicunt D C O 7. ducuntur *corr. Wolfius.* 9. bonorum et malorum G *at signis
ordo inuersus.* 10. aut in bonis aut in malis R V P G B 1-3 K 1 S E 1 2
W 1 2 M 2 J O 1-3 7. aut in malis aut in bonis M 1 D C. 12. maleuolus
R G K S. maliuolus V B E.
§ **66**, 14. maxume R V B. maxumae G *in* maxume *ead. man. mut.*
v
maximae K *eod. atr.* 15. adfici R V G K. affici B S. 16. sint sane R P G
B 1-3 K 1 S E 2 W 1 2 M 2 J O 2 3 7. sin sane M 1. sunt sane
V E 1 D C O 1. 17. diutiae G. ‖ cetera R V P G K E 1 2 W 2 J O 17.
&   q3
cetera B 1 *in ras. superscr.* et cetera W 1 M 1. cetera S. ceteraq· M 2.
&c̈ ed. H.

'huius rei error, h. e., error in quo
homines in hac re uersantur' (Küh.), as
haec opinio will then have to be explained
as 'huius rei opinio,' which is absurd,
unless we take *opinio* to mean *opinio praua*
which cannot be defended even by the
proximity of *error.*
    ut in malis...ducuntur, 'just as in the
case of what is looked upon as evil, such
things are to be shown to be tolerable, so
in the case of what is good, things considered important and pleasurable are to
be shown to be less emotional.' Erasm.
followed by Dav. altered *tolerabilia* to
tolerabiliora to correspond to *sedatiora*
below : the mss reading is defended, not
very convincingly, by Wopkens (*op. cit.*
p. 299) as a case of *enallage graduum*,
but the exx. he quotes are not to the
point. The meaning of the sentence is
perfectly intelligible and no laboured explanations are required. As a subject for
tolerabilia efficienda sunt Küh. supplies
by *συνεξευγμένον ea quae grauia et tristia
ducuntur* from *ea quae m. et l. d.* below ;
it seems simpler to assume a pronominal
subject to be supplied from *malis opinatis*;
in *sedatiora* Cic. has by a not uncommon

figure used a word appropriate to the
feelings to describe the objects which
excite such feelings ; for the meaning of
efficere here cf. i 8, 16 n.
    amator : 12, 27 n.
    § **66. erat** : Roby § 1535.
    sequentem : of an indefinite subject i
38, 91 n. ; iii 17, 38 n.
    eam rationem : sc. *Stoicorum.*
    negare unquam...boni : Cicero has
here in his mind a famous paradox of
Chrysippus reported by Plut. de St. rep.
c. 25 p. 1046 B 'τὴν ἐπιχαιρεκακίαν'
ὅπου μὲν 'ἀνύπαρκτον εἶναί' φησιν· 'ἐπεὶ
τῶν μὲν ἀστείων οὐδεὶς ἐπ' ἀλλοτρίοις
κακοῖς χαίρει, τῶν δὲ φαύλων οὐδεὶς χαίρει
τὸ παράπαν'; since χαρά proceeded only
from τὸ ἀγαθόν, and the only ἀγαθόν was
ἀρετή, which the *insipientes* lacked, it
followed that they could not enjoy the
Stoic χαρά : but it was quite possible for
them to enjoy the ἄλογος ἔπαρσις of ἡδονή
which was its counterpart. Yet towards
the end of the § Cic. clearly distinguishes
between *gaudere* as the word appropriate
to the noble, and *laetari* as appropriate to
the ignoble, feeling. He has here carelessly put *laetitia* for *gaudium.*

in iis ipsis potiundis exsultans gestiensque laetitia turpis est, ut, si
ridere concessum sit, uituperetur tamen cachinnatio. eodem enim
20 uitio est ecfusio animi in laetitia, quo in dolore contractio, eademque leuitate cupiditas est in appetendo, qua laetitia in fruendo, et,
ut nimis adflicti molestia, sic nimis elati laetitia iure iudicantur
leues; et, cum inuidere aegritudinis sit, malis autem alienis uoluptatem capere laetitiae, utrumque inmanitate et feritate quadam
25 proponenda castigari solet; atque, ut prouidere decet, timere non

18. potiundis R 1 6 7 17   V   B 1 2   K 1 2   E 1   W 1 2   M 1   DC O 1 2.

potiundus G dus *in* dis *alt. man. mut.*   potiendis P.   potiendis B 3   S   E 2
M 2 Π O 3 ed. H.   pociēdis O 7.   ‖   exultans R V G B K S E.
19. cachinnatio R V.   chachinnatio G B E.   ‖   eodem enim uitio R 1 2 10 16
V P G   B 1–3   K 1   E 1 2   L 2 6   W 1 2.   in eodem uitio C.   20. ecfusio
R V G.   h,ecfusio K 1 *at* h, *atr. nigriore script.*   hec fusio D.   hẹc fusio E.
h'fusio C.   et fusio B 2.   effusio B 1 *eod. ut uid. atr.*   effusio P B 3   S   W 1
M 1 2   J   O 1–3 7.   21. appetendo R V G *h. l.* B K S E.   22. afflicti R 6 7
B 3   E 2   W 1   M 1 2   D C Π   O 2 3 7.   aflicti E 3.   afflictiọ S *eod. atr.*
afflictio P 1.   adflictio R V G K ed. H.   afflictio R 17   B 1 2   E 1   O 1.
afflict'o W 2.   afflicto J.   ‖   molestia R 1 6 7   V P G   B 1–3   K 1   S E   W 1 2
M 1 2   D C Π J   O 2 3 7.   molesta R 17   O 1 ed. H.   ‖   ạnimis B 1 *alio atr.*
puncto adpos.   animis R G   B 2   K 1   E 1.   animiṣ V.   animis S *litt. post*
mi *eras.*   animi R 6   K 2   E 2   M 1 2   D C Π   O 1–3.   āi R 7 17   P B 3
J   O 7.   ‖   iure iudicantur R P G   B 3   K 1   W 1   M 1 2   C Π J.   iudicare
iudicantur B 2.   iure dicantur V S.   24. immanitate R V G B K S.
inmanitate E 1.   25. confidere decet R 1 6 7 17   V P G   B 1–3   K 1 2   S
E 1–3   L 2–6   W 1 2   M 1 2   D C Π J   O 1–3 ed. H.   uirtus fidei decet O 7.
prouidere *corr. Tregder.*

cetera: for the asyndeton cf. iii 34, 81;
Off. iii 10, 43 'honores, diuitiae, uoluptates, cetera generis eiusdem.'
gestiens, 'impatient,' 'restless': for a
good ex. of the force of the word cf. Plaut.
Mil. Glor. 1214 'PY. at gestio; PA. at
modice decet : moderare animo.'
eodem...uitio: abl. of descr. as *eadem
leuitate* below: Ern. inserted *in*, unnecessarily; for though Cic. uses elsewhere
the phrase *in uitio esse* (iii 9, 19; Fin. v
11, 31) there is no reason why *uitium*,
any more than *leuitas*, should not be
used as an abl. of description.
ecfusio ... contractio = διάχυσις, συ-
στολή: Mo. compares Lael. 13, 48 'ut et
bonis amici quasi diffundatur et incommodis contrahatur': see n. on 6, 14
above, and Plat. Symp. p. 206 D quoted
by Küh. Cf. also Seneca, de Const. 9, 3
'ad offensiones rerum hominumque non
contrahitur.'
adflicti molestia: is contrasted with
elati laetitia in meaning and corresponds
to it in construction; to both classes of
persons the word *leues* is applied, as
leuitas in Off. i 26, 90 'nam ut aduersas
res sic secundas inmoderate ferre leuitatis

est': 'notent tirones,' says Ern. (*Clav. Cic.*
s.v. *leuitas*), 'leuitatem tribui omnibus
uehementibus et inanibus cupiditatibus et
perturbationibus animi quod in his nulla
est constantia, nulla grauitas; unde etiam
leues dicuntur, qui iis dediti sunt.' Bentley's corr. *molles* adopted by Bouh. Dav.
F. A. W. Or. neglects this meaning of *leues*
and spoils the symmetry of the clause.
proponenda: instr. abl. 'by setting
forth their barbarous and (one may say)
savage nature'; *quadam* modifies the
preceding word. For the constr. cf. i 30,
72 n. and Draeger, *Syntax* ii § 799, 2.
castigari: iii 27, 64 n.
prouidere, Tregder's conj. for the MSS
confidere, has been accepted by Wes. Ba.
Sff. Küh. TS. Sch. and undoubtedly
supplies the meaning required by the
argument, which turns entirely upon the
distinction between permissible and non-
permissible feelings of an analogous
nature, and between the permissible and
non-permissible expressions of such mental
states; thus *ridere* is allowable, *cachinnatio* is not; *gaudere* is allowable, *laetari*
is not; but *confidere* is not analogous in
the same way to *timere*, whereas *prouidere*

decet, sic gaudere decet, laetari non decet, quoniam docendi causa a gaudio laetitiam distinguimus; **67** illud iam supra diximus, contractionem animi recte fieri numquam posse, elationem posse. aliter enim Naeuianus ille gaudet Hector:

30 Laétus sum laudári me abs te, páter, a laudató
uiro,

aliter ille apud Trabeam:

Léna deleníta argento nútum obseruabít meum,
Quíd uelim, quid stúdeam; adueniens dígito in-
35 pellam iánuam,
Fóres patebunt; de ínprouiso Chrýsis ubi me as-
péxerit,

§ **67**, 28. contractionem G M 1 D O 1 2.   contractionē B 1 3 S W 1 2 J.
contractionē V *linea supra* e *atr. uiridi ducta.*   contractione R B 2 K 1 E 1 2
M 2 O 3.   curationem O 7.   29. hector B.   haector G.   hetor E.
30. a laudato R 1 6 10 V P G B 1–3 K 1 E 1 2 W 1 2 M 2 D C Π J O 1–3 7.
laudato M 1 a *om.*   patria laudato R 7.   33. delenita R V P G K E 1 2 Gr.
                                                                                          i
delinita R 6 7 B 1 3 W 1 M 1 2 D C Π J O 1–3.   delenita S.   de lenitate B 2.
declinata O 7.   36. inprouiso R V G K E.   improuiso B S. ‖ chrysis R G K.
chrisis B 2 S.   crisis E 1.   chysis V. ‖ aspexerit R V G B 1 2
K S E D O 1.

is, the exercise of the εὔλογος ἔκκλισις which is analogous to, but distinct from, fear. Dav.'s conj. *cauere* adopted by F. A. W. Or. Ml. Hasper, Hei. gives a similar sense and Dav. has no difficulty in proving from 6, 13 above, Sen. Epp. 85 and Aug. C.D. xiv 8 that *cautio* was a term in recognised use in this sense; but it is hard to see how *cauere* could have been corrupted into *confidere.* Lamb. followed by Bentley read *diffidere*, but the passage quoted by Dav. from Stobaeus (Ecl. p. 183 (ii 6, 11)) τούτοις δ' ἀκολούθως οὐκ ἀπιστεῖν [sc. τὸν σοφόν], τὴν γὰρ ἀπιστίαν εἶναι ψεύδους ὑπόληψιν, τὴν δὲ πίστιν ἀστεῖον ὑπάρχειν, εἶναι γὰρ κατάληψιν ἰσχυρὰν βεβαιοῦσαν τὸ ὑπολαμβανόμενον seems decisive against it. Kl. and Mo. defend the MSS reading, on the ground that Cic. is merely concerned to emphasise the broad distinction between the un-ruffled placidity of the *sapiens* and the various morbid emotions (and the expression of them) characteristic of the *insipiens*, without going too closely into subtle de-tails; and it must be admitted that Cic. is not always so careful of his philosophical vocabulary as to make us absolutely cer-tain that he cannot have expressed himself loosely here.

The corruption, if such it be, is as old as Nonius Marcellus who quotes (de diff. s.v. *laetari* p. 444 M.) our passage with the reading *confidere*; Müller in his edn. of Non. Marc. (ii p. 35) suggests that *non confidere* should be read here.

gaudere: the distinction between *gaudere* and *laetari* seems to be observed in Lucan vi 792 and 795.

§ **67. supra**: in 6, 14. Cicero's point is that the approach of *bonum* induces in the mind of the *sapiens* a feeling of elation which is *placida atque constans*; whereas the approach of imagined evil, which in the case of the *insipiens* causes *aegritudo*, leaves the mind of the *sapiens*, to whom no external event is an evil, absolutely unmoved.

Naeuianus, 'in Naevius,' cf. iii 26, 62 'Accianus.'

Hector: in the Hector proficiscens, Ribbeck, *Scaen. Rom. P. Rell.* I² p. 8; the line is quoted again by Cic. Fam. v 12, 7; xv 6, 1 and in Sen. Epp. 102, 16.

ille, 'the character in Trabea': the name of the comedy is unknown: the lines are to be found in Ribbeck, *op. cit.* II² p. 31 and form the largest extant frg. of Trabea. For another quotation from Trabea see 15, 35. These and the pre-ceding lines are trochaic tetrameters catalectic.

digito: Küh. compares Ter. Eun. ii 2, 53 (284) 'uno digitulo foris aperis.'

fores: Bent. followed by Dav. wished to read 'foris (fori') patebunt' here *metri*

Álacris ob uiám mihi ueniet cómplexum exoptáns
meum,
40   Míhi se dedet.

quam haec pulchra putet, ipse iam dicet:

Fórtunam ipsam anteíbo fortunís meis.

XXXII. 68. Haec laetitia quam turpis sit, satis est diligenter attendentem penitus uidere. et ut turpes sunt, qui ecferunt se laetitia tum cum fruuntur Veneriis uoluptatibus, sic flagitiosi, qui eas inflammato animo concupiscunt. totus uero iste, qui 5 uolgo appellatur amor (nec hercule inuenio quo nomine alio possit appellari), tantae leuitatis est ut nihil uideam quod putem conferendum. quem Caecilius

38. complexum R V G B K S.   cōplexū P.   40. se dedet R G   B 1 2
                                                              dedet
E W 2 M 2 J O 1.   se dedit K 1.   sedet V D.   se   S cum ras.
sed debet M 1.   se deceret O 3.
XXXII. § 68, 1. haec laetitia..... effe habet V marg. atr. uiridi adscr. e cont.
om.; in cont. rūt se, at atr. uiridi scr.   2. attendentem G.   adtendentem K. ||
ecferunt B.   hecferunt K 1.   hęc ferunt P E.   haec ferunt G.   hc ferunt B 2.
hec fēr P marg. ef.   efferunt R at ef in ras. B 3   S   W 2   M 1 2   D J.
3. ueneriis R V G ex correct. alt. fort. man. B K S E   M 2   D C J.   uenereis
R 6   P E 2   W 2   Π   O 1-37.   uenereis W 1 at e ante i mut.   ueneris
                                        o
B 2 3   M 1.   5. uolgo R V G B K.   uulgo E al. atr. superscr.   uulgo S. ||
appellatur R G B K S E.   appellaņtur V.   uocatur J. || hercule R V G K S E.
6. appellari R V G B K S E.

gratia; the second syllable in the line, it is true, must be short, but the law of breuis breuians accounts for the scansion of fores as a pyrrhic.

Fortunam...meis is the completion of the line beginning 'mihi se dedet.' For the play upon words Küh. compares Cornif. ad Herenn. iv 17, 24; p. Sull. 21, 62 'cum commoda colonorum a fortunis Pompeianorum rei publicae fortuna disiunxerit.'

XXXII. §68. satis...uidere: i.e. 'satis est diligenter attendere ut penitus quis uideat,' an easily intelligible brachylogy. Bent. followed by Dav. and Ern. altered satis to facile. For attendentem, referring to an indefinite subject, cf. 31, 66 n. on ' sequentem.'

Veneriis: for the spelling see Neue, Formenlehre I³ pp. 160, 188.

flagitiosi, 'scandalous'; see note on flagitio in 33, 70.

amor: Latin has only one word to translate the two Gk words, φιλία and ἔρως, the former denoting 'friendship,' 'affection,' the latter 'passion'; in 33, 70 Cic. uses 'amor amicitiae' as a translation of φιλία. The distinction between

ἔρως and φιλία is observed by Maximus Tyrius xviii 3 (ed. Hobein) πρᾶγμα διττόν κτλ. while Dio Chrysostom iv 168 R. uses them together in a good sense.

An echo of the Stoic distinction and of Cicero's phraseology is to be found in St Thomas Aquinas, Summa Theol. Sect. Sec. Quaest. xxvi fin. who distinguishes amor amicitiae from amor concupiscentiae.

Caecilius: iii 23, 56 n. The lines in the text are obviously an adaptation of the fragment of Euripides' Auge (Nauck, frag. 269) quoted by Stobaeus, Floril. 63, 11 (p. 387)

Ἔρωτα δ᾽ ὅστις μὴ θεὸν κρίνει μέγαν
καὶ τῶν ἁπάντων δαιμόνων ὑπέρτατον
ἢ σκαιός ἐστιν ἢ καλῶν ἄπειρος ὤν
οὐκ οἶδε τὸν μέγιστον ἀνθρώποις θεόν.

Dav. conjectured that Menander, who constantly imitated Eur. (Quint. x 1 69), may have taken over these lines into his Συναριστῶσαι and that Cic. quotes the lines in the text from a translation of this comedy by Caecilius. A fragment of Caecilius' Synaristosae has been preserved by Aul. Gell. xv 15, 2. Ribbeck, however, while he notes the similarity between the present passage and a known fragment

'déum qui non summúm putet,
Aut stúltum aut rerum esse ínperitum' existimat,
10 'Cui ín manu sit, quem ésse dementém uelit,
Quem sápere, quem sanári, quem in morbum ínici,

.   .   .   .

Quem cóntra amari, quem éxpeti, quem arcéssier.'

69. o praeclaram emendatricem uitae poëticam! quae amorem
flagitii et leuitatis auctorem in concilio deorum conlocandum

9. imperitum R V K.   imperium G *alt. man. superscr.* ‖ existumet R V G K.
existimat M 1 ed. H.   existimet R 6 7 17 P B 1–3 K 2 S E 1–3 L 2–6
W 1 2 M 2 D C II J O 1–3 7.   10. cui R V P G B 1–3 K S E 1 2 W 1 2
M 1 2 J O 1 3.   cuius D C.   cū O 7.   quia illi O 2. ‖ demente V *atr.*
uiridi superscr.   demente R G.   11. insanāre K 1 *atr. nigriore corr.*
insanire R 1 2 6 7 10 V P G B 1–3 S E 1 2 W 1 2 M 1 2 D C II J O 3 7.
sanari *corr. Manutius.* ‖ inici R V P G B 1–3 K E 1 2 W 2 M 1 2 D C J
O 1 3.   iniici S W 1.   12. quem R V P G K.   quam B E. ‖ arcessiri
R 1 2 10 G B K Gr. S *marg.* accersiri.   arcesciri V *al. atr. superscr.*
accersiri R 6 P B 2 3 E 2 W 1 2 M 1 2 D C II J O 1 3.   arcersiri R 17.
accessiri R 16 E 1.   acersiri O 7 *fuerat* arcersiri.   accersi O 2.   arcessier
corr. Erasmus.
§ **69,** 13. amorem M 1.   amorē M 2   B *at linea atr. nigriore duct.*   amore
R V G.   amoreſ K 1 ſ *ex parte eras.*   14. flagitii R V G B K S E D. ‖
concilio R V G B E.   consilio S.   ‖ conlocandum R V B K E G *ex corr.*
alt. man., fuerat ut uid. conlocari dum.   collocandum S.

of Menander's Συναριστῶσαι (ἔρως δὲ τῶν
θεῶν | ἰσχὺν ἔχων πλείστην ἐπὶ τούτου
δείκνυται· | διὰ τοῦτον ἐπιορκοῦσι τοὺς
ἄλλους θεούς) does not think the evidence
sufficient to warrant him in placing it
among the frgg. of Caecilius' Synaristosae
(*op. cit.* II² pp. 68, 76).

existimat: the subject is Caecilius:
no doubt the word here in the play was
existimo.

cui : Ern. followed by F.A.W. and
Ba. reads here *cuius* which must be
scanned as a monosyllable. The change
on metrical (or any other) grounds is
unnecessary as *cui* can be scanned as a
dissyllable with elision of the second
syllable.

sanari: Manutius' emendation, adopted
by Lamb. Bent. Dav. Or. and all recent
edd. (except Küh.) for the MSS *insanire*
which, as Bent. shows, introduces confusion into the enumeration: *dementem
esse* is answered by *sapere*, and *sanari* by
in morbum inici; the scribe thought
that *sapere* should be followed by its
opposite and wrote *insanire.*

Bentley saw that after this line one had
been lost, as is shown by *contra* in the
last line. He supplied the lacuna with
'quem odio esse, quem contemni, quem
excludi foras.'

§ **69. praeclaram**: ironical, as in i
21, 49; Lael. 13, 47 'o praeclaram sapientiam: solem enim e mundo tollere
uidentur, qui amicitiam e uita tollunt.'

emendatricem uitae: cf. ii 11, 27 ;
iii 2, 3 for similar complaints about the
poets. Xenophanes was, it seems, the
first to set the fashion in this; cf. his
lines quoted by Sext. Emp. Math. ix
193 πάντα θεοῖς ἀνέθηκαν Ὅμηρός θ'
Ἡσίοδός τε | ὅσσα παρ' ἀνθρώποισιν ὀνείδεα
καὶ ψόγος ἐστίν | κλέπτειν μοιχεύειν τε καὶ
ἀλλήλους ἀπατεύειν. Plato's outburst in
the third book of the Republic is well
known. It was the attempt to save the
poets (and especially Homer) from the
charge of teaching immorality that gave
rise to the allegoric system of interpretation, which the Stoics seem to have
largely adopted in their attempt to fit
their theology on to the framework of
popular religion. On this question, cf.
Decharme, *La Critique des traditions
religieuses chez les Grecs,* pp. 270 ff.
Cicero here, of course, as the following
words show, is referring especially to the
later Greek poetry, principally comedy,
and its imitations in Roman literature,
which no ingenuity could defend against
his criticism.

in concilio deorum, 'amongst the num-

15 putet. de comoedia loquor, quae, si haec flagitia non probaremus, nulla esset omnino; quid ait ex tragoedia princeps ille
Argonautarum?

> Tú me amoris mágis quam honoris séruauisti
> grátia.

20 quid ergo? hic amor Medeae quanta miseriarum excitauit in-
cendia! atque ea tamen apud alium poëtam patri dicere audet
se 'coniugem' habuisse

> Íllum, Amor quem déderat, qui plus póllet potior-
> que ést patre.

XXXIII. **70.** Sed poëtas ludere sinamus, quorum fabulis in
hoc flagitio uersari ipsum uidemus Iouem. ad magistros uirtutis
philosophos ueniamus, qui amorem negant stupri esse et in eo

---

15. nos probaremus R G K S *marg.* non.   probaremus B non *om.*
                    †ait
16. ait R 1 16   V G K S.   aut B.   aut R 2 10   E.   17. argonautarū V
at rū *in ras.*: *post* argonautarum *habet* S *in marg.* iason *man. ant. script.*
18. seruasti R V G   B1–3   K S   E1–3   L2–6   W1 2   M2   D C Π J   O2 3 7
ed. H.   seruastri O 1.   seruauisti *ed. Cratand.*   21. audet sed V B.
audet sed R G K.
XXXIII. § **70,** 2. at *in* ad *alt. man. corr.* G.

---

ber of the gods'; for this use of *concilio*
cf. Plaut. Mil. Gl. 249 'sed si ambas
uidere in uno miles concilio uolet.'

loquor : for the expression cf. i 15, 34
'loquor de principibus; quid? poetae
nonne post mortem nobilitari uolunt?'
Fin. v 11, 33.

non : Bentley with some inferior MSS
read *nos* here and altered *si* above to *nisi* :
this would lay an emphasis upon *nos*
'their readers' or 'their hearers' as distinguished from 'the authors' (*poetae*)
which the context will not bear.

ex tragoedia, 'in tragedy'; the quotation is from Ennius' play Medea exul
(Ribbeck, *op. cit.* I², p. 49). Jason's
words in Euripides are (Med. 530) ὡς
ἔρως σ' ἠνάγκασε | τόξοις ἀφύκτοις τοὐμὸν
ἐκσῶσαι δέμας.

quid ergo? generally followed (as *quid
igitur* in i 25, 61) by another question,
cf. Ac. i 4, 13; ii 29, 92 'quid ergo?
istius uiti num nostra culpa est?' Off. iii
18, 73; Fin. v 26, 76, etc. : in Or. ii
14, 60 as here there is no question
following.

alium poëtam : Accius, who wrote a
Medea, and Pacuvius, who dealt with the
story in his Medus, have been suggested.
Ribbeck (*op. cit.* I² 261) classes the fragment among the *incerta.*

illum...patre : a trochaic tetrameter
catalectic.

XXXIII. § **70. sed poetas** : so according to the Epicurean Velleius the poets
'ipsa suauitate nocuerunt, qui et ira in-
flammatos et libidine furentes induxerunt
deos,' Cic. N.D. i 16, 42.

ludere, 'to wanton': the word seems
here to combine the amatory implication
found, e.g. in Ovid (A.A. i 91, ii 389)
with the idea of poetic trifling (e.g. Cat.
50, 2 multum lusimus in meis tabellis).

fabulis = μῦθοις ; had 'dramas' been
meant *in fabulis* would have been required.

flagitio : the original meaning of this
word is 'shame,' 'disgrace' (Plaut. Poen.
965, Trin. 1035); the meaning 'disgraceful conduct' is one which arose later and
was perhaps developed from phrases like
flagitium facere 'to bring disgrace upon';
the adj. *flagitiosus* always has the meaning 'shameful' 'disgraceful.' See Usener's
exhaustive discussion in *Rhein. Mus.* LVI
(1901), pp. 1 ff.

stupri, 'say that love is not a matter
of sensuality,' for the gen. cf. Madv. *Gr.*
§ 282. This was the Stoic view, reported
by Diog. Laert. vii 130, τὸν ἔρωτα...μὴ
εἶναι συνουσίας ἀλλὰ φιλίας.

litigant cum Epicuro non multum, ut opinio mea fert, mentiente.
5 quis est enim iste amor amicitiae? cur neque deformem adulescentem quisquam amat neque formosum senem? mihi quidem
haec in Graecorum gymnasiis nata consuetudo uidetur, in quibus
isti liberi et concessi sunt amores. bene ergo Ennius:

Flágiti princípium est nudare ínter ciuis córpora.

10 qui ut sint, quod fieri posse uideo, pudici, solliciti tamen et
anxii sunt, eoque magis quod se ipsi continent et coërcent.

5. adulescentem R V B 2 K.   adulestentem G.   adolescentem P B 1 S E.
7. gymnasiis R V G B.   gynnasiis S.   gmgnasiis E.   9. flagitii E 1.
flagitii K 1 *atr. nigriore corr.* flagitii R V G B 1 2 S E 2 3 D. ‖ ciuis V B K E.

ciuis R e *super* i *eod. atr.*   ciues G S.   11. coercent R V G K.   cohercent
R 2 10 16 P B.

Epicuro : cf. Hermias in Plat. Phaedr.
p. 76 [Usener, *Epicurea* 483] οἱ μὲν γὰρ
ὑπέλαβον ἁπλῶς φαῦλον τὸ ἐρᾶν ὡς 'Επίκουρος ὁρισάμενος αὐτὸν σύντονον ὄρεξιν
ἀφροδισίων μετὰ οἴστρου καὶ ἀδημονίας; the
same definition is also quoted from Epic.
by Alexander Aphrod. and Dionysius
Thrax [Usener, *l.c.*].
amor amicitiae, i.e. φιλία; the genitive is like that in *nomen uirtutis, uirtus
continentiae* and similar phrases, Madv.
Gr. §286.
cur neque...senem: the sneer as Dav.
notes is repeated in [Lucian] Amores 23
ψυχῆς γὰρ ἔρωτα πλάττονται καὶ τὸ τοῦ
σώματος εὐμορφον αἰδούμενοι φιλεῖν, ἀρετῆς
καλοῦσιν αὐτοὺς ἐραστάς...τί γὰρ παθόντες
ὦ σεμνοὶ φιλόσοφοι τὸ μὲν ἤδη μακρῷ χρόνῳ
δεδωκὸς ἑαυτοῦ πεῖραν ὁποῖόν ἐστιν, ᾧ
πολιὰ προσήκουσα καὶ γῆρας ἀρετὴν μαρτυρεῖ, δι' ὀλιγωρίας παραπέμπετε, πᾶς δὲ
ὁ σοφὸς ἔρως ἐπὶ τὸ νέον ἐπτόηται;
The Stoics had themselves with characteristic candour noted the apparent inconsistency; Plut. de Comm. not. c. 28
quotes them as saying αἰσχροὺς μὲν γὰρ
εἶναι τοὺς νέους, φαύλους γ' ὄντας καὶ
ἀνοήτους, καλοὺς δὲ τοὺς σοφούς· ἐκείνων
δὲ τῶν καλῶν μηδένα μήτ' ἐρᾶσθαι μήτ'
ἀξιέραστον εἶναι. We may infer their explanation from other passages; Diog.
Laert. vii 129 quotes Zeno and Chrysippus
for the statement ἐρασθήσεσθαι δὲ τὸν
σοφὸν τῶν νέων τῶν ἐμφαινόντων διὰ τοῦ
εἴδους τὴν πρὸς ἀρετὴν εὐφυίαν. This
σπουδαῖος ἔρως then inferring mental
capability for virtue from physical charm
(εἶναι δὲ καὶ τὴν ὥραν ἄνθος ἀρετῆς) was
attracted to nascent ἀρετή with the desire
at once to associate with it and to perfect
it; as Stobaeus (Ecl. ii 65) puts it the
Stoics παραλαμβάνουσιν εἰς τὰς ἀρετάς
(τὴν ἐρωτικήν) considering it to be ἐπιστή-

μην νέων θήρας εὐφυῶν προτρεπτικὴν οὖσαν
ἐπὶ τὴν κατ' ἀρετήν: and Plut. (*l.c.*) θήρα
γάρ τις, φασίν, ἐστὶν ὁ ἔρως, ἀτελοῦς μέν,
εὐφυοῦς δὲ μειρακίου πρὸς ἀρετήν. In the
case of the perfected or nearly perfected
σοφοί the ἔμφασις κάλλους does not exist
to furnish the occasion, nor the imperfec-
tion to furnish the object, for ἔρως.
in Graecorum gymnasiis : edd. refer
to de Rep. iv 4, 4, Corn. Nep. praef. § 4.
See Girard, *L'Éducation Athénienne*,
pp. 40 f. According to Thuc. (i 6) the
practice of exercising in a state of nudity
was introduced at Olympia shortly before
his time and was an invention of the
Lacedaemonians : the Schol. to Iliad
xxiii 683 says the practice was due to a
competitor's περίζωμα becoming loose and
tripping him up. It flattered the Roman
national pride to assume that their virtues
were their own and their vices imported
from abroad : so Salvian (de Gub. Dei
vii 20, 88) speaking of the *uiri molles* of
Carthage describes them as 'Graecis
quam Romanis similiores'; Lucan vii
270 ff.
isti, i.e. *adulescentium,* cf. for instances
of the fact Plut. Demetr. 24 ; Xen. Eph.
iii 2 ; Parthenius, Erot. c. 7 *ad init.*
Ennius : it is not certain from what
work of Ennius the quotation is taken ;
Ribbeck (*op. cit.* I², 70) puts it among the
uncertain fragments from the tragedies.
The line is a trochaic tetrameter catalectic. For the sentiment cf. Off. i 35,
129 scaenicorum quidem mos tantam
habet uetere disciplina uerecundiam ut in
scaenam sine subligaculo prodeat nemo ;
uerentur enim ne si quo casu euenerit ut
corporis partes quaedam aperiantur, aspi-
ciantur non decore. nostro quidem more
cum parentibus puberes filii, cum soceris
generi non lauantur. Plut. Cato, c. 20

71. atque, ut muliebris amores omittam, quibus maiorem licentiam natura concessit, quis aut de Ganymedi raptu dubitat quid poëtae uelint, aut non intellegit quid apud Euripidem et loquatur et
15 cupiat Laius? quid denique homines doctissimi et summi poëtae de se ipsis et carminibus edunt et cantibus? fortis uir in sua re publica cognitus quae de iuuenum amore scribit Alcaeus! nam Anacreontis quidem tota poësis est amatoria. maxime uero omnium flagrasse amore Reginum Ibycum ap-
20 paret ex scriptis.

XXXIV. Atque horum omnium libidinosos esse amores uidemus. philosophi sumus exorti, et auctore quidem nostro Platone, quem non iniuria Dicaearchus accusat, qui amori auc-

§ 71, 12. adque K. ‖ muliebris R V B 1 K E. muliebris G is *ex* es

ead. man. corr. muliebres B 2 S. 13. ganymedi R. $\overset{ga}{}$nymedi G

alt. man. superscr. ganumedi K. ganimedi E 1. ganimedi$^{\overset{\scriptstyle \iota}{}}$ $\overset{de}{}$ B 1 *atr. nigr.* *superscr.* ganymedis V B 3 M 2 O 1. ganymedis S i *in* y *al. atr. mut.* ganimedis P B 2 K 2 W 1 2 D J O 3 ed. H. ganimed M 1. g animedis II r *inter* g *et* a *eras.* 14. euripidem R G B 1–3 K S. euripidē P E J. eurupidem V. $\overset{d}{}$ 15. quidenique G *ead. man. superscr.* 16. edunt M 1. edant R 1 6 7 17 V G B 1–3 K 1 2 S E 1–3 L 2 4–6 W 2 M 2 D C II J O 1–3 7 ed. H. edeant L 3. edant W 1. 17. scribit R 1 7 17 G B 1 2 K 1 2 E 1 3 W 1 2 M 1 D C J O 2. scripsit R 6 P B 3 S E 2 M 2 II O 3 ed. H. scripxit O 7. 19. maxume R V G B K. maxime S E. ‖ reginum R V P G B 1 3 K S E W 1 2 M 2 D C J O 1 2. reginā II. regnū B 2. regium O 3. *om.* M 1. ‖ ibycum R G K. ibÿcum V. hibycum O 1. ibicum B 1 3 W 1 D C. ybicum W 2 J. ibi cum B 2 S E 1 O 3. Ibicum II *fuerat* ibi cum. ibi O 2. ‖ apparet R V G B K E. XXXIV. 1. lubidinosos R V G B K J. libidinosos B 2 W 1. 3. accussat G.

φησὶν...τὰ αἰσχρὰ τῶν ῥημάτων...εὐλαβεῖσθαι τοῦ παιδὸς παρόντος...συλλούσασθαι δὲ μηδέποτε· καὶ τοῦτο κοινὸν ἔοικε Ῥωμαίων ἔθος εἶναι.

qui, i.e. *amantes* to be supplied out of *amores* above.

§ 71. muliebris, i.e. *mulierum*. For the adj. taking the place of an objective genitive cf. Nägelsbach, *Stil.* § 20, 3 (a) and exx. quoted there.

Ganymedi: for the form cf. *Vlixi* i 41, 98 and Neue, *Formenlehre* 1³, pp. 508 ff.

Euripidem : apparently in his Chrysippus which dealt with the relationship of Laius and Chrysippus, the son of Pelops; cf. Aelian V.H. xiii 5 ἐρασθῆναι πρῶτον γενναίων παιδικῶν λέγουσι Λάιον ἁρπάσαντα Χρύσιππον τὸν Πέλοπος.

carminibus ... cantibus, 'poems ... songs'; for the distinction cf. 2, 3 'ex quo perspicuum est et cantus tum fuisse discriptos uocum sonis et carmina.'

Alcaeus of Mitylene in Lesbos flourished at the beginning of the sixth century B.C.

Cf. Quint. x 1, 63 'Alcaeus in parte operis aureo plectro merito donatur...sed et lusit et in amores descendit, maioribus tamen aptior.'

nam...quidem : 23, 52 n.

Anacreontis : Anacreon of Teos lived through nearly the whole of the sixth century B.C. The poems in the Anthologia Graeca which bear his name are later forgeries, and his works, divided by the Alexandrian critics into five books, are extant only in fragments.

Ibycum. Ibycus of Rhegium *flor.* c. 544 B.C. : Suidas (s.v. Ἴβυκος) γέγονε δὲ ἐρωτομανέστατος περὶ μειράκια. He wrote in the Doric dialect and his poems were divided into seven books, of which only fragments are extant.

XXXIV. Atque marks the transition to a fresh point in the argument, the contrast between the actual facts with regard to *amor*, and the *auctoritas* with which philosophers had invested it.

Platone : Cic. is referring probably to passages like Symposium 210 A, Phaedrus

toritatem tribueremus. **72.** Stoici uero et sapientem amaturum
5 esse dicunt et amorem ipsum 'conatum amicitiae faciundae ex
pulchritudinis specie' definiunt. qui si quis est in rerum natura
sine sollicitudine, sine desiderio, sine cura, sine suspirio, sit sane;
uacat enim omni libidine; haec autem de libidine oratio est. sin
autem est aliquis amor, ut est certe, qui nihil absit aut non mul-
10 tum ab insania, qualis in Leucadia est:

> Sí quidem sit quisquám deus,
> Cui égo sim curae.

73. at id erat deis omnibus curandum, quem ad modum hic
frueretur uoluptate amatoria!
15　　Heu me ínfelicem!
nihil uerius. probe et ille:

§ **72,** 5. faciundae R 6　M 2.　　faciunde B 3　J　O 1.　　faciendae G　E 1　O 2.
faciendę R　V P　B 1　W 1　O 3.　　faciende R 7 17　B 2　K 1　S　E 2　M 1
D C Π　O 7 ed. H.　　faci de K 2.　　facande W 2.　　6. qui si quis R G K.
quinquis V.　　8. libidine (*bis*) R V G B K.　　lubidine J.　　12. cui R V P G
B 1–3　K 1 2　S　E 12　W 1 2　M 2　D C Π J　O 1–37 ed. H.
§ **73,** 13. at id R P G　B 3　K 1 2　W 1 2　M 1 2　D J　O 1 3.　　ad id V　B 2.
aditerat E 1. ‖ deis B 3　M 2　O 2.　de is *litt. ante* i *eras.* V B.　dehis R P　E 1.
de his G　B 2　K 1　S　E 2　W 2　J　O 1 7.　　de hiis K 2　D Π.　diis W 1　M 1.

14. frueretur R G K *alii.*　　rfueretur V *atr. uiridi superscr.*

251 A, and to gossip such as is reported
by Diog. Laert. iii 29 who quotes several
epigrams ascribed to Plato. Christian
controversialists like Tertullian (de An.
54) eagerly repeated the charges. It may
be sufficient to quote on the other side
the frank acknowledgment of S. Augustine (C.D. ii 14) that in Plato's life 'no
base deed' could be found.

Nothing is known, except from the
reference here, of Dicaearchus' contribu-
tion to the indictment of Plato.

§ **72. Stoici**: see the passage from
Diog. Laert. quoted above.

conatum: Diog. Laert. *l.c.* εἶναι δὲ τὸν
ἔρωτα ἐπιβολὴν φιλοποιίας διὰ κάλλος
ἐμφαινόμενον.

qui: sc. *amor.*

in rerum natura, 'in actual fact' as
opposed to philosophic theory, cf. v 1, 4
'nosautem…rerumnaturamquam errorem
nostrum damnare malumus'; v 37, 107.

sine sollicitudine: Plato applies even
to his ideal passion for beauty such
phrases as ἀδημονεῖ τε τῇ ἀτοπίᾳ τοῦ
πάθους καὶ ἀποροῦσα λυττᾷ καὶ ἐμμανὴς
οὖσα οὔτε νυκτὸς δύναται καθεύδειν οὔτε
μεθ' ἡμέραν οὗ ἂν ᾖ μένειν, Phaedr. 251 D.

sin autem: the apodosis (e.g. *plane
reiciendus est*) is omitted after the parenthesis of quotations which occupy the rest
of the §. For the anacoluthon cf. 36, 77.

Leucadia, 'The Maid of Leucas,' a
comedy by Sextus Turpilius, adapted
from a comedy by Alexis (or Menander)
with the same title. As Ribbeck (*Gesch.
der röm. Dicht.* 1, p. 165) points out, the
subject was a favourite with the writers
of the Middle and New Comedy. The
plot turned upon the hopeless passion
inspired by an old man called Phaon to
whom Aphrodite in return for a service
had given an ointment which made all
the women he met fall in love with him.
The frgg. of Turpilius' comedy are collected in Ribbeck (*Scaen. Rom. Poes.
Frag.* 11², pp. 97 ff.); see also Servius
on Aen. iii 279.

§ **73. at**: ironical; for this use cf.
Hand, *Turs.* 1, pp. 432 ff.

uerius: sc. *quam quod dixisti te in-
felicem esse.*

et ille, 'the other character too makes
a sound remark'; for *et* (=*etiam*) cf. iii
13, 28 'ex hoc et illa iure laudantur': often
in Cicero; Draeger, *Syntax* II § 312.

Sánusne es, qui témere lamentáre?

hic insanus uidetur etiam suis.   at quas tragoedias efficit!

Te, Apóllo sancte, fér opem, teque, omnípotens
20   Neptune, ínuoco,
Vosque ádeo, ucnti!

mundum totum se ad amorem suum subleuandum conuersurum
putat, Venerem unam excludit ut iniquam:

nam quíd ego te appellém, Venus?

25 eam prae libidine negat curare quicquam; quasi uero ipse non
propter libidinem tanta flagitia et faciat et dicat.

XXXV. **74.** Sic igitur adfecto haec adhibenda curatio est,

17. sanusne es R V P G   B 3   K 1 2   S   E 2   W 1 2   M 2   Π J   O 1-3 7.
    ɫ es
sanusne est B.   sanusne est B 2   E 1   M 1   D.   insanusne est C.   ‖ lamentare
                                                                                    ris
R V P G B 1 2   K 1 2   S   E 1 2   W 1 2   M 2   Π   O 1 2 7 ed. H.   lamentare
B 3.   lamentari D C.   lamtat M 1.   laudare O 3.   18. sic insanus R V G
B 1-3.   sicut insanus M 1   D.   hic *corr. Maduigius.*   ‖   at quas V P G.
                                                          efficit
adquas R K.   ‖   efficit W 1   M 2   O 1 7.   fecit S.   effecit R 1 6 7 17   P
                                                                                   e
B 1-3   K 1 2   E 1 3   W 2   M 1   D C J   O 2 3 ed. H.   affecit V *atr. uiridi*
            ef
superscr.   fecit Π *al. atr. suppl.*   feffecit G f *ante* ef *expunx. alt. man.*
fecit E 2.   19. et apollo R 1 10   V P B   K 1 2   E 1-3   L 2-6   O 1 7.   *om.* ed. H.
et appollo sanctae G p *post* a *et* a *ante* e *expunx. alt. man.*   te Apollo *corr. edd.* ‖
                                                                                    o
teque V P   K 2   E 2   W 1   O 1 7.   tequea R G K.   teque a B 1.
teque ea E 1.   24. appellem V G K S.   25. lubidine R G B K J.   libidine
V S E   W 1.   26. lubidinem R G B K J.   libidinem V E   W 1.
XXXV. § **74**, 1. adfecto R V G K E.   affecto B S.

---

hic, 'our friend'; *hic* is Madv.'s conjecture, adopted by nearly all recent edd.
(except Küh.) for the MSS. *sic.*
tragoedias : cf. Or. i 51, 219 'neque
uero istis tragoediis tuis...perturbor,' *ib.*
53, 228; ii 51, 205. A similar use of
τραγῳδία is found in Gk. Hyperid. iii 26
(ed. Blass), ἐὰν δ' ἐπὶ τοῦ γεγενημένου
ἐῶμεν, τὰς τραγῳδίας αὐτῆς καὶ τὰς κατη-
γορίας ἀφῃρηκότες ἐσόμεθα.
Te, Apollo : an iambic tetrameter
acatalectic.
sancte = ἀγνέ, a ritual epithet of Apollo.
omnipotens : 'cum...*omnipotens* Iouis
epitheton sit, non Neptuni, *amnipotens*
uidetur restituendum esse, quae est optima
huius dei propter potestatem eius in
fluuios appellatio' Rossbach (*Philol.* LXIII
N.F. p. 100), who is possibly right.
adeo, 'too' : for this use Hei. quotes
Enn. Medea 237 (Ribb.) 'Iuppiter, tuque
adeo, summe Sol' : cf. Hand, *Tursell.*
I 145.

flagitia...dicat: 'is guilty of such im-
proper conduct and language.' *flagitium*
is used here in the later sense of 'im-
proper act,' cf. Augustin. de doctr. christ.
3, 16 'quod autem agit indomita cupiditas
ad corrumpendum animum et corpus
suum, flagitium uocatur' (quoted by
Usener, *Rhein. Mus.* LVI 5 n.). Mo.
quotes also N.D. iii 38, 91 'utrum poetae
Stoicos deprauarint an Stoici poetis
dederint auctoritatem non facile dixerim ;
portenta enim ab utrisque et flagitia
dicuntur.'
XXXV. § **74. haec...ut** : Madv. *Gr.*
§ 374.
et: a second *et* might have been
expected to follow, but the construction
is changed, and instead of a clause *et
abducatur* dependent upon *ut* we have
abducendus etiam est. Or. proposed to
get rid of the anacoluthon by reading *ei,*
unnecessarily.

ut et illud quod cupiat ostendatur quam leue, quam contemnendum, quam nihili sit omnino, quam facile uel aliunde uel alio
modo perfici uel omnino neglegi possit. abducendus etiam est
5 non numquam ad alia studia, sollicitudines, curas, negotia, loci
denique mutatione tamquam aegroti non conualescentes saepe
curandus est; **75** etiam nouo quidam amore ueterem amorem

2. ut et illud R V P G B 1 2 K 1 2 S E W 1 2 M 1 J O 1 2 7 ed. H.
ut et id B 3 M 2 O 3. et ut illud II E 2. ut et ostenda q̂m leue sit illud C.
ut et ostendat q̂m leue sit illud D. ‖ ostendatur E 2 M 1 II. ostendat
R 1 6 7 1 7 V P G B 1–3 K 1 2 S E 1 W 1 2 D O 1 3 7. ostenda C. ‖
contemnendum R V. conte*n*ēdum S p *eras*. contempnendum G.
continendum E 1. 3. nihili R G B K M 1. nichili R 7 K 2 E 2 II.
nichili P. nihil R 6 V S M 2 O 1–3. nichil R 17 B 2 C O 7.
quam nihili *om*. W 1 2 J. ‖ uel aliunde uel R 1 17 V P B 1 3 K 1 S E 1 2
W 1 2 M 1 2 D J O 1–3 7 ed. H. uell aliende uel G *uidetur fuisse* uel habende
uel: l *ante* a *eras. et* u *superscr. ead. man.* i *ex corr. alterius man.* uel aliunde et
B 2. *om*. C. 4. neglegi R V G B K E. negligi S. ‖ etiam est R V P G
B 1–3 K 1 2 S E 1 2 W 1 M 2 II J O 1 2. est etiam W 2 M 1 D C
O 7. etiam *om*. O 3. 5. luci V. 6. aegroti non R V G B 1–3 K 1 S
E 1 2 W 1 2 M 1 2 D C J O 1–3 7.
§ **75**, 7. quidam R 1 17 P G B 1–3 K 1 D C. quidam V (*sic*).
quidam M 2. quidē E 1. quidem O 7. quidē E 2. quid̂ O 2.
q̂dē S *marg*. quodam. quodam R 6 K 2 W 1 2 M 1 J O 1 3. quodē II
o *alio ut uid. atr. mut.*

cupiat : subj. because dependent upon
another subj., *ostendatur*; Roby, § 1778.
ostendatur : this correction of Dav.'s
(confirmed by three MSS.) has been
accepted by most recent edd.; *ostendat*
the reading of the majority of the MSS. is
retained by Or. who supplies as subject
is qui curaturus est implied in *curatio*;
Bouh. with one MS. reads *ostendas*,
comparing *nolis* and *omittas* in § 75.
uel aliunde uel alio modo, 'attained
from some other quarter or in some other
way.' There is no necessity either (with
Hei.) to reject *uel alio modo* as a gloss or
(with T.S.) to assume that *adripi* (cf.
Or. i 59, 252) has dropped out after
aliunde.
ad alia studia : Mo. compares Ov. de
rem Am. 151 sqq. sunt fora, sunt leges,
sunt quos tuearis amici : | uade per
urbanae splendida castra togae. | uel tu
sanguinei iuuenalia munera Martis |
suscipe ; deliciae iam tibi terga dabunt.
loci...mutatione : cf Sen. de Tranqu.
17, 8 'aliquando uectatio iterque et
mutata regio uigorem dabunt.'
aegroti non conualescentes, 'patients
who are not recovering their strength'
(sc. by other methods of treatment). Ern.
deleted *non*, referring to Celsus, de Med.

iv 32 (25) 'ex quocumque autem morbo
quis conualescit, si tarde confirmatur...
debet...loca, caelum, cibos saepe mutare.'
Ern. took *conualescere* as equivalent to
melius se habere coepisse as in N.D. ii
4, 12 'ne aegri quidem quia non omnes
conualescunt, idcirco ars nulla medicinae
est,' and if this were its only meaning
we should have to follow him in deleting
non ; but the word can be used of the
whole process of convalescence up to
complete recovery, as is seen by the
phrase of Celsus a few lines lower down
'cum uero ex toto conualuerit' and Sen.
de Ira ii 19, 4 'senes difficiles et queruli
sunt, ut aegri et conualescentes'; Cic.
pro Sulla 27, 76 'ut...conualescere aliquando et sanari ciuitas posset'; Liv.
v 5, 12 'qui curari se fortiter passus
extemplo conualescere possit.' Bei. proposed *modo* in place of *non*, but no change
is required.
§ **75. nouo...amore** : Mo. quotes
Nonnus, Dionys. xi 356 ἄλλῳ λῦσον ἔρωτι
τεῶν σπινθῆρας ἐρώτων | ......παλαιοτέροιο
γὰρ αἰεὶ | φάρμακόν ἐστιν ἔρωτος ἔρως
νέος.
clauo clauum : the Gk form of the
proverb is ἥλῳ τὸν ἥλον ἐκκρούειν or
πάτταλον παττάλῳ ἐκκρούειν. Cf. Arist.

tamquam clauo clauum eiciendum putant; maxime autem admonendus est quantus sit furor amoris. omnibus enim ex animi
10 perturbationibus est profecto nulla uehementior, ut, si iam ipsa
illa accusare nolis, stupra dico et corruptelas et adulteria, incesta
denique, quorum omnium accusabilis est turpitudo, — sed ut
haec omittas, perturbatio ipsa mentis in amore foeda per se est.
76. nam ut illa praeteream quae sunt furoris, haec ipsa per sese
15 quam habent leuitatem, quae uidentur esse mediocria,

> Iniúriae,
> Su p ciones, ínimicitiae, indútiae,
> Bellúm, pax rursum! incérta haec si tu póstules
> Ratióne certa fácere, nihilo plús agas,
20 Quam sí des operam, ut cúm ratione insánias.

haec inconstantia mutabilitasque mentis quem non ipsa prauitate
deterreat? est etiam illud, quod in omni perturbatione dicitur,
demonstrandum, nullam esse nisi opinabilem, nisi iudicio
susceptam, nisi uoluntariam. etenim si naturalis amor esset,

8. clauo R G B W 1 2 *alii.* claua V. ‖ eiciendum R 1 6 7 17 V P G
B 1 3 K 1 2 E 1 2 W 1 2 M ɪ D C J O 7. eŷciendum S i *in* ŷ *mut.* ‖
maxume R V G B K. maxime S E. ‖ admonendus quantus R 1 6 7 V P G
B 1–3 K 1 2 S E 1 W 1 2 M 1 2 J O 1–3 7. ammonendus quantus E 2

C II. amouendus quantus D. est *inseruit Baiter.* 12. ut hẹc çomitas V
atr. uiridi corr.

§ 76, 14. futuris K. ‖ per sese G K. peṣṣe V. 15. mediocṛɪa E 1.
mediocra G. 17. suspiciones R K S G *at* c *in* t *alt. man. mut.* suspitiones E.
18. sit u B *litt. post* u *eras.* sit ut V. sit *ut* E. siʈ uʈ S. sit ut R G K.
22. est enim illud R V P G B 1–3 K 1 2 S E 1 2 W 1 2 M 1 2 D C II J
O 1–3 7. etiam *corr. Manutius.*

Pol. viii 1314a, 5 καὶ χρήσιμοι οἱ πονηροὶ
εἰς τὰ πονηρά· ἥλῳ γὰρ ὁ ἧλος, ὥσπερ ἡ
παροιμία.

ex: for *ex* in place of the partitive gen.
cf. Nägelsbach, *Stil.* § 124, 5.

ut, si iam...per se est, another anacoluthon, again due to a parenthesis. Mo.
thinks that *ut* can be taken here as
equivalent to *uelut*, 'zum Beispiel.' For
si iam = etiam si, cf. 31, 65.

corruptelas: cf. Lact. Inst. Diu. vi 19,
'utuntur libidine ad capiendas tantum
uoluptates : hinc stupra, hinc adulteria,
hinc corruptelae omnes exstiterunt.'

accusabilis est, 'furnishes ground for
accusation'; *accusabilis* is ἅπαξ εἰρημένον
in Cicero: it is found again in Salvianus
(de Gubern. Dei, viii 1, 3).

§ **76. furoris**: 'which fall under the
head of insanity'; the *illa* are *stupra*,
corruptelae and *adulteria*, which are only
committed when the mind has fallen so

much under the dominion of passion as
to be no longer master of its own actions.

haec ipsa, 'even the following'; in
this sense *illa* would be more usual than
haec, but it has just been used in the
sense of 'the former.'

iniuriae: Ter. Eun. i 1, 14 sqq. Dav.
compares Hor. Sat. ii 3, 260 sqq.

suspiciones: for the lengthening of the
second syllable cf. Enn. 266, 281; Afran.
317 (Ribbeck).

postules, 'expect': for this meaning
cf. Plaut. Men. 443 'sed ego inscitus qui
domino me postulem moderarier.'

ratione certa...cum ratione, 'on a
fixed principle...with all your wits about
you': *cum ratione insanire* is, as the
Schol. Bemb. notes, an oxymoron.

est etiam introducing a further consideration: *etiam* is the conjecture of
Manutius (adopted by Tr. Ba. Sff. T.S.
etc.) for the MSS *enim*, retained by Küh.

25 et amarent omnes et semper amarent et idem amarent, neque
alium pudor, alium cogitatio, alium satietas deterreret.
XXXVI. 77. Ira uero, quae quam diu perturbat animum
dubitationem insaniae non habet, cuius inpulsu exsistit etiam
inter fratres tale iurgium :

> *A.* Quís homo te exsuperáuit usquam géntium
> 5   inpúdentia?
> *M.* Quis aútem malitiá te?

nosti quae sequuntur; alternis enim uersibus intorquentur inter
fratres grauissimae cóntumeliae, ut facile appareat Atrei filios
esse, eius qui meditatur poenam in fratrem nouam:

25. *Post* et amarent omnes *habent* et amarentur et semper R 16 L 2 ed. H.
et amarentur omnes et semper R 17.   amarentur omnes et semper K 2.   *post*
amarent *om.* omnes L 5.   26. satietas R G B K.   sacietas V.
    XXXVI. § 77, 1. ira uero quae R V *at* ae *in ras.* G B K E 1 W 1 M 2 O 2 3.
ira uero que B 2 3 S E 2 M 1 D C II J O 1 7.   ira uero q̄ P.   ira uero q̄ W 2.
2. inpulsu V G B 2 E.   impulsu R P B K. ‖ existit R V G B K S E.
4. exsuperauit R G B K E 2 M 2. ‖ umquam R V P G K E 2 M 1 D ed. H.
unquam B 1–3 K 2 S L 3–6 W 1 C II J O 1–3 7.   ūquam E 1 W 2.
nũq̃ L 2.   usquam *corr. Bentleius.*   5. inpudentia R V G K E J.   inprudentia
B 2 S.   impudentia B.   6. quis autem R V P G B 1–3 K 1 2 S E L 2–6
M 2 C II J O 1–3 ed. H.   quis aūt E 2 W 1 M 1 D O 7.   quis aut' R 17.
quis aut R 6 7.   quis āt W 2.   7. sequuntur B 1 2 S W 1 2 M 1 D C II J *alii.*
                                                                             v
secuntur R V P G B 3 K.   8. grauissimae R V G K.   gratissimę E.
                                                                                 t
gratissimę B. ‖ appareat R V G B K E.   9. meditatur R G.   mediatur V
atr. uiridi superscr.

cogitatio, 'reflexion,' perhaps sug‐
gested by the context of the passage
quoted from the Eunuchus, e.g. i 1,
19 'et quod nunc tute tecum iratus
cogitas,' etc.
XXXVI. § 77. **ira uero**: another
anacoluthon: the apodosis (deferred by
the digression in this and the subsequent paragraph) would have been (as
we see from the beginning of § 79)
something like *quomodo utilis esse dici
potest?*
Dav. following Lamb. and Man.
avoided the anacoluthon by omitting
quae, and he is follọwed by Tr. and Kl.
Bentl. proposed in' addition to change
quam to *cum*.
dubitationem...habet: cf. i 49, 119 n. ;
Off. iii 2, 9 ; Fin. v 12, 34, and Nägelsbach, *Stil.* § 95, p. 257.
fratres: Agamemnon and Menelaus.
The lines are assigned by Ribbeck (*Scaen.
Rom. Poes. Fragg.* I², 41) to the Iphi-
geneia of Ennius ; earlier critics had

assigned them to the Atreus of Accius ;
the metre is iambic octonarius.
usquam: Bentley's emendation for
unquam of nearly all MSS ; he compared
Plaut. Poen. 825, Pseud. 98.
autem: Fleckeisen (followed by Küh.
T.S. Sff. Hei.) proposed *item*, taking the
metre to be trochaic tetrameter ; but, as
Ribbeck (*op. cit.* p. xxvii) points out, 'in
responsis uel interrogatis uel exclamatis
ubi quid augetur uel intenditur, sollemne
est *autem*' : he compares Plaut. Cas. 165 ;
Pseud. 305 ; Amph. 901 ; Ter. Eun.
798 ; Hec. 817 ; Phorm. 775, etc.
intorquentur: cf. iii 26, 63 n. and Sil.
Ital. Pun. xi 340 si uiso intorserit ense |
diram, qua uertit per campos agmina,
uocem.
fratrem: sc. 'Thyestem': the lines
following are from the Atreus of Accius
(Ribbeck, *op. cit.* I², p. 162) and are
quoted again in Or. iii 58, 219 and de
Nat. Deor. iii 26, 68: the metre is iambic
trimeter.

10   Maiór mihi moles, máius miscendúmst malum,
Qui illíus acerbum cór contundam et cónprimam.
quo igitur haec erumpit moles? audi Thyestem:
Ípsus hortatúr me frater, út meos malís miser
Mánderem natós....
15 eorum uiscera apponit. quid est enim quo non progrediatur
eodem ira, quo furor? itaque iratos proprie dicimus exisse de
potestate, id est de consilio, de ratione, de mente; horum enim

10. miscendum malum R16717 VPG B1–3 K12 S E12 L2–6
W12 M12 DC IIJ O23. miscendum est malum O1. miscēdis malū
O7. miscendumst malum *corr. Wolfius.* 11. conprimam G. cōprimam
RPBE. comprimam VKS. 12. quo RV P1–6 G K12 E12 J O3.
quę S *at* ę *fuerat* o *ut uid.* W1. que II O1. quae O2. qui C. ‖
haec RGK. hęc VBE. hęc O1. ħ P. h' O7. hae R6 O2.
hee II O3. hęę R10. he P56 B3 E2 *litt. post* e *eras.* J ed. H.
hec R717 P24 K2 M1. hic C. eę P3 S *at* h *eras., fuerat ut uid.* hec. ‖
erupit M1 ed. H. erunt R16 V P345 GB K12 S E1 L2–6 O13
Urs. 3240. erūt R7 P6 B23 W2 M2 J O2. erut E3.
      i
erunt P1. eruit P2. eī R17. erit W1 DC O7 Gr. ferunt E2 II.
erumpit *corr. Bentleius teste Dauisio.* ‖ thyestem RVG K. thiestem S E.
13. ipsum R16 VGBKS L3 W1 M2 DC O13. ipsū PEII.
ipum Ħ3 L46. ip̄m R717 B3 E2 L25 W2 J O27 ed. H. ip̄e B2.
istum K2. 14. manderem R117 V P4 GB K12 E12 M1 DCJ O7.
                                                          e
manderem R67 P12 B3 W1 M2 O1–3. mandᵃrem W2. mandᵃre S.
mandere ed. H. maderem B2. 15. uiscera B1–3 E23 W1 M12 DC
O237 ed. H. uisceræ V. uiscera O1. uiscere RGKE W2. ‖
                                                                    d
apponit RVGBKSE. ‖ quo RGK. quo V *atr. uiridi superscr.*
16. eodem R16717 V P3 G B23 K12 W1 M2 J O12 ed. H.
eo ē W2 *litt. post* o *eras.* eorum P124 B1 S E12 M1 DCII O3.
eorūdē O7.

moles: sc. *mouenda* out of *miscendum*;
for the metaphor in the latter cf. Cat. iv 3, 6.
quo...erumpit, a correction of the MSS.
attributed by Dav. to Bentley, though in
Bentley's *notae ineditae* printed at the end
of Dav.'s edition the word is *erupit.*
For *erumpere* cf. Q. Fr. i 2, § 2
'sentire potuit sermones iniquorum in
suum potissimum nomen erumpere,' pro
Mur. 38, 81 'omnia...in hos dies, in
hos mensis, in hoc tempus erumpunt.'
Lael. 21, 76 'erumpunt saepe uitia amicorum tum in ipsos amicos tum in alienos.'
ipsus hortatur: Ribbeck, *op. cit* I²,
p. 165: the lines are quoted again in Or.
iii 58, 217, whence the correction *ipsus*
of the MSS. reading *ipsum* here is derived.
manderem: this reading which has
less MSS. support here than *mandarem* is
read by the majority of MSS. in Or. *l.c.*
and adopted by Ribb. who quotes Sen.
Thyest. 779 'artusque mandit ore funesto
suos': *mandarem* is supported by Lucr.
ii 638 'ne Saturnus eum malis mandaret
adeptus.'

uiscera, 'flesh,' cf. ii 7, 19 n. For
other exx. cf. N.D. ii 6, 18 'terrenam
ipsam uiscerum soliditatem'; Seru. ad
Aen. i 211, iii 622 'uiscera proprie carnes
sunt'; Lucan. vi 545, ix 1052; Salu. de
Gub. Dei vi 2, 10; vii 1, 3 and (metaphorically) Amm. Marc. xxiv 4, 9 'miles
uisceribus hostium pascebatur.'
quo: 'what length is there to which
anger may not go, just as readily (lit. just
as far) as madness': *quo...eodem* may be
compared (with Mo.) to such expressions
as *quod idem* Ac. ii 17, 52, Diu. i 45, 102;
quam eandem Off. i 7, 20, *quem eundem*
Lael. 18, 65.
Hand in a note to Wopkens, *Lect.*
Tull. p. 143, explains *quo* as equivalent to
quare; which, even were it supported by
parallels, would give a poor sense. Bentl.
proposed 'quid enim est quo n. p. ira?
eo demum quo furor,' arriving at the
same sense as the MSS. reading by an
unnecessarily circuitous route.
exisse de potestate: cf. iii 5, 11 n.
horum: sc. *consilii, rationis, mentis.*

potestas in totum animum esse debet. **78.** his aut subtrahendi
sunt ii in quos impetum conantur facere, dum se ipsi colligant
20 (quid est autem se ipsum colligere nisi dissipatas animi partis
rursum in suum locum cogere?), aut rogandi orandique sunt ut,
si quam habent ulciscendi uim, differant in tempus aliud, dum
deferuescat ira. deferuescere autem certe significat ardorem
animi inuita ratione excitatum. ex quo illud laudatur Archytae,
25 qui cum uilico factus esset iratior, 'Quo te modo,' inquit,
'accepissem, nisi iratus essem!'
    XXXVII. **79.** Vbi sunt ergo isti, qui iracundiam utilem

§ **78,** 19. ei R V G B S E *plerique.*   ii M 1 *h. l.*   hi W 2 *in ras.*   eis P. ‖
impetum R V G B 1 2 K S E.   ‖   se ipsi B 1–3 S E 1 2 W 1 2 M 1 2
D C J O 2.   ipse ipsi V P.   ipse ipsi R G K.   se illi O 1. ‖ conligant
R V G *h. l.* B K E.   colligant P S *alii.*   20. colligere R V G B K S E. ‖
dissupatas V K.   dissipatas G i *ex* u *ead. man. mut.* R i *ex* u *ras. mut.*
dissipatas B 1 2 S E.   ‖   partis V G B K E.   partes R i *in e mut.*
24. archytae R G.   archyte K.   archite S E.   25. uilico R V G B 1 2.
1
uilico E 1 *al. atr. superscr.*   uillico S J O 1. ‖ inquit R G B.   inquid V K.

§ **78. dissipatas...cogere.** Anger according to Stoic doctrine was primarily
due to an *agitatio animi* (Sen. de Ira ii
3, 4) or ψυχῆς κίνησις caused inevitably
by *oblata species iniuriae* : when this was
transformed by the will into an *impetus*
(ὁρμή) out of control of the reason it
became anger. From another point of
view the phenomenon was expressed in
purely physical language: anger was
defined (e.g. by Nemesius, de nat. hom.
c. 19 *ap.* Arnim, *St. vet. frgg.* iii § 416)
as ζέσις τοῦ περὶ καρδίαν αἵματος ἐξ ἀνα-
θυμιάσεως τῆς χολῆς ἢ ἀναθολώσεως
γινομένη or as a dissipation of the vital
heat of the soul towards the periphery
(Galen in Hippocr. de hum. I, vol. xvi,
p.'174 K *ap.* Arnim *l.c.* ἐν γὰρ τῇ ὀργῇ καὶ
τῷ θυμῷ ἡ ἔμφυτος αὐτῇ [sc. τῇ ψυχῇ]
θερμασία ἐκτείνεται· καὶ χολὴ τότε γίνεταί
τε καὶ αὐξάνεται). This scattering of the
vital heat from the heart explained the
rubor and other physical effects of anger.
But there was always the danger that it
might lead to a permanent weakening of
the intellectual centre, the life of which
was the fire or vital heat that was of the
essence of the soul; for this reason excessive anger often led to madness, cf.
Sen. de Ira ii 36, 5 'nulla celerior ad insaniam uia est: multi itaque continu-
auerunt irae furorem nec quam expularunt
mentem umquam receperunt.' To recover
then from a fit of anger was to recall to
the centre the *partes animi* which had
been temporarily disturbed and scattered.

differant: cf. Sen. de Ira iii 12, 4
'maximum remedium irae dilatio est, ut
primus eius feruor relanguescat et caligo
quae premit mentem aut residat aut
minus densa sit.' Plut. de cohib. ira,
c. 11, p. 459 E ὅ τε γὰρ χρόνος ἐμποιεῖ
τῷ πάθει διατριβὴν καὶ μέλλησιν ἐκ-
λύουσαν ἥ τε κρίσις εὑρίσκει καὶ τρόπον
πρέποντα καὶ μέγεθος ἁρμόττον κολάσεως.

Archytae. Archytas of Tarentum, a
statesman and Pythagorean philosopher,
flourished 400—365 B.C. R. and P. § 61.
The story here told of him occurs again
in a slightly different form in Rep. i 38, 59
and Val. Max. iv 1, 1 ext. Seneca, de Ira i
15, 3, tells the same story of Socrates, and
in iii 12, 5 has a precisely similar tale
about Plato, who, being in a rage, asked
the obliging Speusippus to flog his slave
for him; the latter story is repeated by
Plut. adu. Col. 2, p. 1108 A, while Diog.
Laert. (iii 26) attributes Archytas' saying
to Plato (μεμαστίγωσο ἂν εἰ μὴ ὠργιζόμην).
It is impossible to say of whom the story
was originally invented.

accepissem: see ii 14, 34 n. on *uerberibus accipiuntur.* This use of *accipere*
is found in Lucilius (vi 667) and is
according to Marx *ad loc.* derived from
the *sermo uolgaris*: cf. also Plaut. Aul.
630 and Cic. Verr. ii 1, 54, 140.

XXXVII. §**79. isti:** sc. 'Peripatetici,'
cf. 19, 43.

magis iracundus: Cicero's argument
seems to be this: if anger were a natural
effect of certain impressions, then an im-

H.   13

dicunt (potest utilis esse insania?) aut naturalem? an quicquam
est secundum naturam quod fit repugnante ratione? quo modo
autem, si naturalis esset ira, aut alius alio magis iracundus esset,
5 aut finem haberet prius quam esset ulta ulciscendi libido, aut
quemquam paeniteret quod fecisset per iram? ut Alexandrum
regem uidemus, qui cum interemisset Clitum familiarem suum,
uix a se manus abstinuit; tanta uis fuit paenitendi. quibus cognitis quis est qui dubitet quin hic quoque motus animi sit totus
10 opinabilis ac uoluntarius? quis enim dubitarit quin aegrotationes
animi, qualis est auaritia, gloriae cupiditas, ex eo, quod

XXXVII. § 79, 2. aut naturalem R V P 1 4 G B 1 2 K E 2 O 7.
aut naturalē R 10 E 1. aut naturale R 7 16 17 K 2 W 2 M 1 D C J O 1.

aut naturale est B 3. aut naturalis L 3. aut naturalis II *al. atr. superscr.*
et is in ras. aut naturalis est R 6 E 3 L 6 W 1 M 2 O 2 3. an naturale
ed. H. ‖ an quicquam (quidquam) R 2 6 10 B 3 E 3 L 6 W 1 M 2 II O 2 3.
an potest quicquam L 3. hâñc quicquam P *marg.* an. ~~hanc~~ quicquam E 1.
hac quicquam S *at in ras.; marg. at eras.* naturalis? an. hanc quicquam R
V P 4 G B 1 2 K E 2 O 7. hanc quicqd R 17. hoc quicquam R 16
L 5 J O 1 ed. H. h' quicquam W 2. ñ quicquam K 2. hoc aut quicquam
R 7 L 2. quicquam M 1 D C an *om.* 3. est E 1 W 1 C. es R L 2–6.
ēē R 10 V P 1 4 B 1 2 E 2 W 2 J O 1 7. esse G K 1 ed. H.
ēē‸ S *marg.* p̄t‸. ēē E 3 *al. atr. superscr.* esse‸ II esse potest
R 6 B 3 M 2 O 3. est et D. esse et M 1. potest esse O 2 *om.* K 2. ‖
fit R V P G B 1 2 K 1 2 S E 1 2 W 1 2 M 1 D C J O 1 3 ed. H. sit B 3
E 3 M 2 O 2 7. 5. ulla R 1 6 7 10 16 V P 1 3 4 G B 1–3 K 1 2 S
E 1–3 L 2–6 W 1 2 M 1 2 D C II J O 1–3 7 Gr. ull'a R 17. ulta *corr.*
Manutius. ‖ lubido R V G K J. libido P B S E. 6. peniteret B S.

peniteret R V G K E O 1. poeniteret W 1. ‖ qd̄ fecisse V *atr. uiridi superscr.*
8. penitendi S. penitendi R V G K E. poenitendi B 1 W 1.

pression, which angers any one, ought to
produce the same kind and amount of
effect upon every one; but as it is notori-
ous that some men are angered by, and
others are indifferent to, the same occurrence, it follows that anger is not *secundum
naturam.*

Cicero forgets for the moment the
'mixtura elementorum,' which was the
work of nature, and yet was responsible
for 'uarietates morum' so that Seneca can
say 'natura quosdam procliues in iram
facit' (de Ira ii 20, 1).

finem : if anger were *naturalis*, it would
be an *appetitus* or impulse directed towards some end, which would last until
the end was attained, the attainment being
accompanied by a feeling of satisfaction.
Cic. seems, by this argument, to class all
natural impulses together and draw no
distinction between emotions and appe-
tites.

uidemus: 22, 50 n.

Clitum : the incident is told in Arrian,

Anab. iv 8, and with great variations in
detail in Plut. Alex. 50 and 51.

quis enim dubitarit : from these words
down to *perturbatio erroris est* in § 80
is bracketed as spurious by TS. and
Hasper on the grounds chiefly that it
interrupts the argument, and that the
reasoning is illogical. It is true that it is
more or less a digression and repeats in
substance what has been already said in
7, 14 sqq. But Cicero is rather fond of
digressions and repetitions and the reasoning is not so illogical as to justify the
wholesale condemnation of the passage.
The special difficulties are dealt with below.

unde intellegi debet … in opinione.
This sentence, according to TS., should
have been preceded by a statement that
the *aegrotationes animi* are due to *perturbationes* : but in a summary repetition
Cicero was entitled to assume that his
readers could remember what had been
taken as proved throughout the whole
book.

magni aestimetur ea res ex qua animus aegrotat, oriantur? unde intellegi debet perturbationem quoque omnem esse in opinione. **80.** et si fidentia, id est firma animi confisio, scientia quaedam 15 est et opinio grauis non temere adsentientis, metus quoque est diffidentia [exspectati et inpendentis mali], et, si spes est exspectatio boni, mali exspectationem esse necesse est metum. ut igitur metus, sic reliquae perturbationes [sunt in malo]. ergo

12. magni aestumetur G.   magnia estumetur R K.   magni estumetur B. magni estimetur P 1.   magna estumetur V B 2.   magna estimetur K 2. magni a existimetur M 1 a *indistincte script.*: magni estimetur E 2 3   D C   O 1. magni existimetur Π ed. H.   magni extimetur W 1 2   M 2   O 2.   magis

extimetur O 3.   magnis extimetur B 3.   ‖   oriantur K 2   O 7.   oria∧t B 1.

oriaȝt E 1.   oriatur R V P G   B 2   K 1   E 2   W 2   O 1 3.   13. intellegi V B K.   intelligi R G S E. § 80, 15. adsentientis R V P G   K 1   E 1.   assentientis B 1–3   S   W 1 2 M 1   D C Π J   O 1–3.   16. diffidentia B 3   K 2   E 2   W 1 2   M 1 2   D C Π J O 1–3.   deffidentia S *i.e.* ef *in* iff *mut.*   defidentia E 1.   difidentia K 1. difidentiae V.   defidentia R P G   B 1 2.   ‖   expectati, -tatio, -tationem R V B G K S.   exspectati, -tatio, -tationem E.   ‖   inpendentis V G E. impendentis R B K S.   17. esse necesse est R 1 6   V P G   B 1 3   K 1   S   E 1 2 W 1   M 2   D C Π.   necesse est esse J   O 1 3.   esse *om.* B 2   M 1   O 2 7

W 2 *marg.* necesse est esse.   ‖   mecum V *atr. uiridiore superscr.*   mecum G c *in* t *alt. man. mut.*

§ 80. et si fidentia … necesse est metum. The interpretation and meaning of this sentence involve special difficulties: it is a trifle that *fidentia* only occurs again in Cic. in de Invent. ii 54, 163, and that *confisio* is ἄπαξ εἰρημένον—neither can be seriously urged against the genuineness of the sentence : the real crux is in the clause *metus quoque est diffidentia exspectati et inpendentis mali.* Heine (*Posen Progr.* pp. 19 f.) asserts that *diffidentia* with a gen. can only mean 'distrust of,' quoting Suet. Otho, 9 'desperatione ulla aut diffidentia copiarum,' and Plin. Epp. v 1, 7 'non diffidentia causae sed metu temporum,' and proposes to read *opinio* in its place. But this only introduces fresh difficulties : in the first place as TS. and Hasp. point out the proper antithesis to the feeling of *metus* in relation to an *exspectatum et inpendens malum* is (acc. to 6, 13) not *fidentia* but *cautio* ; and one feels that *fidentia* has only been used in the clause before to lead up to *diffidentia* here : besides the description of the object of *metus* (or of the feeling of *diffidentia*) destroys the balance of the clause (*fidentia* having been defined as it is in itself without reference to external circumstances) and anticipates the statement of the following clause *si spes…necesse est metum.*

The words *exspectati et inpendentis mali* are probably due to a marginal gloss that has crept into the text. If they are omitted, the discussion (in Küh.) as to whether *metus* or *diffidentia* is the subject of their clause and Dav.'s proposal to interchange the words become unnecessary.

Cicero's argument, then, is this : if self-reliance is a kind of knowledge in a mind that does not come to rash conclusions, and fear is the opposite of this, and further if hope is an expectation of good (hope being the feeling excited when the mind has quietly come to the conclusion that the circumstance impending is not a *malum*) then *metus* resolves itself into the expectation that what is impending is evil. The discussion of the force of *quoque* in Dav. and Hei. (*l.c.*) is avoided by taking the protasis to extend to 'exspectatio boni.'

ut igitur metus … in malo. This sentence is condemned as spurious by Wesenberg, who says 'Obscurius, praesertim post *mali* aliter positum, est *sunt in malo.* Vulgo intellegitur esse idem quod *sunt in uitio, uitiosae.* sed ut hoc ita sit, quomodo ex iis quae praecedunt concludi potest?' (*Em.* III p. 14), and in this he is followed by Hei. and Ba. Both contentions are sound, but both can be

ut constantia scientiae, sic perturbatio erroris est. qui autem
20 natura dicuntur iracundi aut misericordes aut inuidi aut tale
quid, ii sunt constituti quasi mala ualetudine animi, sanabiles
tamen, ut Socrates dicitur, cum multa in conuentu uitia conlegisset in eum Zopyrus, qui se naturam cuiusque ex forma
perspicere profitebatur, derisus est a ceteris, qui illa in Socrate
25 uitia non agnoscerent, ab ipso autem Socrate subleuatus, cum
illa sibi insita, sed ratione a se deiecta diceret. 81. ergo ut

21. ei sunt constituti R V P G B K   E 2   W 1   Π J O 1   S *marg.*   eis ii sunt
constituti O 3.   ei sint constituti O 7.   hii sunt constituti W 2 *at* hii
in ras. et al. atr.   eis sunt constituti E 1   D C.   eis modi sunt constituti M 1.
ii sunt eius modi constituti M 2.   ‖   ualetudine R G K.   ualetudini V.

ualitudine P B S E.   ‖   sanabiles R 16   B 3   W 2   D   O 1 ed. H.   sanabile est
R 1 2 10   V G   B 1 2   K 1 2   S   E 1 2   O 7.   22. ut R 1 2 10 16   V G   B 2 3
K 1 2   D.   aut E 1.   aut B 1.   ‖   Socrates R V P G   B 1-3   W 2   D J.‖
conlegisset R V   B 1   K.   collegisset G *h. l.* B 2.   collegissent P.
                                                                          h
23. zopyrus R V   B 1 3   O 1.   zopirus G   B 2   E 1   W 2.   zopᴧirus S.
zophirus D.   zephyrus W 1.   25. agnoscerent R V G *h. l.* B K S E   W 2   D.
26. sibi signa sed R 1 17   V P G   B 1   K 1 2   E 1-3   L 2 3 5   J ‾ O 1-3.
                                                                              ēē
sibi signaᴧsed S *marg.* essent.   sibi signa sed W 1 *marg.* fuisse.   sibi signa sed R 7.
        inesse
sibi signa sed Π.   sibi signa (sed *om.*) B 2 3   L 6   M 2.   sibi signa W 2
at sed *post* signa *eras. et spat. relict.*   sibi inesse signa sed L 4.   sibi signa
inesse sed R 6   D C.   sibi uitia in esse sed M 1.   sibi signa uitia inesse sed ed. H.
sibi insita *corr. Bentleius.*   ‖   a se V G   B 2   K 1   E 2   W 1   M 2   J.   ab se S.
aᴧlse R *eod. atr.*   adse E 1.   adse Π.

removed by omitting *sunt in malo* : they
are just the sort of explanatory addition
one would expect to find to a sentence
like ' ut igitur metus, sic reliquae perturbationes,' 'the statement about fear applies to other emotions as well.'
   ii : for this, which is the reading of
the best MSS, Bentley proposed *eis*,
necessitating the further alteration of
Socrates to *Socratis*, in which he is followed by Dav. Mo. Bouh. F.A.W. Or.
   constituti: cf. ii 4, 11 'ita animo ac uita
constitutus'; pro Sest. 65, 137 'a bonis
uiris sapientibus et bene natura constitutis.'
   dicitur : Bake is surely right in his
contention that to end the sentence with
dicitur makes the opening of the following sentence rather abrupt, and that the
natural complement to *dicitur*, when we
take the following words into account, is
de se dixisse, not *constitutus fuisse* (Or.) or
sanabilis fuisse. He is followed in his
assumption of an anacoluthon (the construction being broken with *derisus est*)
by Ba. TS. and Hei., the latter however
contending that Cic. meant to complete
the construction of *dicitur* by some words
like *subleuasse Zopyrum*.
   conlegisset : Dav. conjectured *coniecis-
set*, alleging that *colligere in aliquem* was

bad Latin : but as Wopk. (*op. cit.* p. 332)
points out it is equivalent to *collecta
memorare in aliquem* : *colligere uitia* occurs
again in Fin. i 19, 62. For the pregnant
constr. see Nägelsb. *Lat. Stil.* § 102.
   Zopyrus : ὁ φυσιογνώμων, cf. de Fato 5,
10 : Maximus Tyr. xxv 3 (p. 299 ed.
Hobein) ; Orig. c. Cels. i 33 quoted by
Dav. who denies, however, the identification of this Zopyrus with Alcibiades'
Thracian παιδαγωγός made in Spencer's
note to Orig. and thinks him to have
been the Syrian μάγος who is said by
Diog. Laert. (ii 5, 24) to have foretold
Socrates' death. This view is adopted
by Förster (*Scriptores Physiognomici* i
p. vii n.).
   The story is told in Alexander Aphro-
disiensis, de Fato, quoted by Eusebius,
Praep. Evang. vi 9, 22, where Socrates'
reply is given as ἦν γὰρ ἂν τοιοῦτος ὅσον
ἐπὶ τῇ φύσει, εἰ μὴ διὰ τὴν ἐκ φιλοσοφίας
ἄσκησιν ἀμεινων τῆς φύσεως ἐγένετο, and
by Cassian, Conl. xiii 5, 3, where quoting
perh. from Phaedo's lost dialogue Zopyrus
(Diog. Laert. ii 9, 2) he gives Socrates'
words as παύσασθε, ἑταῖροι· εἰμί γάρ,
ἐπέχω δέ.
   insita : Bentley's emendation for the
meaningless *signa* of the MSS is adopted

optima quisque ualetudine adfectus potest uideri uel natura ad
aliquem morbum procliuior, sic animus alius ad alia uitia pro-
pensior. qui autem non natura sed culpa uitiosi esse dicuntur,
30 eorum uitia constant e falsis opinionibus rerum bonarum et
malarum, ut sit alius ad alios motus perturbationesque procliuior. inueteratio autem, ut in corporibus, aegrius depellitur
quam perturbatio, citiusque repentinus oculorum tumor sanatur
quam diuturna lippitudo depellitur.

XXXVIII. **82**. Sed cognita iam causa perturbationum, quae
omnes oriuntur ex iudiciis opinionum et uoluntatibus, sit iam
huius disputationis modus. scire autem nos oportet cognitis,

§ **81**, 27. optuma R V G B K.   ‖   quisque R V P G   B 1–3   K 1   S   E 1 2
W 1 2   M 2   D C J   O 1–3 7.   ‖   ualetudine V G K.   ualitudine R B S E. ‖

adfectus V G.   adfectos Ė.   affectus R B K S.   ‖   uideri ut natura R 1 6 7 17
V P G   B 2 3   K 1 2   S   E 1–3   L 3–6   W 2   M 2   D C J   O 1–3 7 ed. H.
uideri ut natura W 1.   uideri utru̅ natura L 2.   uideri an̄ M 1.

uideri ut natura Π *alio atr. superscr.*   uideri ut natura B 1 *cum ras. post* ut.
uideri uel natura *corr. Seyffertus*.   30. bonarum et R 1 7 17   V P G   B 1–3   K 1
S   E 1 2   W 1 2   M 1 2   D C J   O 1–3.   bonarum ac R 6   Π.   et *om.* K 2   O 7.
34. lippitudo depellitur R V P G *plerique*.   lippitudo diuturna depellitur O 1.

XXXVIII. § **82**, 3. nos B 2 3   S   M 2   C Π (*at* n *mut. esse uid.*) O 1 2 7.
uos R V P G   B 1   K 1 2   E 1 2   W 1 2   M 1 (*non ut Küh.*) D J   O 3.

by CFWM. Bait. TS. Hei. Sch.; Sff.
prefers *innata*, which he wrongly credits
to Nissen; it is due to Bentl. who wrote
'probo conjecturam cujusdam, quam
Gebhardus memorat illa sibi INGENITA:
nisi forte mauis INSITA uel INNATA'
(*Emend. ad. Tusc. Disp.* p. 477 in Dav.'s
edn. Ox. 1805). It is possible that *signa
sed* of the MSS is a corruption of *sic natura*
(*n̄a*) *esse sed*, which would reproduce the
contrast between φύσις and ἄσκησις in the
version quoted above from Eusebius.

§ **81**. **quisque**. 'Accordingly, just as
every man, though in the enjoyment of
excellent health, may show signs of being
naturally prone to contract some one
disease more than another, in the same
way one mind is more inclined to one
fault, another to another'; for the position of *quisque* cf. Off. i 31, 113; Bent.
(followed by Dav.) altered *quisque* of the
MSS to *quis* and read *at* before *natura* for
the MSS *ut*; but not merely is *quisque* the
reading of all the MSS, but it is essential
to Cicero's argument, which is, that every
one is liable to some natural bodily and
mental bias, which varies from one individual to another; in the second place
there is no such opposition between good
health and a natural liability to some
particular ailment as *at* implies: Hei.
TS. Ml. Sch. who retain *quisque* omit *ut*

before *natura*, but it is hard to see how it
came to be inserted. Sff.'s conjecture
uel (ut) gives an excellent sense and lays
the proper emphasis upon *natura*.
culpa: cf. iii 30, 73 'sunt enim ista
non naturae uitia sed culpae.'
inueteratio: ἅπαξ εἰρημένον: here = 'in-
ueteratum uitium,' 'a chronic complaint.'
oculorum tumor: a concomitant of
the ordinary *lippitudo* (described in Cels.
de med. vi 6, 1 ff.) in which 'tument ac
distenduntur cum dolore oculi': the
arida lippitudo is described *ib.* vi 6, 29
'neque tument neque fluunt oculi sed
rubent tantum...quantoque minor generis
huius impetus, tanto finis minus expe-
ditus est.'
depellitur is suspected by Dav. to be
a repetition, due to a copyist, of *depellitur*
above; the word is bracketed by Wes.
Hei. Bait.

§ **82**. **cognita...causa**: this is, as Mo.
notes, a *locutio iudicialis*; cf. de Or. ii 24,
100 'nihil est negotii eiusmodi causam
cognoscere': Or. 42, 143; Brut. 70, 246.
opinionum, 'judgments resting upon
opinions,' as opposed to the *iudicia* proceeding from *scientia* (ὁ ὀρθὸς λόγος).
disputationis: for the gen. cf. ' cala
mitatis praesentis...medicina' iii 22, 54
'finem faciet Tusculanarum disputatio
num' v 1, 1.

quoad possunt ab homine cognosci, bonorum et malorum finibus
5 nihil a philosophia posse aut maius aut utilius optari quam haec,
quae a nobis hoc quadriduo disputata sunt. morte enim contempta et dolore ad patiendum leuato adiunximus sedationem
aegritudinis, qua nullum homini malum maius est. etsi enim
omnis animi perturbatio grauis est nec multum differt ab amen-
10 tia, tamen ita ceteros, cum sunt in aliqua perturbatione aut
metus aut laetitiae aut cupiditatis, commotos modo et per-
turbatos dicere solemus, at eos, qui se aegritudini dediderunt,
miseros, adflictos, aerumnosos, calamitosos. 83. itaque non for-
tuito factum uidetur, sed a te ratione propositum, ut separatim de
15 aegritudine et de ceteris perturbationibus disputaremus; in ea

4. quoad R.   qoad B 1.   q$̈$ ad V *atr. uiridi corr.*   quod ad G K 1 E 1.
6. quadriduo R V G K D.   quatriduo P B 2 3 S E 1 2 W 1 2 M 1 C Π J
O 1–3 7.   quadruuio B 1.   10. tamen ita R 1 6 17 V P G B 2 3 K 1 2 S

E 1 2 W 1 2 M 1 2 D Π J O 1–3 7.   tū ita C.   tamen in B 1 *at fuerat* ita. ||
cum sunt R V G B 1 2 K 1 2 S E 1 2 W 2 D C Π O 1–3.   cum sint R 6

B 3 W 1 M 1 2 O 7.   cum ş P J.   11. commotos R G.   commotus V.

cōmotos K.   12. qui se aegritudini R.   qui se aegritudiniş K.   quisęgritudini V
e *atr. ant. inculc.*   quasaegritudinis G *in* quis aegritudini *ead. man. (ut uid.) mut.*
13. adflictos V G E.   afflictos R B K S.

quoad...cognosci: Cic. intends by these
words to safeguard his position as an
adherent of the New Academy; for a
similar qualifying expression, cf. Fin. ii
25, 80 'si haec uera sunt, nihil enim
affirmo.'
    bonorum...finibus: the treatise de
Finibus had been finished shortly before
(v 11, 32), probably by the end of June
45 B.C. See Introd. vol. i pp. xv f.
    ad patiendum, 'so that it can be en-
dured'; for the constr. cf. 17, 37 'aut
intolerabile ad demittendum animum aut
nimis laetabile ad ecferendum' and n.
there.
    ita ceteros: *ita* is bracketed by most
edd. and Nissen includes *tamen* in his
condemnation, arguing that *tamen ita*
is but a repetition of *amentia* preceding.
Klotz defends *ita*, remarking (*Quaest.
Tull.* i 124 sq.) 'ut magis illud quod ante
dictum erat legenti adhaeresceret parti-
culam istam adiecit qua illud denuo
repeteret'; Mo. and Küh. adopt the
more satisfactory explanation of Stueren-
burg, who takes *ita* with the following
cum, as in Brut. 62, 222 'grauem oratorem ita dumtaxat cum de re publica
diceret.' Sff. conjectures *in uita*, thus
making a contrast between the true philo-

sophic doctrine enunciated in the preceding clause and the view adopted by
the ordinary man—a contrast which is
sufficiently well brought out by *dicere
solemus* following.
    Cicero's point is that whereas in theory
every *perturbatio* is practically insanity, yet
in practice and common usage we draw a
distinction between various kinds of *perturbatio*, reserving for those suffering from
aegritudo our most emphatic expressions
of pity; *ceteros* refers to all *perturbati*
with the exception of those *aegritudini
deditos*; trans. 'we nevertheless in all the
other cases, namely when people are
suffering from a mental disturbance such
as fear or joy or desire, in this case (*ita*)
merely say usually that they are excited
and disturbed, while in the case of those
who have surrendered themselves to
aegritudo we say that they are wretched,
despairing, miserable, undone.'
    metus: gen. of definition, cf. i 15,
34 n.; i 45, 109; iv 15, 34.
    § 83. propositum: in iii 4, 7 'uidetur
mihi cadere in sapientem aegritudo' where
the interlocutor limited his assertion to
aegritudo, reserving his statement about
the other *perturbationes* for the following
day's discussion (iv 4, 7).

est enim fons miseriarum et caput. sed et aegritudinis et reliquorum animi morborum una sanatio est, omnis opinabilis esse
et uoluntarios ea reque suscipi quod ita rectum esse uideatur.
hunc errorem quasi radicem malorum omnium stirpitus philo-
20 sophia se extracturam pollicetur. **84.** demus igitur nos huic
excolendos patiamurque nos sanari. his enim malis insidentibus
non modo beati, sed ne sani quidem esse possumus. aut igitur
negemus quicquam ratione confici, cum contra nihil sine ratione
recte fieri possit, aut, cum philosophia ex rationum conlatione
25 constet, ab ea, si et boni et beati uolumus esse, omnia adiumenta
et auxilia petamus bene beateque uiuendi.

§ 83, 16. sed et aegritudinis R G.   sed ẹgritudinis V.   17. omnis R V G
B 1   K.   omnes B 2.   om̄s S E.   ‖ opinabilis R V G B K.   opinabiles
B 2   S E.   18. ea re que V   B 1 2   J.   ea req; R 17   W 2.   ea re q3 S
at q3 *in ras. et spatio post relicto.*   ea re q̄ P *marg.* q3.   ea re quae R G K.
                                                   b   a
ea re quoque O 7.   ea quẹ re E 1 *atr. ant. superscr.*   eaq; re R 6   B 3   K 2
E 2   W 1   M 2   D C Π   O 1–3 ed. H.   eaq; nec R 7.   eaq; de re M 1.

§ 84, 20. igitur nos R 17 17   V P G   B 1 3   K 1 2   S   E 1 2   W 1 2   M 1 2
Π J   O 1–3 7 ed. H.   nos igitur D C.   ergo nos R 6   B 2.   22. nommodo G.
23. ratione confici P.   rationͥ confici V *al. atr. superscr.*   rationi confici
R 1 2 10 16   G   K 1.   24. conlatione G B.   collatione R P K E 2 *alii.*
consolatione V.   collocatione S *marg.* collatione.   *om.* E 1.

enim: for the order of words cf. i 27,
66 n.; 'in his est enim' i 32, 78.

fons...et caput, 'fountain head and
source': this is nearly always the meaning of *caput* as applied to streams and
rivers, but cf. Liv. xxxiii 41, 7; Caes.
B.G. iv 10; for the phrase here edd.
compare de Or. i 10, 42; Fin. v 6, 17;
pro Planc. 23, 57.

omnis opinabilis esse: for the acc.
and inf. in loose explanation of *sanatio*

est cf. Ac. ii 38, 120 'quanti libertas ipsa
aestimanda est non mihi necesse esse quod
tibi est?' with Reid's note.

ea re...quod: for the constr. cf. Ac. ii
34, 111 'illud ea re a se esse concessum
quod uideretur esse quaedam in uisis
differentia'; Off. iii 13, 53 'ea re, quia
turpe sit, non esse faciendum.'

stirpitus is ἅπαξ εἰρημένον in Cicero.

§ 84. **non modo**: cf. i 36, 87 n.

M. TVLLI CICERONIS
TVSCVLANARVM DISPVTATIONVM
LIBER QVINTVS

I. 1. Quintus hic dies, Brute, finem faciet Tusculanarum disputationum, quo die est a nobis ea de re quam tu ex omnibus maxime probas disputatum. placere enim tibi admodum sensi et ex eo libro quem ad me accuratissime scripsisti et ex 5 multis sermonibus tuis uirtutem ad beate uiuendum se ipsa esse contentam. quod etsi difficile est probatu propter tam uaria et tam multa tormenta fortunae, tale tamen est ut elaborandum sit quo facilius probetur. nihil est enim omnium quae in philosophia tractantur quod grauius magnificentiusque dicatur. 10 2. nam cum ea causa inpulerit eos qui primi se ad philosophiae

uerba uirtutem ad beate uiuendum se ipsa esse contentam om. R V P B   E 1 2 W 1   M 1. *glossatoris manu subscr. habet* II.
    I. § 1, 2. ea de re R V P G   B 2 3   K 1 2   E 2   L 5   W 2   M 1 2   Π J   O 1 3. ea dere S *at* ea *in lit.*   addere B 1   E 1   D C   O 7.   de ea re W 1   O 2.
3. maxime R V B K S. *habet* G *alt. man. superscr.*   4. accuratissime R V G B K.
5. semmonibus G *in* sermonibus *alt. man. mut.*   6. contentam R V K.
conten tam B 1 *ras. ante et post* n.   contentam G n *ex* mp *alt. man. mut.*
                                       f
contēptā P. ‖ difficile P K.   difficili R V.   dificili G *alt. man. superscr.*
8. quod G *at* d *ead. man. deleto.* ‖ probetur R V G B K.   probætur E 1.
     r   n
pet P.   9. tractatur G *ead. man.*
    § 2, 10. impulerit R V P G B K S.   inpulerit E 1.

I. § 1. **finem faciet...disputationum**: for the gen. cf. iv 18, 41 n. on *uitio* and Madv.'s note on Fin. ii 9, 27 'qualis ista philosophia est, quae non interitum afferat prauitatis' and Madv.'s *Lat. Gr.* § 241, 3, § 242, 2.
    quo die: for the repetition of the antecedent in the relative clause for the sake of clearness (a usage frequent in legal formulae) cf. p. Mil. 20, 53 'ante fundum Clodi, quo in fundo, etc.'; Q.F. iii 3, 1 'diem scito esse nullum quo die non dicam'; Rep. i 26, 41 'ad eam causam referendum est, quae causa genuit ciuitatem.'
    ea de re: for the order of the words cf. i 27, 66 n.
    admodum goes with *sensi*, acc. to the usual Ciceronian rule: see Reid's n. on Lael. 1, 2.

eo libro: i.e. his de Virtute, cf. Fin. i 3, 8 'quamquam a te ipso id quidem facio prouocatus gratissimo mihi libro quem ad me de uirtute misisti'; Sen. ad Helu. 9, 4 quotes 'Brutus in eo libro quem de uirtute composuit.' Quintilian's criticism on Brutus' philosophical style is well known (x 1, 123) 'suffecit ponderi rerum: scias eum sentire quae dicit.'
    ad me...scripsisti, 'wrote and dedicated to me'; i.e. *ad me scriptum misisti*, the form of expression employed in 4, 11; cf. Lael. 1, 4 'in Catone maiore qui est scriptus ad te de senectute.'
    § 2. **ea causa**: Küh. and Hasp. are clearly wrong in taking this to mean 'the foregoing consideration,' a meaning which Cicero would have expressed by *quae causa cum*; *ea* is explained by the clause *ut...conlocarent*; the 'primi qui se ad

studium contulerunt ut omnibus rebus posthabitis totos se in
optimo uitae statu exquirendo conlocarent, profecto spe beate
uiuendi tantam in eo studio curam operamque posuerunt. quodsi
ab iis inuenta et perfecta uirtus est, et si praesidii ad beate
15 uiuendum in uirtute satis est, quis est qui non praeclare et ab
illis positam et a nobis susceptam operam philosophandi arbi-
tretur? sin autem uirtus subiecta sub uarios incertosque casus
famula fortunae est nec tantarum uirium est ut se ipsa tueatur,
uereor ne non tam uirtutis fiducia nitendum nobis ad spem beate
20 uiuendi quam uota facienda uideantur. 3. equidem eos casus in

---

12. optumo R V G B K. ‖ conlocarent R V G B K E.   collocarent S.
                                                                     ru
14. ab his R V P G B K S E. ‖ praesidii R V G B K S E   O 3 7.   18. tantam
R *eod. ut uid. atr.*

'philosophiae studium contulerunt' are
not the early physicists, as this would
make 'totos se in optimo uitae statu exquirendo conlocarent' hopelessly unhis-
torical (a blunder which Hei. is content
to attribute to a lapse of memory on
Cicero's part), nor Socrates and his
followers (Küh.), which would involve an
equally serious lapse in *primi*, but the
σοφοί 'a quibus uita hominum instructa
primis sit' (§ 6) and the others mentioned in §§ 7 sq. ; the *optimus uitae
status* will then have a meaning primarily
political and social, not ethical.

Sff., while rightly rejecting Bentley's
aliqua for *ea* as palaeographically unlikely,
and Bake's *nam quaecumque causa* as bad
grammar with *compulerit*, proposes to
omit *ea* as a dittography of the *ca* in
causa. But as his object is to get rid of
the historical difficulty in the interpretation of the words *qui primi...conlocarent*,
a difficulty which does not exist if the
passage be interpreted (as above) in view
of §§ 6 and 7, the emendation becomes
unnecessary; his proposal further involves the awkwardness of taking the
clause *ut ... conlocarent* as limiting the
application of *primi se contulerunt* in
the preceding clause, a case in which
Cic. would almost certainly have used
ita...ut.

Transl. 'For since the motive impel-
ling those who first devoted themselves
to the study of philosophy was such that
...they gave their whole attention to the
discovery of the ideal state of existence,
it must certainly have been from the expectation of a happy life that they devoted
so much care and attention to the pursuit
of it.'

inuenta et perfecta, 'discovered and
elaborated, thoroughly discussed'; for
this use of *perficere* cf. 25, 72 'sequentia
adiungit, perfecta concludit'; iv 5, 9
'erit enim hoc totum, quod quaero, ex
utroque perfectius' ('more thoroughly
discussed'); Legg. i 13, 35; Diu. ii 1, 3
'quae (sc. quaestio) ut plane esset cumu-
lateque perfecta.' Generally *perfecta*, when
applied to *uirtus*, means 'thoroughly performed,' e.g. pro Sest. 40, 86 'et sentire
uero et facere perfectae cumulataeque
uirtutis'; cf. Off. iii 3, 14 'illud autem
officium, quod rectum idem appellant,
perfectum atque absolutum est.' Cicero
seems fond of contrasting *inuenire* and
perficere, e.g. de Or. i 4, 13 'Athenas, in
quibus summa dicendi uis et inuenta est
et perfecta'; Brut. 18, 71 'nihil est enim
simul et inuentum et perfectum.'

positam: used here to recall *operamque
posuerunt* above : Nissen strangely takes
it as equivalent to *depositam* forming a
contrast with *susceptam.*

subiecta, 'brought under the power
of': Madv. in his n. on Fin. ii 15, 48
shows that *subicere* is followed either by
the dative, as in Off. ii 6, 22; pro domo
40, 106; or by *sub* with the acc. as here,
and in iv 7, 16; iv 8, 19; Ac. ii 23, 74.

tantarum uirium: Mo. notes that
the gen. plur. is more rarely used in this
constr. than the abl. plur.; he quotes
Plin. N.H. vii 2 'gens...stridoris horrendi,
hirtis corporibus.'

§ 3. eos casus: his political disappoint-
ments and domestic troubles which had
been increasing since 47 B.C.; see vol. I,
Intr. pp. xiv sq.

in quibus: Lamb. deleted *in* which is
supported by pro Arch. 11, 28 'quid est

202 *TVSCVLANARVM DISPVTATIONVM* [I. 3

quibus me fortuna uehementer exercuit mecum ipse considerans
huic incipio sententiae diffidere interdum et humani generis inbecillitatem fragilitatemque extimescere. uereor enim ne natura,
cum corpora nobis infirma dedisset iisque et morbos insanabilis
25 et dolores intolerabilis adiunxisset, animos quoque dederit et
corporum doloribus congruentis et separatim suis angoribus et
molestiis inplicatos. 4. sed in hoc me ipse castigo, quod ex
aliorum et ex nostra fortasse mollitia, non ex ipsa uirtute, de
uirtutis robore existimo. illa enim, si modo est ulla uirtus,
30 quam dubitationem auunculus tuus, Brute, sustulit, omnia quae
cadere in hominem possunt subter se habet eaque despiciens
casus contemnit humanos culpaque omni carens praeter se ipsam
nihil censet ad se pertinere. nos autem omnia aduersa cum

§ **3, 22.** interdum et R 1 7 V P G B 1 2 K 1 2 S E 1 W 1 M 1 D C
O 3 7. interdum et_A II *al. atr. superscr.* interdum & W 2 O 2.
interdum etiam R 6 B 3 M 2 J O 1. ‖ imbecillitatem R V P G *h. l.* B 2 K.
inbecillitatem B 1 S E 1. 24. hisque R V G B. ‖ insanabilis R V G K.
insanabiles P B 1 2 S E 1. 25. intolerabilis P B E 1. intollerabilis
R V G K. intolerabiles S. 26. congruentis R V G B 1 K E.
congruentes B 2 S. 27. implicatos R V G B K S. implicatos E 1.
§ **4.** in hoc R 1 6 V P G B 1-3 K 1 2 S E 1 2 W 1 2 M 1 2 D C II J
O 1-3 7. hoc Gr. in *om.* 29. existumo R G B K. existumē V.
30. auunculis tuis E 1. ‖ sustulit R G B K. sustu lit V *litt. erasa.*
31. in hominem K 1. in hominē V P B. in homine R G. 33. aduersa tum
R 1 6 7 10 17 V P G B 1 3 K 1 2 S E 1-3 L 2-6 W 1 2 M 2 D C II J
O 1-3 7 ed. H. aduersa tamē R 16. aduersa nobis B 2. aduersa M 1 tum *om.*
cum *corr. Dauisius.*

quod...tantis nos in laboribus exerce-
amus': for *exercere* edd. compare pr.
Planc. 32, 78; Fam. xii 4, 1; p. Mil. 2, 5.
congruentis, 'responsive to': cf. de Or.
iii 59, 222 'est enim actio quasi sermo
corporis, quo magis menti congruens esse
debet'; Wopkens, *op. cit.* p. 143, defends
the reading of the MSS. against Davies'
conjecture *conruentes* and Lambinus'
coaegrentes. For the thought cf. Ov. Tr.
v 13, 3 'aeger enim traxi contagia corpore
mentis.'
§ **4. in hoc,** 'in speaking of this'; cf.
in eo libro 9, 24 n.
castigo, 'rebuke,' the usual (but not
invariable) meaning of the word in class.
Lat. Cf. ii 21, 50 'uidesne ut obmutuerit
non sedatus corporis sed castigatus animi
dolor'; Liv. xxvi 35, 8; xxvii 34, 14;
xxviii 26, 3; xxxi 6, 5, etc.
auunculus: M. Porcius Cato Uticensis:
Brutus' mother was Servilia, Cato's ὁμομή-
τριος ἀδελφή (Plut. Cat. 1, Brut. 2). For
Cicero's opinion of Cato's character cf.
Att. ii 5, 1 'Cato ille noster qui mihi

unus est pro centum milibus'; Phil. xiii
14, 30 'quorum princeps M. Cato idemque omnium gentium uirtute princeps.'
Quintilian (xii 7, 4) couples the uncle and
nephew 'quorum alter appellatus sapiens,
alter nisi creditur fuisse uix scio cui reli-
querit huius nominis locum.'
subter: only here and in i 10, 20 in
Cicero, it is found also in Varro, R.R. iii
3, 5, but is almost entirely confined to
poetry before the time of Livy; the abl.
after *subter* is found only in Catullus and
Virgil; Draeger, *Synt. d. Lat. Spr.* i p.
621; Neue, *Formenl.* ii³ pp. 931 sqq.
Detlefsen (in *Philol.* XLII p. 181) sees in
subter the influence of poetry, and suggests that *despiciens...humanos* is the conclusion of a hexameter line from Cicero's
Laus Catonis; in a later number (*ib.*
p. 413) he withdraws the unhappy suggestion that 'contemnit humanos' can
end a hexameter, but makes the fresh
conjecture that a word has been omitted
in quotation and that *humanos* is the first
word of the following line.

uenientïa metu augentes, tum maerore praesentia rerum naturam
35 quam errorem nostrum damnare malumus.

II. 5. Sed et huius culpae et ceterorum uitiorum pecca-
torumque nostrorum omnis a philosophia petenda correctio est.
cuius in sinum cum a primis temporibus aetatis nostra uoluntas
studiumque nos compulisset, his grauissimis casibus in eundem
5 portum ex quo eramus egressi, magna iactati tempestate confugimus. o uitae philosophia dux, o uirtutis indagatrix expultrixque uitiorum! quid non modo nos, sed omnino uita hominum
sine te esse potuisset? tu urbis peperisti, tu dissipatos homines

---

34. naturarum G *in* naturam *alt. man. corr.*   naturā͢rū̄ E 1.   35. damnare
om. G *in marg. alt. man. adscr.*

II. § 5, 2. correctio R V P G K.   correptio E 1.   4. compulisset R V P G
B 2 K 1 2 S M 1 D C O 1–3 Gr.   cōpulisset B 1 E 1 W 2 II.
conpulisset R 7.   9pulisset O 7.   cōpulisset E 2.   contulisset R 6 W 1 J.
contulisset M 2 *at marg. al. manu* compulisset.   ‖   grauissimis R V G B.
grauisimis K.   6. expultrixq; V P B 1 S E 2 W 1 2 M 1 2 J O 1–3 7.
expultrixque R *at fuerat* excultrixque.   excultrixque G B 2 K.   expultrix
excultrixq3 D.   expultrix excultrix C.   expultrixq; excultrixq; E 1.

7. quid non modo R G.   quinonmodo V.   quiñm P.   8. urbis V G B K.

urbis R *eod. atr.*   urbes P. ‖ dissipatos R V G B.   disipatos K.

---

cum...praesentia : cf. iii 7, 14 'quarum
enim rerum praesentia sumus in aegritudine, easdem impendentia et uenientis
timemus'; *cum* is Dav.'s correction of
the MSS *tum* and is adopted by all recent
edd. except Or.; *tum...tum* can only
mean 'at one time...at another time,'
whereas here *uenientia* and *praesentia*
being in apposition to *omnia* require the
meaning 'both...and.'
    II. § 5. **sinum**, 'protection,' a com-
mon meaning of the word ; the literal and
metaphorical uses are happily blended in
Virg. Aen. viii 711 sqq. 'contra autem
magno maerentem corpore Nilum | pan-
dentemque sinus et tota ueste uocantem |
caeruleum in gremium latebrosaque flu-
mina uictos.'
    a primis temporibus : cf. Off. ii 1, 4
'in his studiis ab initio uersatus aetatis
existimaui honestissime molestias posse
deponi si me ad philosophiam rettulis-
sem'; pro Arch. 6, 14; Brut. 91, 315.
    aetatis : cf. i 39, 93 n. on 'exacta
aetate.'
    compulisset : Dav. preferred here the
reading *contulisset* found in some MSS
but (as Küh. points out) the word *com-
pellere* is used 'ad summum uehement-
issimumque animi impetum, quo Cicero
ad philosophiae studium deferretur, exprimendum.'

portum : for the metaphor edd. quote
Eur. Med. 768 οὗτος γὰρ ἀνὴρ ἧ μάλιστ'
ἐκάμνομεν | λιμὴν πέφανται τῶν ἐμῶν βου-
λευμάτων ; Anthol. Pal. ix 49 ἐλπὶς καὶ
σὺ τύχη, μέγα χαίρετε, τὸν λι. 'ν' εὗρον :
the metaphor is common in Cicero; see i
49, 119 n.
    o uitae...dux : Cicero's apostrophe is
sharply criticized by Lactantius, Instit.
Diu. iii 13 fin. 'potuit eodem modo
gratias agere cibo et potui, quia sine his
rebus uita constare non possit.'
    indagatrix, like *expultrix*, is ἅπαξ
εἰρημένον in Cicero. For the metaphor
Mo. compares Diog. Laert. viii 1, 6,
where Pythagoras is said to have called
philosophers θηραταὶ τῆς ἀληθείας, and
Didymus ap. Stobaeum, Ecl. Eth. ii 1, 18
ἡ μὲν γὰρ φιλοσοφία θήρα τῆς ἀληθείας
ἐστὶ καὶ ὀρέξις: cf. also Iamblichus,
Protrept. c. 5 p. 72 K αἱ μὲν ἄλλαι πᾶσαι
ἐπιστῆμαι θηρευτικαί τινές εἰσι...τῶν ἀγαθῶν, and N.D. i 30, 83 'physicum, id est
speculatorem uenatoremque naturae.'
    quid : cf. iv 23, 52 n. on 'quid...
foedius.'
    tu urbis peperisti. With this para-
graph cf. Or. i 8, 32, where the institution
of civil society is ascribed to the *uis
oratoria,* and pro Sest. 42, 91, where it is
ascribed to those 'qui primi uirtute et consilio praestanti exstiterunt'; de Rep. vi

in societatem uitae conuocasti, tu eos inter se primo domiciliis,
10 deinde coniugiis, tum litterarum et uocum communione iunxisti,
tu inuentrix legum, tu magistra morum et disciplinae fuisti; ad
te confugimus, a te opem petimus, tibi nos, ut antea magna ex
parte, sic nunc penitus totosque tradimus. est autem unus dies
bene et ex praeceptis tuis actus peccanti inmortalitati ante-
15 ponendus. cuius igitur potius opibus utamur quam tuis, quae et
uitae tranquillitatem largita nobis es et terrorem mortis sus-
tulisti? **6.** ac philosophia quidem tantum abest ut proinde ac

---

14. peccanti R 2 7 10 17 V P G B 1 2 K W 2 O 1.   peccan&i R *eod. atr.*
peccandi O 7.   pene toti R 6 16. ‖ inmortalitati R V K S.   immortalitati G
h. l. B.   immortalitate E 1.   15. quae uitae G *alt. man. superscr.*
§ 6, 17. ac R V P G B 1 K 1 2 E 1 M 1 D C O 3 7.   at R 6 B 3 S
M 2 J O 1 2.   a W 1 c *post* a *eras.*   a W 2 *al. atr. superscr.*   at II t *al.*
man. inculc.   a R 7 E 2.   ex B 2. ‖   proinde R V P G B 1 2 K 1 2
S E 2 W 2 M 1 D C Π J O 2 7.   proinde B 3.   perinde W 1 M 2 O 1 3.
pro ac E 1.

13, 13 'nihil est enim illi principi deo,
qui omnem mundum regit, quod quidem
in terris fiat, acceptius quam concilia
coetusque hominum iure sociati, quae
ciuitates appellantur,' Hor. A.P. 396 sqq.
Though each state owed its inception to
some lawgiver, yet the universality of
organized communities is due to the
natural law, 'nos ad coniunctionem con-
gregationemque hominum et ad naturalem
communitatem esse natos,' Fin. iii. 20,65.
Hei. thinks that the statement here is
probably due to the formulation of the
Stoic view by Posidonius as quoted by
Sen. Epp. 90, 5.
  Lucretius seems to express a similar
view in v 1105 sqq. 'inque dies magis hi
uictum uitamque priorem │ commutare
nouis monstrabant rebus benigni │ ingenio
qui praestabant et corde uigebant.' But
the Epicurean doctrine of the origin of
society was diametrically opposed to that
of the Stoics : the view of Epicurus is
quoted in Epictet. diss. ii 20, 7 οὐκ ἔστι
φυσικὴ κοινωνία τοῖς λογικοῖς πρὸς ἀλλήλους.
  penitus totosque: for the connection of
adj. and adv. by means of a conj. cf.
Plaut. Trin. 268 'sunt tamen quos miseros maleque habeas,' and Bacch. 474 'tu
Pistoclerum falso atque insontem arguis';
Sall. Iug. 5, 4 'magnum ac late imperium
ualebat' (quoted by Ussing, *ad loc.*);
cf. also Panegyricus Messallae 201 'quod
tibi si uersus noster, totusue minusue, │ uel
bene sit notus'; Quintil. ii 10, 5 'haec
supra fidem et poetica...themata.'

unus dies ... anteponendus: for the
sentiment Dav. compares Posidonius ap.
Sen. Epp. 78, 28 'unus dies hominum
eruditorum plus patet quam imperitis
longissima aetas'; Philo, Quis rer. diu.
her. p. 522 A μίαν γὰρ ἡμέραν ὑγιεινῶς
εἶπε προφήτης ἀνὴρ βούλεσθαι βιῶναι μετ'
ἀρετῆς ἢ μυρία ἔτη ἐν σκιᾷ τοῦ θανάτου,
σκιὰν τὸν φαῦλον αἰνιττόμενος βίον: add to
these reff. Plut. Cons. ad Apoll. 17 p. 428
οὐχ ὁ μακρότατος βίος ἄριστος ἀλλ' ὁ σπου-
δαιότατος. The passage quoted by Mo.
from Julian's letter to Oreibasios (ep. 17,
p. 498, 4 Hertl.), ἄμεινον γὰρ ὀλίγον
ὀρθῶς ἢ πολὺν κακῶς πρᾶξαι χρόνον, is not
parallel (cf. *Philol.* LXII pp. 586 ff.).
  The Stoics held that the happiness
produced by virtue was so great that no
prolongation could make it greater ; cf.
Fin. iii 14, 46 'Stoicis non uidetur opta-
bilior nec magis expetenda beata uita si
sit longa quam si breuis,' and the reff.
given in Zeller, *Stoics, etc.* p. 225 n. 1.
A similar view was held by Epicurus
ὁ ἄπειρος χρόνος ἴσην ἔχει τὴν ἡδονὴν καὶ ὁ
πεπερασμένος, Diog. Laert. x 145 ; Fin. i
19, 63. Later sophistic writers sometimes
contrast the happiness of a moment's
pleasurable experience with the happiness
supposed to attach to immortality as such,
e.g. Charit. Aphr. vi 7, 12 οὐδὲ ἀθανασίαν
προυτίμησεν ἂν ἡμέρας μιᾶς τῆς μετὰ Χαιρέου.
  §6. ac...quidem: a formula of transition, ii 2, 4 n.; iii 13, 28 n.
  proinde ac: i 36, 86 n.; Draeger,
Synt. der Lat. Spr. II § 315, 13 (6).

de hominum est uita merita laudetur, ut a plerisque neglecta
a multis etiam uituperetur. uituperare quisquam uitae parentem
20 et hoc parricidio se inquinare audet et tam impie ingratus esse,
ut eam accuset quam uereri deberet, etiamsi minus percipere
potuisset? sed, ut opinor, hic error et haec indoctorum animis
offusa caligo est, quod tam longe retro respicere non possunt nec
eos a quibus uita hominum instructa primis sit fuisse philosophos
25 arbitrantur.

III. 7. Quam rem antiquissimam cum uideamus, nomen
tamen esse confitemur recens. nam sapientiam quidem ipsam
quis negare potest non modo re esse antiquam, uerum etiam
nomine? quae diuinarum humanarumque rerum, tum initiorum
5 causarumque cuiusque rei cognitione hoc pulcherrimum nomen

18. neglecta G.   neglẹta V.   neclecta R K.   20. parricidio R P G S E.
paricidio R *atr. nigriore superscr.*   paricidio V. ‖ impie R V G K. *ante* impie
habet V *ras. duarum fere litt.*   24. primis sit V B 2 K 1 2 E 2 W 2 Gr.
primiss& R *eod. atr. superscr.*   primi sit G.   primị sit P.   primum sit R 17
B 1 W 1 J O 1.   primo sit B 3 E 1 M 2 Π O 2 3.   primitus sit S M 1.
prius sit R 6.   i primis sit R 7.   primo instructa sit D C.
III. § 7, 1. antiquissimam R V P G.   antiquissimạ̄ș K *atr. nigriore corr.*
4. nomineque G. ‖ *uerba* rerum...causarumque *in marg. habet* G *alt. man. adscr.*
5. cuiusque rei R 2 6 7 10 16 P B 1–3 E 1 2 M 1 2 D C Π O 1 3.   cuius rei
V *ead. man.* cuiusque W 1 rei *om.*   cuius rei R 1 17 K 2 W 2.   cuiu rei G
alt. man. superscr. cuius reg K 1.   rei cuiusque O 2 7. ‖ pulcherrimum R G B K.

parentem, 'mother,' as is shown by
eam below. For this, the original, meaning of *parens,* cf. Phil. ii 20, 49 'aude
dicere te prius ad parentem tuam uenisse
quam ad me'; Catullus lxii 28; Ciris
68; Consol. ad Liuiam 81; Tac. Ann.
xiii 13.

caligo: a metaphor from the darkness
which sometimes swims before the eyes
as the result of nervousness; the phrase
is used literally in Liv. xxvi 45, 3 'quidam
stantibus scalis cum altitudo caliginem
oculis offudisset, ad terram delati sunt';
the same metaphor is found in Fin. v 16,
43; Tac. H. ii 80 'tantae altitudinis
obfusam oculis caliginem disiecit'; cf.
also Plaut. Mil. Gl. 405 'nunc demum
experior mi ob oculos caliginem obsti-
tisse'; Plat. Soph. 264 C καὶ τοῦθ' ἡμῶν
ἀπορουμένων ἔτι μείζων κατεχύθη σκοτο-
δινία; Theaet. 155 C ἐνίοτε ὡς ἀληθῶς
βλέπων εἰς αὐτὰ σκοτοδινιῶ.
Cic. here probably intends *longe retro
respicere* to convey the idea of looking
back after having mounted to a considerable height rather than after having
advanced a considerable distance.

III. § 7. antiquissimam: according
to Diog. Laert. (prooem. § 1) τὸ τῆς φιλοσοφίας ἔργον ἔνιοί φασιν ἀπὸ βαρβάρων
ἄρξαι...; § 3 λανθάνουσι δ' αὐτοὺς τὰ τῶν
Ἑλλήνων κατορθώματα, ἀφ' ὧν μὴ ὅτι γε
φιλοσοφία ἀλλὰ καὶ γένος ἀνθρώπων ἦρξε,
βαρβάροις προσάπτοντες. But Cic. would
hold that the philosophy of which he is
speaking here arose independently wher-
ever men became civilized.
nomen: the word σοφίη occurs once in
Homer (Il. xv 412); the word σοφός
occurs first in Archilochus (*frg.* 45); the
earliest use of the word φιλοσοφεῖν is in
Herod. i 30, where it is applied to Solon.
In Latin the word was borrowed as early
as the time of Ennius, 'sophiam, sapientia quae perhibetur' (Ann. vii 218 ed.
Vahl., acc. to the certain emendation of
Scaliger), and it occurs in Afranius' Sella
(Ribb. *Scaen. Rom. p. fragm.* II² p. 202)
and in the fabulae Atellanae (*id. ib.*
p. 274); cf. Sen. Epp. 89, 6.
quae...cognitione: for this definition
of *sapientia* cf. iv 26, 57 n.
tum, 'as well as,' cf. Phil. iii 3, 7
'ueteranorumque, fortissimorum uirorum,

apud antiquos adsequebatur. itaque et illos septem qui a Graecis σοφοί, sapientes a nostris et habebantur et nominabantur, et multis ante saeculis Lycurgum, cuius temporibus Homerus etiam fuisse ante hanc urbem conditam traditur, et iam heroicis aetati-
10 bus Ulixem et Nestorem accepimus et fuisse et habitos esse

6. adsequebatur R V G K E.   assequebatur B S.   7. et habebantur
R 2 6 7 10 17   V P   B 1–3   E 1 2   W 1 2   M 2   Π   O 1–3 7.   habebantur
D C et *om.*   et habeantur R K.   et et habeantur G.   8. saeculis R G K.

seculis S E.   ‖   lygurgum R V G.   lygilu̧rgum K *eod. atr.*   ligurgum B E. ‖
etiam R V P G   B 1 2   K 1   S D J.   ēt W 1.   2̄ W 2.   et M 1.
10. ulixem R P   B 1–3   K 1   S   E 2   W 2   M 1 2   D J   O 1 3.   ulixem G
i *ex correct. alt. man.*   uxē E 1.   ulyxem V.   ‖   nestorem R V G S J.

nestora E 1.   ‖   fuisse & R G K.   fuisse V *atr. ant. superscr.*

tum legionis Martiae quartaeque mirabilis consensus.'

septem. The list of the Seven Wise Men as given by Plato (Protag. p. 343 A) is Thales of Miletus, Pittakos of Mytilene, Bias of Priene, Solon the Athenian, Kleoboulos of Lindus, Myson ὁ Χηνεύς and Chilon of Sparta. Other authorities differ both as to the number of the Wise Men and as to their names; cf. Grote, *Hist. of Greece* iii pp. 316 ff.

The claims of these men to the title of σοφοί or *sapientes* would have been disputed by the strict Stoics, their wisdom being merely φρόνησις, the 'rerum expetendarum fugiendarumque scientia,' not σοφία, the 'rerum diuinarum et humanarum scientia' (Off. i 43, 153), which comprised the virtues. Cicero himself in other passages takes the strict view with regard to their claims, e.g. Off. iii 4, 16 'nec ii qui sapientes sunt habiti et nominati, M. Cato et C. Laelius, sapientes fuerunt, ne illi quidem septem, sed ex meliorum officiorum frequentia similitudinem quandam gerebant speciemque sapientium'; Lael. 2, 7. In the present passage as in Rep. i 7, 12 they seem to be mentioned mainly for their political activities; and it was political virtue only which Dicaearchus admitted them to have, Diog. Laert. i 1, 14 Δικαίαρχος οὔτε σοφοὺς οὔτε φιλοσόφους φησὶν αὐτοὺς γεγονέναι, συνετοὺς δέ τινας καὶ νομοθετικούς.

saeculis, 'generations,' γενεαῖς; cf. the Panegyricus Messallae ll. 50, 112, where Nestor's three γενεαὶ μερόπων ἀνθρώπων are referred to as 'terna saecula.' Censorinus (de die nat. c. 17 pp. 30 ff. ed. Hultsch) defines *saeculum* as 'spatium uitae humanae longissimum partu et morte definitum,' or more accurately, according to the 'rituales Etruscorum libri, in quis scriptum esse fertur

initia sic poni saeculorum, quo die urbes atque ciuitates constituerentur, de his qui eo die nati essent eum qui diutissime uixisset die mortis suae primi saeculi modulum finire, eoque die qui essent reliqui in ciuitate, de his rursum eius mortem, qui longissimam egisset aetatem, finem esse saeculi secundi.' The Roman authorities preferred, for practical purposes, the round number of one hundred years (cf. Kukula, *Römische Säkularpoesie*, pp. 2 ff.).

Lycurgum: the claims of Lycurgus were not admitted by the Stoic authorities, any more than those of the Seven; Cleisthenes, Lycurgus and Solon were all φαῦλοι καὶ ἀνόητοι (Plut. de St. rep. 3 p. 1033 F) and neither their laws nor those of the Twelve Tables were anything more than *scripta* (Ac. ii 44, 136).

Homerus: Dav. in a learned note has collected the ancient authorities for the dates of Homer and Lycurgus, e.g. Plut. Lyc. i 4; Strab. x p. 482 c; Clem. Alex. Strom. i p. 322, who thinks Lycurgus and Solon were μακρῷ νεώτεροι than Homer and Hesiod.

A slightly different chronology is adopted by Cic. in Rep. ii 10, 18 'Homerum autem, *qui minimum dicunt*, Lycurgi aetati triginta annis anteponunt fere. ex quo intellegi potest permultis annis ante Homerum fuisse quam Romulum.'

Modern criticism, holding it doubtful whether such a person as Lycurgus ever existed (cf. Gilbert, *Greek Constitutional Antiq.* p. 15 and authorities quoted there), and being equally doubtful with regard to Homer, leaves the question to one side.

Ulixem et Nestorem: πολύμητις is one of the Homeric epithets for Ulysses, and Nestor's wise counsel was as proverbial as his garrulity; cf. ii 21, 48, where Ulysses is called 'sapientissimus Graeciae.'

sapientis. **8.** nec uero Atlans sustinere caelum nec Prometheus adfixus Caucaso nec stellatus Cepheus cum uxore, genero, filia traderetur, nisi caelestium diuina cognitio nomen eorum ad errorem fabulae traduxisset. a quibus ducti deinceps omnes qui 15 in rerum contemplatione studia ponebant sapientes et habebantur et nominabantur, idque eorum nomen usque ad Pythagorae manauit aetatem, quem, ut scribit auditor Platonis Ponticus Heraclides, uir doctus in primis, Phliuntem ferunt uenisse,

i
11. sapientis R 2 V G B 1 K E.   sapientes R *eod. atr.*   sapientes B 2 S.
§ 8. Atlans K 1.   at}{lans R *eod. atr.*   athlans V B 2 D.   athalans G
in athlans *alt. man. mut.*   atlant̃ E 1.   athlas P B 1 3 K 2 S E 2 L 5
W 1 2 M 1 2 J O 1 3.   athalas O 7.   12. adfixus R V G K E.   affixus B S.
14. traduxisset B 3 W 1 2 M 1 2 J O 1-3.   traduxisset V.   traduxissent
n
B 1.   traduxisset G *ead. man.*   traduxissēt O 7.   traduxissent R K 1 S
E 1 2 D C II. ‖ ducti R V P G B 1-3 K 1 S E 1 W 2 M 1 2 D C II J
O 1 3.   15. sapientes R V P G K.   16. pythagorẹ W 1.   pytagorẹ V.
phitagore G E 1.   18. phliuntem R 6.   philuntem R V G B 1 K 1 E 1 2
D C O 1 3.   philontem K 2 S W 2 M 1 2 J O 2.   philunthem R 17.
philnutē II.   phylontē W 1 O 7.   philătem B 3.   philumem B 2.
silontem R 7.

Atlans: in Homer, Atlas appears to be a divinity of the sea ὅς τε θαλάσσης | πάσης βένθεα οἶδεν (Od. i 52); according to Professor T. D. Seymour, *Life in the Homeric Age*, p. 441 'he does not appear to be a mountain; the columns which support both earth and heaven appear to be the sea itself.' In Hesiod, Theog. 517 ff., 746 ff., he is a giant supporting the heaven upon his head and hands, the schol. at the latter passage drawing attention to the discrepancy between Hom. and Hesiod; cf. Aesch. P.V. 348. In Ovid, Met. iv. 626, he is identified with the African Mt. Atlas, into which he is said to have been metamorphosed; so Virg. Aen. iv 247, where see Servius' note. The view that he was an astronomer, about whose personality myths were formed, is not put forward earlier than Cicero's time (Hoffter quoted by Mo.), and is probably due to the combined influence of Euhemerus and the Stoic allegorizing doctrines. It appears in Virgil, Aen. i 741; Diod. Sic. iii 60; cf. Paus. ix 20, 3.

There is a long astronomical explanation of the myth in the Hesiodic Ἀλληγόριαι p. 475 (Gaisford, *Poetae Minores Gr.* ii 579 sq.) in which Atlas is regarded as an allegory for ἡ τοῦ παντὸς περιφορὰ ἐπὶ τῷ ἄξονι; Cornutus, Theol. Gr. c. 26 (p. 48, 9 ed. Lang), regards Atlas as a synonym for ὁ ὅλος κόσμος.

Prometheus: cf. Hesiod, Theog. 251 ff.; Aesch. (P.V. 457, 484) represents Prometheus as having taught mankind astronomy and μαντική. Cornutus, Theol. Gr. c. 18 (p. 31, 19 ed. Lang), allegorizes him in the Stoic fashion into ἡ προμήθεια τῆς ἐν τοῖς ὅλοις ψυχῆς.

stellatus: here in the sense of καταστερισθείς, Milton's 'starr'd' (*Il Penseroso* 19), cf. Manilius, Astron. i 341; for the usual meaning cf. Virg. Aen. iv 261 'stellatus iaspide fulua | ensis.'

Cepheus, with his wife Cassiopeia, his daughter Andromeda, and their son-in-law Perseus, were transformed into stars; Cassiopeia had incurred the wrath of Juppiter Ammon and the nymphs by boasting of her beauty (Ovid, Met. iv 607; Cic. Aratea 442 ff.; Manil. Astr. i 350 ff.).

traduxisset: for *traducere* cf. iii 17, 37 where, as here, it bears the sense of bringing into another sphere of ideas or thought.

ducti, 'descended': cf. *ducere genus, progeniem* (Virg. Aen. v. 568; vi 835; i 19).

ad Pythagorae...aetatem: Pythagoras' life may be set between 572 B.C. and 500 B.C.; v. R. and P. § 54.

Heraclides: in his treatise περὶ τῆς ἄπνου (Diog. Laert. prooem. 12). Heraclides was a pupil of Speusippus ἀλλὰ καὶ τῶν Πυθαγορείων διήκουσε καὶ τὰ Πλά-

eumque cum Leonte, principe Phliasiorum, docte et copiose
20 disseruisse quaedam; cuius ingenium et eloquentiam cum admiratus esset Leon, quaesiuisse ex eo, qua maxime arte confideret;
at illum artem quidem se scire nullam, sed esse philosophum.
admiratum Leontem nouitatem nominis quaesiuisse quinam
essent philosophi et quid inter eos et reliquos interesset;
25 **9.** Pythagoram autem respondisse similem sibi uideri uitam
hominum et mercatum eum qui haberetur maximo ludorum

19. phliasiorum R K1 M2 O1.   philiasiorum G *at* i *ante* l *exp. alt. man.*
philiasiorum V B13 E2 C O2.   phliasicorum J.   philasiorum M1.
philiasorum O3.   phyliasiorum O7.   phorum B2.   20. admiratus R V P G.
ammiratus B.   21. maxime R V B K S.   maximae G a *ante* e *exp. alt. man.*
23. admiratum R K.   atmiratum G.   ammiratum B.   24. essent G K.
n
ess& R *et* V *atr. ant. suppl.*
§ **9,** 25. pythagoram R V G K.   phytagorā B.   Phitagorā E1. ‖ uitam W1.
uitā P B D.   uitā V *at linea alt. man. supraduct.*   uita R G K.
26. maxumo R V G B K.   maximo S.

τωνος ἐζηλώκει; the Athenians called him
Πομπικός because ἐσθῆτί τε μαλακῇ ἐχρῆτο
καὶ ὑπέρογκος ἦν τὸ σῶμα (Diog. Laert. v
6, 1—3). For the inversion of the name
and the adjective cf. 32, 90 'Scythes
Anacharsis'; i 24, 59 'Scepsius Metrodorus'; Ac. ii 45, 137 'Stoicus Diogenes'
with Reid's n.

Phliuntem: there was a difference of
opinion as to the place where this conversation took place; some authorities
said Sicyon (Diog. Laert. prooem. 12);
Sosicrates (*id.* viii 1, 8) agreed with
Heracleides.

eumque: for the so-called transition
from the relative to the demonstrative cf.
ii 25, 61 n. Dav. denied the possibility
of this transition here, reading *uenisse
cumque Leonte.* It must be admitted that
none of the passages adduced in support
of the reading by Küh. on either edd. (*ad
loc.*) or Wopkens (*op. cit.* p. 144) is really
parallel; they merely prove (what Dav.
would not have denied) that it is common
in Latin instead of repeating a relative
with an alteration of the case either to
omit it or to substitute a demonstrative, as
in 13, 38; iii 8, 16, etc.; in the present
passage a demonstrative in the same case
as the relative is needlessly inserted, as in
Plaut. Capt. 555 'quibus insputari saluti
fuit atque is profuit'; it is, of course,
possible that *eumque* is a corruption for
(e.g.) *tumque* or *diuque.*

illum: sc. *respondisse* to be supplied
κατ' ἀντίθεσιν from *quaesiuisse.* The
story is told in Diog. Laert. viii 1, 6
Σωσικράτης δ' ἐν Διαδοχαῖς φησιν αὐτὸν
ἐρωτηθέντα ὑπὸ Λέοντος τοῦ τῶν Φλιασίων

τυράννου τίς εἴη, φιλόσοφος, εἰπεῖν· καὶ
τὸν βίον ἐοικέναι πανηγύρει· ὡς οὖν εἰς
ταύτην οἱ μὲν ἀγωνισόμενοι, οἱ δὲ κατ'
ἐμπορίαν, οἱ δέ γε βέλτιστοι ἔρχονται θεαταί,
οὕτως ἐν τῷ βίῳ οἱ μὲν ἀνδραποδώδεις, ἔφη,
φύονται δόξης καὶ πλεονεξίας θηραταί, οἱ δὲ
φιλόσοφοι τῆς ἀληθείας.

admiratum, 'astonished at,' a less
common meaning of the word; cf. Cic.
Att. vi 9, 1 'admiratus sum, ut uidi
obsignatam epistulam, breuitatem eius.'

nouitatem nominis, 'the novel name,'
which, according to the tradition, was
of Pythagoras' invention; Diog. Laert.
prooem. 12 φιλοσοφίαν δὲ πρῶτος ὠνόμασε
Πυθαγόρας καὶ ἑαυτὸν φιλόσοφον; Iamblich.
uita Pyth. viii 44.

§ 9. similem...mercatum: cf. Iambl.
uita Pyth. xii 58 ἐοικέναι γὰρ ἔφη τὴν εἰς
τὸν βίον τῶν ἀνθρώπων πάροδον τῷ ἐπὶ τὰς
πανηγύρεις ἀπαντῶντι ὁμίλῳ· ὡς γὰρ
ἐκεῖσε παντοδαποὶ φοιτῶντας ἄνθρωποι
ἄλλος κατ' ἄλλου χρείαν ἀφικνεῖται, ὁ μὲν
χρηματισμοῦ καὶ κέρδους χάριν ἀπεμπολῆσαι
τὸν φόρτον ἐπειγόμενος, ὁ δὲ δόξης ἕνεκα
ἐπιδειξόμενος ἥκει τὴν ῥώμην τοῦ σώματος·
ἔστι δὲ καὶ τρίτον εἶδος καὶ τό γε ἐλευθεριώ-
τατον, συναλιζόμενον τόπων θέας ἕνεκα καὶ
δημιουργημάτων καλῶν καὶ ἀρετῆς ἔργων
καὶ λόγων, ὧν αἱ ἐπιδείξεις εἰώθεσαν ἐν ταῖς
πανηγύρεσι γίνεσθαι· οὕτω δὴ κἂν τῷ βίῳ
παντοδαποὺς ἀνθρώπους ταῖς σπουδαῖς εἰς
ταὐτὸ συναθροίζεσθαι· τοὺς μὲν γὰρ χρημάτων καὶ τρυφῆς αἱρεῖ πόθος, τοὺς δὲ ἀρχῆς
καὶ ἡγεμονίας ἵμερος φιλονεικίαι τε δοξο-
μανεῖς κατέχουσιν· εἰλικρινέστατον δὲ εἶναι
τοῦτον ἀνθρώπου τρόπον, τὸν ἀποδεξάμενον
τὴν τῶν καλλίστων θεωρίαν, ὃν καὶ προσ-
ονομάζειν φιλόσοφον. For the sentiment,

apparatu totius Graeciae celebritate; nam ut illic alii corporibus
exercitatis gloriam et nobilitatem coronae peterent, alii emendi
aut uendendi quaestu et lucro ducerentur, esset autem quoddam
30 genus eorum, idque uel maxime ingenuum, qui nec plausum nec
lucrum quaererent, sed uisendi causa uenirent studioseque per-
spicerent quid ageretur et quo modo, item nos quasi in mercatus
quandam celebritatem ex urbe aliqua sic in hanc uitam ex alia
uita et natura profectos alios gloriae seruire, alios pecuniae; raros
35 esse quosdam, qui ceteris omnibus pro nihilo habitis rerum naturam studiose intuerentur; hos se appellare sapientiae studiosos
(id est enim philosophos); et ut illic liberalissimum esset spectare
nihil sibi adquirentem, sic in uita longe omnibus studiis contem-
plationem rerum cognitionemque praestare.

27. apparatu R V G B K S E. ‖ graeciae G.   gra&iae R K.   grecę E. ‖
illic S W 1 O 1.   illi W 2.   illi R V G B K E O 7.   30. maxime
R V B K S E.   maxume G.   31. luchrum G. ‖ studioseque R V P G K.
studioque B *eod. ut uid. atr.*   32. item R V G B 3 K 1 2 S E 2 W 2 M 1 2
C II O 3.   itē P B 1 E 1 D J O 1 2 7.   ite B 2.   ita W 1. ‖
mercatus R 2 10 G.   maercatus R.   mercatos K.   mercatum W 1 O 3.
meatu R 16.   33. quandam R V G B 1 2 K 1 M 1.   quamdam D C.
quādā E 1.   quadam R 6 7 17 K 2 S W 1 2 M 2 II J O 1-3 7.   quadā
R 2 10.   q̃dā E 2.   q̃&̃ R 1 6. ‖ celebritatem M 1 C.   celebritatē V B
E 1 D.   celebritate R 1 2 6 7 10 16 17 P G B 23 K 2 S E 2 W 1 2 M 2
II J O 1-3 7.   caelebritate K 1.   37. enim R 1 7 V G B 13 K 1 E 1
W 1 2 M 2 J O 1-3 7.   enim S *marg.* nomine id enī P *marg.* id est.
enim *om.* B 2 E 2 M 1 D C II. ‖ liberalissimum R V P G B.   liberalissḭmū K.
38. adquirentem R V G B K E.   acquirentem S.   39. cognitionemque R 6
B 3 W 1 2 M 1 2 D C J O 1-3 7.   cogNItionemq; V *eod. atr.* at NI *in ras.*
cogitationemque R 1 7 17 P G B K 1 2 S E 1 2 II. *uerba* rerum cognitione mqu
om. B 2.

which became a commonplace, Dav.
quotes Menander, *frag.* 481 K; Alexis
ap. Athenaeum xi 9 p. 463 d; Dio Chrys.
xxvii p. 287; Arrian, Epict. ii 14, 23;
Synes. de prouid. 128 (col. 1280 Migne);
Sen. Epp. 118, 3.

For **similem...et** : in place of the more
usual *atque (ac)* cf. de leg. agr. ii 17, 46
'simile uero est multa committi et con-
donari omnia'; Fin. ii 7, 21 'dicit
absurde similiter et si dicat.'

mercatum eum qui...celebritate : the
periphrasis is probably intended, not to
provide an equivalent for πανήγυρις, but
to avoid the mention of the particular
Greek festival which Cic. found specified
in his authority for the story.

corporibus exercitatis : abl. instr. ' by
their athletic frames.'

emendi : the religious festivals in Greece
gave an opportunity for the holding of

annual fairs; cf. Becker, *Charicles* (E.T.)
p. 292 and the authorities quoted there.

uisendi : cf. i 19, 44 n.

item, 'so' for the more usual *ita*; cf.
Or. 60, 202 'non item in oratione ut in
uersu'; II Verr. iv 9 21 'item ut prae-
dones solent.'

quasi...sic: Mo. compares Cato M.
19, 71 'et quasi poma ex arboribus, cruda
si sunt, uix euelluntur, si matura et cocta,
decidunt, sic uitam adulescentibus uis
aufert'; Lael. 17, 63.

ex alia uita et natura, 'another life
and mode of existence,' a reference to
Pythagoras' doctrine of μετεμψύχωσις.

id est enim philosophos, a paren-
thetical comment of Cicero's: for *id est*
explanatory of the following, instead of,
as is more usual, the preceding, word
cf. the exx. quoted in iii 27, 65 n.

H.   14

IV. 10. Nec uero Pythagoras nominis solum inuentor, sed rerum etiam ipsarum amplificator fuit. qui cum post hunc Phliasium sermonem in Italiam uenisset, exornauit eam Graeciam quae magna dicta est et priuatim et publice praestantissimis et 5 institutis et artibus. cuius de disciplina aliud tempus fuerit fortasse dicendi. sed ab antiqua philosophia usque ad Socraten, qui Archelaum, Anaxagorae discipulum, audierat, numeri motusque tractabantur, et unde omnia orerentur quoue reciderent, studioseque ab iis siderum magnitudines, interualla, cursus anquirebantur

IV. § 10, 1. pythagoras R V G K W 1.   pytagoras B 1.   phitagoras E 1.
2. amplicator G. ‖ phliasium R V G B 3 K.   philiasium B 1 2 E 1 W 1.
phyliasium S.   3. sermonem R.   4. prae(pre)stantissumis R G K.
p̄stantissumis V *at* su *in ras. et spatio inter* u *et* m *relicto.*   p̄stantissummis B.

p'stantiſimis P.   6. socraten B 1.   socratem R V G K S W 1 O 1 3.
8. orerentur R V G.   orirentur R 6 7 17 P B 1–3 K 2 S E 1 2 W 2 M 1 2

D C J O 1–3 7.   orientur Π.   orarentur K 1.   exorirentur W 1. ‖

recederent V *atr. ant. superscr.*   ʼrecederent R 1 6 7 10 16 17 P G B 1 3 K 1 2
S E 1–3 L 2–6 W 1 2 M 1 2 D C Π J O 1–3 7.   redēt B 2.   9. ab iis
O 3 S *at fuerat* his.   ab hiis D.   ab his R V P G B 1 2 K E 1 W 2 M 1
J O 1 7. ‖ siderum R 1 2 10 16 V G.   syderum P B. ‖ currus G r *in* s
alt. man. corr. ‖ anquirebantur R V P B K E.   antiquirebantur G.

inquirebantur E 2 W 1 2 M 2 D J O 2 3 7.   ac|quirebantur S.   in querebantur

M 1.   querebantur B 2.   requirebantur O 1.

IV. § 10. **rerum…amplificator**, ' not merely devised a name for philosophy, but also extended its scope,' i.e. by the inclusion of politics and psychology ; cf. the fragment of Herakleitos quoted in Diog. Laert. viii 1, 6 Πυθαγόρης Μνησάρχου ἱστορίην (i.e. philosophical enquiries) ἤσκησεν ἀνθρώπων μάλιστα πάντων.
in Italiam : to Croton, Diog. Laert. viii 1, 3. The date of his arrival is given by Cicero (Rep. ii 15, 28) as the fourth year of Tarquinius Superbus. On Pythagoras and his work in Italy see Burnet, *Early Greek Phil.* pp. 96 ff.
quae magna dicta est : cf. i 16, 38 n.
fuerit : fut. perf. used in postponing the consideration of a question ; cf. Roby, *Gr.* § 1485. Hei. conjectures that Cic. intended to devote a book to Pythagoreanism to which his translation of the Timaeus was a preliminary.
Archelaum : cf. Diog. Laert. ii 4, 16 οὗτος πρῶτος ἐκ τῆς Ἰωνίας τὴν φυσικὴν φιλοσοφίαν μετήγαγεν Ἀθήναζε καὶ ἐκλήθη φυσικός, παρὸ καὶ ἔληξεν ἐν αὐτῷ ἡ φυσικὴ φιλοσοφία, Σωκράτους τὴν ἠθικὴν εἰσαγαγόντος· ἔοικε δὲ καὶ οὗτος ἅψασθαι τῆς

ἠθικῆς· καὶ γὰρ περὶ νόμων πεφιλοσόφηκε καὶ καλῶν καὶ δικαίων· παρ' οὗ λαβὼν Σωκράτης τῷ αὐξῆσαι αὐτὸς εὑρεῖν ὑπελήφθη. Clem. Alex. Strom. i. 301 A (quoted by FAW) τοῦτον (i.e. Anaxagoras) διαδέχεται Ἀρχέλαος, οὗ Σωκράτης διήκουσεν· " ἐκ δ' ἄρα τῶν ἀπέκλινε λαόξοος ἐννομολέσχης | Ἑλλήνων ἐπαοιδός," ὁ Τίμων φησὶν ἐν τοῖς Σίλλοις, διὰ τὸ ἀποκεκλικέναι ἀπὸ τῶν φυσικῶν ἐπὶ τὰ ἠθικά. According to Gomperz (*Gk Thinkers* i 378) A. was employed ' in building a serviceable bridge between the doctrines of Anaxagoras and Anaximenes.'
numeri motusque, 'mathematics and the theories of motion'; cf. Fin. v 29, 87 ' cur Plato Aegyptum peragrauit ut a sacerdotibus barbaris numeros et caelestia acciperet?'; *ib.* i 21, 72 'aut se, ut Plato, in musicis, geometria, numeris, astris contereret.' The following words refer to the earlier physicists, such as Thales, who sought for a universal principle (e.g. air) out of which the universe arose and into which all things were resolved (*reciderent*) : in support of *recidere* against the MSS. Bentley quotes N.D. ii 26, 66; Lucr. i 857; v 280.

10 et cuncta caelestia. Socrates autem primus philosophiam deuocauit e caelo et in urbibus conlocauit et in domus etiam introduxit
et coëgit de uita et moribus rebusque bonis et malis quaerere.
11. cuius multiplex ratio disputandi rerumque uarietas et ingenii
magnitudo Platonis memoria et litteris consecrata plura genera
15 effecit dissentientium philosophorum, e quibus nos id potissimum
consecuti sumus quo Socraten usum arbitrabamur, ut nostram
ipsi sententiam tegeremus, errore alios leuaremus et in omni disputatione quid esset simillimum ueri quaereremus. quem morem
cum Carneades acutissime copiosissimeque tenuisset, fecimus et
20 alias saepe et nuper in Tusculano ut ad eam consuetudinem
disputaremus. et quadridui quidem sermonem superioribus ad

10. deuocauit R 17   V P G   B 1-3   K 1   S   E 1 2   W 1   M 1 2   D C Π
O 2 3 7.   euocauit W 2   J   O 1.   11. e caelo R 7   V G   W 1 2   M 1   O 1 7.
ex caelo B 2.   a caelo S.   a caelo P B 1 3   E 1 2   M 2   D C   O 3. ‖
conlocauit R V G K. ˙ collocauit B 1 2   S   E 1   W 1.   ‖   domus R V P G   K 1
S E 1.   domos R 6 7   B 1-3   E 2   W 1 2   M 1 2   D C Π J   O 1 2 7.
domibus O 3 Gr.
§ 11, 13. ïngenii R V G B K S E.   15. effecit R 7   K 2   E 1-3   M 1 2
D C   O 3 ed. H.   efficit B 3.   efficit R 1 6 1 7   V G   B 1 2   K 1   W 1 2   O 1 7.
effic̄ V P.   fecit O 2.   ‖ dissentientium G ten *in* tien *alt. man. corr.*   ‖   potissimum
R V P G B K.   16. consecuti R 1 2 7 10 17   P G   B 1-3   K 1   S   E 1   W 2
M 1   D C J   O 1 7 Gr.   consequuti R 16   K 2   E 2   Π   O 3.   consectati R 6.
*ₜₒₚ*secuti V *atr. ant. mut.*   consecuti M 2.   secuti W 1.   ‖   socratem
R V P G K S.   socratē B 1 2   E 1   W 2   Π J.   ‖   arbitrabamur R P G B K S
E 2   Π   O 7.   arbitra̦bamur V *atr. ant.*   arbitramur R 6 7 17   B 2 3   E 3
L 5   W 1 2   M 1 2   D C J   O 1-3 ed. H.   ʳΧabitam̄ E 1.   18. simillimum
R V G B K.   ‖   quaeremus G *in marg.* re *ead. manu.*   ‖   mouerem G *in* morem
alt. man. mut.   19. acutissime copiosissimeque R V G B K.   20. ut ad eam
V P G B K.   ut ad ea*ᵈᵉ*m R.   21. quadridui R V G K.   quadridui P
al. atr. superscr.   qua̦tridui B 2.   quatridui B 1 3   S   W 1 2   Π J   O 1 2 7.
*ⁱ*quatriduo E 1.   quatriduo C.

Socrates: cf. Ac. i 4, 15 'S. mihi
uidetur, id quod constat inter omnis,
primus a rebus occultis et ab ipsa natura
inuolutis, in quibus omnes ante eum
philosophi occupati fuerunt, auocauisse
philosophiam et ad uitam communem
adduxisse,' with Reid's note there.
e caelo: Sff.'s correction *a caelo* though
apparently supported by Ac. i 4, 15,
quoted above, is unnecessary and misses
the point. Cicero means to say that
Socrates made philosophy a denizen of
earth, while before she had been a denizen of heaven. Sff.'s objections against
the use of *e* here are in reality objections
against Cicero's judgment in the use of
metaphors.
§ 11. **multiplex ... uarietas,** 'many-
sided genius for argument and wide range

of topics,' referring to the perpetually
recurring unexpected turns of the Socratic
dialogue. The word *multiplex* may be
used in either a good or a bad sense ; see
Reid's n. to Ac. i 4, 17.
consecrata, 'enshrined in the records
of literature.' Billerbeck compares ad
Qu. Fr. i 1, 44 'non neglegeres, praesertim cum amplissimis monumentis con-
secrare uoluisses memoriam nominis tui.'
genera, 'schools,' αἱρέσεις, the Mega-
rians, Academicians, Peripatetics, Cynics,
etc.
arbitrabamur: cf. ii 18, 43 n. on
excellebat.
Carneades, a native of Cyrene, succeeded Lacydes as head of the New
Academy (Diog. Laert. iv 9, 62). His
eloquence and dialectical powers were

te perscriptum libris misimus, quinto autem die cum eodem in loco consedissemus, sic est propositum de quo disputaremus:

V. **12.** Non mihi uidetur ad beate uiuendum satis posse uirtutem.

At hercule Bruto meo uidetur, cuius ego iudicium, pace tua dixerim, longe antepono tuo.

5 Non dubito, nec id nunc agitur, tu illum quantum ames, sed hoc, quod mihi dixi uideri, quale sit, de quo a te disputari uolo.

Nempe negas ad beate uiuendum satis posse uirtutem?

Prorsus nego.

Quid? ad recte, honeste, laudabiliter, postremo ad bene 10 uiuendum satisne est praesidi in uirtute?

Certe satis.

Potes igitur aut, qui male uiuat, non eum miserum dicere aut, quem bene fateare, eum negare beate uiuere?

Quidni possim? nam etiam in tormentis recte, honeste, lauda-15 biliter et ob eam rem bene uiui potest, dum modo intellegas, quid

---

22. libri mi̱s̱simus G *alt. man. corr.* ‖ eodem in loco R 1 6 7 V P G B 1–3 K 1 S E 2 3 L 5 W 1 2 M 1 2 J O 1 2. in eodem loco R 17 Π O 7. eodem loco *om.* in E 1 D C O 3. V. §12. *Litteras* A *et* M *habent* W 1 O 3: M *et* D *habent* W 2 D. Dis (Di) *et* M *habet* O 1: *non habent* R V G K E 1 O 7. 1. at R G B 1 2 K. ad V *atr. uiridi superscr.* 5. sed hoc R 6 W 1 M 1. sed de hoc R 1 17 V P G B 1–3 K 1 2 S E 1–3 L 5 W 2 M 2 D C Π J O 1–3 7 *om.* R 7. 6. de quo R V P G B 1 2 K 2 S E 1 2 W 2 M 1 2 D C Π J O 1 2 7. de quo B 3. de eo K 1 *om.* R 7 W 1. 10. presidi R G. p̄sidi E 1. pre̱sidi V *eod. atr. fort.* praesidii *uel* pre̱s. *uel* pres. *uel* p̄sidii P B 1–3 K 1 2 S E 2 W 1 2 M 1 2 J O 1–3 7 *om.* D. 14. laudabiliter V. 15. intellegas R V G B K. intelligas S E.

---

famous (Or. i 11, 45; Ac. ii 45, 139). His embassy to Rome in 155 B.C. along with Diogenes and Critolaus is well known.

V. § 12. On A and M to distinguish the interlocutors in Cicero's dialogues see an article by Pohlenz in *Hermes* LXIV pp. 627 ff. He holds that A and M were originally Δ and M standing for *Discipulus* and *Magister* and that they were first used in a translation of an exegetical treatise by Paulus, a Persian of Nisibis, made for African Christians by Junilius Africanus.

uirtutem: for the (unusual) acc. and inf. after *uidetur* cf. 8, 22: it is defended by edd. on the analogy of the Gk construction after δοκεῖ; so after *dicitur* in Fin. iii 18, 60, quoted by Nipperdey in his note on Tac. Ann. i 69.

pace tua dixerim, 'by your leave,' for the formula cf. Legg. iii 12, 29; Off. iii 10, 41; Ov. Tr. v 12, 45.

nec: adversative, 'still,' 'and yet,' as in i 24, 58; and Att. xiv 14, 5 'nos et liberati ab egregiis uiris nec liberi sumus' where as here *neque = neque tamen*.

hoc: sc. *agitur*.

nempe: ironical, as in iii 20, 49; Brut. 3, 14.

postremo = denique, 'in short,' an unusual use: Hei. compares II Verr. iii, 2, 4, where after the mention of avarice, cruelty, lust is added 'omnia postremo quae uindicaris in altero tibi ipsi uehementer fugienda sunt.'

et, 'and accordingly,' summing up the force of the previous adverbs, cf. iii 2, 3 n. on *et inhaerescunt.*

nunc dicam 'bene.' dico enim constanter, grauiter, sapienter, fortiter. **13.** haec etiam in eculeum coiciuntur, quo uita non adspirat
beata.

Quid igitur? solane beata uita, quaeso, relinquitur extra
20 ostium limenque carceris, cum constantia, grauitas, fortitudo,
sapientia reliquaeque uirtutes rapiantur ad tortorem nullumque
recusent nec supplicium nec dolorem?

Tu, si quid es facturus, noua aliqua conquiras oportet; ista
me minime mouent, non solum quia peruulgata sunt, sed multo
25 magis quia, tamquam leuia quaedam uina nihil ualent in aqua,
sic Stoicorum ista magis gustata quam potata delectant. uelut
iste chorus uirtutum in eculeum inpositus imagines constituit
ante oculos cum amplissima dignitate, ut ad eas cursim perrec-

§ 13, 17. eculeum R V P G   B 2   K 1   S   E 1 2   D Π   O 1 3 7.   ẹculeum
B 1   M 1.   equuleum B 3   W 2   M 2   J.   aculeum W 1.   ‖ coiciuntur V P
B 1   K 1   E 1   M 1.   coitiuntur R G.   coniciuntur B 3   M 2   D J   O 7.
9iciuntur B 2.   9niciuntur W 2.   conitiuntur C.   cōniciuntur O 3.
cōijciuntur S *at* j *fort. postea add.*   ‖   adspirat R G.   aspirat V B S.
20. ostium R V   B 1 *alii.*   hostium G S   E 1 2 *alii.*   21. reliquaeque
(reliquẹque, reliqueque) R V P G   B 1-3   K 1 2   S   E 1 2   W 1   M 2   Π J   O 1 3.
                                                                        nec
reliq̄ q3 W 2   O 2 7.   relique q; M 1   C.   relique R 6.   22.   supplicium G
alt. man. superscr.   23. facturas G *as in* us *alt. man. corr.*   24. minime R 1 2
V P G B K.   memini R 10 16.   ‖ peruulgata R V P G K S J.   puulta E 1.
26. stoicorum R G K E.   istoicorum V.   ‖   potata R 1 16   V P G K *alii.*
      ta   h
pota S.   pota R 2 10   B 1 2   E 1.   27. corus V *atr. ant. superscr.*
corus R G K.   ‖   impositus R V G B K S.   inpositus E 1.   28. amplissima
R V G B K.   ‖   cursim R V G   B 3   K   E 2   M 1 2   D J Π   O 3.   cursī W 2
                                                                        im
ex cursū *ras. mut.*   cursum P   B 1 2   S   W 1   C   O 7.   cursū   E 1.
cursụ̄m O 1.   cursin O 2.   ‖ perrecturas G s *exp. alt. man.*

§ 13. haec, 'qualities like these,' i.e.
constantia, grauitas, sapientia, fortitudo,
to be supplied out of the advv. in the preceding sentence.

eculeum: Fin. iv 12, 31; Mil. 21, 57,
an instrument of torture, of the precise
nature of which we have no direct evidence; the sufferer was possibly made to
sit astride upon a sharp ridge of wood
with weights attached to his hands and
feet. See Rich, *Diction. of Rom. and
Gk. Ant. s.v.*

adspirat: 9, 27; p. Quinct. 29, 89;
Sull. 18, 52; II Verr. i 54, 142; edd. note
that the verb is used in Cicero only in
negative sentences, or in questions im-
plying a negative.

Quid igitur, used as in i 25, 61 to
introduce a supposed *reductio ad absurdum*:
so *quid ergo* in iii 32, 78; *quid enim* i 25, 60.

ostium ... carceris, carrying on the
imagery of *in eculeum coiciuntur.*

nullumque, more emphatic than *neque*

ullum, the emphasis being further increased by the repetition of the negative
nec...nec: cf. *nihilque* for *nec quicquam*
in i 49, 118.

facturus, 'if you are to make any im-
pression.'

tamquam with the indicative in the
sense of *ut* is not very common, cf. i
36, 88 n.; iii 10, 23; Quint. Fr. i 1, 46.

in aqua, 'mixed with water.' Cicero
seems to mean that as a connoisseur
judges a wine, not only by its taste, but
by its suitability for mixing with water
and making a sound drink, so a philosopher should judge a proposition not by
its attractiveness in the abstract, but by
the manner in which it works out in
practice.

uelut, 'As, for example,' αὐτίκα; this
use of *uelut* is common in Plautus, v. Brix
and Lorenz on Plaut. Mil. Gl. 25.

chorus uirtutum: for the phrase cf.
Stob. Ecl. Eth. ii p. 268 πᾶς ὁ τῶν ἀρετῶν

tura nec eas beata uita a se desertas passura uideatur; **14** cum
30 autem animum ab ista pictura imaginibusque uirtutum ad rem
ueritatemque traduxeris, hoc nudum relinquitur, possitne quis
beatus esse quam diu torqueatur. quam ob rem hoc nunc quaeramus; uirtutes autem noli uereri ne expostulent et querantur se
a beata uita esse relictas. si enim nulla uirtus prudentia uacat,
35 prudentia ipsa hoc uidet, non omnis bonos esse etiam beatos,
multaque de M. Atilio, Q. Caepione, M'. Aquilio recordatur,
beatamque uitam, si imaginibus potius uti quam rebus ipsis
placet, conantem ire in eculeum retinet ipsa prudentia negatque
ei cum dolore et cruciatu quicquam esse commune.

§ **14,** 31. nudum R 16 7 17 V P G B 1–3 K 1 2 S E 1 2 W 1 2 M 1 2
D C Π J O 1–3 7.   33. uerereri R V G K. ‖ quaerantur se beata G *alt. man.*
superscr.   36. matilio R 1 10 16 G B 1 2 K 1.   m̄atilio V til *in ras.*
M. Attilio R 6 B 3 W 2 M 2 O 2.   .m. attilio R 2 E 2.   m. atilio P S O 1.
marco attilio O 7.   attilio W 1.   malitio E 1. ‖ Q. B 3 W 1 M 1 2 D C O 1–3.
Qu. R 6.   quinto R 1 2 10 V P G B 1 2 K 1 2 E 1 2 W 2 Π O 7.
~~quinto~~ S *marg.* Q.   quitto R 16.   q3 R 17. ‖ caepione M. aquilio R 6.
cepione m. aquilio B 3 M 2 D C O 2 3.   caepionē aquilio V *marg.* m̄.
cepione m. aquilo R 2 10.   caepionemaquilo R G.   coepionem aquilio K 1.
cipione .m. aquilio P.   cepionē aquilo E 1 2.   cepionē aquilio S *marg.*
Q. Scipione.   scipione M. aquilio Π.   cepione aquilio O 1.   cepione aquilo
R 16 17 B 1.   cepioe aliq W 2.   scipione aquilo B 2.

θεῖος χορός ; Plat. Phaedr. 247 A φθόνος
γὰρ ἔξω θεῖου χοροῦ ἵσταται.

ante oculos, 'presents to our eyes an
extremely impressive spectacle'; the *oculi*
are those of the spectators, not of the
supposed *chorus virtutum.*

beata uita: the subject is sometimes
(and often in poetry) placed in the second
half of a double sentence : cf. Ac. i 8, 30
(quoted by Wopkens, *op. cit.* 148),
'quamquam oreretur a sensibus, tamen
non esse iudicium ueritatis in sensibus'
where Lamb. thinks that *iud. uer.* should
come immediately after *oreretur*, as Ern.
here proposes to put *beata uita* after
porrectura. Sff. thinks that *beata uita*
has been inserted between *eas* and *a se* to
prevent the possibility of *se* being taken
to refer to *eas.*

§ **14. nudum**, 'the abstract difficulty
remains.' Hei. compares Parad. 3, 24
' nuda ("in the abstract") ista si ponas,
iudicare qualia sint non facile possum.'

nulla uirtus prudentia uacat : *prudentia* though usually employed in Cic.
(e.g. iii 8, 17) as a translation of φρόνησις
is here used as equivalent to ἐπιστήμη,
scientia, the knowledge which enters into
the definition of all virtues (Stob. Ecl. ii
59, 4 W.). Cf. Off. i 43, 153 where the

distinction between the *sapientia* (σοφία)
common to all virtues and the particular
virtue *prudentia* (φρόνησις) is clearly drawn.

M. Atilio : M. Atilius Regulus, 'the pro-
totype of heroic misfortune' (Mommsen)
with the Romans, cons. 256 B.C., defeated
and captured by the Carthaginians in
255, and according to the legend put to
death with tortures, cf. Off. iii 26, 99 ;
Hor. C. iii 5, 13 sqq. ; Mommsen, *R.H.*
II 178 ff.

Q. Caepione : Q. Servilius Caepio, cos.
106 B.C., defeated by the Cimbri at
Arausio in 105, deprived of his office, of
his seat in the senate, and of his property,
does not seem to have been such a
striking example of virtue struggling
against misfortune as Cicero thinks.
Mommsen, *R.H.* III 436 ff.

M'. Aquilio : M' Aquilius the younger,
cos. 101 B.C., despatched as Roman
ambassador to Asia in 90 B.C., induced
Nicomedes of Bithynia to declare war on
Mithradates and was captured and put to
death by Mithradates the following year.
Mommsen, *R.H.* IV 24 ff.

ipsa prudentia, expunged unnecessarily by Dav. and Ern. A number of
similar exx. of repetition are quoted by
Wopkens, *op. cit.* D. 359.

VI. **15.** Facile patior te isto modo agere, etsi iniquum est
praescribere mihi te quem ad modum a me disputari uelis.
sed quaero utrum aliquid actum superioribus diebus an nihil
arbitremur.

5　Actum uero, et aliquantum quidem.

Atqui, si ita est, profligata iam haec et paene ad exitum
adducta quaestio est.

Quo tandem modo?

Quia motus turbulenti iactationesque animorum incitatae et
10 impetu inconsiderato elatae rationem omnem repellentes uitae
beatae nullam partem relinquunt. quis enim potest mortem aut
dolorem metuens, quorum alterum saepe adest, alterum semper
inpendet, esse non miser? quid, si idem, quod plerumque fit,
paupertatem, ignominiam, infamiam timet, si debilitatem, caeci-
15 tatem, si denique, quod non singulis hominibus, sed potentibus
populis saepe contigit, seruitutem? potest ea timens esse quis-

---

VI. § **15**, 1. ito G *in* isto *alt. man. corr.*　‖　agere P　W 1　D C　O 1 3 7.

egere V *et* B *atr. ant. superscr.*　　aegere K 1.　　egere R G　B 2　E.
2. praescribere R G.　　p̄scribere V.　　10. impetu R G B K S.　　impetuм V.
inpetu E (*h. l.*).　‖　aelate R V K G a *ante* e *exp. alt. man.*　‖　omnem *alt. man.*
superscr. habet G.　　13. inpendet G E.　　impendet R V B K S.　‖　quid si
R V P G　B 1–3　S　E 2　M 2　Π　O 2.　quod si E 1　W 1　D C J.　　Q si
M 1　O 3.　qđ si K 1　O 1.　qd' si W 2.　qui si O 7.　14. infamia R G
　　　　　　　　　　　　　　　　　　　　　　　　　　　　　　　modo
alt. man. superscr.　　infamia K *atr. nigriore mut.*　　15. non singulis V.
16. contingit G *at* n *post* i *exp. alt. man.*

VI. § **15. facile patior,** 'I am quite
content that,' i 23, 55, p. Planc. 25, 62 ;
Att. xv 2, 2.

aliquid : cf. i 20, 45 'etenim si nunc
aliquid adsequi se putant ' and n. there.

et aliquantum quidem: cf. iii 20, 48 n.

profligata : 'virtually finished.' Aul.
Gell. N.A. xv 5 devotes a chapter to the
castigation of writers who used the word
profligare in the sense in which Cic. uses
it here and in Fam. viii 9, 2 ; xii 14, 2 ;
30, 2 'qui profligato bello ac paene
sublato renouatum bellum gerere cona-
mur,' prou. cons. 14, 35 ; according to
him it should always be used in the sense
of *ad perniciem interitumque deducere* ;
the proper Latin for the meaning given
to *profligata* here is, he asserts, *adfectus*
for which he quotes Cicero prou. cons.
8, 19 ' bellum adfectum uidemus ' and *ib.*
12, 29 : it seems clear that the scruples
felt by Aul. Gell. were unknown to
Cicero and Livy (iii 50, 10 ; ix 37, 1 ;
xxi, 40, 11 ; xxxv 6, 3).

alterum...alterum, 'the latter (i.e. *dolor*)

...the former (i.e. *mors*)' as in i 38, 91 :
the neuter is used, since *quorum*, referring
to nouns of different genders, is neuter :
for other neuters referring to masc. and
fem. nouns cf. i 24, 56 ; iii 4, 7.

ignominiam, infamiam, 'disgrace, de-
gradation,' cf. de Rep. iv 6, 6 ' censoris
iudicium nihil fere damnato nisi ruborem
adfert : itaque...animaduersio illa ignominia dicta est' whereas *infamia* involved
the loss of civil rights ; the same climax
in iv 20, 45.

non...sed differs from *non modo...sed
etiam* : in *non...sed* the speaker definitely
excludes from consideration an idea
which, whether true or false, is not relevant or is inadequate : in *non modo...
sed etiam* he includes both statements in
order to emphasize the greater importance
of the second : cf. Ac. ii 23, 73 ; Off. ii
8, 27 ; Fin. i 2, 6. Contrast the expression in Fin. i 13, 43 'cupiditates...quae
non modo singulos homines, sed uni-
uersas familias euertunt, totam etiam
labefactant saepe rem publicam.'

quam beatus? **16.** quid, qui non modo ea futura timet, uerum
etiam fert sustinetque praesentia? adde eodem exsilia, luctus,
orbitates; qui rebus his fractus aegritudine eliditur, potest tan-
20 dem esse non miserrimus? quid uero? illum quem libidinibus
inflammatum et furentem uidemus, omnia rabide adpetentem
cum inexplebili cupiditate, quoque affluentius uoluptates undique hauriat, eo grauius ardentiusque sitientem, nonne recte
miserrimum dixeris? quid? elatus ille leuitate inanique laetitia
25 exsultans et temere gestiens nonne tanto miserior quanto sibi
uidetur beatior? ergo ut hi miseri, sic contra illi beati quos
nulli metus terrent, nullae aegritudines exedunt, nullae libidines
incitant, nullae futtiles laetitiae exsultantes languidis liquefaciunt
uoluptatibus. ut maris igitur tranquillitas intellegitur nulla ne
30 minima quidem aura fluctus commouente, sic animi quietus et
placatus status cernitur cum perturbatio nulla est qua moueri
queat. **17.** quodsi est qui uim fortunae, qui omnia humana, quaecumque accidere possunt, tolerabilia ducat, ex quo nec timor

§ 16, 18. adde V S E 1 3.   at de R G   K 1 2   L 5 ed. H.   at de P *marg.*
adde. acde B 1.   ‖ exilia R V G B K S E.   20. miserrimus R V G B K. ‖
libidinibus R V G B K.   21. adpetentem R V G K E.   appetentem B S.
22. affluentius R V G B K S E.   24. miserrimum R V G.   miꞩserrimum K. ‖
elatus V P G B S E.   eleuatus R K   25. exultans R V G B K S E. ‖
temere J.   temē P.   tꞮmere V i *in e mut.*   tꞮmere R 1 i *in e mut.*
                                                                                        c
timere G K S E.   timore B.   26. sic contra R G S.   sicontra V *eod. atr.*
sicontra K.   27. libidines R V G B K.   28. futtiles R V G K.   futiles
B 1 W 1. ‖ exultantes R V G B K S E. ‖ liquaefaciunt G.   29. intellegitur
R V G B K.   intelligitur S E.   30. minima R V P G B K.
    § 17, 32. quaecumque R 6 7   W 1   J   O 1 3.   quae cuique R V P G B 1–3
                                                                                        a
K 1   S E 1 2 M 1 2 D C Π O 2 7.   q̅c̅3 W 2.   33. tolerabili V *eod. atr.*
tollerabilia G.

§ 16. eliditur, 'is crushed'; the word is
used of ships broken up in a storm (Caes.
B.C. iii. 27), of strangling (*elisa fauce*
Ov. M. xiv 738; ix 198; xii 142), of
grinding between the teeth (Ov. M. xiv
196 *elisi sub dentibus*), of being crushed in
a crowd (Ov. Epp. ex Pont. iv 9, 21
turba quamuis eliderer).

sitientem, often used metaphorically
in Cic. pro Planc. 5, 13 'sitientem me
uirtutis tuae deseruisti' Q. Fr. iii 5, 3;
Phil. v 7, 20.

futtiles: 'futtiles dicuntur qui silere
tacenda nequeunt sed ea effundunt; sic et
uasa futilia a fundendo uocata' Fest.
p. 89 M.

liquefaciunt: cf. ii 22, 52; iv 17, 37.

§ 17. **Quodsi est qui**: 'But if there is
such a character...what is there to prevent his happiness?' The form of the

conclusion does not throw any doubt
upon the existence of such characters as
are described; but as the discussion has
turned not upon their existence, but upon
their happiness in misfortune, the hypothetical form of the conclusion is appropriate.

Many edd. follow F.A.W. in punctuat-
ing 'quod si est, qui...' 'if this is so, the
person who, etc.': but this makes an
extremely harsh anacoluthon (*qui ducat...
idemque si nihil concupiscat*), and as Küh.
points out, Cic. never elsewhere uses
quod si est in this sense but *quod si ita
est*, or *id si est*, or *id si ita est*, or *quod ut
ita sit* or *quod cum ita sit*.

quaecumque accidere possunt, an
emphatic amplification of *omnia*; the
reading *quae cuique* adopted by Kl. and
C.F.W.M. introduces a distributive idea

eum nec angor attingat, idemque si nihil concupiscat, nulla
35 ecferatur animi inani uoluptate, quid est cur is non beatus sit?
et si haec uirtute efficiuntur, quid est cur uirtus ipsa per se non
efficiat beatos?

VII. Atqui alterum dici non potest quin ii qui nihil metuant,
nihil angantur, nihil concupiscant, nulla inpotenti laetitia ecfe-
rantur, beati sint, itaque id tibi concedo; alterum autem iam
integrum non est. superioribus enim disputationibus effectum
5 est uacare omni animi perturbatione sapientem.

18. Nimirum igitur confecta res est; uidetur enim ad exitum
uenisse quaestio.

Propemodum id quidem.

Verum tamen mathematicorum iste mos est, non est philo-
10 sophorum. nam geometrae cum aliquid docere uolunt, si quid ad
eam rem pertinet eorum quae ante docuerunt, id sumunt pro
concesso et probato, illud modo explicant de quo ante nihil
scriptum est; philosophi quamcumque rem habent in manibus, in
eam quae conueniunt congerunt omnia, etsi alio loco disputata
15 sunt. quod ni ita esset, cur Stoicus, si esset quaesitum satisne
ad beate uiuendum uirtus posset, multa diceret? cui satis esset
respondere se ante docuisse nihil bonum esse, nisi quod honestum

---

35. ecferatur R V G B.   efferatur P B 3 W 1 2 J O 7.   hœcferatur K 1.
feratur O 1.

VII. 1. quin hi G B.   2. agantur V *atr. ant. superscr.* ‖ impotenti
R V G B S.   inpotenti E.   in potenti O 3. ‖ ecferant V B 1.   ecferant
R G.   hęcferant K 1 ec in hęc *atr. nigr. mut.*   efferantur P B 3 S E 2
W 1 2 M 1 2 C II J O 1–3 7.   efferant R 10.   et ferant E 1.   efferentur R 6.
ferantur B 2.   5. uacari G.
§ 18, 9. uerumtamen R V G K.   ueruntamen B S.   16. beatae G.
17. se ante docuisse R 6 7 17 K 2 E 3 L 5 W 1 2 O 3 ed. H.   se ante docuisset
II t *ex parte eras.*   se ante C docuisse *om.*   se aūt docuisse D O 7.
se satis ante docuisse J O 1.   sed ante docuisset P *marg.* se ante docuisse.

sed ante docuisset R G B 1 2 K 1 E 1.   sęd ante docuisset V *atr. uiridi mut.*
si ante docuisset B 3 E 2 M 1 2 O 2.

which is quite out of place ; the reading
favoured by Bentl. *quae cuiquam* is
superior to *quae cuique* but lacks adequate
MSS. support.

ex quo=*ut ex eo*, 'so that, as a result.'

idemque si=*et si idem*; the construction is *quodsi est qui...ducat, et si idem
nihil concupiscat*, the second *si* being a repetition after the parenthesis, and *idem*
being put at the beginning of the clause
to make clear that the second *si*-clause
relates to the same subject.

VII. **dici non potest quin**: for the
constr. cf. Phil. iii 8, 21 'quid potest dicere

quin...se hostem confesssus sit'; Fin. iv
13, 32 quoted by Draeger, *Synt.* II p. 641.

alterum...integrum non est: 'the
second point is no longer open to discussion': for *integrum* cf. 21, 62, Liv. xxvi
15, 9, p. Ligar. i 1 'confitendum est,
opinor, praesertim cum meus necessarius
Pansa fecerit ut id integrum iam non esset.'

§ 18. **ad eam rem** refers to *aliquid* :
ea res is used to avoid the repetition of *id*.

conueniunt, 'are pertinent'; cf. Inu. ii
5, 16 'hoc autem...oportebit attendere
non omnis [sc. locos communes] in
omnem causam conuenire.'

esset, hoc probato consequens esse beatam uitam uirtute esse
contentam, et quo modo hoc sit consequens illi, sic illud huic, ut,
20 si beata uita uirtute contenta sit, nisi honestum quod sit, nihil
aliud sit bonum. 19. sed tamen non agunt sic; nam et de
honesto et de summo bono separatim libri sunt, et cum ex eo
efficiatur satis magnam in uirtute ad beate uiuendum esse uim,
nihilo minus hoc agunt separatim. propriis enim et suis argu-
25 mentis et admonitionibus tractanda quaeque res est, tanta
praesertim. caue enim putes ullam in philosophia uocem emis-
sam clariorem ullumue esse philosophiae promissum uberius
aut maius. nam quid profitetur? o di boni! perfecturam se, qui
legibus suis paruisset, ut esset contra fortunam semper armatus,
30 ut omnia praesidia haberet in se bene beateque uiuendi, ut esset
semper denique beatus. 20. sed uidero quid efficiat; tantisper
hoc ipsum magni aestimo quod pollicetur. nam Xerxes quidem

                    uita
    18. beatauirtute V B 1.   beata uitaute E 1.   beata uirtute R G   B 2   K 1.
    19. contentam R 2 10   V P G B 1 E 1   O 1.   contemptam R 1   K 1.
conc̊atam (sic) R 16.   20. contenta R 2 10 G O 1.   contempta R 1 16 K 1   E 1.
    § 19, 24. nihilo minus V.   nicħlo minus P.   nihilhominus R eod. atr.
nihilhominus G.   25. admonitionibus R.   ammonitionibus B 1 S.
am̄onitionibus V.   ām̄monitionibus E 1.   amonitionibus G.   26. ullam in
                                                                              a
R 1 7 P B 1–3   K 1 2   S   E 1 2   W 1 2   M 1 2   D C Π J   O 1–3.   ullam in V
atr. ant.   ullam a G.   ullam ph'ye O 7.   27. ullaue G in ullumue
alt. man. corr.   28. dii R V P G B 1–3   K 1   S   E 1   J   O 7.
                                                             n
    § 20, 32. magni V P.   magi G alt. man. superscr.   magi R K. ‖
aestumo R V G.   estumo B K.   estimo P.

sit: the change from secondary to
primary sequence is due probably to the
fact that in the writer's mind *cui satis
esset respondere* was practically equivalent
to *qui respondebit.*
    § 19. libri: thus Chrysippus wrote both
περὶ ἀρετῶν (Diog. L. vii 127) and
περὶ ἀγαθῶν (Plut. St. rep. p. 1048 A),
Cleanthes both περὶ καλῶν and περὶ
ἀρετῶν (Diog. L. vii 175).
    ex eo, the identity of *honestum* and the
summum bonum, which is proved by the
Stoics in two separate lines of argument.
    hoc, the sufficiency of virtue to promote
happiness, which though virtually proved
in the discussion on *honestum* and again
in that on the *summum bonum* is made
the subject of a separate treatise.
    propriis...et suis: cf. i 29, 70 'quae
est ei natura? propria, puto, et sua';
Or. ii 10, 39 'adsumpto aliunde uti bono,
non proprio nec suo.'
    paruisset...esset : for secondary se-

quence depending upon a primary tense
(*profitetur*) cf. iii 15, 32 n. on *uenisset.*
    §20. uidero: cf. i 11, 23 n. on *uiderit.*
    nam Xerxes quidem : *nam* here intro-
duces a clause giving not so much an
intellectual as an emotional reason for the
preceding statement : 'the promise of
happiness is not to be despised, because
one would give a great price to be persuaded it could be realized' is perhaps
not a logical but certainly a comprehen-
sible statement. The following sentence
falls into two parts (*Xerxes quidem...
praemium proposuit* and *nos uellem
praemio elicere possemus*) forming the
statement of a contrast ; *quidem* (like
μὲν) points forward to the second part
which might have contained an *autem* or
sed to correspond : cf. Lael. 8, 26 'an
esset hoc quidem proprium amicitiae, sed
antiquior...alia causa ;...nam utilitates
quidem...percipiuntur...in amicitia autem
nihil fictum est.'

refertus omnibus praemiis donisque fortunae, non equitatu, non
pedestribus copiis, non nauium multitudine, non infinito pondere
35 auri contentus praemium proposuit qui inuenisset nouam uoluptatem; qua ipsa non fuit contentus; neque enim umquam finem
inueniet libido. nos uellem praemio elicere possemus qui nobis
aliquid attulisset quo hoc firmius crederemus.

VIII. **21.** Vellem id quidem, sed habeo paulum quod
requiram. ego enim adsentior eorum quae posuisti alterum
alteri consequens esse, ut, quem ad modum, si quod honestum
sit, id solum sit bonum, sequatur uitam beatam uirtute confici,
5 sic, si uita beata in uirtute sit, nihil esse nisi uirtutem bonum.
sed Brutus tuus auctore Aristo et Antiocho non sentit hoc; putat
enim, etiamsi sit bonum aliquod praeter uirtutem.

33. donisque R 1 2 10 16   G K.   doníque V *atr. ant. superscr.*

34. nonnauium K.   nonauium V *atr. ant. superscr.*   nonauium R G.
35. *uerba* praemium......contentus *om.* E 1.   ‖ proposuit qui R V P G B 1–3
K 1 2 S E 2 W 1 2 M 1 2 D C J O 1 7.   ‖ inuenisset R V P G B 1–3 K 1 2 S
E 2 W 1 2 M 1 2 D C Π J O 1–3 7.   ‖ uoluntatem G B.   36. non fuit
R 1 10 16 V G L 4.   non fuerit E 3.   fieret L 2 non *om.*   37. inueniet R 1 7
V P G B 1–3   K 1   E 2 W 2   M 2 D Π J   O 1–3 7.   inueníſet M 1.
inuenit W 1 C.   ‖ libido R V G B 1 2 K S E.   38. attulisset R S E.
adtulisset V d *in* t *eod. atr. mut.*   adtulisset G.   atulisset K 1.

VIII. § 21, 1. paulum R V G B 1 K 1 E 1 W 1 2 D C J O 1.   paululum
P B 2 3 S E 2 M 1 2 O 2 3 7.   2. adsentior V G E.   assentior R B K S.
6. aristone R 1 6 7 10 16 17 V P G B 1–3 K 1 2 S E 1–3 L 2–5 W 1 2 M 1 2
D C Π J O 1–3.   aristore O 7.   antione R 2.   Aristo *corr. Lambinus.*
7. *post* praeter uirtutem *habet* V *manu ant. in marg. script.* taᵐ ad beate uiuendũ
satis pose uirtutē, *quae uerba scribae qui grassabatur in* § 24 *libri tertii tribuenda
uidentur.*

praemiis: Lamb. altered to *muneribus*
and Bentl. who thought *muneribus* too
wide a departure from the MSS. tradition
himself proposed *corporis bonis et fortunae*: for *praemium* in the sense of
' advantage.' Hei. compares Lucr. iii. 956
' omnia perfunctus uitai praemia marces.'
proposuit qui inuenisset, i.e *prop. ei
qui inuenisset*: for the omission of the
antecedent Wopkens (*op. cit.* p. 250)
quotes amongst other passages iv 23, 51
' qui rem publicam saluam esse uellent
se sequi iussit,' Fin. ii 28, 90 ' qui...
loquitur ut Frugi ille Piso non audio ':
Ern. and Dav. unnecessarily insert *ei*.
fuit contentus: Bentl. followed by
Ern. and Bait. read *fuisset* and Kl. *fuerit*.
There is no necessity for any alteration.
It is true that none of the other authorities who tell this story either of Xerxes
(Val. Max. ix 1, 3 ext.) or of Darius Codo-
mannus (Clearchus ap. Athen. xii 539 B)
or of the Persian kings in general

(Theophr. ap. Athen. iv 144 F) has any
corresponding statement with regard to
the result of the new pleasure upon the
king's happiness. But Cicero may either
have made the assertion on his own
responsibility or have regarded Xerxes'
attempt to conquer Greece as sufficient
evidence of a continued dissatisfaction
with his fortunes.
hoc, ' our present contention' sc. *philosophiam omnia praesidia habere in se
bene beateque uiuendi.*
VIII. § **21. sic**: sc. *sequatur.*
Aristo: that this and not *Aristone* is
the right reading here is proved by the
fact that Cic. elsewhere refers to Aristus,
the brother of Antiochus of Ascalon, as
being the teacher of Brutus (Brut. 97,
332 ; Ac. i 3, 12 ; Fin. v 3, 8) ; also the
coupling of the two names here in apposition to a singular noun *auctore* implies a
closer connexion between them than we
know to have existed between Antiochus

Quid igitur? contra Brutumne me dicturum putas?
Tu uero, ut uidetur; nam praefinire non est meum.

10   **22.** Quid cuique igitur consentaneum sit, alio loco. nam
ista mihi et cum Antiocho saepe et cum Aristo nuper, cum
Athenis imperator apud eum deuersarer, dissensio fuit. mihi
enim non uidebatur quisquam esse beatus posse, cum in malis
esset; in malis autem sapientem esse posse, si essent ulla corporis
15   aut fortunae mala. dicebantur haec, quae scriptitauit etiam Antiochus locis pluribus, uirtutem ipsam per se beatam uitam efficere
posse neque tamen beatissimam; deinde ex maiore parte plerasque

8. brutumne R 6 7 17 B 3 S E 2 W 1 2 M 1 2 D C II O 1 2 7.   brutum
ne*t* V *atr. ant. corr.*   brutum nec R 1 P G B 1 2 K 1 E 1 J *om.* O 3.
§ **22,** 11. aristone R 1 6 10 17 V P B 1–3 K 1 S E 1–3 L 3–6 W 1 2
M 1 2 D C II J O 1–3 7 ed. H.   aristhone G.   aristono L 2.   Aristo *corr.*
Lambinus.   12. dissentio G.   15. scriptasit R 1 10 G B K E S *marg.* scripsit.
scrip*t*sit V *atr. ant. mut.*   scripsit R 6 7 17 P B 3 E 2 L 2–46 W 1 M 1 2
II O 2 3.   scripta sunt B 2 L 5 D C J O 1 7 ed. H.   scripta sint K 2.
scripsit su̧nt E 5.   scripsit W 2 *at in ras.*   sc̦pta s̊ R 16.   scriptitauit
corr. Klotzius.   16. efficere posse R 6 V P G B 1–3 K 1 S E 1 2 W 1 2
                                                              posse
M 1 2 D C II J O 1–3 7.   efficere R 1 *eod. atr.*   efficere R 7 posse *om.*
17. beatissimam R V G K. ‖   maiore (*hic et infra*) R V G B 1 2 K 1 S E 1 2
W 1 2 M 1 2 J O 1–3.   maiori (*hic et infra*) D O 7.   maiori *hic, infra*
maiore C.

and Aristo. It is true that Plut. Brut.
c. 2 calls Antiochus' brother Aristo
(though many edd. (after Dav.) alter
Ἀρίστωνα to Ἄριστον); those who read
Aristone here are compelled to assume
either that Plut. is right as against Cicero's
repeated statements with regard to the
form of the name or that Cic. is here referring to Aristo the Peripatetic (see
Reid's n. on Ac. ii 4, 12) with whom
there is no evidence that Brutus had
anything to do.

Antiocho : cf. iii 25, 59 n.

putat enim : sc. *uitam beatam uirtute
confici.*

tu uero : sc. *agas*; cf. i. 9, 17 'tu, ut
uidetur.'

praefinire non est meum, a good-
humoured reference to the remonstrance
in 6, 15 , '*iniquum* est praescribere mihi
te quemadmodum a me disputari uelis.'

§ 22. **ista...dissensio,** i.e. ' eadem dissensio quae nunc est mihi tecum ': for
dissensio cum cf. Brut. 49, 185 ; Off. iii
13, 56.

saepe, during his residence as a student
in Athens in 79 B.C. Cf. iii 25, 59 n.

nuper, during his visit to Athens in
50 B.C. when returning from Cilicia
where he had been saluted as *imperator*
by his army, Att. v 20, 3 : on this
occasion he was entertained by Aristus,

cf. Brut. 97, 332 'Aristus hospes et
familiaris meus ' Att. v 10, 5.

It seems almost incredible that Küh.
should read *Aristone* here ; it is perfectly
clear from the passages referred to that
Cic. was the guest of Aristus, not Aristo,
during his stay in Athens. Küh. finds support for his reading in the ref. in Ac. ii
4, 12 where the speaker after mentioning
Heraclitus, Aristus, Aristo and Dio says
' multum temporis in ista una disputatione
consumpsimus ' ; Küh. seems to think
this a proof that Cic. and Aristo once
discussed this subject : a glance at the
context would have shown that the
speaker there is not Cic. but Lucullus,
who is describing a discussion in which
he engaged at Alexandria.

sapientem : for the change from the
personal to the impersonal constr. cf.
Or. ii 74, 299 (after *dicitur*) Cato M.
18, 63 (after *dicuntur*) : a somewhat
similar change of constr. is seen in N.D.
i 12, 31 'facit enim...Socratem *disputantem*...eundemque et solem et animum
deum *dicere.*'

scriptitauit : Kl.'s emendation for the
corrupt *scripta sit* of many mss. has been
adopted by Hei. Sff. and Küh.: the reading *scripsit* is adopted by Bai. T.S.
C.F.W.M. and Schiche ; in the latter
case it is necessary to assume that *scripta*

res nominari, etiamsi quae pars abesset, ut uires, ut ualetudinem,
ut diuitias, ut honorem, ut gloriam, quae genere non numero
20 cernerentur; item beatam uitam, etiamsi ex aliqua parte clauderet,
tamen ex multo maiore parte obtinere nomen suum. **23.** haec
nunc enucleare non ita necesse est, quamquam non constantissime dici mihi uidentur. nam et qui beatus est, non intellego
quid requirat ut sit beatior (si est enim quod desit, ne beatus
25 quidem est), et quod ex maiore parte unam quamque rem appellari spectarique dicunt, est ubi id isto modo ualeat; cum uero
tria genera malorum esse dicant, qui duorum generum malis
omnibus urgeatur ut omnia aduorsa sint in fortuna, omnibus
oppressum corpus et confectum doloribus, huic paulumne ad
30 beatam uitam deesse dicemus, non modo ad beatissimam?

---

18. si quae R G B K S   E 1 2 D.   si q̄ P.   si qua B 2 3   W 1 2   M 1 2
J   O 1–3 7.   si q̄ C.   ‖   ualetudinem R V G.   ualitudinem B S E.
ual&itudinem (*sic*) K 1.   20. clauderet R 1 17   P G   B 1   K 1   S   E 1 2   D C
        ca
O 7.   claud*g*ret V *atr. ant. mut.*   claude_Λret Π *eod. atr.*   cluderet B 2.
claudicaret R 6 7   P *marg.*   B 3   S *marg.*   W 1   M 1 2   O 1–3 ed. H.   claudicet
W 2   J.   21. obtinere K 1   E 2   W 1   M 1.   optinere R V G   B 1 2   S E 1.
§ **23,** 22. enucleare R G K.   enunc leare V.   ‖   constantissime R V G B K.
23. uidentur P.   uidetur R V G K.   ‖   intellego R V G B K.   intelligo S E.
25. maiore R V G B K.   ‖   quamque partem G.   quamque S rem *om.* ‖
appellari R V G B K.   28. aduorsa R G   B 1   K E.   aduersa V   B 3   Π   O 1.
adûsa P S   W 2   M 1   J.   adursa B 2.   29. paulumne R V G   B 1 2   K 1
W 1 2   J   O 3.   paululumne P   B 3   S   E 2   M 1 2   Π   O 1 2.   paulum
E 1   D C.   paululum O 7.   30. ad beatissimam R V G K.

---

was written in the archetype for *scripsit*
and the mistake rectified by adding the
proper form of the final syllable; the
error may have been rendered easier as
Bai. suggests by the two syllables *scrip-*
and *-sit* being divided in the archetype.

ex maiore parte: cf. Fin. v 30, 92
'semper enim ex eo quod maximas partes
continet latissimeque funditur tota res
appellatur.'

genere non numero, 'which are distinguished as belonging to a particular
class, not by occupying a certain position
in it,' i.e. one does not think of denying
the title of 'wealthy' or 'healthy' to a
man because some one else is healthier or
wealthier; so a life may deserve the title
of 'happy' although one may conceive a
life happier still. For the use of *genere*
here cf. De opt. gen. or. 1, 3 'non genere
differunt...sed in eodem genere non sunt
pares' and 'haec ut alius melius quam
alius concedendum est ; uerum id fit non
genere sed gradu'; for the use of *numerus*
as equivalent to *locus* or *gradus* cf. Diu.

in Caec. 19, 62 'cum is tibi parentis
numero fuisset.'

clauderet, a word used in Ter. And.
573, and by Cic. in Or. 51, 170 ; Brut.
59, 214: *claudicaret* of some MSS. adopted
by Bentl. is due to the substitution of a
more familiar for an unusual word.

enucleare, 'analyse in detail;' cf. Part.
Or. 17, 57 'nec quicquam in amplifica-
tione nimis enucleandum est': in Planc.
5, 10 'enucleata suffragia' means 'votes
given after careful consideration'; cf. also
Wilkins' note to Or. iii 9, 32.

non ita = *non admodum*: 'only occurs
in Cicero and the older writers before
adjectives and adverbs' Reid on Ac. ii 2, 5.

est ubi like the Gk. ἔστιν ὅπου; T.S.
cf. Plaut. Pseud. 1325 'erit ubi te
ulciscar si uiuo.'

tria genera: for the τριλογία τῶν
ἀγαθῶν and (consequently) τῶν κακῶν into
bona (and *mala*) *mentis, corporis* and
externa cf. Reid's n. to Ac. i 5, 19.

non modo = *ne dicam,* 'to say nothing of
the supremely happy life'; cf. i 38, 92 n.

IX. **24.** Hoc illud est quod Theophrastus sustinere non potuit. nam cum statuisset uerbera, tormenta, cruciatus, patriae euersiones, exsilia, orbitates magnam uim habere ad male misereque uiuendum, non est ausus elate et ample loqui cum humiliter 5 demisseque sentiret; quam bene, non quaeritur, constanter quidem certe. itaque mihi placere non solet consequentia reprehendere, cum prima concesseris. hic autem elegantissimus omnium philosophorum et eruditissimus non magnopere reprehenditur cum tria genera dicit bonorum, uexatur autem ab omnibus primum 10 in eo libro quem scripsit de uita beata, in quo multa disputat, quam ob rem is qui torqueatur, qui crucietur, beatus esse non possit. in eo etiam putatur dicere in rotam (id est genus quoddam tormenti apud Graecos) beatam uitam non escendere.

IX. § **24,** 1. teophrastus R V G B.   teoph rastus K 1 a *eras*.   teoprastus E 1.
3. exilia R V G B K S E.   7. elegantissimus R V G B.   eligantissimus K.
8. eruditissimus R V G B K. ‖   magnopere R V P G B K S.   9. dicit J.
dĭc W 2.   dici V *et* B *atram. ant. superscr.*   dici R G K E.   12. id est genus quoddam tormenti apud graecos R 2 10 17   V P G B 1 2   K 1   S   E 1 2   L 2–4 D C Π O 1 7 Gr.   quod genus tormenti est apud graecos W 1.   .i. in genus *cett.* M 1.   id est in genus *cett.* O 3.   uel genus *cett.* ed. H.   E 3 *sed punctis not.* *habet* R 1 *at linea subducta atr. recenti. non habent* R 6 16   B 3   K 2   L 5 6   W 2 M 2   J   O 2.   13. escendere V.   escenderet R G.   ascendere R 6   P   B 1 3 S   E 2   W 1   M 1 2   Π   O 2 3 7.   adscenderet B 2.   ascenderet K 1.
scandere W 2   J   O 1.   scand R 16.   attingere D.   attingeret E 1. actingere C.

IX. §**24.** **sustinere**: 'this is the very point which Theophrastus was unable to maintain': Theophrastus saw that the logical result of the τριλογία τῶν ἀγαθῶν was an abandonment of the doctrine that virtue alone was capable of conferring happiness; therefore he frankly refused to maintain an impossible position: for *sustinere* cf. Att. vii 7, 5; II Verr. i 4, 10 'sustinebunt tales uiri se tot senatoribus... non credidisse.' For Theophrastus's views cf. Fin. v 5, 12; Ac. i 9, 33.
cum...sentiret, 'with such abject and spiritless views,' referring to *cum statuisset...uiuendum*.
elegantissimus: cf. Ac. i 9, 33 'Theophrastus...uir et oratione suauis et ita moratus ut prae se probitatem quandam et ingenuitatem ferret,' Brut. 31, 121 'quis...Theophrasto dulcior?'
uexatur, 'is assailed'; cf. Flacc. 20, 48 'probris omnibus maledictisque uexat.' Mo.: cf. Aul. Gell. ii 6, 3 'qui fertur et raptatur atque huc atque illuc distrahitur, is uexari proprie dicitur'; Macr. Sat. vi 7 (where the same explanation is given).

in eo libro, '*for* the book which he wrote': after verbs denoting to praise or to blame, *in* can be used to express the grounds of the action : edd. cf. Q. Fr. ii 4, 5 'Pompeius noster in amicitia P. Lentuli uituperatur'; Planc. 33, 82 'quem qui reprehendit in eo reprehendit,' etc. Bentl. declared that the sentence made nonsense, as *in* here could only mean 'in' and read 'quod in eo libro, quem...beata, multa disputarit.'
Theophrastus wrote (acc. to Diog. Laert. v 2, 43, 49) a work περὶ εὐδαιμονίας and another περὶ τῆς θείας εὐδαιμονίας. It is probably the former to which Cic. refers here and in Fin. v 28, 85.
rotam: Aristoph. Pax 451 ἐπὶ τοῦ τροχοῦ στρεβλοῖτο μαστιγούμενος where the Sch. notes οἱ γὰρ δοῦλοι σφαλλόμενοι ἐπὶ τροχοῦ δεσμούμενοι καὶ συρόμενοι ἐτύπτοντο ἀνακλώμενοι ἐν αὐτῷ: cf. also Antiph. de caede Her. 40 ; Andoc. de Myst. 43 ; Dem. contr. Aph. 48. Many editors bracket *id est...Graecos* as an obvious gloss. But it is doubtful whether

non usquam id quidem dicit omnino, sed, quae dicit, idem ualent.

15 **25.** possum igitur, cui concesserim in malis esse dolores corporis, in malis naufragia fortunae, huic suscensere dicenti non omnis bonos esse beatos, cum in omnis bonos ea quae ille in malis numerat cadere possint? uexatur idem Theophrastus et libris et scholis omnium philosophorum quod in Callisthene suo lau-
20 darit illam sententiam:

　　　Vitám regit fortúna, non sapiéntia.

negant ab ullo philosopho quicquam dictum esse languidius. recte id quidem, sed nihil intellego dici potuisse constantius. si enim tot sunt in corpore bona, tot extra corpus in casu atque
25 fortuna, nonne consentaneum est plus fortunam, quae domina rerum sit et externarum et ad corpus pertinentium, quam consilium ualere? **26.** an malumus Epicurum imitari? qui multa praeclare saepe dicit; quam enim sibi constanter conuenienterque dicat,

14. non usquam R V P G B₁₂ K S E₁₂ W₁₂ M₁₂ C Π J O₁₃₇.
§ **25**, 16. suscensere R K E.　　s[c]censere V s *in c mut.*　　succensere P G
B₁₂ S E₂ W₁₂ M₁₂ D C Π J O₁₃₇. ‖ omnis (*bis*) R V B G K.
18. theophrastus R.　　thephrastus G *alt. man. superscr.*　　theofrastus V.
teophrastus B E.　　teopharastus K.　　19. scholis B.　　scolis R V G K S E. ‖
callisthene V P G B K.　　calisthene R.　　22. languidius R G B K.　　languidus V.
23. intellego R V G B K.　　intelligo S E.
§ **26**, 28. quam enim R V P G B 1–3 K S E₁₂ W₁₂ M₁₂ D Π J
O 1–3 7.　　qm C.

the phrase 'in rotam escendere' would have been intelligible to a Latin reader without explanation; and it is significant that in the two passages in Apuleius where the wheel of torture is mentioned (Apul. Met. iii 9 'nec mora cum ritu Graeciensi ignis et rota...inferuntur,' and x 10 'nec rota uel eculeus more Graecorum tormentis eius apparata iam deerant'), the fact of its being a Greek form of punishment is emphasized. References to Ixion's wheel are common in the poets (e.g. Tib. i 3, 74; Verg. Aen. vi 616; Ov. M. iv 461, etc.), and such a reference would not have required explanation here: but *rota* cannot stand for *rota Ixionis* any more than *taurus* could stand in ii 7, 17 for *taurus Phalaridos*. In Plaut. Cist. 208 'iactor, crucior, agitor, stimulor, uorsor in Amoris rota' the metaphor would be quite intelligible even to an audience to whom the *rota* as a form of punishment was unfamiliar; but there are no such qualifying words here as in Plaut. to help the reader's understanding.

omnino goes closely with the negative though it is often thrown to the end of the clause or phrase for the sake of emphasis, cf. Fin. ii 31, 100; N.D. iii 27, 69; Ac. ii 15, 48; trans. 'This particular phrase he certainly never makes use of.'

naufragia, a favourite metaphor for disaster, both in prose and in poetry, cf. Phil. xii 8, 19; Fam. i 9, 5; Ov. Tr. i 6, 8.

scholis: cf. i 4, 7 n.

Callisthene: cf. iii 10, 21 n.

sententiam, 'sentiment' = γνώμην: cf. Or. ii 8, 34 'quid autem subtilius quam crebrae acutaeque sententiae?' with Wilkins's note.

The Gk form of the sentiment is τύχη τὰ θνητῶν πράγματ' οὐκ εὐβουλία: it is quoted by Stobaeus, Ecl. Phys. p. 196 [i 6, 7], as from the *Achilleus Thersitoktonos* of Chairemon, and it forms the text for Plutarch's tract περὶ τύχης.

§ 26. enim: Bentl. proposed to delete *enim* and Dav. to replace it by *autem*: neither saw that *enim* here introduces the

non laborat. laudat tenuem uictum. philosophi id quidem, sed
30 si Socrates aut Antisthenes diceret, non is qui finem bonorum
uoluptatem esse dixerit. negat quemquam iucunde posse uiuere,
nisi idem honeste, sapienter iusteque uiuat. nihil grauius, nihil
philosophia dignius, nisi idem hoc ipsum 'honeste, sapienter,
iuste' ad uoluptatem referret. quid melius quam fortunam ex-
35 iguam interuenire sapienti? sed hoc isne dicit qui, cum dolorem
non modo maximum malum, sed solum malum etiam dixerit,
toto corpore opprimi possit doloribus acerrimis tum cum maxime
contra fortunam glorietur? quod idem melioribus etiam uerbis
Metrodorus: **27.** 'Occupaui te,' inquit, 'Fortuna, atque
40 cepi omnisque aditus tuos interclusi, ut ad me adspirare non posses.' praeclare, si Aristo Chius aut si Stoicus

---

29. laudat tenuem B 3   E 2   W 1 2   M 1 2   D II   O 1–3 7.   laudatenuem V
        l at
atr. ant. superscr.   lauda tenuem B 1.   lauda tenuem R G E.   laudetenuae K 1
                                                                                v
om. B 2.   31. iucunde R K.   iucundae G *at a conf. ead. man.*   iocunde V
atr. ant. superscr.   iocunde P S E.   33. dignius nisi idem dignius nisi idem G.

                                                                         d
34. quid melius R 6   B 3   W 1 2   D C J   O 1 2 7.   qui melius V *atr. ant.* B.
qui melius R P G   B 2   K   E 1 2   O 3.   35. hisne V *atr. ant. corr.*   hisne R G.
                                                                                 ut
36. maximum R V G B.   maximum K S E.   37. toto corpore V *atr. ant.*
superscr. ‖ acerrumis R V G B K. ‖ maxime R V G B K S E.
§ **27**, 40. cepi K e *in* e *mut. atr. nigriore.*   coepi V G. ‖ omnisque
R V G B K E. ‖ adspirare R V K.   aspirare G B S.   41. posses R 1 6 7 17
V P G   B 1–3   K 1   S   E 1   W 1 2   M 1 2   J   O 1 7.   possi°s O 2.   possis
E 2   D C II.   possit O 3. ‖ Aristo Chius R 6.   aristochius V P B.
                                                                                                 c
aristonchius R 16.   aristocchius R 1 2.   aristochius E.   aristhochius G
alt. man. superscr.   ristochius R 17.

---

reason for the preceding statement ; Epicurus could not express a noble sentiment
were it not that he is entirely careless as
to its consistency with his main principle,
which is radically base.
   tenuem uictum : cf. iii 20, 49 n.
   si...diceret : 'in the mouth of Socrates
or Antisthenes'; the imperf. subj. here
does not denote a supposition contrary to
fact in present time, but represents in past
time the 'pure supposition' expressed in
present time by *si* with the present subj.:
for other exx. see Sonnenschein, *Unity
of the Latin Subj.* p. 42.
   Antisthenes, the founder of the Cynic
School; he was a pupil of Socrates παρ'
οὖ καὶ τὸ καρτερικὸν λαβὼν καὶ τὸ ἀπαθὲς
ξηλώσας κατῆρξε πρῶτος τοῦ κυνισμοῦ
Diog. L. vi 1, 2. Zeller, *Socrates* and
the Socratic Schools, E.T. pp. 284 ff.
   negat quemquam...uiuat : cf. iii 20,
46, 49 and nn. there.
   iusteque : cf. 14, 41 n. on *atque*.

fortunam...sapienti : a translation of
Epicurus' saying βραχεῖα σοφῷ τύχη
παρεμπίπτει quoted by Diog. Laert. x
144; Stob. Ecl. Eth. p. 199 [ii 7, 28];
Plut. περὶ τύχης, p. 99 A: the same
transl. occurs Fin. i 19, 63; ii 27, 89:
Seneca, De Const. 15, 4 translates 'raro
sapienti fortuna interuenit': in the adverbial use of *exiguam* Cic. adheres
closely to the Gk idiom. Usener (*Epicurea*, p. 74) reads βραχέα not βραχεῖα,
and holds that Cic. wrote *exiguum* both
here and in Fin. *ll. cc.*
   Metrodorus : cf. iii 3, 8 n.
   §27. occupaui te : προκατείλημμαί σ', ὦ
τύχη, καὶ πᾶσαν τὴν σὴν ἀφῄρημαι παρείσ-
δυσιν, quoted by Plut. περὶ εὐθ. p. 476 c
but without the author's name.
   Aristo, son of Miltiades of Chios, a
pupil of Zeno but inclined towards the
practice of the Cynics. According to
Diog. Laert. vii 160 he taught τέλος εἶναι
τὸ ἀδιαφόρως ἔχοντα ζῆν πρὸς τὰ μέταξυ

Zenon diceret, qui, nisi quod turpe esset, nihil malum duceret;
tu uero, Metrodore, qui omne bonum in uisceribus medullisque
condideris et definieris summum bonum firma corporis adfec-
45 tione explorataque <eius> spe contineri, Fortunae aditus inter-
clusisti? quo modo? isto enim bono iam exspoliari potes.

X. 28. Atqui his capiuntur imperiti, et propter huius modi
sententias istorum hominum est multitudo; acute autem dispu-
tantis illud est, non quid quisque dicat, sed quid cuique dicendum
sit, uidere. uelut in ea ipsa sententia quam in hac disputatione
5 suscepimus omnis bonos semper beatos uolumus esse. quos

42. zenon R 12 16 17 P G B 1 2 K 1 S E 1 2 W 2 D J O 17 zenoℵ
V *atr. ant.*   zeno R 6 W 1 M 1 2 O 3. ‖ nisi quod R G.   nisi quid B 1
al. atr. mut.   nisi quid E 1.   44. corporis R 6 7 17 B 3 E 2 W 1 2 M 1 2
                                                          f   s
D C Π O 1–3 7.   corpori V *ead. man.*   corpori B 1 *atr. ant. alia man.*
superscr.   corpori R 1 P G B 2 K 1 S E 1. ‖ adfectione R V G K E.
affectione R 2 P B 1 3 S.   45. explorataque spe R V P G B 1–3 K 1 S
E 1 2 W 1 2 M 1 2 D C Π J O 1–3 7.   explorataque eius spe *corr.*
Lambinus.   46. expoliari R 6 17 P S E 2 C Π O 7.   expoliare R G
                                                                              f   i
B 1–3 K 1 E 1 W 1 2 J O 1 2.   expoliare V *atr. ant. superscr.*   exspoliari D.

explorari O 3.   expolicei M 1 (*sic*). ‖ potes B 3 E 2 3 W 1 2 M 1 2 D C Π J
                                                              tes
O 1–3.   potes S *at* t *post* s *eras.*   poẗ P *al. atr. superscr.*   potesꞇ V *atr. ant.*
potest R 16 17 G B 1 2 K 1 E 1 O 7.   te potest R 7.
     X. § 28, 1. atqui R 1 7 V P G B 2 3 K 1 W 1 2 M 1 2 D C Π J O 1–3 7.
atquis B 1.   atq; ed. H. ‖ imperiti R V G B K.   5. omnis R V G B K.
                                                                                    s
omnes S. ‖ quos R 6 M 1. Π *at* os *multa in ras.* ed. H.   quod V S.
quod R 1 G B 1 2 K.   quid R 7 17 P B 3 E 1 3 L 5 W 1 2 M 2
D C J O 1–3 7.   quid E 2 *at* id *in ras.*

ἀρετῆς καὶ κακίας μηδ' ἡντινοῦν ἐν αὑτοῖς
παραλλαγὴν ἀπολείποντα ἀλλ' ἐπίσης ἐπὶ
πάντων ἔχοντα. In his views of the importance of Logic and Physics he differed
sharply from the official Stoic view. See
Zeller, *Stoics*, etc. E.T. pp. 59 ff. and
authorities quoted there. Cf. also Cic.
Fin. ii 13, 43; iv 25, 69; *Ac.* ii 42, 130.
    nisi quod turpe esset: cf. ii 12, 29
'nihil est, inquit [sc. Zeno], malum, nisi
quod turpe atque uitiosum est': for the
attraction of mood and tense in *esset*, cf.
i 5, 9 n.
    definieris: cf. ii 6, 17 'Metrodorus
quidem perfecte eum beatum putat cui
corpus bene constitutum sit et exploratum
ita semper fore' with n. there.
    explorataque (eius) spe: the analogy
of Off. iii 33, 117 'uita omnis beata
corporis firma constitutione eiusque con-
stitutionis spe explorata, ut a Metrodoro
scriptum est, continetur,' and the necessity of the sense require the insertion
either of *eius* (Lamb. followed by all
recent edd. except Küh.) or of *eius* ad-

fectionis; the latter would be more
likely to drop out after the preceding
corporis adfectione than would *eius* by
itself.
    X. § 28. **his**, 'sayings like these,'
i.e. like those of Epicurus and Metrodorus quoted above.
    capiuntur, 'are attracted': for this
use cf. § 31 and ii 12, 29; pro Cluent.
5, 13 'pellexit eis omnibus rebus quibus
illa aetas capi ac deleniri potest.'
    istorum hominum, 'persons of that
way of thinking'; the phrase is inten-
tionally contemptuous.
    uelut, cf. 5, 13 n. The example intro-
duced by *uelut* is discussed down to the
end of § 31.
    uolumus, 'wish to make out,' i 18, 42 n.
N.D. i 11, 26 'mentem istam quasi
animal aliquod uoluit esse.' Liv. xxi
10, 8 'nec puer hic dux erat, sed pater
ipse Hamilcar, Mars alter, ut isti uolunt.'
    quos: most MSS. have either *quid* or
quod; a few have *quos* which has been
adopted by Lamb. Tr. Kl. Ba. and most

H.   15

dicam bonos perspicuum est; omnibus enim uirtutibus instructos et ornatos tum sapientis, tum uiros bonos dicimus. uideamus qui dicendi sint beati. equidem eos existimo qui sint in bonis nullo adiuncto malo; **29** neque ulla alia huic uerbo, cum beatum

10 dicimus, subiecta notio est nisi secretis malis omnibus cumulata bonorum complexio. hanc adsequi uirtus, si quicquam praeter ipsam boni est, non potest. aderit enim malorum, si mala illa ducimus, turba quaedam, paupertas, ignobilitas, humilitas, solitudo, amissio suorum, graues dolores corporis, perdita ualetudo,

15 debilitas, caecitas, interitus patriae, exsilium, seruitus denique. in his tot et tantis (atque etiam plura possunt accidere) potest esse sapiens; nam haec casus inportat, qui in sapientem potest incurrere. at si ea mala sunt, quis potest praestare semper sapientem beatum fore, cum uel in omnibus his uno tempore esse

7. tum (*prius*) R V P G B 1 2 K 1 S E 1 W 1 2 M 1 (*non ut Küh.*) II J O 1–3 7. tum E 2 *at* t *in ras.* cum B 3 M 2 C. ‖ sapientis R V P G B 1 K E 1 J. sapientes B 2 S. 8. equidem hos R V P G B 1–3 K 1 S E 1 2 W 1 2 M 1 2 C J O 1–3 7. ‖ existimo R V G B K.

§ **29**, 11. assequi R V B S E. asequi G *alt. man. superscr.* aessequi K.‖ praeter ipsam V P K. praeter ipsa R G. 13. ducimus R V P G Gr.

dicimus K 1 *atr. nigriore superscr.* dicimus R 1 6. 14. ualetudo J.

ualitudo R V G B K S E. 15. interius G *alt. man. superscr.* ‖ exilium R V P G B K S E. 16. etiam plura possunt R 1 7 10 V P G B 1 2 K 1 S E 1 2 M 1 C II O 3. etiam plura quae possunt B 3 W 1 2 M 2 J O 1 2. etiam quae plura possunt R 6. et que etiam plura possunt D. 17. importat

R V G B K S E. 18. incurrere R G K. incurere V *manu ant. superscr.*‖ semper sapientem R 1 7 V P G B 1–3 K 1 E 1 W 1 2 M 1 2 D C J O 1 3 7. sapientem semper R 6 E 2 II O 2.

edd., and is supported by *uideamus qui dicendi sint beati* below : Or. reads *quid* and explains 'quid intelligam quum beatos dico'; but though *quid est bonitas?* is good Latin, it is more than doubtful whether Cicero would have used *quid est* (*sunt*) *boni?* in the sense 'what are good men?'

in bonis, 'in possession of good things': for *in* cf. ii 21, 49 *in uolnere=uolneratus,* v 26, 73 *in cruciatu atque tormentis*; Fin. i 10, 32 'in ea uoluptate uelit esse.'

§**29. complexio,** 'the accumulation and combination of good things and the exclusion of bad things'; for *complexio* in the sense of combination of things of different kinds cf. Fin. i 6, 19 'ita effici complexiones et copulationes et adhaesiones atomorum inter se' where it is a translation of συμπλοκή. The word is rare in Cic. in this sense.

turba quaedam, 'a rabble, so to speak'; for the force of *quaedam* see i 12, 27 n. For a similar list of the *turba malorum* cf. iii 34, 81.

dolores corporis: Diog. L. vii 37 enumerates amongst Zeno's pupils a certain Dionysius ὁ μεταθέμενος εἰς τὴν ἡδονήν· διὰ γὰρ σφοδρὰν ὀφθαλμίαν ὤκνησεν ἔτι λέγειν τὸν πόνον ἀδιάφορον.

perdita: 'bad health' cf. Phil. viii. 10, 31 'cum esset summa senectute et perdita ualetudine,' pro Rab. perd. 7, 21 'perditus morbo.'

in his…sapiens: 'a philosopher may be confronted with all these, many and serious as they are': Cic. purposely avoids the use of the word *malis*, as he did not regard these afflictions as really evils. For the order of the words *potest esse* cf. i 46, 110 n.

praestare: cf. iii 16, 34 n. and Madvig, *Opuscula Acad.* 1 p. 151.

20 possit? 30. non igitur facile concedo neque Bruto meo neque communibus magistris nec ueteribus illis, Aristoteli, Speusippo, Xenocrati, Polemoni ut, cum ea quae supra enumeraui in malis numerent, idem dicant semper beatum esse sapientem. quos si titulus hic delectat insignis et pulcher, Pythagora, Socrate, 25 Platone dignissimus, inducant animum illa, quorum splendore capiuntur, uires, ualetudinem, pulchritudinem, diuitias, honores, opes contemnere eaque quae his contraria sunt pro nihilo ducere; tum poterunt clarissima uoce profiteri se neque fortunae impetu nec multitudinis opinione nec dolore nec paupertate terreri, 30 omniaque sibi in sese esse posita, nec esse quicquam extra suam

§ **30, 21.** nec R V P G B ι 2 Κ ι S E ι 2 W 2 D C II J. neque W ι M ι 2 O 2 3 7. ‖ speusippo R V P B K. spe·usippo G. 23. idem R ι 2 ι ο ι 6 V G B ι 2 Κ ι E ι 2 W 2 M ι D J O 2 7. ijdem S at j postea inculc. iidem W ι M 2 O 3. ‖ quos si R 6 P B ι–3 S E ι 2 M ι 2 D C II O 2 3. quod si R ι 17 V G Κ ι 2 W ι 2 J O ι. qui si R 7 O 7. 24. delectat B ι W ι. dilectat R V G K. 25. inducant animum R ι 6 17 P B ι–3 Κ ι E 2 W 2 M ι 2 D C II J O 2 3 7. inducant in animum G at ι ante animum eras. ut uid. inducant animum V atr. ant. superscr. inducat animum O ι. inducā animum W ι. 26. ualetudinem R V G K J. ualitudinem B S E. 27. contem/nere S. contempnere G E. ‖ contraria K. ra ri ~ contria R eod. atr. contrịa G alt. man. superscr. contria B 2. contria V. ‖ sunt B ι W ι 2 J O ι 27. sint R V P G B 3 Κ ι S E ι 2 M 2 D C II. 28. impetu R V G B K S E.

§ **30. communibus,** i.e. whose lectures Brutus and I attended. Cic. is referring to philosophers like Antiochus and Aristus, whose point of view is here under discussion. Ha. curiously takes communibus as = mihi et Academicis Peripateticisque communibus, a meaning which (however true of Antiochus and Aristus the words may be in point of fact) cannot be got out of the context.
ueteribus illis: Antiochus though calling himself an Academic attempted on the one hand to minimize the differences between the Academics and Peripatetics and on the other hand to show that the Stoic doctrines were really to be found in Plato : hence he regarded not merely the heads of the Academy (Speusippus, Xenocrates, Polemo) but Aristotle as his teachers in philosophy; cf. Fin. v 3, 7 ; Ac. ii 45, 137. See Hirzel, Untersuchungen zu Cicero's philosophischen Schriften III 242.
quos : for the relative attracted into the construction of the nearer clause cf. iii 31, 76 'ut Prometheus ille Aeschyli, cui cum dictum esset...respondit', iv 19, 43 'sine aculeis iracundiae, quae etiamsi non adsit, tamen uerbis atque

motu simulandam arbitrantur' : see also i 34, 84 n.
Pythagora : Hirzel (loc. cit.) points out that the coupling of Plato and Pythagoras was characteristic of the later developments of Platonism.
Cic. implies here, though he does not definitely say so, that Pythagoras, Socrates and Plato adopted the Stoic view upon the sufficiency of virtue as against that of the Peripatetics and Academics. Elsewhere he claims Socratic authority for the Stoic παράδοξα, iii 5, 10 ; Ac. ii 44, 136. Antiochus, on the point, ἐπεδείκνυε ὅτι παρὰ Πλάτωνι κεῖται τὰ τῶν Στωϊκῶν δόγματα, Sext. Emp. Pyrrh. Hypot. i 33 fin. But it is more than doubtful whether either Socrates or Plato would have subscribed to the Stoic formula.
inducant animum : this and not inducere in animum is Cicero's usual phrase, Diu. i 13, 22 ; pro Cluent. 15, 45 ; even in pro Sulla 30, 83 (where see Reid's n.) the right reading is almost certainly animum inducam.
omniaque : for -que connecting contrasted clauses see i 29, 71 n. on adhibuitque.

potestatem quod ducant in bonis. **31.** nunc et haec loqui, quae
sunt magni cuiusdam et alti uiri, et eadem, quae uulgus, in malis
et bonis numerare concedi nullo modo potest. qua gloria commotus Epicurus exoritur; cui etiam, si dis placet, uidetur semper
35 sapiens beatus. hic dignitate huius sententiae capitur, sed numquam id diceret si ipse se audiret. quid est enim quod minus
conueniat quam ut is qui uel summum uel solum malum dolorem esse dicat idem censeat 'Quam hoc suaue est!' tum, cum
dolore crucietur, dicturum esse sapientem? non igitur ex singulis
40 uocibus philosophi spectandi sunt, sed ex perpetuitate atque
constantia.

XI. **32.** Adducis me ut tibi adsentiar. sed tua quoque uide
ne desideretur constantia.

Quonam modo?

§ **31**, 31. nec hunc et haec R V P G B 1 K 1 E 1 L 4 5 D.   nec hunc
et hoc O 7.   nec hunc et h^c B 2 K 2 L 2.   nec hunc et h' R 17 W 2 C J.
neque hunc et haec R 6.   nec hinc et haec S.   nec huic et haec R 7.
neq; huic et hec ed. H.   nam hunc et haec E 2 L 3 M 12 II O 2 3.
nam hinc et haec L 6.   nam huic et haec E 3.   nunc et haec *corr. Wesenbergius.*

32. uulgus R G S E.   uulgás V *atr. ant.*   34. si dis placet G B K.

si displacet R.   si displacet V *marg.* si diis placet.   si displicet P S E 1 2
D C O 7.   si diis placet W 1 2 M 1 2 J O 1–3.   36. si ipse se audiret V
at se audiret *in ras. et in marg. excurr.*   si ipse audiret G.   38. idem R 6 17

V *at* m *in ras.* P B E 2 W 1 M 1 2 D C II O 1–3 7.   id÷ ^em E 1 *al. atr. superscr.*
id÷ K.   id est R G.

XI. § **32**, 1. adducis V P B K.   aducis R.   *uerba* adducis...constantia *habet* G
in marg. infer. alt. manu adscript. || adsentiar R V K E.   assentiar G B S.

§ **31. nunc**: for *nunc* adversative (often
nunc autem, or *nunc uero*) cf. ii 19, 45;
iii 1, 2 n.

qua gloria = *gloria huius rei* sc. *loquendi quae sunt magni cuiusdam et alti
uiri*: for this use of the pron. cf. i 19,
45 n. on *haec*; and for the subjective use
of *gloria* cf. ii 20, 46.

si dis placet: expressing indignant
surprise; cf. Ter. Eun. 919, where Don.
says 'proprium est exclamantis propter
indignitatem alicuius rei'; cf. Fin. ii 10,
31; Or. iii 24, 93, with Wilkins' note.

audiret, 'if he were to go to his own
school'; for *audire* in the sense of to
'attend the lectures of' cf. N.D. i 14, 37
'Cleanthes...qui Zenonem audiuit'; Off.
i 1, 1 'te, Marce fili, annum iam audien-
tem Cratippum...abundare oportet praeceptis institutisque philosophiae,' Fin. i 5,
16; from this is developed the sense seen
in i 26, 65 'nec Homerum audio,' 'nor do
I accept Homer's authority,' Fin. i 13, 42

'errore maximo, si Epicurum audire uoluerint, liberabuntur' and here.

quam hoc suaue est: cf. ii 7, 17; Lact.
Diu. Inst. iii 27 'Epicurus multo fortius;
sapiens, inquit, semper beatus est; et uel
inclusus in Phalaridis tauro hanc uocem
emittet: suaue est et nihil curo. quis eum
non irriserit? maxime quod homo uoluptarius personam sibi uiri fortis imposuit,'
a passage evidently modelled upon this.

uocibus, 'isolated sayings'; for *uox*
in this sense cf. pro Planc. 14, 34; II Verr.
v 65, 168 'in hac uoce, "ciuis Romanus
sum."'

spectandi, 'are to be judged,' cf. Q.
Rosc. Com. 10, 28 'nemo enim illum ex
trunco corporis spectabat'; Att. xii 39,
1: and the use of the word *spectatus*,
'approved.'

perpetuitate, 'the general tenor and
consistency of their doctrines'; cf. Off. i
33, 119 'ut constare in perpetuitate uitae
possimus nobismet ipsis.'

Quia legi tuum nuper quartum de finibus; in eo mihi uidebare
5 contra Catonem disserens hoc uelle ostendere, quod mihi quidem
probatur, inter Zenonem et Peripateticos nihil praeter uerborum
nouitatem interesse. quod si ita est, quid est causae quin, si
Zenonis rationi consentaneum sit satis magnam uim in uirtute
esse ad beate uiuendum, liceat idem Peripateticis dicere? rem
10 enim opinor spectari oportere non uerba.

33. Tu quidem tabellis obsignatis agis mecum et testificaris
quid dixerim aliquando aut scripserim. cum aliis isto modo qui
legibus inpositis disputant; nos in diem uiuimus; quodcumque
nostros animos probabilitate percussit, id dicimus, itaque soli
15 sumus liberi. uerum tamen, quoniam de constantia paulo ante
diximus, non ego hoc loco id quaerendum puto uerumne sit
quod Zenoni placuerit quodque eius auditori Aristoni, bonum
esse solum quod honestum esset, sed, si ita esset, † tum ut totum

6. probatur R 6 7 V P G B 1 2 S E 1 W 1 2 M 1 2 D C O 1–3 7.
probare R.   probares E 2 Π.   probare' K 1.   probaretur J.   7. quin si
R V P B.   qui si G *alt. man. superscr.*   qui nisi E 1.   quin S si *om.*
§ 33, 13. impositis R V G B K E.   impositis V.   15. uerumtamen
R V G K.   ueruntamen B S.   16. quaerendum R G.   querendum V B S.
querendum K (i *in* ꬲ *mut.*)   17. audituri G.   18. esset tum ut totum hoc
R 1 17 P G B 1 K 1 2 E 1 L 2–4 W 1 2 M 1 J O 1 ed. H.   esset tum
ut totum hoc V *atr. ant.*   esset tum ut hoc totum R 6 D C.   esset tum totum
hoc S E 2 3 L 5 6 M 2 Π O 7. esset tum hoc totum O 3.   esset cum ut
totum hoc B 2 O 2.

XI. § 32. **nuper**: the five books of
the de Finibus were completed by the
end of June 45 B.C.; Att. xiii 19, 4. The
reference in the text is to Fin. iv 20, 56 sqq.

probatur: Bentl. Dav. Ern. read here
probare, with which *uidebare* must be
supplied. Kl. points out that the inf.
probably arose from the copyist mistaking
the contraction for *probatur*.

inter Zenonem...interesse: cf. 41, 120;
Fin. iv 20, 57 'hic [sc. Zeno] loquebatur
aliter atque omnes, sentiebat idem quod
ceteri'; v 8, 22 'restant Stoici, qui
cum a Peripateticis et Academicis omnia
transtulissent, nominibus aliis easdem res
secuti sunt.' Carneades seems to have
been the first to take this view of the
case; cf. Fin. iii 12, 41 'Carneades...
pugnare non destitit in omni hac quaestione, quae de bonis et malis appelletur,
non esse rerum Stoicis cum Peripateticis
controuersiam, sed nominum.'

rationi, 'system,' cf. ii 27, 65 n.

§ 33. **tabellis obsignatis.** Depositions
and affidavits were made in the presence
of witnesses who affixed their seals (*ob-
signare*) to the written record: pro Quinct.
21, 67 'eius rei condicionisque tabellas
obsignauerunt uiri boni complures,' Att.

ii 12, 1 'emittat ad me Publius qui
obsignet: iurabo Cnaeum...Antii mihi
narrasse se in auspicio fuisse.' Such a
document when sealed became legal evidence, and legal advisers were supposed
to see that their clients in such affidavits
stated nothing which could be used
against their case. Or. i 38, 174 'cum
obsignes tabellas clientis tui quibus in
tabellis id sit scriptum quo ille capiatur.'

Cic. here humorously protests against
his statements in the de Finibus being
regarded as a sworn deposition, for the
truth of which he could be held responsible. A similar metaphorical use of the
phrase is found in Pis. 28, 69 'retinere
quod acceperat, testificari, tabellas obsig-
nare uelle, Epicurum diserte dicere ex-
istimare.'

Transl. 'You are conducting your
argument with me as if depositions had
been sworn in the case, and you are putting in evidence what I said or wrote
some time or other.'

isto modo: sc. *agas*; cf. 8, 21 *tu uero.*

quodcumque...dicimus: cf. 29, 82;
iv 4, 7.

Aristoni: cf. 9, 27 n.

sed si ita...poneret: the reading *tum*

hoc beate uiuere in una uirtute poneret. **34.** quare demus hoc
20 sane Bruto ut sit beatus semper sapiens; quam sibi conueniat
ipse uiderit; gloria quidem huius sententiae quis est illo uiro
dignior? nos tamen teneamus ut sit idem beatissimus.

XII. Et, si Zeno Citieus, aduena quidam et ignobilis uerborum opifex, insinuasse se in antiquam philosophiam uidetur,
huius sententiae grauitas a Platonis auctoritate repetatur, apud
quem saepe haec oratio usurpata est ut nihil praeter uirtutem
5 diceretur bonum. **35.** uelut in Gorgia Socrates, cum esset ex eo
quaesitum, Archelaum, Perdiccae filium, qui tum fortunatissimus

19. poneret R 1 6 7 10 16 17   V G   B 1 2   K 1 2   S   E 1–3   L 2–6   W 1   M 1 2
D C Π J   O 1–3 7 ed. H.   posuit W 2.

§ **34, 21.** ipse B 1   E 2   M 1 2.   ipsa V.   ipsa R G K   E 1.
22. beatissimus R V P G B K.
XII. 1. zeno citieus G   B 1.   zenociti̯eus V.   zeno eitiens B 2.
zenoticieus R K.   zenotici̯ ej̯ P.   zenocio eius E 1.   zenonici eius S.
zenoticius ed. H.   ‖ quidam R V G   B 1   M 2   O 7.   quidei S ē *in* ā *mut.*
quidem E 2 J.   2. insinuasse se in R 1 6 7 17   V P G   B 1 2   K 1   S   E 1–3
W 1 2   M 2   D C Π J   O 1 3.   insinuasse se ad O 7.   insinuasse in M 1   O 2.

§ **35, 5.** uelut V P G.   uelud R K.   6. archelaum B.   arcelaum V *atr. uiridi*
superscr.   arcaelaum G.   arcelaum R K E.

ut totum of nearly all MSS can only be
defended either by supplying (with Or.)
postulandum (from *quaerendum*) before
ut, and taking the subject of *poneret* to be
(not *Zeno* or *Aristo*, but) *Peripateticus*—
on which Sff. comments 'haec a sano
homine scribi aut probari potuisse uix
credibile uidetur'—or (with T.S. and
Ha.) by making *ut...poneret* depend upon
uerum sit in the sense of 'whether it is
proper that he should etc.,' the tense of
the subj. being supposed to be due to the
attraction of the preceding *honestum esset.*
Hei. inserts *uolui* before *ut*. Bentl. followed by Dav. proposed *ni ita esset,*
utrum totum hoc, and this line of emendation is followed with unimportant variations by F.A.W. Küh. Sff. (who inserts
recte before *poneret*); Schiche reads *sed*
ni ita esset, num consentaneum esset tum
ut totum...poneretur.

It is perhaps possible that Cicero wrote
'sed si ita esset tum hoc...poneret,' that
tum was corrected in the archetype by
uel (*ut*) *totum*, and that the gloss was
copied into the text after *tum* in the form
ut totum : 'I do not consider that the
point now to be discussed is whether
Zeno's view is correct, but if it were, then
he would make the life of happiness to
depend solely upon virtue.'

§ **34. demus** : for *dare* in this sense
cf. i 11, 25 'dasne aut manere animos
post mortem aut morte ipsa interire' :
here the clause 'ut...sapiens' is explanatory of *hoc*.
teneamus ut : cf. i 42, 100 n.
XII. **aduena**, 'an outsider, so to speak,
and in literature a vulgar artisan.' The
word *aduena* is used not simply because
Zeno being a native of the Phoenician
town of Citium was supposed not to be of
Greek blood (so Küh. and edd. generally)
but because he was, as a foreigner, an
intruder into Greek philosophy; for this
metaphorical use of the word (emphasized
here by *quidam*) cf. Or. i 58, 249.
For other criticisms, always unfavour-
able, upon Zeno's style cf. Fin. iii 2, 5 ;
iv 3, 7 and Zeller, *Stoics, etc.* E.T. p. 40.
§ **35. uelut** : 5, 13 n.
in Gorgia, p. 470 D and E : it was a
favourite passage with later moralists;
Dav. refers to Plut. de lib. educ. p. 6A,
Dio Chrys. Or. iii p. 102 R ; Julian,
Or. ii p. 79.
Archelaum : he was king of Macedonia
from 413 B.C. to 399 B.C. ; a patron of
art and letters, he entertained Greek
poets, artists and musicians at his court :
cf. Holm, *History of Greece* III p. 203.

haberetur, nonne beatum putaret, Haud scio, inquit; numquam enim cum eo conlocutus sum. — ain tandem?
aliter id scire non potes? — nullo modo. — tu igitur
10 ne de Persarum quidem rege magno potes dicere beatusne sit? — an ego possim, cum ignorem quam sit
doctus, quam uir bonus? — quid? tu in eo sitam uitam
beatam putas? — ita prorsus existimo, bonos beatos,
improbos miseros. — miser ergo Archelaus? — certe,
15 si iniustus. — Videturne omnem hic beatam uitam in una
uirtute ponere? **36.** quid uero? in Epitaphio quo modo idem?
'nam cui uiro,' inquit, 'ex se ipso apta sunt omnia quae
ad beate uiuendum ferunt, nec suspensa aliorum aut
bono casu aut contrario pendere ex alterius euentis
20 et errare coguntur, huic optime uiuendi ratio comparata est. hic est ille moderatus, hic fortis, hic sapiens, hic et nascentibus et cadentibus cum reliquis

7. nonne R16 VPG B12 K1 S E12 W12 M12 DCΠJ
O127.   non O3.   8. conlocutus R V G B K E.   collocutus P S. ||
i
an tu aliter Π *al. atr. superscr.*   an tu an aliter V *atr. ant. superscr.* B1 *atr.*
nigriore superscr.   an tu aliter R67 E2 L236 M12 DCJ O12 ed. H.
an tu an aliter S L4.   an tu an aliter P.   an tu   aliter W2 an *post* tu *eras.*
an tu an aliter R117 G B2 K12 E13 L5 O7.   an tu id aliter W1.
an tu aliter tu id O3.   ain tandem? aliter *corr. Seyffertus.*   10. magno R G B K
o
E2 C O27.   magna V.   11. possim R17 VPG B12 K12 S
E1-3 W1 M12 DCΠJ O37.   p'si W2.   possem O2.   possum O1.
13. existimo R V G B K E.   14. improbos R V G B K S E. || archelaus
R V G B K.   arcelaus E.
§ 36, 17. e se ipso V *ras. inter* e *et* s.   esse ipso R G B K E.   in se ipso P.
18. beate R B J.   beate *ex* beatae *alt. man. mut.* G.   beatae V.
ex
19. alterius Π *al. atr. superscr.*   alterius E2 ex *om.*   20. optume R V G B K. ||
comparata R V G K.   cōparata B.   22. cadentibus B K *plerique.*
candentibus R G B2 E1.

Ain tandem? aliter: Sff.'s correction
of *an tu an aliter* of the best MSS seems
most satisfactory, *tandem* having been in
his view corrupted through the contraction
tan into *tu an.* *Ain tu?* *an* (Mo.) which
seems nearer the MSS is less satisfactory,
as *ain tu?* never seems to be followed by
any but a simple question (Hand, *Tursell.*
III p. 495). The reading *ain tu? aliter,*
adopted by Küh. Hei. Sch., does not
account for the second *an* of the MSS.
Ain tandem? translates τί δαί; of the
Gk. which lower down is translated again
by *quid?* For further exx. of the use of
the phrase Küh. refers to Cic. Fam. ix
21, 1; Fin. iv 1, 1; Legg. i 20, 53.
uideturne: for this ironical use of *ne*

where *nonne* might have been expected
cf. ii 11, 26 n.
§ 36. in Epitaphio: from the Menexenus
p. 247 E. The Menexenus was composed
by Plato in ironical imitation of such λόγοι
ἐπιτάφιοι as the funeral speech of Pericles
in Thuc. ii, 35 sqq.
ex se ipso apta: a translation of εἰς
ἑαυτὸν ἀνήρτηται: cf. Parad. ii. 17 'nemo
potest non beatissimus esse, qui est totus
aptus ex sese' and n. to 14, 40 below.
suspensa: Küh. compares Fam. v. 13, 1
'quam quidem laudem sapientiae statuo
esse maximam, non aliunde pendere nec
extrinsecus aut bene aut male uiuendi
suspensas habere rationes,' written in the
same year.

commodis, tum maxime liberis parebit et oboediet
praecepto illi ueteri; neque enim laetabitur umquam
25 nec maerebit nimis, quod semper in se ipse omnem
spem reponet sui.' Ex hoc igitur Platonis quasi quodam
sancto augustoque fonte nostra omnis manabit oratio.

XIII. **37.** Vnde igitur ordiri rectius possumus quam a communi parente natura? quae, quicquid genuit, non modo animal,
sed etiam quod ita ortum esset e terra ut stirpibus suis niteretur,
in suo quidque genere perfectum esse uoluit. itaque et arbores
5 et uites et ea quae sunt humiliora neque se tollere a terra altius
possunt alia semper uirent, alia hieme nudata uerno tempore

23. tūmaxime V.   tumaxime R G.   ‖ oboediet R V G K.   obędiet B 1.
obediet B 2 S E 1 J.   24. umquam nec R V P G B K S E 1 2 W 1 M 1 2
C J O 1 3 7.   umquam n3 W 2.   25. quod semper R G B E 1 2 W 1 D.
quod semper V *atr. uiridi superscr.*   qui semper W 2 M 2 O 2.   quid semper
M 1.   26. reponet R 1 7 V P G B 1 2 K 1 S E 1 2 W 1 2 M 1 2
D C Π J O 1–3 7 ed. H.   27. manabit P B 1 K W 1 M 1 J.   manębit V.
manebit R G B 2.

XIII. § **37**, 1. ordiri R 6 7 W 1 M 1 2 D C O 2 3 ed. H.   oriri V
atr. uiridi superscr. W 2 Π.   oriri R 1 17 P G B 1 2 K 1 2 S E 1 2 J
O 1 7. ‖ rectius *post* ordiri (oriri) *habent* R 1 7 V P G B 1 2 K 1 E 1 2 M 1 2
D C O 2 3 7. *ante* ordiri (oriri) *habent* R 6 W 1 2 J O 1 ed. H.   3. ortum esset
R V P G B 1 2 K 1 E 1 2 W 1 2 M 1 2 D C Π J O 1 2 7.   esset ortum O 3.
4. quidque R V P G K 1 E 1 M 2.   quicque B 2 E 2.   quodque W 2
M 1 D C J O 1.   quocque W 1.   quidquid S *marg.* quodque.   6. uiuerent
G *at* ue *ead. man. expunx.*

tum maxime liberis : Cic. seems to
have mistaken the Gk slightly, οὗτος
γιγνομένων χρημάτων καὶ παίδων καὶ
διαφθειρομένων μάλιστα πείσεται τῇ παροι-
μίᾳ, where μάλιστα has no special reference to παίδων.

neque enim...sui : Victorius followed
by Bentl. and others regarded these words
as two iambic senarii ; Bentl. mending
the metre by reading *aut* for *nec* before
maerebit and *ponet* for *reponet*. Ribbeck
in *Trag. Rom. Frag.* 1 p. 211 considered
the words *quod...sui* to be a fragment of
the *Teucer* of Pacuvius, a suggestion which
he withdrew tacitly in his second edition.
Or. notes that Cic. is not likely to have
translated Plato's last sentence into verse
on his own account, and that if the words
be verse it must be assumed that some
one else had done so and that Cicero
preferred this translation to his own—a
doubly hazardous supposition.

fonte: for the metaphor cf. i 3, 6
'philosophiae fontes aperiemus, e quibus
etiam illa manabant.' Or. i 10, 42 'ab
illo fonte et capite Socrate,' and for the
collocation of *anctus* and *augustus*, Tac.

Dial. 4 'sanctiorem illam et augustiorem
eloquentiam colam.'

XIII. § **37. unde...ordiri** : cf. ii 18,42 n.

communi parente natura: for the
Stoic conception of Nature as only another
term for the Divine Being cf. Zeller,
Stoics, etc. E.T. pp. 145 ff. and the reff.
given there.

quod ita ortum...niteretur, 'the vegetable world'; a similar periphrasis in
N.D. ii 10, 26 'omnia quae terra con-
cipiat semina, quaeque ipsa ex se generata
stirpibus infixa contineat'; but T.S. are
surely wrong in saying that there is no
single word in Latin to express this idea.
Cic. uses *stirpes* alone in this sense in
N.D. ii 13, 36 'neque enim si stirpium
similis sit [sc. natura], aut etiam bestiarum, optima putanda sit.' Fin. v 4,
10 'persecutus est...Theophrastus autem
stirpium naturas omniumque fere rerum,
quae e terra gignerentur, causas atque
rationes,' where *stirpium naturas* is a
translation of φυτικαὶ αἰτίαι and the other
words refer to such books as περὶ ἁλῶν,
νίτρου, στυπτηρίας, περὶ λίθων, περὶ μετάλ-
λων mentioned by Diog. L. v 2, 13.

tepefacta frondescunt, neque est ullum quod non ita uigeat
interiore quodam motu et suis in quoque seminibus inclusis ut
aut flores aut fruges fundat aut bacas, omniaque in omnibus,
10 quantum in ipsis sit, nulla ui inpediente perfecta sint. **38.** facilius
uero etiam in bestiis, quod iis sensus a natura est datus, uis ipsius
naturae perspici potest. namque alias bestias nantis aquarum
incolas esse uoluit, alias uolucres caelo frui libero, serpentis quasdam, quasdam esse gradientis; earum ipsarum partim soliuagas,
15 partim congregatas, inmanis alias, quasdam autem cicures, non
nullas abditas terraque tectas. atque earum quaeque suum
tenens munus, cum in disparis animantis uitam transire non
possit, manet in lege naturae. et ut bestiis aliud alii praecipui
a natura datum est, quod suum quaeque retinet nec discedit ab

---

7. uigeat E 2 M 1 2 II *alii.*   uigea⁻t B 1 n *ex parte eras.*   uigeant R V G
K 1 E 1.   10. sit R V P G B 1 2 K 1 S E 1 2 W 1 2 M 1 2 D C Π J
O 1-37. ‖ ui P B 1 2 K 1 E 2 W 2 M 1 2 D C O 37.   uim V.
uim R G. ‖ impediente R V G B K S.   inpediente P E. ‖ perfecta sint
R V G B 1 2 K 1 S E 2 W 1 2 M 1 2 Π J O 2 3.   perfecta sunt E 1
D C O 1.   perfecta sit O 7.

§ 38, 11. quod iis M 2 O 2.   quod iis S *ex* his *ras. mut.*   quod his
R V P G B 1 2 K 1 E 1 2 W 1 M 1 O 1.   quod hiis D C Π O 3.
quod is W 2 J.   si his O 7.   12. nantis V P G B 1 2 K E 1.

nantis R *eod. atr. ut uid.*   nantes S.   13. uolucres R V P G B 1 2 K S E 1. ‖
serpentis G B 1 2 K 1 L 3 O 1.   sepentis V P E 1.   serpentés R 1 i *in* e
mut. eod. atr. ut uid.   serpentes S W 1 M 1 J O 1 2 7. ‖ quasdam quasdam
R 1 7 V G B 1 K 1 L 4.   quasdam *semel tantum* R 6 17 P B 2 K 2 S
E 1 2 L 2 5 6 W 2 M 2 D C Π O 3 7 ed. H.   quasdam serpentes quasdam
L 3 W 1 M 1 J O 1 2.   14. gradientis R 2 V P G B K.   gradientés R 1
e *in* i *mut. et postea* i *paene eras.*   gradientes R 10 16 B 2 S O 7.
15. inmanis R V P G B 2 K.   immanis B 1 E.   immanes S.
inmanes O 7. ‖ quasdam autem R G.   quasdam aū V.   quasdam aut E 1.
quasdam uero S.   17. disparis R V G B 1 2 K E.   dispares S. ‖ animantis
R V G B.   animantés S e *in* i *mut.*   18. praecipui R V P G B 1 K 1 2 S
E 1 2 W 2 M 1 2 Π J O 1-3.   p̄cipuị⊦ B 2.   praecipue D C.
praecipuum W 1 O 7.   19. discedit P E 2 W 1 M 1 D C Π O 1-3 7.
discedat M 2.   discendit B 1.   discendit R V G B 2 K.

---

fundat: this word denotes an easy or
an abundant production ; cf. Nägelsbach,
Stil. § 130, 3, who compares N.D. ii 51,
129 '[oua] fetum fundunt,' Or. iii 50, 194
' solitus est uersus hexametros...fundere
ex tempore.'
sit...sint: attracted into the construction of the clause immediately preceding ;
the clause beginning with *omnia* is parallel
in thought to the clause *neque est ullum
...bacas.*
§ **38. etiam** qualifies *facilius* : for
etiam thus placed after, and separated
by another word from, the word it qualifies cf. II in Verr. iii 88, 206 ' cetera quae
forsitan alii quoque etiam fecerint,' and
Madvig, *Gr.* § 471.

partim...partim = *alias...alias* : cf. 33,
93 ; N.D. i 37, 103 'bestiarum autem
terrenae sunt aliae, partim aquatiles, aliae
quasi ancipites'; Liv. xxvi 21, 16; Roby,
Lat. Gr. §§ 1264, 1429.
quaeque suum: for the order (which
is here perhaps influenced by the construction) see Draeger, *Syntax* § 33 and
the exx. quoted there from Livy (e.g. v
20. 8 'quod quisque sua manu ex hoste
captum domum rettulerit'; vi 25, 9
'huc atque illuc euntium qua quemque
suorum usuum causae ferrent'), and the
poets.
discedit ab eo: for the transition
from relative to demonstrative cf. ii 25,
61 n.

20 eo, sic homini multo quiddam praestantius; etsi praestantia
debent ea dici quae habent aliquam comparationem, humanus
autem animus decerptus ex mente diuina cum alio nullo nisi
cum ipso deo, si hoc fas est dictu, comparari potest. **39.** hic
igitur si est excultus, et si eius acies ita curata est ut ne cae-
25 caretur erroribus, fit perfecta mens, id est absoluta ratio, quod
est idem uirtus. et, si omne beatum est cui nihil deest et quod
in suo genere expletum atque cumulatum est, idque uirtutis
est proprium, certe omnes uirtutis compotes beati sunt. et hoc
quidem mihi cum Bruto conuenit, id est cum Aristotele, Xeno-
30 crate, Speusippo, Polemone. sed mihi uidentur etiam beatissimi.
40. quid enim deest ad beate uiuendum ei qui confidit suis
bonis? aut, qui diffidit, beatus esse qui potest? at diffidat necesse est qui bona diuidit tripertito.

XIV. Qui enim poterit aut corporis firmitate aut fortunae

---

21. comparationem R V G B K. 23. comparari R V G K. cōparari B.
§ **39**, 24. caecaretur R V P G B i 2 K i 2 E i 2 W i 2 M i 2 D C Π J
O 1–3. cēcaretur S *at car in lit.* cecetur O 7. 25. quod est idem uirtus
R V G B i 2 K i S E i–3 L 5 W i 2 M 2 D C Π J O i 3 7. quod idem
est uirtus K 2 M i O 2. q̄ est idem qd uirtus ed. H. 28. omnes R 6 17
G B i 2 S *alii.* omnis R V P K i E i 2 W i 2. omnis *in* omnes *mut.* Π. ‖
compotes R V G. cōpotes B K. 29. id est R V G B 2 K M 2 C.
id P B i. idē W i 2 J O 7. idē S *spat. post* ē *relict.* 30. speusippo
P W i. pseusippo R V B i. pseu·sippo G. ~~pseu~~usippo S *marg.* speusippo.
pseupsippo K i E i. ‖ beatissimi R V G B K.
§ **40**, 33. triptito E. tripertilio G. tripertio R V K.
XIV. 1. firmitate R K. firmitati V G B i 2 S.

---

etsi: introducing a correction, sometimes followed by an adversative con-
junction, as here and i 42, 99, sometimes
alone as in iii 8, 17.

habent, 'admit of,' cf. i 49, 119 n.; iv
36, 77 n.

decerptus, 'a fragment of,' an attempt
to translate ἀπόσπασμα, a *uox technica* in
Stoic writers; cf. Marc. Aur. v 27 ὁ δαίμων
ὃν ἑκάστῳ...ὁ Ζεὺς ἔδωκεν, ἀπόσπασμα
ἑαυτοῦ· οὗτος δέ ἐστιν ὁ ἑκάστου νοῦς καὶ
λόγος and the parallels quoted by Gale
ad loc. especially N.D. i 11, 27 'Pythagoras...censuit animum esse per naturam
rerum omnem intentum et commeantem,
ex quo nostri animi carperentur.'

§ **39**. **ut ne**: cf. i 32, 78 n. and Madv.
Lat. Gr. § 456 obs. 4.

caecaretur: the impft. here expresses
not the result, but the result aimed at in
past time. Küh. on i 4, 7 compares Somn.
Scip. 3 (15, 15 Or.) 'homines sunt hac
lege generati qui tuerentur illum globum';
Bentley's *caecetur*, adopted by Or., is not
merely unnecessary but spoils the sense.

quod est idem: we should have expected *quae est eadem*, and the fem. would
have been more in accordance with Cic.'s
usage: the neuter *quod* is perhaps due (as
Küh. suggests) to the gender of *id* in *id
est* immediately before.

§ **40. Quid enim deest...qui potest?**
Cf. Arist. Nic. Eth. I, 1100 a 4 δεῖ γὰρ
[sc. πρὸς τὴν εὐδαιμονίαν], ὥσπερ εἴπομεν
καὶ ἀρετῆς τελείας καὶ βίου τελείου· πολλαὶ
γὰρ μεταβολαὶ γίνονται καὶ παντοῖαι τύχαι
κατὰ τὸν βίον, καὶ ἐνδέχεται τὸν μάλιστ'
εὐθενοῦντα μεγάλαις συμφοραῖς περιπεσεῖν
ἐπὶ γήρως, καθάπερ ἐν τοῖς Τρωϊκοῖς περὶ
Πριάμου μυθεύεται· τὸν δὲ τοιαύταις χρησά-
μενον τύχαις καὶ τελευτήσαντα ἀθλίως οὐδεὶς
εὐδαιμονίζει, where Aristotle proves Cic.'s
contention that the result of reckoning
other things than virtue as conducive to
happiness, destroys all assurance of the
continuance of happiness. The same
argument is urged in Fin. ii 27, 86.

tripertito: i.e. into *bona animi, bona
corporis* and *bona externa.*

stabilitate confidere? atqui nisi stabili et fixo et permanente
bono beatus esse nemo potest. quid ergo eius modi istorum est?
ut mihi Laconis illud dictum in hos cadere uideatur, qui glorianti
5 cuidam mercatori, quod multas nauis in omnem oram maritimam
dimisisset, 'Non sane optabilis quidem ista,' inquit, 'rudentibus apta fortuna.' an dubium est quin nihil sit
habendum in eo genere quo uita beata compleatur, si id possit
amitti? nihil enim interarescere, nihil exstingui, nihil cadere
10 debet eorum in quibus uita beata consistit. nam qui timebit ne
quid ex his deperdat, beatus esse non poterit. **41.** uolumus
enim eum qui beatus sit tutum esse, inexpugnabilem, saeptum
atque munitum, non ut paruo metu praeditus sit, sed ut nullo.

2. stabilitate R G　B 2　K 1　W 1.　　stabili R 16　W 2.　　stabilitate V.
stabilitati R 2 10　S.　　　stabilitatē B 1　E 1.　　5. nauis R V G　B 1　K.
naues B 2　S　E 1.　　　6. quidem ista R 1 17　V P G　B 2　K 1　S　E 1 2
W 1 2　M 1　D C Π J　O 2 3 7.　　ista quidem O 1.　　ista quidem est R 6
M 2.　　quidem est ista R 7.　　7. qui nihil G *alt. man. superscr.*
8. quo uita R G　B 1 2　K 1　E 2　W 1　J　O 1 7 Gr.　　qui V *atr. ant.*
quod P 2　S　E 3　M 1　O 2 3. ‖ compleatur O 7.　　complectitur R 1 67 10 16 17
V　P 1 2　G　B 1 2　K 1 2　S　E 2 3　L 2 3 5 6　W 1 2　M 1 2　D C Π J
O 1-3 Gr. ed. H.　　completitur L 4.　　cōpletit E 1.　　9. extingui
R V G B K S E.　　11. ex his R V P G B K S E　W 1 2　M 1　J　O 1 7.
ex iis M 2　O 2.　　ex hiis D C II.　　ex eis O 3.
§ **41**, 12. septum G *h.l.*

XIV. glorianti: Cicero has, as Dav.
points out, either followed a slightly
different version to that followed by
Plutarch, or repeated the story inaccurately. Plutarch's version is (Apophth.
Lac. p. 234 F) πρὸς δὲ τὸν μακαρίζοντα
Λάμπιν τὸν Αἰγινήτην διότι ἐδόκει πλουσι-
ώτατος εἶναι ναυκλήρια πολλὰ ἔχων, Λάκων
εἶπεν, 'οὐ προσέχω εὐδαιμονίᾳ ἐκ σχοινίων
ἀπηρτημένῃ.'
　apta: cf. Lucilius x 389 (Marx) 'ualidis
in funibus aptas,' where see Marx's note;
the abl. without a preposition is found in
Ennius 'fides alma apta pinnis,' quoted
in Off. iii 29, 104; in Enn. 340 (Vahlen)
'uinclis uenatica uelox apta'; and in
Lucil. xxx 1060 (Marx) 'restibus aptus';
cf. also Leg. i 21, 56 'uita apta uirtute';
the word is derived from the root in
adipiscor and literally means 'caught,'
'attached,' 'conexus et conligatus' as
Nonius explains it (p. 235, 2).
　compleatur: the reading *quo...com-
plectitur* of nearly all MSS was defended
by Lamb. as an example of the passive
use of the deponent found in Rosc. Am.
13, 37 'quo uno maleficio scelera omnia

complexa esse uideantur' and by Dav.
as an example of 'Hellenismus' (or attraction of the relative) in Auct. ad
Herenn. i 7, 11 'aperte rationibus quibus
perscripsimus.' Bentl. proposed to read
compleitur, in which he is followed by Tr.
and Ba. Wopkens (*op. cit.* p. 148) proposed *compleatur* (found in one Oxford
MS), accepted by Or. Kl. Küh. Sff., which
is undoubtedly right; cf. 16, 47 'iis uitam
beatam compleri negant.' The subj.
comes under the head of 'class-subjunc-
tives.'
　§ 41. atque: according to the rules
laid down by Madv. in his note to Fin. iv
20, 56 *saeptum* and *munitum* should here
be taken closely together as forming the
third phrase in the series, as according to
him Cic. never in an enumeration of three
or more terms puts a copula between the
last two if they form independent terms
in the series. But, as Küh. points out,
though the rule may be generally true it
is not universal, and breaks down (e.g.)
in 9, 26 where no such distinction can be
drawn between 'honeste, sapienter, iuste'
and 'honeste, sapienter iusteque.'

ut enim innocens is dicitur, non qui leuiter nocet, sed qui nihil
15 nocet, sic sine metu is habendus est, non qui parua metuit, sed
qui omnino metu uacat. quae est enim alia fortitudo nisi animi
adfectio cum in adeundo periculo et in labore ac dolore patiens,
tum procul ab omni metu? **42.** atque haec certe non ita se
haberent, nisi omne bonum in una honestate consisteret. qui
20 autem illam maxime optatam et expetitam securitatem (securitatem autem nunc appello uacuitatem aegritudinis, in qua uita
beata posita est) habere quisquam potest cui aut adsit aut adesse
possit multitudo malorum? qui autem poterit esse celsus et
erectus et ea quae homini accidere possunt omnia parua ducens
25 qualem sapientem esse uolumus, nisi omnia sibi in se posita cen-

           si
15. sicne G *ead. man.* ‖ parua metuit R 1 6 10 17 V P G B 1 2 K 1 2 S
E 1 3 L 3-5 W 1 M 1 2 Π O 2 3 ed. H. parū metuit D C. parūa
metuit O 1. pua metuit R 16 E 2 L 6 W 2 J *marg. e cont. om.* O 7.
parua non metuit R 7. non parua non metuit L 2. 16. quae est enim R V P G
E 1 2 W 1 M 1 2 D C Π J O 1 2 7. quẹd est enim K 1. que enim est O 3.
quae est B 2 enim *om.* 17. adfectio R V G K E. affectio B S. ‖ cum in
adeundo R V P G B 1 2 K 1 E 1 2 W 1 2 M 2 D C Π J O 1 3. tum in
adeundo K 2 M 1 O 2 7 ed. H.
§ **42,** 18. atquae G a *ante* e *exp. alt. man.* 20. maxume R V B K.
illa maxúme G u *ex* i *mut.* maxime S E. ‖ expetitam M 1 O 1. expeditam
R 1 6 7 10 16 17 V P G B 1 2 K 1 2 S E 1-3 L 2 4-6 W 1 2 M 2 D C Π J
O 2 3 7. expectatam L 3. 21. appello G K. apello R V.
                                                 ad   e
22. adsitaut V a *ante* u *alio atr. inculc.* sitaut G *ead. man.* 23. et rectus
G *ead. man.* 25. omnia sibi in se R V P G B 1 2 K 1 2 E 1 2 W 1 2
                                                  in se
D C Π O 1 3 7 ed. H. omnia in se L 5. omnia s̶i̶b̶i̶ J. omnia∧sibi
in se S *marg.* bona. omnia bona sibi in se M 2. omnia is in se
M 1 O 2.

parua metuit, ' whose fears are of small things,' i.e. who though secure against serious apprehensions may yet have small troubles to expect. This, which is the reading of the best (and most) MSS. is retained by Tr. Ml. Kl. Ba. and is defended by Madv. on Fin. v 30, 91; Fabr. and Or. with some MSS. read *parum*: Ba. alters *parua* to *pauca*; Sff. conjectured *parce* and T.S. (followed by Küh.) alter to *qui paruo metu est.* Sff.'s objection that the man who fears *parua* is really full of fears, not practically free from them, while true as a statement of practical experience and of Peripatetic doctrine (cf. Stob. Ecl. Eth. ii 296 τὸν δ' ἔμπαλιν πάντα φοβούμενον, ὥστε καὶ τὴν σκιάν, ἀγεννῆ καὶ δειλόν) ignores the fact that we are here dealing with hypotheses. Cic. is arguing that no one can be said to be *sine metu* who is afraid of any-

thing whatever, and assumes the case of a man who, secure against serious disaster, can have no fear of any but insignificant mischances; his being afraid of the latter is only a proof that he has nothing worse to fear, not that he is constitutionally a coward.

    procul: the adverbial clause is here equivalent to an adj. Edd. quote as parallels N.D. ii 66, 166 'ipsorum deorum *saepe* praesentiae,' Or. iii 47, 183 'a breuibus *deinceps* tribus.'

    § **42. omnia sibi in se posita** : Bentl. followed by Dav. altered *sibi* to *sua* which, Wopkens (*op. cit.* p. 148) points out, he need not have done if he had remembered 10, 30 'omniaque sibi in sese esse posita.' Ter. Ad. 958 'suo sibi gladio hunc iugulo' quoted by Or. is not parallel.

sebit? an Lacedaemonii Philippo minitante per litteras se omnia
quae conarentur prohibiturum quaesiuerunt, num se esset etiam
mori prohibiturus; uir is quem quaerimus non multo facilius
tali animo reperietur quam ciuitas uniuersa? quid? ad hanc
30 fortitudinem de qua loquimur temperantia adiuncta, quae sit
moderatrix omnium commotionum, quid potest ad beate uiuendum deesse ei quem fortitudo ab aegritudine et a metu uindicet,
temperantia cum a libidine auocet, tum insolenti alacritate gestire
non sinat? haec efficere uirtutem ostenderem, nisi superioribus
35 diebus essent explicata.

　　XV. **43.** Atque cum perturbationes animi miseriam, seda-
tiones autem uitam efficiant beatam, duplexque ratio perturbationis sit, quod aegritudo et metus in malis opinatis, in
bonorum autem errore laetitia gestiens libidoque uersetur,

26. lacedaemonii G.　　lacedaimoni E 1.　　lacedemonii B 1.　　lacedemoni B 2.
lace demonii R V.　　lacedomonii K.　　‖　philosopho militanti V *marg. alio atr.*
adscr. t philippo minitanti.　　minitanti R 6 7　L 2　W 1　M 1 2　D C J　O 1–3 7.
militanti W 2.　　militanti S *marg.* minitanti.　　militante R 1 2 10 17　V P G
B 1 2　K 1 2　E 1 2　L 5　II.　　minitante *corr. Bentleius.*　　29. reperietur
P B K　W 1.　re*p*perietur R *eod. atr.*　　repperietur V G　E 1.　　30. loquimur
R 6 7 17　K 2　E 2　L 5　W 1 2　M 1 2　D C II　O 1–3 ed. H.　　loqui*m* V
at m *in ras.*　　loquitur B 1 *al. atr. superscr.*　loqt S *marg.* loqm.　　loquitur
R P G　B 2　K 1　E 1　O 7.　　‖　quae sit R 1 2 6 10 16　V P G　B 1 2　K 1 2　S
E 1 2　W 1 2　M 1 2　D C J　O 7.　　31. commotionum ∠ V *marg. atr.* uiridi
adscr. addi po*t.*　　‖　beatae G.　　33. cum a K 2.　　*t*um a J *fuerat fortasse* cum.
tum a S *at* t *ex* c *mut.* uidetur.　　tuma P.　　tum a R 1 6 7 17　V G　B 1 2
K 1　E 1–3　W 1 2　M 1 2　D C II　O 1–3 7 ed. H.　　‖　libidine R V P G K.
　　XV. § **43**, 1. atque cum S.　　atqui cum P 2　K 2　E 3　L 2–4 6　W 1 2
M 1 2　J　O 1–3.　　atquicumqu*ę* V.　　atq3 cumq3 E 2　II.　　atquicumque
R G　K 1.　　atqui*c*q; P *marg.* atq cū.　　adquecūque O 7.　　at quicunque
B 1 2　L 5.　　at quecumque D C.　　at q*c*q; E 1.　　‖　miseriam R V P G　B 1 2
K 1　S　E 1 2　W 1 2　M 1　D C II J　O 2.　　miseram M 2　O 1 3 7.
4. uersetur R V P G　B 1 2　K 1　S　E 1 2　W 1 2　M 1 2　D C II J　O 1–3 7.

minitante: Bentley's reading for the
MSS *minitanti* is adopted by nearly all
recent edd. Of those who retain the MSS
reading Kl. and Or. regard the abl. form
in *-i* as permissible in participles in the
abl. absolute construction; while Küh.
following a suggestion of F.A.W. takes
minitanti as a dative, and the sentence as
an anacoluthon, Cic. having intended to
write *responderunt* but having written
quaesiuerunt instead. Confusion between
-i and *-e* is common enough in MSS.
　　The story is told with many variations
by Val. Max. vi 4, 4 ext.; Plut. Apophth.
Lac. p. 235 B, and Stob. Ecl. iii 7, 69.

XV. § **43. Atque**, 'and further'; this
use of *atque* in passing to a fresh set of
considerations is common in Cicero; cf.
Sff.'s note to Lael. 15, 54. Sff. proposes
to read here *cumque*, supposing *atque* to
have arisen from a dittography of the
preceding two syllables.
　　duplex ratio: explained in iv 6, 11—12.
　　quod...uersetur: the subjunct. is perhaps best explained as due to the influence
of the subjunctives preceding; cf. Roby,
Lat. Gr. II § 1778. T.S. alter *quod* to
cum, comparing iv 19, 44 'quod somnum
capere non posset,' which is not really
parallel; see n. there.

5 cum omnia <ea> cum consilio et ratione pugnent, his tu tam grauibus concitationibus tamque ipsis inter se dissentientibus atque
distractis quem uacuum, solutum, liberum uideris, hunc dubitabis
beatum dicere? atqui sapiens semper ita adfectus est; semper
igitur sapiens beatus est. atque etiam omne bonum laetabile
10 est; quod autem laetabile, id praedicandum et prae se ferendum;
quod tale autem, id etiam gloriosum; si uero gloriosum, certe
laudabile; quod laudabile autem, profecto etiam honestum; quod
bonum igitur, id honestum. **44.** at quae isti bona numerant, ne
ipsi quidem honesta dicunt; solum igitur bonum, quod hones-
15 tum; ex quo efficitur honestate una uitam contineri beatam.
non sunt igitur ea bona dicenda nec habenda quibus abundantem licet esse miserrimum. **45.** an dubitas quin praestans
ualetudine, uiribus, forma, acerrimis integerrimisque sensibus,

5. cum omnia cum R 1 7 1 7   V P G   B 1 2   K 1   E 1 2   L 3 5   W 1 2   D C J
O 1 3 7.   cum ōīa cum L 4.   cum ōīa L 2.   cum hc omīa S *at* hc *in marg.*
haec
excurrit.   cum omnia cum E 3 *et* II *alio atr. superscr.*   cum haec omnia cum
R 6   L 6   M 2   O 2 ed. H.   cum omnia haec cum M 1.   cum q3 omīa cum K 2.
cum omnia ea *corr. Seyffertus.*   6.   tamque in ipsis G *at* in *exp. alt. man.*
8. adfectus R V G K E.   affectus B S.   9. atque etiam R V   P 1 2   G
K 1   E 1.   at quae etiam W 1   O 2.   atqui etiam K 2 ˙M 1   O 1.
§ **44,** 13.   at que isti D   O 1.   atq̄: isti V.   atque isti R G   B 1   K 1
q
C   O 7.   atq; isti P.   atq3 quę S *at* quę *in marg. ad init. lineae.*   atqui isti
i
K 2   E 2   W 2   M 1 2.   15.   unam uitam G.   ‖ contineri B 1.   continere V.
continere R G   B 2   K 1.   16.   abundantem R V S *at lit. ante* ab.   habun-
dantem G B K E.   17.   miserrimum R V G B K.
§ **45,** 18.   ualetudine R V G K.   ualitudine B S E.   ‖ acerrimis R V G B.
r
acerumis K *eod. atr.*   ‖ integerrumisque B.   integerrimisque L 6.   integerum
er   e
hisque R K.   integrum hisque V *atr. uiridi superscr.*   integrum hisque G.

cum omnia <ea>: Sff.'s addition of
ea seems to be the best emendation of
this passage. Bentley's *quae* for *cum* has
been adopted by Sch. Ba. and T.S., the
latter two also altering *pugnent* to *pugnant.* Or. and Küh. prefer *cum <haec>
omnia.*
atqui: as often, introducing the minor
premiss of the syllogism; cf. Fin. i 18, 58
with Madv.'s note.
atque etiam, 'and further still,' stronger
than *atque* in transitions. For the 'chain-
argument' which follows cf. Fin. iii 8, 27
'quod est bonum, omne laudabile est;
quod autem laudabile est, omne est honestum; bonum igitur quod est, honestum
est' and Plut. Stoic. rep. 1039 c; and
for the Stoic 'chain-argument' in general,
Zeller, *Stoics*, etc. p. 115.
§ **44. at:** like *atqui,* sometimes introduces the minor premiss; cf. iii 7, 15,

where the syllogism is 'sapiens numquam
est perturbatus; *at* aegritudo perturbatio
est; semper *igitur* ea sapiens uacabit';
so in 16, 48 below; N.D. iii 17, 43; Fin.
i 11, 39.
numerant, 'reckon as'; cf. N.D. iii
16, 40 'singulas enim stellas numeras
deos'; pro Mur. 24, 49 'Sulpicium
accusatorem suum numerabat' and the
other passages quoted by Wopkens, *op.
cit.* p. 183.
abundantem, ' of which one may have
plenty and yet be miserable'; for the acc.
and inf. after *licet* and the use of the
participle as equivalent to a relative clause
with an indefinite antecedent cf. i 38, 91
'quare licet etiam mortalem esse animum
iudicantem aeterna moliri' and n. there.
§ **45. an dubitas quin...dicere:** the
sentence is an anacoluthon; Cic. might
have written ' an dubitas quin praestans

adde etiam, si libet, pernicitatem et uelocitatem, da diuitias,
20 honores, imperia, opes, gloriam: si fuerit is qui haec habet
iniustus, intemperans, timidus, hebeti ingenio atque nullo, dubi-
tabisne eum miserum dicere? qualia igitur ista bona sunt, quae
qui habeat miserrimus esse possit? uideamus ne, ut aceruus ex
sui generis granis, sic beata uita ex sui similibus partibus effici
25 debeat. quod si ita est, ex bonis quae sola honesta sint efficiendum est beatum; ea mixta ex dissimilibus si erunt, honestum
ex iis effici nihil poterit; quo detracto quid poterit beatum
intellegi? etenim, quicquid est quod bonum sit, id expetendum
est; quod autem expetendum, id certe adprobandum; quod
30 uero adprobaris, id gratum acceptumque habendum; ergo etiam
dignitas ei tribuenda est. quod si ita est, laudabile sit necesse
est; bonum igitur omne laudabile. ex quo efficitur ut, quod sit
honestum, id sit solum bonum.

---

19. si lubet R V G B K.   21. hebeti G *ead. man. superscr.* (n)   23. miserrimus
R V G B K.   24. effici *et* efficiendum R V G B K.   25. efficiendum est
beatum R 1 7 V G B 1 2 K 1 W 2 D O 1 3 7.   efficiendum esse beatum
W 1 O 2.   efficien~~ß~~ est beatū K 2.   efficiendus est beatus R 17 M 1.
26. emixta G *ead. man. superscr.* (a)   27. ex iis M 2.   ex hiis R 16 D II.
ex his R 1 2 10 V P G B 1 K 1 E 1 2 W 1 2 M 1 C J O 1-3 7. ‖ quo
detracto R P G B 1 K 1 S M 1 2 C J O 1-3 7.   quod detracto V.
qd̄ detracto E 1.   29. adprobandum R V G K E.   approbandum B S.
30. adprobaris R V G K.   approbaris B S E.   31. tribuenda G da *ex* dū
alt. manu mut.

---

u2letudine...si fuerit iniustus...miser sit';
the change of construction is due to the
length and varied construction of the
clause immediately following *praestans*.
   pernicitatem et uelocitatem: for the
distinction between these words cf. i 19,
43 n. on *uelocius*.
   atque, 'dull and even wanting in
intellect'; for the intensive use of *atque*,
often strengthened by *adeo* or *potius*, cf.
Hand, *Turs.* I 406.
   uideamus ne: for this 'formula urbana
monendi et dubitandi,' cf. the Gk ὅρα μή,
and the use of *uide ne* in (e.g.) i 34, 83.
   beatum: 'happiness,' τὸ μακάριον, a
meaning for which Cic. generally prefers
the phrase *uita beata*; cf. Fin. v 28, 84
'uirtutem in qua sit ipsum etiam beatum.'
F.A.W. quoted by Mo. notes that Cic.
later in N.D. i 34, 95 suggested *beatitas*
and *beatitudo*, 'aut ista siue beatitas siue
beatitudo dicenda est—utrumque omnino
durum, sed usu mollienda nobis uerba

sunt,' which Quint. viii 3, 32 implies
were not universally received even in
his time.
   ea mixta ex dissimilibus si erunt, 'if
they (i.e. the *bona* which are relied upon
to produce happiness) are made up of a
mixture of dissimilar elements'; for the
phrase cf. Off. iii 33, 119 'nec uero finis
bonorum, qui simplex esse debet, ex dis-
simillimis rebus misceri et temperari
potest.' In the text Cic. uses *bona* in
rather a non-committal way to cover all
objects which are reckoned usually to
deserve that title, whether in his own
judgment they really do so or not. It is
necessary therefore in the preceding clause
to read 'quae sola honesta sint,' ' only
such *bona* as are honourable,' the intention
of the clause being to define a certain
class of *bona*.
   etenim: introducing a further argument as in iii 9, 20; iv 17, 40; Fin. i 9,
30, etc.

XVI. **46.** Quod ni ita tenebimus, multa erunt quae nobis bona dicenda sint; omitto diuitias (quas cum quiuis quamuis indignus habere possit, in bonis non numero; quod enim est bonum, id non quiuis habere potest), omitto nobilitatem famam-
5 que popularem stultorum inproborumque consensu excitatam; haec, quae sunt minima, tamen bona dicantur necesse est: candiduli dentes, uenusti oculi, color suauis et ea quae Anticlea laudat Ulixi pedes abluens:

> Lénitudo orátionis, móllitudo córporis.

10 ea si bona ducemus, quid erit in philosophi grauitate quam in uolgi opinione stultorumque turba quod dicatur aut grauius aut grandius? **47.** at enim eadem Stoici 'praecipua' uel 'producta' dicunt, quae 'bona' isti. dicunt illi quidem, sed iis uitam beatam

---

XVI. § **46**, 2. sint R V J.   sunt G B E.   5. inproborumque V G E.
improborumque R B K.   6. minima R V G B K.   7. et ea quae R 6 7
M 2   O 3.   et ea que̜ W 1.   et ea que M 1   O 1.   et ea q̄ E 3   J.
ea
et que II *al. atr. superscr.*   S *litt. ante* q *erasa.*   et eq; P *marg.* ea q̄.   et aeque
R G K.   et e̜que V B 1.   et eque R 17   B 2   E 12   L 5   W 2   C O 2 7.
et e quant ea D. || anticlea R V P G   B 12   L 6   M 12   J   O 3.   anticle
E 1   O 2.   antidea E 2   L 2–5   C II.   anticlia O 1.   ‖ laudat R 6
II *al. atr. superscr.* om. R 1 7 17   V P G   B 12   K 1 ,E 1–3   L 2–6   W 1 2
M 12   D C J   O 1–3 7 ed. H.   8. ulixi R V P G   B 12   K 12   S   E 2 3
L 2–6   W 2   M 12   D C II J   O 1 3 7 ed. H.   Ulyssi W 1.   auxilii E 1   O 2.
10. ducemus R V G   B 12   K 12   S   E 2   M 2   II Gr.   dicemus R 6 7   P
                                                                                    v
E 1   W 12   M 1   D C J   O 1 7.   11. uolgi V G B.   uolgi R *indistincte*
at atr. ant. superscr.   uulgi E 1   S.
§ **47**, 13.   sed iis M 2   O 2.   sed hiis K 2   D C II.   sed his R V P G
B 12   K 1   S   E 12   W 12   M 1   J   O 13 ed H.   *Claus.* om. O 7.

XVI. **46. indignus**: ii 5, 14 n.

minima: i.e. *minimi pretii* (Küh.): Neide's correction *minime* (sc. *bona*) is unnecessary.

candiduli: found only here and Juv. x 355 in class. Latin: the use of the diminutive imparts a slight shade of contempt.

color: cf. iv 13, 31 'apta figura membrorum cum coloris quadam suauitate' and n. there.

Anticlea: a μνημονικὸν ἁμάρτημα on Cicero's part. Anticlea was Ulysses' mother (Od. xi 84); it was his nurse Euryclea who, when washing his feet, recognized him by a scar (Od. xix 380 sqq.). It is better to assume that Cicero made a slip than to read *Eurycleia* here, as no plausible reason can be given to explain the substitution of the wrong name for the right one by a copyist. It is possible that the blunder was a common mistake and not Cicero's own. Ribbeck (*Röm. Trag.* p. 274) seems to think it possible,

relying on the evidence of a figured and inscribed vase from Chiusi, that Pacuvius in his play Niptra gave the name of Antiphata to the character who washed Ulysses' feet.

Ulixi: for the form of the gen. cf. i 48, 98; *Callistheni* in iii 10, 21; *Aristoteli*, Fin. i 5, 14 (with Madvig's note); *Herculi*, Ac. ii 34, 108; *Lacydi*, Ac. ii 6, 16 (with Reid's n.).

lenitudo...corporis: a trochaic tetr. catalect. from the Niptra of Pacuvius, for which see ii 21, 48 n. and Ribbeck, *Scaen. Rom. Poes.* I² pp. 107 sqq.

quam: for the *quam*-clause preceding the comparative cf. iii 22, 52 'maris subita tempestas quam ante prouisa terret nauigantes uehementius.'

§ **47. praecipua...producta**: tentative translations of the technical Stoic term προηγμένα, for which see Fin. iii 15, 50 sqq.; Diog. Laert. vii 105; Sext. Emp. iii 24 p. 174 (who defines προηγμένα as

compleri negant; hi autem sine iis esse nullam putant aut, si sit
15 beata, beatissimam certe negant. nos autem uolumus beatissimam, idque nobis Socratica illa conclusione confirmatur. sic
enim princeps ille philosophiae disserebat: qualis cuiusque animi
adfectus esset, talem esse hominem; qualis autem homo ipse
esset, talem eius esse orationem; orationi autem facta similia,
20 factis uitam. adfectus autem animi in bono uiro laudabilis, et
uita igitur laudabilis boni uiri, et honesta ergo, quoniam laudabilis. ex quibus bonorum beatam uitam esse concluditur.
48. etenim, pro deorum atque hominum fidem! parumne cogni-
tum est superioribus nostris disputationibus, an delectationis et
25 otii consumendi causa locuti sumus sapientem ab omni concita-
tione animi, quam perturbationem uoco, semper uacare, semper
in animo eius esse placidissimam pacem? uir igitur temperatus,
constans, sine metu, sine aegritudine, sine alacritate ulla, sine

---

14. sine hiis E 3. sine his S. si his R V G. si is B E 1.
15. beatissimam (*bis*) R V P G B K. 18. adfectus R V G K E. affectus B S. ||
homo ipse R V P G K 1 E 1 W 1 2 M 1 2 D C J O 1 3 7 ed. H. S *marg.*,
e cont. claus. om. ipse homo R 6 7. ipse esset homo E 2 Π. ipse B 2
homo *om.* *claus. om.* B 1 O 2. 19. orationem R 6 K 2 O 3. orōnē S
at o extra init. lineae. orōnem L 4 *at o postea add.* rationem R 1 7 17 V P G
B 1 2 K 1 E 1–3 L 2 3 5 6 W 1 2 M 1 2 D C Π J O 1 7 ed. H. *claus. om.* O 2. ||

 o
orationi R 6 O 3. oRationiṣ S *at o postea add.* Rationis Π. rationi E 3
L 2 6 M 1 2 D C ed. H. rōniṣ P. rationi R 7 *litt. post ni erasa.* rationis
R 1 17 V G B 1 2 K 1 2 E 1 2 L 3–5 W 1 2 J O 1 2 7. 20. adfectus
R V G K E. affectus B S.
§ **48**, 23. fidem R 6 M 1 2 D C Π O 1–3 7. fidē B 1 E 2 W 1.
fide R V G B 2 K 1 E 1. uitam W 2 (*sic*). 24. an delectationis B 1 E 2
W 1 M 1 2 O 1 3. an delectacionis K 1. an dilectationis R G.
an dilectationibus V. 27. placidissimam R V P G B K. 28. alacritate ulla
R 1 6 7 V P G B 1 2 K 1 2 S E 1–3 L 5 W 1 2 M 1 2 Π J O 1–3 7.
alacritudine ulla D C.

τὰ ἱκανὴν ἀξίαν ἔχοντα ὡς ὑγίειαν πλοῦτον)
and the other authorities quoted in Zeller,
Stoics etc. pp. 263—267.
sic enim: Cic. is apparently (as Dav.
notes) referring to Plat. *Rep.* iii p. 400 D
τί δ' ὁ τρόπος τῆς λέξεως, ἦν δ' ἐγώ, καὶ ὁ
λόγος; οὐ τῷ τῆς ψυχῆς ἤθει ἕπεται; Πῶς
γὰρ οὔ; Τῇ δὲ λέξει τὰ ἄλλα; Ναί. But
the idea is a commonplace from the
time of Solon who is credited (Diog.
Laert. i 58) with the saying τὸν μὲν λόγον
εἴδωλον εἶναι τῶν ἔργων, as may be seen
from the quotations collected by Dav.
pro deorum...fidem: an exclamation
found in Lael. 15, 52 in the form ' pro
deorum fidem atque hominum '; Cicero
notes in *Or.* 46, 156 that the form *deum*
(which is found in Ter. *Andr.* 246) is
also permissible in this phrase.
delectationis: cf. iii 34, 81.

sine alacritate ulla: the MSS reading
has been objected to here upon two
grounds: first that *alacritas* is not in
itself a word of evil signification, and
secondly that even if it were there is no
particular reason for emphasizing it by
the addition of *ulla*. The first objection
may be met by the testimony of Nonius
Marcellus (p. 456 M.) who quotes our
passage for proof that *alacritas* is to be
reckoned *in malis*; Bentley, however,
followed by Sff. reads *futili* for *ulla* and
Bouh. (with greater palaeographical probability) *stulta*. Many edd. who accept
Nonius' testimony take exception to *ulla*:
Nissen proposes *illa*; Sauppe (followed
by He.) reads *sine aegritudine, nulla
libidine*, a reading accepted by L. Müller
(*ad* Non. Marc. *l.c.*) in preference to the
testimony of the MSS of Nonius : C. Ph.

H.   16

libidine nonne beatus? at semper sapiens talis; semper igitur
30 beatus. iam uero qui potest uir bonus non ad id quod laudabile
sit omnia referre quae agit quaeque sentit? refert autem omnia
ad beate uiuendum; beata igitur uita laudabilis; nec quicquam
sine uirtute laudabile; beata igitur uita uirtute conficitur.
XVII. 49. Atque hoc sic etiam concluditur: nec in misera
uita quicquam est praedicabile aut gloriandum nec in ea quae
nec misera sit nec beata. et est in aliqua uita praedicabile aliquid
et gloriandum ac prae se ferendum, ut Epaminondas:

5   Consiliis nostris laus est attonsa Laconum,
ut Africanus:

29.   libidine R V P G B K.   ‖   at semper P B.   a τ semper V ras. inter
a et τ).   aut semper R G K.   32.   nec quicquam R 1 2 10 16   B 1   K 1.
ne quicquam V G.
XVII. § 49, 3.   est praedicabile aliquid et gloriandum ac prae se ferendum G
cett. om. aliquid et interpunxit et aut suberscr. alt. man.   4. ac prae se
ferendum R V P.   ac preferendum K 1.   5. attonsa R V G S E.
adtonsa K 1.

Wagner proposed *sine aegritudine, alacritate nulla, nulla libidine.* There is no
objection, however, to *ulla* on the score
of Ciceronian usage. Cic. is rather fond
of series of ablatives with *sine* and often
adds *ullus* to one of them; it is true that
the qualified noun is usually either the
first or last of the series but not invariably;
cf. N.D. ii 29, 74 'hominem sine arte,
sine litteris, insultantem in omnes, sine
acumine ullo, sine auctoritate, sine lepore.' Similarly in Leg. Agr. i 9, 26
'nullum externum periculum est, non rex,
non gens ulla, non natio pertimescenda
est.'

iam uero: Küh. compares Stob. Ecl.
Eth. ii p. 138 τέλος δέ φασιν [sc. οἱ Στωϊ-
κοί] εἶναι τὸ εὐδαιμονεῖν, οὗ ἕνεκα πάντα
πράττεται, αὐτὸ δὲ πράττεται μὲν οὐδενὸς
δὲ ἕνεκα, τοῦτο δ' ὑπάρχειν ἐν τῷ κατ'
ἀρετὴν ζῆν, ἐν τῷ ὁμολογουμένως ζῆν, ἔτι,
ταὐτοῦ ὄντος, ἐν τῷ κατὰ φύσιν ζῆν'...
κέχρηται δὲ καὶ Κλεάνθης τῷ ὅρῳ τούτῳ...
καὶ ὁ Χρύσιππος...τὴν εὐδαιμονίαν εἶναι
λέγοντες οὐχ ἑτέραν τοῦ εὐδαίμονος βίου...
δῆλον οὖν ἐκ τούτων ὅτι ἰσοδυναμεῖ τὸ κατὰ
φύσιν ζῆν καὶ τὸ καλῶς ζῆν.
XVII. § 49. et: for *et* introducing the
minor premiss (here of a disjunctive syllogism) cf. iii 8, 18.

aliqua: emphatic, 'there *is* a life in
which, etc.'; for the truth of this premiss
Cic. appeals to experience. If there is
some life to which nobility and glory
attaches, and that is neither the unhappy
life nor the life that is neither happy nor

unhappy, it follows that it must be the
happy life.
Epaminondas: sc. *prae se fert.* The
quotation is a translation of the first line
of an epigram said by Pausanias (ix 15, 4)
to have been inscribed on the base of
the statue of Epaminondas in Thebes:
ἡμετέραις βουλαῖς Σπάρτη μὲν ἐκείρατο
δόξαν | Μεσσήνη δ' ἱερὰ τέκνα χρόνῳ δέ-
χεται. | Θῆβαι δ' ὅπλοισι μεγάλη πόλις
ἐστεφάνωται | αὐτόνομος δ' 'Ελλὰς πᾶσ' ἐν
ἐλευθερίῃ. Plut. non p. suau. uiui sec.
Ep. p. 1098 A quotes the same line in
illustration of his thesis ταῖς μέντοι τῆς
ψυχῆς χαραῖς ὁμολογουμένως μέγεθος
ὑποκεῖσθαι δεῖ πράξεων καὶ κάλλος ἔργων
ἀξιολόγων εἰ μέλλουσι...ἐμβριθεῖς ἔσεσθαι
καὶ βέβαιοι καὶ μεγαλοπρεπεῖς.
Africanus: i.e. P. Scipio Africanus,
the elder. The lines quoted are from
Ennius (Vahlen, *Enn. Poes. Rell.*[2] p. 216).
Scaliger (*Catal.* p. 187) saw that they
were the opening of an epigram of which
the two following lines are given by
Seneca, Epp. 108, 34 (from a lost portion
of Cic. de republica) 'si fas endo plagas
caelestum ascendere cuiquam est | mi soli
caeli maxima porta patet.' The last two
lines are also quoted by Lactantius, Diu.
Inst. i 18, 10, with many expressions of
dissent from their theology. The reading
of the first line given by Mamertinus in
his Genethliacus Maximiano (16, 3) is 'a
sole exoriente adusque Maeotis paludes,'
thus mistaking the sense, which is that
from Rome to where the sun rises over

A sole exoriente supra Maeotis paludes
Nemo est qui factis aequiperare queat.

50. quod si <est>, beata uita glorianda et praedicanda et prae
10 se ferenda est; nihil est enim aliud quod praedicandum et prae
se ferendum sit. quibus positis intellegis quid sequatur; et quidem, nisi ea uita beata est quae est eadem honesta, sit aliud
necesse est melius uita beata; quod erit enim honestum, certe
fatebuntur esse melius. ita erit beata uita melius aliquid; quo
15 quid potest dici peruersius? quid? cum fatentur satis magnam
uim esse in uitiis ad miseram uitam, nonne fatendum est eandem
uim in uirtute esse ad beatam uitam? contrariorum enim
contraria sunt consequentia. **51.** quo loco quaero quam uim
habeat libra illa Critolai, qui cum in alteram lancem animi bona
20 inponat, in alteram corporis et externa, tantum propendere
illam lancem putet ut terram et maria deprimat.

8. aequiperare V G Gr.   equiperare B 1 W 1.   equiperare R P K E
W 2 J O 1 3.   equiparare S.   qui me factis uituparare M 1. ‖ quaeat G.
§ **50,** 9. quod si beata R 1 6 7 17 V P G B 1 2 K 1 2 S E 1–3 W 1 2
M 1 2 D C Π J O 1–3 7 ed H.   quod si est, beata *corr. Lambinus.* ‖ prae se
ferenda R G K.   et p̄ferenda R 17 E 1.   10. prae se ferendum R G.
et p̄eferendum V.   et p̄ferendum R 17.   11. intellegis R V G B K.
intelligis S E.   16. eandem R V G B 1 K 1 S.   eamdem E 1.
17. uim in uirtute R 6 K 2 E 2 W 2 M 1 II O 1 2.   uim i uirtute J ed. H.
                                                in
uim uirtute B 1 *al. atr. superscr.*   uim uirtute O 7.   uim uirtutem R V P G
B 2 K 1 S E 1 D C.   uim uirtutum R 7 17 E 3 W 1 M 2 O 3.
§ **51,** 19. habeat R G K J.   haberet V.   20. imponat R V P G B K S E.
21. illam lancem W 2.   illam   lancem S boni *eras. et spat. relict.*   illam boni
lancem R 1 6 7 17 V P G B 1 2 K 1 2 E 1 3 L 2–6 W 1 M 1 2 D C Π O 1 3 7
ed. H.   illam lancem boni J.   illam bona lancem E 2.   illa boni lancem O 2.

the marshes of Maeotis Scipio has no
equal.

For the scansion of *Maeotis* as *Maeoti'*
cf. i 5, 10 n. and for the form of the genitive (instead of *Maeotidis*) edd. refer to
leg. agr. ii 19, 52 where Cic. has the abl.
Maeote; Bouh. also compares Plaut.
Epid. 35 *Theti* for *Thetidi.*
In the second line Dav. and Or. insert
me after *factis,* unnecessarily, since the
object is easily supplied.

§ **50. quod** : sc. *praedicabile aliquid*
(Küh.)

et quidem, 'and furthermore,' introducing a new argument, an extension
of the more frequent use in which it
amplifies a preceding statement by the
addition of a word or clause, e.g. 18, 53 ;
i 11, 24 'feci mehercule, et quidem
saepius'; iii 16, 35 'diceres aliquid et
magno quidem philosopho dignum.'

§ **51. quam uim habeat,** 'what is involved in,' cf. i 22, 52 'hanc habet uim

praeceptum Apollinis'; Off. iii 9, 39
'haec est uis huius anuli et huius exempli';
Sull. 13, 39.

Critolai: Critolaus succeeded Aristo as
head of the Peripatetic School. For his
celebrated visit to Rome in company with
Diogenes and Carneades cf. Or. ii 37, 155;
Zeller, *Aristotle etc.* II pp. 479 sqq.

Cicero seems to be the earliest author
who mentions Critolaus' illustration of
the relative merits of the *bona animi* and
the *bona corporis et externa*: cf. Fin. v
30, 92 where, however, Critolaus' name
is not given. The Emperor Julian may
have had it in his mind when he wrote
(Or. iii p. 119 A, p. 152 Hertl.) ἀνδρῶν
γὰρ ἀγαθῶν φημι ξυντυχίαν πρὸς χρυσίου
πλῆθος ὁσονδηοῦν ἐξεταζομένην καθέλκειν
τὸν ζυγὸν καὶ οὐκ ἐπιτρέπειν τῷ σώφρονι
κριτῇ οὐδὲ ἐπ' ὀλίγον ῥοπῆς ἐπιστῆσαι.

propendere illam lancem, 'that the
former scale is so much the weightier':
for *propendere* cf. 31, 86 and Plaut. Asin.

16—2

XVIII. Quid ergo aut hunc prohibet aut etiam Xenocratem,
illum grauissimum philosophorum, exaggerantem tantopere
uirtutem, extenuantem cetera et abicientem, in uirtute non
beatam modo uitam sed etiam beatissimam ponere? quod qui-
5 dem nisi fit, uirtutum interitus consequetur. **52.** nam in quem
cadit aegritudo, in eundem metum cadere necesse est; est enim
metus futurae aegritudinis sollicita exspectatio; in quem autem
metus, in eundem formido, timiditas, pauor, ignauia; ergo, ut
idem uincatur interdum nec putet ad se praeceptum illud Atrei
10 pertinere:

> Proinde íta parent se in uíta ut uinci nésciant.

hic autem uincetur, ut dixi, nec modo uincetur sed etiam seruiet;
at nos uirtutem semper liberam uolumus, semper inuictam; quae

---

XVIII. 2. grauissumum R G B K. grauissimum V. ‖ tantopere
R G B S E. tanto opere V. 3. abicientem R V P G B 1 2 K 1 W 1
J O 3 7. abitientem E 1. abícientem S. 4. beatissimam R V G B K.
5. fit R V P G B 1 2 E 2 M 1 2 Π O 3 Gr. sit K 1 W 2 D C J O 1 2 7.

§ **52**, 7. exspectatio R E. expectatio V G B K S. 11. ut uicinesciant
V (*sic*) *marg.* ‡ uinci *atr. uiridi adscript.* 13. at nos R 6 7 P K 2 E 2 L 2–6
W 1 2 M 1 2 D C Π J O 1 2 ed. H. at nos autem V. at nos át E 3.
at nos autem R 1 17 G B 1 2 K 1 S E 1 O 3 7.

---

305. The word *boni* inserted in so many
MSS is apparently a careless gloss, and
Ba. and Ml. suspect *lancem* as well; *boni*
is inaccurate as the difference between
the scales was not that one contained *bona*
and the other *mala*, but each a different
kind of *bonum*. Be. followed by Dav.
changed one gloss into another by reading
animi for *boni*, and Bouh. does no better
with *honesti*; Ern. (followed by Mo. Kl.
Sch.) amplifies *boni* into *bonorum animi*,
which if *boni* be not a gloss is the best
emendation (cf. Vahlen, *Opusc. Acad.* ii
pp. 353 ff.), and Sff. rewrites the words
altogether, reading *praeponderare illam
hanc lancem.*

deprimat, ‘outweighs’; this, the same
phrase, is found in *Fin.* v 30, 92. As
Dav. points out, the use of the word is
technically incorrect if applied to the
effect of a heavier scale upon a lighter
one: but *premo* and its compounds had
acquired the secondary sense of ‘to be too
heavy for,’ ‘to be superior to,’ and this
meaning possibly influenced the use here.
It is also possible that Cic. used *deprimere*
as a translation of καθέλκειν, which may
have been the word used in the Greek
source, and which passed from the meaning of ‘drag down the scale,’ seen in

Aristoph. *Ran.* 1398 and the passage
from Julian quoted above, to the meaning
‘ outweigh ’ seen, e.g. in Diog. Laert. vii
18.

XVIII. **Xenocratem:** cf. i 10, 20 n.
Dav. suggests that the ref. here may be
to his work περὶ ἀρετῆς in two books
mentioned by Diog. Laert. iv 12.

exaggerantem, ‘extolling,’ as in 30,
85; iii 19, 45.

§ **52. nam in quem cadit:** cf. iv 6,
14 sqq.

ergo ut idem uincatur: i.e. *ergo in
eundem cadit, ut uincatur.*

illud Atrei : the quotation is usually
assigned to the Atreus of Accius, but
Ribbeck, *Scaen. Rom. Poes. Frgg.* 1² p. 251
assigns it to the ‘incertae incertorum
fabulae.’ The line is an iambic senarius,
proinde being scanned as a disyllable,
with elision of the last syllable.

hic: sc. *in quem cadit aegritudo*: the
autem following contrasts the character
under discussion with the style of character
implied by the advice of Atreus.

at nos: many edd. (including Dav. Tr.
Mo. Kl. Küh. Sff.) adopt the reading *nos
autem*, and Mo. conjectures that *at* is due
to dittography of the final syllable of the
preceding word. Wesenb. who reads *at*

nisi sunt, sublata uirtus est. **53.** atque si in uirtute satis est
15 praesidii ad bene uiuendum, satis est etiam ad beate; satis est
enim certe in uirtute ut fortiter uiuamus; si fortiter, etiam
ut magno animo, et quidem ut nulla re umquam terreamur
semperque simus inuicti. sequitur ut nihil paeniteat, nihil desit,
nihil obstet; ergo omnia profluenter, absolute, prospere, igitur
20 beate. satis autem uirtus ad fortiter uiuendum potest; satis ergo
etiam ad beate. **54.** etenim ut stultitia, etsi adepta est quod
concupiuit, numquam se tamen satis consecutam putat, sic sapientia semper eo contenta est quod adest neque eam umquam
sui paenitet.

14. nisi sunt R V P G   B 2   K 1   E 1 2   W 2   M 2   D C Π J   O 1 3.
      ͥ
nisi sunt S.   nisi st B 1.   st' W 1.   nisi sint M 1   O 2 7.
nisi ita est R 6.
§ **53.** atq; M 1   O 2.   atq R 17.   atqui R 1 6 7   V P G   B 1 2
K 1 2   S   E 2 3   L 5   W 1 2   M 2   Π J   O 1 3 7 ed. H.   *claus. om.* E 1   D C.
15. praesidii R G.   presidii V.   presidii K 1.   18. paeniteat R.
peniteat B.   peniteat V G K.   20. uirtus ad fortiter uiuendum R V P G   B 1 2
K 1   S   E 1 2   W 1 2   M 1 2   D C Π J   O 3 7 ed. H.   *claus. om.* O 1 2.
§ **54,** 22. consecutam K.   consecutā B V *atr. uiridi superscr.*   consecuta
                                                       a
R G.   ‖ putat R G K.   putet V *atr. uiridi superscr.*   23. conta G.
      t   bi
24. paeni& R *atr. ant.*   penitet B.   penite^t S.   penitet V P G K.

thinks it equally probable that *autem* was
repeated from the preceding clause, and
T.S. argue that *at* is more appropriate, as
it expresses a stronger antithesis. As a
matter of fact, either of the two is equally
appropriate here. Cic. having proved that
a man subject to *aegritudo* will allow
himself to be overcome, proceeds to use
that statement as the major premiss of a
syllogism, of which this sentence forms
the minor premiss (which may be introduced by *atqui, at, autem* or *et*): 'the
man who is subject to *aegritudo*, is not a
free man; virtue is free and independent;
ergo, in the man who is subject to *aegritudo* virtue there is none.' The syllogistic
nature of the reasoning is somewhat obscured by Cicero's method of expressing
the conclusion.
quae nisi sunt, 'unless these qualities
exist, virtue there is none.' The conclusion brings us back by another route to
the preceding conclusion 'quod quidem
nisi fit, uirtutum interitus consequetur.'
The neuter *quae* refers loosely to *libera*
and *inuicta*; Wesenberg's correction of
sunt to *est* is hardly necessary.
§ **53. Atque**: introducing a fresh line
of argument; *atqui* adopted by Schiche

alone amongst recent edd. is inappropriate.
The following sentences form a 'con-
structive conjunctive syllogism. 'If virtue
is sufficient for a good life, it is sufficient
for a happy life; virtue is sufficient for a
good life [proved in *satis est enim certe...
uiuendum potest*]; ergo, it is sufficient for
a good life.' The proof that virtue is
sufficient for a good life is based upon a
proof of the identity of *bene uiuere* and
fortiter uiuere; but all that Cic. succeeds
in proving is not the identity but that
fortiter uiuere is an indispensable condition of *bene uiuere.*
et quidem: cf. 17, 50 n.
nihil paeniteat, 'nothing causes regret,'
cf. 28, 81 'quod paenitere possit' and
Madv. *L. Gr.* § 218 (*a*) obs. 2.
omnia: sc. *se habebunt, fiunt* (Ern.)
which seems preferable to Küh.'s *ad-
sint.*
absolute = *perfecte*, cf. *Fin.* iii 7, 26
'sequitur omnes sapientes semper feliciter,
absolute, fortunate uiuere.'
§ **54. eo contenta est quod adest**: cf.
Hor. *Carm.* iii 29, 32 'quod adest
memento componere aequis' and the Gk
στέργειν τὰ πάροντα, Herod. ix 117 and
often.

XIX. Similemne putas C. Laelii unum consulatum fuisse, et eum quidem cum repulsa (si, cum sapiens et bonus uir, qualis ille fuit, suffragiis praeteritur, non populus a bono consule potius quam ille a bono populo repulsam fert) — sed tamen utrum 5 malles te, si potestas esset, semel ut Laelium consulem an ut Cinnam quater? 55. non dubito tu quid responsurus sis; itaque uideo cui committam. non quemuis hoc idem interrogarem; responderet enim alius fortasse se non modo quattuor consulatus uni anteponere sed unum diem Cinnae multorum et clarorum 10 uirorum totis aetatibus. Laelius si digito quem attigisset poenas

XIX. 1. similemne R6 M1 D C. simile ne S. simile̅ ne R7
B1 O1. simile̅ ne Π *alio fort. atr.* e *in* e̅ *mut.* similene R1 17 V P G
B2 K12 E1-3 L5 W12 M2 J O237 ed. H. ‖ c. laelii R K1 W1.
c. le̅lii V. c. lelii G B12 S E1 W2 M12 D C O13. ‖ consulatum
R6 B1 E2 M1 Π O12. consolatum R V G B2 O7. ‖ fuisse P C Π.

fuiss& V. fuisset R G K E1. 2. si cum R12 10 G K. si$_Λ$ cum V
B1 'S. sic cum R16 D C J O17. sed cum W1. 3. consulae G.
4. a bono populo R V P G B12 K12 S E1-3 L24-6 W1 M12 D C Π J
O23 ed. H. bono populo O7 a *om.* ab uno populo L3 O1. a uano
populo R6. a bono populo W2 *marg., e cont. om. om.* R7 17. ‖ *post* repulsam
fert *denuo inculcant* suffragiis praeteritur R12 10 V P G K E13 L2-5.

6. cinnam R G K. cinam V *atr. ant.* cinam E1.
§ 55, 7. committam R12 16 V G. co̅mittam R10 K. ∂mittam P.

8. consulatus R6 P B1 K1 W12 C O1-37. consolatus R *eod. atr.*
consolatus V G B2. 10. attigisset R V G B K S E.

XIX. **unum consulatum**: in the year 140 B.C. along with Q. Servilius Caepio; he had been unsuccessful in his candidature for the consulship of the previous year. A *repulsa* was looked upon as more or less of a disgrace; cf. Plut. Cato Min. c. 50 on Cato's conduct on a similar occasion φέροντος τοῦ πράγματος οὐκ αὐτοῖς μόνοις τοῖς ἀποτυχοῦσιν ἀλλὰ καὶ φίλοις αὐτῶν καὶ οἰκείοις σὺν αἰσχύνῃ τινὶ κατήφειαν καὶ πένθος ἐφ' ἡμέρας πολλάς. Cic. Off. i 21, 71 'uidentur...offensionum et repulsarum quasi quandam ignominiam timere atque infamiam.'

a bono populo: Cicero's point is that the *repulsa* of a man of Laelius' character (which could not be impeached) proves, not that the *populus* had too high a standard for him, but that he had too high a standard for them; 'the electors are repulsed by the virtue of the candidate, not the candidate by the virtue of the electors.' The corrections miss the point: Mdv. Tr. Ba. omit *bono* before *populo*: Erasm. followed by Be. Or. F.A.W. Küh. altered it to *uano*, and

Dav. to *malo*: Sff. reads *a <non> bono populo.*
Cicero's view of the high standard expected by the people in candidates for the consulship is well known.

ut Laelium consulem: sc. *esse*; cf. 23, 66; Fin. v 5 13 'Strato physicum se uoluit'; Inu. i 31, 52 'tuumne equum malis [sc. habere] quam illius?' and Madv.'s note on Fin. ii 31, 102.

§ 55. **committam**, 'in whose hands I am putting myself'; this absolute use of *committere* is common from Plautus onwards. Hei. compares II Verr. iii 60, 137; Leg. Agr. ii 8, 20 'uniuerso populo ...committit.'

unum diem: cf. 2, 5 n. Victorius (*Variae Lect.* xii 10) compares the lines quoted in Plut. Solon 14 καὶ τυραννεύσας 'Αθηνῶν μοῦνον ἡμέραν μίαν | ἀσκὸς ὕστερον δεδάρθαι καὶ ἐπιτετρῖφθαι γένος.

digito...attigisset, 'laid a finger upon.' Turn. (*Adv.* vii 16) compares the line of Porcius Licinus quoted in Aul. Gell. xix 9, 6 'si digito attigero, incendam siluam simul omnem.'

dedisset; at Cinna collegae sui, consulis Cn. Octauii, praecidi
caput iussit, <iussit> P. Crassi, L. Caesaris, nobilissimorum
hominum, quorum uirtus fuerat domi militiaeque cognita, M.
Antonii, omnium eloquentissimi quos ego audierim, C. Caesaris,
15 in quo mihi uidetur specimen fuisse humanitatis, salis, suauitatis,
leporis. beatusne igitur qui hos interfecit? mihi contra non
solum eo uidetur miser quod ea fecit, sed etiam quod ita se
gessit ut ea facere ei liceret. etsi peccare nemini licet; sed
sermonis errore labimur; id enim licere dicimus quod cuique
20 conceditur. **56.** utrum tandem beatior C. Marius tum, cum
Cimbricae uictoriae gloriam cum collega Catulo communicauit,

11. collegę R V.　　college G K E. ‖ CN. Octaui L 3.　　·CN· Octauii
M 1 2　O 1.　　GN. Octaui V　B 2　E 1.　　GN. octauii R G　B 1　K 1
S　W 1 2.　　GN. octai 1 1 1 P *marg.* octauii.　　cnei octauii D.　　gnei octauii E 2.
Gn. Ottauii O 3.　　12. iussit R 1 6 7 17　V P　B 1 2　K 1 2　S　E 1-3　L 2-6
W 1 2　M 1 2　D C Π J　O 1-3 ed. H.　　lussit G.　　iubssit O 7.　　iussit,
iussit *corr. Seyffertus*. ‖ p̄. crassi G.　　post crassi O 2. ‖ l. caesaris V G.
　　　　　　　　　　　　　　　　　　　　　　　　uci
L　Cęsaris S. ‖ nobilissimorum R V P G B K.　　13. M. Antonii
R P G K S E.　　m̄ antonii V.　　14. C. caesaris B 1　E 2　M 1.　　G. caesaris
R V G　B 2　K 1　M 2.　　15. specimen fuisse R 1 17　V P G　B 1 2　K 1
E 1 2　W 1 2　M 1　D C Π J　O 1 2 7 ed. H.　　fuisse specimen R 6 7　M 2.
　　　　　　　　　　　　　　　　　　　　　　　　　　　　　ih
fuisse spem O 3.　　16. qui hos S　E 2　M 1 2　Π　O 2 3.　　qu͵os V
atr. uiridi corr.　　quos P *marg.* q̨ hos.　　q̨, hos E 3.　　quos R G　B 1 2
K 1　E 1.　　quia hos K 2　L 5　W 1 2　J　O 1.　　qui eos O 7 ed. H.
quia eos D C.　　18. & si peccar & V.　　& si peccaret R G K.
§ 56, 20. c. marius V P G　B 1·　K 1　S　E 1 2　W 1　O 3.　　G. marius
R　W 2.　　21. cimbrice G. ‖ collega R V G B K S E. ‖ catulo R V G B
W 1　J.　　catullo S.

consulis Cn. Octauii: Manut. considered
consulis to be a gloss upon *collegae*, and
he is followed by Lamb. Hei. Bak. Bai.,
but Kl. and Küh. are no doubt right in
regarding it as used for emphasis. Dav.
compares Liv. xxxi 14, 2 and Vell.
Pat. ii 22, 2 : but in the former passage
Weissenborn reads not *consulis* but *Cn.*
For the consulship of Cn. Octavius in
87 B.C. and his relations with Cinna cf.
Mommsen, *R.H.* iv 58 ff.

P. Crassi: i.e. P. Licinius Crassus cos.
in 97 B.C.; cf. Appian, B.C. i 72 Κράσσος
δὲ μετὰ τοῦ παιδὸς διωκόμενος, τὸν μὲν
υἱὸν ἔφθασε προανελεῖν αὐτὸς δ᾽ ὑπὸ τῶν
διωκόντων ἐπανῃρέθη ; the account in
Livy's Epitome lxxx is 'Crassus filius
ab equitibus Fimbriae occisus; pater
Crassus ne quid indignum uirtute sua
pateretur, gladio se transfixit.'

L. Caesaris : i.e. L. Iulius Caesar
Strabo, cos. in 90 B.C. ; he and his
brother, mentioned below, ἐν ὁδῷ κατα-
ληφθέντες ἀνῃρέθησαν (Appian, *l.c.*); their
heads were placed on the rostrum
(Livy, *l.c.*).

militiae: Crassus had commanded
during the Spanish and Social wars,
and Caesar had distinguished himself in
the Social war at Acerrae (Mommsen,
R.H. iii 479, 509 ff.).

M. Antonii: the celebrated orator, interlocutor along with Crassus in Cicero's
de Oratore ; for his life see Wilkins'
edition of the dialogue i pp. 13 ff. The
story of his betrayal to Marius and his
murder is told in Appian, *l.c.* and in
Plut. Marius 44.

audierim: subj. of limitation; cf. i 16,
38 n. on *exstet.* Kühn. *Lat. Gr.* 11 p. 862, 8.

C. Caesaris: for his charm and wit
cf. Off. i 37, 133 'sale et facetiis...uicit
omnes.' Or. ii 23, 98 'inusitatum nostris
quidem oratoribus leporem quendam et
salem...consecutus est.' Brut. 48, 177,
'nemo unquam urbanitate, nemo lepore,
nemo suauitate conditior.'

etsi...sed : cf. i 42, 99 n. ; iv 29, 63 ;
for *etsi* in this sense without *sed* following
cf. iii 8, 17.

§ 56. **communicauit:** cf. Plut. Mar. c.
27 *fin.* μάλιστα δὲ οἱ πολλοὶ κτίστην τε

paene altero Laelio (nam hunc illi duco simillimum), an cum
ciuili bello uictor iratus necessariis Catuli deprecantibus non
semel respondit sed saepe: 'Moriatur'? in quo beatior ille
25 qui huic nefariae uoci paruit quam is qui tam scelerate imperauit. nam cum accipere quam facere praestat iniuriam, tum
morti iam ipsi aduentanti paulum procedere ob uiam, quod fecit
Catulus, quam quod Marius, talis uiri interitu sex suos obruere
consulatus et contaminare extremum tempus aetatis.

XX. **57**. Duodequadraginta annos tyrannus Syracusanorum
fuit Dionysius, cum quinque et uiginti natus annos dominatum
occupauisset. qua pulchritudine urbem, quibus autem opibus
praeditam seruitute oppressam tenuit ciuitatem! atqui de hoc
5 homine a bonis auctoribus sic scriptum accepimus, summam

22.   poene G.   ‖ hunc illi R 7 17   K 2 L 2 4 5   W 1   D C.   huic illum
R 6 L 3 6   M 1 2   O 1–3 ed. H.   huic illi R 1   G   B 1 2   K 1   E 1 2   W 2
                                                                    v̄
Π J.   huic illum S *marg.* hūc illi.   huic illi P *marg.* illū.   huic illi V
atr. uiridi superscr.   huc illi O 7.   ‖ simillimum R V G B K.   ‖ annum G
in an cum *alt. man. mut.*   23. deprecantibus V K.   depraecantibus R G.
  r
depcantibus P.   25. nefariae V G.   nefarię R 1 2 10   P.   ne/farię B 1
duabus litt. eras.   ‖ quam is R 1 2 10 16   G K.   quam his V.   ‖ imperauit
R V G B K S E.   28. quam quod R G K.   "quod" quam V.   ‖ interitus
ex suos R V P G K.   interitus & suos B.
XX. § **57**, 2.   dyonisius R G   B 1 2.   dionisius V K S E.   4. atqui
R V G   B 1 2   K 1 2   E 2   W 2   M 1 2   D C Π J   O 1–3 ed. H.   adqui P.
at quidem E 1.   atque W 1   O 7.   atq E 3.

'Ρώμης τρίτον ἐκεῖνον ἀνηγόρευον...οὐ μὴν
ἐθριάμβευσεν οὕτως ἀλλὰ μετὰ τοῦ Κάτλου,
μέτριον ἐπὶ τηλικαύταις εὐτυχίαις βουλό-
μενος παρέχειν ἑαυτόν· ἔστι δὲ ὅτι καὶ
τοὺς στρατιώτας φοβηθεὶς παρατεταγμένους,
εἰ Κάτλος ἀπειλγοιτο τῆς τιμῆς, μηδὲ
ἐκεῖνον ἐᾶν θριαμβεύειν. Juv. viii 253
with Mayor's n.

paene altero Laelio: cf. for Cicero's
opinion of Catulus, Brut. 35, 132 where
he attributes to him 'multae litterae,
summa non uitae solum atque naturae
sed orationis etiam comitas, incorrupta
quaedam Latini sermonis integritas,' and
ib. 21, 84 where he credits Laelius with
'ingenium, litterae, eloquentia, sapientia.'

moriatur: Plut. Mar. 44 πρὸς τοὺς
δεομένους ὑπὲρ αὐτοῦ καὶ παραιτουμένους ὁ
Μάριος τοσοῦτον μόνον εἶπεν, 'Ἀποθανεῖν
δεῖ.

accipere...iniuriam: a commonplace
of Socrates' ethical teaching; cf. Plat.
Gorg. 469 c ἑλοίμην ἂν μᾶλλον ἀδικεῖσθαι
ἢ ἀδικεῖν; Aristotle says much the same
in Nic. Eth. v 11 § 7 φανερὸν δὲ καὶ ὅτι
ἄμφω μὲν φαῦλα καὶ τὸ ἀδικεῖσθαι καὶ τὸ
ἀδικεῖν...ἀλλ' ὅμως χεῖρον τὸ ἀδικεῖν· τὸ

μὲν γὰρ ἀδικεῖν μετὰ κακίας καὶ ψεκτόν...τὸ
δ' ἀδικεῖσθαι ἄνευ κακίας καὶ ἀδικίας.

ob uiam: Catulus closed himself up in
a room and πολλοὺς ἄνθρακας ἐκζωπυρήσας
ἀπεπνίγη. Plut. Mar. 44; App. B.C. i 74.

obruere: cf. Or. i 25, 116 'ita quicquid est in quo offenditur, id etiam illa
quae laudanda sunt obruit.'

XX. § **57**. **Dionysius**, the elder, tyrant
of Syracuse 405—367 B.C. ; for his career
v. Holm, *Hist. of Greece* (E.T.) iii pp.
130 ff. ; Grote viii pp. 403 ff.

pulchritudine: cf. Rep. iii 31, 43 'urbs
illa praeclara quam ait Timaeus Graecarum maximam, omnium autem esse
pulcherrimam.' II Verr. iv 52, 117, where
there is a long description of the city.

autem: for this use Hei. refers to iv 2,
5 'quot et quanti poetae, qui autem
oratores'; Mur. 13, 29 'magna res,
magna dignitas, summa autem gratia.'

de hoc homine: for the construction
'de hoc accepimus fuisse uirum acrem'
Wopkens (*op. cit.* p. 75) compares Fam.
x 20 1 'de te tamen fama constans nec
decipi posse nec uinci'; on the other
hand in iv 22, 50 we find 'de Africano...

fuisse eius in uictu temperantiam in rebusque gerundis uirum
acrem et industrium, eundem tamen maleficum natura et iniustum. ex quo omnibus bene ueritatem intuentibus uideri necesse
est miserrimum. ea enim ipsa quae concupierat, ne tum quidem,
10 cum omnia se posse censebat, consequebatur. **58.** qui cum esset
bonis parentibus atque honesto loco natus (etsi id quidem alius
alio modo tradidit) abundaretque et aequalium familiaritatibus
et consuetudine propinquorum, haberet etiam more Graeciae
quosdam adulescentis amore coniunctos, credebat eorum nemini,
15 sed iis quos ex familiis locupletium seruos delegerat, quibus
nomen seruitutis ipse detraxerat, et quibusdam conuenis et feris

6. gerundis R 1 17   V G   B 1 2   K 1   S   E 3   L 4 5   W 2   J   O 1.
e e
gerendis R 6 7   P   E 2   L 3 6   W 1   M 1 2   D C II   O 2 3 7 ed. H.   g₁randis E 1.

ꞇ
gerōdis L 2.   8. intuentibus B 1.   inuentibus V atr. ant.   inuentibus R G
B 2   K 1.   9. miserrimum R V P G B K.
§ 58, 12.   abundaretque R V K II.   habundaretque G B E D   O 1 7 ed. H. ‖
et aequalium R 6   W 1   M 2   II   O 2 3.   eī aequalium B 1 ei in et atr.
nigriore mut.   ei aequalium R V P G   B 2   K 1   S   E 1 2.   aequalium om. et
R 7 17   K 2   W 2   M 1   D C J   O 1 7.   13.   amore gretiae G a ante m
e
exp. alt. man.   more gratię V atr. uiridi superscr.   14.   adulescentis R G K.
e
adualescentis V.   adolescentis B.   adolescentis E 1.   adolescentes P S. ‖
iis
credebat nemini W 1 eorum om.   15.   sed iis M 2.   sed his S.   sed hiis II.
sed his R V G K.   sed si is E 1.   sed si is B 1.   ‖   quos ex R 6 17   P   K 2
ꞓ
E 2   W 1 2   M 1 2   D C II   O 1–3 7 ed. H.   quod ex V atr. uiridi mut.
quod ex R G   B 1   K 1   E 1.   om. R 7.   ‖   locupletium R 1 17   V P G   B 1 2
K 1 2   E 1   W 1 2   M 2   D C J.   locupletum R 6   S   E 2   M 1   O 1–3 ed. H.
locuplectum O 7.   ‖   delegerat R V P G   B 2   K 1 2   W 1 2   D C J   O 1 3 7.
delegarat S at a ante r mut. fuerat delegerat.   delegarat B 1.   delegaret E 1.
16.   traxerat G marg. de alt. man. adscr.   ‖   conuenis et feris R 6 17   P   B 1   W 1
M 1 2   D C   O 2 3 ed. H.   conuenis et feris II at s ante et in ras.   conuenisset
feris R 1   V G   B 2   K 1   O 7.   coinuenisset feris E 2.   cum uenisset feris E 1.
conuenisse feris O 1.   cū uenis et feris S.   cū in lit. et o ante u uideri potest.
conuenis feris W 2 at nis in ras.

iurare possum non illum...fuisse'; 11 Verr.
iv 18, 38 'de hoc Verri dicitur habere eum
perbona toreumata.'
    For the character of Dionysius here
given cf. Corn. Nep. de regibus 2 ' et manu
fortis et belli peritus fuit et id quod in
tyranno non facile reperitur, minime libidinosus, non luxuriosus, non auarus,' and
Grote, Hist. of Gr. ix pp. 44 ff. ; Freeman,
Hist. of Sicily iv pp. 5 ff.
    ueritatem, ' the facts of life '; cf. 5, 13
and Or. i 34, 149 'dicatis quam maxime
ad ueritatem adcommodate' with Wilkins'
note.
    § 58. altus alto modo : Diodorus
Siculus xiii 96 says his father was a
γραμματεύς ; Isocrates, Or. v. 73, refers
to him as πολλοστὸς ὢν Συρακοσίων καὶ

τῷ γένει καὶ τῇ δόξῃ καὶ τοῖς ἄλλοις ἅπασιν
and as οὐκ ἔνδοξος (ib. 75).
    more Graeciae : cf. iv 33 70 n. on ' in
Graecorum gymnasiis.'
    credebat : Erasm. followed by Bentl.
wished to insert se, wrongly, as the contrast intended by sed is not that between
appointing the serui and barbari to be his
bodyguard, and rejecting the adulescentes :
but between his want of all real confidence
in the adulescentes and his action in en-
trusting the care of his person to strangers ;
cf. Plat. Epist. vii p. 332 D Διονύσιος...
πιστεύων οὐδενί. Wopkens' defence of the
MSS reading (op. cit. p. 149) misses the
point.
    nomen seruitutis : according to Diod.
Sic. xiv 7, Dionysius seems to have ad-

barbaris corporis custodiam committebat. ita propter iniustam dominatus cupiditatem in carcerem quodam modo ipse se incluserat. quin etiam, ne tonsori collum committeret, tondere 20 filias suas docuit. ita sordido ancillarique artificio regiae uirgines ut tonstriculae tondebant barbam et capillum patris. et tamen ab his ipsis, cum iam essent adultae, ferrum remouit instituitque ut candentibus iuglandium putaminibus barbam sibi et capillum adurerent. **59.** cumque duas uxores haberet, Aristomachen, 25 ciuem suam, Doridem autem Locrensem, sic noctu ad eas uentitabat ut omnia specularetur et perscrutaretur ante. et cum

17. committebat R V P G.   cōmittebat K.   18. dominatus domi G *eod. atr.*   19. committeret R V G.   cōmitteret P K.   20. filias lias G *at* lias *exp. alt. man.* ‖ sordido ancillarique R 7 16 17   K 2   E 3   L 2–5   W 1 2
                                                         q:
M 1   D C   O 1 2.   sordido ancilariq; J.   sordido ancillari B 1 *ras. post* o.
                                                                                 at
sordidoque ancillari R V G   B 2   K 1   E 1   Π.   sordidoq; ancillari P.
                                                                       q:
sordidoque artificio ancillari E 2.   sordidoque artificio ancillari‸ Π *al. atr. superscr.* sordido atque ancillari R 2 10   S   L 6   M 2   O 3 7 ed. H.   ancillari sordidoque
                                   i
R 6. ‖ artificio R 1 6 7   G.   artifico V *atr. uiridi superscr.*   officio R 16 17. 23. iuglandium R G   B 1 2   K 1   S   E 1 2   W 2   M 2   J.   iu glandium C.
                                                            i
iuglandium W iu *ante* g *in ras.*   iuglandum V *atr. ant.*   iuglandum M 1   O 2. inglandium D   Π   O 1 ed. H.   inglandiū P *marg.* iuglandiū.   in gladium O 3 7.
  § **59,** 24. aristomachen L 2 4   W 1   O 1 ed. H.   aristomachē P   B 1 E 1   O 7.   aristomachem R V   B 2   K S   E 2   L 3 5 6   M 1 2   D   O 3.
                                                              c
aristhomachem G.   25. noctu R P G.   notu V *atr. ant.* K *eod. atr.*

mitted freedmen to the roll of citizens and to have given them the title νεοπολῖται; Dionysius' first bodyguard was chosen from the Syracusan army (Diod. xiii 95); to them were afterwards added a body of Spaniards who refused to lay down their arms after the battle of Daskon in 397 (*id.* xiv 75); shortly after ἄλλους μισθοφόρους ξενολογήσας τούτοις τε καὶ τοῖς ἠλευθερωμένοις οἰκέταις ἐνεπίστευσε τὴν ἀρχήν (*id.* xiv 78).

feris: altered by Lamb. and Fabr. to *fere*; but (as Dav. puts it) 'non tantum *fere* sed omnino barbari fuerunt hi satellites'; Dav. also illustrates the use of *barbari* as a substantive.

Victorius (*Variae Lectiones* XI 13) draws attention to the similarity between Cicero's language here with regard to Dionysius and Plato's in describing the τυραννικὸς ἀνήρ in the ninth book of the *Republic*: Cicero's 'in carcerem quodam modo ipse se incluserat' is like Plato's ἆρ' οὖν οὐκ ἐν τοιούτῳ μὲν δεσμωτηρίῳ δέδεται ὁ τύραννος, Rep. ix 579 B. Vict. thinks it possible that Cicero may have had Plato's passage in mind, but the resemblances are not so

close as to make this a very likely supposition.

tonstriculae is ἅπαξ εἰρημένον. For women as barbers edd. quote Plaut. Truc. 405 'tonstricem Suram nouisti nostram'; Mart. ii 17, 1 'tonstrix Suburae faucibus sedet primis.' For the story cf. Ammian. Marcell. xvi 8, 10 'semper se feriri sperabat, ut Dionysius tyrannus ille Siciliae qui ob hoc idem uitium et tonstrices docuit filias ne cui alieno ora committeret leuiganda'; *Off.* ii 7, 25 'superiorem illum Dionysium...qui cultros metuens tonsorios candente carbone sibi adurebat capillum'; Val. Max. ix 13, *ext.* 4. A somewhat different version in Plut. Dio. 9 τῶν πλαστῶν τις ἐπιφοιτῶν ἄνθρακι τὴν κόμην περιέκαιεν.

Lampridius says that the Emperor Commodus did the same 'adurens comam et barbam timore tonsoris' (Vita, Comm. 17, 3).

duas uxores: he married them on the same day, according to a story reported by Plutarch (Dio. 3) and Aelian V.H. xiii 10; Diod. Sic. xiv 45 says merely περὶ δὲ τὸν αὐτὸν χρόνον ἀμφοτέρας γήμας.

fossam latam cubiculari lecto circumdedisset eiusque fossae
transitum ponticulo ligneo coniunxisset, eum ipsum, cum forem
cubiculi clauserat, detorquebat. idemque cum in communibus
30 suggestis consistere non auderet, contionari ex turri alta solebat.
60. atque is cum pila ludere uellet (studiose enim id factitabat)
tunicamque poneret, adulescentulo quem amabat, tradidisse
gladium dicitur. hic cum quidam familiaris iocans dixisset:
'huic quidem certe uitam tuam committis,' adrisissetque
35 adulescens, utrumque iussit interfici, alterum quia uiam demon-
strauisset interimendi sui, alterum quia dictum id risu adprobauisset. atque eo facto sic doluit nihil ut tulerit grauius in uita;

27. fossam latam R 6 E 2 M 2 C O 3. fossam latā D Π. fossā latā P
E 3 B 1 at a in ā alio atr. bis mut. fossa lata R 1 2 7 10 16 17 V G B 2 K 1 2
S E 1 L 5 W 1 2 M 1 J O 1 2 7 ed. H. ‖ cubiculari lecto R 6 E 2 M 2
D C Π O 3. cobiculari lecto E 3 O 7. cubiculari lecto B 1 at ῑ post ri eras.
cubiculariṣ lecto P. cubicularis lecto R 1 V G B 2 K 1 E 1. cubicularis
lectum R 17 K 2 L 5 W 2 J O 1 2. cubicular' lectum M 1. cubicularem
lectum R 7 W 1. cubiculaῤ lectum R 16. cubiculares lecto R 10 S.
28. forem R V P G B 1 2 K 1 E 1 2 D C Π O 3 7. forē S marg. fores.
fores R 6 7 17 W 1 2 M 1 2 J O 1 2 ed. H.
§ 60, 31. atque is R V P B 1 K 1 W 2 D O 7 ed. H. atque is (h eras.)
S W 1. atque his G E 1. 34. adrisissetque G B 1 2. adrisisseque V
atr. ant. adrisisetque R K 1 E 1. arrisissetque S. 35. Iussit G.
36. adprobauisset R V G K E. approbauisset B S. 37. eo facto R P G K.
eo facta V atr. uiridi superscr.

cubiculari lecto, 'the couch in his
bedchamber': the same phrase occurs in
Diu. ii 65, 134: the lectus cubicularis is
distinguished from the lectus tricliniaris
by Varro, L.L. viii 32.
The conjecture tecto (Gesn. Tr.) is contradicted by the following words which
imply that the fossa was inside the door
of the chamber, as the bridge was dis-
connected after shutting the door; cf.
also Val. Max. ix 13, ext. 4 'cubicularem
lectum perinde quasi castra lata fossa
cinxit, in quem se ligneo ponte recipiebat,
cum forem cubiculi extrinsecus a custodi-
bus opertam, interiorem claustro ipse
diligenter obserasset.' Ammian Marc.
xvi 8, 10 supposes the fossa to have been
outside the chamber 'aedemque breuem,
ubi cubitare sueuerat, alta circumdedit
fossa, eamque ponte solubili superstrauit;
cuius disiectos asseres et axiculos secum
in somnum abiens transferebat, eosdemque
compaginabat lucis initio processurus.'
ipsum, 'even that,' small as was the
chance of any one being able to cross it.
O. Rossbach in Phil. LXIII N.F. (1904)
p. 100 n. conjectured ipse, remarking
'neque enim id premitur ponticulum duc-
tilem detorqueri, sed regem ipsum hoc
humili officio fungi,' which completely
misses the point.

detorquebat: i.e. 'in alteram partem
deflectebat, ut introitus esset interclusus'
(Beorald.). Cic. assumes that the only
way to reach the bed from the door was
over the bridge which spanned the fossa;
the bridge was supposed to swing on a
pivot which permitted of its being swung
to the side when not in use.
§ 60. poneret, 'laid aside'; so ponere
librum i 11, 24.
gladium: cf. the similar story in Plut.
Dio. 9 ἐπεὶ δὲ Λεπτίνης ὁ ἀδελφὸς αὐτῷ
ποτε χωρίου φύσιν ἐξηγούμενος λαβὼν
λόγχην παρά τινος τῶν δορυφόρων ὑπέ-
γραψε τὸν τόπον, ἐκείνῳ μὲν ἰσχυρῶς
ἐχαλέπηνε τὸν δὲ δόντα τὴν λόγχην ἀπέ-
κτεινεν. Dav. suggested that the young
man of this story may be Leon, whose
fate is told in Aelian, V.H. xiii 34, τὸν
Λέοντα ὁ Διονύσιος μετὰ τὴν πρόσταξιν τὴν
κατ' αὐτοῦ ἀνευρὼν ἐς τρὶς τοῖς δορυφόροις
ἐκέλευσεν ἀπάγειν καὶ μετέγνω τρίς, καὶ
καθ' ἑκάστην μεταπομπὴν κατεφίλει κλάων
καὶ καταρώμενος αὐτῷ ὅτι ἔλαβε τὸ ξίφος.
τελευτῶν ἥττηται τῷ φόβῳ καὶ προσέταξεν
ἀποσφαγῆναι εἰπὼν ὅτι ' οὐκ ἔστιν, ὦ Λέον,
σοι ζῆν.'
quidem certe: Küh. points out that in
this combination, quidem emphasises the
preceding word, while certe is attached
more closely to the verb.

quem enim uehementer amarat, occiderat. sic distrahuntur in
contrarias partis inpotentium cupiditates. cum huic obsecutus
40 sis, illi est repugnandum.

XXI. **61.** Quamquam hic quidem tyrannus ipse iudicauit
quam esset beatus. nam cum quidam ex eius adsentatoribus,
Damocles, commemoraret in sermone copias eius, opes, maie-
statem dominatus, rerum abundantiam, magnificentiam aedium
5 regiarum negaretque umquam beatiorem quemquam fuisse,
'uisne igitur,' inquit, 'o Damocle, quoniam te haec uita
delectat, ipse eadem degustare et fortunam experiri
meam?' cum se ille cupere dixisset, conlocari iussit hominem

38. amarat R V G B 2 K S E Gr. Vict.   amaret O 7.   39. partis
R V G K O 1.   partes S E. ‖ impotentium R V G K S.   inpotentium E. ‖
obsecutus sis R G B 1 2 K 1 2 E 3 L 2–6 W 1 2 M 1 2 D C J O 1 2 7.
obsequutus sis Π O 3.   assecutus sis ed. H.
XXI. § **61**, 1. iudicauit R 1 6 7 1 7 V P G B 1 2 K 1 S E 1 W 1 M 1
C Π O 1–3 ed. H.   indicauit K 2 E 2 W 2 M 2 D J O 7.
2. adsentatoribus R V G K.   3. commemoraret R V G K.   ∂memoraret P.
                                                                         inquit
5. regnarum G *at* n *in* i *alt. man. mut.*   6. inquit K 1.   R *eod. atr.*
superscr.   inquid V.   inquid G *at* d *in* t *alt. man. mut.* ‖ damocle R V P G
B 1 K 1 2 S E 1 W 1 2 M 1 2 D C J O 1 2 7.   damode B 2 O 3.
damoclee E 2 Π. ‖   te haec uita R V P G B 1 2 K 1 S E 2 M 1 2 Π
O 2 3 7.   haec te uita R 6 K 2 W 1 2 J O 1.   haec uita te E 1.
h' uita D C te *om.*   7. ipse eadem R 1 7 1 7 V G B 1 2 K 1 2 E 1 2 W 2.
D C Π O 3 7.   ipse eandem R 6 S W 1 M 2 O 1.   ipse eãdem P J.
                                                                         ri
ipse in eadem dignitate fortunam M 1   ‖   experiri R G B K.   experri V
atr. ant. superscr.   8. conlocari V G B.   collocari R K S E.

obsecutus sis: the 2nd pers. of the
subj. expresses an indefinite subject;
Madv. *Lat. Gr.* § 370. Sff. reads *es*,
relying upon the doctrine laid down
by Madvig in his *Opusc. Acad.* ii p. 243
and his note to Fin. v 15, 41 'ubi enim
aliquid certo tempore fieri solere signifi-
catur, idque tempus actionis praegressae
absolutione notatur...ibi Latini sic loqu-
untur: *cum* (id est, quotiens) *huc ueni,*
etc....Coniunctiuo modo nullus locus est
in hac simplici temporis notatione,' which
(though true) is here not to the point.
XXI. § **61. iudicauit**: the MSS reading has been defended by Wopkens (*Lect.
Tull.* p. 149) and by Mo. who quotes
Off. iii 22, 86 'quamquam id quidem cum
saepe alias, tum Pyrrhi bello a C. Fabricio
consule iterum et a senatu nostro iudicatum
est,' where, as here, the idea seems to be
that of 'giving one's verdict': Man. and
Lamb. relying upon *declarasse* in the next
paragraph read *indicauit* here, unnecessarily, and they are followed by Be. Dav.
Or. F.A.W.

Damocles: for the story of Damocles
Dav., in a learned note, quotes Hor. C.
iii 1, 17; Pers. iii 40; Macr. Somn. Scip.
i 10; Philo ap. Eus. Praep. Euang. viii
14, 29; Amm. Marcell. xxix 2, 4.
copias eius, opes: for the asyndeton cf.
i 14, 31 n. and Heine, *Posen. Progr.* p. 8.
Damocle: for the formation of the voc.
see ii 21, 49 n. on *Ulixes*.
eadem: the neuter plur. seems (as in
i 24, 56: ii 26, 62) to give a more com-
prehensive sense than either *eandem* (Dav.
Or.) or *eam* (Ern. Kl. Ba. Sff.) would
have done; cf. Sen. Tro. 1143 (of the
dying Polyxena) 'et fere cuncti magis |
peritura laudant.' Sff. justifies *eam* by
the hypothesis that *eadem* is due to dittography of the first syllable of *degustare.*
For the use of *degustare* here edd. quote
Sen. Epp. 33, 5 'depone istam spem
posse te degustare ingenia summorum
hominum'; Quint. iv 1, 14 'degustanda
tamen haec prooemio non consumenda.'
hominem: more emphatic than *eum* as
in i 21, 49.

in aureo lecto strato pulcherrimo textili stragulo, magnificis
10 operibus picto, abacosque compluris ornauit argento auroque
caelato. tum ad mensam eximia forma pueros delectos iussit
consistere eosque nutum illius intuentis diligenter ministrare.
62. aderant unguenta, coronae, incendebantur odores, mensae
conquisitissimis epulis exstruebantur; fortunatus sibi Damocles
15 uidebatur. in hoc medio apparatu fulgentem gladium e lacunari
saeta equina aptum demitti iussit, ut inpenderet illius beati
ceruicibus. itaque nec pulchros illos ministratores aspiciebat nec
plenum artis argentum nec manum porrigebat in mensam, iam
ipsae defluebant coronae; denique exorauit tyrannum ut abire

9. pulcherrimo R V P G B K. || textili R V G B 2 W 1 2 D Π O 3 7.
textilis P. 　 textilis K 1. 　 10. picto R G K. 　 pi cto V *litt. eras.* ||
compluris R V G K O 1. 　 cōpluris B 1 E 1. 　 complures S.
　　　　que
12. eos 　 G *alt. man. superscr.* || intuentis R V G K E O 1. 　 intuent ĕs S
e *in* i *mut.* 　 intuentes B 1.
§ 62, 14. conquisitissimis R V G B K. 　 cū quisitissimis E 1. || epulis P K.
epulis V. 　 aepulis R G. || extruebantur R V G B K S E. 　 15. apparatu
R V G B K S E. 　 16. saeta V K. 　 seta R 2 P. 　 seta R 6 7 10 16 17
B 1 2 S E 1 2 W 1 2 M 1 2 D C Π J O 1–3 7. 　 sa&aequina R 1.
lacunaria et aequina G *in* lacunarī saeta equina *alt. man. corr.* || aptum R 1 2 10
V P G K E 1 Gr. S *marg.* appēsū. 　 appensum R 6 7 16 17 E 2 L 5 W 1 2
M 2 O 1 ed. H. 　 apensū E 3. 　 apprehensum M 1. || demitti V P G.
dimitti R K. || impenderet R V G B 1 2 K 1 S. 　 ipenderet E 1.
17. pulchros R V P G B K S E. || aspiciebat R V G B K S E. 　 19. ipse G.

strato...picto: for the chiastic arrangement see Nägelsbach, § 169; *textili stragulo* being equivalent to a single noun (*peristroma*) can take another adj. *pulcherrimo* without the addition of a copula.

Embroidered couch covers are called *peristromata Campanica* in Plaut. Pseud. 146: the *magnifica opera* remind one of the similar description in Catullus lxiv 47 ff., 'puluinar uero diuae geniale locatur | sedibus in medis, Indo quod dente politum | tincta tegit roseo conchyli purpura fuco. | haec uestis priscis hominum uariata figuris | heroum mira uirtutes indicat arte.'

ministrare: used of waiting at table (i 26, 65) or of the attendance of servants generally (Fin. ii 21, 69).

§ 62. **odores:** the effect for the cause; the same expression occurs in iii 18, 43: *odores* is often thus used, cf. Plaut. Men. 354, Pseud. 1248 (with Lorenz's n.).

epulis, 'dishes' as in Plaut. Trin. 471 'si illi congestae sint epulae a cluentibus'; compare Ellis's n. to Avianus Fab. 30, 10. For *exstruebantur* cf. Lucil. xiii 442 (Marx) 'extructa ampliter...mensa' where Marx quotes Cato M. 13, 44; Pis. 27, 67; Ov. Met. xi 120.

fortunatus, 'in luck'; so in Ov. F. iii 540 the word is used by jealous bystanders of revellers returning home drunk.

saeta, not necessarily 'a horse's hair' but 'a horse hair line,' cf. Avianus Fab. 20, 1 'piscator solitus praedam suspendere saeta'; for the Gk ὁρμίης ἀφ' ἱππείης (Babr. vi 3): see Ellis's n. *ad loc.* who refers to Ov. Hal. 35; Mart. i 55, 9; x 30, 16 for this use of *saeta.* Amm. Marc. xxix 2, 4 speaks also of a *saeta equina,* but Philo (ap. Eus. *P.E.* viii 14), having changed the sword into an axe, is compelled to change the *saeta* into a μήρινθος.

For **aptum** see n. to 'rudentibus apta' in 14, 40 above.

illius beati, 'our fortunate friend'; the expression is sarcastic.

defluebant, 'threatened to fall from his head'; his alarm was disturbing all his movements; for *defluere,* which is not very common in classical writers in this sense, cf. Ov. Met. vi 141 'tristi medicamine tactae | defluxere comae'; Liv. ii 20, 3 'moribundus Romanus labentibus super corpus armis ad terram defluxit'; for another sense cf. i 25, 62 n.

20 liceret quod iam beatus nollet esse. satisne uidetur declarasse
Dionysius nihil esse ei beatum cui semper aliqui terror inpendeat? atque ei ne integrum quidem erat ut ad iustitiam remigraret, ciuibus libertatem et iura redderet; iis enim se adulescens
inprouida aetate inretierat erratis eaque commiserat ut saluus
25 esse non posset, si sanus esse coepisset.

XXII. 63. Quantopere uero amicitias desideraret, quarum
infidelitatem extimescebat, declarauit in Pythagoriis duobus illis,
quorum cum alterum uadem mortis accepisset, alter, ut uadem

21. dyonisius V G B K.   dionisius R E. ‖ aliqui terror B 1 E 1.
aliquid error R 1 G B 2 K 1 E 2.   aliqderror P *marg.* aliqſ terror.
aliquis terror R 2 6 7 10 17 K 2 W 1 M 2 D O 3 7.   aliquid terror V *at* t
postea atr. uiridi inculc.   aliquid terror Π *at* t *postea inculc.*   aliquid terroris
E 3 M 1 O 2.   aliquis error W 2 *al. atr. superscr.* ‖ impendeat R G B K S.
impendat V *atr. ant.*   inpendeat E 1.   22. remigraret R G K.   remigaret V
atr. uiridi superscr.   23. ciuibusque libertatem R 6 ed. H. ‖ his G. ‖
adulescens R V G B 2 K 1 O 1.   adolescens P B 1 S E.   24. inprouida
R V P G B 1 2 K 1 Π.   improuida S W 2 D C O 1. ‖ inretierat
R V G B K E.   irretierat S. ‖ ea quae G. ‖ commiserat V G.   cōmiserat
B K.   comiserat R.
XXII. § 63, 2. pythagoriis R 1 K 1 W 2.   pytagoriis G B.   pythagoris V.
pytagorius P.   pitagoriis B 2.   phitagoriis E 1.   pythagoreis R 6 W 1 O 1.
pithagoreis S *at spatio post* pi *relict., fuerat ut uid.* pijthagoreis.   3. uadem K 1 2
E 2 W 1 M 1 2 D Π O 1–3 ed. H.   uadē P W 2 C O 7.   uadē V
at > *atr. uiridi suppl.*   uadē B 1 *at* e *in* ē *al. atr. mut.*   uade R B 2 E 1.
uade G *at lineam super* e *duxisse uid. alt. man.* ‖ alter ut P K 2 E 3 L 2–6
W 1 2 ed. H.   alterum R V G B 1 2 K 1 S E 1.   alterum ut O 7.
alter D C O 2 ut *om.* ‖ uadem R V G B 2 W 1 2 O 3 7.   uadē P B 1
E 1 D C.   uadā S a *in* e *mut.*

nollet : subj. of reported reason, cf. iv
19, 44 n.
aliqui : cf. i 11, 23 n. ; i 34, 82 n.
ut, ' it was not open to him to ' ; the
inf. is more usual after *integrum*, cf. iii
29, 73 n.
inprouida aetate : Dav. proposed to
insert *in*, which he supposed had fallen
out by haplography ; but the simple abl.
seems to be intended to express cause as
well as time.
XXII. § 63. **in Pythagoriis**, ' in the
case of ' ; for *in* cf. 9, 24 n. on *in eo
libro*.
The two Pythagoreans were Damon
and Phintias, whose story is told in Off. iii
10, 45 ' Damonem et Phintiam Pytha-
goreos ferunt hoc animo inter se fuisse ut
cum eorum alteri Dionysius tyrannus diem
necis destinauisset et is qui morti addictus
esset paucos sibi dies commendandorum
suorum causa postulauisset, uas factus sit
alter eius sistendi, ut si ille non reuertisset,

moriendum esset ipsi. qui cum ad diem se
recepisset, admiratus eorum fidem tyrannus petiuit, ut se ad amicitiam tertium
ascriberent.' Cf. also Diod. Sic. x 4 ;
Val. Max. iv 7 *ext.* 1. According to
Aristoxenus, whose account is given in
Iamblichus, Vit. Pythag. c. 33, the whole
thing was a cruel experiment of Dionysius
the younger and his friends to test the
reality of Pythagorean professions.
The story is told in varying forms and
with varying names, and seems to have
been invented for purposes of edifica-
tion in Pythagorean circles. See ' Die
Novelle von der Bürgschaft im Altertum,'
by H. Gasse, in *Rh. M.* LXVI pp. 607 ff.
uadem mortis : Scheibe wished to
delete *mortis* here as ' ineptum ' and as
interpolated from *horam mortis* below.
Heine (*Posen. Progr.* p. 5) shows by a
comparison of Off. iii 10, 45 ; Fin. ii 24, 79
that a defining genitive or prepositional
phrase after *uadem* is regular.

suum liberaret, praesto fuisset ad horam mortis destinatam,
5 'utinam ego,' inquit, 'tertius uobis amicus adscriberer!'
quam huic erat miserum carere consuetudine amicorum, societate
uictus, sermone omnino familiari, homini praesertim docto a
puero et artibus ingenuis erudito! musicorum uero perstudiosum, poëtam etiam tragicum (quam bonum, nihil ad rem; in
10 hoc enim genere nescio quo pacto magis quam in aliis suum
cuique pulchrum est. adhuc neminem cognoui poëtam (et mihi
fuit cum Aquinio amicitia), qui sibi non optimus uideretur. sic
se res habet: te tua, me delectant mea) — sed ut ad Dionysium

4. ad horam R P G.　　　adoram V E.　‖ mortis R 1 6 7 17　V G　B 1 2　K 1
S　E 1 2　M 1 2　C II　O 2 3 7 ed. H.　　mortiş P.　　morti K 2　W 1 2　J　O 1.
5. adscriberer R V G B K E.　　asscriberer II.　　ascriberer S.　　7. docto
R G K.　　dato V.　　8. ingenuis R 6 7　V P G　B 1　E 2　W 1 2　M 1 2
D C　O 1 3.　　ingenuus O 2.　　ingeniis R 1 17　B 2　K 1　E 1　II　O 7. ‖
musicorum P　K 2　E 1–3　W 1 2　D　O 1–3 7 ed. H.　　musicū B 1.
　　　　　　　　　　　　　　　　　　　　　　　o
misicorum R V G　B 2　K 1.　　‖ uero V G.　　u P　B 1.　　u￪ro R i *ex* e
al. atr. mut.　　‖ perstudiosum poetam (*om.* accepimus) R 1 7　V P G　B 1　K 1 2
E 1–3　L 2 3 5 6　W 1 2　M 2　D C J　O 2 7 ed. H.　　perstudiosum_A poetam S
　　　　　　　　　　　accepimus
marg. accepimus.　　perstudiosum poetam II *al. atr. superscr.*　　perstudiosum
accepimus poetam O 3.　　perstudiosum poetam etiam tragicum accepimus L 4
M 1　O 1.　　11. pulcrum G *h. l.*　　12. aquinio R 1 7　V P G　B 2　K 1　S
　　　　　　　　　　　　　　　　　　taliquo
　　　　　　　　　　　　　　　　　　i
E 1 2　W 2　M 1 2　D C II J　O 1 7.　　aqnio B 1.　　aquino K 2　W 1
O 2 3 ed. H.　‖ optumus R V G B K.　　13. dyonisium R 1 16　V P G　B 1　K 1.
dionisium R 2 10.

horam mortis : the genitive is paralleled by 'diem necis' in Off. iii 10, 45,
quoted above : Lamb.'s *morti*, adopted
by Tr., is unnecessary.
　musicorum uero perstudiosum : for
Dionysius' love of music and poetry cf.
Diod. Sic. xiv 109 (σφόδρα γὰρ εἰς τὴν
ποιητικὴν ὑπῆρχε μεμηνώς), xv 6, 74 ;
Aelian, V.H. xiii 18 ; Amm. Marcell. xv
5, 37·
　The accusatives *perstudiosum* and *poetam* are out of construction. Had the
parenthesis not interrupted the thought
Cic. might have ended his sentence with
fuisse accepimus or some such phrase ; for
similar ἀνάκολουθα cf. iii 8, 16; Fin. ii 33,
107. Bentley followed by Dav. altered
the accusatives (including *bonum*) to the
dative ; and many edd., including Kl.
He. Sff. Sch., insert *accepimus* with some
MSS ; Lamb. added *fuisse* as well; Sff.
and Sch. read ' erudito, musicorum uero
perstudioso. poetam etiam tragicum accepimus.' For *bonum*, attracted into the
case of the preceding adj. (instead of *quam
bonus fuerit, nihil ad rem*), cf. Fin. ii 27,
88 ' ne dolorem quidem ' with Madvig's
note.

neminem : cf. i 41, 99 n. on *hominem,
neminem.*
　For this cynical view of the character
of poets edd. refer to ad Att. xiv 20, 3
' nemo unquam neque poeta neque orator
fuit qui quemquam meliorem quam se
arbitraretur ' and Arist. Eth. Nic. ix 7
(1168 a) μάλιστα δ' ἴσως τοῦτο περὶ τοὺς
ποιητὰς συμβαίνει, ὑπεραγαπῶσιν γὰρ οὗτοι
τὰ οἰκεῖα ποιήματα στέργοντες ὥσπερ τέκνα.
　Aquinio : if this poet is identical with
Catullus' *Aquinus* (xiv 18) we must either
(with some MSS. and Ern. Bouh. F.A.W.
and Or.) read *Aquino* here or else suppose
that *Aquinius* and *Aquinus* are different
forms of the same name (Ellis, *Comment.
on Cat. ad loc.*). It is just possible, the
supply of bad poets being then (apparently) what it always is, that Cic. and
Catullus are speaking of different persons.
　se res : for the order of these two
words, which varies, see Madvig's note
to Fin. i 7, 25.
　te tua...mea : Cic. quotes in a similar
context (Att. xiv 20, 3) a line of Atilius
to the same effect 'suam cuique sponsam,
mihi meam ; suum cuique amorem, mihi
meum,' adding the comment ' non scite.'

redeamus, omni cultu et uictu humano carebat; uiuebat cum
15 fugitiuis, cum facinerosis, cum barbaris; neminem, qui aut libertate dignus esset aut uellet omnino liber esse, sibi amicum
arbitrabatur.

XXIII. 64. Non ego iam cum huius uita, qua taetrius,
miserius, detestabilius excogitare nihil possum, Platonis aut
Archytae uitam comparabo, doctorum hominum et plane sapientium; ex eadem urbe humilem homunculum a puluere et radio
5 excitabo, qui multis annis post fuit, Archimedem. cuius ego
quaestor ignoratum ab Syracusanis, cum esse omnino negarent,
saeptum undique et uestitum uepribus et dumetis indagaui sepulcrum. tenebam enim quosdam senariolos, quos in eius
monumento esse inscriptos acceperam, qui declarabant in summo

---

15. facinerosis R V G B 2 K 1. facinorosis P B 1 K 2 S E 1 2
W 1 2 M 1 2 D C II J O 1–3 7 ed. H.
XXIII. § 64, 1. non ego R G B K O 1 Gr. none/go V *litt. post* e *eras.*
3. uitae uitam V B. uitae uitam R G K. uite uitam B 2. ‖ comparabo
R V G K S. cōparabo B. 5. archimedem R G K. archimedē V
B 1 2 S E. 6. ignoratum ab R V G B K E M 2. ignoratum ab S.

ignoratum a W 1 2 J O 7. ‖ negaret septum G *ead. man. superscr.*
7. uestitum R 1 2 10 G K. uestitutum V *atr. uiridi corr.* uestatū R 16. ‖
sepulchrum R 2 V G B E. sepulc)rum R 1 *eod. atr.* sepulc/rū S h *eras.*
sepulcrum K.

XXIII. § 64. Archytae: cf. iv 36,
78 n.

humilem homunculum, 'an obscure
individual,' i.e. in comparison either with
the more celebrated Plato or Archytas,
whom everyone had heard of, or with
Dionysius. The expression can hardly
be ironical as Mayor (Juv. iii 76 n. on
geometres) assumes. The rhetorical expression used by Sil. Ital. Pun. xiv 343
'nudus opum' in describing Archimedes
(quoted by Dav. and subsequent edd.)
ought not to be appealed to as an interpretation of *humilis* here. Archimedes,
according to Plutarch, Marc. c. 14, was
Ἱέρωνι τῷ βασιλεῖ συγγενής...καὶ φίλος,
and can scarcely have been in poverty.

puluere et radio, 'from his drawing
board and pencil'; an *abacus* covered
with fine sand was used by mathema-
ticians, and diagrams were made on it
with a *radius* or sharp-pointed rod. Cf.
Fin. v 19, 50; Pers. i 131; Sen. Epp.
74, 27.

It seems better to take *a puluere* with
excitabo (the idea being that of metaphorically summoning Archimedes to leave
his geometry for the moment) than with
homunculum on the analogy of such
phrases as *seruus ab epistulis*.

Archimedem: the celebrated mathematician and inventor who was said to
have assisted by his warlike machines in
the defence of Syracuse in 212 B.C.; he
was killed by Marcellus' soldiers while
engaged in solving a mathematical prob-
lem (Liv. xxv 31, 9; Plut. Marc. 19);
for his orrery see i 25, 63 and n.

quaestor: as Cicero was quaestor
(75 B.C.) of the W. part of Sicily,
with his headquarters at Lilybaeum, his
visits to Syracuse can only have been
occasional.

sepulcrum: cf. Livy xxv 31, 10 (of the
death of Archimedes) 'aegre id Marcellum
tulisse sepulturaeque curam habitam et
propinquis etiam inquisitis honori prae-
sidioque nomen ac memoriam eius fuisse.'

tenebam: sc. *mente*, cf. Off. iii 16, 67
'qui id, quod emerat, quo iure esset
teneret'; the usage is common in Plautus,
e.g. Epid. 292 'hic poterit cauere recte,
iura qui et leges tenet'; Most. 171 'ut
lepide omnis mores tenet.'

The iambic lines referred to are not
extant. By the diminutive *senariolos* Cic.
does not seem to mean to express depre-
ciation of their quality but to indicate
their length as contrasted with that of the
hexameter.

10 sepulcro sphaeram esse positam cum cylindro. 65. ego autem cum omnia conlustrarem oculis (est enim ad portas Agragentinas magna frequentia sepulcrorum), animum aduerti columellam non multum e dumis eminentem in qua inerat sphaerae figura et cylindri. atque ego statim Syracusanis (erant autem principes 15 mecum) dixi me illud ipsum arbitrari esse quod quaererem. inmissi cum falcibus multi purgarunt et aperuerunt locum. 66. quo cum patefactus esset aditus, ad aduersam basim accessimus. apparebat epigramma exesis posterioribus partibus

10. sepulchro V G B E.   sepulchro R 1 *eod. atr.*   sepulc⸝ro S h *eras.*
sepulcro K.   sepulcrho R 2. ‖ spheram R V G B K.   sperā P E.

§ 65, 11. conlustrarem R V G B K.   conlustrarem S.   collustrarem E. ‖
ad portas R 2 10 16   P   K 1 2   E 2 3   W 2   M 1 2   D C II   O 1–3 7 ed. H.
                      d
a portas R 1   G.   aporta V *atr. uiridi superscr.*   a porta B 1 2   E 1. ‖
agragianas R 1   G   K 1 2   W 2   O 2   S *at litt. ad init. eras.*   sagragianas R 10
V P   B 2   E 2   D C II   O 3 7.   agraginas E 3   M 2.   sagragiana B 1   E 1.
ag̃ gianas R 16.   agg̃gianas O 1.   fagg̃inas M 1.   aggregianas W 1.
fegragianas R 2.   agregianas ed. H.   12. sepulchrorum V G B E   W 2.
sepulchrorum R *eod. atr.*   sepulc⸝rorum S h *eras.*   sepulcrorum K. ‖ animum
                                                  aduerti
aduerti R V P G   B 1 2   K   E 1.   animū﹏   S *marg.* anīadu'ti.
animaduerti E 2   W 1 2   M 1 2   D C II J   O 1 2. ‖ columellam R G B K S *marg.*
                                                          o
colūnellā W 2   O 3.   colūmellam V u *in* ū *atr. uiridi mut.*   calumellam E 1
al. atr. superscr.   13. sphęrae B 1.   sphaere G K.   spherae R V.
      h
spere P.   15. illud ipsum R V P G   B 1 2   K 1   E 1–3   L 4–6   M 1 2   J   O 7.
illud L 3   O 1 ipsum *om.*   16. inmissi cum R 7 17   K 2   C.   inmissi
tum ed. H.   īmissi cum E 3   M 2.   immissi cum E 2   L 5   W 2   D J
O 1–3.   imissi cum W 1   M 1.   immisi cum R 6.   immisse cum II.
  í
inmusicum V *atr. uiridi mut.*   inmusicū P *in* in imis cū *mut.*   inmusicum
R 1   G.   in musicū B 1 2   E 1   O 7.   in musicū R 10 S *marg.* immisi cū.
inmuscum K 1. ‖ falcibus R 1 2 10 16   V P G   B 1 2   L 5   W 1 2   M 1   D C II J
         c
O 1 3.   faltibus K 1 *atr. nigriore superscr.*   faucibus E 1.   facibus K 2. ‖
multi R 1 2 7 10 16   V P G   B 1 2   K 1 2   S   E 1–3   W 1 2   M 1 2   D C II J
O 1–3 ed. H.   tulii O 7.
§ 66, 17. patefactus R 6 17   K 2   E 2   W 1 2   M 1 2   D C II   J   O 1–3 7 ed. H.
        s   s   s
patefactu P.   patefactū B 1 ū *in* us *mut.*   patefactum S.   patefactum R 1   V
G   K 1   B 2   E 1. ‖ addit' G *at prius* d *confod. alt. man. et post* t *duae litt. eras.* ‖
basim R 6 17   P   B 1   K 2   E 1 2   W 1 2   M 1 2   D C II   O 1 3 7.   bassim
R 1   V   B 2   K 1   O 2   G *at prius* s *expunx. ead. man. ut uid.*   18. apparebat
R V G K S E. ‖ epigramma G.   epygramma R V K. ‖ exesis R G   K 1
W 1 2   D   O 1 7.   exęsis V.   exeis B 1   E 1.

sphaeram : cf. Plut. Marc. 17 πολλῶν δὲ καὶ καλῶν εὑρετὴς γεγονὼς λέγεται [sc. ὁ Ἀρχιμήδης] τῶν φίλων δεηθῆναι καὶ τῶν συγγενῶν ὅπως αὐτοῦ μετὰ τὴν τελευτὴν ἐπιστήσωσι τῷ τάφῳ τὸν περιλαμβάνοντα τὴν σφαῖραν ἐντὸς κύλινδρον ἐπιγράψαντες τὸν λόγον τῆς ὑπεροχῆς τοῦ περιέχοντος στερεοῦ πρὸς τὸ περιεχόμενον. Archimedes' treatise on this point περὶ σφαίρας καὶ κυλίνδρου is still extant.

This *sphaera* is to be distinguished from that spoken of in i 25, 63, where see n. de Rep. i 14, 22.

animum aduerti : cf. iii 20, 48 n.

multi, 'a number of men'; the emendations *tumuli* (Scheibe), *famuli* (Lattmann) and *milites* (Sff.) are quite unnecessary.

exesis : a common word, especially in poetry, for the effects of weathering. Sen.

H.   17

uersiculorum dimidiatis fere. ita nobilissima Graeciae ciuitas,
20 quondam uero etiam doctissima, sui ciuis unius acutissimi monu-
mentum ignorasset, nisi ab homine Arpinate didicisset. sed
redeat, unde aberrauit oratio. quis est omnium, qui modo cum
Musis, id est cum humanitate et cum doctrina, habeat aliquod
commercium, qui se non hunc mathematicum malit quam illum
25 tyrannum?× si uitae modum actionemque quaerimus, alterius
mens rationibus agitandis exquirendisque alebatur cum oblec-
tatione sollertiae, qui est unus suauissimus pastus animorum,
alterius in caede et iniuriis cum et diurno et nocturno
metu. age confer ʾDemocritum, Pythagoram, Anaxagoram; quae
30 regna, quas opes studiis eorum et delectationibus antepones?

---

19. nobilissima...doctissima...acutissimi R V G B K.   22. reddeat R V K
                                                                                i
G *at prius* d *expunx. ead. man. ut uid.* ‖ qui modo R G B 2 K 1.   quomodo
V *atr. uiridi superscr.*   24. qui se non hunc mathematicum malit R 1 10 V P G
B 1 2 K 1 2 S E 1–3 L 2–5 W 1 2 M 1 Π J O 1–3.   qui non se hunc
math. malit D.   qui nunc non se hunc math. malit C.   qui non hunc math.
malit M 2 L 6.   qui se non ad hunc m. malit O 7.   qui se non hunc
                                                                           cū
mathematicum esse malit ed. H.   qui se non habet mathe malit R 16.
                                i
26. exquirendisque G.   exquǿrendisque R *eod. atr.*   exquirandisque K.
27. suauissimus R V G B.   suauisimus K.   28. in caede R V P B 2
K 1 2 S E 1–3 W 1 2 M 2 C Π J O 3.   in cede G B 1 D O 1.
cede M 1.   caede O 2.   etiam cede O 7. ‖ et iniuriis R V P G B 1 2 K 1 2
S E 1 2 D C Π.   et in iuriis O 7.   et in iniuriis O 3.   et in uitiis O 1.
                                                                                       h
et in uiciis W 1 2 J.   29. pythagoram R K.   pythagorā V.   phytagoram
G *ead. man.*   pytagorā P B.   phitagorā E. ‖ anaxagoram R 1 2 V G.
anaxagorā R 10 16 P B.

Phoen. 72 'partes lapsi montis exesas.'
Virg. G. iv 419 'exesi latere in montis.'
    dimidiatis, 'almost to the middle of
the line'; strictly speaking *dimidiatis*
should have agreed with *uersiculorum*,
but Bentley's *dimidiatum* (adopted by
Dav.) seems unnecessary.
    For the adjectival use of *dimidiatus* cf.
Aul. Gell. iii 14.
    Graeciae: not 'Greece' in the narrow
sense, but including Magna Graecia, 'the
Greek world' as in pro Arch. 5, 10. It
is no doubt the implied superiority of
Syracuse to Athens which has induced
some edd. here to take *Graeciae* as a
synonym for *Magnae Graeciae*, for which
there seems to be no sufficient authority;
but Cicero's language here is no stronger
than in II Verr. 4, 52, 117, where he
speaks of Syracuse as 'maxima Graecarum
[urbium], pulcherrima omnium.'

    ignorasset: the suggestion of Freder-
king (*Philol.* LX p. 637) *ignoraret*, 'would
still be ignorant' would make Cicero say
that no one but himself would ever have
discovered the monument.
    se...malit: see n. on 18, 54 above;
Lamb. here inserts *esse* after *hunc*, unnecessarily.
    oblectatione sollertiae: cf. Plut. non
p. suau. uiu. sec. Ep. 11 [p. 1093 E]
τίνας οἰόμεθα καὶ πηλίκας ἡδονὰς ἀπὸ
γεωμετρίας δρέπεσθαι καὶ ἀστρολογίας...
Ἀρχιμήδην ἀνευρόντα τῇ γωνίᾳ τὴν διά-
μετρον τοῦ ἡλίου κ.τ.λ.
    pastus: cf. Fin. v. 19, 54 'animi
cultus ille erat ei quasi quidam humanitatis cibus.'
    in caede: some word like *uersabatur*
is to be supplied from *alebatur*. Ma. and
La. omit *in*, while Ba. proposes to repeat
it before *iniuriis*.

67. etenim, quae pars optima est in homine, in ea situm esse necesse est illud, quod quaeris, optimum. quid est autem in homine sagaci ac bona mente melius? eius bono fruendum est igitur, si beati esse uolumus; bonum autem mentis est uirtus; 35 ergo hac beatam uitam contineri necesse est. hinc omnia quae pulchra, honesta, praeclara sunt, ut supra dixi, sed dicendum idem illud paulo uberius uidetur, plena gaudiorum sunt. ex perpetuis autem plenisque gaudiis cum perspicuum sit uitam beatam exsistere, sequitur ut ea exsistat ex honestate.

XXIV. **68.** Sed ne uerbis solum attingamus ea quae uolumus ostendere, proponenda quaedam quasi mouentia sunt, quae nos magis ad cognitionem intellegentiamque conuertant. sumatur enim nobis quidam praestans uir optimis artibus, isque animo 5 parumper et cogitatione fingatur. primum ingenio eximio sit necesse est; tardis enim mentibus uirtus non facile comitatur; deinde ad inuestigandam ueritatem studio incitato. ex quo triplex ille animi fetus exsistet, unus in cognitione rerum positus et in explicatione naturae, alter in discriptione expetendarum

---

§ 67, 31. optuma...optumum R V G B K. ‖ in homine...necesse est *om.* G *in marg. inf. add. alt. man.* 32. quaeris R V P G B 1 K 1 2 S W 1 2 M 2. queris É 1 2 M 1 D C II J O 1–3 7 ed. H. queri9 B 2. ‖ omnium optimum W 1. ‸optimum II *al. atr. superscr.* omnium *non habet* Gr. 34. si beati esse R G B 1 E 1 2 J. si esse beati S. si beati V esse *om.* 36. pulchra R G B. pulcra K. 39. existere...existat R V G B K S E.
XXIV. § 68, 1. attingamus R V G B K S E. ‖ ea quae G. ea͞q V que *in* quae *atr. uiridi corr.* eaque R K. 3. intellegentiamque R V G B K. intelligentiamque S E. 4. optimis R V G B K. optimis S. obtimis E. 6. uirtutis G *at* ti *exp. ead. man.* 8. fetus R 7 17 P B 2 K 1 2 L 2–6
‡ flexus
W 2 M 1 D C J O 1–3 7. f&us R 1. fętus E 1. fętus S. faetus M 2. factus V G. foetus R 6 B 1 E 3 W 1. flexus P 4 E 2 II. affectus ed. H. ‖ existet R 1 V P 1 4 G B 1 2 K 1 2 S E 1–3 W 1 2 M 1 2 D C II J O 1–3 7. existit R 7 ed. H. 9. discriptione R V G K. descriptione B 1 *et* E 1 di *in* de *mut.* descriptione R 7 P B 2 S E 2 W 1 2 D C II J O 2. discretione O 1. discrepatione O 7.

---

§ 67. **ut supra dixi**: in 15, 43 above.

XXIV. § 68. **mouentia**: probably a translation of some such word as κινοῦντα or κινητικά (or ὁρμητικά); for this use of κινοῦν in Stoic phraseology cf. Stob. Ecl. II 6, 6, p. 175, 8 τὸ δὲ κινοῦν τὴν ὁρμὴν οὐδὲν ἕτερον εἶναι λέγουσιν ἀλλ᾽ ἢ φαντασίαν ὁρμητικὴν τοῦ καθήκοντος αὐτόθεν.

nobis: cf. ii 1, 2 n. on *mihi*.

comitatur: for the dative with *comitari* cf. 35, 100.

triplex: for the threefold division of philosophy into τὸ φυσικόν, τὸ ἠθικόν and τὸ λογικόν cf. Ac. i 5, 19; ii 36, 116; Fin. v 4, 9; it continued to be a commonplace of philosophical discussion as e.g. in Julian, Or. vii 215 D (p. 279 Hertl.): *triplex fetus* is here equivalent to *tres fetus*, as is shown by *unus*, *alter*, *tertius*.

10 fugiendarumque rerum *et in ratione* uiuendi, tertius in iudicando
quid cuique rei sit consequens, quid repugnans, in quo inest
omnis cum subtilitas disserendi, tum ueritas iudicandi. 69. quo
tandem igitur gaudio adfici necesse est sapientis animum cum
his habitantem pernoctantemque curis! ut cum totius mundi
15 motus conuersionesque perspexerit sideraque uiderit innumera-
bilia caelo inhaerentia cum eius ipsius motu congruere certis

10. fugiendarumque rerum R 1 *ante* rerum *est ras. duarum fere litt. et post* rerum
be
in ras. apparet uiuendiue *litteris paene euanidis.*   fugiendarumque ue̦ rerumneuiuendi
V *atr. uiridi mut.*   fugiendarumque ue rerumne uiuendi G K 1.   fugiendarumque
rerumne uiuendi R 16 17 B 1.   fugiendarumque ueterumne uiuendi R 2.
rerum
fugiendarumque∧   uiuendi S *marg.* rerū 1 9munione.   fugiendarumque uererunt
ne uiuendi E 1.   fugiendarumque rerumue uiuendi K 2 L 3 5 W 2 J.
fugiendarumque rerum uiuendi P 4 O 17.   fugiendarumque rerum in communione
uiuendi W 1.   fugiendarumque rerum bene uiuendi L 4.   fugiendarumque
uiuendi rerum E 2 II.   fugiendarumque rerum in ratoē uiuendi L 2.
fugiendarumque ne rerum ne uiuendi B 2.   fugiendarumque ne uiuendi P 5.
fugiendarumque ue uiuendi Urs. 3240.   fugiendarumque......uiuendi R 10 *spatio
duodecim fere litterarum relicto.*   fugiendarumue rerum uiuendi P 3 L 6 M 2.
fugiendarumue rerumne uiuendi P 1.   fugiendarumue rerumue uiuendi P 6.
fugiendarumue rerum in munere uiuendi O 2.   fugiendarumue rerum bn̄ uiuendi E 3.
∧ue
fugiendarumq; rerum inmune uiuendi M 1.   fugiendarumue rerum R 6 O 3.
fugiendarumne rerum uiuendi P 2.   fugiendarum rerum in rōē uiuendi R 7.
fugiendarum rerumue in munere uiuendi D C.   fugiendarumque rerum arte ue
uiuendi ed. H. ‖ iudicando quid R 6 V P G B 1 2 K 2 S E 1–3 W 1 M 1 2
D II O 7.   iudicando qui O 1.   iudicando qđ ed. H.   iudicando ne quid
R 1 K 1 W 2 J.   iudicanda quid O 2.   12. omnis cum R 1 17 V G B 2
K 1 E 1 2 W 2.   omnis tum P B 1 S E 3 W 1 M 1 2 D C II J O 1–37. ‖
ti
subtilitas G K.   sublitas V *atr. ant. superscr.*
§ 69, 13. adfici R V G K E.   affici B S. ‖ necesse est R 6 7 17 V P 2
D C.   necesse ēēt E 3.   necesseēet K 1 ē et *in* ēēt *alio atr. mut.*   necesse
esset R 1 P 1 3–6 G B 1 2 K 2 S E 1 2 W 1 2 M 1 2 II J O 1–3 7 ed. H.
14. ut cum R 1 7 V P G B 1 2 K 1 2 S E 1–3 W 1 2 M 1 2 D C II J
O 1–3 7 Gr. ed. H.   & cum R 6.

disserendi…iudicandi : referring to the
subdivision of τὸ λογικόν into ἡ ῥητορική
and ἡ διαλεκτική (Diog. Laert. vii 41).

§ 69. habitantem : cf. iii 34, 83 n.
curis, 'pursuits,' like the Gk μελέται ;
cf. Diu. i 42, 93 'Aegyptii et Babylonii
…omnem curam in siderum cognitione
posuerunt.'

ut, ejected by Be. and Dav., may be
taken either in the sense of 'as for example' (Küh. T.S. etc.), in which case *perspexerit* and *uiderit* will be future perfect
indic. or (with Sff.) as meaning ' so that,'
in which case the sentence will be anacolu-
thistic, the verb intended to follow upon
ut being omitted owing to the length of
the subordinate clause *cum…definiant.*
Sff. supposes that Cic. would have written
*ut cum…definiant, ipse se agnoscat con-
iunctumque cum diuina mente se sentiat,*

as he does when he finally picks up the
broken thread in § 70 : it seems simpler
to find the missing clause in the next
sentence and supply *horum aspectus im-
pellat et admoneat ut plura quaerat.*

mundi, 'the heavens'; a translation of
κόσμος in the second of the three senses in
which it was used (according to Diog. Laert.
vii 138) by the Stoics καὶ αὐτὴν δὲ τὴν
διακόσμησιν τῶν ἀστέρων κόσμον εἶναι
λέγουσι; Cic. uses *mundus* in the same
sense in his translation of the Phaenomena
of Aratus, ll. 224, 237 (ed. Bait.).

caelo: the sphere of the fixed stars or
οὐρανός ; cf. Diog. Laert. *l.c.* ἀνωτάτω μὲν
οὖν εἶναι τὸ πῦρ, ὃ δὴ αἰθέρα καλεῖσθαι, ἐν
ᾧ πρώτην τὴν τῶν ἀπλανῶν σφαῖραν γεννᾶ-
σθαι, εἶτα τὴν τῶν πλανωμένων…οὐρανὸς
δέ ἐστιν ἡ ἐσχάτη περιφέρεια ἐν ᾗ πᾶν
ἵδρυται τὸ θεῖον.

infixa sedibus, septem alia suos quaeque tenere cursus multum
inter se aut altitudine aut humilitate distantia, quorum uagi
motus rata tamen et certa sui cursus spatia definiant. horum
20 nimirum aspectus inpulit illos ueteres et admonuit ut plura
quaererent. inde est indagatio nata initiorum et tamquam
seminum unde essent omnia orta, generata, concreta, quaeque
cuiusque generis uel inanimi uel animantis uel muti uel loquentis
origo, quae uita, qui interitus quaeque ex alio in aliud uicissi-
25 tudo atque mutatio, unde terra et quibus librata ponderibus,
quibus cauernis maria sustineantur, qua omnia delata grauitate

17. suos quaeque R 1 G. suos queque R 10 V S. suos queque R 2 K.
suos quoque R 16. suoseque B 1. suoseque E 1. suosq̄: P.
20. aspectus R V G B K S E. ‖ impulit R V G B K S. inpulit E. ‖
admonuit R V G K. ammonuit R 2 B. admouit P. 21. inde est enim G
at enim *exp. ead. man.* ‖ indagatio R V P G K. inadatio B E. 23. loquentis
B K. loquentẹs R *eod. atr.* loquentes G. 24. qui interitus K 1 E 2
W 1 M 1 J O 2. qui interitus Π *al. atr. superscr.* q̄ interitus K 2.
q̣ interitus E 3. quis interitus M 2 D C O 3. quịi interitus R 1 *eod. atr.*
quẹ. interitus V *atr. uiridi mut.* quẹ interitus B 1. quẹ interitus E 1.
que interitus R 16 B 2. q̄ interitus P *marg.* qs. quae interitus G.
qua interitus R 2. 25. et quibus R 1 2 6 7 10 16 17 V P G E 12 L 2–4 6
plerique. e quibus L 5. quibus W 1 et *om.* 26. sustineantur R 2 6 S E 2
L 2 5 M 1 Π O 2 3 7 ed. H. sustineant R 10 P. sustineaȓ R 16.
sustineant R 1 17 G B 2 K 1 E 1. sustineaṇt V B 1. sustineat K 2 E 3
L 3 4 6 M 2 DC O 1. sustinuịt J. substineat W 1 2. substinuit R 7. ‖
in qua R 1 6 7 V P G B 1 K 1 S E 1 2 L 2 3 5 6 W 1 M 1 Π J O 1–3 7
ed. H. qua E 3 *eod. atr.* in quo L 4. in quā D. inq K 2 W 2.
inquam C. inq3 B 2. in quo R 17. qua *corr. Dauisius.*

septem : the seven planets, i.e the Sun,
the Moon, Mercury, Venus, Mars, Jupi-
ter and Saturn; cf. i 25, 63 n.
rata : a 'uox usitatissima in commemorandis rebus caelestibus,' as Wopkens
remarks (*op. cit.* p. 230); he compares
N. D. ii 38, 97 'qui cum tam certos caeli
motus, tam ratos astrorum ordines...
uiderit.'
horum...quaererent : for the thought
cf. i 19, 45 'haec enim pulchritudo...
philosophiam cognitionis cupiditate in-
censam excitauit.'
initiorum...seminum : cf. Tac. Dial.
c. 33 'initia et semina ueteris eloquentiae,'
where Gudemann quotes Quint. ii 20, 6
'initia quaedam ac semina sunt concessa
natura.'
uicissitudo : referring to the evolution
of air, water and earth by successive con-
densations from fire; cf. the passage
quoted from Chrysippus in Stob. Ecl. i
10, 16 τὸ δὲ πῦρ κατ' ἐξοχὴν στοιχεῖον

λέγεσθαι, διὰ τὸ ἐξ αὐτοῦ πρώτου τὰ λοιπὰ
συνίστασθαι κατὰ μεταβολὴν καὶ εἰς αὐτὸ
ἔσχατον πάντα χέομενα διαλύεσθαι...πρώ-
της μὲν γιγνομένης τῆς ἐκ πυρὸς κατὰ
σύστασιν εἰς ἀέρα μεταβολῆς, δευτέρας δ' ἀπὸ
τούτου εἰς ὕδωρ, τρίτης δ' ἔτι μᾶλλον κατὰ
τὸ ἀνάλογον συνισταμένου τοῦ ὕδατος εἰς
γῆν.
quibus...ponderibus, 'by what forces
it is held in equilibrium'; the earth being
the κέντρον of the universe was held in
position by the resultant of the centripetal
and centrifugal forces; cf. i 17, 40 nn.
and Achilles, Isagoge 4 (quoted in von
Arnim, *Stoic. vet. frag.* ii p. 175), para-
phrasing Chrysippus and others, καὶ τὴν
γῆν δὲ πανταχόθεν ὑπὸ τοῦ ἀέρος ὠθουμένην
ἰσορρόπως ἐν τῷ μέσῳ εἶναι καὶ ἑστάναι...
ὥσπερ εἴ τις λαβὼν σῶμα δήσειε πανταχόθεν σχοινίοις καὶ δοίη τισὶν ἰσορρόπως ἕλκειν
ἐπ' ἀκριβείας· συμβήσεται γὰρ πανταχόθεν
ἐπίσης περιελκόμενον στῆναι καὶ ἀτρεμῆσαι;
Plut. de Stoic. repugn. p. 1053.

medium mundi locum semper expetant, qui est idem infimus in rotundo.

XXV. 70. Haec tractanti animo et noctes et dies cogitanti exsistit illa a deo Delphis praecepta cognitio, ut ipsa se mens adgnoscat coniunctamque cum diuina mente se sentiat, ex quo insatiabili gaudio compleatur. ipsa enim cogitatio de ui et natura 5 deorum studium incendit illius aeternitatem imitandi neque se in

27. expetant E 2 L 4 6 ed. H.　　　expeçtant E 3.　　　expectant R V P G
K 1 2 S L 2 3 5 W 1 M 1 O 3.　　　exspectant E 1.　‖　infimus R V P G K.

28. rotundo V P B 1 K 1 E 1 W 1 2 M 1 J O 1 3 7.　　　rotondo S.
rutundo R *h. l.* G B 2.

XXV. § 70, 1. tractanti R 6 7 17　P B 1　E 2　W 1 2　M 1 2　D C Π
O 1–3 7.　　　tractandi V *atr. uiridi superscr.*　　　tractandi R 1　G B 2 E 1.
tractand*ǫ̇* K 1.　‖　cogitanti R 1 6 7 17　P G B 1 E 1 W 1 2 M 1 D C O 2 3 7.

cogitandi V *atr. uiridi superscr.*　cogitandi B 2 K 1.　2. existit R V P G B S E. ‖
illa a deo delphis R 6　P 2　K 1 2　E 2　W 2　M 1 2　Π J　O 1 2.　　　illa deo
delphis R 1 7　V B 1 2 G.　　illa deeo delphis E 1.　　illa de adelphis D C O 3 7.
illa de adelphis S *marg.* a deo.　　illa de adhelphis P 1.　　illa de delphis W 1
litt. eras.　　　3. agnoscat R V P G *h. l.* B K S E.　　4. compleatur R G K.
cōpleatur V P B.　　5. incendit P B 1.　　incedit R G B 2.　‖　aeternitatis
R V P G　B 1 2　E 2　W 1 2　D C Π　O 1–3 7.　　　externitatis M 1.
aeternitatem *corr. Seyffertus.*　‖　imitandi R 1 7 17　V P 1–6　G B 1 2 K 1 2
E 1–3 L 2–6 W 2 M 1 2　D C Π J　O 2 3 7 Urs. 3240.　　　imitandae R 6.
imitand*ę* S　W 1.　　imitande O 1 ed. H.

cauernis, 'hollows'; water being lighter than earth, the sphere of water originally lay above the earth; later, by a process which is differently explained, the sea became confined to certain deep hollows and channels on the surface of the earth; cf. N.D. ii 45, 116; Manilius, Astron. i 163 'et saccata magis struxerunt aequora terram | adiacuitque cauis fluidum conuallibus aequor.'
sustineantur, 'are held'; for the use of *sustinere* cf. Sen. de breu. uit. 19, 1 'quid sit quod huius mundi grauissima quaeque in medio sustineat'; for the change from secondary to primary sequence cf. 7, 18 above, and for the reverse change iii 15, 32.
medium ... rotundo: the statement often occurs, e.g. N.D. ii 45, 116; Manil. Astr. i 170 'medium totius et imum est.' Sen. de breu. uit. 19, 1 (quoted in preceding n.); Plut. de Stoic. repugn. p. 1054: Sallustius, de diis et mundo c. 7 (Mullach, *Frgg. Phil. Gr.* iii p. 37) σφαίρας δὲ οὔσης τοῦ κόσμου...ἐπειδὴ σφαίρας πάσης τὸ κάτω μέσον ἐστί, πανταχόθεν γὰρ πλεῖστον ἀφέστηκε· τά τε βαρέα φέρεται κάτω, φέρεται δὲ εἰς γῆν.
The matter of the preceding paragraph has been derived in all probability from Posidonius; see Capelle, in *Neue Jahrb.* 1905, p. 534[4].

XXV. § 70. Haec tractanti: Cicero passes here from the consideration of the first of the *tres animi fetus* of § 68, viz. *cognitio rerum* (which has occupied § 69) to the second, the *discriptio expetendarum fugiendarumque rerum* which occupies this and the next paragraph.
noctes et dies: Madv. notes on Fin. i 16, 51 that Cic. always uses either *noctes diesque* or *noctes et dies* or *et dies et noctes* or *dies noctesque.*
praecepta: cf. i 22, 52 and nn. there.
compleatur: the subj. is consecutive; Bentley's *completur* is adopted only by Dav. and Ern.
illius: sc. *mentis.*
aeternitatem: Sff.'s emendation of *aeternitatis* (the reading of nearly all the mss) has been accepted by Hei. T.S. and Sch.; the gen. seems to be due to the influence of the preceding *illius*: a few mss have *aeternitatis imitandae*, adopted by Dav. Or. Tr. Wes., while Madv. (on Fin. i 18, 60) proposed *aeterni status imitandi*: the reading of the mss *aeternitatis imitandi* is kept by Kl. Mo. Ha. and Küh., and is defended by reference to Ter. Hec. 372 'ego eius [sc. mulieris] uidendi cupidus recta consequor,' and Cic. Phil. v 3, 6 'facultas...agrorum suis latronibus condonandi.' Madv. (*l.c.*) points out that while such a construction

breuitate uitae conlocatam putat, cum rerum causas alias ex aliis
aptas et necessitate nexas uidet, quibus ab aeterno tempore flu-
entibus in aeternum ratio tamen mensque moderatur. **71.** haec
ille intuens atque suspiciens uel potius omnis partis orasque
10 circumspiciens quanta rursus animi tranquillitate humana et
citeriora considerat! hinc illa cognitio uirtutis exsistit, efflore-
scunt genera partesque uirtutum, inuenitur quid sit quod natura
spectet extremum in bonis, quid in malis ultimum, quo referenda
sint officia, quae degendae aetatis ratio deligenda. quibus et
15 talibus rebus exquisitis hoc uel maxime efficitur, quod hac disputatione agimus, ut uirtus ad beate uiuendum sit se ipsa
contenta. **72.** sequitur tertia, quae per omnis partis sapientiae
manat et funditur, quae rem definit, genera dispertit, sequentia

---

6. conlocatam B 1 K 1.   conlocatā V.   collocatam R 6 E 2 M 2
D C Π O 1–3.   collocatā P B 2 S W 1 2 M 1 J.   conlocata R G E 1.
collatam R 17 O 7.
§ **71,** 9. omnis partis R V P G B K E.   ōms partes S.   11. existit
R V P G B S E.   existit K *ex* extitet *mut.*   13. spectet R V P B K S.
spectat E.   expectet G *at* ex *expunx. et* s *superscr. alt. man.*   expectetur Gr. ‖
quid in malis R V P G B.1 2 K 1 S E 1 2 W 2 M 1 2 D Π O 1 3.
in malis quid O 2.   quod in malis W 1 O 7.   qđ' in malis J. ‖ ultumum
R V G K.   ultimum P B.   14. degendę R E.   degende P S O 7.
degente G *at* t *expunx. et* d *superscr. ead. man.* ‖ deligenda M 1 2 O 1 2 7.
diligenda R V P G B 1 2 K 1 É W 2 D J.   dirigenda O 3.   15. maxime
R V P G R.^h ‖ quod ac G *ead. man.*
§ **72,** 17. omnis partis R V P G B K.   ōms partes B 2 S.   18. definiụịt V.
definiuit R G.   difiniuit K.   diffinit P W 1 M 1 2.

---

as *agrorum condonandi* is well attested
with plural nouns, being a mixture of
agros condonandi and *agrorum condonan-
dorum*, a similar construction is never
found with a singular noun. See also
Roby, *Lat. Gr.* ii p. lxviii.
  conlocatam : for which Dav. (followed
by Ba. and Wes.) reads *conlocatum*, agrees
in gender with the personified *cogitatio*,
which ‘makes the mind eager to imitate
the eternal existence of the gods and
refuses to regard mortality as its natural
sphere.’
  quibus : sc. *rebus* ; for this attempt to
reconcile natural law with a guiding providence, Küh. quotes Chrysippus, ap.
Stob. Ecl. Phys. i 5, 15 p. 180 εἱμαρμένη
ἐστὶν ὁ τοῦ κόσμου λόγος ἢ λόγος τῶν ἐν
τῷ κόσμῳ προνοίᾳ διοικουμένων.
  rursus : i 17, 40 n. on *rursum.*
  citeriora : τὰ κατωτέρω τοῦ οὐρανοῦ :
‘mundane affairs,’ i.e. everything on this
side of the moon, which occupied the
lowest of the celestial spheres.

  genera partesque : i.e. the four cardinal virtues and their subdivisions.
  efficitur: cf. i 8, 16 n. on *efficies ut.*
  § **72. tertia** : the final division of the
discussion commenced in § 69.
  definit, ‘forms a definition’; the importance assigned by the Stoics to definition
is well known ; Diog. Laert. vii 41.
  genera : for the Stoic categories (γένη)
cf. Zeller, *Stoics* (E.T.) pp. 97 ff. and
authorities there quoted.
  sequentia adiungit: not ‘makes inferences’ but ‘forms hypothetical judgments’ (συνημμένα) ; cf. Diog. Laert. vii
71 τῶν δ' οὐχ ἁπλῶν ἀξιωμάτων συνημμέ-
νον μέν ἐστι...τὸ συνεστὸς διὰ τοῦ Εἰ
συναπτικοῦ συνδέσμου· ἐπαγγέλλεται δ' ὁ
σύνδεσμος οὗτος ἀκολουθεῖν τὸ δεύτερον
τῷ πρώτῳ. Cicero’s phrase might be
translated into Greek by ἀκολουθοῦντα
συνάπτει. These hypothetical judgments
play a large part in constructing the
favourite Stoic ‘chain-argument’ so often
exemplified in these books.

adiungit, perfecta concludit, uera et falsa diiudicat, disserendi
20 ratio et scientia. ex qua cum summa utilitas exsistit ad res pon-
derandas, tum maxime ingenua delectatio et digna sapientia.
sed haec otii. transeat idem iste sapiens ad rem publicam tuen-
dam. quid eo possit esse praestantius, cum contineri prudentia
utilitatem ciuium cernat, iustitia nihil in suam domum inde
25 deriuet, reliquis utatur tot tam uariisque uirtutibus? adiunge
fructum amicitiarum, in quo doctis positum est cum consilium
omnis uitae consentiens et paene conspirans, tum summa iucunditas e cotidiano cultus atque uictus usu. quid haec tandem uita

20. existit R V P G B S E.   extitit K.   21. maxume R V B.
maxime P G S E. ‖ sapientia R 16 7 17 V P 1–6 G B 12 K 12 S E 1–3
L 2–6 W 12 M 12 D C J O 1–3 7 Urs. 3240.   sapiencia Π.   22. otii R G K.
ocii V P.   23. cum contineri R V P G B 12 K 12 S E 12 W 12 M 12
D C Π J O 1–3 7 ed. H.   26. positum est cum R 16 V P G B 12 K 1 E 1
W 12 M 12 Π J O 1 3 7.   positum est tum S E 2 O 2.   positum est in
D C.   27. poene G. ‖ iucunditas R V G B.   iocunditas P S E.
                                                                    ex
28. e cotidiano R P G B K W 1.   ex quotidiano M 1 O 1.   & cotidiano V
atr. uiridi superscr.   et cotidiano B 2 E 1.   et quotidiano O 7.

in cotidiano D. ‖ atque uicturus R P 4 G B 1 E 1.   atque uic9 B 2.
atque uicturus V *atr. uiridi corr.*   atque uictus K 1.   atque uirtute P 6.
atque uictu R 6 7 17 P 1–3 K 2 S E 23 L 2–6 W 12 M 2 D C Π J O 37
                                                    c
Urs. 3240 ed. H.   atque uita M 1 *al. atr. superscr.*   atque uita O 2.
uel uictu O 1.   e cotidiano cultus atque uictus usu *corr. Seyffertus.* ‖ tantdem G
t *ante* d *del. alt. man.*

perfecta concludit, 'draws the conclusions which have been arrived at,'
perficere referring to the bringing of the
argument to its conclusion, *concludere* to
the formal drawing of the conclusion, cf.
Fin. i 7, 22 'quomodo efficiatur concluda-
turque ratio'; for *concludere* cf. i 32, 78 n.
uera...diiudicat, 'detects fallacies,' cf.
Galen, de an. pecc. dign. 3 (in v. Arnim,
Stoic. uet. frgg. ii p. 90) ἀναγκαῖον δ' ἐστὶ
τὸν ἐξαίφνης προσελθόντα κρίσει λόγου
ἀδυνατεῖν διαγνῶναί τε καὶ διακρῖναι τοὺς
ψευδεῖς ἀπὸ τῶν ἀληθῶν· ἐναργὲς δὲ τούτου
τεκμήριόν ἐστι τὰ καλούμενα σοφίσματα,
λόγοι τινὲς ὄντες ψευδεῖς εἰς ὁμοιότητα τῶν
ἀληθῶν πεπανουργευμένοι.
haec otii: Cicero often expresses his
aversion to the Stoic insistence upon logic,
Ac. ii 35, 112, Fin. iv, 3, 6; Seneca also
declaims against it as useless or even in-
jurious, Ep. 45, 10; 48, 6 'o pueriles ineptias! in hoc supercilia subduximus'; *ib*.9
'utinam tantum non prodessent! nocent.'
ad rem publicam: cf. Diog. Laert. vii
121 πολιτεύεσθαι φασὶ τὸν σοφὸν ἂν μή τι
κωλύῃ, ὥς φησι Χρύσιππος ἐν πρώτῳ περὶ
βίων; Stob. Ecl. Eth. ii. 6, 6 ἔφαμεν δ'
ὅτι καὶ πολιτεύεσθαι κατὰ τὸν προηγούμενον λόγον οἷόν ἐστι.

contineri: the philosopher 'sees that
the public interests can only be secured
by wise judgment'; it is idle to object,
as Heine (*Pos. Progr.* p. 13) does, that
Cicero must have said either that the
philosopher sees what is to the advantage
of the community or that the interests of
the community depend upon the wise
judgment of the philosopher, and that
therefore *contineri* should be omitted
with Lamb. Or. Ba. Tr. He. T.S. etc.
It is to be assumed that the philosopher
will act upon his opinions and an opinion
that the public interests depend upon
prudentia will produce in the end the
same effect upon his conduct, as the
opinion that a certain course is in the
public interest. Kl.'s conj. *communem*
and Sff.'s *fidens* in place of *contineri* are
entirely unnecessary.
in suam domum, 'into his house'; for
the preposition cf. Off. i 39, 138 'ille in
suam domum consulatum primus attulit.'
Roby, *Lat. Gr.* ii § 1108.
uictus usu: Sff.'s emendation provides
the only explanation of *uicturus* of so
many good MSS; *cultus* naturally became
cultu after *cotidiano*.

desiderat, quo sit beatior? cui refertae tot tantisque gaudiis
30 Fortuna ipsa cedat necesse est. quodsi gaudere talibus bonis
animi, id est uirtutibus, beatum est omnisque sapientes his
gaudiis perfruuntur, omnis eos beatos esse confiteri necesse est.

XXVI. **73**. Etiamne in cruciatu atque tormentis?

An tu me in uiola putabas aut in rosa dicere? an Epicuro,
qui tantum modo induit personam philosophi et sibi ipse hoc
nomen inscripsit, dicere licebit, quod quidem, ut habet se res,
5 me tamen plaudente dicit, nullum sapienti esse tempus, etiamsi
uratur, torqueatur, secetur, quin possit exclamare: 'quam pro
nihilo puto!' cum praesertim omne malum dolore definiat,
bonum uoluptate, haec nostra honesta, turpia inrideat dicatque
nos in uocibus occupatos inanis sonos fundere, neque quicquam

29. quod sit G *in* quo sit *corr. alt. man.* ‖ cui referte R 7 E 2 C.
rei   at referte
cui referte II *al. atr. superscr.*   cui p fecte D *al. atr. superscr.*   cui rei referte S.
cui rei refertae R G K 1 O 2 Gr.   cui rei referte B 1 L 4 W 1.   cui rei
referte R 6 P 1 2 6 E 1 3 L 5 M 1] ed. H.   cui rei referta et V B 2.
cui rei refertae e P 4.   cui rei referctae L 3   M 2.   cui rei refercte P 5 O 1 3.
cui rei perfecta L 2.   cui recte perfecte O 7.   cui rei refferre L 6.
32. omnis eos R V P G B K.   ‖ beatos esse confiteri R V P G B 1 2 K 1 S
E 1 W 1 2 M 2 D C J O 1 3 ed. H.   confiteri beatos esse M 1 O 2.
beatos confiteri K 2 O 7 esse *om.*   esse beatos confiteri E 2 II.
XXVI. § **73**, 1. &iam R ne *eras.*   3. qui tantum W 1 D C O 1 3 7.
                 a
qui G *alt. man. superscr.*   quia R V P B 1 2 K 1 S *marg.* E 1 2 W 2 M 1 2
II J O 2.   5. etiamsi R V G B 1 2 K 1 S E 1 2 II J O 3.   et si P
K 2 W 1 2 M 1 O 1 2 7.   et si M 2 D C.   8. inrideat R V G B K.
irrideat P S E.   9. inanis R V P G B K.   inanes S E.

XXVI. § **73**. **in uiola…in rosa**: i.e.
uiolis, rosis circumfusum, cf. Fin. ii 20, 65
'potantem in rosa Thorium,' where Madv.
quotes Sen. Ep. 36, 9 'in rosa iacere': for
the use of the collective sing. cf. iii 18, 43.

an Epicuro: the sentence might have
have been expected to assume the form
'an Epicuro…dicere licebit…Stoicis immo
Peripateticis etiam non idem dicendum
erit?' as Madv. *Emm. in Cic. lib. phil.* i
44 sq. (quoted by Mo.) suggests; but the
structure of the sentence changes as the
thought developes, and the contrast, which
is not mentioned before § 75, loses its
sharpness.

qui: Kl. adopts *quia*; but as Wopkens
(*op. cit.* p. 150) says, the following words,
so far from giving a reason, 'nihil ad rem
faciunt nisi ut Epicuri mentioni odii ac
uituperationis notam apponant.'

personam, 'the mask of a philosopher';
Cic. sometimes quotes to dispute Epicurus'
title to rank as a philosopher on the
ground of his want of culture (Fin. i 7,
26; N.D. i 26, 72), his contempt of logic
(Fin. i 7, 22; Ac. ii 30, 97) and his incon-

sistencies (Off. iii 33, 117); but he praises
his clear and straightforward style (Fin.
i 5, 14; ii 5, 15).

inscripsit: Dav. quotes Fin. ii 3, 7
' qui [sc. Epicurus] se unus, quod sciam,
sapientem profiteri sit ausus.'

uratur…secetur: cf. Sen. Ep. 71, 23
'quid miraris si uri, uolnerari, occidi,
alligari iuuat, aliquando etiam libet'; Mo.
notes that the expressions seem to be
borrowed from the oath taken by gladiators, and compares Sen. Ep. 37, 1, 'eadem
honestissimi huius et illius turpissimi auc-
toramenti uerba sunt, uri, uinciri, ferroque
necari'; cf. also Petr. 117 'in uerba
Eumolpi sacramentum iurauimus, uri,
uinciri, uerberari ferroque necari.'

quam…puto: cf. ii 7, 17. Sen. Ep.
66, 18, where Epicurus' phrase is given
as 'dulce est et ad me nihil pertinet';
cf. Tertullian's 'nihil crus sentit in neruo,
cum animus in caelo est' (ad Mart. 2).

cum praesertim: iii 21, 51 n.

sonos fundere: cf. iii 18, 42; Ac. ii
23, 74 (with Reid's n.); Fin. ii. 15, 48
'uoce inani sonare.'

10 ad nos pertinere, nisi quod aut leue aut asperum in corpore
sentiatur: huic ergo, ut dixi, non multum differenti a iudicio
ferarum obliuisci licebit sui et tum fortunam contemnere, cum
sit omne et bonum eius et malum in potestate fortunae, tum
dicere se beatum in summo cruciatu atque tormentis, cum con-
15 stituerit non modo summum malum esse dolorem, sed etiam
solum? **74.** nec uero illa sibi remedia comparauit ad toler-
andum dolorem, firmitatem animi, turpitudinis uerecundiam,
exercitationem consuetudinemque patiendi, praecepta fortitudinis, duritiam uirilem, sed una se dicit recordatione adquiescere
20 praeteritarum uoluptatium, ut si quis aestuans, cum uim caloris
non facile patiatur, recordari uelit sese aliquando in Arpinati
nostro gelidis fluminibus circumfusum fuisse. non enim uideo

11. differenti a G.   differentia R V P.   differentiᵗⁱa a S.   12. et tum
R 16 V P G B 1 K 12 S E 23 W 2 M 12 Π J O 1–3.   et cum B 2
E 1.   et tantum W 1.   et tñ D.
§ 74, 16. comparauit R V G K S.   cōparauit P B E.   ‖ tollerandum
R V K G *at ex* tollendum *ead. man. mut.*   tołandū P.   18. praecepta
fortitudinis R 17 V P G B 12 K 12 S E 1–3 W 12 M 12 D C Π J
O 1–37 ed. H.   19. duritiam R V G.   duritiem S. ‖ adquiescere
R V P G B E.   adquéescere K.   acquiescere S *at* c *ex* d *mut.*
20. uoluptatium R V G B 1 K E 1.   uoluptatum P B 2 S E 2 W 12
M 12 C Π J O 1–37.   21. sese R 7 17 M 1 D C O 27 S *at pr.*
se *in ras.*   ᶠᶠ   ee B 1 ēē *in* sese *mut.*   eṣse V *atr. uiridi mut.*   ēē P *marg.* se.
se R 6 M 2 Π J O 13 W 2 *at indistincte in ras.*   esse R 1 G K 1.
ēē B 2 E 13 L 5 W 1. ‖ aliquando se E 2.   om. K 2.   se uelit aliquando
esse ed. H. ‖ arpinati P G B 12 K 12 W 12 M 12 D C Π O 1–37 ed. H.
apinati R V E 1.   alpinati E 2.

leue aut asperum : according to Epicurus all pleasure was in the last resort
of physical origin ; Plut. non p. suau. 4
p. 1088 E ἐπ᾽ οὐδενὶ ψυχῇ τῶν ὄντων
πέφυκε χαίρειν καὶ γαληνίζειν πλὴν ἐπὶ
σώματος ἡδοναῖς παρούσαις ἢ προσδοκωμέ-
ναις. Physical pleasure or pain depended
upon the smooth or rough character of
the atoms composing the objects which
gave pleasure or pain ; Lucr. ii 402 ff.
where the words *leuia* and *aspera* are used
to express the contrast.
a iudicio ferarum : Epicurus relied
upon alleged facts with regard to animals
(which he called 'specula naturae,' Fin.
ii 10, 31) for proof of his assertion that all
living beings naturally desired pleasure ; cf.
the passage quoted in Usener, *Epicurea*
§ 398 ; for the *comparatio compendiaria*
in 'differenti a iudicio ferarum'='cuius
iudicium non multum differt a iudicio
ferarum' cf. i 1, 2 n. Wopk. *op. cit.* p. 189.
§ 74. una...adquiescere : the ref. is
to Epicurus' letter written on his death-

bed to Idomeneus, Diog. Laert. x 22 ;
Fin. i 30, 96 in which, after enumerating
his disorders, he says ἀντιπαρετάττετο δὲ
πᾶσι τούτοις τὸ κατὰ ψυχὴν χαῖρον ἐπὶ τῇ
τῶν γεγονότων ἡμῖν διαλογισμῶν μνήμῃ.
Epicurus had, however, laid down that
the prospect of a speedy cessation of extreme pain ought to be an additional
source of consolation ; cf. iii 17, 38 ;
Fin. ii 28, 93.
uoluptatium : for the termination of
the gen. plur. cf. Neue, *Formenl.* I³
p. 410.
gelidis fluminibus : Cic. probably has
in view such a scene as he describes in
the preface to the second book of the
De Legibus, where the interlocutors are
seated in the *insula* enclosed by two
arms of the Fibrenus, just above where
it falls into the Liris ; the Fibrenus was
exceptionally cold. Legg. ii 3, 6 'nec
enim ullum hoc frigidius flumen attigi,
cum ad multa accesserim, ut uix pede
temptare id possim.'

quo modo sedare possint mala praesentia praeteritae uoluptates. **75.** sed cum is dicat semper beatum esse sapientem,
25 cui dicere hoc, si sibi constare uellet, non liceret, quidnam faciendum est iis qui nihil expetendum, nihil in bonis ducendum,
quod honestate careat, existumant? me quidem auctore etiam
Peripatetici ueteresque Academici balbutire aliquando desinant
aperteque et clara uoce audeant dicere beatam uitam in Phalaridis
30 taurum descensuram.

XXVII. 76. Sint enim tria genera bonorum, ut iam a laqueis
Stoicorum, quibus usum me pluribus, quam soleo, intellego, re-
cedamus, sint sane illa genera bonorum, dum corporis et externa
iaceant humi et tantum modo, quia sumenda sint, appellentur
5 bona, alia autem illa diuina longe lateque se pandant caelumque
contingant; ut ea qui adeptus sit, cur eum beatum modo et non

§ 75, 24. cum his V G.   25. sibi P G *alt. man. superscr.*   sibi S si *om.* ‖
faciendum R V P G K 1   E 1 2   L 2 3 4 6.   faciundum O 1.   26. iis W 1
M 2 O 3.   hiis D C Π O 7.   his R V P G   B 1 2   K 1   E 1 2   W 2   M 1
J O 1 2.   eis S *at ex* his *mut.*   27. careant G n *exp. ead. man.* ‖ existumant
R 2 V G K.   existumânt R 1.   existimant P B.   28. academici G.
academici V *atr. ant.*   achademici R P B K E.   ‖ balbutire R 2 16 P.
balbutire V *atr. ant.*   balbuttire R 1 10 G.   30. decensuram V *atr. uiridi*
superscr. de⌃cēssurā P.   decensuram R G B 2 K 1.
XXVII. § 76, 1. sint enim R 1 2 10   V P G B 1 K 1 E 2 M 2 D C O 1.
sint enim S.   sit enim E 1.   sunt enim R 16 K 2 W 1 O 7.   sùnt O 2
enim *om.*   3. sint sane R V G B 2 K 1 2 M 1 J ed. H.   sint sane S.
sunt sane E 1 W 1 O 7.   š sane P.   ‖ corporis et externa R 6 7 W 1
O 3 7 ed. H.   corporis⌃externa Π *al. atr. corr.*   corporis externa R V P G
B 1 2 K 1 2 E 1–3 W 2 M 1 2 D C J O 1 2.   *om.* R 17.   4. sumenda sint
R 1 7   V G B 1 2 K 1 2 S E 1–3 W 1 M 1 C Π J O 1 2 7 ed. H.
sumenda sunt R 6 P W 2 M 2 D O 3.   ‖ appellentur R G   B 1 2 K 1
W 1 2 M 1 2 Π J O 1 2 7.   appelent V *atr. uiridi superscr.*   appellantur
P S E 1.   5. alia R 16 7 10 16 17 V P 1 2 G B 1 2 K 2 S E 2 3 L 2–6
W 1 2 M 1 2 D C Π J O 1–3 7 ed. H.   alii K 1 E 1.   ‖ illa G *alt. man.*
superscr. 6. ut ea R V P G B 1 2 K 1 2 S E 1–3 W 1 2 M 1 2 D C Π J
O 1 2 7 ed. H.

§ 75. balbutire, 'to give an uncertain
sound'; this seems to be the only passage
in which this sense occurs : Diu. i 3, 5,
quoted by Or. and others, is (as Küh.
points out) not really parallel, nor is
Ac. ii 45, 137, quoted by Ern. *Clau.* s.u.
Phalaridis taurum : ii 7, 17 n.
XXVII. § **76. laqueis** : cf. Or. i 10,
43 'Stoici uero nostri disputationum
suarum...laqueis te inretitum tenerent.'
pluribus : sc. *uerbis*, 'at greater
length'; cf. Famm. ii 3, 1 'scribam ad
te postea pluribus'; Diu. ii 2, 7 'sed

haec alias pluribus'; Quint. v 13, 14 ;
xi 3, 153.
sumenda : i.e. τὰ προηγμένα, the 'quae
aestimanda sunt' of Fin. iii 15, 51 ; cf.
Stob. Ecl. Eth. ii 6, 6 προηγμένον δ' εἶναι
λέγουσι ὃ ἀδιάφορον ὃν ἐκλεγόμεθα κατὰ
προηγούμενον λόγον.
alia : i.e. *bona animi* ; Jeep (followed
by Küh.) proposes to read *animi* in place
of *alia*.
ut ea qui adeptus sit... : 'so that the
man who succeeds in winning them (sc.
the *bona animi*)—why should I merely

beatissimum etiam dixerim? dolorem uero sapiens extimescet? is enim huic maxime sententiae repugnat. nam contra mortem nostram atque nostrorum contraque aegritudinem et reliquas 10 animi perturbationes satis esse uidemur superiorum dierum disputationibus armati et parati; dolor esse uidetur acerrimus uirtutis aduersarius; is ardentis faces intentat, is fortitudinem, magnitudinem animi, patientiam se debilitaturum minatur. 77. huic igitur succumbet uirtus, huic beata sapientis et con-15 stantis uiri uita cedet? quam turpe, o di boni! pueri Spartiatae non ingemescunt uerberum dolore laniati. adulescentium greges

7. beatissimum R V P G B K.   8. maxime R V P G B K S E. 11. acerrumus R B K G *ex* acerrimus *ead. man. mut.* acerrum; V. acerrimus P S. a**d**cerrimus E 1.   12. uirtuti R 1 6 7 10 16 V P G B 1 2 K 1 2 S E 1–3 L 2–6 W 1 2 M 1 2 D C Π J O 1–3 7 ed. H.   uirtu R 17.   uirtutis *corr. Wesenbergius.* ‖ ardentis R V P G B 1 K E 1 O 1.   ardenti B 2. ardentes S.

§ 77, 15. cedet P G B 1 2 K 1 S E 1 M 1 D Π O 1–3 W 2 *marg. e cont. om.*   caedet R V M 2.   dicet J. ‖ dii R V P G B 1 K 1 S E 1 W 2 D C J O 1 2 7.   16. ingemescunt V G B 2.   ingemescunt R *eod. atr.* ingemiscunt P B 1 K 1 S E 1 W 2 D O 7. ‖ adulescentium R V G B 2.

adolescentium P B 1 S E. ‖ greges P G B K.   reges V *al. atr. superscr.* graeges R.

say that he is happy and not supremely happy?' Cicero doubtless, as Hand (in Wopkens, *op. cit.* p. 152) points out, had intended to end his sentence, 'beatus sit dicendus,' but substituted a question for the direct statement. Wopkens (*l.c.*) quotes a close parallel from *Fin.* ii 21, 67 'nunc uero, quoniam haec nos etiam tractare coepimus, suppeditabit nobis Atticus noster e thesauris suis quos et quantos uiros.'

Küh. alone among recent edd. retains *ut* here, Lamb. being almost universally followed in deleting *ut* as due to dittography of the last two letters of *contingant*. Heine (*Pos. Progr.* p. 12) retracting his former opinion (*Halle Dissert.* p. 30) argues against *ut* on the ground that the words 'ea qui adeptus sit, etc.' contain the ἀπόδοσις, the *propositio* of which is contained in the preceding subjunctives. But this is not so; the clause beginning *ut ea* is dependent upon 'alia autem... contingant,' to the subject of which alone *ea* can refer; if Heine's view of the construction were correct, it would have to be taken to refer to all three *genera bonorum*, which is absurd. The argument is: let us assume that the *bona corporis*, as well as the *bona externa*, deserve to come under the same category as the *bona animi*, i.e the category of *bona* ; but we

must make the proviso that they are to occupy an admittedly and markedly inferior position, and that the *bona animi* are to cover practically the whole field and tower over everything else, and so enable their possessor to be called not *beatus* merely but *beatissimus*.

huic sententiae: sc. *sapientem beatissimum esse.*

uirtuti: Wes. seems right in changing *uirtuti* of the MSS here to the genitive, as the noun is dependent entirely upon *aduersarius*, not on the verb or on the general construction of the sentence.

faces: ii 25, 61 n.

§ 77. Spartiatae: for the διαμαστίγωσις see nn. on ii 14, 34; 20, 46. The example of endurance furnished by the Spartan youths was a favourite topic in ethical exhortations, cf. Sen. de prouid. 4, 11 'numquid tu inuisos esse Lacedaemoniis liberos suos credis, quorum experiuntur indolem publice uerberibus admotis?... quid mirum, si dure generosos spiritus deus temptat?' Musonius rell. p. 112 (Hense) τεκμήρια δὲ τούτων αἱ τῶν ἐφήβων ἐκεῖ καρτερήσεις, ἐθιζομένων φέρειν λιμὸν τε καὶ δίψος καὶ μετὰ τούτων ῥῖγος, ἔτι δὲ πληγὰς καὶ πόνους ἄλλους.

uerberum dolore laniati, 'while being flogged with cruel blows till the blood comes'; for *uerb. dolore = uerberibus qui*

Lacedaemone uidimus ipsi incredibili contentione certantis pug-
nis, calcibus, unguibus, morsu denique, cum exanimarentur prius
quam uictos se faterentur. quae barbaria India uastior aut
20 agrestior? in ea tamen gente primum ei qui sapientes habentur
nudi aetatem agunt et Caucasi niues hiemalemque uim perferunt
sine dolore, cumque ad flammam se adplicauerunt, sine gemitu
aduruntur. **78.** mulieres uero in India, cum est cuius earum uir
mortuus, in certamen iudiciumque ueniunt, quam plurimum ille
25 dilexerit (plures enim singulis solent esse nuptae); quae est
uictrix, ea laeta prosequentibus suis una cum uiro in rogum

17. contentione M 1 2   †ten contione B.   ten con‸tione P.   ’ con‸tione E 1.
contione R V K.   conditione G di *exp. alt. man.* ‖ certantis R V G B 1 2
K 1 E 1.   certantis P (e).   certantes S.   18. cum exanimarentur R V P G
B 1 2 K 2 E 1 2 L 2 3 5 6 W 1 2 M 1 2 D C Π J O 1–3 7. ut cụm exanimarentur
L 4.   tum exanimarentur S.   ut exanimarentur ed. H *om.* E 3.   19. uictos se
R V P G B 2 K 1 S E 1 2 D C Π O 3 7.   se uictos B 1 K 2 W 1 2
M 1 2 J O 1 2.   20. ei R V P G B 2 K 1 S E 1 2 W 2 M 1 2 D C Π J
O 7.   ii O 2.   hi W 1 O 3.   21. nudi aetatem R G B 1 W 1 M 2.
nudietatem V E 2 M 1 D C Π O 1 3 7.   nuditatem B 2 (e).   nuditatem S
W 2 J O 2.   nudi‸e'tatem P.   22. adplicauerunt G.   applicauerunt R V
B 1 K 1 E 1 Gr.   applicuerunt J.   applicauerint B 2 S E 2 W 1 M 1
D C Π O 1 2.   applicuerint P M 2 O 3 W 2 *marg. e cont. om.*
applicaueĭt O 7.

§ **78,** 23. cuius R 1 P G B 1 2 K 1 S W 2.   cuius V i *atr. uiridi superscr.*
cui⁹ libet E 1 *al. atr. superscr.*   cuius uir R 17 K 2 O 7 earum *om.*   earum
cuius uir E 2 II.   cuiusque R 6 M 2 O 3 ed. H.   cuiusque uir W 1 earum *om.*
cuius libet M 1 D C O 2.   cuiusuis J.   alicuius O 1.   a uiuis R 7.
24. plurumum R V G B K.   plurimum P S.   26. leta G. ‖ una cum
P G K.   unaṃ cum V.

dolorem afferunt cf. iii 5, 11 n.; for the
perf. part. used to express time con-
temporaneous with the time of the principal verb, as the aor. part. sometimes in
Greek (Goodwin, *M. and T.* §§ 148 ff.),
cf. Cat. lxiii 15 'sectam meam exsecutae
duce me mihi comites | rapidum salum
tulistis,' with Friedrich's n., who compares Prop. i 3, 26; iv 3, 14.
  greges: i.e. ἀγέλαι (Plut. Lyc. 16),
which was the ordinary Gk word for the
correct Spartan βοῦαι (Gilbert, *Gk Const.
Ant.* p. 63).
  uidimus ipsi: probably when as a
young man he spent some time in the
Peloponnesus, iii 22, 53.
  prius quam, 'rather than'; for *prius
=potius* cf. i 8, 16 n.
  barbaria=*barbarorum terra*, as always
in Cic.
  ei qui sapientes: the Brahmins or
γυμνοσοφισταί; see ii 22, 52 n. on

'Calanus' and compare the description
of their mode of life given in Philo-
stratus, Apoll. Tyan. iii 15 p. 94 (Kayser)
where they are said to go barefoot, and
ὑπαίθριοι δοκοῦντες αὐλίζεσθαι...ὔοντος οὐ
ψεκάζονται καὶ ὑπὸ τῷ ἡλίῳ εἰσιν, ἐπειδὰν
αὐτοὶ βούλωνται; cf. also Lucan iii 240;
Quint. Curt. viii 9, 32.
  Caucasi: the Himalayas; cf. ii 22,
52 n. on *Caucasi.*
  adplicauerunt: cf. ii 23, 54 n. on
restiterunt.
  § **78. cuius**, 'the husband of any of
them'; there is no necessity to change
cuius to *communis* with Geel, or to
rewrite (with Jeep) *cum est coniunx
earum uix mortuus.* The desire to alter
cuius is due to a misunderstanding of
mulieres, which refers, not to a group of
women married to a particular man, but
to the married women of India, each of
whom was the wife of some man.

inponitur, illa uicta maesta discedit. numquam naturam mos
uinceret; est enim ea semper inuicta; sed nos umbris, deliciis,
otio, languore, desidia animum infecimus, opinionibus maloque
30 more delenitum molliuimus. Aegyptiorum morem quis ignorat?
quorum inbutae mentes prauitatis erroribus quamuis carnificinam
prius subierint quam ibim aut aspidem aut faelem aut canem aut
crocodilum uiolent, quorum etiamsi inprudentes quippiam fecerint, poenam nullam recusent. **79.** de hominibus loquor; quid?
35 bestiae non frigus, non famem, non montiuagos atque siluestris
cursus lustrationesque patiuntur? non pro suo partu ita propug-

im
27. imponitur R V B K S.   ponitur G *alt. man. superscr.*   Iponitur P E 1. ‖
i
maesta R.   mesta V P G J.   maiesta E.   28. deliciis P   delicis V.
delitiis R G K.   29. langore G.   30. delenitum R G B 2 K 1.
† linitū
delenitum V i *in* e *mut., ut uid.*   delinitum M 2 D C O 1.   deuictum P
alio atr. superscr.   deuictum E 2 II.   deuinctu S *marg.* delinitū.
demotum Gr. *marg.* deuictum.   demotum B 1 E 1.   31. inbutae R V G
h. l. K E.   imbutae B S.   ‖ prauitatis R V P G B 2 K 1 2 S E 3 W 1 2
D C II J O 1-3 7.   prauitatibus B 1 E 1 ed. H.   ‖ canifici nam G.
32. felem V P G B 1 2 E 1 2 W 1 M 1 D O 1 2 7.   faelem R K 1 W 2
M 2 J.   33. crocodillum M 1.   crochodilon O 2.   crocodrillum D C.
r
croc∧odillum P.   corcodillum R V G B 2.   corcodrillum R 2 16 B 1 K 1.
corcodrillum S.   cocodrilum M 2 O 7.   cocodrillum K 2 E 1 2 W 1 2
II J O 3.   coccodrillum O 1.   ‖ inprudentes R V G K E.   imprudentes B S. ‖
quippiam R V P G B K S E.
§ 79, 35. siluestris R V P G B K.

illa, 'the rival wife'; as there were
generally several rivals to the favourite
wife, Bentl. and Dav. proposed to alter
all the words in the sentence to the
plural; Scheibe proposed *turba* for *illa*,
and Schiche changed *illa* to *quae* to
make the sentence exactly parallel to
the preceding.

Cicero expresses himself as if the
victorious wife established her claim in
opposition to the claims of some definite
rival, and Cicero's authority may have
described some means by which this
selection was made, in which this would
have been the case: whether this be so or
not, Cicero's use of *illa* is both intelligible
and idiomatic; for the idiom cf. Hor. S. i
1, 115 'instat equis auriga suos uincenti-
bus, *illum* | praeteritum temnens extre-
mos inter euntem.'

umbris, 'idle hours,' i.e. time spent in
the shade instead of at work in the open
air; cf. pro Mur. 14, 30 'cedat...forum
castris, otium militiae, stilus gladio,
umbra soli.'

Aegyptiorum: the history and religious
rites of the Egyptians had been an object
of interest to the Greeks since the time
of Herodotus and Pythagoras (Isocr. Bus.
30); in the Hellenistic period increased
attention was directed to Egyptian religion through the work of Hekataios
and Manetho (Gruppe, *Die Griech. Culte
u. Mythen* I pp. 422 ff.).

prauitatis, 'arising from a distorted
mind'; for the gen. cf. Fin. iii 10, 35
'omniaque ea sunt opiniones ac iudicia
leuitatis'; some of the other exx. adduced
in support of the MSS. reading here by
Wopkens (*op. cit.* 152 ff.) are not parallel.

quorum, 'any of these things,' i.e. acts
of aggression against any of the animals
named, cf. Her. ii 65 τὸ δ' ἄν τις τῶν
θηρίων τούτων ἀποκτείνῃ ἥν μὲν ἑκών, θάνατος ἡ ζημίη· ἥν δ' ἀέκων ἀποτίνει ζημίην
τὴν ἄν οἱ ἱρέες τάξωνται· ὃς δ' ἄν ἴβιν ἤ,
ἱρηκα ἀποκτείνῃ ἥν τε ἑκὼν ἥν τε ἀέκων
τεθνάναι ἀνάγκη. Cic. N. D. i 29, 82 'ne
fando quidem auditum est crocodilum aut
ibim aut faelem uiolatum ab Aegyptio.'

§ 79. montiuagos: the word seems to
be ἄπαξ εἰρημένον in prose; it occurs in
Lucretius i 404; ii 597, from whom Cicero
may have borrowed it.

nant ut uulnera excipiant, nullos impetus, nullos ictus reformi-
dent? omitto quae perferant quaeque patiantur ambitiosi honoris
causa, laudis studiosi gloriae gratia, amore incensi cupiditatis.
40 plena uita exemplorum est. XXVIII. **80.** Sed adhibeat oratio modum et redeat illuc
unde deflexit. dabit, dabit, inquam, se in tormenta uita beata
nec iustitiam, temperantiam in primisque fortitudinem, magnitudinem animi, patientiam prosecuta, cum tortoris os uiderit,
5 consistet uirtutibusque omnibus sine ullo animi terrore ad cruciatum profectis resistet extra fores, ut ante dixi, limenque carceris.
quid enim ea foedius, quid deformius sola relicta, < a > comitatu
pulcherrimo segregata? quod tamen fieri nullo pacto potest; nec
enim uirtutes sine beata uita cohaerere possunt nec illa sine
10 uirtutibus. **81.** itaque eam tergiuersari non sinent secumque
rapient, ad quemcumque ipsae dolorem cruciatumque ducentur.
sapientis est enim proprium nihil quod paenitere possit facere,
nihil inuitum, splendide, constanter, grauiter, honeste omnia, nihil

37. uulnera R V P G *h. l.* B K S E.   ‖   impetus R V P G K.   Ipetus S.

inpetus E.   38. omittoquę R.   omittoq; G *ead. man. superscr.*   omittoq̄; V
linea al. atr. superduct.   omitto q̣ P.   40. plena P K.   plana R G.

XXVIII. § **80,** 2. deflexit R P G K 1 M 1   D   O 3.   deflexit S.
defluxit M 2 J.   fluxit O 1.   ‖ dabit dabit R 6   P 1.   dabit (*semel tantum*)
R 1 7 17 V P 2–6 G B 1 2 K 1 2 S E 1–3 L 2–6 W 1 2 M 1 2 D C Π J
O 1–3 7 Urs. 3240 ed. H.   4. patientiam R 6 K 1.   patientiā W 1 M 1 O 2.
patientiā B 1 *linea al. atr. superduct.*   patienciā Π *linea fort. al. atr. superduct.*
patia B 2.   paciā R 7.   patientia R 1 17   V P G S   E 1 2   W 2 M 2 D C J
O 1 3 7 Gr.   6. fores R P G B K.   7. comitatu (a *deest*) R 1 6 7 17   V P G
B 1 2 K 1 2   S E 1–3 W 1 2 M 1 2 D C Π J O 1–3 7 ed. H.   a comitatu
corr. Lambinus.   8. pulcherrimo V P S E.   pulcherrumo R K.
  § **81,** 10. non sinent P.   non sinenti V.   non sinenti R G K.
12. pęnitere B.   penitere R V P G K.   13. constanter grauiter V P G B 1 2
K 1 2 S E 1 2 W 1 2 M 1 2 Π J O 1–3 7.   grauiter constanter R D C.

cupiditatis: sc. *gratia*. Vrs. Gron.
and Dav. delete *gratia* after *gloriae* and
make all three genitives depend upon
causa.
   XXVIII. § **80. illuc unde deflexit,** i.e.
to the discussion of c. xxvi.
   dabit, dabit: Dav., Or., Mo. and Küh.
seem right in retaining the repetition
found in some MSS., and the use of *inquam*
is more usual with the repeated, than with
the single, word : cf. i 49, 119 n.
   ut ante dixi : in 5, 13 above.
   cohaerere: cf. iii 25, 61 n.
   § **81. tergiuersari,** 'hang back'; cf.
iii 18, 41 n.
   quod paenitere possit, ' which could
cause regret'; Lambinus' proposal of

cuius for *quod* is unnecessary; cf. 18,
53 n.
   ut...uideatur, 'as seeming novel and
unexpected' : the point of view which
the action of the verb (*admirari*) serves
to bring out is represented as the result
of the action : so in negative sentences
e.g. Or. i 25, 115 ' neque haec ita dico ut
ars aliquos limare non possit' : ' this
statement does not prevent the possibility
of etc.' i.e. ' this statement is made from
a point of view which recognizes the
possibility of etc.' For the attitude of
the wise man towards the accidents of
fortune cf. iii 14, 30.
   stare, ' abide by his principles'; cf. ii
26, 63 n.

ita exspectare quasi certo futurum, nihil, cum acciderit, admirari,
15 ut inopinatum ac nouum accidisse uideatur, omnia ad suum
arbitrium referre, suis stare iudiciis. quo quid sit beatius, mihi
certe in mentem uenire non potest. 82. Stoicorum quidem facilis
conclusio est; qui cum finem bonorum esse senserint congruere
naturae cumque ea conuenienter uiuere, cum id sit in sapientis
20 situm non officio solum uerum etiam potestate, sequatur necesse
est ut, cuius in potestate summum bonum, in eiusdem uita beata
sit. ita fit semper uita beata sapientis. habes quae fortissime de
beata uita dici putem et, quo modo nunc est, nisi quid tu melius
attuleris, etiam uerissime.

XXIX. Melius equidem adferre nihil possum, sed a te impetrarim libenter ut, nisi molestum sit, quoniam te nulla uincula
inpediunt ullius certae disciplinae libasque ex omnibus quod-

---

14. exspectare R G E.   expectare V P B K S.   ‖   admirari R V P G K.
                              i
ammirari B.   16. beatius R P G K.   beatus V *atr. ant.*
  § **82,** 19. in sapiente R V P G B K *plerique.*   in sapiētē W 1.   in sapientis
corr. Lambinus.   22. ita fit R P G K.   ista fit V.   ‖   fortissime R V P G B K.
24. attuleris R V P G B K S E.   ‖   uerissime R V P G B K.
XXIX. 1. impetrarim R V G B K S.   inpetrarim E 1.   impetrari E 2
O 1 7 Gr. Vict.   impetrare M 2.   impetrarē P   B 2.   2. lubenter
R V P G B K   L 5 Gr.   ‖   ut nisi R 1 17   V P G B 1 2   K 1   S   E 1   M 1
D C   O 2 3 7.   uelim nisi R 6   E 2   M 2   Π   O 1.   nisi R 7   K 2   L 5
W 1 2   J ed. H.   ‖   molestum sit R V P G B K *plerique.*   sit molestum L 5
W 2   J   O 1 ed. H.   3. impediunt R V G B K S E.   ipediunt P. ‖
                                                              v
ullius R 6 7   E 2 3   W 1   M 1 2   C Π   O 1–3 ed. H.   illius V *atr. uiridi superscr.*
  u   u   +i
illius B 1 *alio atr. superscr.*   illius P.   vllius E 1 i *in* v *alio atr. mut.*   ullius D.
illius R 1 17   G   B 2   K 1   S   L 5   W 2   J   O 7.

---

§ **82. senserint** = *censuerint* as in i.
17, 39 'Platonem ferunt...non solum sensisse idem quod Pythagoram sed rationem
etiam attulisse'; Ac. i 6 22 'philosophia
sensit in una uirtute esse positam beatam
uitam,' where see Reid's n.
congruere...uiuere: a translation of
the Stoic ὁμολογουμένως τῇ φύσει ζῆν; for
the varying versions and interpretations
of the formula cf. Diog. Laert. vii 87 ff.
and Zeller, *Stoics etc.* E. T. p. 215.
sapientis: Lambinus's emendation is
probably correct: *sapiente* of the MSS.
(retained by Or., Tr., Kl., Mo., Küh.)
gives an awkward, though not impossible,
construction to *officio* and *potestate* 'from
the point of view of his duty,...ability,'
and is probably due to the influence of
the *in* preceding.
habes: cf. i 49, 119; iii 17, 38; iv 14, 33.
fortissime, 'most consistently with
fortitude'; *fortis* is thus sometimes pre-

dicated of words or actions natural to a
person of courage; cf. iii 10, 22 'qui
maxime forti et, ut ita dicam, uirili utuntur ratione.'
XXIX. **ut**, omitted by Dav. and Ern.;
another instance of anacoluthon; instead
of *impetrarim ut...audiam*, the construction with which he begins, Cicero puts
uelim id audire after the long parenthesis,
uelim repeating and replacing *impetr.*
and *id audire* taking the place of the *ut*-
clause.
sit is altered to *est* by Halm and Ba.:
but, as Küh. says, 'coniunctiuus optime
respondet antecedenti *impetrarim.*'
ullius...disciplinae: cf. ii 11, 33; iv 4, 7.
libas: the word combines the ideas of
a fastidious as well as a capricious selection; in its application here and elsewhere
(Or. i 35, 159 etc.) to mental studies the
metaphor suggested is probably that of
the bee (Lucr. iii 11): in Tac. Dial. c. 31 it

cumque te maxime specie ueritatis mouet (quod paulo ante
5 Peripateticos ueteremque Academiam hortari uidebare, ut sine
retractatione libere dicere auderent sapientis esse semper beatissimos)— id uelim audire quem ad modum his putes consentaneum
esse id dicere. multa enim a te contra istam sententiam dicta
sunt et Stoicorum ratione conclusa.

10   **83.** utamur igitur libertate, qua nobis solis in philosophia licet
uti, quorum oratio nihil ipsa iudicat, sed habetur in omnis partis,
ut ab aliis possit ipsa per sese nullius auctoritate adiuncta
iudicari. et quoniam uideris hoc uelle ut, quaecumque dissentientium philosophorum sententia sit de finibus, tamen uirtus
15 satis habeat ad uitam beatam praesidii, quod quidem Carneadem
disputare solitum accepimus; sed is, ut contra Stoicos, quos
studiosissime semper refellebat, et contra quorum disciplinam
ingenium eius exarserat, nos quidem illud cum pace agemus. si

---

4. maxime R V P G B K S E.   5. achademiam R V P G B K E.
6. retractatione R V P G K E.   retractione L 2 5 6 Gr. ‖ dicere P B K.
dicerent V *atr. uiridi corr.*   dicerent G *ead. man. corr.*   dicerent R. ‖

                                                                            e
sapientis R V G B K O 1.   sapientis P. ‖ beatissimos R V P G B K E.
§ 83, 11.   omnis partis R V P G B K E.   omnes partis O 1.   omnes partes S.
15. praesidii R V P G B 1 2 K S.   praesidiū E 1. ‖ carneadem R V G K.

                                                     o   of
carneadē P B S E.   16. quos R 1 G K.   qſ B 1 *ex* qđ *mut.*   qđ E 1 *al. atr.*
superscr.   qˌ P.   quod R 2 10.   17. studiosissime R V P G B K.
18. exarserat P K E.   exasserat R V G. ‖ nos illud quidem R V G   B 1 2
K 1 2   E 1   W 1   M 1 2   J   O 1 7.   nos illius quidem P   E 2   D C Π   O 2 3.
nos illius quidem S *marg.* illud *alia man. adscr.*   nos quidem illud *corr.*
Wesenbergius.

---

is contrasted with *haurire*, denoting the
exhaustive studies of the specialist 'eum
qui quasdam artes haurire, omnes libare
debet.'
  paulo ante: in 26, 75 *supra*.
  retractatione: practically equivalent to
tergiuersatio above; cf. i 31, 76 n. on
retractabis.
  istam: i.e. 'the view of your friends,'
the followers of the Academy: Cic. had
said that they need not beat about the
bush any longer but should declare for
the all-sufficiency of virtue in procuring
happiness. True, is the retort; but you
yourself have already argued the Stoic
position against them so strongly, and
shown the absurdity of their premisses
from that standpoint so well, that you
put it beyond doubt that their principles
cannot possibly lead to the position you
wish to be established.
  § 83. **nobis**: i.e. *Academicis*.
  habetur...partis, 'puts the case for all
sides impartially'; *orationem h. in utram-
que partem* = 'to state a case both ways':

in omnis partis often equals 'all round,'
'from every point of view'; cf. *Off.* i 3,
7 'quibus in omnis partis usus uitae con-
formari potest'; *Fam.* v. 10*b* [10, 6]
'meam causam agas meque tibi in omnis
partis defendendum putes.'
  adiuncta: Bentley's *adiuta* is unnecessary as is shown by Wopkens (*op.
cit.*, p. 155) who quotes Diu. ii 55, 113
'auctoritatem quidem nullam debemus
nec fidem commenticiis rebus adiungere.'
  quod quidem...agemus: the first *quidem* emphasizes *quod*, 'as indeed'; the
clause *sed...agemus* introduces an amplification of the nature of a parenthesis,
while the *quidem* after *nos* serves to draw
attention to the preceding word in contrast to *is*: 'but he conducted the dispute
(sc. *disputauit* from preceding clause) as
might have been expected from him in
dealing with the Stoics, whom he used to
criticize with great vigour, and whose
tenets had roused him to a white heat;
we indeed shall discuss the matter (*illud
agemus* = *disputabimus*) with moderation.'

H.   18

enim Stoici finis bonorum recte posiuerunt, confecta res est:
20 necesse est semper beatum esse sapientem. **84.** sed quaeramus
unam quamque reliquorum sententiam, si fieri potest ut hoc
praeclarum quasi decretum beatae uitae possit omnium sententiis
et disciplinis conuenire.

XXX. Sunt autem haec de finibus, ut opinor, retentae de-
fensaeque sententiae: primum simplices quattuor, nihil bonum
nisi honestum, ut Stoici, nihil bonum nisi uoluptatem, ut
Epicurus, nihil bonum nisi uacuitatem doloris, ut Hieronymus,
5 nihil bonum nisi naturae primis bonis aut omnibus aut maximis frui, ut Carneades contra Stoicos disserebat. haec igitur
simplicia, illa mixta: **85** tria genera bonorum, maxima
animi, secunda corporis, externa tertia, ut Peripatetici nec
multo ueteres Academici secus; uoluptatem cum honestate

Lamb. proposed to read *hoc quidem...
nos autem*, though the clause beginning
with *nos* is contrasted not with the *hoc*-
clause but with *is...exarserat*; Vrs. read
with some MSS. *nos illius* (or *illorum*) *quidem*; Bouh., Tr. and Kl. read *nos illud
idem*; Sch. and Küh. with some MSS. *nos
illud quidem*. Sff. proposes *nos illud quiete
et* while Bentl. proposed *nos illud quidem
omnium*, which alterations are entirely
unnecessary.

For Carneades' attitude to the Stoics
cf. iv 24, 53 n.; for *ut* cf. i 8, 15 n.

accepimus: it is possible that Cic. may
have in mind the *Consolatio* of Clitomachus, which he quotes in iii 22, 54 for
the views of Carneades.

posiuerunt, a form of the perf. which
occurs often in Plautus and Inscrr. and
is found in Cato, Catullus (xxxiv 8) and
Fronto: see Neue, *Formenl.* III³, pp. 397
sqq., who prefers here the spelling of some
MSS. *possiuerunt*. Küh. follows Or. and
Tr. in reading *posuerunt*, with many MSS.

§ **84. decretum**: cf. ii 4, 11 n.
XXX. **haec**: cf. i 11, 22 n. The following résumé of the tenets of the principal
schools of philosophy with regard to the
summum bonum is closely paralleled in
Fin. ii 11, 34 f.; v 7, 18 ff.; Ac. ii 42,
129 ff.

Hieronymus: cf. ii 6, 15 n. and Zeller,
Aristotle, etc. (E.T.) ii p. 475.

naturae primis bonis: the πρῶτα κατὰ
φύσιν, called *prima naturae commoda* in
Fin. v 21, 58 and Ac. ii 45, 138; though
the phrase *prima naturae* is more usual
(Fin. iii 9, 30; iv 16, 43; v 8, 21) yet
there is no necessity for deleting *bonis*
here with Wes.

It was a matter in dispute between the
Stoics and the Peripatetics what should
come under this title: the latter included
'incolumitatem conseruationemque omnium partium, ualetudinem, sensus inte-
gros, doloris uacuitatem, uiris, pulchritudinem, cetera generis eiusdem' (Fin. v
7, 18); the Stoics would not include any-

10 Dinomachus et Callipho copulauit, indolentiam autem hones-
tati Peripateticus Diodorus adiunxit. hae sunt sententiae quae
stabilitatis aliquid habeant; nam Aristonis, Pyrrhonis, Erilli
non nullorumque aliorum euanuerunt. hi quid possint obtinere
uideamus omissis Stoicis, quorum satis uideor defendisse senten-
15 tiam. et Peripateticorum quidem explicata causa est praeter
Theophrastum, et si qui illum secuti inbecillius horrent dolorem
et reformidant; reliquis quidem licet facere id quod fere faciunt,
ut grauitatem dignitatemque uirtutis exaggerent. quam cum
ad caelum extulerunt, quod facere eloquentes homines copiose
20 solent, reliqua ex conlatione facile est conterere atque contemnere. nec enim licet iis qui laudem cum dolore petendam esse

10. callipho R P G   B 1   K 1   S   W 2   ʃ J. $\overset{l}{\text{calipho}}$ V.   calippho E 1.
calipho B 2   W 1   M 1   O 1 7.   11. peripateticus R V P K.   peripatheticus B.
peripaticus G.   ‖   hae R 1 6   G.   he̜ P   B 1   W 1   O 3.   he̜ S c *eras.*
he E 2   W 2   J.   he̜c V *atr. uiridi mut.*   he̜c E 1.   hec B 2   K 2   II ed. H.
haec K 1.   hee D.   12.   pyrroniſ erilli V.   pyrronis erilli J   L 4.
pyrronis erilli E 3   O 3.   pirronis erilli R 17.   pyrrhonis herilli R 6   P 5
L 3   W 1.   pyrroni ferilli R 1 2 10 16   G   B 1   K 1   L 5   Urs. 3240.
                                                                      ſ
pyrroniſer_illi P 1 *marg.* pirronis herilli.   pironiſer_illi E 1.   pyrroni ferilli S.
pyroni ferilli P 4   E 2.   pyroni ferelli P 6.   pirronio herilli P 3   M 2.
pirronis herili L 6.   pirroni ferilli B 2.   pirroni ferilli R 7.   pyrrhonis
herylli O 1.   pirronis perilli M 1.   pironis perilli O 2.   pirronis pherilli L 2.
                                                 h
pironis pherilli P 2.   pyronis erilli II *at* s *alio, ut uid., atram.*   pyrronis b erilli
W 2.   pironis hereli O 7.   et erilli pironis D C.   *claus. om.* K 2.
13.   optinere R V P G B K E.   14.   omisis K.   16.   imbecillius R V P G K.
inbecillius B E.   19.   extulerunt W 2 *marg.* extulerit.   extulerint R 1 6 7 17
V P G   B 1 2   K 1   S   E 1 2   W 1   M 1 2   D II J   O 2 3 7.   extulerit C.
abstulerint O 1.   20.   conlatione R V G B K.   collatione P.   ‖   contemnere
R B K.   contempnere P G E.   21.   licet iis M 2.   licet hiis O 7.   licet his
                                                                                 h
R V P G   B 1 2   K 1   E 1   W 2 · M 1   O 1.   licet is S *eod. atr.*

thing of the nature of pleasure (Fin. iii 5,
16). The whole question is treated in
Excursus IV to Madvig's edition of the
De Finibus.

§ 85. **Dinomachus et Callipho**: of these
two, though they are often mentioned by
Cicero (e.g. Off. iii 33, 119; Fin. v 8, 21;
Ac. ii 45, 139) little else is known.
    indolentiam: cf. iii 6, 12 n.
    Diodorus of Tyre (Stob. *Ecl. Phys.*
i 1, 29) was a pupil of the Peripatetic
Critolaus (Or. i 11, 45).
    Aristonis, Pyrrhonis: ii 6, 15 n.
    Erilli: Erillus of Carthage was a pupil
of Zeno (Diog. Laert. vii 166; Ac. ii 42,
129); he is frequently mentioned by Cicero
(Fin. ii, 13, 43, etc.); for the spelling
Erillus as against Herillus see Madvig's

note on Fin. ii 11, 35. According to him
the *summum bonum* was ἐπιστήμη (Diog.
L. *l.c.*).
    obtinere: i 12, 26 n.
    explicata, 'unambiguous'; for the ad-
jectival use edd. quote Or. i 2, 4; pro
Planc. 2, 5; Att. ix 7, 2.
    Theophrastum: cf. 9, 25 above and
Fin. v 5, 12 'Theophrasti...liber in quo
multum admodum fortunae datur.'
    exaggerent: cf. 18, 51 n.
    extulerunt: cf. ii 23, 54 n. on *resti-
terunt.*
    conterere, 'disparage,' an unusual
meaning; cf. Plaut. Poen. 537 'est domi
quod edimus ne nos tam contemptim
conteras.'

dicant negare eos esse beatos qui illam adepti sint. quamquam enim sint in quibusdam malis, tamen hoc nomen beati longe et late patet.

XXXI. **86.** Nam ut quaestuosa mercatura, fructuosa aratio dicitur, non si altera semper omni damno, altera omni tempestatis calamitate semper uacat, sed si multo maiore ex parte exstat in utraque felicitas, sic uita non solum si undique referta
5 bonis est, sed si multo maiore et grauiore ex parte bona propendent, beata recte dici potest. **87.** sequetur igitur horum ratione uel ad supplicium beata uita uirtutem cumque ea descendet in taurum Aristotele, Xenocrate, Speusippo, Polemone auctoribus nec eam minis, blandimentis corrupta deseret. eadem

22. dicant R 1 7 10 16 17 V P G B 1 2 K 1 2 S E 1–3 L 2–6 W 1 2 M 1 2 D C Π J O 1–3 7 ed. H.   dicunt R 6. ‖ adepti sunt R 1 6 10 16 17 V P G B 1 2 K 1 2 S E 1 2 L 2–6 W 1 M 1 2 D C Π J O 1–3 7.

adepti ſꜩ R 2.   adepti ∫̃ W 2.

XXXI. § 86, 1. aratio R 6 P 3 L 3 6 W 1 M 2 O 3.   ara E 3 *fort.*^tio

eod. atr.   arratio P 5. ^a ratio Π *al. atr. superscr.*   rō P 1 *marg.* aratio. ꝶ W 2 *marg.* aratio.   ratio R 1 7 17 V P 4 G B 1 2 K 1 2 E 1 L 5 D C J O 1 2 7 ed. H.   ſatio E 2 *at* ſ *in litura.*   rō S *marg.* nō.   non L 4. ideo L 2.   tum M 1. 2. altera omnis R 1 6 7 17 V P 1–6 G B 1 2 K 1 2 E 1–3 L 2–6 W 1 2 M 2 D C Π J O 1 3 7 Urs. 3240 ed. H.   altera oms̄ S. omni damno et tempestates et calamitate M 1 O 2.   omni *corr.* Ursinus. 3. ex parte R V P G B.   expartae K. 4. exstat R V B 2.   extat P G B 1 K 1 E 1 2 M 1 2 D C O 2 3 7.   existat S J O 1.

§ 87, 6. horum R 1 7 L 4 O 7.   horū Π *at* ū *in ras.*   bo2ꜩ E 3no horum *in* bonorum *fort. eod. atr. mut.*   honorum R 1 V P 1 2 6 G B 2 K 1 2. bonorum R 6 7 16 P 3–5 B 1 S E 1 2 L 3 5 6 W 1 M 1 2 D C J O 1–3 ed. H. eorum bonorum R 10.   bō2ꜩ W 2.   bto2ꜩ L 2. 9. minimis blandimentis R 1 6 7 17 V P G B 1 K 1 2 S E 1–3 L 3–6 W 1 M 1 2 D Π J O 1–3 ed. H. minĩs blandimentis B 2.   m̄imis blandimentis L 2 W 2 C O 7.   minis, blandimenti *corr. Klotzius.*

dicant...sint: the subj. seems to be required in both clauses because the first clause, though referring to definite persons already mentioned, describes them as a class concurring in a view by which alone they are of importance in the argument, and the second clause describes a class *simpliciter*: 'it is not open to these philosophers, though asserting that that renown is worth seeking at the cost of pain, to refuse to give the name of happy to any who have secured it': Kühner's statement 'indicatiuus necessarius est quia certi philosophi intelleguntur' misses the point. Edd. are divided between *dicunt... sint*, and *dicant...sunt*.

quamquam...sint: the subj. is concessive, 'though they may be granted to be': see i 45, 109 n. on *abierit.*

nomen beati, 'the term happiness'; for *beatum* cf. 15, 45 n.

XXXI. § 86. **maiore ex parte:** cf. 8, 22 'ex maiore parte plerasque res nominari.'

propendent: cf. 17, 51 n. Edd. note that *praeponderari* is found only in the passive voice in Cic.

§ 87. **horum:** i.e. the Peripatetics and the Old Academy (30, 85); Aristotle is mentioned *infra* as representing the former, and the latter is represented by Xenocrates and Speusippus (i 10, 20 n.) and Polemo, the successor of Xenocrates (Diog. L. iv 16).

minis, blandimentis: for the asyndeton Hei. (*Pos. Progr.* p. 8) compares 31, 87; i 14, 31; iii 3, 6 (where see nn.); with *minis* it seems best to supply some word like *territa* from *corrupta*, though for Caesar (B.C. iii 64, 2) has *id corruptum timore.* The MSS. have *minimis bland.*; Be. followed by Dav., Or., Ba., Küh. read

10 Calliphontis erit Diodorique sententia, quorum uterque honestatem
sic complectitur ut omnia quae sine ea sint longe retro ponenda
censeat. reliqui habere se uidentur angustius, enatant tamen,
Epicurus, Hieronymus, et si qui sunt qui desertum illud Carneadeum curent defendere. nemo est enim quin eorum bonorum
15 animum putet esse iudicem eumque condocefaciat, ut ea quae
bona malaue uideantur possit contemnere. **88.** nam quae tibi
Epicuri uidetur, eadem erit Hieronymi et Carneadis causa et
hercule omnium reliquorum. quis enim parum est contra mortem
aut dolorem paratus? ordiamur ab eo, si placet, quem mollem,
20 quem uoluptarium dicimus.

10. calliphontis B 1 2 K.　　callipontis V.　　callifontis P G.　　calipphontis
E 1. ‖ diodorique P B 1 W 1 2 M 1 2 O 1 7.　　diodori q; S *ras. post* ri.
diodorisq; E 1.　　diodorisque R V G B 2.　　diodoloris K 1 lo *ex parte eras.*
11. complectitur R V G K S.　　conplectitur E.　　cõplectitur B P. ‖

longe retro M 1 O 2 3.　　longe 2 tro W 2 *marg.* ret.　　longe et retro R 1 6 7 17
V P G B 1 2 K 1 2 S E 1-3 L 2-6 W 1 M 2 D C Π J O 17 ed. H.
13. illum R 1 2 10 16 V P G B 1 2 K 1 2 E 1 3 W 1.　　illud *corr. Bakius.* ‖
carneadeum R G K.　　carne ad eũ B 2.　　carneadeụm V *atr. uiridi mut.*
carneadem R 2 10 16 P B 1 K 2 S E 1 3 W 1 2 M 2 D O 1 2 7 ed. H.
carneadent L 5.　　14. quī eorum P 2 B 1 S D.　　qui eorum R 1 6 7 V G
K 1 2 E 1-3 L 2-6 W 1 2 M 1 2 Π J O 1 2 7.　　qui bonorum P 1 *marg.* eo2ᵤ.
q' eorum B 2.　　qui bonorum eorum O 3.　　qui bonorum animum eorum C.
qui eorm ed. H.　　16. contemnere R V K.　　contempnere P G E.
§ **88.** nam quae R 6 L 3 M 2.　　q̄ W 2.　　que L 6 Π O 1 ed. H.
q̄ J E 3 E 2 *at fuerat ut uid.* q3.　　φ P 1 B 2 M 1.　　quod S *marg.* quẹ.
quod R 1 7 17 V G B 1 K 1 E 1 L 4 W 1 D C O 2 3 7.　　qd' K 2 L 2 5.
17. epicuri R 6 E 2 L 3 6 M 2 Π J O 1 ed. H.　　epicuri' W 2 (*sic*).
epicurus R 1 7 17 V P B 1 2 K 1 2 S E 1 L 2 4 5 M 1 D C O 2 3 7.
epycurus G.　　epycurhus W 1. ‖ hieronymi R.　　hieronimi V G B E.
hyeronimi K. ‖ carneadis R V P G B 1 2 K 1 S E W 1 2 *alii.*　　18. hercule
R V P G B 1 2 K 1 S E 1 W 2 M 1 2 D Π J O 1-3 7.　　hercle W 1.
19. ordiamur P B S *plerique.*　　ordiṇamur K 1 E 1.　　ordiṇamur V.
ordinamur R G B 2 ed. H.

minis aut ; Sch. conj. *nimiis,* which
may very possibly be right; Wes. read
minis nec bland. ; the reading in the text
is due to Kl. and Sff.

enatant, 'swim ashore'; the word does
not seem to be used elsewhere in this
metaphorical sense, which is usually expressed by *emergere.*

illud Carneadeum, 'Carneades' well-
known thesis,' i.e. 'nihil bonum nisi
naturae primis bonis aut omnibus aut
maximis frui' (30, 84 supr.). This doctrine is called *desertum* as the attitude
of the Old Academy had been pretty
generally abandoned; cf. N. D. i 3, 6 ;
i 5, 11 quoted by Bentley.
The reading is Bake's correction of the
MSS. ; Küh. alone among recent edd. reads
illum Carneadem.

nemo...quin eorum: 'Every single one
considers that the mind is the judge of

these several goods, and each impresses
upon it the lesson of acquiring the capacity
to despise seeming goods and seeming
evils'; *quin* is Lambinus' emendation
confirmed by four MSS. of the MSS. *qui.*
There is no necessity with Dav., Ern.,
Or., etc. to put *eorum* before *quin,* as
the range within which *nemo* applies is
sufficiently defined by the context, as is
the case with *quis...paratus* below, where
no one proposes to insert *eorum.* Bentl.
followed by Küh. changed *eorum* to *uer-
orum,* unnecessarily, since the idea of a
right decision is sufficiently expressed by
iudicem.

condocefaciat seems to occur in Cicero
only here and in N. D. ii 64, 161. Mo.
erroneously supposes it to be ἅπαξ
εἰρημένον.

uoluptarium: cf. ii 7, 18, 'Epicurus,
homo, ut scis, uoluptarius,' iii 18, 40.

quid? is tibi mortemne uidetur aut dolorem timere? qui eum diem quo moritur beatum appellat maximisque doloribus adfectus eos ipsos inuentorum suorum memoria et recordatione confutat nec haec sic agit ut ex tempore quasi effutire uideatur? 25 de morte enim ita sentit ut dissoluto animante sensum extinctum putet, quod autem sensu careat, nihil ad nos id iudicet pertinere. item de dolore certa habet quae sequatur, cuius magnitudinem breuitate consolatur, longinquitatem leuitate. **89.** quid tandem?

21. uidetur aut W 1.   uidetur an R 1 6 7 17   V P G   B 1 2   K 1 2   S   E 1–3   L 2–6   W 2   M 1 2   D C Π J   O 1–3 7 ed. H.   22.   appellat R V G B K S.‖ maximisque R V G B K.   ‖ adfectus V G E.   affectus R P B K S. 24. nec haec R V G   B 1   E 1.   nec hec E 2   C ed. H.   naec hec K 1.

nec hec S.   nec h (o) B 2   D.   nec h (c) P 1   K 2.   nec h' W 2   J.   nec hoc II at o *ut uid. mut.*   nec hoc E 3   M 1 2   O 1–3.   nec his W 1.   nec hic

(*pro* haec sic) O 7.   ‖ effutire R 2   V.   effute P.   effuttire R 1   G K. 25. ita sentit L 3   W 1.   ista sentit B 1 *marg.* ita.   ista sentit R 1 6 7 10 16 17 V P G   B 2   K 1 2   S   E 1–3   L 2 4–6   W 2   M 1 2   D C Π J   O 1–3 7 ed. H. ‖

extinctum R V P G B K S E.   27. de dolore L 2 3 6   W 1   O 1 3 7.   (de) dolore E 3 *eod. ut uid. atr.*   dolore S *et* W 2 *marg.* de.   dolore R V P G   K 1   E 1 L 4 5.   dolorē B 1.   dolorum K 2.   in dolore D C ed. H.   ‖ quorum magnitudinem R 1 6 7 10 16 17   V P G   B 1 2   K 1 2   S   E 1–3   L 2–6   W 1 2 M 1 2   D C Π J ed. H.   cuius *corr. Bentleius.*   28. leuitate B 2   E 2   W 1 M 2   C Π   O 7.   lenitate V P G   B 1   E 1   W 2   M 1   D J   O 1 2 ed. H. laenitate R K.

§ **89.** quid tandem R 6 7   L 6   W 2   M 1 2   O 2 ed. H.   qui (d) tandem II. qui tandem R 1 17   V P G   B 1 2   K 1 2   S   E 1–3   L 5   W 1   D C J   O 1 3 7.

eum diem...appellat : in the letter said (by Diog. Laert. x 22) to have been written on his deathbed to Idomeneus; τὴν μακαρίαν ἄγοντες καὶ ἅμα τελευτῶντες ἡμέραν τοῦ βίου, ἐγράφομεν ὑμῖν ταυτί. Cic. gives a translation of it in *Fin.* ii 30, 96, but says it was addressed to Hermarchus. Usener (*Epicurea*, p. 139 n.) thinks that copies may have been sent to several friends.

doloribus: στραγγουρία καὶ δυσεντερικὰ πάθη (Diog. Laert. *l.c.*): 'uesicae et torminum morbi,' Fin. ii 30, 96.

memoria et recordatione, 'lively recollection' ; 'memoria is the mere recollection of something in the past, produced by the *mens et cogitatio* : *recordatio* is the representation and laying to heart of the past *cum animo et affectu*' (Wilkins on Or. i 53, 228).

confutat : the reading *compensat* (adopted by Be.) which Urs. says he found in a manuscript is probably a conjecture of his own in an attempt to better Cicero's translation of ἀντιπαρετάττετο in the original.

For the use of the word cf. Cato, ap. Aul. Gell. vi (vii) 3, 13 'iniuriis atque imperiosis minationibus confutare' and

Titinius 128 (Ribbeck, *Scaen. Rom. Poes. Frag.* II² 151) 'cocus magnum ahenum, quando feruit, paula confutat trua.'

ex tempore : i.e. *tempori conuenienter* 'to suit the occasion.'

effutire : explained by Nonius (s. u.) by 'commenticia dicere'; he quotes Ter. Phorm. 746 and Lucr. v 910; cf. also N. D. i 30, 84; ii 37, 94.

de morte: cf. Diog. Laert. x 125 συνέθιζε δὲ ἐν τῷ νομίζειν μηδὲν πρὸς ἡμᾶς εἶναι τὸν θάνατον· ἐπεὶ πᾶν ἀγαθὸν καὶ κακὸν ἐν αἰσθήσει στέρησις δέ ἐστιν αἰσθήσεως ὁ θάνατος; Sext. Emp. *Pyrrh. Hypot.* iii 229 καὶ ὁ Ἐπίκουρος δέ φησιν, ὁ θάνατος οὐδὲν πρὸς ἡμᾶς· τὸ γὰρ διαλυθὲν ἀναισθητεῖ, τὸ δὲ ἀναισθητοῦν οὐδὲν πρὸς ἡμᾶς. A. Frederking points out in *Philol.* LX p. 637 that the reasoning requires ἀναισθητοῦν to be read in the latter passage in place of ἀναισθητοῦν, though Cic. is probably translating ἀναισθητοῦν in 'quod sensu careat.' It is obvious that what is 'nihil ad nos' must be 'what we do not perceive' not 'what lacks feeling.'

ita: the reading *ista* is defended by Wopkens (*op. cit.*, p. 155 f.) by parallels which would be equally good for *ita*.

de dolore: cf. ii 19, 44 and nn. there.

isti grandiloqui contra haec duo, quae maxime angunt, melius se
30 habent quam Epicurus? an ad cetera quae mala putantur non
et Epicurus et reliqui philosophi satis parati uidentur? quis non
paupertatem extimescit? neque tamen quisquam philosophorum.
XXXII. Hic uero ipse quam paruo est contentus! nemo de
tenui uictu plura dixit. etenim, quae res pecuniae cupiditatem
adferunt ut amori, ut ambitioni, ut cotidianis sumptibus copiae
suppetant, cum procul ab his omnibus rebus absit, cur pecuniam
5 magnopere desideret uel potius cur curet omnino? **90.** an
Scythes Anacharsis potuit pro nihilo pecuniam ducere, nostrates
philosophi facere non poterunt? illius epistula fertur his uerbis:
'Anacharsis Hannoni salutem. mihi amictui est

29. quae maxime R G K.   quę maxume B.   quę haec maxime V. ‖
melius se R V P G   K 1   B 1 2   S   E 1 2   W 1   M 1 2   D C Π   O 1 3 7.
melius (se *om.*) K 2   L 5   W 2   J   O 2 ed. H.
XXXII. 3. adferunt R V P G K.   afferunt B S E.   4. ab his R V P G
B 1 2   K 1   S   E 1 2   L 5   W 1 2   M 1   J   O 1.   ab iis M 2   O 2 3.   ab hiis
K 2   D C Π   O 7.   5. magnopere R V P G B K S E.
                                                        h
§ **90, 6.** scythes R P B K.   scytes E.   schytes V *atr. ant.*   sythes S.
cythes G.   ‖   anacharsis R V P B K.   anacahrsis G.   anatharsis S.
7. facere R 1 6 7 17   V P G   B 1 2   K 1 2   S   E 1-3   W 1 2   M 1 2   D C Π J
O 1-3 7 ed. H.   ‖   poterunt L 3   W 1   M 2   O 1.   potuerunt V *alio atr. corr.*
potḥerunt E 1.   potuerunt R 1 6 7 10 16 17   P G   B 1 2   K 1   S   E 2 3   L 2 4-6
W 2   M 1   D C Π J   O 2 3 7 ed. H.   potïnt K 2.   ‖   epistula G K.   epistḷla R
u *in* o *alio atr. mut.*   epistola B E.   epḷa V P S.

§ **89. grandiloqui**: the Stoics; Cicero in putting the argument from the Epicurean standpoint adopts dramatically the Epicurean tone in referring to the Stoics. It seems unnecessary to suppose that he is directly quoting some Epicurean source.

neque tamen quisquam: it is hard to see why Lamb. proposed to insert *non* after *tamen*: Cicero's contention is that while the ordinary man feared poverty, there was no single philosopher of any school whose tenets did not enable him to despise it.

XXXII. **tenui uictu**: cf. iii 20, 49 n. on 'tenuem uictum.'

§ **90. Anacharsis**: a Scythian prince who visited Athens in the time of Solon and was said to have been put to death for introducing Greek customs into Scythia: he was counted by some authorities as one of the seven wise men: cf. Herod. iv 76; Strab. vii p. 303 A; Diog. Laert. i 101 ff. For the gentile adj. preceding the noun cf. 3, 8 n.
For the form of the *argumentum a minore* 'an potuit ducere...poterunt' cf. i 14, 31 n.

facere, 'to do so,' cf. iv 14, 31 n. for this use of *facere*; Man. and Dav. omit the word, and Sorof unnecessarily inserted *idem*.

poterunt, adopted by Lamb. Or. Tr. Küh. Sff. as against *potuerunt* (Kl. Ba. Wes.), is undoubtedly right. The argument is not an inference from one fact in the past (*Anacharsis potuit*) to another fact in the past (*nostrates philosophi potuerunt*), but a confident prediction as to the conduct of *nostrates philosophi* based upon the knowledge of the action of a barbarian. *Nostrates* (contrasted with *Scythes*) includes both Greeks and their Roman followers, not the Greeks alone (Wes.) nor the Romans alone (Küh. Sff.).

epistula: Cicero's translation is loose in places; the Greek is Ἀνάχαρσις Ἄννωνι. ἐμοὶ μὲν περίβλημα χλαῖνα Σκυθική, ὑπόδημα δέρμα ποδῶν· κοίτη δὲ πᾶσα γῆ, δεῖπνον καὶ ἄριστον γάλα καὶ τυρὸς καὶ κρέας ὀπτόν, πιεῖν ὕδωρ· ὡς οὖν ἀγοντός μου σχολήν, ὧν οἱ πλεῖστοι ἕνεκεν ἀσχολοῦνται, παραγενοῦ πρός με, εἴ τινα χρείαν ἔχεις· δῶρα δὲ οἷς ἐντρυφᾶτε, ἀντιδωροῦμαί σοι, ὑμεῖς δ' ὅσοι Καρχηδονίων, εἰς χάριν σὴν ἀνάθεσθε θεοῖς.

Scythicum tegimen, calciamentum solorum callum,
10 cubile terra, pulpamentum fames, lacte, caseo, carne
uescor. quare ut ad quietum me licet uenias. mu-
nera autem ista quibus es delectatus uel ciuibus
tuis uel dis immortalibus dona.' omnes fere philosophi
omnium disciplinarum, nisi quos a recta ratione natura uitiosa
15 detorsisset, eodem hoc animo esse potuerunt. **91.** Socrates, in
pompa cum magna uis auri argentique ferretur, 'Quam multa
non desidero!' inquit. Xenocrates, cum legati ab Alexandro
quinquaginta ei talenta attulissent, quae erat pecunia temporibus
illis, Athenis praesertim, maxima, abduxit legatos ad cenam
20 in Academiam; iis apposuit tantum quod satis esset nullo
apparatu. cum postridie rogarent eum, cui numerari iuberet,
'Quid? uos hesterna,' inquit, 'cenula non intellexistis
me pecunia non egere?' quos cum tristioris uidisset, triginta

Scythicum tegimen, i.e. skins; cf. Sen.
Ep. 90, 16 'non hodieque magna Scy-
tharum pars tergis uulpium induitur ac
murum.'

delectatus is not a very close translation of ἐντρυφᾶτε, but the slight inaccuracy is due probably to Cic. and not to
a copyist. Lamb.'s *delicatus* or *deliciatus*
is unnecessary.

detorsisset : Sff., who declares that the
form of a conditional sentence is out
of place here, reads *detorsit*: with this
reading the sentence means 'almost all
philosophers of every school were able
to accept this attitude except those whom
natural depravity turned aside.' But the
conditional *detorsisset* which alone has
MSS. authority yields a perfectly satisfactory sense 'all would have been of
this mind (*potuerunt esse=fuissent*) had
not depravity turned some aside,' *quos*
being not a relative, but an indefinite,
pronoun.

§ **91. Socrates** : in iii 23, 56 Socrates
and Diogenes have already been introduced as types of philosophic poverty.

The story about Socrates is told in Diog.
Laert. ii 25 πολλάκις δ' ἀφορῶν εἰς τὰ
πλήθη τῶν πιπρασκομένων ἔλεγε πρὸς αὑτὸν
Πόσων ἐγὼ χρείαν οὐκ ἔχω. Victorius (*Var.
Lect.* xiv 18) notes that *quam multa* is
more appropriate to Diogenes' version of
the story in which Isocrates is represented
as looking at many different things than
to Cicero's, where he is looking at a large
quantity of the same thing.

Xenocrates : the story is told sub-
stantially in the same form in Val. Max.
iv 3, 3 ext. Diog. Laert. iv 8 has simply
Ἀλεξάνδρου γοῦν καὶ συχνὸν ἀργύριον
ἀποστείλαντος αὐτῷ τρισχιλίας Ἀττικὰς
ἀφελὼν τὸ λοιπὸν ἀπέπεμψεν εἰπὼν ἐκείνῳ
πλειόνων δεῖν πλείονας τρέφοντι; it is often
mentioned, e.g. in Plut. Alex. c. 8 de fort.
Alex. i c. 10.

cui numerari, 'into what bank he
wished it paid': *cui* sc. *argentario*; both
at Athens and at Rome monetary trans-
actions of importance were generally
carried out through the agency of a
banker (τραπεζίτης, *argentarius*), cf. pro
Caec. 6, 16.

minas accepit, ne aspernari regis liberalitatem uideretur. **92.** at
25 uero Diogenes liberius, ut Cynicus, Alexandro roganti ut diceret,
si quid opus esset, 'N u n c q u i d e m p a u l u l u m,' inquit, 'a s o l e.'
offecerat uidelicet apricanti. et hic quidem disputare solebat
quanto regem Persarum uita fortunaque superaret; sibi nihil
deesse, illi nihil satis umquam fore; se eius uoluptates non desi-
30 derare, quibus numquam satiari ille posset, suas eum consequi
nullo modo posse.

XXXIII. **93.** Vides, credo, ut Epicurus cupiditatum genera
diuiserit, non nimis fortasse subtiliter, utiliter tamen, partim esse
naturales et necessarias, partim naturales et non necessarias,
partim neutrum ; necessarias satiari posse paene nihilo ; diuitias
5 enim naturae esse parabiles ; secundum autem genus cupiditatum nec ad potiendum difficile esse censet nec uero ad
carendum ; tertias, quod essent plane inanes neque necessitatem
modo, sed ne naturam quidem attingerent, funditus eiciendas
putauit. **94.** hoc loco multa ab Epicureis disputantur, eaeque

---

§ 92, 26. si quid R P G K. siquiṣ V *atr. uiridi superscr.*
28. fortunaque
R G. fortuneque V *atr. uiridi superscr.* 29. eī V *i.e.* eius.
XXXIII. § 93, 2. subtiliter R P G K. _ suptiliter B. ‖ *Verba* partim
esse naturales et n&essarias partī naturales et N̄ N&essarias partī *habet* V *glossatoris
manu inculc.*; *uerba* partim naturales et non necessarias *om.* K 1. 3. naturales
R P G B K E. naturalis O 1. ‖ naturales R P G K S E O 1. 5. esse parabiles
R V G K. parabiles esse R 2 P B S. 8. attingerent R V P G B K S E.‖
eiiciendas R V P G B 1 2 K 1 2 E 1 W 2 M 1 2 D J O 7. eijciendas S.
eiiciendas R 6 W 1 Π O 3. § 94, 9. eaeque R 2 G B K. Çaeq̨ue R 1. eaque V E. ꝗeq; P.

Diogenes : Diog. Laert. vi 38 ἐν τῷ
Κρανείῳ ἡλιουμένῳ αὐτῷ 'Αλέξανδρος
ἐπιστάς φησι, Αἴτησόν με ὃ θέλεις· καὶ
ὅς, 'Αποσκότησόν μου, ἔφη. Dav. quotes
also Plut. de exil. 605 D; Dio Chrys.
Orat. iv p. 61 M.

ut : cf. i 8, 15 n.

offecerat : Mo. compares N. D. ii 19,
49 'ipsa enim umbra terrae soli officiens
noctem efficit.'

regem Persarum : Dav. quotes Dio
Chrys. Or. vi p. 93 M (of Diogenes)
ὥστε οὐκέθ' αὐτὸν ἠξίου τῷ Περσῶν βασιλεῖ
παραβάλλειν· πολὺ γὰρ εἶναι τὸ μεταξύ·
τὸν μὲν γὰρ ἀθλιώτατον ἁπάντων τυγχά-
νειν κ.τ.λ.

XXXIII. § 93. **uides :** cf. use of *uideo*
in iii 25, 59.

subtiliter : for Cicero's mingled praise
and criticism cf. Fin. i 13, 45 'quae est
enim aut utilior aut ad bene uiuendum

aptior partitio quam illa qua est usus
Epicurus'; Fin. ii 9 26 'primum diuisit
ineleganter; duo enim genera quae erant,
fecit tria. hoc est non diuidere sed frangere.' According to Cicero in the latter
passage, the division should have been
'duo genera cupiditatum, naturales et
inanes; naturalium duo, necessariae et non
necessariae.' Cic. is quoting one of the
κύριαι δόξαι of Epicurus (Diog. Laert. x
149) τῶν ἐπιθυμιῶν αἱ μέν εἰσι φυσικαὶ καὶ
ἀναγκαῖαι· αἱ δὲ φυσικαὶ καὶ οὐκ ἀναγκαῖαι·
αἱ δὲ οὔτε φυσικαὶ οὔτε ἀναγκαῖαι, ἀλλὰ
πρὸς κενὴν δόξαν γινόμεναι.

partim...partim = *alias...alias*, cf. 13,
38 n.

neutrum : i.e. *neque naturales neque
necessarias*, cf. Madv. ad Fin. iii 17, 56.

ad potiendum : for this use of *ad* with
the gerund cf. iv 17, 37 n.

neque...modo : cf. i 36, 87 n.

10 uoluptates singillatim extenuantur quarum genera non contemnunt; quaerunt tamen copiam. nam et obscenas uoluptates, de quibus multa ab illis habetur oratio, facilis, communis, in medio sitas esse dicunt, easque si natura requirat, non genere aut loco aut ordine, sed forma, aetate, figura metiendas putant, ab iisque abs-
15 tinere minime esse difficile, si aut ualetudo aut officium aut fama postulet, omninoque genus hoc uoluptatum optabile esse si non obsit, prodesse numquam. **95**. totumque hoc de uoluptate sic ille praecipit ut uoluptatem ipsam per se, quia uoluptas sit, semper optandam et expetendam putet, eademque ratione

10. singillatim R V P G   B 1 2   K 1   E 1   C S *marg.* singulati.   sigillatim E 2   Π   O 7.   singulatim W 1   M 1 2   J   O 1 2.   singlati W 2.   ‖   non *ante* contemnunt *om.* D   O 2.   12.   facilis communis R V G B K S E.   facit communis P.   14.   metiendas R P G   B 1 2   K 1 2 *plerique.*   mentiendas V.

metßiendas E 1.   ‖   ab hisque G B S.   ab hisque^q; E.   ab hisque R 1.

ab hisqur V i *in e mut.*   ab his quae K.   ab his q̄^q3 P.   15.   difficile R V P K.

diffile^ci G *alio atr. superscr.*   16.   optabile R G B K.   obtabile V P.

§ **95**, 19.   optandam et expetendam R 7   L 2 4   D C   O 3.   optandam 7 expetendam E 1 *at 7 fort. alio atr. scr.*   optandam expetendam R 1 17   V P G   B 1 2   K 1   S   E 2   W 2 *marg.* M 1   O 7.   optandam expetendamque L 3 5 6

M 2   O 1   Π *at* q; *extra lineam alio atr. scr.*   optandam expetendam^q; E 3 *fort. eod. atr.*   optandam W 1.   expetendam J   O 2.   *claus. om.* K 2. optandam expectandamque ed. H.

§ **94**. **extenuantur**, 'are belittled'; cf. Fin. ii 10, 30 'hanc in motu uoluptatem... interdum ita extenuat ut M' Curium putes loqui.'

The words *eaeque...extenuantur* form a hexameter line (as was noted by Muretus) if *eaeque* be scanned as a disyllable.

quarum...copiam: the interpretation of these words has given rise to much needless discussion; the meaning and relation of the clauses are made clear by the punctuation adopted in the text 'those pleasures, which they admit to belong to honourable categories [i.e. the first two classes] are belittled when discussed severally; though for all that they wish them to be easy of attainment': *copiam* here = *facilem copiam*; *genera* is contrasted with *singillatim*.

Madv. (on Fin. i 13, 45) proposed to omit *non* before *contemnunt*, and he is followed by Tr., Usener (*Epicurea* § 440) and Hei. (*Posen. Progr.* pp. 13 f.): Bentley followed by Ern. and F. A. W. inserted *non* before *quaerunt*; both emendations destroy the meaning, which is that the Epicureans who regard true pleasure as the chief good, and who therefore naturally wish it to be easy of attainment, in discussing the several pleasures make them out to consist of such simple feel-

ings, and speak so temperately about them that their point of view is not so very far removed after all in practice from that of more grandiloquent philosophers.

et obscenas uoluptates: these belonged to the second class, *naturales et non necessariae*; the *et* would, had the treatment of this section not been prolonged, have been followed by another *et* and a clause dealing with *uictus* and *epulae* which now forms a separate section.

Cicero elsewhere (e.g. Fin. ii 10, 29) speaks much less indulgently of Epicurean views on this point.

non genere...putant: Hor. Sat. i 2, 27 ff. is an unblushing commentary upon this sentiment.

optabile esse...nunquam: a mistranslation of the Epicurean sentiment quoted in Diog. Laert. x 118 συνουσίη δέ, φασίν, ὤνησε μὲν οὐδέποτε· ἀγαπητὸν δέ, εἰ μὴ καὶ ἔβλαψεν: the latter clause means 'one might consider oneself fortunate, if it did not actually do one harm.' Cicero takes it to mean 'desirable, unless it did harm.'

§ **95**. **totumque**: cf. i 34, 82 n. on *totumque hoc.*

et expetendam: unless one is prepared to assume an awkward asyndeton here, one must read either *et expetendam* with

20 dolorem ob id ipsum, quia dolor sit, semper esse fugiendum ;
itaque hac usurum compensatione sapientem ut et uoluptatem
fugiat, si ea maiorem dolorem effectura sit, et dolorem suscipiat
maiorem efficientem uoluptatem, omniaque iucunda, quamquam
sensu corporis iudicentur, ad animum referri tamen. 96. quo-
25 circa corpus gaudere tam diu dum praesentem sentiret uoluptatem, animum et praesentem percipere pariter cum corpore et
prospicere uenientem nec praeteritam praeterfluere sinere. ita
perpetuas et contextas uoluptates in sapiente fore semper, cum
exspectatio speratarum uoluptatum perceptarum memoriae
30 iungeretur.
   XXXIV. 97. Atque his similia ad uictum etiam trans-

21. ut et R 17 E 3 L 3 4 W 1 J O 7. et ut M 1 O 2. ⁊ ᵘᵗ W 2.
et R 1 V P G B 2 K 1 E 1 L 5. ut R 6 7 B 1 S E 2 L 26 M 2

D C II ed. H. ut et uoluptatem om. K 2. 23. iucunda B K. iocunda R
eod. atr. iocunda V P G S E.
   § 96, 25. sentiret R V P G B K plerique. J marg. e cont. om. sentire O 2.
28. cum expectatio R 1 7 V P B 1 2 K 1 S E 2 W 1 D O 1 2 3 ed. H.
cum exspectatio E 1 C. cum expectatione G at ne exp. ead. man. cum
                                                                     ne
expectatione R 1 7 P 2 M 1. cum exspectatione O 7. cum expectatio Π
                                                                       ni
al. atr. suppl. cum expectationi R 6 M 2. cum expectatio E 3 fort. eod. atr.
cum expectatiōi W 2 o in ōi alio atr. mut. cum expt̄acō K 2. 29. memorię W 1.
memorie R 1 7 O 7. memoriæ B 1 a in ae alio atr. mut. memoria
R 1 2 10 16 V P G B 2 K 1 E 1-3 L 5 6 W 2 M 1 2 D C II O 1-3 ed. H.
memō K 2.
   XXXIV. § 97, 1. atque his R V P G B 1 2 K 1 S E 1 2 W 1 2 M 1
(non ut Küh.) J. atque iis O 2. atque hiis C II O 7.

Wes. Sff. etc. or expetendamque with
Or. Ba., etc.: the former is preferable as
et may easily be lost before ex-.
   compensatione: Mo. compares N. D.
i 9, 23 'ita multa sunt incommoda in uita
ut ea sapientes commodorum compensatione leniant.'
   ut...efficientem uoluptatem: cf. Epicurus' words in his letter to Menoiceus
ap. Diog. Laert. x 129 ἀλλ' ἔστιν ὅτε
πολλὰς ἡδονὰς ὑπερβαίνομεν, ὅταν πλεῖον
ἡμῖν τὸ δυσχερὲς ἐκ τούτων ἔπηται· καὶ
πολλὰς ἀλγηδόνας ἡδονῶν κρείττους νομίζο-
μεν, ἐπειδὰν μείζων ἡμῖν ἡδονὴ παρακολουθῇ,
πολὺν χρόνον ὑπομείνασι τὰς ἀλγηδόνας.
   § 96. quocirca corpus...: Diog. Laert.
x 137 τὴν γοῦν σάρκα διὰ τὸ παρὸν μόνον
χειμάζειν· τὴν δὲ ψυχὴν καὶ διὰ τὸ παρελ-
θὸν καὶ τὸ παρὸν καὶ τὸ μέλλον; Fin. i 17,
55 'nam corpore nihil nisi praesens et quod
adest sentire possumus, animo autem et
praeterita et futura.'

   sentiret: for the tense cf. iii 15, 32 n.
on uenisset: Bentley's sentiat has not
been adopted except by Dav.
   cum expectatio...iungeretur: the
reading of the best MSS. here involves
construing iungeretur with the simple
abl. memoria which (though defended by
Küh.) seems impossible. The insertion
of cum before perceptarum adopted by
Ba. Ml. Sff. Sch. TS. Hei. is credited
generally to Madv.: it is really due to
Bentley: memoriae was tentatively proposed by Urs. and adopted by Lamb.;
Dav. proposed expectationi in place of
expectatio.
   XXXIV. § 97. uictum: cf. Fin. ii 8,
24—26. Some idea of what one of these
treatises must have been like may be
formed from the περὶ τροφῆς of the Stoic
Musonius (C. Musonii Rufi Reliquiae ed.
Hense, pp. 99 ff.).

feruntur, extenuaturque magnificentia et sumptus epularum,
quod paruo cultu natura contenta sit. etenim quis hoc non
uidet, desideriis omnia ista condiri? Darius in fuga cum aquam
5 turbidam et cadaueribus inquinatam bibisset, negauit umquam
se bibisse iucundius. numquam uidelicet sitiens biberat. nec
esuriens Ptolomaeus ederat; cui cum peragranti Aegyptum
comitibus non consecutis cibarius in casa panis datus esset, nihil
uisum est illo pane iucundius. Socraten ferunt cum usque ad
10 uesperum contentius ambularet quaesitumque esset ex eo quare
id faceret, respondisse se, quo melius cenaret, obsonare ambu-
lando famem. **98.** quid? uictum Lacedaemoniorum in philitiis
nonne uidemus? ubi cum tyrannus cenauisset Dionysius, negauit

2. extenuaturque R 16 7 17   V P G   B 1 2   K 1 2   S   E 1   W 2   M 1   D C J
O 1 3 7.   extenuāturque M 1.   extenuātur II *alio atr. mut.*   extenuatur E 2.
extenuanturque W 1.   et extenuantur O 2.   6. iucundius R V G B K.
iocundius P S E.   7. ptolomeus R G S E J *alii.*   ptoloms̄ K.   ptholomeus
V B.   tholomeus P D.   8. cibarius K 2   L 5 6   J.   cybarius L 3.
cibaris̶ E 2 *alio atr. corr.*   cibariis R V G   E 1   L 2 4.   cibariis P *marg.* cibarᵱ.
cibariís S *litt. inter* r *et* i *eras.*   cybariis B.   9. iucundius R V G B K.
iocundius P S E.   ‖ socraten R V P G   B 1 2   K 1   S.   socratē K 2   E 1 2
W 1 2   D II J.   socratem L 5 6   M 1 2   O 1–3 7.   11. obsonare R 10   B 1 2
S   E 1–3   W 1   M 1 2   D   O 1 3.   opsonare R 2 P.   obsạnare V
atr. uiridi corr.   obsạnare R 1 *atr. nigriore mut.*   obsanare G   K 1   J   O 7.
absanare K 2.
§ 98, 12. philitiis R 1   V   P 2   G   B 1   M 1 2   C   O 3.   phȳlitiis R 2.
philiciis R 10   K 1   S   E 1   W 1 2   D II J   O 1 ed. H.   philidiis E 2 *at* d
ex c *mut.*   pyliciis P 1.   phidiciis R 6.   13. cenauisset P K E.
cẹnauisset R V S.   caenauisset G.

Darius: Maximus Tyrius xxxiv 6
(p. 397, ed. Hobein) tells a similar story
of Ἀρτοξέρξης ὁ Περσῶν βασιλεύς who
ἡττηθεὶς ἔφευγεν ἐπὶ ψιλὸν λόφον ὅπου τῆς
νυκτὸς ἀναπανόμενος ἐδίψησεν ὁ δύστηνος
πρῶτον τότε...καὶ ἠγάπησεν παρὰ ἀνδρὸς
Μάρδου λαβὼν ἐν ἀσκῷ ὁδωδὸς ὕδωρ. A
similar story is found in Plut. Art. 12 and
Apophth. p. 174 A. The story was no
doubt first invented to point the moral
of such comparisons as that in 32, 92 and
then told of more than one king, whether
of Persia or of Egypt.
consecutis: for the rare use of the perf.
part. of deponents with an active meaning in the abl. absol. construction cf.
Draeger, *Synt. d. lat. Spr.* ii p. 765
(§ 583).
cibarius: cf. Isid. Orig. xx 2 '[panis]
cibarius est qui ad cibum seruis datur nec
delicatus.'
Socraten: Socrates is often quoted in
favour of *tenuis uictus,* Finn. ii 28, 90;

Musonius, *l.c.* p. 102 ἔφη τοὺς μὲν πολλοὺς ἀνθρώπους ζῆν ἵνα ἐσθίωσιν αὐτὸς δὲ
ἐσθίειν ἵνα ζῇ, Aul. Gell. xix 2, 7. Dav.
quotes Athen. iv p. 157 E; Xen. Mem.
i 3, 5; Porphyr. de abst. iii 26.
contentius: Nonius, p. 264 M. quotes
this passage in support of the meaning of
continuus, perseuerans given to *contentus.*
§ 98. **philitiis:** the common meals
(συσσίτια) of the Spartans were known
as φιδίτια or φιλίτια, the latter form
being no doubt due to a popular derivation from φίλος; on the derivation of
φιδίτια see (for different views) Vaniček,
Etym. Wört. p. 1010; Gilbert, *Gk. Const.
Antiq.* p. 66¹.
Dionysius: a somewhat similar story
is told in Stob. Flor. iii 29, 100 [vol. ii
p. 22 Gaisf.] Διονύσιος Λακωνικὸν μάγει-
ρον πριάμενος ἐκέλευσεν αὐτὸν σκεύασαι
τὸν Λακωνικὸν ζωμόν· καὶ σκευάσαντος οὐκ
ἤσθιεν· ἤρετο δὲ κατὰ τί αὐτῷ ἥδονται
ἀηδεστάτῳ ὄντι οἱ Λάκωνες· ὁ δὲ οὐκ ἔχειν

se iure illo nigro, quod cenae caput erat, delectatum. tum is qui
15 illa coxerat: 'Minime mirum; condimenta enim defuerunt.' 'quae tandem?' inquit ille. 'labor in uenatu,
sudor, cursus ad Eurotam, fames, sitis. his enim rebus
Lacedaemoniorum epulae condiuntur.' atque hoc non ex
hominum more solum, sed etiam ex bestiis intellegi potest, quae,
20 ut quicquid obiectum est, quod modo a natura non sit alienum,
eo contentae non quaerunt amplius. **99.** civitates quaedam
uniuersae more doctae parsimonia delectantur, ut de Lacedaemoniis paulo ante diximus. Persarum a Xenophonte uictus

---

14. cene V P B 2 E 1 L 5 O 1.　　　çenę K 1.　　　　caene R G.
coenae R 6 W 1 O 2.　‖ caput erat R 6 W 1 M 2 O 3 ed. H.　caρ̄ erat R 7.
　　　　　　　　　　　　　　　　　　　　　　　　　　　　　　　　　t
caput cene erat D C.　　capud erat K 2.　　capuderat O 1.　　capuerat V
atr. uiridi corr. S *fort. eod. atr.* E 1 *et* W 2 *alio atr. mut.*　　capuerat R 1 17 G
　　　　　　　　　a ⌣
B 1 2 K 1 L 5 J.　　cuρ̄ˈferat P *marg.* caput.　　ceperat O 2.　　cepat E 2 Π.
aᵗ caput
　copia erat E 3.　　copia erat O 7.　*om.* M 1.　‖ delectatū...coxerat *habet in marg.*
V *atr. uiridi adscr.*　　15.　minime R V P B K.　　mineiurum G *in* minime mirum
　　　　　　　　　　　　　　　　　　　　　　　　　　　u
ead. man. mut.　　17. sudor P B K E.　　sodor R *fort. eod. atr.*　　sodor V G.‖
ad eurota L 2 5.　　ab eurota R 1 6 V P G B 1 2 K 1 2 S E 1 2 L 3 4 6
W 1 2 M 1 2 D C Π J O 1–3 7 ed. H.　　　　ad Eurotam *corr. Bentleius.*
18. epulę R 10 B 1 E 1.　　epule P E 2.　　epulę V.　　aepulę R 1 K 1.
aepulae G.　　19. intellegi B.　　intelligi R V P G K S E.　　20. ut quicquid
R 1 6 V P G B 1 K 1 2 S E 1 2 W 1 M 1 D J O 1–3.　　　ut quidquid
W 2 Π O 7.　　ut quitqq̣̇' C.　　ut quid M 2.　*om.* B 2.　‖ quod modo R 6
　　　　　　　　　　　　　　　o　　　　　　　　　　　　　　d
K 2 E 2 M 1 D C Π O 1–3 7.　　ǫ̣m B 1.　　　quo₁modo R 1 *atr. nigriore*
superscr.　　quomodo P G B 2 K 1 S E 1 W 2 M 2 J.　　quomodǫ̣ V
atr. uiridi mut.　　dūmo W 1 ed. H. ‖ a natura R 1 6 V P G B 1 2 K 1 2 S
E 1 2 W 1 2 M 1 2 D C Π J O 1–3 7.

　　§ 99, 23. persarum R P G K E.　　parsarum V *atr. uiridi superscr.*

ἔφη τοῦτον τὰ ἡδύσματα ἃ ἐκείνους ἔχειν, διὰ
τοῦτο αὐτῷ μὴ ἀρέσαι· καὶ ὃς ἐπύθετο τίνα
εἴη ταῦτα...ὁ δ' εἶπεν ἃ μὴ ἔστι παρὰ σοί,
οἱ πρὸ τοῦ δείπνου πόνοι καὶ τὸ ἐν τῷ Εὐρώτῃ
λουτρόν, cf. also Plut. Inst. Lac. p. 236 E.
A similar story is found in Plut. Lyc. 12
of one of the kings of Pontus.
　iure illo nigro: ὁ μέλας ζωμός, also
called αἱματία; among the ingredients
were blood, pork, vinegar and salt; see
Gilbert *op. cit.* p. 67² and reff. there.
　cenae caput, 'principal dish,' cf. Fin.
ii 8, 25 and the Gk phrase κεφαλὴ δείπνου,
occurring in a fragment of Alexis (*Fragg.
Com. Gr.* iii p. 462 Mein.). Mo. compares
Mart. x 31, 4.
　cursus ad Eurotam, 'running beside
the Eurotas,' where the δρόμος was;
Bentley's emendation for *ab Eurota* adopted by Wes. Ba. Me. TS. Hei. Sff.
and Schiche. Ern. keeps *ab E.* and ex-

plains 'cursus uidetur initium cepisse a
ripa Eurotae ad quam sedebant specta-
tores' and he is followed by Mo. and
Küh. But it is to be noted that the
versions of the story quoted above all
refer to *bathing* in the Eurotas as one of
the main sources of the appetite required
for appreciation of the *ius nigrum*, and
it is possible that *cursus ab Eurota* is
right and refers to a run taken after the
bath in the river.
　Sff. unnecessarily makes *cursus* qualify
sudor, to provide a better parallel to *labor
in uenatu*. Bak. brackets as a gloss *his
en m ..condiuntur.*
　ut quicquid: cf. iv 19, 44 n.
　§ 99. a Xenophonte: in Cyr. i 2, 8
διδάσκουσι δὲ καὶ ἐγκράτειαν γαστρὸς καὶ
ποτοῦ...φέρονται δὲ οἴκοθεν σῖτον μὲν ἄρτον,
ὄψον δὲ κάρδαμον· cf. Fin. ii 28, 92.

exponitur, quos negat ad panem adhibere quicquam praeter
25 nasturcium. quamquam, si quaedam etiam suauiora natura
desideret, quam multa ex terra arboribusque gignuntur cum
copia facili, tum suauitate praestantia! 100. adde siccitatem,
quae consequitur hanc continentiam in uictu, adde integri-
tatem ualetudinis; confer sudantis, ructantis, refertos epulis tam-
30 quam opimos boues; tum intelleges, qui uoluptatem maxime
sequantur, eos minime consequi, iucunditatemque uictus esse in
desiderio, non in satietate.

XXXV. Timotheum, clarum hominem Athenis et principem
ciuitatis, ferunt, cum cenauisset apud Platonem eoque conuiuio
admodum delectatus esset uidissetque eum postridie, dixisse:
'Vestrae quidem cenae non solum in praesentia, sed
5 etiam postero die iucundae sunt.' quid, quod ne mente
quidem recte uti possumus multo cibo et potione completi?
est praeclara epistula Platonis ad Dionis propinquos, in qua

25. nasturcium R V P G B 1 K: S E 1 2 W 1 M 2 D C O 1-3.
nasturtium R 6 W 2 Π J O 7. nastrutium M 1. 26. cum copia R 1 6 17
V P G B 1 K 1 E 1 2 M 2 D C J O 1 3 7. tum copia R 7 W 1 2 Π
O 2 ed. H. 27. praestantia R 1 6 7 17 V P G B 1 2 K 1 S E 1 2 L 2-4
W 1 2 M 1 2 D C J O 1-3 7. prestancia Π.
§ 100, 29. ualetudinis R V G. ualitudinis P B K S E. ‖ sudantis ructantis
R V P G B K E. sudantes ructantes S. 30. intelleges R V G B K.
intelliges P S E. ‖ maxime R V P G K. maxume B. 31. minime
R V P G B K.
XXXV. 2. cenauisset P G K E *alii.* cęnauisset R B. 3. postridie V.
ï
post͜die P *marg.* .p̣'t'die. p̣tridie B K. posttridie R G. posteridie E.
4. uestrae equidem R 1 2 6 7 10 16 17 V P B 1 K 1 2 E 1-3 L 2 4-6' W 1 2
M 2 D C Π O 1 3 7 ed. H. uestreae quidem G. uerū equidem M 1 J.
uere quidem O 2. equidem S *marg.* uestrę. et quidem L 3. ‖ cenę R 2.
cene K. cęnę R V P. caene G. 5. postero die R V P G B *alii.* ‖
d͡
quiquod R *atr. nigriore superscr.* quiqd̄ V P G K E. 6. completi R 1 P G.
cōpleti R 2 V K. copleti E. 7. epistula G. epistūla R 1 u *in* o *mut. atr.*
nigriore. epistola V B K E. epła P S J.

nasturcium: cf. Suidas s.v. κάρδαμα·
ἐπισχετικὰ οὔρων τὰ κάρδαμα καὶ πτύσμα-
τος καὶ διὰ τοῦτό φασι τοὺς Πέρσας χρῆσθαι·
φυλάττουσι γὰρ πολλὰ πτύειν καὶ οὐρεῖν
καὶ ἀπομύττεσθαι.
cum...praestantia: Lamb. (followed
by Ba. Wes. T.S. Schiche) read *praestanti*, and Bentl. followed by Dav. changed
facili into *facilia*; but Mo. Küh. Hei. Sff.
are no doubt right in keeping *praestantia*
of the MSS.
§ **100. siccitatem**, 'a dry habit of
body.' Cato M. 10, 34 'summam esse in eo
corporis siccitatem.' Catull. xxiii 12 atqui
corpora sicciora cornu ‖ aut siquid magis
aridum est habetis ‖ sole et frigore et esuri-
tione...a te sudor abest, abest saliua ‖
mucusque et mala pituita nasi. Salu. de

gub. iii 14 'opinor enim omnes omnino
homines cibis ac poculis fortes esse,
infirmos autem abstinentia, ariditate,
ieiuniis' where *ariditas* seems to denote
an excess of *siccitas*.
XXXV. **Timotheum**: son of Konon,
recovered Athenian naval supremacy
in the Aegean in 376 and the following years: v. Holm, *Hist. of Gr.* iii
89 ff.
principem, 'statesman,' i 15, 34 n.
ferunt: the story is told with slight
variations in Athen. x 419 D; Aelian
V. H. ii 18; Plut. de tuenda san. praec.
127 B (quoted by Dav.).
epistula: the passage occurs in the
seventh epistle p. 326 B; the reference
is to his first visit to Italy and Sicily:

scriptum est his fere uerbis : 'Quo cum uenissem, uita illa
beata, quae ferebatur, plena Italicarum Syracusiarum-
10 que mensarum, nullo modo mihi placuit, bis in die
saturum fieri nec umquam pernoctare solum ceteraque
quae comitantur huic uitae, in qua sapiens nemo
efficietur umquam, moderatus uero multo minus.
101. quae enim natura tam mirabiliter temperari potest?'
15 quo modo igitur iucunda uita potest esse a qua absit prudentia,
absit moderatio? ex quo Sardanapalli, opulentissimi Syriae
regis, error adgnoscitur, qui incidi iussit in busto :

> Haec habeo quae edi, quaeque exsaturata lubido
> Hausit; at illa iacent multa et praeclara relicta.

9. syracusiarum R V B 1.   syracusyṛịarum G.   siracusiarum P 1 K 2
E 1 W 2 D C.   siracusarum J.   sirracusiarum B 2.   syracusarum R 7
K O 2.   siracusarum S M 2 O 1.   syracusanarum R 6 W 1 O 3 ed. H.
siracusanarum R 17 P 2 E 2 M 1 Π O 7.   10.   *post* Syracusiarum *habent*
que R 1 *alio atr.* que *in* q, *mut.* P.   quae G.   que *om.* P 2 W 2.
11. ceteraq. quę K.   ceteraq; q̄ P.   ceteraque quae R.   caeteraque quae G.
cętaq; B 1 quae *om.*   cetera quę E 1.   ceteraq; ed. H quae *om.*
12. in qua P G.   in quae R B.

§ **101**, 15. prudentịę V *atr. uiridi corr.*   16. sardanapalli R V G B 1 2
K 1 S E 1 W 2 M 1 D J O 1 2.   sardịnapalli P.   sardanapali E 2 W 1
M 2 O 3 7 ed. H.   ‖ opulentissimi R V G B K E.   17. adgnoscitur R V K.
adgnoscitur G *eod. atr.*   agnoscitur P B S E.   18. exsaturata R V G B K.
ex
7saturata P.   ‖ lubido J.   libido R V P G B K E *alii.*   19. hausit P K E.
h
ausit R V *atr. uiridi superscr.*   ausit G.

ἐλθόντα δέ με ὁ ταύτῃ λεγόμενος αὖ βίος
εὐδαίμων Ἰταλιωτικῶν τε καὶ Συρακουσίων
τραπεζῶν πλήρης, οὐδαμῇ οὐδαμῶς ἤρεσε·
δὶς τε τῆς ἡμέρας ἐμπιμπλάμενον ζῆν καὶ
μηδέποτε κοιμώμενον μόνον νύκτωρ· καὶ
ὅσα τούτῳ ἐπιτηδεύματα ξυνέπεται τῷ
βίῳ· ἐκ γὰρ τούτων τῶν ἐθῶν οὔτ' ἂν
φρόνιμος οὐδείς ποτε γενέσθαι τῶν ὑπὸ τὸν
οὐρανὸν ἀνθρώπων ἐκ νέου ἐπιτηδεύων δύναιτο
οὔθ' οὕτως θαυμαστῇ φύσει κραθήσεται·
σώφρων δ' οὐδ' ἂν μελλήσαι ποτὲ γενέσθαι.
Italicarum...mensarum: the luxury
of Magna Graecia and Sicily was proverbial, cf. Plato, Rep. iii 404 D ; Gorg.
518 B. For the Gk form of the adj.
Syracusius in place of the usual Latin
Syracusanus see Wilkins' n. to Or. ii 13,
57; it occurs also in Or. iii 34, 139; Off.
i 44, 155; Diu. i 20, 39.
bis in die: cf. Virg. G. iii 527 'non
illis epulae nocuere repostae' with Conington's n.
uitae: for the dat. with *comitari* cf. 24,
68 n. Cic. is translating ὅσα τούτῳ ἐπιτηδεύματα ξυνέπεται τῷ βίῳ.

temperari, 'what disposition could
show such a remarkable combination,'
οὔθ' οὕτως θαυμαστῇ φύσει κραθήσεται.
§ **101. Sardanapalli**: the legend of
Sardanapallus (as told by Ktesias), generally supposed to be a distortion of the
history of Assurbanipal who was king of
Assyria 668—625 B.C., is given by Diod.
Sic. ii 23 ff., who represents him as the
last king of Assyria : Prof. Sayce (*Encycl.
Brit.* s.v.) thinks that the name is derived
from that of Assur-danin-pal, the rebel
son of Shalmaneser I, whose reign ended
with the fall of Niniveh in 823, while his
supposed fate is an echo of that of Samas-
tum-yukin, brother of Assur-bani-pal. The
latter was 'luxurious and indolent...but
a magnificent patron of art and literature.'
Syriae: Greek and Latin writers habitu-
ally confused Assyria and Syria : cf. Herod.
vii 63 ὑπὸ μὲν Ἑλλήνων ἐκαλέοντο Σύριοι,
ὑπὸ δὲ τῶν βαρβάρων Ἀσσύριοι ἐκλήθησαν ;
Strabo xvi p. 737 A ; Fin. ii 32, 106.
The lines said to have been inscribed
on the tomb of Sardanapallus are given

20 'Quid aliud,' inquit Aristoteles, 'in bouis, non in regis
sepulcro inscriberes? haec habere se mortuum dicit
quae ne uiuus quidem diutius habebat quam fruebatur.'
102. cur igitur diuitiae desiderentur, aut ubi paupertas beatos
esse non sinit? signis, credo, tabulis, ludis—si quis est, qui his
25 delectetur, nonne melius tenues homines fruuntur quam illi qui
iis abundant? est enim earum rerum omnium nostra in urbe
summa in publico copia. quae qui priuati habent, nec tam multa
et raro uident, cum in sua rura uenerunt; quos tamen pungit

20. inquit R P G.   in<u>t</u>qd V *atr. uiridi corr.*   inquid K. ‖ aristoteles
V G K.   aristot<u>é</u>les R e in i *atr. nigriore mut.*   aristotiles P.   21. sepulcro

R P G.   sepulchro V B K S E.   22. <u>u</u>ius R *atr. nigriore superscr.*
§ 102, 24. non sinit R V P G B K *plerique.*   non sinitur L 5.   non sunt
B 2 ed. H. ‖ tabulis ludis R 1 6 7 17 V P G B 1 2 K 1 2 S E 1–3 L 2–6
W 1 2 M 1 2 D C Π J O 1–3 7 ed. H.   26. abundant R *atr. <u>h</u>nigro superscr.*
habundant P G. ‖ earum rerum omnium R 1 17 V P G B 1 2 K 1 S E 1 2
W 1 M 1 2 Π O 2 3 7.   omnium earum rerum R 7 K 2 W 2 D C J O 1.

earum omnium rerum R 6. ‖ nostra in urbe R 6.   nostra <u>in</u>urbe Π.
nostrae urbe G *ead. man. mut.*   nostra urbe R 1 7 17 V P B 1 2 K 1 2 S
E 1 2 W 2 M 1 2 J O 1–3 7.   in nostra urbe W 1   D C ed. H.
27. priuati R 1 10 16 V P G B 1 2 K 1 S E 2 L 2–6 W 1 2 D C J
O 2 7 ed. H.   prau<s>i</s>tati E 1.   28. uenerunt R V P G B 1 2 K 1 S E 1 2
W 2 M 1 2 D C Π J O 1–3 ed. H.   ueniunt O 7.   peruenerint W 1.

with some variations in Athen. viii p.
336 A; Strabo xiv p. 672 B; Diod.
Sic. ii 23. Cic. translates only the last
two ταῦτ' ἔχω ὅσσ' ἔφαγον καὶ ἐφύβρισα
καὶ μετ' ἔρωτος | τέρπν' ἔπαθον, τὰ δὲ
πολλὰ καὶ ὄλβια κεῖνα λέλειπται. These
two are printed among the ἀδέσποτα of
the Palatine Anthology vii 325, and are
often quoted, e.g. Dio. Chrys. iv p. 81 M.
The verses are attributed to Choerilus;
see Madv. on Fin. ii 32, 106: Suidas (s.v.
Σαρδανάπαλος) says they were composed
by κόλακες καὶ μιμηταὶ τῆς ἐκείνου φιλοσαρ-
κίας καὶ γαστριμαργίας καὶ οἰστρηλασίας.
Aristoteles, quoted again in Fin. ii 32,
106. The passage does not occur in any
of the extant works, which contain two
other reff. to Sardanapallus, Eth. Nic. i
5, 3; Pol. viii p. 1312a 1 (where some
doubt is thrown upon the truth of the
legend). Athenaeus *l.c.* quotes another
saying of Aristotle with regard to Sardanapallus, ὃν ἀδιανοητότερον εἶναι κατὰ τὴν
προσηγορίαν τοῦ πατρὸς [i.e. 'Ανακυνδαρά-
ξεω] 'Αριστοτέλης ἔφη.
§ 102. **ludis**: that this, and not any of
the conjectures, is the right reading here
is rendered probable by the enumeration

in Fin. ii 32, 107 'signum, tabulae, locus
amoenus, ludi, uenatio,' where also the
argument is somewhat similar. The sentence is an anacoluthon: as the paren-
thetical *credo* shows, Cicero had begun
his sentence as an ironical statement of
the opposite of what he wished to enforce,
'signis, credo, tabulis, ludis...minus tenues
homines fruuntur,' but altered the construction to the form in the text. Sff.
proposed *signis credo et tabulis studeo.*
nostra in urbe: the reading of G,
nostrae, seems to have arisen from **nostra** i,
and to be decisive in favour of inserting
in before *urbe*, and not before *nostra*:
Mo. endeavours to defend the MSS. reading by citing exx. of *media urbe* and *tota
urbe* which are not really parallel.
priuati, 'in their own homes' = *priuatim*; for the use of the adj. in place of an
adverb cf. the use of *occultus* and *secretus*
in Liv. ii 11, 7; xxv 30, 4 (quoted by
Naegelsb. *Lat. Stil.* p. 224); it is unnecessary (with Lamb. Wes. Or. Ba. Sff.
T.S. Hei.) to alter here to *priuatim.*
nec...et: cf. i 4, 7 n.
uenerunt: cf. ii 23, 54 n.

aliquid, cum illa unde habeant recordantur. dies deficiat, si
30 uelim paupertatis causam defendere. aperta enim res est et
cotidie nos ipsa natura admonet, quam paucis, quam paruis
rebus egeat, quam uilibus. XXXVI. 103. Num igitur ignobilitas aut humilitas aut
etiam popularis offensio sapientem beatum esse prohibebit?
uide ne plus commendatio in uulgus et haec quae expetitur
gloria molestiae habeat quam uoluptatis. leuiculus sane noster
5 Demosthenes, qui illo susurro delectari se dicebat aquam ferentis
mulierculae, ut mos in Graecia est, insusurrantisque alteri: 'hic
est ille Demosthenes.' quid hoc leuius? at quantus orator!
sed apud alios loqui uidelicet didicerat, non multum ipse secum.
104. intellegendum est igitur nec gloriam popularem ipsam per
10 sese expetendam nec ignobilitatem extimescendam. 'ueni
Athenas,' inquit Democritus, 'neque me quisquam ibi
adgnouit.' constantem hominem et grauem, qui glorietur a

29. deficiat V G B1 E1. deficiat P ^e alio atr. superscr. deficiăt B2
ā in a mut. deficiet R1 K12 S E23 W12 M2 D C II J O1-3 ed. H.
deficiēt O7. defitiet M1.
XXXVI. § 103, 3. commendatio R V G B. cōmendatio K E. || uulgus
R V P G B K S E. 5. demosthenes P. demostenes R V G K E. ||
susurro V G B12 K1 alii. susurr_io R atr. nigriore superscr. susurrio P. ||
aquam R6 E3 W1 M12 D C O12 ed. H. aquam E2 at a alio atr. add.
quam V ^a atr. uiridi superscr. quam II ^a alio atr. superscr. quam R P G B12
K1 E1 W2 J O7. q, K2 om. O3. 6. insusurrantisque G E1.
insusurrantisq3 P K2 S E3 D O1. insusurrantisq; K1. insusurrantisq̯ue R.
insusurrantisqu̯e V. insusurrantis q̄ B2. 7. at quantus R P G B E.
aut quantus V. aut quantus K. an quantus R2.
§ 104, 9. intellegendum R V G K. intelligendum P S E. 11. quisquam
ibi R167 V G B12 K12 S E1-3 W2 M1 D C II J O1 ed. H.
ibi quisquam R17 P W1 M2 O237. 12. adgnouit R V K. agnouit
P G B S E.

dies deficiat, si uelim: for the phrase
Mo. quotes N. D. iii 32, 81.
XXXVI. § 103. leuiculus is ἅπαξ
εἰρημένον in Cicero.
sane: cf. iv 21, 48 n.
noster: the word is used either as =
'quem in deliciis habeo' (Küh.) or 'quia
eius orationibus lectitandis familiaritatem
quasi cum eo contraxerat' (Mo.); cf. iii
10, 22 'Peripatetici, familiares nostri.'
Demosthenes: the story is found again
in Aelian V. H. ix 17; cf. Plin. Epp. ix
23, 5 'D. iure laetatus est quod illum
anus Attica ita noscitauit οὗτός ἐστι
Δημοσθένης.'
ut mos in Graecia est: this parenthetic
exclamation may serve as an argument

for the retention of 'id est genus quoddam
tormenti apud Graecos' in 9, 24.
secum: i.e. 'to indulge in reflexion
and self-criticism'; cf. Off. iii 1, 1 where
Cato is praised for his habit 'et in otio de
negotiis cogitare et in solitudine secum
loqui'; cf. Epictet. Dissert. iv 4, 26 ἀλλ'
ἂν μὲν οὕτω φέρῃ τὰ πράγματα ὥστε
μόνον ἢ μετ' ὀλίγων διεξαγαγεῖν...λαλεῖ
σεαυτῷ.
§ 104. Democritus: cf. Diog. Laert. ix
36 ἦλθον γάρ, φησίν, εἰς Ἀθήνας καὶ οὔτις
με ἔγνωκεν and Val. Max. viii 7, 4 ext.
ibi is omitted by Urs. Vict. Fabr. for
the insufficient reason that there is nothing
to correspond to it in the Greek of Diogenes (Vict. Var. Lect. XIX 22).

gloria se afuisse! an tibicines iique qui fidibus utuntur suo, non
multitudinis arbitrio cantus numerosque moderantur, uir sapiens,
15 multo arte maiore praeditus, non quid uerissimum sit, sed quid
uelit uulgus, exquiret? an quicquam stultius quam, quos singulos
sicut operarios barbarosque contemnas, eos aliquid putare esse
uniuersos? ille uero nostras. ambitiones leuitatesque contemnet
honoresque populi etiam ultro delatos repudiabit; nos autem eos
20 nescimus, ante quam paenitere coepit, contemnere. 105. est
apud Heraclitum physicum de principe Ephesiorum Hermodoro;
uniuersos ait Ephesios esse morte multandos quod, cum ciuitate
expellerent Hermodorum, ita locuti sint: 'Nemo de nobis
unus excellat; sin quis exstiterit, alio in loco et apud
25 alios sit.' an hoc non ita fit omni in populo? nonne omnem
exsuperantiam uirtutis oderunt? quid? Aristides (malo enim

13. afuisse G B 2.   afuisse R V *atr. uiridi add. E alio atr. add.* S.
abfuisse B 1 f *in* b *mut.*   affuisse P *marg. alio atr. adscr.* ab.   affuisse K 1 2.
abfuisse R 6 7   E 2   W 1 2   M 1 2   D II J   O 1–3 ed. H.   affugisse R 17   O 7.||
hiique R 7.   hique R 2 10 16   V P G   B 1   K 1   S E.   hiq,ue R 1 q *in* q,
alio atr. mut. || qui *om.* V *habent* R P G B K E.   15.   praeditus R G.
p̄ditus P.   p̄dit' K E.   pred̨ictus V. || uerissimum R V P G B K.

16. uulgus R V P G B K S E.   17. contemnas R 2 V.   contemnas R 1

eod. atr.   contempnas R 10 16   P G K.   18. contemnet V.   contemnet R 1

eod. atr.   contempnet P G.   ctẽpnat K 1 *eod. atr.*   20. paenitere M 2.
peq̨nitere K 1   B 1   S.   penitere P É 1 2   M 1   II J   O 1 7.   poenitere
R V G   O 2.   p̄nit⁹ B 2.

§ 105, 21.   Verba a Ephesiorum *usque ad* non sine causa igitur Epicurus (§ 110)
desunt in P 1, *pagina amissa.*   23.   locuti sint R 1   V   B 2   G *ex* sunt *eod. atr.*
mut.   locuti sunt R 17   B 1   K 2   S   E 1 2   L 5   M 1 2   D C II   O 1–3 7 ed. H.

locuti ʃ K 1.   locuti s̃t W 1 2   J.   24.   sin quis R 1 17   V G   B 2   K 1 2
O 1 7.   si quis R 7   B 1   E 1   W 2   J.   et si quis S   E 2   W 1   M 2   D C II
O 3 ed. H.   sed si quis R 6.   et quisquis M 1   O 2.   26.   exsuperantiam
R V G K.   exuperantiam B S E.

gloria = φιλοδοξία; cf. ii 20, 46 n.
multo arte maiore: for the order of
the words cf. (with Mo.) N. D. iii 27, 69,
pro Sest. 23, 52 'multo alia maiora.'
singulos: Dav. quotes Aelian, V. H.
ii 1, where Socrates is quoted as saying
to Alcibiades, εἰ τῶν [leg. τοιούτων] καθ'
ἕνα καταφρονεῖς, καταφρονητέον ἄρα καὶ
τῶν ἠθροισμένων; Diog. Laert. ii 34 and
Xen. Mem. iii 7, 6 where similar advice
is given to Charmides.
barbarosque: a pupil of N. Wecklein
in *Philol.* XLIII p. 677 conjectured *fabros-
que.*
aliquid: cf. i 20, 45 n.
§ 105. **Hermodoro**: cf. Musonius Rufus
ix p. 47 (ed. Hense) ἤδη τινὲς ἄνδρες ἀγαθοὶ
ὄντες ἐξηλάθησαν ὑπὸ τῶν πολιτῶν · ὥσπερ

'Αθήνηθεν μὲν 'Αριστείδης ὁ δίκαιος, ἐξ
'Εφέσου δὲ 'Ερμόδωρος, ἐφ' ᾧ καὶ 'Ηράκλει-
τος ὅτι ἔφυγεν ἠβηδὸν ἐκέλευεν 'Εφεσίους
ἀπάγξασθαι, where Hense notes that Cic.
here and Musonius are probably using the
same authority.
Hermodorus, according to Pliny, N. H.
xxxiv 11, was the *interpres* of the laws of
the Twelve Tables.
nemo: ἡμέων μηδὲ εἷς ὀνήϊστὸς ἔστω· εἰ δέ
τις τοιοῦτος, ἄλλῃ τε καὶ μετ' ἄλλων (Diog.
Laert. ix 2): the unusual *nemo* for *ne
quis* is probably intended to reproduce
the emphasis of μηδὲ εἷς.
exsuperantiam: another ἅπαξ εἰρημένον.
Aristides: cf. the passage of Musonius
Rufus cited above and Plut. Aristid. 7.

Graecorum quam nostra proferre) nonne ob eam causam expulsus est patria, quod praeter modum iustus esset? quantis igitur molestiis uacant qui nihil omnino cum populo contrahunt! quid
30 est enim dulcius otio litterato? iis dico litteris quibus infinitatem rerum atque naturae et in hoc ipso mundo caelum, terras, maria cognoscimus.

XXXVII. **106.** Contempto igitur honore, contempta etiam pecunia quid relinquitur quod extimescendum sit? exsilium, credo, quod in maximis malis ducitur. id si propter alienam et offensam populi uoluntatem malum est, quam sit ea contem-
5 nenda secunda paulo ante dictum est. sin abesse patria miserum est, plenae miserorum prouinciae sunt, ex quibus admodum pauci in patriam reuertuntur. **107.** at multantur bonis exsules. quid tum? parumne multa de toleranda paupertate dicuntur? iam uero exsilium, si rerum naturam, non ignominiam

---

30. iis dico M 2 O 3.   hiis dico D C II.   his dico R V G B 1 K 1 S
E 1 2 W 1 2 M 1 J O 1 2 7. *om.* B 2.
XXXVII. § 106, 2. exilium R V G B K S E.   3. maxumis R V G B K.
maximis E.   4. contemnenda] sicuta R G.   sĩc a V.   sĩc a P 4 B 2.
sicut ɟ S.   sic a E 1.   sicuti R 17 O 7.   sicut P 2 K 1 M 1.   sicut E 3.
sicuti B 1 *at ras. post* ti.   sicut E 2 a *post* t *eras.*   sic um P 6.   ut O 2.
om. R 6 7 P 3 5 K 2 L 2-6 W 1 2 M 2 D C J O 1 3 ed. H. *habet* II *marg.*
adscr. clausula e cont. om.   secunda *correxi.*   5. abesse patria R 1 7 17 V
P 2-6 G B 1 2 K 1 2 S E 1-3 L 6 W 1 2 M 1 2 D C J O 1-3 7 ed. H.
abesse_ᴀ patria II *alio atr. superscr.*   abesse a patria R 6.

§ **107,** 7. at multantur R G B K.   ad multantur V *atr. uiridi superscr.*
8. exules...exilium R V G B K S E.

Graecorum...nostra: sc. *exempla.*
contrahunt, 'have dealings with': cf. Off. i 2, 4 'neque si tecum agas quid, neque si cum altero contrahas.'
iis dico litteris: for the (alleged) attraction to the case of the preceding Küh. compares Phil. viii 7, 20 'quam hesternus dies nobis, consularibus dico, turpis inluxit': pro Cael. 13, 32 'cum istius mulieris uiro, fratre uolui dicere,' where however *fratrem* is the better reading. It is more than doubtful whether these are parallel, or whether there is any attraction at all here: it is better to take *iis dico litteris* as equivalent to *iis dico litteratum* (or *ornatum*) *litteris,* the words *iis litteris* being not an equivalent to *litterato otio* but a qualifying abl. attached to a participle unexpressed, the whole phrase being an amplification of *litterato.*
XXXVII. § **106. contemnenda**: the words *sicut a* or *sic uti* which follow in many MSS are simply omitted by most

edd. Heine (*Pos. Progr.* 9) thinks they are a corruption of *sapienti,* Kühn. a corruption of *ac uana* and Sff. of *ac leuicula.* It seems more probable that they are a corruption of *secunda,* used predicatively 'how much it ought to be regarded with indifference when favourable': *secŭda* might easily become *sicuta.*
ante: in 36, 104.
abesse patria: the abl. without the preposition *a* seems well attested here and in Fam. iv 6, 2; v 15, 4; in Ac. i, 1, 1 'cum eius uilla abessemus' is the reading of all the MSS. though Reid inserts *ab,* as Wes. here reads *a patria.*
prouinciae: the reference is probably to Roman *mercatores* or *publicani* whose business compelled them to take up an abode outside Italy.
§ **107. quid tum**: cf. ii 11, 26 n.
rerum naturam, 'actual facts': cf. iv 34, 72 n. Bentley's *rei* for *rerum* is uncalled for.

10 nominis quaerimus, quantum tandem a perpetua peregrinatione
differt? in qua aetates suas philosophi nobilissimi consumpserunt,
Xenocrates, Crantor, Arcesilas, Lacydes, Aristoteles, Theophrastus, Zeno, Cleanthes, Chrysippus, Antipater, Carneades,
Clitomachus, Philo, Antiochus, Panaetius, Posidonius, innumera-
15 biles alii, qui semel egressi numquam domum reuerterunt. at
enim sine ignominia...adficere sapientem? de sapiente enim haec
omnis oratio est, cui iure id accidere non possit; nam iure

---

10. tandem a R 7 L 2.   demum a R 6 E 3 L 3 6 W 2 M 2 O 3.
damna R 1 P 2 G B 1 M 1 O 2 S *marg.* demū a.   dāna B 2 K 1.

damna V *atr. uiridi superscr.*   damna a O 1.   damnū_A II *alio atr. add.*

danna L 4.   dāpna R 17   O 7.   dāpna E 1 *alio atr. superscr.*   dāpna a J.
dampna a K 2   L 5.   dampnū E 2.   a D C ed. H.   nā a W 1.
11. nobilissimi R G K.   nobilissimi V B.   12. archesilas R V G B 1 2 K.||
lacydes R G K.   lacides V B 1 2.   laudes E 1.   13. cleantes R V G B K E.

14. Clitomachus *et* Panaetius *om.* R 1.   carneades philo antiochus possidonius
V *marg.* paneatius clitomachus carneades.   *post* carneades *addit* G *in marg.*
eod. atr. panaetius clitomachus carneades *pergitque in textu* philo antiochus (*ex*
anthichus *corr.*) possidonius.   carneades panaetius clitomachus carneades philo
antiochus possidonius B 1 2 E 1   O 2.   carneades panaetius clitomachus philo
antiochus posidonius R 6 7 17   E 2 3   W 1 2   M 1 2 D C Π J   O 1–3 7 ed. H.
carneades "S *marg.*" panetius clitomacus.   possidonius *habent* R 1 K 1 2 E 1. ||
innumerabiles alii qui R 1 2 6 7 10 16 17   V G B 1 K 1 2 E 1 2 W 1 M 1 2
O 1 7 ed. H.   15. reuerterunt R V G B 1 2 K 1 S E 1 2 W 1 2 M 1
D C Π O 1 3 7.   reuertere O 2.   reuertunt^r J.   16. sine ignominia adficere
(adficere) R 1 17   V G B 1 2 K 2 E 1 2 L 5 6 W 2 M 1 D C J O 1 2.
si ignominia adficere K 1.   sine ignominia afficere ^Λ S *marg.* poterit_Λ.   sine
                                                                            non
ignominia afficere poterit R 6 M 2 O 3.   ^Λ sine ignominia afficere poterit
II *alio atr. suppl.*   sine ignominia affici poterit R 7.   sine ignominia efficere
poterit O 7 ed. H.   ^sine^ ignominia afficere E 3 *marg.* poterit.   17. accidere R 6 7 17
K 2 E 2 3 L 5 W 1 2 M 1 D C Π O 1 2 7.   accipere V p *in* d *alio atr. mut.*
accip^de E 1 *alio atr. mut.*   accipere R 1 G B 1 2 K 1.

---

tandem: Dav.'s conjecture (confirmed
by two MSS) for *demum* (retained by Or.
Tr.) has been accepted by Wes. Küh.
Sff. etc.; *demum* is (as Wes. points out)
never used in questions of this kind.

Xenocrates: Hei. notes that the names
ought to be arranged in pairs according
to the schools of philosophy represented;
(1) the Old Academy (Xenocrates, Krantor); (2) the Middle Academy (Arcesilas,
Lacydes); (3) the Peripatetics (Aristotle
and Theophrastus); (4) the Stoics: (*a*) the
original Stoa (Zeno and Cleanthes): (*b*) the
Middle Stoa (Chrysippus, Antipater);
(5) the New Academy (Carneades, Clitomachus); then follow the two contemporary representatives of the New
Academy, Philo and Antiochus, and the

two representatives of the Stoa best
known to the Roman world, Panaetius
and Posidonius.

Panaetius at any rate revisited his
native Rhodes in after life as appears
from Rep. iii 35, 48 (Schmekel, *Phil.
der. mittl. Stoa*, p. 6 n.).

sine ignominia: it seems better (with
Tr. Kl. Mo. Ba. Ml. Schiche) to
mark a lacuna here than to adopt any
of the numerous conjectures for filling
up the sentence between *ignominia* and
sapientem, such as *ignominia afficiet
sapientem* (Küh.), an *potest ignominia
afficere sapientem?* (Wes. and TS., the
latter however inserting *exilium* after
potest) or to rewrite the sentence with
Man. (*at enim non erit sine ign.*: *igno-*

exsulantem consolari non oportet. **108.** postremo ad omnis
casus facillima ratio est eorum qui ad uoluptatem ea referunt
20 quae sequuntur in uita, ut quocumque haec loco suppeditetur, ibi
beate queant uiuere. itaque ad omnem rationem Teucri uox
accommodari potest:

> Pátria est, ubicumque ést bene.

Socrates quidem cum rogaretur cuiatem se esse diceret, 'mun-
25 danum' inquit; totius enim mundi se incolam et ciuem arbitrabatur. quid? T. Albucius nonne animo aequissimo Athenis
exul philosophabatur? cui tamen illud ipsum non accidisset, si
in re publica quiescens Epicuri legibus paruisset. **109.** qui
enim beatior Epicurus quod in patria uiuebat quam quod

---

18. exulantem R G B K E *alii.*   exultantem V.
§ **108.** omnis R V G B K.   19. facillima R V G B K.   20. sequuntur S
E 2 W 1 M 1   D Ⅱ J   O 3 7.   sequuntur B 1.   secuntur R V G B 2 K 1
E 1 W 2 M 2.   ‖ suppeditetur R 1 10 17   V   P 2   G   B 2 K 1 D C.
suppeditētur S.   suppeditet R 2 B 1.   subpeditet E 1.   suppeditent R 6
E 2 3 M 1 2 Ⅱ O 1–3 ed. H.   suppeditent̂ W 1   O 7.   suppeditentur R 7.
suppeditet̀ J.   suppeditaretur W 2.   subpeditet̀ R 16.   21. queant R E.
queant V K.   quaeant G.   22. accommodari R G K E.   accŏmodari V.
                                                              d
26. quid T̂. R G B 1 K 1.   quit V *atr. uiridi superscr.*   quidt B 2. ‖
aequissimo R G B K.   ȩquissimo V.

---

minia *adf. potest sap. ?*) or Bent. (*at est
in nomine ign.; an ea adf. poterit sap. ?*)
or Sff. (*at est non sine ign.; eamne attingere sap. !*).

§ **108. ratio,** 'method' sc. *consolandi*;
the reason for the superior ease of the
Epicurean method is given in the clause
ut...queant uiuere.

sequuntur: Mo. and Küh. take *sequuntur* as equivalent to *accidunt,* but one
can hardly be said *referre ad uoluptatem*
anything except one's own states of mind
or actions; it is better to take *sequuntur*
in the sense of 'pursue,' governing *quae.*

ad omnem rationem, 'to every system,'
Epicurean and Stoic or Peripatetic alike,
each school giving its own meaning to
'ubicumque est *bene.*' Heine's explanation 'jeder Lebenslage' is quite wrong.
Nissen's 'ad omnem rationem consolandi,'
i.e. omnes philosophi hac consolatione
uti possunt' is unsatisfactory; Teucer's
reflexion is a 'ratio consolandi' which
all schools can use, not a statement which
can be adapted to every method of consolation.

Patria est: Ribbeck classes the line
among the fragments of the *incertae
incertorum fabulae* (*Scaen. Rom. poes.
Frag.* I² p. 248) though it is generally
assigned to the *Teucer* of Pacuvius.

The sentiment in various forms is common in both Greek and Latin literature;
Arist. Plut. 1151 πατρὶς γάρ ἐστι πᾶσ' ἵν'
ἂν πράττῃ τις εὖ; Eurip. fr. 1047 N.
ἅπασα δὲ χθὼν ἀνδρὶ γενναίῳ πατρίς; Ov.
F. i 493 'omne solum forti patria est.'

quidem: cf. i 48, 116 n.

mundanum, 'a citizen of the world,'
a translation of κόσμος. The phrase is
attributed to Socrates in Arrian, Epict. i
9, 1 and Plut. de exilio 5 (p. 600 F.), to
Aristippus in Diog. Laert. ii 99 and to
Diogenes (*ib.* vi 63). The idea became
a commonplace of Stoicism; cf. Marc.
Aurel. vi 44 πόλις καὶ πατρίς, ὡς μὲν
Ἀντωνίνῳ μοι ἡ Ῥώμη, ὡς δὲ ἀνθρώπῳ ὁ
κόσμος with Gataker's n. *ad loc.* Musonius
Rufus ix p. 42 (ed. Hense) οὐχὶ κοινὴ
πατρὶς ἀνθρώπων ἀπάντων ὁ κόσμος ἐστίν;

Albucius was condemned for extortion
in Sardinia and went into exile at Athens
in 103. He had studied Epicurean philosophy when a young man at Athens
(Brut. 35, 131) and was mocked at for his
imitation of Greek ways (Lucil. quoted in
Fin. i 3, 8).

Epicuri legibus: Epicurus discouraged
political activity in a philosopher (Diog.
Laert. x 119).

§ **109. patria:** Epicurus was supposed
by some to be an Athenian of the deme

30 Athenis Metrodorus? aut Plato Xenocratem uincebat aut
Polemo Arcesilam, quo esset beatior? quanti uero ista ciuitas
aestimanda est ex qua boni sapientesque pelluntur? Damaratus
quidem, Tarquinii nostri regis pater, tyrannum Cypselum quod
ferre non poterat, fugit Tarquinios Corintho et ibi suas fortunas
35 constituit ac liberos procreauit. num stulte anteposuit exsilii
libertatem domesticae seruituti?

XXXVIII. 110. Iam uero motus animi, sollicitudines aegritudinesque obliuione leniuntur traductis animis ad uoluptatem.
non sine causa igitur Epicurus ausus est dicere semper in pluribus
bonis esse sapientem, quia semper sit in uoluptatibus. ex quo
5 effici putat ille, quod quaerimus, ut sapiens semper beatus sit.
111. etiamne, si sensibus carebit oculorum, si aurium? etiam; nam
ista ipsa contemnit. primum enim horribilis ista caecitas quibus
tandem caret uoluptatibus? cum quidam etiam disputent ceteras
uoluptates in ipsis habitare sensibus; quae autem aspectu perci-

§ 109, 30. aut W 1 M 1 O 1 2.   aut V *at* a *in marg. atr. uiridi adscr.*

ut E 1 2 *alio atr. superscr.*   ut R G B 1 2 K 1 L 5 6 W 2 M 2 D C Π J
O 3 7.   āt S *marg.* ut.   ‖   xenocratem R V G B K S E 2.   xenocratē E 1.

31. polemo R V K.   palemo B E.   plemo G *eod. atr.*   polemon J. ‖
arcesilam R V G B 2   arcesilā K 1.   arcessidam B 1 E 1.   33. tarquinii
R 10 K 2 E 1 L 3 4–6.   tarquiᴀi R 1 *eod. ut uid. atr.*   tarqnii K 1 E 2.
tarquini L 2 O 2 3 ed. H.   tarqni E 3.   tarqtii V.   tarquii G. ‖
nostri regis R V G B 1 2 K 1 S E 1 2 W 1 M 1 2 Π O 2 3.   regis nostri
K 2 L 3 5 6 W 2 D C J O 1 ed. H.   nostri pater tyranni L 2.   35. exilii
R V G B K S E.
XXXVIII. § 111, 7.   contemnit R v B.   contempnit V P G K. ‖
horribilis R v P G K.   orribilis V *atr. uiridi superscr.*   9. aspectu
R V P G B K S E.

Gargettus; others said that he was born
in Samos, of a family of Athenian cleruchs,
and did not come to Athens till he was
eighteen (Diog. Laert. x 1).
Metrodorus, a native of Lampsacus:
cf. ii 3, 8 n. The statement of some
edd. here that another tradition made him
an Athenian rests upon an old reading in
Diog. Laert. x, 22.
aut...aut: the conjecture of Lamb. *an
...an* is unnecessary, as is the substitution
of *ut* for the first *aut* (proposed by
Dav.).
quo...beatior, 'in the means for securing greater happiness'; Xenocrates
and Arcesilas were both foreigners, the
former being a native of Chalcedon (Diog.
Laert. iv, 6) and the latter of Pitane
(D. L. iv 28).

Damaratus: cf. Republ. ii 19, 34;
Liv. i 34, 2; Dion. Hal. iii 46 (Dav.).
Cypselum: tyrant of Corinth from 657
to 625 B.C.; Herod. v 92; Arist. Pol.
viii (v) 1310 b 29.
stulte anteposuit: cf. iii 16, 34 n. on
'male reprehendunt.'
XXXVIII. § 110. The matter of this
and the succeeding paragraphs is probably
derived from some Epicurean source, now
lost: cf. Usener, *Epicurea* § 599.
effici...ut: cf. i 8, 16 n.
§ 111. **quidam...disputent**: for the
view of sensation referred to here cf.
Aetius iv 23, 2 p. 414 D. Ἐπίκουρος καὶ τὰ
πάθη καὶ τὰς αἰσθήσεις ἐν τοῖς πεπονθόσι
τόποις, τὸ δ' ἡγεμονικὸν ἀπαθές quoted by
Usener *op. cit.* § 317; Lucr. iii 350 sqq.
and the nn. to i 20, 46.

10 piantur, ea non uersari in oculorum ulla iucunditate, ut ea quae
gustemus, olfaciamus, tractemus, audiamus, in ea ipsa ubi sentimus
parte uersentur. in oculis tale nil fit; animus accipit quae uidemus.
animo autem multis modis uariisque delectari licet, etiamsi non
adhibeatur aspectus. loquor enim de docto homine et erudito,
15 cui uiuere est cogitare. sapientis autem cogitatio non ferme ad
inuestigandum adhibet oculos aduocatos. **112.** etenim si nox
non adimit uitam beatam, cur dies nocti similis adimat? nam
illud Antipatri Cyrenaici est <id> quidem paulo obscenius, sed
non absurda sententia est; cuius caecitatem cum mulierculae
20 lamentarentur, 'quid agitis?' inquit, 'an uobis nulla uidetur
uoluptas esse nocturna?' Appium quidem ueterem illum,
qui caecus annos multos fuit, et ex magistratibus et ex rebus
gestis intellegimus in illo suo casu nec priuato nec publico
muneri defuisse. C. Drusi domum compleri a consultoribus

10. non uersari R v G.   ñ uersari P K.   çonuersari V *atr. uiridi superscr.*||
iucunditate R V G B K.   iocunditate v P S E.   11. gustemus R v P G B K.
gestemus V *atr. uiridi superscr.*   12. uersentur R 16 7 17   V P G   B1 2   K1 2
S   E1 2   L 5 6   W 2   M1 2   D C II J   O 1–3 ed. H.   uersantur W 1.||
tale nil R V G K.   tale n'l B 2   W 2.   tale nihil B 1   M1 2   O 2 3.
tale nichil R 7   P   E1 2   L 5   D II J.   nil tale O 1.   nihil tale W 1.
nichil tale C.   13. dilectari V G.   14. aspectus R V P G B K S E.
§ **112**, 16. etenim R v P G B.   eşt enim V *atr. uiridi corr.*   18. antipatri
R V P G K   E 2.   antiprī B 2.   antipari E 1.   antipatris S s *postea add.*||
est quidem R 16 7   V P G   B1 2   K1 2   S   E1–3   L 2 3 4 6   W 1 2   M 2
D C II J   O 1 3 ed. H.   est q̃ M 1.   est q̃ O 2.   quidem R 17.
est id quidem *corr. Seyffertus.*   20. quid agitis R V̂ P G   B1 2   K1   S   E1 2
L 5 6   W 2   M1 2   D C II J   O 1–3 ed. H.   quid agit K 2.   quid aegit B 2.
quid aitis W 1. || nulla uidetur V P G   B 1   E 1.   uĩla uidetur B 2.
ulla uidetur R K.   uidetur nĩla S.   22. annos multos R 1 2 10 16   V P G
B1 2   E1 2   W 2   M1 2   D C J   O 3.   multos annos R 17   v   K 1   O 1 2.
23. intellegimus R V G.   intelligimus P B K S E.   24. C drusi W 1.
G drusi v.   Ç atrusi V C *in* G *alio atr. mut.*   G. atrusi R   B 1   E 1   P *marg.*
C aî drusi.   C atrusi S   E 2   Catrusi B 2.   Gatrusi G.   Cratusi K 2.
Gratusi R 16   K 1   L 5   J.   Gratū si R 17.   cn. drusii O 1.   c. autem drusi
R 6   L 6   M 2   O 3.   G tusi W 2 *marg.* C aũt drusi. || compleri R V G.
cõpleri K. || a consultoribus R 1 7   V P G   B1 2   K1 2   S   E1 2   W 2   M1 2
J   O 1–3.   a *om.* R 6   L 6   W 1.

uersari in: cf. iv 18, 42 'in magna
parte pestis uersantur.'
fit...accipit: for the change to oratio
recta cf. ii 7, 17; iv 10, 24. For the
thought F. A. W. compares the line of
Epicharmus quoted in Plut. fort. 3 νοῦς
ὁρῇ καὶ νοῦς ἀκούει· τἄλλα κωφὰ καὶ τυφλά.
aspectus: cf. i 30, 73 n.
aduocatos: for the legal metaphor Mo.
compares iv 23, 52; Ac. ii 27, 86.
§ **112. nam**: cf. iii 16, 35 n.
Antipatri: for Antipater of Cyrene, the
follower of Aristippus, cf. Diog. Laert. ii 86.

id quidem: the insertion of *id* proposed by Sff. seems necessary: cf. Madv.
Gr. § 489 b.
agitis, 'what are you thinking of?,'
'what ails you?' F. A. W. and Mo. read
aitis, which is a doubtful form. For the
meaning of the phrase cf. the retort of
Granius to M. Drusus quoted in pro
Planc. 14, 33 'immo uero tu, Druse, quid
agis?'
Appium: iv 2, 4 n.; Cato M. 11, 37.
C. Drusi, brother of M. Drusus, the
opponent of C. Gracchus (Brut. 28, 109):

25 solitam accepimus; cum, quorum res esset, sua ipsi non uidebant, caecum adhibebant ducem. pueris nobis Cn. Aufidius praetorius et in senatu sententiam dicebat nec amicis deliberantibus deerat et Graecam scribebat historiam et uidebat in litteris.

XXXIX. **113**. Diodotus Stoicus caecus multos annos nostrae domi uixit. is uero, quod credibile uix esset, cum in philosophia multo etiam magis adsidue quam antea uersaretur et cum fidibus Pythagoreorum more uteretur, cumque ei libri noctes 5 et dies legerentur, quibus in studiis oculis non egebat, tum, quod sine oculis fieri posse uix uidetur, geometriae munus tuebatur uerbis praecipiens discentibus unde quo quamque lineam scriberent. Asclepiaden ferunt, non ignobilem Eretricum

26. CN M I 2　O I　S *at mut. est.*　ⓖN P　W I　J.　GN R V v G　B 2
K　O 2 3.　GH W 2.　gn̄ B I　E I.　gneus E 2　II.　‖　aufidius R I 6
P v　E 2　W I 2　II J　O 1-3.　autfidius R V G　B 2　K.　aut filius B I　E I.
28. uidebat R I 6 7 17　V P　B I 2　K I 2　S　E I 2　L 2-6　W I 2　M I 2
　　　　　　　　　　　　　　　　　　　　an
D C II J　O 1-3 ed. H.　uidebt　G *eod. atr.*

XXXIX. § **113**, 2. nostrae domi R I 2 10　v P　G　B I 2　K I　S　E I 2　W I 2
M I 2　II J　O 2.　domi nostrae R 16　D C　O I 3.　nr̄ē domi iuixit V u *in i ras. mut.*
nostrae domui R 17.　3. adsidue G.　adsiduę V.　assidue R v P B K S E.
8. Asclepiaden K.　　Asclepiadem R V G　K 2　S E　L 5 6　M I 2.
asclepiadē P B.　‖　ignobilem R I 6　K I　M I 2　D C　O 2 3.　ignobilē R 7 17
P　B 2　E I 3　W I　II.　　ignobile V v G.　‖　eretricum R 10　K.
ceterorū
er&ricum　R *atr. ant.*　ereticū E.　Heretricum S *marg.* nec Iscitū.
heretricum R 16　K 2　E 2 *marg. atr. ant.* L 5 6　W 2　M 2　J　O I ed. H.
　　　　　　　　　　　　h　　　　　　　　　　　　ᵊ
mer&ricum V G.　meretricū P *al. atr. mut.*　metricum B 2.　metricum
R 7 17 v　L 2 4　W I　II　O 3.　medicum L 3.　creticum B I　M I　D C
marg. ereticū.　nec inexercitum R 6　O 2.

Val. Max. viii 7, 4 'Livius Drusus...aetatis uiribus et acie oculorum defectus ius ciuile populo benignissime interpretatus est, utilissimaque discere id cupientibus monumenta composuit.'

Cn. Aufidius: Fin. v 19, 54 'equidem e Cn. Aufidio, praetorio, erudito homine, oculis capto, saepe audiebam, cum se lucis magis quam utilitatis desiderio moueri diceret.' He was praetor in 108 B.C. The history composed by him was probably a Roman history, though written in Greek (v. Peter, *Hist. Rom. rell.* i pp. ccxxxvi f.).

uidebat in litteris: almost = 'neque uidebat nisi in litteris,' 'all the sight he had was literary insight': *uiuebat* which Urs. said he found in one MS and which Bentl. adopted, is a peculiarly unhappy conjecture; it overlooks the fact that except for *uidebat* here there would be no mention made of Aufidius' blindness, the only title he had to appear in the context.

For the metaphorical use of *uidere*, edd.

following Vict. refer to Soph. O.T. 388 ἐν τοῖς κέρδεσιν | μόνον δέδορκε, τὴν τέχνην δ' ἔφυ τυφλός.

XXXIX. § 113. Diodotus, mentioned by Cic. in N.D. i 3, 6 along with Philo, Antiochus and Posidonius as one of his teachers: cf. Ac. ii 36, 115 'Diodoto quid faciam, Stoico, quem a puero audiui, qui mecum uiuit tot annos, qui habitat apud me, quem et admiror et diligo': Brut. 90, 309; Fam. xiii 16, 4; he died in 59 B.C. (Att. i. 20, 6).

domi: this form of the locative has the almost unanimous support of the MSS here, though in i 22, 51 the best MSS have *domui*; the latter is read here by Sch., with the *prima manus* of V.

esset, sc. *nisi ipse uidissem* (Kühn.); Bake's conj. *est*, adopted by Ti., is unnecessary: cf. Brut. 70, 246 'quod mirabile esset.'

cum...tum: cf. iii 13, 27 n.

Asclepiaden, of Phlius, the friend of Menedemus of Eretria, whom he was said to have imbued with his own philo-

philosophum, cum quidam quaereret quid ei caecitas adtulisset,
10 respondisse, puero ut uno esset comitatior. ut enim uel summa
paupertas tolerabilis sit, si liceat quod quibusdam Graecis
cotidie, sic caecitas ferri facile possit, si non desint subsidia ualetudinum. **114.** Democritus luminibus amissis alba scilicet discernere et atra non poterat, at uero bona mala, aequa iniqua,
15 honesta turpia, utilia inutilia, magna parua poterat, et sine
uarietate colorum licebat uiuere beate, sine notione rerum non
licebat. atque hic uir impediri etiam animi aciem aspectu
oculorum arbitrabatur, et cum alii saepe quod ante pedes esset
non uiderent, ille in infinitatem omnem peregrinabatur, ut nulla
20 in extremitate consisteret. traditum est etiam Homerum caecum

9. philosophum D O 2.　　　phm W 1　L 2.　　　ph'm C.　　　phum M 1.

　　　　　　　　　　　　　　　　　　　　　　　um
philosophum B 1 *marg.* philosopho24.　　　philosopho24 S.　　　philosophorum
R 1 6 7 10 17　V v P G　B 2　K 1 2　E 1 3　E 2 *marg. atr. ant.* L 3–6　W 2　M 2
Π J　O 1 3 ed. H.　‖　adtulisset K.　　attulisset R V P G B S E.　　10. respondisse
v P B K.　　　respondissē R.　　respondisse& V.　　12. cotidie R V P G B E.
cottidie K.　　quotidie v.　‖　ualetudinum V G.　　ualitudinum R P B K S E.
§ **114,** 13.　discernere et atra R V G　B 2　K 1　S　E 1 2　W 2　M 1　Π J
　　　　　　　　　　/.　　/.
O 1 ed. H.　et atra discernere B 1.　　et atra discernere R 6 7 17　P　K 2　L 6
W 1　M 2　D C　O 2 3.　　17. impediri R V P G B K S E.　‖　etiam animi
R V P G　B 1 2　K 1 2　S　E 1 2　W 1 2　M 1 2　D C J　O 1 2.　　animi etiam
R 6　E 2　Π. *om.* O 3.　‖　aspectu R 6 17　v B 1　K 2　S　E 1 2　W 1 2　M 1 2
　　　　　　　　　　　　　　　　　　　₩
D C Π J　O 1–3.　aspectum R 1.　　aspectu P.　　aspectū K 1.　　aspectm̄ B 2.
aspectum V.　　aspectus G *in* aspectū *eod. atr. mut.*　　18. cum alii P v.
cum aliis R G.　　cum aliis V K.　　19. ille in infinitatem S　E 2　M 1　Π.
ille infinitatem v P　B 1　E 3　W 1　M 2　O 1 2 ed. H.　　illa infinitatem R G
　　　　　　　　e
K 1 2.　　illa infinitatem V *atr. uiridi superscr.*　　illam infinitatem W 2.
illā Ifirmitatem J.　　ille finitatem W 2.　　illā finitatem B 2　E 1.　　ille p
finitatem D C.　　ille *an* illa *incert. ante* infinitatem F.　‖　peregrinabatur R 1 2
V P　B 1　K 1　E 1　W 2　D　O 1 2　F.　　perigrinabatur G.　　peruagabatur W 1.

sophy (Diog. L. ii 137 ἀλλὰ πρεσβύτερος
’Ασκληπιάδης, ὡς λέγεσθαι ποιητὴν μὲν
αὐτὸν εἶναι, ὑποκριτὴν δὲ Μενέδημον).

quod...cotidie: i.e. *parasitari.*

ualetudinum, 'attacks of ill-health,'
lit. 'states of health,' the plur. being
understood *in malam partem* as there are
many kinds of ill-health but only one kind
of good health: cf. Tac. A. vi 50 'regere
ualetudines principis.'

§ **114. Democritus:** cf. Fin. v 29, 87
'Democritus, qui (uere falsone non quaeremus) dicitur se oculis priuasse'; Plut.
de curiosit. 12 p. 521 D. ἐκεῖνο μὲν ψεῦδός
ἐστι τὸ Δημόκριτον ἑκουσίως σβέσαι τὰς
ὄψεις; Decimus Laberius, *Restio* 1 (Ribbeck, *Scaen. Rom. Poes. Frgg.* II²p. 291)
'Democritus Abderites physicus philo-
sophus | clipeum constituit contra ex-
ortum Hyperionis | oculos effodere ut
posset splendore aereo.'

licebat...non licebat: cf. i 48, 116 n.
on 'defuerunt...non defuit.'

notione rerum, 'an apprehension of
realities'; for *notione* Usener (*Epicurea*
p. 336 n.) suggests *notatione.*

cum alii...consisteret: for the reading
in the text Bentl. (followed by Dav.)
conjectured *cum hi saepe...illa infinitatem
omnem peragrabat,* where *hi = oculi* and
illa = mens: the reading *illa* is found in
many MSS., but the conjecture misses the
point, which is not to contrast Democritus' mind with his eyes or with the
eyes of other people, but to contrast the
blind philosopher with other people ; *alii*
then is necessary and consequently *ille.*

For *quod ante pedes esset* cf. Ennius *ap.*
Diu. ii 13, 30 'quod est ante pedes nemo
spectat, caeli scrutantur plagas' Ter. Ad.
386; and for the expression *peregrinabatur ... consisteret* cf. N.D. i. 20, 54,

fuisse; at eius picturam, non poësin uidemus. quae regio, quae
ora, qui locus Graeciae, quae species formaque pugnae, quae
acies, quod remigium, qui motus hominum, qui ferarum non ita
expictus est ut, quae ipse non uiderit, nos ut uideremus effecerit?
25 quid ergo? aut Homero delectationem animi ac uoluptatem aut
cuiquam docto defuisse umquam arbitramur? **115** aut, ni ita se
res haberet, Anaxagoras aut hic ipse Democritus agros et patri-
monia sua reliquissent, huic discendi quaerendique diuinae
delectationi toto se animo dedissent? itaque augurem Tiresiam,
30 quem sapientem fingunt poëtae, numquam inducunt deplorantem
caecitatem suam. at uero Polyphemum Homerus cum inmanem
ferumque finxisset, cum ariete etiam conloquentem facit eiusque

21. poesin R V P G   B 1 2   K 1   E 1   F.   poesï W 2.   poesim v W 1
M 1 2   D C *plerique.*   22.   qui locus V P G K F.   quilocus R *alio atr. superscr.* ‖
graeciae v G *marg.* F.   greçiȩ R.   greciȩ R 2   V P   O 3.   grecie W 2
D   O 1.   ‖ formaq; pugne D C.   formȩ que pugna K 1.   forme que pugna
R 17   E 2   L 5 6   Π J   O 1.   forme q̄ pugna B 2   K 2   W 2.   formae q̄ pugna
L 2.   fortune que pugna M 1.   fortune q̄ pugna E 3.   formȩ quȩ pugna P
B 1   S   E 1   L 4   O 3.   forme quȩ pugna V.   formȩ quae pugna R 1.
formae quae pugna R 6   G   L 3   M 2   O 2   F.   quae pugna quae species
formae v.   quȩ formȩ quȩ pugnȩ W 1.   24.   expictus R V P G   B 1   E 1 2   F.
expict' K 1.   expictum v.   ‖ effecerit R v P G   E 1 2   F *plerique.*   efficerit
V K.   25.   ac uoluptatem R 6   P   B 1   E 1 3   L 6   M 2   C O 2 3.
aut uoluptatem R 1 17   V G   K 1 2   E 2   L 2–5   W 1 2   M 1   D Π   O 1   F
ut uidetur.   26.   defuisse R V P G B K E F.   fuisse v.
§ **115**, 28.   reliquissent V P B K E.   relinquissent R G.   29.   dedissent
R 1 6 17   V P G   B 1 2   K 1 2   S   E 1 2   W 2   M 1 2   D C Π J   O 1–3   F.
dedidissent W 1.   dedisset O 2 ed. H.   31.   polyphemum R V G.
poliphemum P B K F.   ‖ inmanem R V P G K F.   immanem B S E.
32.   finxisset v P   B 1   E F.   fixisset B 2.   fixisset R V G.   ~~fuisset~~ S

marg. finxisset.   ‖ conloquentem V F.   conloquentem R.   cloquentem K.
colloquentem P   B 1   S.

'animus...ita late longeque peregrinatur
ut nullam tamen oram ultimam uideat, in
qua possit insistere'; with *peregrinabatur*
we must supply *animo* or *mente*.

picturam: so Athenaeus v p. 182A
Ὅμηρος ὥσπερ ἀγαθὸς ζωγράφος and
Luc. Imagg. c. 8 τὸν ἄριστον τῶν
γραφέων Ὅμηρον (quoted by Dav.).

poësin: this form of the accusative ending seems best attested here though Wes.
and Sff. read *poësim*.

§ **115. Anaxagoras...reliquissent**: for
the alleged facts see Diog. Laert. ii 6 [of
Anaxagoras] οὗτος...πλούτῳ διαφέρων ἦν
...τὰ πατρῷα παρεχώρησε τοῖς οἰκείοις and
ix 35 [of Democritus] τρίτον τε ὄντα
ἀδελφὸν νείμασθαι τὴν οὐσίαν...ὁ δὲ Δημή-
τριος ὑπὲρ ἑκατὸν τάλαντά φησιν εἶναι
αὐτῷ τὸ μέρος ἅπαντα δὲ καταναλῶσαι.

dedissent: cf. i 30, 72 n. on *dedissent*;
Or. here prefers *dedidissent*.

Polyphemum in Od. ix 447 ff. Cicero's
recollection of the passage is hazy, as
Polyphemus is not there represented as
contrasting the ram's freedom with his
own helplessness, but the ram's present
slowness with his former freedom of
movement. It seems hardly necessary to
suppose that Cic. has in his mind a
passage from some other poet whom he
is confusing with Homer.

conloquentem...laudare: for the change
of construction cf. N.D. i 12, 31 'facit
enim...Socratem disputantem...eundem-
que...dicere'; cf. also Prop. ii 8, 33
'uiderat informem multa Patroclon arena |
porrectum et sparsas caede iacere comas,'
where however there is a change of subject: so after *spectare* in Prop. ii 19, 11,
iv 12, 53: the emendation *laudantem*
(Lamb.) is therefore unnecessary.

laudare fortunas quod, qua uellet, ingredi posset et, quae uellet,
attingere. et recte hic quidem ; nihilo enim erat ipse Cyclops
35 quam aries ille prudentior.

XL. 116. In surditate uero quidnam est mali? erat surdaster

M. Crassus, sed aliud molestius, quod male audiebat, etiamsi, ut
mihi uidebatur, iniuria. Epicurei nostri Graece fere nesciunt nec
Graeci Latine. ergo hi in illorum et illi in horum sermone surdi,
5 omnesque nos in iis linguis quas non intellegimus, quae sunt

33. qua uellet R 1 7 v G B 1 2 K 1 E 1 2 L 2 3 6 W 1 M 2 D C II
O 1 3 F. q̃ uellet P. qua uellet S. q; uellet V. q̄ uellet K 2 L 4 5
W 2 J. q̄ uellet O 2. quo uellet R 17 M 1 ed. H. ‖ et quae M 2 O 2.
et quȩ P W 1 M 1 O 3. et que R 7 L 6 J O 1. et q̄ L 2 ed. H.
et quem̧ L 4. et quem B 1. et quȩ S ē *in* ȩ *mut.* et q̄, B 2. et quē G
K 1 2 E 1. et quem R V L 3 5 D C F. et quo W 2. 34. attingeret
R 1 6 1 7 V P G B 1 2 K 1 2 S E 1 L 2-6 W 1 M 1 D J O 1-3 F ed. H.
actingeret C. attīge W 2. contingeret II E 2. attingere et recte
corr. Lambinus.

XL. § 116, 3. epicurei R 1 2 6 7 1 0 1 6 V P 1 G B 1 2 K 1 S E 1 2
L 2-6 M 1 2 D C II J O 1-3 F. epycurei W 2. epicuri R 17 P 2.
epycurhei W 1. ‖ graece R v O 2 F. grece B K. gce P. grecȩ V.
graecae G. ‖ fere R V P G B 1 2 K 1 E 1 D C F. fari R 6 v K 2
E 2 3 L 2-6 W 1 2 M 1 2 II J O 1 3 ed. H. rari O 2. 5. omnesque nos
R 6 P 2 W 1 J O 1 F. omnesque id nos R 1 7 V P 1 G B 1 2 K 1 2
E 1-3 L 5 6 W 2 M 1 2 D C II O 2 3 ed. H. omnesque id nos S.
omnisque nos v. ‖ in iis v L 6. in hiis K 2. in eis F. in his R V P G
B 1 2 K 1 E 1 2 L 5 W 1 2 O 1-3. in illis D. ‖ intellegimus R V G B K F.
intelligimus v P S E.

fortunas: for the plur. Mo. compares
pro Sull. 23, 66 'secundas fortunas amit-
tere coactus est.'

attingere. et recte: this reading (Lamb.
Wes. Schiche) seems to explain best on
the whole the reading *attingeret* which is
attested by nearly all the MSS. and is
accepted by Tr.: the reading *attingere:
recte* adopted by Küh. Sff. and others is
less satisfactory as it assumes as a cause
for the reading *attingeret* the influence of
the preceding subjunctives, which is less
likely than a purely mechanical error.

XL. § 116. surdaster, 'hard of hearing,' is ἅπαξ εἰρημένον.

male audiebat, κακῶς ἤκουεν, 'had a
bad reputation': cf. Plut. Crass. c. 2
'Ῥωμαῖοι μὲν οὖν λέγουσι πολλαῖς ἀρεταῖς
τοῦ Κράσσου κακίαν μόνην ἐπισκοτῆσαι
τὴν φιλοπλουτίαν· ἔοικε δὲ οὐ μία, πασῶν
δ' ἐρρωμενεστέρα τῶν ἐν αὐτῷ κακιῶν
γενομένη τὰς ἄλλας ἀμαυρῶσαι; he had
been accused of corrupting a Vestal
Virgin, but was acquitted on the plea
that the attentions he paid her were of a
purely commercial nature, as he wished
to buy her property cheaply.

Epicurei: all recent edd. except Kl.

and Sff. expunge or bracket the word,
which Madv. calls a 'foedum additamen-
tum'; but it seems futile to resist the
unanimous testimony of the MSS. in a case
where there is no plausible explanation of
how the word came to be inserted (as
there is e.g. in Lucr. ii 42), and where
the reading as it stands gives a good sense.
It is characteristic of Cic. to gibe at the
want of Greek scholarship shown by the
Roman Epicureans (cf. i 3, 6; ii 3, 7;
iv 3, 7, etc.), and there is a grim humour
in selecting the coterie who laid such
stress upon pleasures of the senses, as
examples of persons deprived of pleasure
(and wisdom) 'at one entrance.' *Epicurei nostri* and *Graeci*, moreover, give
a better point to *omnes nos* below.

Latine: *sciunt* is to be supplied from
nesciunt: cf. Ac. ii 47, 145 'tu nunc,
Catule, lucere nescis, nec tu, Hortensi, in
tua uilla nos esse' with Reid's n. and
Fin. ii 8, 25 'recte ergo is negat unquam
bene cenasse Gallonium, recte miserum,'
where Lamb. inserts *dicit*, an excusable but
erroneous proceeding, as Madv. remarks.

omnesque nos: many MSS have *omnesque id nos*, which Kl. Wopk. and Küh.

innumerabiles, surdi profecto sumus. at uocem citharoedi non audiunt. ne stridorem quidem serrae tum cum acuitur, aut grunditum cum iugulatur suis nec, cum quiescere uolunt, fremitum murmurantis maris; et si cantus eos forte delectant, 10 primum cogitare debent ante quam hi sint inuenti multos beate uixisse sapientis, deinde multo maiorem percipi posse legendis his quam audiendis uoluptatem. 117. tum, ut paulo ante caecos ad aurium traducebamus uoluptatem, sic licet surdos ad oculorum. etenim, qui secum loqui poterit sermonem alterius 15 non requiret.

Congerantur in unum omnia, ut idem oculis et auribus captus sit, prematur etiam doloribus acerrimis corporis. qui primum

---

6. at R 2 10 v P E 2 W 1 M 2 C J O 1–3.   aut R 1.   aut E 1.
aut R 17 V G K M 1. ‖ citharoedi R F.   citaroedi V G.   citharedi P K.
cytaredi E 1 *atr. ant.*   7. serrae R 6 v L 3 M 2 O 2 F.   serre L 2 6
W 1 M 1 O 1.   ferre Π *at* re *in ras. et fuerat* fer.   fere W 2 *marg.* serre.
fere E 2 *at* f *in ras.*   ferre R 7.   fere R V P G B 1 2 K 1 2 E 1 L 5 O 3.
ferri E 3 D C.   fieri R 17 L 4.   ferari ed. H.   8. grunditum R 17
V G B 2 K 1 E 1.   grunditum R 1 *atr. nigriore mut.*   grunditū E 1.
grunnitum B 1.   grunnitum R 2 7 16 v P E 2 3 L 5 W 2 M 2 D C Π J O 1.
grunitum R 6 L 6 O 2 3.   gr‖ nitum F.   grinnitum W 1 ed. H.   grunntū K 2.
gnnitum S *marg.* grunnitum.   ginnicū R 10.   grunntur M 1. ‖ suis R V P G
B 1 E 1 M 1.   sus K 1 *eod. atr.*   suis C.   sus R 6 7 17 v K 2 S E 2 3
L 5 6 W 1 2 M 2 D Π J O 1–3 ed. H.   om. B 2.   11. sapientis O 2 F.
sapientes R V P G B K E.   12. his R V P G K E.   iis F.
§ 117, 14. qui secum v K 2 W 2 D C Π O 1–3 F ed. H.   que secum V
i *in* e *mut.*   qui secum B 1 *eod. ut uid. atr.*   que secum E 1.   que secum P.
quae secum R G.   que secum K 1.   q̄ secum B 2.   si secum W 1.
16. congerantur R 16 7 17 v P 1 2 G K 1 2 E 2 3 L 5 6 W 2 M 2 Π
O 1–3 ed. H.   congerentur J.   conggerantur B 2.   congregantur V.
congregentur W 1 D C.   cū gerantur M 1.   cogantur B 1 E 1.   rigerantur
F *initio abscisso.*   17. prematur V B 2 E 1.   praematur R *eod. atr.*
p̄matur P K.   praematur G. ‖ acerrumis R V G B K F.

---

retain, explaining *id* as an anticipation of *surdi* following (Wopk. *op. cit.* pp. 159 sqq.); Hand (n. to Wopk. *l.c.*) proposed *iidem*, Man. followed by Lamb. Ml. and Wes. read *item* and Sff. conjectures *denique*; Dav. wrote 'in horum sermone surdi omnes. Quid? nos in iis' etc. The reading in the text is adopted by Tr. Ba. Or.

ante quam...sapientis: a sentiment due to Democritus; cf. Philodemus de mus. V.H.[1] i c 36, 29 (quoted by Usener, *Epic.* p. 337 n.) Δημόκριτος μὲν τοίνυν...

μουσικήν φησι νεωτέραν εἶναι καὶ τὴν αἰτίαν ἀποδίδωσι λέγων μὴ ἀποκρῖναι τἀναγκαῖον ἀλλὰ ἐκ τοῦ περιεῦντος ἤδη γενέσθαι. *sapientis* is bracketed by Dav. and Bentl.

§ 117. paulo ante: in 38, 111.
secum loqui: cf. 36, 103.
captus, as often, = *priuatus*: Diu. ii 3, 9 'oculis captus, ut Tiresias'; Ac. ii 17, 53 'mente captos.'

primum, without *deinde* following, its place being taken by *sin forte*; cf. i 24, 57 n. and Wopk. *op. cit.* p. 73.

per se ipsi plerumque conficiunt hominem; sin forte longin-
quitate producti uehementius tamen torquent quam ut causa sit
20 cur ferantur, quid est tandem, dii boni, quod laboremus? portus
enim praesto est, quoniam mors ibidem est aeternum nihil
sentiendi receptaculum. Theodorus Lysimacho mortem minitanti
'Magnum uero,' inquit, 'effecisti si cantharidis uim consecutus es.' **118.** Paulus Persi deprecanti ne in triumpho
25 duceretur, 'In tua id quidem potestate est.' multa primo
die, cum de ipsa morte quaereremus, non pauca etiam postero,
cum ageretur de dolore, sunt dicta de morte, quae qui recordetur
haud sane periculum est ne non mortem aut optandam aut
certe non timendam putet.

20. dii R V P G B₁₂ K₁ S E₁ DJ O₁ F.   21. quoniam mors
ibidem est R P G B₁ K₁ E₁₂ W₁₂ M₁₂ D C Π O₂₃.   niã m. i. e.

F *initio abscisso.*   quae m. i. e. v.   que O₁.   q̃₃ B₂.   mors ibidem est V
paginae parte abscissa.   23. cantharidis P B K *alii.*   canTharidis G.

cantharidis F.   Taridis V.   ‖ consecutus es P B₁₂ K₁ E₁₂ F *alii.*
con....uf ef V.   consecutus est R *eod. atr.*   consequutus es v.

§ 118, 24.   paulus R V P G B S E.   ‖ persi *paene omnes.*   perse W₁ ed. H.
persę O₁.   persae v.   per se O₃.   25. in tua id quidem R V P G B₂
                                                            /. /.
K₁₂ E₁₋₃ W₂ Π J O₁₂ F S *marg.* inquit ed. H.   id in tua quidem B₁.
in tua id inquit potestate R 6.   in tua inquit id quidem W₁ M₁.   in tua id
quidem inquit M₂ D C.   ‖ primo die v   K₂ E₂ W₁ D C Π O₁ F ed. H.

p die W₂.   prima die E₃ O₂₃.   primordie P E₁.   primordie R V G
B₁₂ K₁.   28. haud sane R v G K.   hau.... V.   haut sane B₂.

h
aut sane E₁.   aut sane F.   hauḍ sane P h *extra lineam adscr. et* t *in* d *mut.*

sin forte...laboremus: the doctrine of
the εὔλογος ἐξαγωγή, professed alike by
Stoics, Epicureans and Peripatetics. There
seems to be no sufficient reason for inserting *tanta* (with Sff.) after *causa*.

portus: the metaphor is common; cf. i
49, 118 n. and Plut. non posse suau. u. sec.
Ep. c. 23 p. 1103 C εἰς μίαν καταφυγὴν
καὶ λιμένα πράττοντες κακῶς, τὴν διάλυσιν
καὶ τὴν ἀναισθησίαν, ἀποβλέπουσι; Epict.
Diss. iv 10, 27 οὗτος δ' ἐστὶν ὁ λιμὴν
πάντων, ὁ θάνατος, αὕτη ἡ καταφυγή.

ibidem, 'at once,' 'on the spot' like
the Gk αὐτόθεν. The word is omitted by
Or. Tr. and Mo. and altered to *quidem*
by Nissen and Wes., the latter placing it
after *quoniam*; many edd. follow Bentl.
and Dav. in regarding *quoniam...est* as a
gloss. Vahlen (*Opusc. Acad.* II 351 ff.)
proposes 'quoniam mors <ubi est>, ibidem est aeternum....' Bake proposed to
delete *mors* and take *ibidem* to mean ἐκεῖ,
i.e. *apud inferos.*

Theodorus: cf. i 43, 102 for another

tale about Theodorus and Lysimachus
and n. there. Similar retorts are also to
be found in Sen. de tranqu. 14, 3 ; Val.
Max. vi 2, 3 ext.

cantharidis, a poisonous beetle or fly,
from which a deadly drug was manu-
factured : cf. Fam. ix 21, 3 'Gaius
accusante L. Crasso cantharidas sum-
psisse dicitur'; Plin. N.H. xxix 30
'ipsarum cantharidum uenenum in qua
parte sit, non constat inter auctores. alii
in pedibus et capite existimant esse, alii
negant. conuenit tantum pennas earum
auxiliari in quacumque parte sit uenenum.'

§ 118. Paulus: Plut. Aem. Paul. c. 34
προσέπεμψε τῷ Αἰμιλίῳ δεόμενος μὴ πομ-
πευθῆναι καὶ παραιτούμενος τὸν θρίαμβον·
ὁ δὲ τῆς ἀνανδρίας αὐτοῦ καὶ φιλοψυχίας,
ὡς ἔοικε, καταγελῶν, ἀλλὰ τοῦτο γ' ἔφη,
καὶ πρότερον ἦν ἐπ' αὐτῷ καὶ νῦν ἐστιν,
ἂν βούληται.

Persi : for the form see iii 22, 53 n.
Or. reads *Persae.*

XLI. Mihi quidem in uita seruanda uidetur illa lex quae in Graecorum conuiuiis obtinetur: 'aut bibat,' inquit, 'aut abeat.' et recte. aut enim fruatur aliquis pariter cum aliis uoluptate potandi aut, ne sobrius in uiolentiam uinulentorum incidat, ante 5 discedat. sic iniurias fortunae quas ferre nequeas defugiendo relinquas. haec eadem quae Epicurus, totidem uerbis dicit Hieronymus.

119. Quodsi ii philosophi quorum ea sententia est ut uirtus per se ipsa nihil ualeat, omneque quod honestum nos et laudabile 10 esse dicimus, id illi cassum quiddam et inani uocis sono decoratum esse dicant, ei tamen semper beatum censent esse sapientem,

---

XLI. 2. obtinetur S E F.   optinetur R v P G B 1 2 K 1.   4. in
uiolentiam V v G B 2 K F.   in uiolentiam R *eod. ut uid. atr.*   in uinolentiam
B 1 E 1 2 *alii.*   in uinulentiā P.   5. discedat v P B 1 E 1 2   F *alii.*
decedat K.   dice^sbat R *atr. nigriore corr.*   dicebat V G.   7. hieronymus R v.
hieronimus V G B 1 2 K E.   hyeronimus F : *ante* hieronymus *inser.* et v P 2
M 2 O 1 2.
§ 119, 8. ii philosophi v M 2.   ii p͞hy L 6.   ii p͞hi W 2 h *ante* ii *eras.*
hii p͞hi P 6 K 2 II.   hi p͞hi W 1.   hi p͞hi P 2 E 2 *at* ſ *post* hi *eras. uidetur
et spatium post* p͞hi *relictum est.*   iis philosophis P 3 5.   eis philosophis F.
hiis philosophis P 4.   I hiis philosophis R 7.   his philosophis R 1 6 V P 1 G
B 1 2 K 1 S E 1 J O 1 3.   suis philosophis O 2.   his p͞his credimus M 1.
hiis credimus p͞his D.   is credimus ph'is C.   9. omneque v E 2 L 6 M 2
D C II O 1.   ōeq; W 2 ſ *eras.*   omnesque R V P G B 1 2 K 1 2 S E 1 3
L 5 W 1 M 1 O 2 3.   omnisque ed. H.   10. dicimus R 6 17 B 1
L 6 W 1.   dicamus R 1 7 V v P G B 2 K 1 2 S E 1-3 L 5 W 2 M 1
D C II J O 1-3 ed. H.   ducamus M 2. ‖ cassum R v P B 1 2 K 1 E 1 *alii.*
casum V.   casus G *in* cassū *eod. atr. corr.* ‖ inani R V G.   inaniſ F.
inan̄ni K.   inanis P.   11. et tamen R 1 6 7 10 16 17 V v P G B 1 2 K 1 2
S E 1 2 L 3-6 W 1 2 M 1 2 D C II J O 1-3.   &_A^{tn} E 3.   et tum L 2.
ei *corr. Wesenbergius.*

XLI. **obtinetur**, for which Dav. Or. Tr. substitute *obtinet*, is the only form possible in the sense required here, ' is in vogue '; cf. i 12, 26 n.

The Gk proverb is quoted by Stephanus ἢ πῖθι ἢ ἄπιθι. The moral application of it referred to by Cic. here is of common occurrence: cf. Lucr. iii 938; Hor. Epp. ii 2, 213, S. i 1, 118; Plut. Cons. ad Ap. c. 34 p. 120 B προαπεφοίτησε τοῦ θνητοῦ βίου, καθάπερ ἐκ τοῦ συμποσίου, πρὶν εἰς τινα παροινίαν ἐκπεσεῖν τὴν τῷ μακρῷ γήρᾳ παρεπομένην.

With *inquit* it is best to understand *lex*; for another use cf. i 39, 93 n.

Epicurus: Buresch gives reasons (in *Leips. Stud.* IX 62) for believing that this idea was developed in the *Consolatio* of Epicurus and borrowed from him by Crantor in his περὶ πένθους, from whom Cic. and Plut. derived it.

Hieronymus: ii 6, 15 n.

§ 119. **ii philosophi**: sc. *Epicurei*. The reading of many MSS *iis* (or *his*) *philosophis* (retained by Kl. and Küh.), if correct, must be explained as an anacoluthon, Cic. having intended to conclude with (e.g.) *licet haec dicere*, and having altered the constr. after the parenthesis *quorum...dicant.*

inani: cf. 26, 73 and iii 18, 42 n.: *inani* is a transl. of Epicurus' own phrase (perh. κενοὶ φθόγγοι as Usener *Epic.* p. 314 n. suggests) as appears from Fin. ii 15, 48 'ait (sc. Epicurus) eos uoce inani sonare (his enim ipsis uerbis utitur).'

ei: Wesenberg's emendation for the MSS. *et* adopted by Kl. Ba. Ml. Küh.; Or. La. Tr. and Sff. prefer to omit *et*.

quid tandem a Socrate et Platone profectis philosophis faciundum
uides? quorum alii tantam praestantiam in bonis animi esse
dicunt ut ab his corporis et externa obruantur, alii autem haec
15 ne bona quidem ducunt, in animo reponunt omnia. **120.** quorum
controuersiam solebat tamquam honorarius arbiter iudicare
Carneades. nam cum, quaecumque bona Peripateticis, eadem
Stoicis commoda uiderentur, neque tamen Peripatetici plus
tribuerent diuitiis, bonae ualetudini, ceteris rebus generis eiusdem
20 quam Stoici, cum ea re non uerbis ponderarentur, causam esse
dissidendi negabat. quare hunc locum ceterarum disciplinarum
philosophi quem ad modum obtinere possint, ipsi uiderint; mihi
tamen gratum est quod de sapientium perpetua bene uiuendi
facultate dignum quiddam philosophorum uoce profitentur.

12. profectis G　B 2　F.　　pfectis R 2　B 1　S　E 1　M 2.　　pfectis J.
pfectis R 7 16 17　P　K 1　E 2　W 1 2　M 1　D C II.　　perfectis R 1 6　v
O 1–3 ed. H.　‖　faciundum O 1.　　faciendum R V P G K E.　　13. uides R 1
P G　B 1 2　K 1 2　S　E 1–3　L 5 6　W 2　M 2　II J　O 1–3 F ed. H.　　ui... V
　　　　　　　　　　　　　　　　　　　　　　　　　　　　　uides
in fine lineae, cett. litt. excussis.　　uidetur v.　　censes D *alio atr. superscr.*
censes C.　　putes R 6 7 17　W 1　M 1.　　14. obruantur F.　　obſiuant B 2.
obſ,uant K 2　L 5.　　obs'uät W 2　J.　　obseruant G K 1.　　obseruänt R 1
a *in e mut. alt. man.*　　obserua... V *litt. aliae sequuntur at obscuratae sunt.*
obſiuet S.　　obſiuent D.　　obseruent R 7 17　P 1　B 1　E 1 2　L 2–4　M 1 2
　　　　　　　　　　　　　　　　　　　　　r
C　O 3.　　obseruet P 2.　　obscurent II *at cur in ras.*　　obscurentur v　R 6
　　　　　　tur　　　　　　　┐
L 6　O 1 2.　　obscurē　E 3.　　obseruent ed. H.　　15. ducunt R V P G　B 1
　　　　　　　　　　　v
E 1 2　W 2　D C II J F *ut uid.*　　dịcunt K 1 *eod. atr. corr.* M 2.　　dicunt B 2
S　E 3　W 1　M 1　O 1–3 ed. H.
§ 120, 19. ualetudini R V G K.　　ualitudini P B S E.　　21. dissidendi R 6.
desid'andi P　E 2.　　desiderandi R 1 7 17　V v G　B 1 2　K 1 2　E 1 3　L 2–6
　　　　　　　　　　　　　　　　　　　　　　　l' desiderandi
W 1 2　M 2　II J　O 1–3 ed. H.　　desiderandi S.　　disserendi D *alio atr. superscr.*
disserendi M 1　C.　　‖　negabat R V G B K *alii.*　　negabant v P S.
22. obtinere P E.　　optinere R V G B K.　　24. quiddā P.　　qddam V.
quidam R G B K E.

quid...faciendum uides ?: i.e. *nonne
idem...faciendum uides?* 'What else do
you see for them to do?'; sc. except to
say *semper beatum esse sapientem* with the
Epicureans. There is no necessity to
change *uides* to *censes* with Küh., or
putas with Madv. Tr. Wes. Kl. Ba., or
iudicas with Sff. and T.S., or *suades*
with Kl.
　alii...alii : i.e. *Peripatetici...Stoici.*
　obruantur: Bentley's brilliant emendation of the MSS has since been confirmed
by the discovery of the Bodleian fragment.
The error may have arisen from a confusion between r and ſ, the contraction
for *ser.*
　§ 120. **honorarius:** i.e. 'quod honoris

causa ad aliquem arbitrium defertur' (Ern.
Clau. Cic. s.v.); cf. Fat. 17, 39 'tamquam arbiter honorarius medium ferire
uoluisse'; and on the position of Carneades
iv 3, 6 n.
　cum : for the *cum*-clause with another
cum-clause in subordination cf. the exx.
of *si...si* quoted in the n. to ii 27, 67.
　commoda: i.e. προηγμένα, *praecipua.*
　dissidendi: cf. Fin. iv 26, 72 'uidesne
igitur Zenonem tuum cum Aristone uerbis
consistere, re dissidere, cum Aristotele et
illis re consentire, uerbis discrepare,' a
passage which Kl. quotes in favour of his
conjecture *discrepandi.*
　uiderint: i 11, 23 n.

25 **121.** Sed quoniam mane est eundum, has quinque dierum disputationes memoria comprehendamus. equidem me etiam conscripturum arbitror (ubi enim melius uti possumus hoc, cuicuimodi est, otio?), ad Brutumque nostrum hos libros alteros quinque mittemus, a quo non modo impulsi sumus ad philo-
30 sophiae scriptiones, uerum etiam lacessiti. in quo quantum ceteris profuturi simus non facile dixerim, nostris quidem acerbissimis doloribus uariisque et undique circumfusis molestiis alia nulla potuit inueniri leuatio.

§ 121, 26. comprehendamus R V G B S. conprehendamus K E.
28. cuicuimodi V P G B 1 2 K 1 2 W 2. cuîcuîmodi R 1 *atr. nigro mut.*
cuimodi R 17 L 5. cuimō J. cuiusmodi R 6 v S E 1 L 3 4 W 1 D C
O 3 ed. H. cuiuscunque modi L 26. 29. inpulsi R V G K. impulsi v B E.‖
         ic
philosophas V G B 1 K 1 E 1. phas B 2 K 2. philosoph,as R 1.
philosophicas R 6 7 17 v P S E 2 W 1 M 1 2 D C Π J O 1-3 Vrs. 3240 ed. H.
phylosophicas W 2. phylosoficas E 3. philosophiae *Nonii codd.*
31. profuturi sumus R 1 2 6 7 10 16 17 V v P G B 1 2 K 1 2 S E 1-3 L 2-6
           l' p futuri sumus
W 1 2 M 1 2 Π J O 1-3 ed. H. p fuerimus D *alio atr. superscr.* p fuerimus C.
profuturi simus *corr. Beroaldus.* ‖ dixerim V P G B 2 S E 1 2 M 1 C Π
O 3 ed. H. dixerimus R 1 *atr. nigro corr.* dixerim¹ R 6 17 K 1 J.
dixerimus B 1 K 2 W 1 2 M 2 O 1 2. ‖ acerbissimis R V P G B K E.

§ 121. **eundum**: sc. *Romam.*
ubi: i.e. *in quo.*
cuicuimodi: used in a depreciatory sense, as often in Cic. 'the leisure I have, if leisure it can be called': cf. iii 34, 83 where the meaning is 'I have leisure enough now if leisure it can be called,' the use of *hoc* there being (not, as Küh. and others say, equivalent to *huius rei* but) the same as here and meaning simply *quod nunc est.*
alteros: he had already dedicated to Brutus the five books *de Finibus.*
philosophiae: this, which is the read-

ing known to Nonius p. 174, 18, is adopted by Tr. Kl. Kuh. Sff. Hei.: *philosophas* is kept by F. A. W. Or. Ba. T. S. It is highly improbable that Cic. would have used *philosophus* as an adj.; cf. Ac. i 2, 8 with Reid's n.
simus...dixerim: for the transition from plural to singular without change of meaning cf. de imp. Cn. Pomp. 16, 47 'de huius autem hominis felicitate quo de nunc agimus hac utar moderatione dicendi' (quoted by Hei.) and for the opposite change Or. ii 35, 150 'complectar uno uerbo quo saepe iam usi sumus.'

INDEX

The Arabic numerals refer to sections.

CPSIA information can be obtained
at www.ICGtesting.com
Printed in the USA
LVOW10s1916200518
577860LV00001B/2/P